Novels
for Students

Novels for Students

Presenting Analysis, Context and Criticism on Commonly Studied Novels

Volume 5

Sheryl Ciccarelli
Marie Rose Napierkowski
Editors

Foreword by Anne Devereaux Jordan, Teaching and Learning Literature

GALE

DETROIT · LONDON

Novels for Students

Staff

Series Editor: Sheryl Ciccarelli and Marie Rose Napierkowski.

Contributing Editors: Sara L. Constantakis, Catherine L. Goldstein, Margaret Haerens, Motoko Fujishiro Huthwaite, Arlene M. Johnson, Paul Loeber, and Diane Telgen.

Editorial Technical Specialist: Karen Uchic.

Managing Editor: Joyce Nakamura.

Research: Victoria B. Cariappa, *Research Team Manager.* Andy Malonis, *Research Specialist.* Julia C. Daniel, Tamara C. Nott, Tracie A. Richardson, and Cheryl L. Warnock, *Research Associates.* Jeffrey Daniels, *Research Assistant.*

Permissions: Susan M. Trosky, *Permissions Manager.* Maria L. Franklin, *Permissions Specialist.* Sarah Chesney, *Permissions Associate.*

Production: Mary Beth Trimper, *Production Director.* Evi Seoud, *Assistant Production Manager.* Cindy Range, *Production Assistant.*

Graphic Services: Randy Bassett, *Image Database Supervisor.* Robert Duncan and Michael Logusz, *Imaging Specialists.* Pamela A. Reed, *Photography Coordinator.* Gary Leach, *Macintosh Artist.*

Product Design: Cynthia Baldwin, *Product Design Manager.* Cover Design: Michelle DiMercurio, *Art Director.* Page Design: Pamela A. E. Galbreath, *Senior Art Director.*

Copyright Notice

National Advisory Board

Table of Contents

The Informed Dialogue: Interacting with Literature

When we pick up a book, we usually do so with the anticipation of pleasure. We hope that by entering the time and place of the novel and sharing the thoughts and actions of the characters, we will find enjoyment. Unfortunately, this is often not the case; we are disappointed. But we should ask, has the author failed us, or have we failed the author?

We establish a dialogue with the author, the book, and with ourselves when we read. Consciously and unconsciously, we ask questions: "Why did the author write this book?" "Why did the author choose that time, place, or character?" "How did the author achieve that effect?" "Why did the character act that way?" "Would I act in the same way?" The answers we receive depend upon how much information about literature in general and about that book specifically we ourselves bring to our reading.

Young children have limited life and literary experiences. Being young, children frequently do not know how to go about exploring a book, nor sometimes, even know the questions to ask of a book. The books they read help them answer questions, the author often coming right out and *telling* young readers the things they are learning or are expected to learn. The perennial classic, *The Little Engine That Could, tells* its readers that, among other things, it is good to help others and bring happiness:

> "Hurray, hurray," cried the funny little clown and all the dolls and toys. "The good little boys and girls in the city will be happy because you helped us, kind, Little Blue Engine."

In picture books, messages are often blatant and simple, the dialogue between the author and reader one-sided. Young children are concerned with the end result of a book—the enjoyment gained, the lesson learned—rather than with how that result was obtained. As we grow older and read further, however, we question more. We come to expect that the world within the book will closely mirror the concerns of our world, and that the author will *show* these through the events, descriptions, and conversations within the story, rather than *telling* of them. We are now expected to do the interpreting, carry on our share of the dialogue with the book and author, and glean not only the author's message, but comprehend how that message and the overall affect of the book were achieved. Sometimes, however, we need help to do these things. *Novels for Students* provides that help.

A novel is made up of many parts interacting to create a coherent whole. In reading a novel, the more obvious features can be easily spotted—theme, characters, plot—but we may overlook the more subtle elements that greatly influence how the novel is perceived by the reader: viewpoint, mood and tone, symbolism, or the use of humor. By focusing on both the obvious and more subtle literary elements within a novel, *Novels for Students* aids readers in both analyzing for message and in determining how and why that message is communicated. In the discussion on Harper Lee's *To*

Kill a Mockingbird (Vol. 2), for example, the mockingbird as a symbol of innocence is dealt with, among other things, as is the importance of Lee's use of humor which "enlivens a serious plot, adds depth to the characterization, and creates a sense of familiarity and universality." The reader comes to understand the internal elements of each novel discussed—as well as the external influences that help shape it.

"The desire to write greatly," Harold Bloom of Yale University says, "is the desire to be elsewhere, in a time and place of one's own, in an originality that must compound with inheritance, with an anxiety of influence." A writer seeks to create a unique world within a story, but although it is unique, it is not disconnected from our own world. It speaks to us *because* of what the writer brings to the writing from our world: how he or she was raised and educated; his or her likes and dislikes; the events occurring in the real world at the time of the writing, and while the author was growing up. When we know what an author has brought to his or her work, we gain a greater insight into both the "originality" (the world of the book), and the things that "compound" it. This insight enables us to question that created world and find answers more readily. By informing ourselves, we are able to establish a more effective dialogue with both book and author.

Novels for Students, in addition to providing a plot summary and descriptive list of characters—to remind readers of what they have read—also explores the external influences that shaped each book. Each entry includes a discussion of the author's background, and the historical context in which the novel was written. It is vital to know, for instance, that when Ray Bradbury was writing *Fahrenheit 451* (Vol. 1), the threat of Nazi domination had recently ended in Europe, and the Mc-Carthy hearings were taking place in Washington, D.C. This information goes far in answering the question, "Why did he write a story of oppressive government control and book burning?" Similarly, it is important to know that Harper Lee, author of *To Kill a Mockingbird,* was born and raised in Mon-

roeville, Alabama, and that her father was a lawyer. Readers can now see why she chose the south as a setting for her novel—it is the place with which she was most familiar—and start to comprehend her characters and their actions.

Novels for Students helps readers find the answers they seek when they establish a dialogue with a particular novel. It also aids in the posing of questions by providing the opinions and interpretations of various critics and reviewers, broadening that dialogue. Some reviewers of *To Kill A Mockingbird,* for example, "faulted the novel's climax as melodramatic." This statement leads readers to ask, "Is it, indeed, melodramatic?" "If not, why did some reviewers see it as such?" "If it is, why did Lee choose to make it melodramatic?" "Is melodrama ever justified?" By being spurred to ask these questions, readers not only learn more about the book and its writer, but about the nature of writing itself.

The literature included for discussion in the *Novels for Students* series has been chosen because it has something vital to say to us. *Of Mice and Men, Catch-22, The Joy Luck Club, My Antonia, A Separate Peace* and the other novels here speak of life and modern sensibility. In addition to their individual, specific messages of prejudice, power, love or hate, living and dying, however, they and all great literature also share a common intent. They force us to *think*—about life, literature, and about others, not just about ourselves. They pry us from the narrow confines of our minds and thrust us outward to confront the world of books and the larger, real world we all share. *Novels for Students* helps us in this confrontation by providing the means of enriching our conversation with literature and the world, by creating an *informed* dialogue, one that brings true pleasure to the personal act of reading.

Sources

Harold Bloom, *The Western Canon, The Books and School of the Ages,* Riverhead Books, 1994.

Watty Piper, *The Little Engine That Could,* Platt & Munk, 1930.

Anne Devereaux Jordan
Senior Editor, *TALL*
(*Teaching and Learning Literature*)

Introduction

Purpose of the Book

The purpose of *Novels for Students* (*NfS*) is to provide readers with a guide to understanding, enjoying, and studying novels by giving them easy access to information about the work. Part of Gale's "For Students" Literature line, *NfS* is specifically designed to meet the curricular needs of high school and undergraduate college students and their teachers, as well as the interests of general readers and researchers considering specific novels. While each volume contains entries on "classic" novels frequently studied in classrooms, there are also entries containing hard-to-find information on contemporary novels, including works by multicultural, international, and women novelists.

The information covered in each entry includes an introduction to the novel and the novel's author; a plot summary, to help readers unravel and understand the events in a novel; descriptions of important characters, including explanation of a given character's role in the novel as well as discussion about that character's relationship to other characters in the novel; analysis of important themes in the novel; and an explanation of important literary techniques and movements as they are demonstrated in the novel.

In addition to this material, which helps the readers analyze the novel itself, students are also provided with important information on the literary and historical background informing each work. This includes a historical context essay, a box comparing the time or place the novel was written to modern Western culture, a critical overview essay, and excerpts from critical essays on the novel. A unique feature of *NfS* is a specially commissioned overview essay on each novel by an academic expert, targeted toward the student reader.

To further aid the student in studying and enjoying each novel, information on media adaptations is provided, as well as reading suggestions for works of fiction and nonfiction on similar themes and topics. Classroom aids include ideas for research papers and lists of critical sources that provide additional material on the novel.

Selection Criteria

The titles for each volume of *NfS* were selected by surveying numerous sources on teaching literature and analyzing course curricula for various school districts. Some of the sources surveyed included: literature anthologies; *Reading Lists for College-Bound Students: The Books Most Recommended by America's Top Colleges;* textbooks on teaching the novel; a College Board survey of novels commonly studied in high schools; a National Council of Teachers of English (NCTE) survey of novels commonly studied in high schools; the NCTE's *Teaching Literature in High School: The Novel;* and the Young Adult Library Services Association (YALSA) list of best books for young adults of the past twenty-five years.

Input was also solicited from our expert advisory board, as well as educators from various areas. From these discussions, it was determined that each volume should have a mix of "classic" novels (those works commonly taught in literature classes) and contemporary novels for which information is often hard to find. Because of the interest in expanding the canon of literature, an emphasis was also placed on including works by international, multicultural, and women authors. Our advisory board members—current high school teachers—helped pare down the list for each volume. If a work was not selected for the present volume, it was often noted as a possibility for a future volume. As always, the editor welcomes suggestions for titles to be included in future volumes.

How Each Entry Is Organized

Each entry, or chapter, in *NfS* focuses on one novel. Each entry heading lists the full name of the novel, the author's name, and the date of the novel's publication. The following elements are contained in each entry:

- Introduction: a brief overview of the novel which provides information about its first appearance, its literary standing, any controversies surrounding the work, and major conflicts or themes within the work.

- Author Biography: this section includes basic facts about the author's life, and focuses on events and times in the author's life that inspired the novel in question.

- Plot Summary: a description of the major events in the novel, with interpretation of how these events help articulate the novel's themes. Lengthy summaries are broken down with subheads.

- Characters: an alphabetical listing of major characters in the novel. Each character name is followed by a brief to an extensive description of the character's role in the novel, as well as discussion of the character's actions, relationships, and possible motivation.

Characters are listed alphabetically by last name. If a character is unnamed—for instance, the narrator in *Invisible Man* the character is listed as "The Narrator" and alphabetized as "Narrator." If a character's first name is the only one given, the name will appear alphabetically by the name. Variant names are also included for each character. Thus, the full name "Jean Louise Finch" would head the listing for the narrator of *To Kill a Mockingbird,* but listed in a separate cross-reference would be the nickname "Scout Finch."

- Themes: a thorough overview of how the major topics, themes, and issues are addressed within the novel. Each theme discussed appears in a separate subhead, and is easily accessed through the boldface entries in the Subject/Theme Index.

- Style: this section addresses important style elements of the novel, such as setting, point of view, and narration; important literary devices used, such as imagery, foreshadowing, symbolism; and, if applicable, genres to which the work might have belonged, such as Gothicism or Romanticism. Literary terms are explained within the entry, but can also be found in the Glossary.

- Historical and Cultural Context: This section outlines the social, political, and cultural climate *in which the author lived and the novel was created.* This section may include descriptions of related historical events, pertinent aspects of daily life in the culture, and the artistic and literary sensibilities of the time in which the work was written. If the novel is a historical work, information regarding the time in which the novel is set is also included. Each section is broken down with helpful subheads.

- Critical Overview: this section provides background on the critical reputation of the novel, including bannings or any other public controversies surrounding the work. For older works, this section includes a history of how novel was first received and how perceptions of it may have changed over the years; for more recent novels, direct quotes from early reviews may also be included.

- Sources: an alphabetical list of critical material quoted in the entry, with full bibliographical information.

- For Further Study: an alphabetical list of other critical sources which may prove useful for the student. Includes full bibliographical information and a brief annotation.

- Criticism: an essay commissioned by *NfS* which specifically deals with the novel and is written specifically for the student audience, as well as excerpts from previously published criticism on the work.

In addition, each entry contains the following highlighted sections, set apart from the main text as sidebars:

- Media Adaptations: a list of important film and television adaptations of the novel, including source information. The list also includes stage adaptations, audio recordings, musical adaptations, etc.

- Compare and Contrast Box: an "at-a-glance" comparison of the cultural and historical differences between the author's time and culture and late twentieth-century Western culture. This box includes pertinent parallels between the major scientific, political, and cultural movements of the time or place the novel was written, the time or place the novel was set (if a historical work), and modern Western culture. Works written after the mid-1970s may not have this box.

- What Do I Read Next?: a list of works that might complement the featured novel or serve as a contrast to it. This includes works by the same author and others, works of fiction and nonfiction, and works from various genres, cultures, and eras.

• Study Questions: a list of potential study questions or research topics dealing with the novel. This section includes questions related to other disciplines the student may be studying, such as American history, world history, science, math, government, business, geography, economics, psychology, etc.

Other Features

NfS includes "The Informed Dialogue: Interacting with Literature," a foreword by Anne Devereaux Jordan, Senior Editor for *Teaching and Learning Literature (TALL)*, and a founder of the Children's Literature Association. This essay provides an enlightening look at how readers interact with literature and how *Novels for Students* can help teachers show students how to enrich their own reading experiences.

A Cumulative Author/Title Index lists the authors and titles covered in each volume of the *NfS* series.

A Cumulative Nationality/Ethnicity Index breaks down the authors and titles covered in each volume of the *NfS* series by nationality and ethnicity.

A Subject/Theme Index, specific to each volume, provides easy reference for users who may be studying a particular subject or theme rather than a single work. Significant subjects from events to broad themes are included, and the entries pointing to the specific theme discussions in each entry are indicated in **boldface.**

Each entry has several illustrations, including photos of the author, stills from film adaptations (when available), maps, and/or photos of key historical events.

Citing Novels for Students

When writing papers, students who quote directly from any volume of *Novels for Students* may use the following general forms. These examples are based on MLA style; teachers may request that students adhere to a different style, so the following examples may be adapted as needed.

When citing text from *NfS* that is not attributed to a particular author (i.e., the Themes, Style,

Historical Context sections, etc.), the following format should be used in the bibliography section:

"Night." *Novels for Students*. Eds. Sheryl Ciccarelli and Marie Rose Napierkowski. Vol. 5. Detroit: Gale, 1998. 34–5.

When quoting the specially commissioned essay from *NfS* (usually the first piece under the "Criticism" subhead), the following format should be used:

Miller, Tyrus. Essay on "Winesburg, Ohio." *Novels for Students*. Eds. Sheryl Ciccarelli and Marie Rose Napierkowski. Vol. 5. Detroit: Gale, 1997. 218–9.

When quoting a journal or newspaper essay that is reprinted in a volume of *NfS,* the following form may be used:

Malak, Amin. "Margaret Atwood's The Handmaid's Tale' and the Dystopian Tradition," in *Canadian Literature* , No. 112, Spring, 1987, 9–16; excerpted and reprinted in *Novels for Students,* Vol. 5, eds. Sheryl Ciccarelli and Marie Rose Napierkowski (Detroit: Gale, 1998), pp. 61–64.

When quoting material reprinted from a book that appears in a volume of *NfS,* the following form may be used:

Adams, Timothy Dow. "Richard Wright: Wearing the Mask," in *Telling Lies in Modern American Autobiography* (University of North Carolina Press, 1990), 69–83; excerpted and reprinted in *Novels for Students,* Vol. 5, eds. Sheryl Ciccarelli and Marie Napierkowski (Detroit: Gale, 1999), pp. 59–61.

We Welcome Your Suggestions

The editor of *Novels for Students* welcomes your comments and ideas. Readers who wish to suggest novels to appear in future volumes, or who have other suggestions, are cordially invited to contact the editor. You may contact the editor via e-mail at: **CYA@gale.com@galesmtp.** Or write to the editor at:

Editor, *Novels for Students*
The Gale Group
27500 Drake Rd.
Farmington Hills, MI 48331–3535

Literary Chronology

1802: Victor Hugo is born on February 26, 1802, to Joseph-Léopold-Sigisbert and Sophie-Françoise Trébuchet Hugo, in Besançon, France.

1812: Charles Dickens is born February 7, 1812, at Portsea near Rochester, England.

1848: After a struggle between the working class and the middle-class government, King Louis Philippe flees his throne and the Second Republic is established with a president and a predominately middle-class national assembly. Victor Hugo is a representative on the assembly but soon becomes disillusioned when the people vote to disband the republic and the president becomes a dictator. After criticizing the government and the president publicly, he is forced to leave France. Hugo writes *Les Misérables* during his exile.

1859: Charles Dickens's *A Tale of Two Cities* appears in weekly parts from April 20, 1859 through November 26, 1859, in a new periodical called *All the Year Round*.

1862: Edith Wharton is born on January 24, 1862.

1862: Victor Hugo completes *Les Misérables* on June 30, 1861. Hugo is considered one of the leading writers of the Romantic movement in France, and *Les Misérables* is one of his major works.

1870: Charles Dickens dies of a stroke on June 9, 1870. He is buried in Westminster Abbey on June 14, 1870. *The Mystery of Edwin Drood* is left unfinished.

1876: O. E. Rölvaag is born April 2, 1876, on Dönna Island off the coast of Norway.

1885: Victor Hugo dies of pneumonia in May, 1885, in Paris, France. He is given a state funeral and buried in the Pantheon on May 31, 1885.

1899: Ernest Hemingway is born in Oak Park, Illinois.

1902: John Steinbeck is born in 1902 in Salinas, California.

1911: Edith Wharton's popular novel *Ethan Frome* is published.

1921: Edith Wharton receives a Pulitzer Prize for her novel *The Age of Innocence*.

1926: Ernest Hemingway's novel *The Sun Also Rises* is published.

1927: O. E. Rölvaag's *Giants in the Earth* is published in America in English translation. The original Norwegian version first appeared in Norway in 1924 as *I de dage*.

1928: Gabriel García Márquez is born March 6, 1928, in Aracataca, Colombia.

1928: Philip K. Dick is born December 16, 1928, in Chicago, Illinois.

1928: In October, 1928, a large group of striking banana workers are fired upon by United Fruit Company troops; some estimates suggest four hundred deaths, although the government officially denies the event ever happened. This massacre plays a pivotal role in Gabriel García Márquez's novel *One Hundred Years of Solitude.*

1931: O. E. Rölvaag dies.

1933: Ernest J. Gaines is born on January 15, 1933, to Mauel and Adrienne J. Colar Gaines, in Point Coupée Parish, Oscar, Louisiana.

1937: Edith Wharton dies of a heart attack on August 11, 1937, in St. Brice-sous-Fort, France.

1944: Alice Walker is born in Eatonton, Georgia, on February 9, 1944.

1947: John Steinbeck's *The Pearl* is published.

1950: Julia Alvarez is born on March 27, 1950, in New York City. She is raised in the Dominican Republic, however, and does not return to New York until 1960.

1950: Susan Eloise Hinton is born in Tulsa, Oklahoma, in 1950.

1951: Orson Scott Card is born on August 24, 1951, in Richland, Washington.

1954: Ernest Hemingway receives the Nobel Prize for Literature in 1954.

1954: Louise Erdrich is born on June 6, 1954, in Little Falls, Minnesota.

1955: Barbara Kingsolver is born in 1955, in Annapolis, Maryland.

1961: Ernest Hemingway dies of a self-inflicted gunshot wound at his home in Ketchum, Idaho on July 2, 1961.

1962: John Steinbeck wins the Nobel Prize for Literature, which recognizes an author whose complete work is of the most distinguished idealistic nature in the field of literature.

1967: Gabriel García Márquez's *Cien años de soledad* is published in 1967; it is translated into English as *One Hundred Years of Solitude.*

1967: Seventeen-year-old S. E. Hinton publishes her first novel, *The Outsiders.*

1968: John Steinbeck dies of a severe heart attack in New York City on December 20, 1968.

1968: Philip K. Dick's novel *Do Androids Dream of Electric Sheep?* is published by Doubleday in 1968.

1971: Ernest Gaines' *The Autobiography of Miss Jane Pittman* is published. In the novel, Gaines portrays the history of African Americans, from slavery to the civil rights movement of the 1960s.

1975: Orson Scott Card publishes the original novella of "Ender's Game" in the science fiction magazine *Analog.*

1982: Philip K. Dick dies of heart failure following a stroke on March 2, 1982.

1982: Gabriel García Márquez is awarded the Nobel Prize for Literature in 1982; *One Hundred Years of Solitude* receives special mention in the Nobel committee's citation.

1982: Alice Walker's *The Color Purple* is published.

1982: The groundbreaking film *Blade Runner,* based on Philip K. Dick's novel *Do Androids Dream of Electric Sheep?,* is released in 1982.

1983: Alice Walker wins the Pulitzer Prize for *The Color Purple.*

1984: Louise Erdrich's *Love Medicine* is published.

1984: Louise Erdrich receives a National Book Critics Circle Award for *Love Medicine* in 1984.

1985: Orson Scott Card publishes the novel *Ender's Game,* expanded and developed from his 1975 novella.

1985: Orson Scott Card's novel *Ender's Game* wins the Nebula Award, given by the Science Fiction Writers of America.

1986: Orson Scott Card's novel *Ender's Game* wins the Hugo Award, given by a vote of fans at the World Science Fiction Convention.

1988: The American Library Association recognizes S. E. Hinton with their first Margaret Edwards Young Adult Author Achievement Award, given for lifetime achievement.

1988: Barbara Kingsolver's novel *The Bean Trees* is published.

1989: Laura Esquivel's first novel, *Como agua para chocolate,* is published in Mexico. It is translated in English as *Like Water for Chocolate* in 1991.

1991: Julia Alvarez's first novel, *How the García Girls Lost Their Accents,* is published by Algonquin Books.

1993: The film version of Laura Esquivel's *Like Water for Chocolate,* filmed by her husband Alfonso Arau from her own screenplay, is released in 1993. It becomes one of the most successful foreign films in the U.S. in the 1990s.

Acknowledgments

The editors wish to thank the copyright holders of the excerpted criticism included in this volume and the permissions managers of many book and magazine publishing companies for assisting us in securing reproduction rights. We are also grateful to the staffs of the Detroit Public Library, the Library of Congress, the University of Detroit Mercy Library, Wayne State University Purdy/Kresge Library Complex, and the University of Michigan Libraries for making their resources available to us. Following is a list of the copyright holders who have granted us permission to reproduce material in this volume of *NfS*. Every effort has been made to trace copyright, but if omissions have been made, please let us know.

COPYRIGHTED EXCERPTS IN *NFS*, VOLUME 5, WERE REPRODUCED FROM THE FOLLOWING PERIODICALS:

American Book Review, v. 14, August-September, 1992. © 1992 by The American Book Review. Reproduced by permission.

American Literature, v. 67, March, 1995. Copyright © 1995 Duke University Press, Durham, NC. Reproduced by permission.

Books Abroad, v. 47, Summer, 1973. Copyright © 1973 by the University of Oklahoma Press. Reproduced by permission.

Commonweal, v. CXIX, April 10, 1992. Copyright © 1992 Commonweal Publishing Co., Inc. Reproduced by permission of Commonweal Foundation.

Critical Survey, v. 3, 1991. Reproduced by permission.

Dickens Studies Annual, v. I, 1970. Copyright © 1970 by Southern Illinois University Press. All rights reserved. Reproduced by permission of AMS Press, Inc.

English Journal, v. 54, January, 1965. Copyright © 1965 by the National Council of Teachers of English. Reproduced by permission of the publisher and the author.

Extrapolation, v. 32, Summer, 1991. Copyright © 1991 by The Kent State University Press. Reproduced by permission.

Journal of American Culture, v. 18, Winter, 1995. Reproduced by permission.

The Midwest Quarterly, v. XXX, Summer, 1989. Copyright © 1989 by The Midwest Quarterly, Pittsburg State University. Reproduced by permission.

Modern Fiction Studies, v. XIV, Autumn, 1968; v. 26, Summer, 1990. Copyright © 1968, 1990 by Purdue Research Foundation, West Lafayette, IN 47907. All rights reserved. Both reproduced by permission of The Johns Hopkins University.

The Nation, New York, v. 235, September 4, 1982. Copyright 1982 *The Nation* magazine/The Nation Company, Inc. Reproduced by permission.

North Dakota Quarterly, v. 48, Autumn, 1980. Copyright 1980 by The University of North Dakota. Reproduced by permission.

Publishers Weekly, v. 243, December 16, 1996. Copyright 1996 by Reed Publishing USA. Reproduced from *Publishers Weekly,* published by the Bowker Magazine Group of Cahners Publishing Co., a division of Reed Publishing USA.

Studies in American Fiction, v. 7, Autumn, 1979; v. 14, Spring, 1986. Copyright © 1979, 1986 Northeastern University. Both reproduced by permission.

Studies in American Indian Literature, v. 4, Spring, 1992 for "Love Medicine: A Metaphor for Forgiveness," by Lissa Schneider. Reproduced by permission of the author.

Studies in Twentieth Century Literature, v. 20, Winter, 1996. Copyright © 1996 by Studies in Twentieth Century Literature. Reproduced by permission.

World Literature Today, v. 69, Winter, 1995. Copyright © 1995 by the University of Oklahoma Press. Reproduced by permission.

COPYRIGHTED EXCERPTS IN *NFS*, VOLUME 5, WERE REPRODUCED FROM THE FOLLOWING BOOKS:

Babb, Valerie Melissa. From *Ernest Gaines.* Twayne Publishers, 1991. Copyright © 1991 by G. K. Hall & Co. Excerpted with permission of Twayne Publishers, an imprint of Simon & Schuster Macmillan.

Daly, Jay. From *Presenting S. E. Hinton.* Twayne Publishers, 1987. Copyright © 1987 by Jay Daly. Excerpted with permission of Twayne Publishers, an imprint of Simon & Schuster Macmillan.

Gwaltney, Marilyn. From *Retrofitting "Blade Runner": Issues in Ridley Scott's "Blade Runner"* and Philip K. Dick's *Do Androids Dream of Electric Sheep?".* Edited by Judith B. Kerman. Bowling Green State University Popular Press, 1991. Copyright © 1991 by Bowling Green State University Popular Press. Reproduced by permission.

Sagarin, Edward. From *Raskolnikov and Others: Literary Images of Crime, Punishment, Redemption, and Atonement.* St. Martin's Press, 1981. Copyright © 1981 by St. Martin's Press, Inc. All rights reserved. Reprinted with permission of Bedford/St. Martin's Press, Inc.

Simmons, John S. From *Censored Books: Critical Viewpoints.* Edited by Nicholas J. Karolides, Lee Burress, and John M. Kean. The Scarecrow Press, Inc., 1993. Copyright © 1993 by Nicholas J. Karolides, Lee Burress, and John M. Kean. Reproduced by permission.

PHOTOGRAPHS AND ILLUSTRATIONS APPEARING IN *NFS*, VOLUME 5, WERE RECEIVED FROM THE FOLLOWING SOURCES:

AP/WIDE WORLD PHOTOS: Gaines, Ernest J. (wearing beret), 1993, photograph by Alex Brandon. AP/Wide World Photos. Reproduced by permission.—Kingsolver, Barbara, photograph. AP/Wide World Photos. Reproduced by permission.—Marquez, Gabriel Garcia, photograph. AP/Wide World Photos. Reproduced by permission.—Walker, Alice (sitting in a gilded Louis XV style chair), photograph. AP/Wide World Photos. Reproduced by permission.—Wharton, Edith, photograph. AP/Wide World Photos. Reproduced by permission.

ARCHIVE PHOTOS: Bay Beach, Mexico, photograph. Archive Photos, Inc. Reproduced by permission.—De Ubrique, Jesulin (biting horn of bull), photograph. Archive Photos, Inc. Reproduced by permission.—Emigrants camp, illustration. Archive Photos, Inc. Reproduced by permission.—Goldberg, Whoopi and Margaret Avery in the 1985 motion picture "The Color Purple," photograph. Archive Photos/Warner Bros. Reproduced by permission.—Massachussets in the winter, photograph. Archive Photos, Inc. Reproduced by permission.—Snow covered mountains (reflecting off body of water), Norway, photograph. Archive Photos, Inc. Reproduced by permission.—Tyson, Cicely, in the 1974 television movie "The Autobiography of Miss Jane Pittman," photograph. Archive Photos, Inc. Reproduced by permission.—Villa, Pancho, (seated on horse, sideways), photograph. Archive Photos, Inc. Reproduced by permission.

JERRY BAUER: Erdrich, Louise (standing in front of a tree, wearing a turtle broach), photograph by Jerry Bauer. Reproduced by permission.—Esquivel, Laura, photograph. © Jerry Bauer. Reproduced by permission.

CARROLL & GRAF: From a cover of *Time Out of Joint,* by Philip K. Dick. Carroll & Graf Publishers, Inc., 1987. Reproduced by permission.

CHAPMAN AND HALL: Browne, H. K., illustrator. From a cover of *A Tale of Two Cities* by Charles Dickens. Chapman and Hall, 1859.

CORBIS-BETTMAN: Black man drinking water at "colored" water cooler, 1939, photograph. Corbis-Bettmann. Reproduced by permission.—"Conquerors of the Bastille," engraving after a painting by Francois Flamena. Corbis-Bettmann. Reproduced by permission.—Dickens, Charles, photograph. Corbis-Bettmann. Reproduced by permission.—Hemingway, Ernest, photograph. Corbis-Bettmann. Reproduced by permission.—Rolvaag, O. E. (wearing black rimmed glasses, tweed jacket), photograph. Corbis-Bettmann. Reproduced by permission.

WILLIAM EICHNER: Alvarez, Julia (dark, sleeveless dress), photograph by Sara Eichner. Reproduced by permission of William Eichner.

FIELD MARK PUBLICATIONS: Saguaro cacti, tall, columnar, candelabra-type cacti, hill in background, photograph by Robert J. Huffman. Field Mark Publications. Reproduced by permission.

FRENCH EMBASSY PRESS: Hugo, Victor (facing left, beard), drawing, French Embassy Press and Information Division.

GALE RESEARCH: Dominican Republic, map by Cartesia Software. Gale Research.

JAY KAY KLEIN: Card, Orson Scott (wearing square tinted glasses), photograph by Jay Kay Klein. Reproduced by permission.

THE KOBAL COLLECTION: Cavazos, Lumi, (holding baby in arms), starring in Alfonso Arau's film "Like Water for Chocolate," photograph. The Kobal Collection. Reproduced by permission.—Cavazos, Lumi with Marco Leonardi, (noses touching), starring in Alfonso Arau's "Like Water for Chocolate," photograph. The Kobal Collection. Reproduced by permission.—Estevez, Emilio, with Rob Lowe, C. Thomas Howell, Matt Dillon, Ralph Macchio, Patrick Swayze, and Tom Cruise, standing in group, in the film "The Outsiders," photograph. The Kobal Collection. Reproduced by permission.—Flynn, Errol, with Ava Gardner, Tyrone Power, Mel Ferrer and Eddie Albert, (at a busy cafe), in the film "The Sun Also Rises," pho-

tograph. The Kobal Collection. Reproduced by permission.—Ford, Harrison, (holding and aiming gun), in the film "Bladerunner," photograph. The Kobal Collection. Reproduced by permission.—Howell, C. Thomas, with Tom Cruise and Emilio Estevez, starring in the film "The Outsiders," photograph. The Kobal Collection. Reproduced by permission.—March, Frederic, in the film "Les Miserables," 1935, photograph. The Kobal Collection. Reproduced by permission.—Neeson, Liam (carrying sled), with Patricia Arquette, starring in the film "Ethan Frome," photograph. The Kobal Collection. Reproduced by permission.—Neeson, Liam with Patricia Arquette (holding each other), starring in the film "Ethan Frome," photograph. The Kobal Collection. Reproduced by permission.

LIBRARY OF CONGRESS: Steinbeck, John (herringbone jacket, plaid bow tie), photograph. The Library of Congress.—Trujillo Molina, Rafael (framed, with flag and shield), photograph. The Library of Congress.

NATIONAL ARCHIVES: Typical Chippewa Indian home, photograph. National Archives (NRE-75-MAO(PHO)-40).

SPRINGER/CORBIS-BETTMAN: Coleman, Ronald, in the film "A Tale of Two Cities," 1935, photograph. Springer/Corbis-Bettmann. Reproduced by permission.

UNITED NATIONS: Men packing bananas for shipment, Ecuador, photograph. United Nations. Reproduced by permission.

UPI/CORBIS-BETTMAN: King, Martin Luther, Coretta King, Ralph Bunche and Ralph Abernathy (starting last leg of Selma to Montgomery March), 1965, photograph. UPI/Corbis-Bettmann. Reproduced by permission.

THOMAS VICTOR: Hinton, S.E., photograph by Thomas Victor. Reproduced by permission.

Contributors

Margara Averbach: Writer and translator with a doctorate from the University of Buenos Aires. Original essay on *The Color Purple*.

Betsy Currier Beacom: Freelance writer, North Haven, CT. Entry on *The Bean Trees*.

Anne-Sophie Cerisola: Instructor at New York University. Original essay on *Les Misérables*.

Jane Dougherty: Freelance writer, Medford, MA. Original essay on *The Outsiders*.

Logan Esdale: Doctoral candidate, State University of New York at Buffalo. Original entry on *The Bean Trees*.

Darren Felty: Visiting instructor, College of Charleston (SC); Ph.D. in Literature, University of Georgia. Original essay on *Giants in the Earth*.

George V. Griffith: Professor of English and philosophy at Chadron State College in Chadron, Nebraska. Original essay on *A Tale of Two Cities*.

Diane Andrews Henningfeld: Professor of English, Adrian College (MI). Original essay on *One Hundred Years of Solitude*.

Jeremy W. Hubbell: Freelance writer, Minneapolis, MN. Entries on *The Autobiography of Miss Jane Pittman, Do Androids Dream of Electric Sheep?, One Hundred Years of Solitude, The Pearl, The Outsiders* and *The Sun Also Rises*.

Jeaninne Johnson: Doctoral candidate at Yale University. Original essay on *The Autobiography of Miss Jane Pittman*.

David J. Kelly: Professor of English, College of Lake County (IL). Original essays on *Do Androids Dream of Electric Sheep?* and *Ender's Game*.

Jeffrey M. Lilburn: Writer and translator specializing in twentieth-century American and Canadian literature; M.A., University of Western Ontario. Original essay on *The Sun Also Rises* and *Ethan Frome*.

Elyse Lord: Doctoral candidate in English, University of Utah; visiting instructor, University of Utah and Salt Lake City Community College. Original essay on *The Bean Trees* and *The Pearl*.

Nancy C. McClure: Educational consultant and freelance writer, Clarksburg, WV; Ed.D, West Virginia University. Entry on *Ender's Game* and *Love Medicine*.

Gail Nelson: Freelance writer and editor, San Francisco, CA; M.A., University of Chicago. Entry on *Les Misérables*.

Wendy Perkins: Assistant Professor of English, Prince George's Community College, Maryland; Ph.D. in English, University of Delaware. Original essays and entries on *How the García Girls Lost Their Accents* and *Like Water for Chocolate*.

Vita Richman: Freelance editor and writer, Phoenix, AZ. Entry on *The Color Purple*.

Ken Shepherd: Freelance writer and editor, Wyandotte, MI. Entry on *A Tale of Two Cities*.

Giselle Weiss: Freelance writer, Basel, Switzerland. Entries on *Ethan Frome* and *Giants in the Earth*.

Donna Woodford: Doctoral candidate, Washington University, St. Louis, MO. Original essay on *Love Medicine*.

The Autobiography of Miss Jane Pittman

Ernest J. Gaines
1971

Heralded by some as the best African American author writing in America today, Ernest James Gaines is best known and celebrated for his novel *The Autobiography of Miss Jane Pittman.* As a black writer, Gaines has taken full advantage of African American culture by writing stories about rural Louisiana. In doing so, Gaines has made himself a "country-boy writer" of folk tales more grown than made. These stories tell of the struggles of blacks to make a living in a land that has not championed the rights of all its people.

The story of Miss Jane Pittman is a supposed interview with a woman who is 110 years old. She has witnessed and been a part of the history of black America since the end of the Civil War. She tells her story to the persistent recorder in her own words and with humor. This "editor" admits that he restructured the narrative so it would be more accessible to a novel reader but he tried to maintain, as much as possible, her voice. A triumph in American literature, the subject of the novel has been taken to the heart of its readers, and was made into an Emmy Award-winning television movie.

Author Biography

Amid the worst times of the Great Depression, Ernest James Gaines was born on a plantation in Oscar, Louisiana, in 1933. At the age of nine, he joined his parents in the field and dug potatoes for

Ernest J. Gaines

fifty cents a day. During this time on the plantation he was heavily influenced by his aunt, Augustine Jefferson. She had no legs but was still able to care for him and other members of the family. It was this aunt who took care of laundry and cooking for the family, even though she had to crawl to perform her chores. She became the model for many of the women in Gaines's novels, such as the title character of *The Autobiography of Miss Jane Pittman,* whose faith and self-sacrifice would enable the next generation to have a better life.

At the age of fifteen, Gaines was taken by his mother and stepfather to Vallejo, California. This was a fortunate move for a boy who was to become a writer. The education to be gained in the Californian school system was better than that on the Oscar plantation, and the library, his favorite retreat, was open to readers of all races. But the books he found did not include rural black people as subjects or authors. He read the next best thing—stories of Russian peasants and immigrants. But while their history paralleled the plight of Southern black slaves, he knew that African Americans had tales of their own, since members of his family were constantly telling stories. Gaines began writing to fill those gaps on the library shelves.

At the age of seventeen, he naively sent his first novel to a publisher, but it was returned. Not easily discouraged, he continued to write. He also read extensively. Some of his favorite writers included Russian author Ivan Turgenev, as well as Americans Willa Cather, William Faulkner (to whom he is sometimes compared), and Ernest Hemingway. His diligence paid off when he met with his first success. In 1956, while a student at San Francisco State College, he published a short story in a small literary magazine called *Transfer.* With this encouragement, he graduated from college, won a Wallace Stegner fellowship and went on to study creative writing at Stanford University from 1958–1959.

He reworked the rejected novel he wrote at the age of seventeen and in 1964 published the work as *Catherine Carmier.* Although the novel was not a critical or financial success, Gaines found his voice for future works. That voice was centered on the world of the plantation and its effect on the creation of black culture. "We cannot ignore that rural past or those older people in it. Their stories are the kind I want to write about. I am what I am today because of them," he said in an interview in 1977.

Having found his voice, his 1967 novel, *Of Love and Dust,* brought him recognition. Four years later, *Miss Jane Pittman* established Gaines as a literary master of American fiction. Since then, he has won numerous awards, including a National Books Critic Circle Award and a MacArthur "genius" grant, and has published several collections of short stories and several novels. A writer in residence at the University of Southern Louisiana, Gaines lives with his wife in San Francisco but makes frequent trips to Louisiana.

Plot Summary

Introduction

The Autobiography of Miss Jane Pittman follows the life of one woman from her emancipation as a slave in the 1860s to her initiation into the Civil Rights Movement of the early 1960s. A work of historical fiction, the *Autobiography of Miss Jane Pittman* takes place in rural Louisiana. It opens with an encounter between the ostensible "editor" of the novel, a high school history teacher, and Miss Jane Pittman, a woman who is about 110 years old. He wants to use her life story to teach his students history as it has affected real people. The editor attests that he has tried to reproduce Jane's story in her own words, and the rest of the novel is narrated from her point of view.

Book I: The War Years

A Union Army corporal and his company stop at the Louisiana plantation on which "Ticey," as Jane is called until she is about eleven years old, is enslaved. (As a slave girl whose parents died when she was very young, Jane is not sure when she was born.) The corporal renames Ticey "Jane Brown," after his own daughter, and thereafter Jane refuses to respond to her original slave name.

A year later, at the end of the Civil War, Jane and some of the other former slaves head north. They run into "patrollers," white men who tracked escaped slaves during the war and returned them to their masters. The patrollers murder everyone in the party but Janc and a young boy named Ned. Though Jane is perhaps only eight years older than Ned, she takes responsibility for him as if she were his mother. Jane gathers up some food, and charges Ned to carry a flint and iron, two small rocklike tools for starting a fire.

The two of them continue to travel toward what Jane hopes is Ohio, but they never make it out of Louisiana. They are fed and aided by several people, black and white, friendly and unfriendly. At one point, they meet a hunter:

> "Who was them other people you seen?" I asked him. "Any of them going to Ohio?"
>
> "They was going everywhere," he said. "Some say Ohio, some say Kansas—some say Canada. Some of them even said Luzana and Mi'sippi."
>
> "Luzana and Mi'sippi ain't North," I said.
>
> "That's right, it ain't North," the hunter said. "But they had left out just like you, a few potatoes and another old dress. No map, no guide, no nothing. Like freedom was a place coming to meet them half way. Well, it ain't coming to meet you. And it might not be there when you get there, either."
>
> "We ain't giving up," I said. "We done gone this far."

Tired and exhausted, Jane and Ned soon settle on a plantation owned by Mr. Bone.

Book II: Reconstruction

On Mr. Bone's plantation, Jane works clearing fields and pays for Ned, whom she now considers her own son, to attend school. For a short time, conditions improve slightly for Jane and the other slaves, but quickly worsen as economic instability and racist organizations come to dominate the South. When Colonel Dye takes over the plantation, Jane comments, "It was slavery again, all right." However, she no longer idealizes the North as a place of opportunity and equality for blacks. She continues to perform field work for Colonel Dye through Reconstruction, a period of about twelve years following the Civil War.

Ned changes his name to Ned Douglass, after the abolitionist and autobiographer Frederick Douglass. When he is about seventeen, Ned becomes an organizer for a group that encourages blacks to leave the South and helps them settle in the North. After he is threatened because of his work, Ned leaves for Kansas. Jane and Joe Pittman then commence a common-law marriage and move with Joe's two daughters to Mr. Clyde's ranch. Jane dreams for years that Joe will be killed trying to break a certain wild stallion. When one day she believes she sees that horse in the corral, she visits the hoo-doo woman (a kind of fortune-teller), who confirms that Jane's dream is accurate. Hoping to prevent disaster, Jane frees the stallion from the corral. However, all the men, including Joe, chase after it, and in the process, Joe is killed. Jane keeps the name Pittman in honor of Joe and moves again, settling near Bayonne.

In the year 1899, she is joined by Ned, now a teacher, and his wife and children. Ned ignites the anger of local white supremacists for speaking publicly about the necessity for black freedom and equality. They hire Albert Cluveau, a mercenary killer and Jane's fishing partner, to murder Ned. Neither Jane nor Ned's family can seek justice because the legal system is controlled by white hate groups. Cluveau dies ten years later, suffering violent hallucinations which he wrongly believes are caused by a curse put on him by Jane.

Book III: The Plantation

Though she wishes to relocate far away and escape her painful memories, Jane is persuaded to move eight miles to Samson, "because memories wasn't a place, memories was in the mind." She works in the fields and later in the main house of the Samson plantation. Jane joins the church and becomes a respected member of the community.

During her time at the Samson plantation, Jane witnesses the cruel fate of Timmy Henderson, the illegitimate black son of plantation owner Robert Samson. He is brought up to the house to be a riding companion for his younger half-brother, Tee Bob, and his father allows him to get away with all sorts of pranks as long as he shows proper respect to whites. When the plantation's white overseer, Tom Joe, begins beating Timmy after Tee Bob is thrown from a horse, Timmy talks back to him and accidentally knocks him over. Robert forces him to leave the ranch, even though his own wife argues Tom Joe should be punished instead. "You pinned medals on a white man when he beat a nigger for drawing back his hand," Robert argues.

Later Tee Bob, the only legitimate son and heir to the plantation, falls in love with Mary Agnes LeFabre, a mulatto schoolteacher. Knowing that social customs in the 1930s South would never permit an interracial marriage, Mary Agnes refuses Tee Bob's proposal. Distraught, Tee Bob commits suicide and Robert Samson blames Mary Agnes. Jules Raynard, a longtime family friend, prevents Robert from harming Mary Agnes and sees that she leaves town immediately.

Book IV: The Quarters

This book begins in the early 1940s, just after the birth of Jimmy Aaron. Jane moves out of the main house and back down to the "quarters," where the black sharecroppers live. Jane does not pay rent, but her house has no electricity and no running water. She, like many others in the parish, believes Jimmy to be "the One"—that is, a future leader of their African American community. As he grows up, they all take special care to instill in him high expectations for himself. Since Jane and many of her neighbors are illiterate, Jimmy writes letters for them. He also reads the comics and sports sections of the newspaper out loud to Jane. Jane's passion for listening to baseball games on the radio results in her being replaced as church mother.

Jimmy leaves Samson to attend school in New Orleans, and when he returns in the early 1960s, he tries to persuade Jane's community to join in some civil rights protests he has organized. Though only a few are inclined to join Jimmy, Robert Samson demands that anyone who participates in civil rights demonstrations leave the quarters (which are on his property).

Jimmy and his group determine to have a young mulatto girl arrested in the nearby city of Bayonne. The girl drinks water from a fountain reserved for whites and is arrested. A few days later, Jimmy and his group begin to protest the arrest by marching on the Bayonne courthouse. Jane, who is now well over one hundred years old, and several others from Samson start toward Bayonne to join the demonstration. Robert Samson intercepts them and tells them that Jimmy has been shot dead. Despite Jimmy's death, they are undeterred. Jane stares down Robert and continues past him with the others towards town.

Characters

Jimmy Aaron

The people in the quarters continually hope for a leader like Moses who will help them leave the plantation. By the time Jimmy Aaron is five or six years old, Jane and the others are already wondering if he is the "One." Jimmy's father is unknown and his mother left to find work in New Orleans shortly after his birth, so Jane and the other women of the quarters are his surrogate mothers. His love for reading and learning inspire the hope that he will be the "One." However, when he returns from schooling in New Orleans and asks the church members to begin demonstrating like Dr. Martin Luther King, they all but refuse. Jimmy is shot for his political activism but his death causes passive people like Jane to take a stand, and so she walks past Robert Samson.

Olivia Antoine

A woman from the plantation quarters who sells smalls items such as seeds and perfume around the parish. Since she has a car, she also runs errands for many of the older folk on the plantation. She takes young Jimmy with her on her runs when he is young, and she says she wishes he was her own son. When Jimmy organizes the demonstration at the courthouse in Bayonne, Olivia volunteers to drive everyone there and pay bus fare for those who cannot fit in her car.

Big Laura

A large woman known as Big Laura takes charge of the freed slaves who have struck out for the north. She carries her baby girl, pulls a little boy named Ned along by the hand, and still carries the most supplies of anyone. She keeps the group orderly and refuses to allow a boy to "stud," or rape, Jane. Consequently, Jane looks upon her as protector. Tragically, a group of Confederate soldiers, called "Secesh" (precursors of the KKK), massacre everyone in the group except Ned and Jane. Unable to bury Big Laura, Jane drapes her with clothing then quickly leaves taking Ned with her.

Harriet Black

See Black Harriet

Black Harriet

A very dark "Singalee" woman who is "queen" of the fields at the Samson plantation. When another worker, Katie Nelson, challenges her for the

Still from the 1974 movie The Autobiography of Miss Jane Pittman, *starring Cicely Tyson as Miss Jane Pittman.*

title, she enters into a "race" of digging up weeds. Harriet eventually cracks and begins digging up cotton instead of weeds. Tom Joe gives her a severe beating, and she is forced to leave.

Mr. Bone

Having failed to make much progress toward Ohio, the newly freed Jane ends up at Mr. Bone's plantation. Mr. Bone was put in charge of the plantation by the Union Soldiers as part of the Reconstruction of the South. He is involved in local politics and assists Republican (the antislavery party) candidates in their run for office. Unfortunately, his days at the plantation end when the federal government decides that Reconstruction has done enough. Mr. Bone gives the plantation back to Colonel Eugene I. Dye, but not before warning his workers that they should no longer count on the "Yankees" to care about their situation.

Etienne Bouie

A Creole yardman at the Samson plantation during Tee Bob's time, he is one of the older folks left on the plantation during Jimmy's time.

Media Adaptations

- *The Autobiography of Miss Jane Pittman* was adapted as a television drama in 1974 by Tracey Keenan for Tomorrow Entertainment Inc. The adaptation aired on CBS starring Cicely Tyson in the lead role. The drama was highly acclaimed and received nine Emmy awards. It is available on video through Prism Entertainment.

- The novel has also been recorded several times into audio-book format. The first time was in 1974 when Claudia McNeil read the work for Caedmon Records. Then in 1987, Roses Prichard read the work for Newport Beack Books on Tape. Most recently, Prince Frederick Recorded Books produced a reading by Lynn Thigpen in 1994.

Jane Brown

See Miss Jane Pittman

Mr. Brown

Ticey has been placed at the roadside to meet the Yankee soldiers and give them water. The soldier who speaks to her is Mr. Brown. He tells her that the Yankees are going to set them free and avenge the inhumanity of slavery. He also tells her that 'Ticey' is a slave name. He calls her Jane Brown in honor of his own daughter at home. This encounter causes Jane Brown to decide to go north in search of her namesake and to be free.

Ned Brown

When Ned's mother, Big Laura, is killed by the Secesh (a part of the Confederate Army), Jane gives him the two flint stones she used for making fire. He carries these in honor of his mother and follows Jane North. As Ned grows up, he goes to school and works for a local committee helping African Americans but he leaves when the Ku Klux Klan comes looking for him. He becomes a teacher, serves in the Army during the Cuban (also known as Spanish-American) war, and begins a family in Kansas.

Eventually he moves his family back to the South to be near Jane and to educate the children of former slaves so that they might have a better life than their parents. He also tries to spread the word about black politics—specifically the teachings of black abolitionist Frederick Douglass, whose name he has taken as his own. His rhetoric is uncompromising and sounds revolutionary to the rigid minds of both black and white folks. Inevitably, he is murdered, but his name takes on the aura of legend and a school for black children is built in his memory. Ned's story is one of Gaines's many pieces of anecdotal evidence that change, even though its slow, will always come.

Jimmy Caya

Jimmy hangs around Robert Samson's son Tee Bob because he wants to be accepted into the legitimate aristocracy. He is ashamed of his background as "white trash"—a distinction given to middle-class whites who have come to money late by working land. Jimmy rides from the University with Tee Bob and on one journey Tee Bob tells about his love for Mary Agnes LeFabre, a mixed-race Creole teacher. Jimmy tries to set Tee Bob straight on the rules of white and black in the South. This only infuriates Tee Bob. Later, when Tee Bob commits suicide, Jimmy tries to ingratiate himself with Raynard and Samson by blaming Mary. This backfires because of Tee Bob's letter. Consequently, Jimmy gains nothing but humiliation as he confesses his part in the matter to the sheriff.

Albert Cluveau

A white man, Albert is a contract killer for the area between Johnville and Bayonne. Strangely, he is a friend of Jane's. They fish together quite often, and he performs small chores for her while she sometime cooks for him. However, he talks endlessly about killing people. When Jane's foster son Ned arrives in the area and insists on pursuing his plan to build a schoolhouse for the children, Albert is asked to kill Ned. He tries to avoid the assignment and even warns Jane, but he eventually does the job because he doesn't want to be killed himself. However, he regrets having done so and tries to avoid Jane. Eventually their paths cross and Jane tells him he will not die pleasantly. From then on he leads an uneasy life. When death finally comes, his screams are heard all over the district.

Mr. Clyde

Mr. Clyde owns the ranch where Joe and Jane come to work after leaving Colonel Dye's plantation. He generously loans Joe the money to pay off Dye and is a fair employer, allowing Joe, who will become his Chief Breaker, to be his own boss.

Edward Stephen Douglass

See Ned Brown

Ned Douglass

See Ned Brown

Vivian Douglass

Vivian is Ned's supportive wife. She explains to Jane that she won't try to change his mind about lecturing because she knew before he started he might be killed. After his death, she wants to continue his work but Jane convinces her to take her family back to Kansas where it is safe.

Colonel Eugene I. Dye

As part of Reconstruction, the federal government agrees to withdraw Northern troops and give back land confiscated at the end of the Civil War. Consequently, Mr. Bone is replaced by the Colonel. "It was slavery again, all right," says Jane. To make matters even more difficult for Jane, the Colonel is a bit crazy. Jane and her husband, Joe Pittman, eventually leave his plantation, but only after paying the Colonel money he says he spent to get the Klan away from Joe.

Madame Eloise Gautier

Madame Gautier is a mulatto "hoo-doo" woman (a type of fortune-teller) from New Orleans. Jane visits her after the dreams she has of Joe's death prevent her from sleeping. Madame predicts Joe's death and gives Jane a powder to keep him away from the horse, but Jane doesn't trust it. Instead she frees the horse, setting in motion the events that lead to his death.

Sheriff Sam Guidry

The local sheriff, Guidry, "didn't ask you for information, he told you he wanted it." He views blacks and whites differently, and when Mary LeFabre is too upset to speak with him after Tee Bob's suicide, he starts slapping her around. Eventually he does accept Jules Raynard's version of events and allows Mary to leave town without violence.

Joe Hardy

The second teacher on the Samson plantation, Joe Hardy swindles extra pay from the plantation workers and tries to romance the older girls. He has to leave town after he wakes up Sheriff Guidry to complain of a beating he received from one girl's father.

Timmy Henderson

"Timmy was nigger," as Jane tells it, but everybody knew he was Robert Samson's son. Samson never denies the child is his, because Timmy looks and acts more like his father than Samson's legitimate son, Tee Bob. Samson allows Timmy to be more than "nigger" but less than white. He gives him the position of companion and stable hand to his younger brother Tee Bob. The half-brothers grow up as best friends, and together they pull pranks on the older people. Timmy is allowed to get away with his tricks as long as he defers to Tee Bob and shows respect to white people. Despite Timmy's privileges, "white trash" still want to be called "mister" by anyone with an ounce of black blood. One such person is Tom Joe, the white overseer on the plantation.

Tom Joe hates Timmy and wants any excuse to come at him. The excuse comes one day when Tee Bob is thrown from his horse and breaks his arm. Timmy carries him home and Tom Joe finds Tee Bob's injury enough to warrant a beating. Timmy can't quite avoid being whipped because Tom Joe is white, although he does insult the man. Afterwards, Timmy is forced to leave the plantation for his own safety. While Robert Samson provides him with money to travel, he won't protect him from white men like Tom Joe. Tee Bob doesn't understand why his beloved brother has to leave.

Mary Hodges

A constant companion of Jane during her old age, Mary Hodges is fiercely loyal and protective of her friend's health. She is suspicious of potentially harmful situations. We first encounter her as the "editor" tries to ask Jane to tell her story. At the end, Mary tries to convince Jane not to go to Jimmy's demonstration in Bayonne. Seeing Jane's determination, however, Mary finally accompanies her.

Hunter

The Hunter is a black man Jane and Ned meet in their first week on the road. He ridicules them for trying to reach Ohio, but he is also engaged in a similarly improbable quest to find his father.

Just Thomas

Just Thomas is the head deacon of the Samson plantation's black church. He demonstrates the conservative nature of the black church community, and adamantly resists the message Jimmy is trying to bring to the community. He and Jane argue over letting Jimmy speak. In resisting Jimmy, Just Thomas shows that those who put their trust in religion without also asserting their political rights—as the Reverend Martin Luther King does—do so in the belief that their reward will be greater in heaven.

Mary Agnes LeFabre

Mary Agnes is one of a class of Southerners known as Creoles—an exclusive, mixed race society that is proud of its French roots, and shuns "white trash" as much as it shuns black ex-slaves. This group is mulatto (of mixed black and white ancestry) and in Mary's case it means that her grandfather kept a black mistress (as did many white men before the Civil War). Mary herself is a "high yaller" Creole—so light-skinned she can pass for white. However, she decides to give up her class advantages and bring her education to a plantation school house. Mary comes to realize, members of the Creole class do little to assist in bridging the gap between white and black. In trying to remedy this, she finds herself embroiled in another boundary crossing that ends tragically.

Tee Bob, Robert Samson's son, falls in love with Mary. She explains to him the reality of their situation—their world won't let them be together because he is white and she is black. Following her rejection, Tee Bob kills himself. In his final letter he releases her of blame but the situation forces her to flee the plantation.

Aunt Lena

See Lena Washington

Miss Lilly

Miss Lilly is the first teacher on the Samson plantation. When she arrives from Opelousas, she tries to improve her students' manners and appearance as well as their minds. The workers don't appreciate her interfering, and she finally leaves.

Molly

Molly is an aging black house servant at the Clyde ranch. She has driven off all of the previous workers sent to help her because she is scared someone might take her place as cook and nanny. Jane is too stubborn to let Molly get the best of her, so Molly leaves the ranch. She eventually dies "of a broken heart."

Old Man

The Old Man is a white man who feeds Jane and Ned during their first week on the road. A sympathetic figure, he tries to point out the difficulty of reaching Ohio, but gives the children assistance when they decide to leave anyway.

Miss Pittman

Miss Jane Pittman is the focus of the narrative, for she has witnessed one hundred years of life in Louisiana, from slavery to the civil rights movement. As a strong candid woman she relates the events of the novel. While she sees little good coming from the federal government or from the white race, as individuals she sees both their faults and their goodness. She acknowledges her own weaknesses as well, saying that disliking some people on first sight is "one of my worse habits, probably the worst I have, but I can't get rid of it." Most of all, Jane is a survivor.

Jane's instincts for survival are hard earned. When she leaves the plantation where she was born, she is stubborn in her faith that the North is a sort of promised land. She is determined to take Ned there even when told it will take her thirty years to get there. By the time Mr. Bone turns his plantation over to Colonel Dye, however, she has learned not to believe in rescue: "I would stay right here and do what I could for me and Ned. If I heard of a place where I could live better, where Ned could get a better learning, I would go there to live. Till then I would stay where I was." Jane realizes she can only depend on herself to make her life better.

But Jane also knows that individuals can make a difference in the lives of many. When Ned is threatened because of his work with the committee, she tells him to "do what you think's right," even if it meant leaving her. She also sees the inspiration successful African-American athletes, like boxer Joe Louis and baseball player Jackie Robinson, give to her community. So, although her foster son Ned was killed for his attempts to improve things for black people, she encourages Jimmy in his own crusade for rights. She warns him to be patient, for she knows that only time and the concerted effort of each person toward change would make the difference. While Jimmy ends up another casualty of racism, by the close of the novel, Jane, now inspired by Jimmy, takes a stand for human rights. Jimmy told her that her example would inspire others.

Thus while Jane's "autobiography" is the story of one individual, it is also the story of a community. Jane embodies the philosophy that today's people must sacrifice so their children will have a better future. The expression of this philosophy, however, is especially successful because it is communicated within an entertaining folk narrative. Jane's story is not simply a biography, but a history—a story, finally, of all of us.

Joe Pittman

Joe has lost his wife and his two half-grown daughters are now without a mother. When he meets Jane while working on Colonel Dye's plantation they begin to live together and Jane changes her name to Pittman. Not believing in the church, the two never officially marry. Shortly after, Joe begins to consider leaving the plantation to break horses. With his skill he hopes to get better pay and better treatment. Eventually, he does find a ranch near the Texas border and so impresses the owner, Mr. Clyde, that he is offered a job and given the money he needs to move his family. Dye tries to thwart the move by bringing up a bogus debt, but Joe pays him anyway and moves to the ranch with Jane and his daughters Ella and Clara.

They live well on the Clyde ranch for seven or eight years until Jane begins to dream of his death. When she sees the horse that kills Joe in her dream, she turns to a hoo-doo woman for help. She eventually sets the horse free and in going after the horse, Joe is killed. Joe's battle with nature can be seen as a parallel to Ned's and Jimmy's battles with a racist society.

Jules Raynard

Jules, Tee Bob Samson's *parrain* (godfather), is a good friend of the Samson family. It seems to him that he has lived as much of his life at the Samson plantation as at his own house. He and Jane are good friends who have long chats in the kitchen whenever he visits. His stature in the family enables him to take charge during the chaos following Tee Bob's suicide. He takes control of the evidence and the investigation. He allows enough truth to come out without wholly compromising the family or causing the death of Mary Agnes LeFabre.

Miss Amma Dean Samson

Married to Robert Samson, Miss Amma Dean is a typical wife of the white southern gentleman. She rules the house with quiet dignity, and accepts that her husband has fathered a child with one of the black workers. While she is quirky enough to expect things of Robert not in his character, she is traditional enough to expect Tee Bob to marry Judy Major. She is bothered by his liking for Mary Agnes and devastated by his suicide.

Tee Bob Samson

See Robert Samson Jr.

Robert Samson

Robert owns the Samson estate where Jane lives when Gaines approaches her for a story. He does many things to begin the process of raising the previously enslaved. He treats his wage earners decently and slowly begins to give land to sharecroppers—although he favors the white Cajuns and mulatto Creoles when doing so. However, he is a harsh follower of the Southern moral code governing black and white relations. When his illegitimate son Timmy fights with his white overseer, for instance, he banishes the boy from his plantation, saying "there ain't no such thing as a half nigger." He is ready to murder Mary LeFabre for her innocent involvement with his son until Jules Raynard stops him. When one of his tenants participates in a demonstration in Baton Rouge, he kicks the man's family off the plantation. As a result, when Jane walks past Robert Samson to go to the courthouse in Bayonne, her act symbolizes a blow against the old racist order.

Robert Samson Jr.

As the son of Robert Samson, Tee Bob stands to inherit the plantation but he cannot accept the Southern code which accompanies this heritage. Consequently, he pursues Mary Agnes LeFabre, a woman he is struck with although she is a mulatto. He fights Jimmy Caya when he suggests Mary Agnes is made for Tee Bob to use, not to love. When Mary refuses his advances repeating Jimmy's argument that black and white cannot mix—he violently attacks her. In the end, he writes a letter to his mother saying he can't "find peace" in such an unjust society, and then kills himself.

Ticey

See Miss Jane Pittman

Tom Joe

Tom Joe is the white overseer on the Samson plantation. Considered "white trash," he takes out his anger and feelings of inferiority on the black workers. He knows he can mistreat black people without fear of punishment. For instance, when he argues with Timmy, he is supported by Robert Samson, Timmy's white father, who gives his son a beating after the argument.

Unc Isom

At the opening of the novel, Unc Isom is advisor and spokesperson for the slaves on the plantation. After emancipation, he advises them to think carefully before setting out for the north and breaking up their community. Rumor has it that once he was a witch doctor. However, he is considered to be too old to be able to put a curse on anyone. Therefore, at the news of freedom, several of the younger people defy him and set out from the plantation for the North.

Lena Washington

Lena, Jimmy's great-aunt, raises him as the hope of the community. She is typical of Gaines's self-sacrificing women—the greatest being Jane. This character makes sacrifices in the present that are not immediately beneficial but later result in the betterment of the whole community. Thus, Lena cares for her great-nephew not just because he has no parents, but with the hope that he will become a leader for his people.

Themes

Custom and Tradition

The social code of the South was a set of rules passed down from father to son from long ago. By this code, black and white people are viewed and treated differently. The distinctions between black and white do not always depend on skin color but on blood—as in the case of Mary Agnes—and class standing. The latter condition fits Jimmy Caya, whom Sam Guidry looks at as less than white because of his poor origins. After the South's defeat in the Civil War, however, this social code no longer stood upon legal ground. So while men of Robert Samson's generation accepted it as their heritage, many of their sons had to come to terms with the reality of a changing world. For Tee Bob, it was too much. As Jules Raynard says to Jane, "these rules just ain't old enough."

What Raynard means is that the corruption of the traditional code in the South has not happened fast enough for all involved. While many people involved with the code still participate in its upkeep, there are a few renegades like Tee Bob. For example, Mr. Raynard and Jane are friends, in every sense of the word, yet they are unable to sit at the same table. Small discrepancies like this friendship are slowly eating away at the traditional code but not doing away with it entirely. Those who

directly challenge the code, like Ned and Jimmy, are killed. Those who might, like Jane and Mary, are not yet ready. Then there is Tee Bob; he is born into a world where blacks are workers, not slaves. Moreover, Tee Bob—perhaps because his half-brother Timmy is black—has never learned the meaning of being a Southern white according to the rules of the code. Thus, he goes where his heart leads and sees nothing wrong with loving a "black" woman.

When he shares his secret with Jimmy Caya he receives a crude response, suggesting Tee Bob treat Mary like a slave. Caya, who aspires to be as socially valued as a Samson, also aspires to maintain the code that gives the Samsons their standing. Caya emphatically attempts to defend what he presumes to be the honor of the Samson family. Tee Bob cannot love this woman and remain in society but, as Raynard says, "He couldn't understand that, he thought love was much stronger than that one drop of African blood. But she knowed better." Tee Bob could not rape Mary, as Caya suggested, because he loved her. When she refuses him, he beats her—thus becoming just like the society who says he should not love her. Not wanting to live in a world of such inconsistencies, he commits suicide.

Choices and Consequences

Freedom, for most people, means the ability to make your own choices. In the novel's opening, the reading of the Emancipation Proclamation presents each particular slave with a choice—stay or go. While those who leave are eager to begin a new life, they soon learn that freedom is not so easily gained. The legal chains binding them have been removed, but they have neither the political power nor economic means to enforce their freedom. Throughout the novel, this reality of being "free" but being constricted by second-class status slowly develops into a series of risk-taking choices. These choices often involve a sacrifice by an individual that serves as a source of inspiration and a step forward. Slowly, the abyss between being a freed slave and being a citizen with rights is crossed. This is done through small moments of choosing to be free.

Jane is aware from the moment she hears the Proclamation that she is free to leave. However, not being a slave is very different from being free. When she says, "So this is freedom?" she has only known of being free from her owners, not true freedom. It is very difficult to be "free" when the Ku Klux Klan exists and men like Albert Cluveau are contracted to kill "uppity" blacks like Ned. Changes do begin to occur, however, as people speak out. After Ned's murder, Jane speaks her mind to Cluveau. The school for black children that Ned was killed over later exists at the Samson plantation, and eventually Jimmy goes to college. The fight to gain one's freedom often consists of a series of small steps. As Jane whispers to Jimmy, claiming their rights will take a lot of time and healing, not "retrick."

In the end, enough time has passed. Jane, a representative of the freed slave, is now able to claim her rightful status as an equal person. Jimmy's murder serves as a catalyst. Jane asserts her freedom for the first time in a moment of defiance. She walks past Robert Samson. Her choice to exercise her freedom validates her life. While she did live before that moment, the act of walking by a representative of those who enslaved her heralds a new dawn in her life.

Politics

Miss Jane's story subtly reflects the political history of America from the Emancipation Proclamation to the early moments of the 1960s. While her century-long story is affected by the great events, she is directly involved in them. This makes her an average person, except for her healthy old age; her uniqueness comes from retelling those events. In other words, world-changing events like Lincoln's Proclamation are not as significant to her story as are acts such as her renaming, which occurred because of her encounter with Mr. Brown.

While the novel presents the life of one ordinary individual, Jane's story represents the untold history of thousands of freed slaves and their descendants. In reading Jane's story, one sees evidence of various historical and political programs designed to empower African Americans. Individual efforts to improve education, hold voter registration drives, and protest inequality are part of a larger political effort. In the end, the novel argues, grand political change can only be made by individuals—and not just great leaders. As Jane tells Jimmy, "the people and time brought [Martin Luther] King; King bring the people. What Miss Rosa Parks did, everybody wanted to do. They just needed one person to do it first because they all couldn't do it at the same time; then they needed King to show them what to do next. But King couldn't do a thing before Miss Rosa Parks refused to give that white man her [bus] seat."

Topics for Further Study

- Ernest Gaines has remarked that modern literature and histories tend to focus on grand events and large cities. Research what he calls the "rural past" and explain how ordinary Americans outside of the city have affected history. Possible time periods to investigate include the American Revolution, the building of the American West, and the eras of World War I, the Great Depression, World War II, and the Vietnam War.

- Explain how the person who is "recording" Jane's story succeeds in making history more exciting. How does Jane's story make it easier to explain what happened from the Civil War to the Civil Rights movement?

- Do some research into the period of American history known as Reconstruction. Which efforts to rehabilitate the South failed and why? Why were men like Colonel Eugene I. Dye allowed to return to their plantations?

- Jane Pittman tells of her fondness for Jackie Robinson, the first African American to play major league baseball. Research the history of African American participation in professional and Olympic sports and write a paper connecting milestones on the playing field with milestones in civil rights for African Americans.

Style

Narration and Dialect

Much of the critical acclaim awarded to Gaines for *The Autobiography of Miss Jane Pittman* centers around his narrative creation—Miss Jane Pittman. Jane's first-person ("I") account of one hundred years of her life in America brings a uniquely personal perspective to this historical novel. An important part of her narration is the use of dialect—a variation in language particular to a region or culture. Jane's retelling is recorded in her own rural black dialect, in this instance the language of Gaines's native Louisiana. This use of dialect brings a realism to both the characterization of Jane and the Louisiana setting of the book. In addition, by allowing Jane's unrestrained frankness to take charge of the story, Gaines maintains the feeling of the conversation of her telling. The novel is experienced more as something heard than as something read.

Jane's frank narrative style also serves to highlight one of the themes of the book, that the ordinary individual can make a difference. For example, she says:

> "Jimmy ... I have a scar on my back I got when I was a slave. I'll carry it to my grave. You got people out there with this scar on their brains, and they will carry that scar to their grave. Talk with them, Jimmy."

In this little speech she bypasses the "retrick" of fancy education as well as any moralizing that might have impeded her story. She simply talks and talks and talks her life to the recorder—Gaines. In turn, he presents her without the "retrick" of social commentary that would have made her into an obvious symbol of history instead of an individual. By allowing Jane Pittman to speak for herself and about herself, Gaines creates an African American experience more powerful than any chronological history might have done. This story told by an old woman as if it were fact recovers a lost history that is as important as the one students read in history books.

Setting

In the history of African American literature, Gaines's novel is very important in terms of its setting. Popular literary works by black authors immediately preceding Gaines set their novels in the locale of big industrial cities. Works like Zora Neale Hurston's 1937 novel *Their Eyes Were Watching God* were set in rural America, but they gained little notice until the 1970s. Gaines used his Louisiana home as background for his novel and stayed within that setting. In this fashion he could fill in the background of black heritage: the inheritance of plantation life after the Civil War. As Gaines explained to an interviewer from *Essence* magazine, not all blacks immigrated to the North. They might have tried, but, like Jane, never made it as far as the county line. More important, he said, "a lot happened in those 350 years between the time we left Africa and the fifties and sixties when [black writers like Richard Wright and Ralph Ellison] started writing novels about big-city ghettos.... We cannot ignore that rural past or those older people

in it. Their stories are the kind I want to write about. I am what I am today because of them." Consequently, many of the novel's metaphors are rural symbols, such as the repeated reference to the power of the river and its tendency to flood, or Joe Pittman's battle with the horse.

Symbolism and Metaphor

Jane touches on many symbols to summarize the experience of her life. When she "gets religion," she testifies before the church of her travels. Her salvation testimony is a metaphor—an image or story that has a deeper meaning beyond its surface—about crossing a river. Jane uses other symbols to explain why her community is not rising up against racism as other African Americans have done in other places. She speaks of a black quilt blinding people to the truth. A quilt has long been held to be a symbol of southern feminine life because the quilt, made and added to over generations, records the stories of whole families. Jane tells Jimmy that the older people "must one day wake up and push that black quilt off his back. Must tell himself I had it on too long." She also uses the metaphor of scar tissue to explain why people are so reluctant to demonstrate: scarred by fear, they do not want to risk being hurt again.

Joe Pittman's job breaking wild horses can also be seen as a symbol or metaphor of a larger theme. His lonely struggle against the powerful forces of nature parallels the individual's struggle against a similarly powerful racist society. His death by wild horse parallels Ned's and Jimmy's deaths by bullet. All three were challenging society in the way they knew best. After all, Joe had to stand up for his right to be free to go and challenge the greater strength of nature. Nature proved to be more powerful, but he earned the legend of being a great horse breaker—skin color not withstanding.

Another powerful symbol is the river. When Jane speaks of the flood of 1927, it provides one of her few moments of obvious sermonizing. Whether a man builds dirt levees or dams of concrete, it amounts to the same thing—a futile attempt to control the power of nature. Eventually the levees break and the water destroys: it "will run free again" says Jane, "You just wait and see." It is the same story with the human spirit, or so Gaines would like us to understand. That spirit can be enslaved, scarred, and beaten but, like the river, it will break through the levees and run free. In this reflection on the river, Jane has also foreshadowed, or hinted at, the coming triumph of spirit in the last section of the novel.

Historical Context

The Civil Rights Movement in Louisiana

In 1971, when Ernest Gaines published *The Autobiography of Miss Jane Pittman,* the United States had just seen a time of great social and political upheaval. Throughout the 1960s, African Americans had been struggling to gain equality. Various types of protests, such as the demonstrations described in the novel, were helping to bring centuries-long practices like segregation and racial discrimination to an end. Civil rights were still in the forefront of many African Americans' minds in 1971. Gaines's home state of Louisiana became famous during the 1960s for two events: the New Orleans school integration crisis and the Bogalusa movement.

In its 1954 *Brown v. Board of Education* decision, the Supreme Court outlawed segregation in public schools. Nevertheless, by 1960 the New Orleans school board had still made no progress toward integrating its schools. That fall, Judge Skelly Wright forced the board to come up with a plan for integration. Although this plan allowed only four black first-grade girls to attend white schools, opposition from local whites was tremendous. Most parents of white students at the two schools chosen for integration pulled their children out; those who did not were taunted and terrorized by anti-integration neighbors. Politicians who supported the integration were also harassed and threatened, but the worst treatment was suffered by the four young black students. Every day they went to school, they were bombarded by spitting, screaming crowds of angry white faces. Without the bravery of these four first-grade girls and the support of the African American community and organizations like the NAACP (National Association for the Advancement of Colored People), the terrorism of these white protesters might have continued to prevent school integration.

Instead, gradual improvements were made in integrating schools and other public facilities across Louisiana. More and more African Americans, inspired by the example of the four girls, began to stand up for their right to equal treatment and an integrated society. Bad publicity about the New Orleans school crisis and a resulting loss of business helped the civil rights movement in Louisiana. Local business people lent their support to integration policies, hoping to drum up lagging business by improving Louisiana's image.

Although slow improvements in civil rights were made in New Orleans and across the state, the racist hatred of many white Louisianians was not easily overcome. In the rural mill town of Bogalusa, for example, movements to register African Americans to vote and to integrate local establishments were met with extreme violence. White and black civil rights workers from the North and politically active Bogalusa blacks were repeatedly threatened, beaten, and even shot by Ku Klux Klan followers. Soon members of Bogalusa's African American population, many of whom were World War II or Korean War veterans, formed an armed self-defense group to protect themselves from the KKK threat because local police would not. This corps eventually attracted enough national attention to force President Lyndon Johnson to declare "war on the Klan." This finally provided Bogalusa and other Southern towns and cities with the military and legal support to enact and enforce civil rights laws.

A History of Black Struggle

Inspired by African Americans' gains in civil rights in the 1960s, Gaines sought to relate the long, hard history of oppression that led to these triumphs. Although the slaves were freed by the Emancipation Proclamation at the end of the Civil War, the transition to independence was difficult. In fact, the prospect of leaving home to start a new life was often too much for former slaves. While some moved out of the South, many chose to stay in the same area—sometimes even on the same plantation—where they had worked as slaves; others returned after failed attempts at starting anew. Although these freedmen and freedwomen often performed the same functions they had before emancipation—plowing fields, picking cotton, cooking meals, caring for white children—they were paid for their work (in land, harvest, or wages) and were expected to pay for their food and shelter. To many former slaves, however, these differences seemed insignificant.

Nevertheless, blacks worked to improve their lot by gaining land, education, and equal civil rights. Meeting in churches and schoolhouses, African American groups provided training and education for one another, published newspapers, and got involved in politics. In Louisiana, African American political action was especially effective in the decade from 1867 to 1877. During that time, newly elected black lawmakers and community leaders led a successful fight to outlaw segregation in public schools, streetcars, bars, and hotels.

Pictured here with arm outstretched and flanked by his wife, Coretta, Ralph Bunche, and Ralph Abernathy, Martin Luther King led a path of peaceful, nonviolent resistance to secure civil rights for African Americans.

Unfortunately, passing laws against segregation did not make it disappear. With the victory of anti-integration Democrats in Louisiana's 1877 elections and the 1896 "separate but equal" *Plessy v. Ferguson* Supreme Court decision, even the political gains made by Louisiana's African Americans were canceled out. Thus, while many African Americans in Louisiana tried to exercise the new rights granted to them by law, the risk of violent responses from angry whites kept most from crossing the color boundaries erected by white society.

Ironically, since they were no longer the valuable property of white slave owners, blacks often faced worse violence than they had when they were enslaved. As a result, during Reconstruction African Americans were often the victims of savage, even deadly, attacks by angry and demoralized white Southerners. The fictional massacre described by Miss Jane in the novel is no worse than many real attacks reported in the South in the decades following the war. Although attacks like this were technically illegal, few Southern whites were punished for crimes against blacks. The white culture of violence was far more powerful in the

postwar era than laws, judges, or Freedmen's Bureau officers, who were appointed by the federal government to ease the transition from slavery to freedom. As a result, white witnesses to such crimes were more inclined to protect guilty fellow whites—especially those who demanded such protection with threats of violence—than to stand up for the rights of African Americans. African American witnesses were also subject to violence if they spoke out against whites, and they faced major legal obstacles as well.

Violence against African Americans became formalized in groups such as the Ku Klux Klan and the Knights of the White Camellia. These hate groups were founded by white Confederates who turned their anger and shame at being defeated by the Union into violence against former slaves. Many members of these groups feared a black revolt against the white people of the South and concluded that the way to prevent it was to beat, maim, or lynch those blacks who contradicted a white person or otherwise sought to exercise their political rights. Although these acts of terrorism became much less common after a federal crackdown in the 1870s, the Ku Klux Klan experienced a huge

Compare & Contrast

- **1870s:** The Emancipation Proclamation ends the legal sanction of slavery. However, many blacks remain in the South either as sharecroppers or subsistence wage laborers.

  1950s and 1960s: The Civil Rights movement slowly spreads across the South. The biggest scenes surround the bus boycotts and marches led by leaders like Martin Luther King. Elsewhere in the South, however, Jim Crow laws remain unchallenged but changing.

  Today: Several federal Civil Rights Acts allow persons unfairly treated due to color, sex, or creed full recourse of the law.

- **1870s:** The sudden disruption to Southern life and identity caused by the release of the slaves and defeat in the Civil War leads to the emergence of terror groups like the KKK. These groups prevent the full implementation of Reconstruction, the realization of equal rights, and

the timely integration of African Americans into society.

1950s and 1960s: Unsatisfied with the rate of progress and inspired by Mahatma Gandhi's campaign in India, nonviolent measures were adopted and sit-ins staged in "Whites Only" establishments across America. Other groups, like the Black Panther Party, were formed and became more direct when progress did not happen immediately.

Today: White supremacist organizations still have a vast following. The membership of the KKK per se is not as large but together with its many branches, sympathizers, and imitators, the number of avowedly racist Americans is worrisome. Fortunately, wherever the KKK appears for membership drives, groups like Can the Klan, remnants of the Black Panther Party, and Amnesty International rally to show opposition to the Klan's hate-filled message.

revival during the civil rights movement of the 1960s.

Louisiana's Unique Culture

Although Louisiana of the late 1800s and early 1900s was a typical Southern state in many ways, it possessed a unique culture made up of four distinct groups: whites, blacks, Creoles, and Cajuns. Cajuns, who were white, came from an earlier settlement in French Canada to settle in the area. They influenced Louisiana with their language, food, and customs. During the one hundred years portrayed in the novel, however, most Cajuns were poorer and less powerful than other white Louisiana residents. They were often hired to do the dirty work for more powerful whites; Albert Cluveau, for instance, must kill Jane's adopted son Ned or face threats to his own safety. Creoles were people of mixed African and European ancestry who shared some of the French heritage of the Cajuns. They usually looked

different, however, because of their mixed ancestry. Nevertheless, some Creoles, such as the teacher Mary Agnes LeFabre, were light enough to pass for white. (Note: while the novel uses the term "Creole" for those with mixed French and African heritage, it has also been used as a term for the exclusively white descendants of Louisiana's original French and Spanish settlers.) The mixed-heritage Creoles generally kept away from Cajuns as well as other whites and from African Americans, speaking their own French-based language and maintaining a unique, sophisticated culture. Before the Civil War, most free people of color were Creole. At the bottom of the Louisiana social ladder during this century were African Americans like Jane Pittman, whose dark skin marked them as inferior in the eyes of most whites, Cajuns, and Creoles. These cultural distinctions often play a pivotal role in *The Autobiography of Miss Jane Pittman,* and give it the special regional flavor that has been praised by so many critics.

Critical Overview

The majority of critics have noted that Ernest Gaines made an unforgettable contribution to American literature with *The Autobiography of Miss Jane Pittman*. Gaines has been seen as a historian, as he pretends to be in the introduction of the novel, who has created "a metaphor of the collective black experience," according to Jerry Bryant in the *Iowa Review*. In serving as this metaphor, Jane Pittman is the story of rural African Americans since 1865. Her final moment in the narrative represents this one hundred-year period as a victorious slow march to freedom. As Josh Greenfield writes in *Life* magazine: "Never mind that Miss Jane Pittman is fictitious, and that her 'autobiography,' offered up in the form of taped reminiscences, is artifice. The effect is stunning."

The novel has been so celebrated that the difference in critical views is often limited to the way reviewers praise the novel. Often, this praise has been for Gaines's ability to integrate historical events and political changes without writing an angry "protest novel" of the type that often appeared in the 1960s. As a result, note these critics, the novel focuses on the literary qualities of the story rather than its message. The ability to avoid outrage and self-pity, according to a *Times Literary Supplement* review, stems from the technique Gaines uses to tell the story. Because many of the events Jane remembers are years past, the graphic pain they inspire is somewhat faded. As the reviewer explains: "Cheerfully free of self-pity or dramatics, taking for granted unspeakable persecutions and endurances, faded into matter-of-factness by the suggestions of old age remembering, the record's implicit revelation of wickedness is nevertheless so hard that one would like to turn away from such truth." Fortunately, not all critics have been so nervous.

Novelist Alice Walker, for example, confronts the issue of "politics" in Gaines's work in her review for the *New York Times Book Review*. "Because politics are strung throughout the novel, it will no doubt be said that Gaines's book is about politics. But he is too skilled a writer to be stuck in so sordid, so small a category." Walker says Gaines is best compared to writers such as Charles Dickens and W.E.B. DuBois, rather than Ralph Ellison and Richard Wright, because his preference is for the story over politics. That is, she says, he "claims and revels in the rich heritage" and customs of the Southern blacks of Louisiana. As a re-

sult, Gaines's work is "open to love and to interpretation."

In another early review of the novel for *Time* magazine, Melvin Maddocks calls Gaines a "country-boy writer." He uses this term not only because Gaines writes about rural Louisiana, but also because his stories are set down as if planted, "spreading the roots deep, wide and firm. His stories grow organically … with the absolute rightness of a folk tale." Maddocks also enjoys the way Gaines does not demand immediate change through revolution. Instead, "he simply watches, a patient artist, a patient man, and it happens for him" in the final moment when Jane walks past Robert. Nevertheless, the novel captures the essence of an entire people, states Martin Amis in *New Statesman*. "Miss Jane's story is a bloody slice of life, a protracted blow-by-blow battle with the moonish ignorance and bestiality of the white Southerner." Because Jane has come out of her cycle victorious, the critic observes, there is no self-pity to reduce the effectiveness of the story. Amis also compares Jane's story to Thomas Berger's novel *Little Big Man*. That tale similarly captures the history of an entire people, the Cheyenne tribe of the Great Plains, through the narrative of a 111-year-old witness. The difference between the two is that Gaines avoids a mythic sweep and simply tells the tale of an individual woman.

In her *CLA Journal* review, Winifred Stoelting examines the characters inhabiting Gaines's literary universe. These characters are "caught in the movement of the changing times, they must make choices, the results often unpredictable, the consequences sometimes tragic." Accordingly, Stoelting continues, these characters embody Gaines's belief in the individual: "the world his characters live in values the independence of the human spirit to survive and change."

Picking up the refrain of praise, Addison Gayle summarizes the formula of Gaines's historic novels in his 1975 work *The Way of the New World: The Black Novel in America:* "Realization precedes action; recognition of the truth of history is a prelude for rebellion and revolution." Gayle also dwells on the influence of Nobel Prize-winner William Faulkner on Gaines's writing. Faulkner wrote of the men trapped, like Samson or Raynard, by the old patterns of the white South. In comparing Faulkner's universe to Gaines's, Gayle says: "to endure in Faulkner's universe is to accept predominance of guilt and redemption, and, thus, to accept too the inevitability of fate. To endure in

Gaines' universe is to minimize such themes, concentrate upon people, and, thus, to struggle endlessly against fate." As a result, the critic concludes, Gaines can focus on character yet create "a novel of epic proportions."

Criticism

Jeannine Johnson

In the following essay Johnson, a doctoral candidate at Yale University, examines how The Autobiography of Miss Jane Pittman *works as historical fiction and how Gaines makes a single character work both as an individual and as a historical symbol.*

Published in 1971, *The Autobiography of Miss Jane Pittman* was Ernest J. Gaines's first major critical and popular success. It exemplifies the author's concerns with the relationship between language, identity, and narrative structure. The novel names itself as an autobiography but it is also generally recognized as a work of historical fiction. Gaines's novel functions as an autobiography in so far as it provides a first-person account of the life of a particular person. However, it differs from conventional autobiography in two ways. First, this is the life history of a fictional character as recreated by a fictional editor. Second, Jane's narrative, unlike those in many autobiographies, does not define her life as a quest toward an inevitable goal. In other words, she does not suggest that her past led in any direct way to her present state. As a historical novel, *The Autobiography of Miss Jane Pittman* places its fictional characters in relation to a known history of African Americans in the South and names specific historical persons and events. But Gaines makes Jane, not history, the central figure in his novel, subordinating the broader historical element to her own personal story. *The Autobiography of Miss Jane Pittman* blends fictional autobiography and the historical novel to create a distinct narrative form.

In the introduction, the editor admits that "even though I have used only Miss Jane's voice throughout the narrative, there were times when others carried the story for her." Of course, it is the author himself who literally carries the story. But continuing in his fictional role as editor, the author suggests an even broader impact of other voices on the autobiography: "In closing I wish to thank all the wonderful people who were at Miss Jane's house through those long months of interviewing her, because this is not only Miss Jane's autobiography, it is theirs as well. This is what both Mary and Miss Jane meant when they said you could not tie all the ends together in one neat direction. Miss Jane's story is all of their stories, and their stories are Miss Jane's."

By linking Jane's story to others' stories, the author does not intend to diminish the uniqueness and individuality of Miss Jane, as the story that follows makes clear. For it is Jane who narrates her own story in her own authentic dialect. Instead, he refers to the contributions of many voices in order to stress that there is no "one neat direction" in which a person's life progresses.

For instance, the first book of the novel imitates the framework of a quest North, common in nineteenth-century slave narratives. But in Jane's story, this framework disintegrates in Book II after Colonel Dye takes over Mr. Bone's plantation. The Union peacekeeping troops have withdrawn and Dye informs those who have stayed on the plantation that the school will close and that he will not be able to pay his workers till the end of the year:

> "If that suit you, stay; if it don't, catch up with that coattail-flying scalawag and the rest of them hotfooting niggers who was here two days ago."

> If Colonel Dye had told me that a week before I would have turned around then and left. But after what Bone had told us I had no more faith in heading North than I had staying South. I would stay right here and do what I could for me and Ned. If I heard of a place where I could live better, where Ned could get a better learning, I would go there to live. Till then I would stay where I was.

Jane's decision to remain in Louisiana rather than continue to Ohio is an act of survival rather than one of submission. Many characters in the novel do resist and even challenge their conditions, but these are mostly men (such as Ned, Joe, and Jimmy) who possess a greater freedom to travel. As a woman and as a pragmatist, Jane feels it less useful to relocate herself even when her situation is difficult. When Ned urges her to leave for Kansas with him, he observes, "You ain't married to this place." "In a way," Jane responds with characteristically few words. The author seems to approve Jane's rootedness since all the events represented in the novel are contained within the state of Louisiana. The story does not follow Ned when he moves to Kansas, nor does it even expand as far as

What Do I Read Next?

- Harriet A. Jacobs's *Incidents in the Life of a Slave Girl, Written by herself* was first published in 1861. Since then, it has remained the classic example of the slave narrative genre. The autobiography tells of her life as a slave and her escape to the north in the 1830s.

- In order to answer the doubt that he was ever a slave, Frederick Douglass wrote his autobiography in 1845. He rewrote this in 1881 as *The Life and Times of Frederick Douglass*. The book has since become a classic of American literature and a source of inspiration to countless American youths.

- The South's most celebrated author is William Faulkner, who told stories of a mythical Mississippi county called Yoknapatawpha. The 1929 novel *The Sound and the Fury* is a most powerful tale of the South's decline, partially narrated by a mentally impaired man named Benjy Compson.

- Zora Neale Hurston recorded as much of the cultural experience of black Americans in the South Eastern United States as she was able. Her most acclaimed novel was her 1937 work *Their Eyes Were Watching God*. The story is that of a woman named Janie who struggles to find equal treatment of others. For a time she has this, but the story ends tragically.

- Harper Lee leaped into the spotlight with her 1960 novel *To Kill a Mockingbird*. This Pulitzer Prize-winning story is told from the perspective of a six-year-old girl whose father defends a black man accused of rape. Despite the lawyer's ability to prove the accused is innocent, the man is still found guilty and is killed in jail.

- *Little Big Man* is a fictitious autobiography told by an 111-year-old white man "recorded" by Thomas Berger in 1964. This novel mythically sweeps up the whole of the Cheyenne Nation's history into the life of an abducted white boy who grew up "indian."

- Alex Haley's Pulitzer Prize-winning novel *Roots: The Saga of an American Family* was published in 1976. The novel told the tale of an African American family through seven generations. It was a runaway best-seller inspiring many blacks and whites alike to try and fill in the genealogical gaps of their own family.

- Gaines's 1993 National Book Critics Circle Award-winner *A Lesson before Dying* is considered by many to be his best work. This novel begins as a young black man is sentenced to death for his unwitting involvement in a robbery where a white store owner is killed. A black teacher reluctantly takes on the task of helping this uneducated convict learn to "die like a man."

New Orleans (still within the state) when Jimmy attends school there.

We may explain this geographical limit by noting that the novel shares its Louisiana setting in common with almost all of Gaines's other works, including most recently *A Lesson Before Dying* (1993). But the geographic boundaries of *The Autobiography of Miss Jane Pittman* also symbolize the novel's interest in community. In the introduction, the author proposes that the life story of an individual is also the life story of a community and

vice versa. And if Jane's history is Louisiana's history, it is also the history of African Americans in the South.

By creating an editor who wants to use Jane's narrative to teach American history to his high school students, Gaines indicates that Jane's experiences are as important in understanding the past as are those of more famous historical figures. For example, the author incorporates Jackie Robinson into the novel in part as a sign of African American achievement. Robinson's presence is also a means by which to illustrate the personal sacrifices involved in progress. Robinson, who in 1947 became the first African American to play major league baseball, appears in the novel without much fanfare when Jane comments on her passion for listening to baseball games.

Jane recognizes Robinson's significance for a larger community: "Jackie and the Dodgers was for the colored people; the Yankees was for the white folks. Like in the Depression, Joe Louis was for the colored." More importantly, Robinson's presence has deeply personal consequences for Jane: "I was the oldest in the church and they called me the church mother. But I liked baseball so much they had to take it from me and give it to Emma." We might say that symbolically Jane is willing to lose some standing in her local community in order to identify with an emblem of a larger community and of a wider history. However, in so doing, we must be careful not to discount the particular effect this historic personage had on Jane as a private individual. She loses her position in the church, but she is compensated for this loss by the great joy she experiences as a baseball fan.

Jane certainly does not conceive of her allegiance to Jackie Robinson and the Brooklyn Dodgers in terms of its public meaning. While Gaines does not deny the power and significance of symbolic actions, he implies that those who do perform them or otherwise act as representatives of their communities risk losing their own identities. Jane's last act in the novel has at the same time enormous public and private meaning, as she defies Mr. Samson and heads to Bayonne with other residents of the quarters.

Some critics have faulted the novel's conclusion as abrupt and as belatedly introducing a new plot direction. In fact, Jane's act decisively completes the plot of this final book in the novel, whose theme is unity and whose structure is unified. This book is the story of "the One" and, appropriately, it is the only book which contains no titled subdivisions. This single purposefulness parallels the northern quest of the novel's first book. Just as a quest narrative subordinates the importance of the individual to her ultimate historic symbolism, Jane's defiance signals the end of her own individual, fictive existence. She moves to join a greater historical dimension that this autobiography cannot contain: "Me and Robert looked at each other there a long time, then I went by him." And Jane literally walks out of her own story.

As we imagine Jane continuing toward the demonstration in Bayonne, we would do well to remember that, with regard to history, she harbors no unrealistic expectations for what an individual can accomplish. She warns Jimmy that "'People and time bring forth leaders,' I said. 'Leaders don't bring forth people. The people and the time brought King; King didn't bring the people. What Miss Rosa Parks did, everybody wanted to do. They just needed one person to do it first because they all couldn't do it at the same time; then they needed King to show them what to do next. But King couldn't do a thing before Miss Rosa Parks refused to give that white man her seat.'"

Jane's attitude toward Rosa Parks parallels that of the author toward Jane. Jane observes that Parks is, to a certain extent, simply a representative of a group, having done what "everybody wanted to do." At the same time, Jane grants Rosa Parks her full individuality and recognizes that the personal pain she suffered was not reduced by the symbolic value of her act. Likewise, the author states that Jane's story is everyone's story, and yet Jane's personality, voice, and experience distinguish this autobiography as fully her own.

Source: Jeannine Johnson, in an essay for *Novels for Students,* Gale, 1999.

Valerie Melissa Babb

In the following excerpt, Babb discusses the theme of leadership and the qualities of Jane Pittman as a leader.

From Jackie Robinson to Marie Laveau to nature, all the elements of Jane's narrative show her life to be a microcosm of the vast panorama of African-American culture—its people, its history, its myth, its vision. She is a personified archive that in the first two books of her narrative records the African-American past and her place in it, and in the third provides an insightful commentary on African-American and larger American society. The fourth and last book of her autobiography, "The Quarters," is not so much a record of the past as a blueprint for the future. Its immediacy is represented through the lack of section titles that divide the other books of the work. Previously, titles set the parameters of Jane's memory, naming the experience she is narrating in terms of an event ("Freedom"), a philosophy ("Man's Way"), a vision ("The Chariot of Hell"), or a person ("Miss Lilly"). Such naming cannot be made for the action in "The Quarters," for it is not as far removed from Jane's present as the other sections, and as such, lacks the distance needed to construct a clear defining perspective. The section leaves the reader feeling that it will be the task of another oral historian to look back on its events from the vantage point of the future and give names to those sections which represent Jane's immediate past.

As Jane's autobiography comes forward in time and prepares to address issues that will reverberate in the future, a theme that Gaines will explore in his last two novels emerges: the nature of leadership. Jane and the people of her community are desperately seeking "the One," a Moses to lead them out of economic and psychological bondage. As Jane describes the community in this portion of her narrative, it consists of people searching for dignity even if they must settle for the vicarious esteem derived from the exploits of black athletes. By following such figures as Joe Louis or Jackie Robinson, Jane and her community experience an affirmation their society denies them:

> When times get really hard, really tough, He always send you somebody. In the Depression ... He sent us Joe. Joe was to lift the colored people's hearts.... I heard every lick of that fight on the radio, and what Joe didn't put on S'mellin that night just couldn't go on a man....
>
> Now, after the war, He sent us Jackie.... He showed them a trick or two. Homeruns, steal bases—eh Lord. It made my day just to hear what Jackie had done. In their own ways, Louis and Robinson are leaders, and in her own way, Jane will become a leader as well.

The communal wish for a figure to do within their parish what Joe Louis and Jackie Robinson have done before the world manifests itself in close examination of each youth in the quarters, to see whether any possesses the qualities that make him or her "the One." At first the people's hope rests in Ned, but the certainty of Ned's martyrdom is expressed through Jane's statement "Both of us knowed that day was coming. When and where we didn't know." When Ned is assassinated, the community must renew its search for "the One." It spends many years waiting and searching, but at long last a possible candidate appears. This time it is Jimmy Aaron, and the community's desperation is reflected in Jane's explanation of why Jimmy was chosen: "People's always looking for somebody to come lead them.... Anytime a child is born, the old people look in his face and ask him if he's the One.... Why did we pick him? Well, why do you pick anybody? We picked him because we needed somebody."

As a youth, Jimmy feels summoned to a cause he cannot yet articulate. As Jane describes him,

"Jimmy would be sitting there on the gallery talking, and all a sudden he would stop listening to what I was saying and start gazing out in the road like he was listening to something else. One day ... [h]e said, 'Miss Jane, I got something like a tiger in my chest, just gnawing and ... want come out.... I pray to God to take it out, but look like the Lord don't hear me.'" The image of an indifferent God crystallizes Jimmy's realization that man, he in particular, must do something to rid himself of the "gnawing" and help his people. Like Ned, he too goes away to be educated, and returns as an active participant in the civil rights movement. And like Ned before him, Jimmy seeks to vanquish racial injustice through peaceful protests modeled after those of Martin Luther King, Jr.

Ned and Jimmy are descendants of characters found in Gaines's earlier fiction: Copper Laurent in *Bloodline,* who in spite of his biracial heritage attempts to reclaim his family legacy; Jackson Bradley in *Catherine Carmier,* who through loving the Creole Catherine seeks to move outside the boundaries set for him by his society; and Marcus in *Of Love and Dust,* who wants to be more than "just a slave." What all these characters share, in addition to a common determination to go against the status quo, is a common failure. None have a lasting impact, and for the most part, the systems they confront remain unchanged. Through their failure Gaines implies that the monolith of racism cannot be easily demolished. Razing it will necessitate a different kind of tactic, a different kind of courage, a different kind of leadership.

Ultimately at the end of the autobiography, it is Jane who emerges as a true leader and effects change, not through rhetoric, or as she terms it "retrick," not through tactics, but through her sheer presence and the symbolism embodied in her life. Her decision to go to Bayonne and carry on the protest begun by Jimmy (actually, in a larger context begun by Ned) is the catalyst that charges the rest of the community. A full circle is completed here, as the novel begins with Jane in a position of leadership, guiding Ned to Ohio and freedom, and ends with Jane in a similar position, leading her people in peaceful protest.

Jane's confrontation with racism is not one bordering on insanity, as is Copper's; it is not one that lacks direction, as does Jackson's; and it is not one that is destined to fail from the beginning, as is Marcus's. Gaines casts it as a simple act of personal dignity that commands respect, and the very simplicity of its nature seems to guarantee its success. When Robert Samson, the owner of her plantation, attempts to stop her from attending the protest in Bayonne by reminding her of Jimmy's death, Jane replies, "Just a little piece of him is dead.... The rest of him is waiting for us in Bayonne." She ends her autobiography by describing a scene of quiet strength and understated defiance as she closes: "Me and Robert looked at each other there a long time, then I went by him." The introductory clause of this sentence is a relatively long one for the phraseology given Jane Pittman and serves to build the suspense that allows us to appreciate the finality of Jane's action in the second clause, "then I went by him."

As Gaines considers the question of leadership, it is evident that for him any real and lasting change must be effected through leaders and actions firmly rooted in a cultural past. What makes Jane such a symbol to her people is her connection to the African-American past and her embodiment of African-American history. The people of the quarters look at Jane and see not a leader in the traditional sense of the word but a woman who has lived 111 years, one whose life has spanned many of the major events of black American history. In Jane they can see themselves, their parents, their grandparents, and their great-grandparents. Her presence personalizes their ancestral and sociopolitical history, while giving them strength to form a positive future.

Paraphrasing William Faulkner, Gaines has often stated, "The past ain't dead; it ain't even passed." *Miss Jane* reminds us that the past is never a distant memory for Ernest Gaines but is instead a constant influence on the present and future. As he listened to the stories of the old folks on his Aunt Augusteen's porch, the past arose, lived again, and donned a mantle of immediacy, and this influence of living cultural repositories was not lost on him. Accounts of what went before shape his creation of present literary experience, and homage to the past is characteristic, leading him to say of his work, "I was writing in a definite pattern.... I was going farther and farther back into the past. I was trying to go back, back, back into our experiences in this country to find some kind of meaning to our present lives." It is this meaning that Gaines embodies in Jane, and it this meaning that empowers her story to complement traditional histories. She recalls her life and that of others with a clarity that fosters an appreciation of the importance of her people's history to American culture. Jane's autobiography is an American history amplified by the many strains of African-American culture that con-

ventional histories of the United States may have muted. Her fictional narrative becomes a timeless American epic as myth, religion, and the recollections of former slaves all accentuate the historicity of her tale and Gaines's vision.

While the actions, patterns, and motifs of the novel are compelling and create a riveting history of America from slavery to the mid-1960s, it is Miss Jane whom we remember. She is the composite of all Gaines characters who embark upon difficult journeys leading to psychic freedom and definitions of self contrary to those their society imposes upon them.

Source: "From History to Her-story: The Autobiography of Miss Jane Pittman," *Ernest Gaines,* Twayne Publishers, 1991, pp. 92–96.

Valerie Melissa Babb

In the following excerpt, Babb examines Gaines's use of fictional character Jane Pittman as a vehicle for his vision of black slavery in American history.

Jane's autobiography gives a detailed, interior view of a familiar epoch, and the uniqueness and veracity of her voice compel the reader into an imaginary union with her historic vision. Her choice of words, selection of details, and inclusion of many asides allow her to capture general, regional, and personal histories. Her recalling the series of teachers employed to instruct the black children of her plantation is an example. As she reviews the nature of education on her plantation, Jane digresses momentarily to tell the story of the Creole family, the LeFabres. By placing a family's experience, views, and values in the middle of a general history of black education on a postbellum plantation, she gracefully includes a supplementary component, the color division within Creole society, that gives her story a distinct Louisiana flavor. Jane also employs temporal markers specific to her Louisiana world to lend order to the diverse events of her history. In recalling larger events, such as the institution of sharecropping and the fight for civil rights, she uses signposts, such as the election and death of Huey P. Long and the floods of 1917 and 1927, as narrative guides. Both her asides and her markers are traditional devices used to structure oral narrative, but they are crafted to give history a regional and personal perspective. Jane's memory unfolds an alternative to the standard and reminds us that history is made up of diverse individuals. Slavery, Reconstruction, and the beginnings of the civil rights movement are all documented through the language, art forms, mythology, spirituals, and folk sermons of one woman and her immediate community.

Book 1 of the narrative of this singular woman begins with the era that has most influenced African-American experience in the United States, slavery. Entitled "The War Years," this section of the work is given over to Jane's concrete descriptions of her life as a bondwoman. The horrendous details of barbarity and dehumanization present in other accounts of the slave system are present here, but Jane's treatment of these details is somewhat different. She reveals not only the facts of slavery but also her personal thoughts and reactions to the experience of bondage. Her account is given greater power by comments and analyses depicting both slavery's inhumanity and the manner in which slaves sought to overcome dehumanization. Every facet of "the peculiar institution" is individualized within Jane's narrative, and historic wrongs against a mass of people that might have remained abstract in other historical documents become keenly felt, immediate wrongs against a character so real she seems alive. Her vivid portraits render the horrors of slavery even more abhorrent because they occur to a character whose psyche we know so intimately.

Jane's descriptions reveal an acute, active mind that immediately counters the stereotype of the ignorant, unfeeling slave. In recounting her experience while bringing water to Confederate soldiers, she articulates a slave's perception of the lack of significance chattel status imposes: "They couldn't tell if I was white or black, a boy or a girl. They didn't even care what I was." Jane's matter-of-fact tone as she details the casual denial of her presence constitutes a vivid reminder that the disavowal of a slave's humanity was routine. A subsequent description of a similar encounter contrasts sharply to this earlier episode in which Jane is objectified. In this account Jane brings water to a thirsty Union legion, and soldiers unsympathetic to her status as a human being are replaced by those who acknowledge her existence. One even confers a symbolic token of that acknowledgment, a name. Through Jane's joy, we see what the act of choosing a name comes to symbolize: the possibility of defining identity. She is so taken with the name and the gallantry of the Union soldier who gives it to her that both become representations of the distant ideal of freedom she subsequently seeks upon emancipation.

The action of the Union soldier tempers the denial of personal identity through the denial of such vital personal rights as the prerogative to choose one's name. Though yet another white man arbitrarily changes her name from Ticey to Jane Brown because, as the soldier says, "Ticey is a slave name," this process is different for Jane. The soldier's altering a label of slavery reveals a new world of control to her, one in which the power of the master, in this case manifested through naming, is not final. A name is chosen for her, but for the first time in her life Jane has the option of deciding whether or not she will retain it. Her jubilation in having a choice and a name she perceives as not being rooted in slavery is expressed when she says, "I just stood there grinning.... It was the prettiest name I had ever heard."

Jane pays a high price for her new appellation, and in her subsequent recalcitrance we see the power of nomenclature to confer personal identity and pride, the very characteristics the system of slavery sought to suppress. As her master and mistress punish her for insubordination, the self-esteem she derives from choosing her own name mitigates the arbitrary brutality used to enforce their power within the slave system:

> I raised my head high and looked her straight in the face and said: "You called me Ticey. My name ain't no Ticey no more, it's Miss Jane Brown...." That night ... she told my master I had sassed her.... My master told two of the other slaves to hold me down.... My master jecked up my dress and gived my mistress the whip and told her to teach me a lesson. Every time she hit me she asked me what I said my name was. I said Jane Brown. She hit me again: what I said my name was. I said Jane Brown.

> My mistress got tired of beating me and told my master to beat me some. He told her that was enough, I was already bleeding.By demanding to be called not only by a new name but also by the title "Miss," Jane demands respect and recognition of an existence apart from that of a slave....

As Jane's narrative continues, she relates one of the most important aspects of black life after slavery, the journey to freedom. In earlier preemancipation African-American literature, fear of jeopardizing the safety of those seeking liberation and those assisting in its attainment made precise descriptions of journeys to freedom a rarity. Though her account unfolds after emancipation, Jane's recall furnishes a possible likeness of this often-absent chapter in slave literature. While she is no longer a slave, her freedom is tenuous at best, and her descriptions of heading north contain perils similar to those alluded to in many slave narratives.

She recalls in detail the former slaves' fear, their hope, and the rather cryptic freedom that existed for them after the Civil War: "We didn't know a thing. We didn't know where we was going, we didn't know what we was go'n eat.... We didn't know where we was go'n sleep that night. If we reached the North, we didn't know if we was go'n stay together or separate. We had never thought about nothing like that, because we had never thought we was go'n ever be free. Yes, we had heard about freedom, we had even talked about freedom, but we never thought we was go'n ever see that day." Not having any hope for freedom, Jane did not need a clear conception of liberty. The systematic debasement of slavery was designed in part to make certain that no slave was prepared for the advent of freedom; therefore, considerations of future action were few because emancipation was a remote ideal rather than a reality. Though very much a realist, Jane falls prey to simplifying freedom, thinking that emancipation included the provision of such basic necessities as food, shelter, and clothing. Ironically, her position comes very close to exemplifying the argument used by "benevolent" slaveholders for the continuance of "the peculiar institution": that slaves were docile, witless innocents incapable of self-preservation. Jane's thoughts and life belie that argument, however, and debunk the popular myth of black helplessness.

The shock of freedom's reality first jars Jane when she discovers that emancipation not only entails heretofore-denied responsibility but also bestows a nebulous freedom that guarantees no human rights. The intoxication of liberation is replaced by the sobriety of a slave's tenuous existence when she hides in a thicket, watching as fellow slaves are massacred by former members of the slave patrols and former Confederate soldiers. In this powerful and moving scene, Jane describes the remnants of the band of slaves in her usual matter-of-fact tone and underscores the similarity between antebellum and postbellum brutality: "I saw people laying everywhere. All of them was dead or dying, or so broken up they wouldn't ever move on their own." The scene gathers power as Jane recalls her reaction and the reaction of the little boy she informally adopts, Ned, to the killing of his mother and little sister.

At this point in her narrative, Jane is a child of 11 and Ned is even younger. One is struck by their stoicism as much as by the violence and brutality of the murder. Both remain collected during the massacre, and Jane has the presence of mind to hide Ned, while he has the presence of mind to remain quiet. As she says of him, "Small as he was he knowed death was only a few feet away." Slavery has forced a mature awareness of death upon the children. Loss of life and fragmentation of family are everyday occurrences, and Jane and Ned are prepared to deal with both as unfortunate eventualities....

Viewing the killing of Laura, her baby, and the other ex-slaves matures Jane and alters her conception of freedom, but only somewhat. She is still unaware of the vast geographical distance that stands between her and Ned and the freedom they seek in the North. Her naïveté is evident in her misguided sense of direction, which tells her Ohio is a week's walk from Louisiana. She sets off, actually walking farther south, and a series of picaresque episodes follow, commenting on segments of southern society during Reconstruction. Each is a symbol, and each teaches Jane of the difficulties of freedom: the black hunter seeking his father symbolizes fragmented families and tells Jane freedom "ain't North"; an eccentric old white man reveals the hypocrisy of Jane's freedom and tells her that at her present rate it will take her "about thirty years. Give or take a couple" to reach freedom; and a poor white farmer who by refusing to fight "their war" symbolizes the class conflict among whites during the Civil War leads Jane and Ned to tenuous shelter on a plantation run by the newly formed Freedman's Bureau. Jane's path from one encounter to the next becomes a circular route returning her to where she began, the plantations of Louisiana, and her circuitous movement back to her origins dramatizes Gaines's concept of freedom and progress. She returns "home" because, in his view, true liberation and the progress it engenders are not an abstract, such as the notion of "freedom," or a spatial entity, such as "the North," but rather a spiritual entity, deeply rooted in a person's character, dignity, and knowledge of his or her history and place. With the exception of one segment, the remainder of Jane's story takes place in the parishes of Louisiana that provide the setting for other Gaines works and details the personal choices she makes to progress toward spiritual freedom.

Book 2 of Jane's memoir, entitled "Reconstruction," achieves exactly that, a reconstruction of significant historical events in a new context. In her rendering of the epoch after the Civil War, the upheaval of the southern social order and the new relationship of North to South shift from a central position and become backdrops for Jane's observations of the similarities between slavery and Reconstruction. In describing sharecropping, Jane reveals it as the reincarnation of slavery. The exploitation, absence of regular education, and denial of human rights that typified one now typify the other: "It was slavery again, all right. No such thing as colored troops, colored politicians, or a colored teacher anywhere near the place.... You had to give Colonel Dye's name if the secret group stopped you on the road. Just because the Yankee troops and the Freedom Beero had gone didn't mean they had stopped riding. They rode and killed more than ever now.... Yankee money came in to help the South back on her feet—yes; but no Yankee troops. We was left there to root hog or die." Jane's characterization of the North contrasts sharply to her early idealized vision of a place filled with citizens sympathetic to the plight of African Americans. She is now clearly aware of a North uninterested in racial equality and seeking only to rebuild a southern economy and reunite it with that of the North. For black Americans still uneducated, still hunted by secret patrols, and still monitored strictly, the "North" as an entity had changed little. Through the institution of sharecropping, economic servitude replaced physical servitude, and the negation of humanity remained constant. In detailing her and her husband Joe's efforts to free themselves from the trap of tenant farming, Jane makes it evident that extricating oneself from economic bondage was almost as difficult as extricating oneself from physical bondage. The intimacy characterizing Jane's view of the slavery epoch is continued in her descriptions of tenant farming....

In book 3, "The Plantation," Jane's narrative moves forward in time, fleshing out life on Samson plantation, her last home. She relates stories of the people of the quarters, and larger historic and current events recede from prominence and assume the place of backdrops. Taken as a whole, these recollections serve as modified allegory, illuminating particular aspects of black culture. In the section entitled "Miss Lilly," for example, Jane tells about the stern Lilly, "a bowlegged mulatto woman," whose aspirations for the children of the quarters force her to impose a value system inappropriate to their day-to-day reality of sharecropping: "She didn't just want lesson, she wanted the girls to come there with their dresses ironed, she wanted ribbons in their hair. The boys had to wear ties, had to shine their shoes. Brogans or no brogans, she wanted them shined." Teachers are a valuable commodity in Jane's world, and rare. Lilly, unfortunately, seems to be more concerned with the outward appearances of her charges than with their inward edification, and Jane uses her to illustrate the belief that education must be utilitarian and relevant to be successful. Lilly's story also signifies the obstacles faced in schooling rural black children who must eke out an education between the harvesting of crops. Further, the number of teachers assigned to the plantation makes clear that the ignorance mandated by law in slavery is now perpetuated in a more benign manner: "After Miss Lilly, then came Hardy. Joe Hardy was one of the worst human beings I've ever met.... Telling poor people the government wasn't paying much, so he would 'preciate it if they could help him out some.... For a year and a half we didn't have a school on the place at all. Going into the second year we got that LeFabre girl." The "LeFabre girl" Jane refers to is Mary Agnes LeFabre, a Creole woman who comes to Jane's plantation to escape the strict doctrines of her Creole society. In recalling her history on the plantation, Jane creates a modified allegory that illuminates the complexities of the color line and the self-hatred that engendered it....

Personal recollections with overtones of social allegory are only part of Jane's commentary. As she continues to divulge the details of her history, she makes larger American history a living and present process. Important figures of the American past are not two-dimensional portraits housed in history books but human beings who impact on the lives of other human beings such as Jane. The immediacy in her description of Frederick Douglass is an instance: "Now, after the Yankee soldiers and Freedom Beero left, the people started leaving again. Not right away—because Mr. Frederick Douglass said give the South a chance. But when the people saw they was treated just as bad now as before the war they said to heck with Mr. Frederick Douglass and started leaving." In Jane's portrait Frederick Douglass is not the great orator, abstracted and removed from his cultural roots. Instead he is demythologized and shown to be part of a people's daily life as they attempt to make decisions that will form their history and future....

The personal interpretation Jane gives to history she also gives to traditional Christian religion, and her religion answers the hollow proclamations of the ministers in previous Gaines works. A spiritual woman, she is not awed by religious conventions. She will as soon sit before the radio to listen to Jackie Robinson play baseball on a Sunday as go to church. Her reverence for religion and its symbols is balanced by day-to-day realism, and she keenly feels that worship should not be divorced from life. The use of biblical images and terminology to mark the daily events of life on Samson plantation underscores Jane's pragmatic spiritualism, and the Bible's language is no longer remote but instead provides a fitting lexicon for describing significant periods in black history. The term *exodus,* for example, is used to refer to black migration: "Droves after droves ... was leaving. If you went to town you would see whole families going by. Men in front with bundles on their backs, women following them with a child in their arm and holding another one by the hand.... They slipped away at night, they took to the swamps, they ... went." Jane is a realist and sees that the stories of the Bible are meant as examples. She discerns its mythic nature, viewing its accounts as attempts to explain natural phenomena, the origin of humankind, traditions, and rituals. It is thus easy for her to see relevancy and importance in both the teachings of the Bible and the myths that derive from her own culture. Figures of African-American lore are given as much prominence as biblical figures in Jane's narrative. The former interact intimately with her community, and the immediacy of their presence is incorporated into her episodes. In Jane's encounter with the hoodoo woman Madame Eloise Gautier, we see that the legendary hoodoo queen Marie Leveau and her daughter are made integral parts of the communal psyche: "The hoo-doo lived on a narrow little street called Dettie street.... She was a big mulatto woman, and she had come from New Orleans. At least that was her story. She had left New Orleans because she was a rival of Marie Laveau. Marie Laveau was the Queen then, you know, and nobody dare rival Marie Laveau. Neither Marie Laveau mama, neither Marie Laveau daughter who followed her. Some people said the two Maries was the same one, but, of course, that was people talk." Consistently, whether recalling historical events, analyzing biblical parables, or recounting the doings of legendary figures, Jane's insights join the folk and the mythic in a unique historic vision.

Source: "From History to Her-story: The Autobiography of Miss Jane Pittman," *Ernest Gaines,* Twayne Publishers, 1991, pp. 80-92.

Sources

Martin Amis, "MacPosh," in *New Statesman,* September 2, 1973, pp. 205-206.

Jerry H. Bryant, "From Death to Life: The Fiction of Ernest J. Gaines," in the *Iowa Review,* Vol. 3, No. 1, 1972, pp. 106-120.

Addison Gayle, Jr., "The Way of the New World Part II," in his *The Way of the New World: The Black Novel in America,* Doubleday, 1975, pp. 287-310.

Josh Greenfield, in a review of *The Autobiography of Miss Jane Pittman,* in *Life,* April 30, 1971.

Melvin Maddocks, "Root and Branch," in *Time,* May 10, 1971, pp. K13-K17.

"Southern Cross," a review of *The Autobiography of Miss Jane Pittman,* in *Times Literary Supplement,* March 16, 1973, p. 303.

Winifred L. Stoelting, "Human Dignity and Pride in the Novels of Ernest Gaines," in *CLA Journal,* March, 1971, pp. 340-358.

Alice Walker, in a review of *The Autobiography of Miss Jane Pittman,* in *New York Times Book Review,* May 23, 1971, pp. 6, 12.

For Further Study

Valerie Melissa Babb, *Ernest Gaines,* Twayne, 1991.
See chapter five in particular, in which Babb examines the role of a woman as narrator. Includes an annotated bibliography of Gaines criticism (including articles, reviews, and interviews) up to the mid-1980s.

Herman Beavers, *Wrestling Angels into Song: The Fictions of Ernest J. Gaines and James Alan McPherson,* University of Pennsylvania Press, 1995.
In the fifth chapter, Beavers contends that Gaines re-envisions William Faulkner's alienated South by promoting storytelling as a power for social rejuvenation and as a means to reinforce community.

B. A. Botkin, editor, *Lay My Burden Down: A Folk History of Slavery,* University of Chicago Press, 1945.
A collection of interviews with ex-slaves conducted by the Work Projects Administration in the 1930s and 1940s. Gaines made use of this text in creating an authentic speech pattern for Miss Jane and other characters in her autobiography.

Keith E. Byerman, "A 'Slow-to-Anger' People: *The Autobiography of Miss Jane Pittman* as Historical Fiction," in *Critical Reflections on the Fiction of Ernest J. Gaines,* edited by David C. Estes, University of Georgia Press, 1994, pp. 107-123.
Byerman, in part responding to Babb (see above), contends that Jane's actions should be understood in terms of her instinct for survival rather than for resistance.

John F. Callahan, *In the African-American Grain: The Pursuit of Voice in Twentieth-Century Black Fiction,* University of Illinois Press, 1988.
A wide-ranging study of speakers and voices in the tradition of African-American storytelling.

Mary Ellen Doyle, "Ernest J. Gaines: An Annotated Bibliography, 1956-1988," *Black American Literature Forum,* Vol. 24, No. 21, Spring 1990, pp. 125-151.

The most comprehensive annotated bibliography at the time of its publication.

David C. Estes, editor, *Critical Reflections on the Fiction of Ernest J. Gaines,* University of Georgia Press, 1994.
A collection of critical essays by various authors on Gaines's major fiction. Includes an extensive bibliography on Gaines and African-American studies to 1994.

Ernest Gaines, in an interview in *Essence,* April 30, 1971.
Gaines rationalized the setting of his novel in rural Louisiana, by saying that 350 years of black experience has occurred in this rural setting. This cannot be ignored, but not much has been written about it. Conversely, authors such as Ralph Ellison, Ann Petry, Langston Hughes, and Richard Wright have already captured one hundred years of experience in ghetto narratives.

Marcia Gaudet, "Miss Jane and Personal Experience Narrative: Ernest Gaines's *The Autobiography of Miss Jane Pittman,*" in *Western Folklore,* Vol. 51, No. 1, January, 1992, pp. 23-33.
Gaudet observes that Gaines uses his experience in oral traditions to create for Jane a truly authentic voice.

Blyden Jackson, "Jane Pittman Through the Years: A People's Tale," in *American Letters and the Historical Consciousness: Essays in Honor of Lewis P. Simpson,* edited by J. Gerald Kennedy and Daniel Mark Fogel, Louisiana State University Press, 1987, pp. 255-73.
Blyden asserts that Gaines records Jane's life as the history of an entire race.

Gayl Jones, *Liberating Voices: Oral Tradition in African American Literature,* Harvard University Press, 1991.
Jones demonstrates Gaines's ability to create distinct, authentic voices for Jane and other characters and his commitment to the literary possibilities of African-American linguistic traditions.

John Lowe, editor, *Conversations with Ernest J. Gaines,* University Press of Mississippi, 1995.
A collection of interviews with Gaines by various persons, 1964-1994.

Lee Papa, "'His Feet on Your Neck': The New Religion in the Works of Ernest J. Gaines," in *African American Review,* Vol. 27, No. 2, Summer, 1993, pp. 187-94.
Papa examines Gaines's African-American reinterpretation of Christianity in his novels. He argues that Gaines's characters develop a very personal interpretation of religion which allows them to make and understand self-sacrifice and to establish a deeper relationship with their community.

Anne Robinson Taylor, *Male Novelists and Their Female Voices: Literary Masquerades,* Whitston, 1981.
A general study of the ways male authors use, create, and alter the voices of female narrators.

H. Nigel Thomas, "The Bad Nigger Figure in Selected Works of Richard Wright, William Melvin Kelley, and Ernest Gaines," in *CLA Journal,* Vol. 39, No. 2, December, 1995, pp. 143-165.
A study of the ways in which Wright, Kelley, and Gaines revise and complicate the figure of an unpredictable, dangerous, or uncompromising African-American male character.

The Bean Trees

Barbara Kingsolver

1988

Barbara Kingsolver demonstrates that politics are personal in *The Bean Trees,* her novel of friendship and survival set in the arid American Southwest. The novel focuses on Taylor Greer's search for a new life as she moves from her dull Kentucky home to exotic Arizona and the lessons that she learns along the way. Taylor's adoption of an abused Cherokee toddler, her friendship with a pair of Guatemalan refugees, and her support system of a small community of women, all contribute to the novel's central conviction that people cannot survive without empathy and generosity. Published in 1988 to an enthusiastic critical reception, *The Bean Trees* won an American Library Association award and a School Library Association award and has found a devoted reading audience around the world. Critics and readers alike relish Taylor's humor and warmth, with her down-home speech and perceptive observations. Like her narrator, Kingsolver grew up in Kentucky, and she draws from the voices she heard in her youth to create Taylor's voice. This voice helps to guide the novel, with its strong humanitarian views, away from simple political correctness toward a rich believability. Kingsolver has been praised for her skill in *The Bean Trees* at walking the fine line between preaching and taking a moral stand, and Taylor's straightforwardness and humor provide the cornerstone to Kingsolver's approach.

Author Biography

Born in 1955 in Annapolis, Maryland, Kingsolver grew up in rural Kentucky. She began writing as a young child, but chose to study biology in college at DePauw University. In her twenties she moved to Tucson, Arizona, where she eventually earned a graduate degree in ecology at the University of Arizona. Following graduate school, Kingsolver turned back to her life-long love—writing—and began writing nonfiction as a technical writer in a scientific program at the university. By the mid-1980s she was writing and publishing short fiction. Her contact in Arizona with people from Latin America, particularly refugees, influenced Kingsolver's choice of subject matter when she turned to fiction. Published in 1988, *The Bean Trees* was her first novel.

Best known as a novelist, Kingsolver also writes poetry, nonfiction, and short fiction. She believes that fiction can be used as an instrument of social change, and her own fiction reflects this belief. Kingsolver describes her political stance as that of a "human rights activist"; to pursue these interests, she belongs to Amnesty International and the Committee for Human Rights in Latin America, two humanitarian organizations that advance the cause of human rights around the world. In 1997 she established a literary prize, the Bellwether Prize, to be awarded every year to a first novel of exceptional literary distinction that also embodies this belief in fiction's power to change the world.

Kingsolver describes herself as a pantheist; pantheism is not an organized religion but is more a doctrine based upon the belief that the natural world is imbued with a divine presence. Rooted in her Kentucky childhood, she credits her interest in nature as having been a major influence on her life, and her work reflects her sense that the environment cannot be ignored. In *The Bean Trees,* the dry Arizona landscape that manages to produce flowers and vegetables is central to the novel, as it reflects the deprived lives of the characters who are able to flourish in spite of their difficult circumstances.

Kingsolver has won several literary awards for her work, among them an American Library Association award and a School Library Association award for *The Bean Trees.* Audiences around the world have responded warmly to *The Bean Trees,* as it has been translated into several languages and published in more than sixty-five countries.

Barbara Kingsolver

Plot Summary

The heroine of *The Bean Trees,* Marietta (otherwise known as Miss Marietta, Missy, and Taylor Greer) is determined to avoid becoming a pregnant teen. Her early years in Eastern Kentucky have been heavily influenced by her perception that Pittman County is "behind the nation in practically every way you can think of, except the rate of teenage pregnancies." She has also been influenced by her supportive mother, and by her work with "blood and pee" in a hospital lab.

After saving enough money to buy a '55 Volkswagon bug, Taylor drives away from Pittman County. She renames herself Taylor Greer when she runs out of gas in Taylorville. Then she acquires an unwanted and abused Cherokee baby girl outside a bar in Oklahoma. She names the baby Turtle, for her habit of "holding on."

Taylor stops at the Broken Arrow motel, where she works as a maid through the Christmas holidays. The work is uninspiring; she says that "the only thing to remind you you weren't dead was the constant bickering between [motel employees] old Mrs. Hoge and Irene."

Taylor adapts to life as a mother and maid, while the novel shifts its focus to Lou Ann Ruiz, another Eastern Kentucky emigre whose husband, Angel, has left her seven months pregnant. Although Angel generally ridicules and rejects Lou Ann, he also shows unexpected kindness by returning home to help Lou Ann keep up appearances when her mother and grandmother visit.

Meanwhile, Taylor leaves the Broken Arrow motel and heads west, finally ending her journey at the Jesus is Lord Used Tires in Tucson, Arizona, with two flat tires. The shop's owner, Mattie, lets Taylor park her car on shop property until she can afford to repair it.

Taylor takes up residence in the Hotel Republic and gets a short-lived job at The Burger Derby. Her co-worker, Sandi, tells her about Kid Central Station, a babysitting service for mall shoppers. Taylor takes advantage of Kid Central Station until she is fired from her job after six days of work.

She decides to find a roommate, which is how she meets up with Lou Ann. The two young women, each parent to a young child, each with a Kentucky accent, become instant friends. Where Lou Ann is fearful, Taylor is confident and vigorous, or so it seems initially.

Taylor begins working for Mattie at Jesus is Lord Used Tires and gradually learns that, besides operating a tire business, Mattie is operating a safe house for Guatemalan refugees. Taylor becomes friends with two of these refugees, Estevan and his wife Esperanza.

When Taylor takes Turtle to Dr. Pelinowsky for a check-up, she discovers that Turtle is probably a three-year-old, even though she is only as developed as a two-year-old. Dr. Pelinowsky explains that Turtle has "failed to thrive in an environment of physical or emotional deprivation."

When Esperanza, who is grieving the loss of her homeland and of her own child, attempts suicide, Taylor responds, somewhat naively, that it is "worse to never have anyone to lose than to lose someone." Despite her inherent optimism, Taylor begins to despair at the violence in the world, and begins to doubt in her own ability to nurture Turtle in the face of so much violence.

Meanwhile, Lou Ann gets a job and begins to gain confidence. As Taylor puts it, Lou Ann stops "comparing her figure to various farm animals." When Angel sends Lou Ann a calfskin belt and says he misses her, Lou Ann hesitates, considering her "new responsibilities" at work, as well as her responsibilities to her husband.

Turtle, too, begins to flourish. Her first sound is a laugh, her first word is "bean," and she is rapidly becoming versed in the language of horticulture. However, when Taylor's blind neighbor and babysitter, Edna Poppy, is attacked, Turtle's eyes instantly grow black. The child retreats into herself, into silence. Taylor begins a parallel retreat, in which she continues to question her own ability to mother when the "whole way of the world is to pick on people that can't fight back."

Enter Cynthia, a social worker who explains to Taylor that she has no legal right to Turtle. As Taylor enters her own period of despair, Lou Ann becomes her advocate, reminding her that there is no alternative world to turn to, and that Taylor may not feel up to motherhood, but then, neither does any other mother.

Taylor decides to fight for the right to adopt Turtle and, in collaboration with Mattie, develops a plan to drive Estevan and Esperanza to sanctuary in Oklahoma, while also searching for Turtle's biological parents. They begin their journey. Every time they pass a cemetery, Turtle shouts, "Mama!"

Although the search does not turn up Turtle's biological parents, the three young adults devise an alternative plan. Estevan and Esperanza will pretend to be Turtle's biological parents, the fictional Steven and Hope Two Two. Playing the roles of Mr. and Mrs. Two Two, they will sign Turtle over to Taylor.

The plan is not as far-fetched as it might sound, for Estevan and Esperanza already look and act the part of Turtle's parents. Furthermore, no one expects a child born to the Cherokee Nation tribal lands to have a birth certificate. Lawyer Mr. Jonas Wilford Armistead believes their story, and helps Taylor to draw up the necessary adoption papers.

Taylor says her good-byes to Estevan and Esperanza and calls up her mother, who, it turns out, has recently been remarried and has begun to take up gardening. Finally, Taylor heads back to her home in Arizona, daughter in tow.

Characters

Cynthia

The social worker who informs Taylor that she has no legal claim to Turtle but encourages her to try to adopt the little girl.

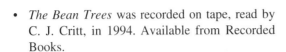

Media Adaptations

- *The Bean Trees* was recorded on tape, read by C. J. Critt, in 1994. Available from Recorded Books.

Esperanza

Esperanza, Estevan's wife, speaks little English and is silent throughout much of the novel; she also has a sad, distant quality about her, which makes Taylor wonder what has happened to her in the past. Upon meeting Esperanza for the first time, Taylor feels Esperanza's depression and notes that she "took up almost no space." Eventually Taylor learns that her sadness is due mostly to the fact that the small daughter she and Estevan had in Guatemala was taken from them by the government in a raid on their neighborhood. Esperanza's brother and two of their friends had also been killed in this raid. Taylor's daughter Turtle reminds Esperanza of her own lost daughter, and Turtle's presence often seems to be painful for Esperanza. When Esperanza tries to kill herself while at Mattie's, and Estevan comes to tell Taylor about the suicide attempt, Taylor learns for the first time from him of the violent political events in Guatemala that led to their escape to the United States. Following this conversation, Taylor begins to see Esperanza and Estevan in a new light, saying that "All of Esperanza's hurts flamed up in my mind, a huge pile of burning things that the world just kept throwing more onto."

Estevan

A gentle, handsome young English teacher who fled with his wife to the United States from Guatemala, Estevan becomes friendly with Taylor and teaches her about real pain and loss when he describes to her the brutal world he and Esperanza left behind them. Estevan and Esperanza have found sanctuary at Mattie's house, and it is through Mattie that they eventually meet Taylor and Lou Ann. As she gets to know him better, Taylor feels herself falling in love with Estevan; she has never known anyone else like him. He has impeccable manners, speaks "perfect English," and is sensitive and wise. He loves Esperanza dearly and is utterly devoted to her, and Taylor respects their relationship. Although Estevan was an English teacher in Guatemala, and also speaks Spanish and his native Mayan dialect, his job in Tucson is as a dishwasher in a Chinese restaurant. Taylor is outraged that such a learned man as Estevan should be reduced to such a lowly position, but he is humble, knowing that he is fortunate to have escaped his dangerous circumstances in Guatemala. Estevan's story of these circumstances teaches Taylor to see her own life in a new way: she realizes that her own life has not really been as hard as she has thought, that her "whole life had been running along on dumb luck and [she] hadn't even noticed."

April Turtle Greer
See Turtle Greer

Taylor Greer

Taylor Greer's wise, colorful voice narrates the novel, and she serves as its central consciousness. A smart and spirited young woman who drives across the country alone to escape the monotony of her hometown, Taylor knows who she is and what she wants, but she is no rugged individualist—she needs other people to be part of her world. Born Marietta Greer in Pittman County, Kentucky, Taylor possessed a strong sense of identity even at a young age. While she was growing up, her Mama cleaned houses for wealthy people, and she heard her Mama call her employers "Miss this or Mister that." At the age of three Taylor knew she too deserved that kind of respect; she insisted on being called "*Miss* Marietta," and then "Miss Marietta" evolved into "Missy."

When Taylor leaves Pittman County for good as a young woman, she decides "that I would get myself a new name" for her new life, and she chooses the name Taylor because her broken-down '55 Volkswagen bug runs out of gas in Taylorville, Illinois. By fleeing her home, Taylor intends to escape the seemingly narrow life that her peers in Pittman County lead. But ironically, in her new life in Arizona she ends up with a child and employed at a used tire repair shop. She tells Estevan that "I spent the first half of my life avoiding motherhood and tires, and now I'm counting them as blessings." Taylor is a survivor and makes the best of her circumstances. She values loyalty and community, and in spite of her long-held desire to avoid motherhood, is fully committed to raising Turtle. She learns about nurturing and mothering from Mattie and Lou Ann, and she discovers through Estevan and Esperanza that her life has not been nearly as difficult as she has often thought—in fact, "even bad luck brings good things."

Taylor's low point comes when the safe world she has created for Turtle is violated, and she begins to feel helplessly that "the whole way of the world is to pick on people that can't fight back." However, when she sees that she can help Estevan and Esperanza, and simultaneously figures out a way to adopt Turtle, she begins to feel more powerful in the face of a cruel world. Taylor ultimately is willing to risk danger to help her friends and to adopt Turtle.

Turtle Greer

Turtle is a silent, needy Cherokee toddler Taylor has foisted upon her by a frightened woman—Turtle's aunt—in the parking lot of a roadside bar in Oklahoma. The woman seems to want to save Turtle from something; she is nervous and appears to be afraid of a man who waits for her in his truck while she gives the baby to Taylor with no explanation: "Just take it," she begs Taylor. Taylor resists at first, telling the woman that "you can't just give somebody a kid," but she finally feels she has no choice, so she takes the baby. Taylor names her Turtle because of "the way that child held on." She tells the baby, "You're like a mud turtle. If a mud turtle bites you, it won't let go till it thunders."

Taylor soon discovers that Turtle has been badly abused and decides that she will keep her and take good care of her. Turtle begins to flourish under Taylor's care. In the dry Arizona weather, she grows and begins to talk, and all of her talk centers on growing things: flowers and vegetables. She loves Mattie's huge garden, learns the names of everything in the seed catalogs, and pretends that she is planting and tending to her own gardens. Taylor eventually must face the fact that she is keeping Turtle illegally, but by then the two feel like a real mother and daughter, so Taylor decides to adopt Turtle. The adoption process Taylor undertakes is unorthodox and not really legal, but it works, and the pair is able to stay together.

Newt Hardbine

Newt is one of the notorious Hardbine clan in Pittman County, Kentucky. Taylor knows Newt as "one of the big boys who had failed every grade at least once and so was practically going on twenty in the sixth grade." Taylor is at work at the hospi-

tal when Newt is wheeled in on a gurney, shot to death by his father, who had once been thrown by an exploding tractor tire up over the top of the Standard Oil sign. Throughout the novel, Newt and the Hardbines represent to Taylor the sordid world she left behind in Pittman County.

Ismene

Ismene is Estevan and Esperanza's young daughter, who was taken from them by the Guatemalan government. Turtle resembles Ismene and reminds Estevan and Esperanza of her.

Granny Logan

Lou Ann's paternal grandmother, who accompanies Lou Ann's mother from Kentucky to visit after Dwayne Ray is born. Granny Logan is suspicious of the Arizona weather—it is hot and dry in January—and of her granddaughter's new life in this strange place. Granny is prickly and is not speaking to her daughter-in-law during their visit.

Ivy Logan

Lou Ann's mother, who travels by bus from Kentucky with her irritable mother-in-law to help Lou Ann after Dwayne Ray is born. Ivy is a hard worker, dispenses maternal advice to Lou Ann about breastfeeding and her weight, and misses her daughter. She and her mother-in-law are not on the best of terms with one another and are not speaking during their visit with Lou Ann; they ask Lou Ann to act as a go-between for them.

Mother Logan

See Granny Logan

Miss Marietta

See Taylor Greer

Missy

See Taylor Greer

Mama

Taylor's Mama is the biggest influence on her as she grows up, and after Taylor leaves her Kentucky home and changes her name from Marietta to Taylor, she can still feel her Mama's support from a distance. Taylor says that Mama "always expected the best out of me…. [and] whatever I came home with, she acted like it was the moon I had just hung up in the sky and plugged in all the stars. Like I was that good."

Mattie

Mattie is the strong, nurturing widow who owns Jesus Is Lord Used Tires, helps Taylor and Turtle when they first arrive in Tucson, and shelters Estevan and Esperanza and other Central American refugees in her home. Mattie is a kind of conductor on the underground railroad-like system that locates such refugees—termed "illegal aliens" by the United States government—and gives them sanctuary. Mattie impresses Taylor at first as a "woman with . . . know-how," and as the two women get to know each other, Mattie becomes a surrogate mother to Taylor and surrogate grandmother to Turtle. Mattie's nurturing personality is also expressed in her garden, "a bright, wild wonderland of flowers and vegetables and auto parts."

Mrs. Parsons

See Virgie Mae Parsons

Virgie Mae Parsons

A sour and stodgy woman, Virgie Mae Parsons lives with Edna next door to Lou Ann and Taylor. She eventually warms up to the young women and their children as she gets to know them. Mrs. Parsons always has a "grip" on Edna's elbow, as she guides her blind friend from place to place.

Edna Poppy

Sweet, kind, and always dressed in red, white-haired Edna lives with Virgie Mae Parsons next door to Taylor and Lou Ann. The two older ladies frequently help their young neighbors by watching the children. After knowing Edna for several months, Taylor is stunned to discover one day that she is blind, but she says to Lou Ann when sharing this information with her, "[Edna] has her own special ways of keeping an eye on things." In spite of her sensitivity to whatever is going on around her, Edna depends largely on her friend Virgie to guide her through the physical world.

Angel Ruiz

Angel is Lou Ann's estranged husband. He left her on Halloween, three years after losing half of his leg—and "something else that was harder to pin down"—in an accident. Angel left Lou Ann when she was pregnant with Dwayne Ray. Lou Ann often has "the feeling that [Angel] didn't really like her or anyone else for that matter. He blamed people for things beyond their control." Angel is from a large Mexican-American family that loves Lou Ann and does not understand why he left her. He

had been a cowboy when Lou Ann met him and dreams of being one again.

Dwayne Ray Ruiz

The infant son of Lou Ann and Angel Ruiz, Dwayne Ray is the object of Lou Ann's extreme, often verging on hysterical, safeguarding.

Lou Ann Ruiz

Before Taylor moves in with her, Lou Ann is abandoned in Tucson by her husband Angel two months before their first baby is born. A country girl at heart, Lou Ann is far away from her own family in Kentucky and has neither friends nor a job. In the wreckage of her marriage, she and her infant son forge a new kind of family life with Taylor, Turtle, and their neighbors and friends. Taylor says that "For Lou Ann, life itself was a life-threatening enterprise. Nothing on earth was truly harmless." Lou Ann reads her horoscope, as well as Dwayne Ray's and Taylor's, every day and worries constantly that terrible things are going to happen, especially to her child. She lacks self-confidence and is always criticizing her appearance, complaining that "I ought to be shot for looking like this" or "I look like I've been drug through hell backwards." But Lou Ann has a kind heart and cares deeply about those who are closest to her, and as much as her self-criticism annoys Taylor, the two women help each other grow into motherhood.

Sandi

The perky teenage mother whom Taylor briefly works with at Burger Derby, Sandi is a survivor. Taylor says that "life had delivered Sandi a truckload of manure with no return address" but that "nothing really seemed to throw" her.

Alice Jean Stamper Greer

See Mama

Hope Two Two

See Esperanza

Steve Two Two

See Estevan

Hughes Walter

Hughes Walter is the handsome young science teacher who helps Taylor get her first real job, working at the Pittman County Hospital.

Mr. Walter

See Hughes Walter

Themes

Friendship

At the center of the novel, friendship is portrayed as having the power to transform even the loneliest and most broken of lives. When they first appear, most of the main characters—Taylor, Turtle, Lou Ann, Estevan and Esperanza—are broke, hurt, lonely, frightened, or just unlucky. However, as their friendships and fierce loyalty to one another grow, these forces begin to sustain the characters' lives. Alone in a city far from their homes, Taylor and Lou Ann make a new home by creating a kind of family with each other and their children. Mattie rescues Taylor and Turtle when they first arrive in Tucson by talking to them sympathetically and by giving Taylor a job. Mattie also rescues Estevan and Esperanza by giving them shelter and keeping them safe. Virgie Mae and Edna Poppy watch out for each other and help Taylor and Lou Ann with the children. Throughout the novel, the characters develop ties with one another by helping each other to survive in a difficult world. The community the characters build grows in the dry Arizona earth, just as the flowers and vegetables in Mattie's garden grow.

Choices and Consequences

Part of learning to survive is learning to make wise choices and realizing that one's choices have consequences. The novel shows how each character has faced important choices and then had to live with the consequences. The choices a character makes can also serve to define that character, showing him or her to be, for example, generous or selfish, strong or weak. The do-or-die moments portrayed in the novel include Taylor's choice to leave Pittman County; her split-second decision to keep Turtle when Turtle's aunt insists she "take this baby"; Estevan and Esperanza's choice not to turn in their friends to the police and also not to pursue Ismene after she was kidnapped; Lou Ann's choice not to return to Angel after he has left her; Taylor's choice to drive Estevan and Esperanza to a new safe house in Oklahoma; and her choice to adopt Turtle for good. Each of these choices is difficult—a viable option exists in each case—but a choice has to be made, and each of these choices has changed the character's life and defined the character.

Human Rights

Human rights involve personal safety and freedom, which most United States citizens take

Topics for Further Study

- Research 1980s U.S. immigration policies for Central American refugees. In what kinds of situations were refugees granted asylum in the United States? What was the nature of United States-Guatemala relations?

- Investigate the political situation in 1980s Guatemala. Who was in power, and what did the government expect of its citizens? Why would Estevan and Esperanza's teachers' union be considered a threat?

- Research weather patterns in Arizona: when and where does the rain fall, and what are the average temperatures throughout the year? Compare actual Tucson weather to its weather in the novel. Compare Tucson weather to Kentucky weather in terms of rainfall and temperatures.

- The teenage Cherokee girl in the bar tells Taylor that "The Cherokee Nation isn't any one place exactly. It's people." Research the Cherokee Nation in terms of its places and people: map its location(s) in Oklahoma, and investigate its values, government, and customs. Why might Taylor, as a white American, be confused about the definition of Cherokee Nation?

- Taylor's narrative often focuses on the vegetation she and her little community find and foster in Arizona. Investigate farming and gardening practices in the Tucson area and compare what you learn with Mattie's garden and other organic vegetation in the novel.

- Research the incidence of child abuse on Indian reservations in the 1970s and 1980s. How did the passage of the Indian Child Abuse Prevention and Treatment Act change the Native American child abuse rate?

for granted. In the novel, Latin American refugees Estevan and Esperanza, whose personal safety and freedom had been denied them in Guatemala, provide the obvious symbol for the theme of human rights. In addition, Turtle, as an abused member of the Cherokee Nation, represents two groups that have been denied human rights: abused children and Native Americans. But Taylor, as a sensitive and empathetic narrator, does not get bogged down in politics when she feels the injustice of human rights violations—she simply worries about people she loves. Her narrative is imbued with concern for human rights regardless of nationality or political views, and her view of the world changes as she becomes more exposed to the reality of human rights violations. Taylor begins to feel overwhelmed by sadness over what Turtle and Estevan and Esperanza have been through, saying to Lou Ann, "There's just so damn much ugliness. Everywhere you look, some big guy kicking some little person when they're down ... it just goes on and on, there's no end to it.... the whole way of the world is to pick on people that can't fight back." Her anger over what she sees as the "way of the world" leads her to try to fight against that way, as she chooses finally to adopt Turtle and to risk danger to deliver Estevan and Esperanza to safety. Taylor's rage and despair over human cruelty transforms her by motivating her to work against cruelty and oppression.

Human Condition

Although not all of the characters in the novel endure human rights violations, all of them find life to be hard in some way. No one in the novel has had an easy life: Taylor has always been poor, Turtle has been abused and abandoned, Lou Ann perceives herself as inadequate, Estevan and Esperanza have lost their child and fled their home country in political danger. But the novel's treatment of the theme of the human condition does not stop with the notion that life is difficult. The humor and friendships generated by the characters in spite of their troubles redeem the novel from presenting a bleak view of the human condition. The novel's stance is that friendship and the support it provides relieves the characters from life's oppressiveness. Mattie provides shelter, work, love, and moral support. Taylor takes care of Turtle. Lou Ann and Taylor make each other laugh and help each other with their children. Taylor and Estevan admire the way each other uses the English language. Virgie Mae and Edna watch Turtle and Dwayne Ray for Taylor and Lou Ann. The characters in the novel have to cope with poverty and may fear for their safety, yet the novel shows that even the most dismal of lives can be transformed by a community of friends.

Style

Point of View

Up until chapter five of *The Bean Trees,* the narrative point of view is split between a first-person narrator and a third-person narrator. In the chapters dealing with Taylor Greer, Taylor tells her own story, but the chapters that focus on Lou Ann Ruiz are narrated in the third person. After Lou Ann and Taylor meet in chapter five, Taylor's point of view takes over and the third-person narrative disappears. Taylor's first-person narration fleshes out her character and puts her at the center of the novel. The third-person narrative in Lou Ann's chapters has limited omniscience, which means that the narrator is able to see into the minds of only some of the characters. In these chapters, the narrative reveals Lou Ann's feelings and motivations, although there is some distance between Lou Ann and the reader. When the two narrative points of view merge in chapter five, a sense of harmony is created, as the chapter's title suggests. Taylor and Lou Ann's decision to make a home together becomes reflected in the unified point of view.

Narrator

Taylor's narrative voice is part of her characterization and the vision of the novel. Her speech is natural, colorful, and often humorous. She describes herself to Lou Ann at their first meeting as "a plain hillbilly from East Jesus Nowhere with this adopted child that everyone keeps on telling me is as dumb as a box of rocks." But Taylor is more than "a plain hillbilly." She is "the one to get away" from her hometown: she flees her familiar surroundings and settles in a new world because she perceives that her options are limited at home. Taylor is bright, articulate, and honest; thus she is able to come to understand and speak for the refugees and lonely souls she encounters in Tucson. As the narrator, her sensitivity to the other characters and openness to new experiences allow Taylor to learn and mature, and the story she tells is really more about her than about the community she helps to create.

Setting

The arid landscape of Arizona, the setting for *The Bean Trees,* is strange and often exotic to Taylor and Lou Ann, who are far away, both geographically and psychologically, from their Kentucky homes. The women often find Arizona beautiful, but they are transplants, and Taylor tells Estevan that sometimes she "feels like . . . a foreigner too.... Half the time I have no idea what's going on around me here." Estevan and Esperanza, as refugees, are also strangers here. As he explains his Guatemalan past to Taylor, Estevan admits, "I don't even know anymore which home I miss. Which level of home." In a way Taylor and Lou Ann are also refugees, fighting to survive. When Lou Ann's mother and grandmother from Kentucky visit her, their reactions to the hot January weather and lack of rain—to them, bizarre weather for January—reflect their belief that Lou Ann has changed since she moved to Arizona. Granny Logan complains, "I don't see how a body could like no place where it don't rain. Law, I'm parched," and Lou Ann replies, "You get used to it," reinforcing Granny's sense that her granddaughter is not the same person she was in Kentucky. The dryness of the Southwestern landscape and the Arizona earth's seeming hostility to growing things serve as a backdrop to the personal struggles of the characters to put down roots and prosper in this new place.

Symbolism

The main symbols throughout the novel concern the improbable growth of things in the dry desert of Arizona. Taylor notices and appreciates the world of flourishing flowers and vegetables throughout the novel; she always seems amazed that anything can grow in the dry earth of this strange place. When Taylor's first spring in Tucson arrives, she is astonished: "You just couldn't imagine where all this life was coming from. It reminded me of that Bible story where somebody or other struck a rock and the water poured out. Only this was better, flowers out of bare dirt." The tenacious natural world symbolizes the difficult courage and tenacious nature of the characters, showing them that they, too, can put down roots and flourish in this dry land. Mattie's garden, part junkyard and part Eden, is an important representation of the persistence of living things. Taylor describes the garden as "a bright, wild wonderland of flowers and vegetables and auto parts. Heads of cabbage and lettuce sprouted out of old tires. An entire rusted-out Thunderbird, minus the wheels, had nasturtiums blooming out the windows." Mattie has made something beautiful and productive out of an ugly, dry landscape, and the characters who create a loving, sustaining community against this same landscape are part of that urge for life and caring. Turtle's interest in all growing things stands in stark contrast to her past abuse, which resulted in her having been a failure-to-thrive baby. She has a fascination with planting seeds and

nurturing them to make them grow, and when she finally begins to talk all she says is the names of plants. Taylor discovers that wisteria vines—the bean trees that Turtle loves—"often thrive in poor soil" and are supported by "a whole invisible system" of "microscopic bugs that live . . . on the roots." This system of bugs, called rhizobia, that help the wisteria by turning nitrogen gas from the soil into fertilizer for the plant, makes Taylor think of people. She tells Turtle, "The wisteria vines on their own would just barely get by . . . but put them together with rhizobia and they make miracles."

Historical Context

Human Rights Struggles in Guatemala

Widespread violence and political upheaval marked a 36-year period in Guatemala that spanned the 1960s through the mid-1990s. During this period, Guatemalans lived in fear and oppression as opposing forces both tore apart the government and terrorized its citizens. Anti-government left-wing guerrilla groups systematically attacked the Guatemalan government on many fronts, assassinating leaders and denouncing the series of governments that rapidly succeeded one another. In reaction to the guerrillas, extreme right-wing groups tortured and killed tens of thousands of citizens—among them teachers, doctors, peasants, students—that they believed were in league with the leftist groups. Many of those tortured and killed in the conflict were Mayans, a people native to the region, and thousands of those persecuted fled the country as refugees, seeking safety in countries like the United States.

Conservatism in the 1980s

Taylor's statement after Turtle is molested in the park that "nobody feels sorry for anybody anymore . . . Not even the President. It's like it's become unpatriotic," addresses the fallout of the 1980s mood of conservatism in the United States. During the Reagan era—the two consecutive terms of the hugely popular conservative president—some conservative groups used words like "patriotism" and "traditional family values" in ways that excluded people and encouraged intolerance. When conservatives celebrated "family values," some critics asserted that they were referring to values culled from a nostalgic, unrealistic view of family life as it supposedly was in the past. Many right-

Saguaro National Monument in Monument Valley, Arizona.

wing conservatives blamed families that did not fit into this stereotype—such as single-parent or blended families—for a host of social ills. Some Christian fundamentalists, believing that what is written in the Bible should guide daily life, condemned any group—homosexuals, liberals, feminists, divorced individuals—that seemed incompatible with their Biblical interpretation. The 1986 Immigration Control and Reform Act included an amnesty program for illegal U.S. immigrants, yet some people seemed to confuse anti-immigrant sentiment with patriotism. Immigrants were often blamed for taking away jobs from "real" Americans.

Division Between Rich and Poor

In 1980s America, the rich got richer while the poor got poorer, and the middle class struggled to hang on. In essence, economic changes were creating a two-tiered society. By the mid-1980s, Wall Street saw the start of the most successful bull market in American history, creating more wealth for investors. Many of those who benefited spent their money showily on expensive cars, designer clothing, and real estate. Yuppies—young urban professionals—emerged in the early 1980s. At the other end of the spectrum, homelessness in the United States rose by about 25 percent a year in the 1980s, due in part to cuts in government spending for low-income housing and mental health services. The price of health care rocketed out of the reach of low-income and many middle-income Americans, and the infant mortality rate in America's inner cities neared and even surpassed those of Third World countries. Drugs and violence tore apart low-income urban neighborhoods, and residents of these neighborhoods saw their educational and employment opportunities shrink.

Child Abuse and Native Americans

The Child Abuse Prevention and Treatment Act passed by the U.S. Congress in 1974 led to a dramatic increase in reporting of child abuse cases. The number of cases reported in 1988 was four times the number reported in 1980, and in 1989 alone, 2.4 million cases were reported. In 1990, hearings before the 101st Congress led to passage of the Indian Child Abuse Prevention and Treatment Act. Congress passed this act after learning how underreported incidents were of child abuse on Indian reservations. The main purpose of the act was to provide Federal enforcement of reporting of child abuse incidents on Indian lands, as well as mental health support and treatment programs for Native American children who had been victimized.

Critical Overview

When *The Bean Trees* was published in 1988, critics received it enthusiastically. Early reviews praised Kingsolver's character development, her ear for voices and dialogue, her portrayal of friendship and community as necessary for survival, and her ability to comment on serious social issues without allowing those issues to overwhelm the story.

A 1988 review of *The Bean Trees* in *Publishers Weekly* called the novel "an overwhelming delight, as random and unexpected as real life." Focusing in part on the character of Taylor, the review referred to her "unmistakable voice" as "whimsical, yet deeply insightful," and it described the novel as "a marvelous affirmation of risk-taking, commitment, and everyday miracles."

Karen FitzGerald, in her 1988 review of the novel in *Ms.,* called *The Bean Trees* "an entertaining and inspiring first novel." She judged the novel's strength as coming from its characters. She perceived Taylor—and the rest of the characters in *The Bean Trees*—as remaining "firmly at the novel's center," in spite of "the large sweep of [its] canvas." FitzGerald asserted that in spite of the novel's strong political views, Kingsolver's characters are vivid and believable enough that they never become "mouthpieces for the party line," causing politics to overshadow plot. She praised Kingsolver's portrayal of women's friendships and placed her within a tradition of women writers—such as Doris Lessing—who have written about women's friendships and communities as being "havens in a hard world."

In his 1988 review in *The New York Times Book Review,* Jack Butler stated admiringly that "Barbara Kingsolver can write" and viewed *The Bean Trees* "an accomplished first novel" that "is as richly connected as a fine poem but reads like realism." But while he praised Kingsolver's clarity and artistry, Butler had reservations about her character development and her skill at creating a plot. Unlike FitzGerald, Butler did not think the characters are wholly believable, seeing them "purified to types" as the novel progresses, and thus lacking depth and color. He was impressed, overall, with Kingsolver's ability to write, but maintained that the novel's problems come from "overmanipulation," or Kingsolver's attempt to make things happen.

Another early reviewer, Diane Manual, wrote in *The Christian Science Monitor* in 1988 that the novel is based upon "character development at its richest, with Taylor growing from happy-go-lucky hillbilly to caring friend and parent." Manual pointed to Taylor as "something that's increasingly hard to find today—a character to believe in and laugh with and admire" and called the novel a "neatly constructed tale." Like FitzGerald and *Pub-*

lishers Weekly, Manual saw the "wonderfully outrageous characters" as being the strongest element of the novel, but added that *The Bean Trees* is not "merely laugh-a-minute fluff." The novel's political views, according to Manual, serve to deepen the characters, particularly Taylor, as she "gradually learns about the suffering some of her newfound friends have endured [and] begins to make her own significant commitment to protecting their hard-won freedom."

Margaret Randall, writing in 1988 in *The Women's Review of Books,* admired the way *The Bean Trees* balances humor with serious topics. She considered the novel "hilariously funny" in spite of its being "a story about racism, sexism and dignity." Like other critics, Randall pointed to Kingsolver's ability to create realistic, human characters: "It's one of those old-fashioned stories ... in which there are heroines and anti-heroines, heroes and anti-heroes, ordinary humans all. They go places and do things and where they go and what they do makes sense for them ... and for us." Randall discussed Kingsolver's treatment of the theme of invasion—"the sexual invasion of a child's body and the political invasion of a nation's sovereignty"—and said that although not new in literature, this theme in Kingsolver's novel "occupies a new territory, that of the commonplace, mostly undramatic, story, told and lived by commonplace people, most of them women."

More recently, assessments of *The Bean Trees* have examined Kingsolver's first novel alongside some of her later works and found trends. In 1993, Michael Neill compared Kingsolver's first three novels and wrote in *People Weekly* that while women's relationships are central to each of these novels—including *The Bean Trees*—the role of male characters is typically insignificant. Neill saw Kingsolver as writing about a different kind of American West more focused on women than on men—than traditionally Western American literature.

In a 1995 article in *Journal of American Culture,* Maureen Ryan derided Kingsolver's first three novels, including *The Bean Trees,* for being conservative at heart in spite of their apparent "political correctness." She asserted that in spite of their stand against human rights violations, they also exhibit an unrealistic and thus dangerous belief that devotion to family and friends can make things all better. Ryan perceived this conservatism cloaked in political correctness as being the reason for Kingsolver's popularity: readers can feel good about reading a socially conscious novel while feeling secure about the novel's underlying message of traditional values.

Criticism

Logan Esdale

A doctoral student at the State University of New York at Buffalo, Esdale reads The Bean Trees *as a lyrical and critical account of family in America.*

Readers and critics of a Barbara Kingsolver novel agree that politics and aesthetics wed in an often inspiring fashion. Reviewers have praised the freshness of the prose and the realism of her characters, who typically battle prejudice and a feeling of dislocation with great determination. Unfortunately, aesthetics and politics usually have a troubled marriage since—in the critic's eye—the one tends to undermine the other: books can be either works of beauty and genius or vehicles for political change. And since Kingsolver's politics are popular or "correct," her work has achieved more popular than critical success. Kingsolver, most likely, would not want it any other way. Leaving this debate to her readers, this essay instead focuses on the politics of names in her first novel, *The Bean Trees,* and how seeing connections between the human and the natural worlds expands our definition of what a name—such as "family"—might mean.

A contemporary poem by the Canadian P.K. Page, "Cook's Mountains," will help introduce the idea that the act of naming says as much about the giver as the receiver. The poem juxtaposes two moments of seeing the Glass House Mountains in Queensland, Australia. First is the scene of Captain James Cook, an eighteenth-century British explorer, naming these mountains "Glass House" because from a distance they appear as "hive-shaped hothouses." Two hundred years later, the poet sees them and is told their name by her driver. Page suggests that although the name is appropriate, "It was his gaze / that glazed each one." The mountains reflect "Cook upon the deck / his tongue / silvered with paradox and metaphor." Learning Cook's name for the mountains compromises Page's appreciation of their natural beauty not only because they become more "man-made" and artificial, but because she is reminded of Australia's past as a British colony. Cook and other explorers actually renamed these lands by effacing the abo-

riginal names. Metaphorically, Cook was in a glass house—was at a remove—when he renamed them. It frustrates Page that by using Cook's name for the mountains she is complicit in the colonial project of wiping out the original inhabitants and their history. Set largely in southern Arizona, ancient Native American country, *The Bean Trees* also explores the politics of naming in the context of Old and New World conflicts. It moves beyond Page's poem because it looks closely at naming in family relationships. The novel asks that we recognize the contiguity between the national and the personal.

Just as the mountains appear more like glass houses once Cook names them, the name we receive at birth instantly becomes central to our identity. We identify with our family name and are identified with it. Within the name are a record of the past and predictions about the future. As well, the act of naming separates one child from another. Some people can afford to ignore the fact that a name says as much about you as your clothing or hair color, but many cannot. For instance, Esperenza and Estevan—Mayan refugees from Guatemala—have to change their names to Hope and Steven so that new American acquaintances, employers and immigration officers will accept them into the American Family. And this name change was not their first: earlier, in Guatemala, their Mayan names were forced into hibernation because of political and racial persecution. This fact emerges in stories only when the cleansing rains of spring occur—only when they are surrounded by friends who offer acceptance and love. And when Lou Ann's family back in Kentucky hears that she has decided to live in Tucson and marry Angel Ruiz, they assume immediately that Angel is "one of those" illegal Mexicans. Angel, Estevan and Esperenza all know that naming is a political act; they know that assumptions are made about a person based on a name, and that sometimes those assumptions can cost you your life. Esperenza and Estevan run from Guatemala for their lives because they refuse to give up the names of 17 friends to a government that feels threatened by a small teacher's union.

This feeling of being threatened by groups of people who have different names and political affiliations circulates freely in America. In the novel, Virgie Mae Parsons—the seeing-eye friend to blind Edna Poppy—feels this threat and mutters: " 'Before you know it the whole world will be here jibbering and jabbering till we won't know it's America.' / 'Virgie, mind your manners,' Edna said. /

'Well, it's the truth. They ought to stay put in their own dirt, not come here taking up jobs.' / 'Virgie,' Edna said." Although Edna's eyes may not allow her to distinguish unaided between a small lemon and a lime, she figuratively sees or reads people much better. Virgie is responding to Estevan, who—though he taught English in Guatemala—is working as a dishwasher for a Chinese family in their restaurant. Estevan has said that only the young daughter speaks English. The irony is, of course, that Virgie is not just talking ignorantly to Estevan, but about Estevan: unlike Angel, Estevan is "one of those" illegal immigrants. Yet the characters confess that in their group he is the most fluent English speaker. Taking our cue from Mrs. Parsons, we can ask: How does a person recognize America? And how does America recognize a person? Virgie believes that language has a transparent logic, that a word means what it says or cannot mean more than one thing. Perhaps surprisingly, this logic is manifest in Edna herself. Edna tells us that when she realized as a young woman that she was named "Poppy," she decided to be one: from that moment on, Edna Poppy has dressed almost entirely in red.

Edna's decision to fashion herself in red was one that embraced chance. Chance also plays its part when the novel's first-person narrator, Taylor Greer, heads west out of Kentucky in an old, weathered Volkswagen Bug, and changes her name. Named "Marietta" but known as "Missy," Taylor exchanges her old name for a new one as part of the process of leaving the old for the new. Before she leaves Pittman County, she decides that where the first tank of gas runs dry, she would find her new name—Taylorville. "Greer" is the last name of a father who left even before she was born. So what can we say about "Taylor Greer" without slowly coming to know her? Very little; or, at least nothing that would not be arbitrary. Taylor's decision teaches us that identity can be multiple. She learns later that these identities do not necessarily conflict with one another. We also learn about the instability of appearances, which can be both frustrating—to the disillusioned immigrant expecting in America the freedom to belong—and rewarding—such as when a withered vine suddenly bursts forth in bloom. Patience, the right conditions, a respect for things you do not yet or may never understand—these are the requirements: "There seemed to be no end to the things that could be hiding, waiting it out, right where you thought you could see it all." Months pass before Taylor dis-

What Do I Read Next?

- *Pigs in Heaven* (1994) is Kingsolver's sequel to *The Bean Trees* and follows Taylor and Turtle as they struggle against an Indian-rights attorney who insists that Turtle be removed from her adopted mother and returned to her people.

- In *Homeland and Other Stories* (1989), a collection of twelve short stories by Kingsolver, characters like an elderly Native American woman and an estranged mother and daughter strive to make places for themselves—to find homes—in the world.

- *Another America/Otra America* (1992), Kingsolver's first book of poetry, treats the subjects of social and political oppression in the lives of ordinary Latin Americans and the prejudices of North Americans towards their neighbors. The book presents each poem in English and Spanish.

- Vince Heptig's color photographs and an introduction by Nobel Peace Prize Laureate Rigoberta Menchu Tum make up *A Mayan Struggle; Portrait of a Guatemalan People in Danger* (1997). Heptig's more than 100 photographs depict the Mayans as a strong people struggling to improve their world as they go about their daily lives in the midst of political strife.

- *Searching for Everardo: A Story of Love, War, and the CIA in Guatemala* (1997) by Jennifer K. Harbury is the author's own story of her three-year search for her Guatemalan husband, Efrain Bamaca Velasquez, who was taken prisoner and eventually killed by the Guatemalan army. Harbury's quest led to her discovery of links between the CIA and the Guatemalan military.

covers that Edna makes her way through the world with plenty of help and indirection.

Out on the road, when a rocker arm on the car demands repair at a rest stop in Oklahoma, near the lands of the Cherokee Nation, Taylor becomes

"Mom" when a small Cherokee baby is put on her passenger seat. The unexpected responsibility of Turtle (named for an unrelenting grip that reminds her of a mud turtle), plus two flat tires and no money to repair them, convince Taylor that if A is Pittman County, Kentucky, then B is Tucson, Arizona. As with Estevan and Esperenza, Taylor and Turtle arrive in Tucson with nothing except each other. Unlike the Mayan immigrants, Turtle and Taylor are not even family. And each of them sees little in this new place that reminds them of family or feels like home. But these people soon discover that underneath the unfamiliar is the familiar. The names may have changed, but given half a chance new places and people soon metamorphose into everything thought gone and dead, and potentially more. "What I really hate," Estevan says, "is not belonging in any place. To be unwanted everywhere." The obstacles for these new Americans are many, but even they, the novel implies, will find a place to call home.

While Esperanza and Estevan wait for the chance to belong—hoping to get past all the roadblocks—Taylor's struggle is more internal and typically American. Once in Tucson, Taylor moves in with Lou Ann, who—because Angel leaves her—is also a single Mom. They quickly discover that while their personalities spark off one another, they have much in common. This growing bond initially contradicts Taylor's sense of independence: "It's not like we're a family, for Christ's sake. You've got your own life to live, and I've got mine. You don't have to do all this stuff for me." Taylor left Pittman County to escape motherhood and domestic servitude. Her escape meant that she was no longer responsible to anyone but herself, and the act of choosing a new name was a function of her desire for independence. "My culture, as I understand it," writes Kingsolver in her collection of primarily autobiographical essays, *High Tide in Tucson,* "values independence above all things—in part to ensure a mobile labor force, grease for the machine of a capitalist economy"; "It took a move to another country to make me realize how thoroughly I had accepted my nation's creed of every family for itself." In *The Bean Trees,* Taylor gradually learns that her independence is not necessarily compromised by motherhood or family. "Everybody behaved as if Turtle was my own flesh and blood daughter," says Taylor. "It was a conspiracy." By the end of the story, once she legally adopts Turtle, Taylor is fully part of it. "Families change, and remain the same. Why are our names for home," Kingsolver asks in *High Tide in Tucson,* "so slow to catch up to the truth of where we live?" Taylor catches this truth when unrelated roommates, employers, children and friends all become part of her new family.

Taylor is employed and adopted by Mattie, who owns a tire sales and repair business. Taylor soon discovers that Mattie's business is more than fixing flat tires, though helping people such as Esperenza and Estevan find new homes corresponds with getting motorists back on the road. Mattie's garden also plays a symbolic role because these people who arrive at her door have been ripped from their home soil; their roots dangle vulnerably and need a gentle transplanting. Mattie is a gardener of people. Kingsolver studied biology and ecology at university, and into her work she weaves this knowledge in bold colors. This metaphor of person as plant is part of a larger system of resemblance between nature and humanity. When an author uses metaphor consistently, as Kingsolver does, the apparently disparate and unrelated elements of the world begin to coalesce. An early instance occurs when Taylor limps into Tucson, and focuses on a discarded cigarette: "Some truck had carried that tobacco all the way from Kentucky maybe, from some Hardbine's or Richey's or Biddle's farm, and now a bunch of ants were going to break it into little pieces to take back to their queen. You just never knew where something was going to end up." There are no metaphors in Virgie's world; Virgie lives in just one world. Taylor understands more about the world when she discovers connections between all the different worlds. What was singular becomes plural.

Taylor's focus, however, usually centers on Turtle. This little girl's first couple of years were full of deprivation, and put her in a condition similar to a desert plant waiting for summer rains. During this drought, Turtle stopped growing, trusting and talking. But under Taylor's care and commitment to her as a daughter, Turtle blooms. Turtle then dramatizes best the overlap between the related worlds by exchanging fluently human names for vegetables ones. As a gardener, Taylor frees herself from a national obsession with family and gender lines, and insularity. She frees herself by becoming more dependent on the people around her. The novel represents women as strong and fulfilled, but also employs identities (gardener instead of mother) that are gender neutral to troubled binary thinking. In this way, a person's family members can speak different languages, have different last names and live in different houses. Taylor learns that a family is not just something that you are born into—that is given to you—but is a collection of people that you make into a home (or a garden). Turtle grounds this argument, and is compared to the wisteria vines that grow out of bare dirt in a park near the house. These vines bloom one anonymous day in March. When the flowers turn to seed, they remind Turtle of beans. To her a wisteria vine is a bean tree. Taylor and Turtle learn later that wisteria vines are indeed part of the legume family, and that they depend on microscopic bugs, or "rhizobia," for food: " 'It's like this,' I told Turtle. 'There's a whole invisible system for helping out the plant that you'd never guess was there.' I loved this idea. 'It's just the same as with people. The way Edna has Virgie, and Virgie has Edna … and everybody has Mattie. And on and on.' / The wisteria vines on their own would just barely get by … but put them together with rhizobia and they make miracles."

Source: Logan Esdale, in an essay for *Novels for Students,* Gale, 1999.

Elyse Lord

Elyse Lord is a writing instructor at the University of Utah and the author of a utopian novel entitled Everything is Lovely and the Goose Honks High. *In the following essay, she defends Kingsolver's use of utopian and feminist ideals in* The Bean Trees.

As excerpts from the reviews will reveal, critics generally rave about Barbara Kingsolver's prose in her first novel, *The Bean Trees.* Kingsolver blends "common language with beautifully constructed images," writes one critic. She "delivers enough original dialogue and wry one-liners to put this novel on a shelf of its own," writes another. "Kingsolver doesn't waste a single overtone. From the title of her novel to its ending, every little scrap of event or observation is used, reused, revivified with sympathetic vibrations," writes another.

What divides, even troubles critics is the novel's utopian impulse. Writes Jack Butler, Taylor Greer (the novel's heroine) "confronts prejudice, trauma, self-abnegation, chauvinism, and always, always has the right attitude.… The other characters are purified to types as well."

Drawing upon Butler, Maureen Ryan describes Kingsolver's fiction as "aggressively politically correct." Kingsolver, she says, "wrestles the beasts of contemporary society: child abuse, labor unrest, political repression, feminism, the disintegration of Native American culture, and environmentalism. But she proffers her medicine sprinkled with Nu-

trasweet." By creating "perfect" mothers, and "intrepid and resilient" women, concludes Ryan, Kingsolver may unwittingly suggest that "if we love our children and our mothers … the big bad world will simply go away."

In other words, neither Butler nor Ryan find the danger in the novel to be "real"; the characters in *The Bean Trees,* despite Kingsolver's careful attention to serious problems, are, in the end, too good to be true. This "lightness" in the novel, suggest the critics, may partially account for its astonishing popularity—more than 400,000 paperback copies were sold in one year.

Though the critical critics may be right that the novel's "happy ending" partially accounts for its popularity, there is much room for speculation as to whether their standards for judgment are fair, or even relevant. For what these critics have failed to discuss is the context of Kingsolver's work, and the historically "male-centered" literary canon that Kingsolver is trying to stretch.

In a Kentucky Educational Television video, Kingsolver describes her own coming of age in the following way. "In the time and place of my adolescence there was enormous pressure on girls to play a kind of Russian roulette with our bodies. And if you won, you could be the most popular girl in the class. But if you lost you were a pregnant 15-year-old girl, way out of luck. I saw this happen to my classmates, beginning in the 7th grade."

Taylor Greer's childhood experiences parallel Kingsolver's and, one might argue, the experiences of many young women. Taylor resists pressures to have sex, manages to, in her own words, escape "getting hogtied to a future as a tobacco farmer's wife," and dreams of living in a place that is not so behind the times. Many of Taylor's classmates, in contrast, are not so lucky. They are "dropping by the wayside like seeds off a poppyseed bun."

Says Kingsolver in the same television interview, "Along about junior high this thing happens to teenage girls. It occurs to you that you're going to be a woman when you grow up. And you start to look around to see what that means. And in the mid-to-late sixties the news was not all that good … You were not gonna drive the car, you were gonna be in the passenger's seat. The voice of reason, the voice of authority and the voice of God were male."

Thus, for Kingsolver, the problems she had to overcome in order to even *imagine* herself writing about Taylor Greer included: How could she write a literary work that was based not on the literature of "old, dead men," but on the experiences of working poor and single mothers? How could she dramatize something so rarely dramatized? How could the threat of unwanted pregnancy, for example, function as a meaningful danger in a literary novel? The questions are not easily answered, particularly when one considers the lack of literary models that Kingsolver had to emulate.

Although Kingsolver does not mention her female influences, one could place her in the context of other popular, literary women writers, all of whom created characters who were "too good to be true," like Mary Lennox in *The Secret Garden,* Pollyanna, Anne of Avonlea, Heidi, and numerous other 19th century paragons of virtue.

One could even speculate that Taylor Greer, evolving consciously or unconsciously out of this "progressive utopian" literature, becomes the first such "too good to be true" female to adopt an abused child. She could be considered the first "too good to be true" female to fear unwanted pregnancy—and the first such "too good to be true" female who, by seeking conversation and communion with other women, begins to reform *herself,* rather than her community.

The problem is not that Kingsolver's "real" social concerns are trivialized by her insistent hopefulness in *The Bean Trees.* The problem is that Kingsolver's readers, trained by reading a male-centered canon, are unable to recognize that Taylor Greer is a wonderfully new and revolutionary character. She is new and revolutionary because she is a mother with a voice, because she is a mother who can tell the tale of her daughter's physical and sexual abuse, because she is a young woman with a "lottery of limited prospects" who feels authorized to author her own life.

Rather than discussing whether or not Kingsolver's fiction meets the not too relevant criteria of realism, critics would be better served by discussing the ways in which it is difficult to dramatize the taboo (such as sexual abuse), and the ways in which it is difficult to dramatize an adventurous female. To reframe this discussion would be to locate Kingsolver's work where it belongs: in the center of a problematic cultural and literary tradition.

At the heart of *The Bean Trees* is a feminist question. How can a young girl, who is good and kind, and yet who resists the idea that her purpose in life is to give birth and raise children, create her own identity? How can this same girl overcome her culture's indifference to her talents, hopes, and as-

pirations? Kingsolver's answer is that Taylor must ultimately learn to author her life in connection with others. This is a new and different answer to a most vexing—and all too familiar—question.

Thus the critics may be correct in viewing Taylor to be a bit too good to be true, insofar as she seems more skilled at authoring her life than the average teenager. However, Taylor's approach to authoring her life is psychologically convincing, and follows patterns familiar to young women in search of self.

In fact, Kingsolver has set up her growth in convincing ways. Taylor may be unusual, but her unusual goodness does not, in the end, undermine her authority, as it might in a less complex story. Specifically, the novel sets up an ongoing dialogue between Turtle's growth, Lou Ann's growth, and Taylor's growth.

Turtle symbolizes the young girl who has not yet left home and begun to develop her own voice. Lou Ann symbolizes the young woman who has left home, but carries with her derogatory internal voices that limit her growth. Taylor symbolizes the young woman who is strong in voice, but seeking to keep her strength and voice while also connecting with—and listening to, hence being changed by—others. All females are at different stages in their development. All face similar (and believable) obstacles.

At the start of the novel, girlhood is seen as a liability, a source of diminishment. Upon discovering that Turtle has been sexually abused, Taylor says, "The Indian child was a girl. A girl, poor thing. That fact had already burdened her short life with a kind of misery I could not imagine." Similarly, Taylor observes that, like many girls, "Turtle's main goal in life, other than hanging on to things, seemed to be to pass unnoticed." And when Turtle and Mrs. Parsons are attacked, Turtle's response is to stop talking. This, according to the logic of the novel, is the danger for all young women—loss of speech, loss of voice, loss of personal authority.

Lou Ann represents a young woman who has not yet developed her voice and, therefore, does not author her own life. She, like Turtle, tries not to attract attention, often by diminishing herself. For example, as she takes the bus home from the doctor's, she notes that it was "pure pleasure not to have men pushing into her and touching her on the bus." Then she rushes home, concentrating on "not being afraid." Meanwhile, though she resents and fears the attention she gets from men, she hates the way she looks. On an "ordinary" day she says, "I look like I've been drug through hell backwards…. Like death warmed over. Like something the cat puked up." Lou Ann is not likely to "create" an alternative self-image to the one she has internalized, for Lou Ann is not the kind of person to correct "anybody on anything." She does not even speak up when the nurse mispronounces her last name.

Both Turtle and Lou Ann begin to flourish and grow in striking ways in the story. Both develop in noticeable ways into speaking, self-creating—rather than self-diminishing—females. Taylor's growth, on the other hand, is more subtle.

At the start of the novel, Taylor has something of a negative identity. She does not want to be like the girls she grew up with, and she has the confidence to try other ways of being—but not the experience.

One obstacle she must overcome is her lack of positive relationships with men, whom she tends to view as dangerous. Early in the novel, Taylor encounters a wounded classmate, Jolene, whose father-in-law has just shot her, killed her husband, and beaten her baby. Jolene tells Taylor that her own father has been "calling me a slut practically since I was thirteen." The implication is that Jolene (like Lou Ann) did not have any alternative to living out a life already scripted for her. Taylor responds "… I didn't have a daddy…. I was lucky that way." The moment is important, because Taylor has recognized that fathers have the power of naming their daughters. Since Taylor is fatherless, she need not fear being named—created—by her father's descriptions of her. However, she needs to overcome the absence in her own identity, and she can only develop this more complete identity in relation to others, including men.

Given the novel's logic, it is appropriate that, at the start of the novel, Taylor carries with her a sense that men are dangerous. For example, she bypasses a motel because "the guy in the office didn't look too promising," and selects instead the Broken Arrow Motor Lodge, where "there was a gray-haired woman. Bingo."

Taylor's journey, then, is concerned with redefining herself so that she has an identity, not a negative identity. She must also recreate her perception of the world as part of her self-authorship, so that she is fully present in the moment. This she begins to do when she renames herself in Taylorsville, when she becomes a mother whose child looks to her for guidance, and, when, in a psychologically convincing journey, she retraces her route

back to Oklahoma, this time with a sense of mastery—and with company.

The point is that Taylor finds believable strength from her connections with others. Without her relationships with Mattie, Lou Ann, Estevan, and Esperanza, Taylor would never have been able to legally adopt Turtle. And without Turtle, she could never have been the "main ingredient" in Turtle's song. Without these connections, Taylor would not have been able to find what she was seeking, a place where she belonged, a place where she could be herself, rather than a young woman whose identity was based largely upon resistance.

This feminist/feminine psychological journey grounds the utopia. Rather than unwittingly suggesting that "if we love our children and our mothers … the big bad world will simply go away," as Ryan worried, Kingsolver is suggesting that a young woman who finds her voice is a powerful force in the world. This power does not make the world any less of a frightening place, but it does make the notion of home and sanctuary possible.

Though critics may take issue with the way that Taylor blithely adopts an abused Cherokee child, as well as the unrealistic way that Estevan and Esperanza take time out from their search for a homeland to help Taylor to adopt Turtle, and the farfetched way that Lou Ann becomes a manager in three weeks of work at a salsa factory, it is clear that Kingsolver's characters are engaged in very recognizable and real growth. It is also clear that, given the literary and social context of her work, Kingsolver is breaking new, and very important ground—and that she paves the way for others to investigate more thoroughly (and perhaps more realistically) the questions and issues that she raises.

Source: Elyse Lord, in an essay for Novels for Students, Gale, 1999.

Maureen Ryan

Ryan dissects Kingsolver's writing style in The Bean Trees *and finds it lacking in substance although well-meaning and "lively."*

Kingsolver's work … consistently floats among the verbiage that vies for our dwindling reading time. Her novels and stories are seductively appealing, offering, as they do, sympathetic, interesting characters; well-paced plots with clear resolutions; and a breezy, colloquial, eminently readable style. That is to say, they give us all the comforting conventions of old-time realistic fiction, flavored with the cool contemporary lingo favored by so many of the truly hip young guns. In short, Barbara Kingsolver's novels and stories are a good read. But I would argue that more importantly—and distressingly—Kingsolver's fiction is so very popular because it is the exemplary fiction for our age: aggressively politically correct, yet fundamentally conservative.

Kingsolver knows what she's about. In the battle that rages in literary magazines for the elusive soul of contemporary American fiction, she unabashedly proclaims herself to be "old-fashioned." It's a popular position: on the attack against so-called minimalist writing and in defense of his very popular behemoth, *The Bonfire of the Vanities,* Tom Wolfe in 1989 bemoaned what he perceived to be the sterility and social irresponsibility of contemporary American fiction and called for a return to the "big, rich" social novel of Dickens and Steinbeck.

Reviewers of Barbara Kingsolver's work perhaps inadvertently betray their sympathies with the call for a return to traditional realistic fiction, generally welcoming her mobilization of political themes and her dissimilarity to the ostensibly clever, narrow, MFA-burdened writers—the Absurdists and Neo-Fabulists and Minimalists—that Wolfe and so many others decry. Karen FitzGerald, for instance, finds *The Bean Trees* to be "refreshingly free of cant and the self-absorption of…overrated urbane young novelists." Diane Manuel applauds *The Bean Trees* for giving readers "something that's increasingly hard to find today—a character to believe in and laugh with and admire." Margaret Randall likes the novel because "it is one of those old-fashioned stories, thankfully coming back onto our literary scene, in which there are heroines and anti-heroines…ordinary humans [who] go places and do things and where they go and what they do makes sense for them…and for us."…

Kingsolver herself makes clear that her commitment to tackle the social issues of our day is conscious—and central to her undertaking. "I only feel it's worth writing a book if I have something important to say," she asserted in a 1989 interview. And she, like Wolfe, dismisses the fashions of contemporary fiction, claiming that she sees "a lot of beautifully written work that's about—it seems to me—nothing." One of the generation that came of age in the 1960s, and consequently believes that "we can make a difference in the world," Kingsolver too laments the "divorce" between "politics and art" in our culture. "I am horribly out of fash-

ion," she boasts. "I want to change the world.… I believe fiction is an extraordinary tool for creating empathy and compassion." Kingsolver wrestles the beasts of contemporary society: child abuse, labor unrest, political repression, feminism, the disintegration of Native American culture, and environmentalism. But she proffers her medicine sprinkled with Nutrasweet. This is fiction for everyone. "I have a commitment to accessibility," she asserts [in an August 30, 1990, *Publishers Weekly* interview], "I believe in plot. I want an English professor to understand the symbolism while at the same time I want one of my relatives—who's never read anything but the Sears catalogue—to read my books." In fact, Barbara Kingsolver's books do appeal to both the literary scholar and the Sears shopper. And why not? The problem is that for all their apparent attention to the pressing social problems of our time, Kingsolver's light and lively books—which purport to give us food that's both nourishing and appetizing—leave all of us feeling just a bit too fine.

Kingsolver's critically acclaimed first novel, *The Bean Trees,* introduced the elements of her fictional world, which she develops in the recent sequel, *Pigs in Heaven.* When plucky, ingenuous Taylor Greer leaves Kentucky and "lights out for the territory" at the beginning of *The Bean Trees,* she sets out on a physical and spiritual journey that thrusts her into a world fraught with danger, evil, and the unexpected. In Oklahoma, enroute to Tucson, Taylor has found herself entrusted with the care of a silent, abused three-year-old Native American child who clings to Taylor with such ferocity that she christens the girl "Turtle." Like it or not, Taylor becomes an instant mother, a "bewildered Madonna," with a new understanding of the hazards of contemporary life. An afternoon at the zoo promises "stories of elephants going berserk and trampling their keepers; of children's little hands snapped off and swallowed whole by who knows what seemingly innocent animal." Taylor wonders "how many…things were lurking around waiting to take a child's life when you weren't paying attention."

Of course, the trip to the zoo is a pleasant afternoon in the park, but there are real dangers in the world that Taylor encounters in her new life. When she first bathes Turtle and discovers the child's "bruises and worse," Taylor acknowledges that "I thought I knew about every ugly thing that one person does to another, but I had never even thought about such things being done to a baby girl."

The Bean Trees and *Pigs in Heaven* are Taylor's story, and they present Taylor's education into the perplexities of contemporary society, as she ventures out of her small, rural Kentucky hometown into a heterogeneous, confusing world. But Taylor's lessons are finally less of the hazards and atrocities of the world than they are about its consolations and strategies for survival. For despite the peril and attendant vulnerability that pervade these characters' lives, real danger is displaced and diffused by the characters' resilience and the inherent goodness of the world. The indifferent aunt who abused, then abandoned Turtle is, for example, only a fleeting, fading presence in *The Bean Trees....* And Taylor, whose commitment to and competence at motherhood develops throughout both novels, puts her worried friend Lou Ann's anxieties into proper perspective: "The flip side of worrying too much is just not caring.... If anything, Lou Ann, you're just too good of a mother."...

Perhaps Taylor has always known that a father and mother and 2.3 children don't necessarily make a family, but she has an important lesson to learn about families nonetheless. When the much-loved Turtle innocently tells a social worker that she has no family, Taylor is astonished and hurt, until she figures out that **feeling** like a family isn't enough; she tells Alice,

> She's confused, because I'm confused. I **think** of Jax and Lou Ann and...of course you,...all those people as my family. But when you never put a name on things, you're accepting that it's okay for people to leave when they feel like it.
>
> They leave anyway, Alice says. My husbands went like houses on fire.
>
> But you don't have to **accept** it, Taylor insists. That's what your family is, the people you won't let go of for anything. [from *Pigs in Heaven*]

Taylor learns what Codi must discover, too; that family—blood or found—must be claimed.

Taylor is right, but so is Alice. Men do leave in Kingsolver's world; and in fact, her protagonists are nearly always women, women confronting the vicissitudes of **being** women in late twentieth-century America. Kingsolver's feminism is unassailable. Writing [in *Utne Reader*, Jan.-Feb., 1993] about her failure to appreciate the current men's movement, she notes that "women are fighting for their lives, and men are looking for some peace of mind.... The men's movement and the women's movement aren't salt and pepper; they are hangnail and hand grenade." Kingsolver's novels are set in an unpredictable, baffling, imperfect world that is always a women's world.

It's not that men are cruel or boorish in *The Bean Trees;* they're simply irrelevant. Taylor's father is "long gone," and Taylor suspects that she's all the better for his absence. Lou Ann's husband slides quietly out of her life, and the novel, as Taylor pulls into Tucson. His absence doesn't matter much either; Lou Ann listens to him packing up his belongings and notices that "his presence was different from the feeling of women filling up the house. He could be there, or not, and it hardly made any difference."

Taylor has spent her life avoiding the likely prospect for a girl like her in Kentucky, getting "hogtied to a future as a tobacco farmer's wife." She knows that "barefoot and pregnant" is not her style. And her (and the novel's) attitude toward men is best articulated by the Valentine's card she sends her mother: "On the cover there were hearts and it said, 'Here's hoping you'll soon have something big and strong around the house to open those tight jar lids.' Inside was a picture of a pipe wrench."...

Kingsolver's is a world, not simply of women, but, significantly, of women and children, **mothers** and children. When Taylor steers her '55 Volkswagen west at the beginning of *The Bean Trees,* she leaves behind her beloved Mama (the Alice who discovers her independence, acquires her own name, and becomes an important character in *Pigs in Heaven*). Mama has struggled to raise Taylor alone, and has always let her daughter know that "trading Foster [Taylor's father] for [her] was the best deal this side of the Jackson Purchase." All of the women in *The Bean Trees* raise children alone; in fact, child-rearing and marriage seem mutually exclusive....

Motherhood—and its concomitant values: family, community, sacrifice, caring—are sacrosanct in Kingsolver's world. In the "different world" that she envisions throughout her fiction, we'd all care for everyone's child; in our world, exhausted, selfless mothers get the nod—and the approbation. Indeed, Kingsolver's apparent appreciation for non-traditional families is compromised by her unrelenting admiration for mothers. And though undoubtedly she means to suggest a vision for improving society; in fact, her privileging of family values works to compromise her message about the injustices of our society, which finally just don't seem all that ominous.

Barbara Kingsolver wants to say something important in her fiction about contemporary society and our responsibility to try to make the world a better place. She wants to challenge us to confront and do something about child abuse, the Native American Trail of Tears, and the American-backed crimes in Central America.... Hers is a considerable and admirable undertaking. As Jack Butler writes in his review of *The Bean Trees* [in *New York Times Book Review,* April 10, 1988], "who can be against the things this book is against? Who can help admiring the things this book is for?" "But," Butler continues, "reality suffers.... At one point late in the book, Turtle experiences a frightening reminder of her early horrors, and much is made of the damage this sort of recurrence can do— but then the subject is dismissed." The problem with Barbara Kingsolver's fiction is that the big subjects, the looming dangers, are always dismissed. Everyone in her books turns out to be inherently good and well-meaning; the men sensitive and sexy, the women intrepid and resilient (and **always** perfect mothers).... The dangers in Kingsolver's novels are not the challenges and perils that her characters all too easily overcome; they are the soothing strains of that old-time religion, lulling us into oblivion with her deceptive insistence that if we love our children and our mothers, and hang in there with hearth and home, the big bad world will simply go away....

The conventions of traditional realistic fiction that Wolfe and Kingsolver's reviewers miss in so much contemporary writing are the meat of Barbara Kingsolver's writing, which she serves with a soupçon of sentimentality for seasoning; and for dessert, the funny, slick patois of so much of that very hip recent fiction. She even gives us a healthy helping of vegetables: we may not like learning of Nicaraguan Contras and child abuse, but we know it's good for us. Finally, however, Kingsolver's work is contemporary American fiction **lite.** It's what we're supposed to eat these days, and it's even fairly tasty, but it's not very nourishing—and we go away hungry....

Source: Maureen Ryan, "Barbara Kingsolver's Lowfat Fiction," *Journal of American Culture,* Vol. 18, No. 4, Winter, 1995, pp. 77–81.

Sources

Jack Butler, "She Hung the Moon and Plugged in All the Stars," in *The New York Times Book Review,* April 10, 1988, p. 15.

Karen FitzGerald, "A Major New Talent," in *Ms.,* Vol. XVI, No. 10, April, 1988, p. 28.

Diane Manual, "A Roundup of First Novels about Coming of Age," in *The Christian Science Monitor,* April 22, 1988, p. 20.

Michael Neill, "La Pasionaria," in *People Weekly,* Vol. 40, October 11, 1993, pp. 109-10.

Publishers Weekly, Vol. 233, No. 2, January 15, 1988, p. 78.

Margaret Randall, "Human Comedy," in *The Women's Review of Books,* Vol. V, No. 8, May, 1988, pp. 1, 3.

Maureen Ryan, "Barbara Kingsolver's Lowfat Fiction," in *Journal of American Culture,* Vol. 18, Winter, 1995, pp. 77-82.

For Further Study

Jack Butler, "She Hung the Moon and Plugged in All the Stars," in *The New York Times Book Review,* April 10, 1988, p. 15.

> Butler admires Kingsolver's poetic style, but derides the novel for only permitting "upbeat" resolutions.

Brenda Daly, *Authoring a Life, a Woman's Survival in and Through Literary Studies,* State University of New York Press, 1998.

> A collection of essays that utilize both personal narrative and feminist theory in order to explore the connection between feminine identity development and language arts studies.

David King Dunaway and Sara L. Spurgeon, "Barbara Kingsolver," in *Writing the Southwest,* edited by David King Dunaway and Sara L. Spurgeon, Plume, 1995, pp. 93-107.

> Dunaway and Spurgeon combine biography, interview and excerpts to give a relatively comprehensive introduction to Kingsolver and her work. Characterized as much as a writer as an activist, Kingsolver fits well in the American Southwest tradition.

Robin Epstein, "Barbara Kingsolver," in *The Progressive,* Vol. 60, No. 2, February, 1996, pp. 33, 35.

> Kingsolver contends that she does not write her books "mainly for women," and discusses how her desire to change the world and how her concern for children, community, politics, and social justice motivate her to write fiction.

Karen FitzGerald, "A Major New Talent," in *Ms.,* Vol. 16, April, 1988, p. 28.

> FitzGerald describes the novel as "vivid and engaging," and praises its exploration of women's friendship—which she links to a contemporary feminist ethic—concluding that the novel is an "entertaining and inspiring" first effort.

Greta Gaard, "Living Connections with Animals and Nature," in *Eco-Feminism: Women, Animals, Nature,* edited by Greta Gaard, Temple UP, 1993, pp. 1-12.

> Gaard discusses how Kingsolver's fiction and the work of other women writers deconstructs the tradition that links woman and nature, categories too often held below man and culture.

Karen M. and Philip H. Kelly, "Barbara Kingsolver's *The Bean Trees:* A New Classroom Classic," in *English Journal,* Vol. 86, No. 8, December, 1997, pp. 61-3.

  The authors maintain that *The Bean Trees* is an "eminently usable text for faculty and an engaging novel for students," and offer strategies for teaching the novel.

Kentucky Educational Television, "Barbara Kingsolver," in *Contemporary Southern Writers,* Annenberg CPB Multimedia Collection, 1996.

  The film features interviews with Kingsolver and her friends, relatives, editors, and critics.

Edward C. Lynskey, "The Bean Trees," in *Library Journal,* Vol. 113, February 1, 1988, p. 76.

  Lynskey finds the novel "refreshingly upbeat," and speculates that subsequent Kingsolver novels will "probably generate more interest than this one."

Diane Manual, "A Roundup of First Novels About Coming of Age," in *The Christian Science Monitor,* April 22, 1988, p. 20.

  Describes *The Bean Trees* as "refreshingly perceptive," and praises the novel for giving readers "a character to believe in and laugh with and admire."

Roger Matuz, editor, "Barbara Kingsolver," in *Contemporary Literary Criticism Yearbook 1988,* Vol. 55, Gale Research, 1988, pp. 64-8.

  Features excerpts from criticism on *The Bean Trees.*

"Briefly Noted," in *New Yorker,* April 4, 1998, pp. 101-02.

  The reviewer finds the parallel growth of Turtle and Taylor "predictable," but the novel as a whole enjoyable.

Donna Perry, "Barbara Kingsolver," in *Backtalk: Women Writers Speak Out,* edited by Donna Perry, Rutgers UP, 1993, pp. 143-69.

  Perry questions Kingsolver on the circumstances of becoming a writer, and then the challenges of being one. Each of Kingsolver's books is discussed in detail, including her book of poems, *Another America/Otra America.*

Margaret Randall, "Human Comedy," in *The Women's Review of Books,* Vol. V, No. 8, May, 1988, pp. 1, 3.

  Randall interprets the novel as a story about invasion, the resolution of which she finds "as believable as it is gratifying." She admires Kingsolver's "deep female consciousness," which she says feels like "bedrock when put up against some of the preachier, more explicitly feminist works."

Patti Capel Swartz, "'Saving Grace': Political and Environmental Issues and the Role of Connections in Barbara Kingsolver's *Animal Dreams,*" in *Isle,* Vol. 1, No. 1, Spring, 1993, pp. 65-79.

  Swartz explores the way that characters' actions lead to personal growth in Kingsolver's "subversive" fiction, and compares Kingsolver to writers like Harriet Beecher Stowe, Charlotte Perkins Gilman, Tillie Olsen, and others who call for social change.

Lisa Schwarzbaum, "Bound for (More) Glory," in *Entertainment Weekly,* No. 429, May 1, 1998, p. 58.

  Schwarzbaum reflects on the popularity of *The Bean Trees,* now out in a 10th-anniversary edition.

Meredith Sue Willis, "Barbara Kingsolver, Moving On," in *Appalachian Journal: A Regional Studies Review,* Vol. 22, No. 1, Fall, 1994, pp. 78-86.

  Willis discusses how the Appalachian traditions of restlessness and a hatred of oppression are influences in Kingsolver's work.

The Color Purple

Alice Walker

1982

The Color Purple, Alice Walker's third novel, was published in 1982. The novel brought fame and financial success to its author. It also won her considerable praise and much criticism for its controversial themes. Many reviewers were disturbed by her portrayal of black males, which they found unduly negative. When the novel was made into a film in 1985 by Steven Spielberg, Walker became even more successful and controversial. While she was criticized for negative portrayal of her male characters, Walker was admired for her powerful portraits of black women. Reviewers praised her for her use of the epistolary form, in which written correspondence between characters comprises the content of the book, and her ability to use black folk English. Reflecting her early political interests as a civil rights worker during the 1960s, many of her social views are expressed in the novel. In *The Color Purple,* as in her other writings, Walker focuses on the theme of double repression of black women in the American experience. Walker contends that black women suffer from discrimination by the white community, and from a second repression from black males, who impose the double standard of white society on women. As the civil rights movement helped shape Ms. Walker's thinking regarding racial issues at home, it also shaped her interest in Africa. During the 1960s, a strong interest in ethnic and racial identity stimulated many African Americans to look for their roots in Africa. The primary theme of *The Color Purple,* though, reflects Walker's desire to project a posi-

tive outcome in life, even under the harshest conditions. Her central character triumphs over adversity and forgives those who oppressed her. This central theme of the triumph of good over evil is no doubt the source of the book's great success.

Author Biography

Alice Walker was born in the rural community of Eatonton, Georgia, in 1944. Most of Eatonton's residents were tenant farmers. When she was eight years old, Walker was blinded in one eye when her brother accidentally shot her with a BB gun. Having grown self-conscious as a result of her injury, Alice withdrew to writing poetry. She began her college education at Spelman in 1961 but transferred to Sarah Lawrence in 1963. After graduating in 1965, she went to Mississippi as a civil rights activist. There she met Melvyn Leventhal, a white civil rights attorney, whom she married in 1967. The Leventhals were the first legally married interracial couple to live in Jackson, Mississippi. They divorced in 1976. Alice Walker's first novel was published in 1970 and her second one in 1976. Both books dealt with the civil rights movement. *The Color Purple* was published in 1982 and brought Walker overnight success and recognition as an important American writer. In 1989 Walker published *The Temple of My Familiar,* in which she used a mythic context as a framework to cover a half million years of human history. In this work, Walker explored the social structure of a matriarchal society and the beginning of patriarchal ones. As in her other works, the author explored racial and sexual relationships. Walker's novel, *Possessing the Secret of Joy,* was published in 1992. Along with novels, Walker has written many collected short stories and books of poetry. Many of her stories have been included in anthologies. An active contributor to periodicals, Walker has had her works published in many magazines, including *Harper's, Negro Digest, Black World, Essence,* and the *Denver Quarterly.* Besides her writing career, Walker has been a teacher of black studies, a writer in residence, and a professor of literature at a number of colleges and universities. She has received numerous awards for her writing, including a National Endowment for the Arts grant, a Guggenheim Award, an O. Henry Award, an American Book Award, and the Pulitzer Prize. She has one daughter and lives in California.

Alice Walker

Plot Summary

First Period

In *The Color Purple,* the story is told through letters. The only sentences outside the letters are the first two: "You better not never tell nobody but God. It'd kill your mammy." Silenced forever, the main character, fourteen year old Celie, writes letters to God. Her father has raped her, and she has two children, a girl and a boy, whom "Pa" took away from her. Celie's mother has died and Pa is looking too much at her little sister, Nettie.

Mr. wants to marry Nettie but Pa rejects him because of the Mr.'s scandals with Shug Avery, a blues singer. Celie manages to get a picture of Shug and falls in love with her. Eventually, Mr. agrees to take Celie instead of Nettie because Pa offers him a cow.

Once she is in his care, Mr. beats Celie all the time. Meanwhile, Nettie runs away from Pa and comes to Mr.'s house, but when she rejects him, he throws her out. Celie advises Nettie to ask her daughter Olivia's new "mother" for help. Nettie promises to write but her letters never arrive.

One day, Shug Avery comes to town, but Mr. does not take Celie to see her. Harpo, Mr.'s son, gets married to Sofia, a strong brave woman, and when he complains that Sofia does not obey him,

Celie advises Harpo to beat her. Sofia finds out, and in the conversation that follows, Celie realizes she is jealous of Sofia: "You do what I can't. Fight," she says.

Second Period

Shug is ill and Mr. brings her to his home. To Celie's surprise, she calls Mr. by his first name, Albert. Celie's love and care make Shug better; Shug starts composing a new song.

Sofia finally leaves Harpo, who turns his house into a juke joint and asks Shug to sing. Shug invites Celie to the performance. Shug sings "A Good Man Is Hard to Find" and then her new piece, called "Celie's Song." Celie discovers that she is important to someone.

Before leaving, Shug says she will make sure Mr. never beats Celie again. She also teaches Celie to love herself. By the time Sofia returns with a new man and six children instead of five, Harpo has a little girlfriend he calls Squeak. Sofia and Squeak hit each other in the juke joint, and finally Sofia leaves.

The mayor's wife sees Sofia in town with the kids and asks Sofia to be her maid. Sofia answers: "Hell no" and hits the mayor when he protests. She is arrested, beaten and left in prison. Meanwhile, Squeak takes care of Sofia's children. When she finds out one of Sofia's wardens is her uncle, Squeak tries to save Sofia. She convinces the warden that working for the mayor's wife would be a better punishment for Sofia. The warden forces Squeak to have sexual intercourse with him. When Squeak goes back home, furious and humiliated, she orders Harpo to call her Mary Agnes, her real name. Sofia starts working for the mayor's wife, but she is treated as a slave.

On her next visit, Shug is married. She and Celie have missed each other, and one night, when the men are away, Celie tells Shug the story of Pa and the children. Shug kisses her, and they make love.

Third Period

One day, Shug asks Celie about Nettie, and together they realize Mr. has been hiding Nettie's letters. They finally recover them from Mr.'s trunk.

Unlike Celie's letters to God, Nettie's letters are written in standard English. The day Nettie left, Mr. followed her and tried to rape her. She fought, and he had to give up, but he promised she would never hear from Celie again. Nettie went to see Corrine, Olivia's new mother, and her husband, the

Reverend Samuel. She also met Celie's other child, Adam. Samuel was a member of a Missionary Society, and Nettie decided to go to Africa with the family. First, they went to New York, where Nettie discovered Harlem and African culture. Then, they went to England and Senegal, where Nettie saw what Europe was doing to Africa: robbing its treasures, using its peoples, and impoverishing the land.

Celie reads Nettie's letters and wants to kill Mr. for having hidden them. To help Celie control herself, Shug suggests that Celie make herself a pair of pants and go on reading the letters.

When the missionary group arrived in Africa, the Olinkas thought Adam and Olivia were Nettie's and Samuel's children. They told Nettie the story about roofleaves:There had been a greedy chief who cut down much of the jungle in order to create more farmland. The plants, which provided the leaves for the roofs of the Olinkas' houses, were destroyed, and many people died. The village began worshipping the leaves. When Nettie looked at the roof of her new house in the village, she knew she was in front of the Olinkas' God.

Olinka girls were not educated. Olivia was the only girl at school. Corrine, jealous and worried by the Olinkas' impressions about her family, asked Nettie to tell the children not to call her Mama. Olivia's only girlfriend, Tashi, could not come to school because her parents forbade it.

After five years of silence, the next letter tells Celie that Adam and Olivia had discovered connections between slave stories and African stories. Tashi's father had died, and her mother had let her go to school. A road was now near the village, and suddenly the Olinkas realized it was going to destroy their sacred place. The chief went to the coast to do something about it, but he discovered that the Olinkas' whole territory now belonged to a rubber company.

When Corrine got ill shortly afterwards, she told Nettie she thought Adam and Olivia were Nettie's and Samuel's kids. Though Nettie swore it was not so, Corrine was not convinced. Nettie and Samuel talked about it, and Samuel told her that Celie's and Nettie's real father was not the man they called "Pa"; their mother had been married before to a man who was lynched by white people. In this way, Celie is freed from the nightmare of believing her children are also her brother and sister.

Fourth Period

For the first time, Celie writes a letter to Nettie. She has visited her old house with Shug and seen her Pa. Meanwhile, she goes on reading Nettie's letters.

Nettie and Samuel tried to convince Corrine of the real story of the children. She believed them only when Nettie made her remember meeting Celie in town. Corrine smiled to them then but died soon afterwards.

"I don't write to God no more, I write to you (Nettie)," says Celie in her next letter. She sees she has been praying to a *white* old *man*. Shug tells Celie she believes God is not a *He* or a *She*, but an *It*. It is everything, and It gets very angry if one walks by the color purple in a field and doesn't notice it.

Shug and Celie decide to leave Mr. together with Mary Agnes, who wants to be a singer. Celie curses Mr. and tells him that everything he did to her, he did to himself. The two women go to Shug's house in Memphis. Then, Shug travels around singing, and Celie starts Folkspants, Unlimited, a family clothing business.

When Celie goes back home to see Sofia and Harpo, she finds Mr. has changed. He cooks and cleans. Now they can talk. Harpo tells Celie his father could not sleep until he sent Celie the last letters he had kept.

The letters say Nettie and Samuel got married in the middle of the Olinka war. The company destroyed the roofleaves. Some of the Olinkas went to the jungle to search for the *mbeles,* a legendary tribe. Samuel and Nettie travelled to England and in the journey, Nettie told the children their real story. They were eager to meet Celie, but Adam missed Tashi. When they got back to Africa, the Olinkas were so desperate that they had marked their children's faces to keep their tradition alive. Tashi had the traditional scars in her cheeks.

In America, Celie's stepfather dies and she inherits the house. She cleans it of its horror with a ceremony and sells her pants there. Shug goes back to Memphis. Celie is very sad and lonely, and she then hears that the ship Nettie had taken to go home was sunk by the Germans.

But Nettie's letters keep arriving. Tashi, her mother, and Adam all disappeared from the village. Meanwhile, Mr. and Celie are united through heartbreak and their love for Shug. Celie discovers that Mr. loves to sew. While they work together, she tells him the Olinkas' version of Adam and Eve's story: Adam and Eve were the first white babies in a black world, rejected because they were different. The serpent represents black people. Whites crush this serpent when they can because they are still enraged. In time, white people will be the new serpent and colored people will crush them. The only way to stop this horror is to worship the serpent and accept that it is our relative.

In her last letter, Nettie tells Celie that Adam and Tashi went to a secret valley where people from different tribes lived together. When they came back, Adam wanted to marry Tashi, but she rejected him. Adam scarred himself to convince her, and then they got married.

Sofia starts working in Celie's store. She is with Harpo again. Mr., who is now called Albert, asks Celie to marry him, but Celie prefers friendship. Shug comes back to them. Celie's last letter in the book is to God, but this time it is Shug's God. Celie is happy: Nettie, Samuel and the children are home at last.

Characters

Adam

Adam is Celie's son who was adopted by the missionary, Reverend Samuel, and his wife, Corrine. When the Reverend and his family return to America, Celie is reunited with her grown son.

Albert

Albert is the widower with four children who buys Celie from her stepfather. Albert treats Celie with cruelty, using her to satisfy his sexual needs and to take care of his children. He really loves Shug Avery, who later comes to live with Albert and Celie when she is sick. Celie appreciates Shug's presence in the house, because Albert treats her better when Shug is around. Albert later in life softens and Celie takes him in as a helper in her business.

Albert's father

Albert's father comes to visit when he hears that Albert has taken Shug Avery into his house. He says many nasty things about Shug and expresses his disapproval of what his son is doing. Albert asks him to leave.

Alphonso

Celie's stepfather. When Celie's mother is sick and dying, he rapes Celie and continues to do so long enough for Celie to have two children, whom he sells to a local missionary and his wife. He

Media Adaptations

- Steven Spielberg directed and produced *The Color Purple* in 1985. The film starred Whoopi Goldberg as Celie, Oprah Winfrey as Sofia, Danny Glover as Albert, Margaret Avery as Shug Avery, and Willard Pugh as Harpo. While the film was nominated in every major category of the Academy Awards, it won no Oscars. It did, however, win awards from the Directors Guild of America, Golden Globes, and the National Board of Reviews. The film also helped launch the careers of Oprah Winfrey and Whoopi Goldberg. It is available as a home video by Warner and Facets Multimedia.

doesn't tell Celie what has happened to the children, and initially Celie thinks he killed them. Celie later learns that he is not her real father. Her real father was lynched years before by a white mob. Alphonso tells Celie not to tell anyone but God about what he has done to her. He warns her that if she tells, it will kill her mother.

Mary Agnes
See Squeak

Shug Avery

Shug, a blues singer, is the woman that Albert loves. She is a sophisticated and liberated woman. After she comes to stay with Albert and Celie, who care for her while she is sick, she and Celie develop a deep relationship. Shug helps Celie gain self-esteem and teaches her to speak up for herself. She finds the letters from Nettie to Celie that Albert has for years kept hidden away from Celie. Shug also helps Celie get started in her business by encouraging her to sew. Later in the story, Shug returns again to Celie and Albert's home, but this time with a husband. Along with Sofia and Nettie, Shug is a role model who helps Celie change her life.

Miss Beasley
See Addie Beasley

Addie Beasley

Nettie and Celie's teacher, who recognizes the girls' intense desire to learn. Their stepfather, Alphonso, is contemptuous of her when she tells him that his daughters are smart.

Carrie

Carrie is a sister of Albert's who comes to visit. She tells Celie that Celie is a much better housekeeper than Albert's first wife.

Celie

Celie is the heroine of the novel. Most of the letters that comprise the book are letters Celie writes to God or, after learning that her sister Nettie is in Africa, to Nettie. Celie does not know about Nettie's attempts to communicate with her until Shug finds the letters from Nettie that Albert has hidden. Through the character of Celie, the author is able to present her message of sexual liberation and self-determination for women. Through Celie's voice, which speaks in black folk English, life in the world of a poor, black, rural sharecropper family unfolds. In the beginning of the story, Celie is a young girl who has been raped by her stepfather, who later sells her to Albert, her husband. Both men treat Celie cruelly and without any regard for her needs or feelings. Celie is forbearing and a hard worker, for which every one praises her. When Albert's mistress, Shug, comes to live with them, Celie becomes liberated from her oppression because of Shug's intervention on her behalf, and because she learns to stand up for herself with Shug's encouragement.

Corrine

Corrine is the Reverend Samuel's wife. Corrine and Samuel are missionaries who adopt Celie's children. Nettie becomes their helper, and the missionaries leave for Africa with Nettie and the children. When Corrine dies in Africa, Nettie marries Samuel. She and Samuel, along with their adopted children, Adam and Olivia, return to America when war breaks out in Africa. Adam's African wife Tashi also comes to America with them.

Fonso
See Alphonso

Grady

Shug Avery's husband, whom she brings to meet Celie and Albert later in the story after some absence from Celie and Albert's home. Shug and Grady return in a sporty car.

Still from the 1985 movie The Color Purple, *starring Whoopi Goldberg (left) as Celie and Margaret Avery (right) as Shug Avery.*

Harpo

Albert's son. Harpo marries Sofia and they have five children. In his relationship with Sofia, Harpo tries to live up to his father's role as the domineering male. Because Sofia is a strong-willed young lady, she becomes disgusted with the way Harpo treats her and leaves him for a time. When she returns with a boyfriend, Harpo is jealous. Eventually, they get back together, but their relationship changes. Harpo accepts her strong character and stops trying to dominate her.

Warden Tom Hodges

The officer in charge of the prison where Sofia is sent after she insults the mayor's wife. When his niece, Squeak, comes to see him in an effort to get Sofia released from prison, Hodges rapes her. Walker uses this scene to illustrate the mentality of racism in the South during the period of the novel. Hodges is the brother of Squeak's white father. Because his niece is black on her mother's side, Hodges has no qualms about sexually assaulting her.

Queen Honeybee

See Shug Avery

Kate

One of Albert's sisters. On one of her visits she tells Albert to buy Celie some clothes.

Livia

See Olivia

Mama

Celie's mother, who is sickly and dies in the early part of the story. When she refuses to have sex with her husband, Albert, he rapes Celie.

Mammy

See Mama

Mayor

The mayor of the town with whom Sofia has a run-in. Sofia is jailed for insulting the mayor and his wife.

Miss Millie

See Millie

Millie

The mayor's wife, with whom Sofia has a run-in. Sofia insults Millie and is arrested. After serving her sentence, Sofia is freed only to become the live-in caretaker of Millie's children.

Mr. ____

See Albert

Mr.'s daddy

See Albert's father

Nettie

Celie's younger sister. Nettie is saved from a fate like Celie's because she has been taken in by the Reverend Samuel and his wife Corinne. When they leave for Africa on missionary work, Nettie goes with them. Nettie's letters to Celie are written in standard English to reflect the fact that she received a better education than Celie. In her letters to Celie, Nettie tells her a great deal about Africa, which comes to represent the larger world as well as African-American ethnic identity in the novel. When the Reverend's wife dies, Nettie marries him. She continues to raise his adopted children, who happen to be Celie's by her stepfather. Nettie returns to America and reunites Celie with her children.

Odessa

Sofia's sister. Odessa takes care of Sofia's children when Sofia is sent to jail.

Olivia

Celie's daughter by her stepfather. Olivia was adopted by the Reverend Samuel and his wife Corinne, along with her brother Adam, who was also one of Celie's children. Olivia returns to America with the Reverend, Nettie, Adam, and his wife, Tashi, and is reunited with Celie, her birth mother.

Old Mr. ____

See Albert's father

Pa

See Alphonso

Pauline

See Olivia

Prizefighter

When Sofia returns home after leaving Harpo for a substantial absence, she brings a prizefighter with her. He is her boyfriend, and Sofia uses him to make Harpo jealous.

Reverend Mr.

See Reverend Samuel

Reverend Samuel

The missionary who adopts Celie's children from Albert. Celie does not know they have been adopted. She thinks Albert killed them. The Reverend, his wife, and Nettie, who has been taken in by them, leave with the children for Africa to do some missionary work there. After the Reverend loses his wife, he marries Nettie.

Sofia

One of the three major female characters in the story who have a positive influence on Celie. Celie sees how Sofia stands up for herself to Harpo and to the white community as well. When Sofia becomes disgusted with Harpo's behavior toward her, she leaves him for awhile. When she returns, she taunts him with her new boyfriend, a prizefighter. Eventually, Sofia and Harpo reunite in a different relationship. When she is insulted by the mayor's wife, she talks back and causes a scene, for which she is arrested and thrown in jail.

Squeak

Squeak becomes Harpo's girlfriend after Sofia leaves him. When Sofia returns she is quite nasty to her, but she also helps Sofia out when she is jailed for standing up for herself from being insulted by whites. When Squeak intercedes for her with her white uncle, Warden Tom Hodges, she is raped by him.

Sugar

See Shug Avery

Swain

The musician who performs at the jukejoint Harpo has built.

Tashi

Adam's African wife, who comes to America with him and the rest of the missionary family when they flee Africa to escape hostilities there.

Tobias

Albert's brother, who comes to visit Shug while she is sick at Albert's house. He brings some chocolate, and they socialize while Celie teaches Shug to quilt.

Uncle Tom

See Warden Tom Hodges

Themes

Sexism

Sexual relations between men and women in *The Color Purple* is a major theme. Alice Walker sets her story of Celie's transformation from a passive female to an independent woman within the culture of southern black rural society from the 1920s to the 1940s. In the beginning of the story, Celie is dominated first by her father, whom she later learns is really her stepfather, then by her husband, Albert (Mr.). The catalyst for the character change in Celie is the relationship she develops with Shug Avery, her husband Albert's mistress. Because Celie has been warned by her stepfather, Alphonso, not to tell anyone but God about how he repeatedly rapes her, she begins to write letters to God. It is through the letters that the reader develops a sense of Celie's being, which at first is self-effacing, but eventually becomes strong and independent.

In the novel there are a number of role reversals that take place between men and women. Harpo, Albert's son, tries to emulate his father and attempts to dominate his strong-willed wife, Sofia. By the end of the story, Harpo and Sofia have reversed traditional male-female roles. Harpo stays home to take care of the house, while Sofia works. Celie and Albert also reverse roles. By the end of the story, Celie is an independent businesswoman, and Albert is her assistant. Celie has also learned to speak up for herself, claiming her house when her stepfather dies. The sexual relationship between Celie and Shug further breaks with the traditional roles of passive women and dominant men that the story challenges. In the relationship between Samuel and Corrine, the missionaries who adopt Celie's children, and later between Nettie and Samuel, Walker presents what could be called a partnership relationship between a man and woman. In these relationships, both the man and the woman share the same goals and work together to realize them. Walker uses the incident between Squeak and her white uncle, the warden at Sofia's prison, to illustrate how sexism and racism were expressed. The warden has no qualms about raping his own niece, which reflects a southern, white, male disregard for the dignity of black women. During the period of the novel, it was a commonly held view among white males that they could do whatever they pleased with black women, a view that many black males shared as well.

Topics for Further Study

- Alice Walker has been criticized for portraying negative male characters in *The Color Purple*. Explain why you agree or disagree with this analysis. Be specific in your discussion by citing passages that support your viewpoint.

- Research the history of the epistolary novel and give three other examples of this form in literature. For each example, include the title, author, date of publication, and a summary of the novel. Many epistolary novels are written from the main female character's point of view. Are there any advantages or disadvantages to using this literary form when the major character is a woman?

- Research colonial rule in Africa. Narrow your scope by focusing on one European country and one African country that was colonized by it. Give a history of the African country before, during, and after European colonization.

- Sexual violence is a major theme in *The Color Purple*. From current media reports write an essay on how sexual violence is presented to the public. Include statistical information on sexual violence, such as the extent of increase or decrease in occurrences over the past 20 years. What are the underlying causes of sexual violence? Are there any methods for combating sexual violence that have been proven effective?

Transformation

Celie's transformation from a young passive girl, who is the object of violence and cruelty from her stepfather and her husband, into an independent woman with self-esteem is at the heart of *The Color Purple*. While the ways in which conflicts are resolved may stretch the imagination at times, they are central to the author's view that goodness can triumph over evil. That Celie is able to forgive Albert by the end of the story and take him in as a helper reflects Walker's insistence on the redeeming quality of the human heart. She shows in transformed relationships that the worst cruelty committed by one person on another does not prohibit a change of heart. Her view is basically that the conditions under which human beings struggle shape their behavior. Albert had a difficult life and took out his frustrations on Celie. When Celie became self-sufficient, she could easily have turned her back on Albert, but it is not within the framework of her character to be uncharitable. In becoming independent, Celie has found happiness. Rejecting Albert would detract from her happiness. Celie's behavior toward Albert reflects Walker's insistence on forgiveness and contributes to the overall religious overtones of the book.

Culture

Cultural difference plays a significant role in *The Color Purple*. Walker effectively uses black folk English in Celie's letters to express the voice of poor, black rural African Americans. Walker presents a clear picture in the book of the economic and social hardships that African Americans faced in the rural south during the early 1900s. She also presents an honest picture of the effects of racial repression. The picture Walker paints of black life is not one-sided. While Celie and Albert are tied to the land and the harsh life it represents, Nettie escapes into a black middle-class life through her missionary friends. Religion in the South played an important role in liberating many African Americans from poverty. As a spin-off for involvement with the church, literacy and education flourished. Celie is embracing a religious literacy through her letters to God, and in her letters to Nettie she comes to grips with the larger world, including Africa, outside her small community. By making the connection to Africa, Walker emphasizes the importance of African Americans' roots.

Style

Point of View

The Color Purple is written in the first person, and the voice is predominately Celie's, but some of the letters that comprise the book are written to Celie by her sister Nettie. The story covers thirty years of Celie's life from childhood to her maturity as an independent woman. By having Celie write in black folk English, Walker brings the reader close to the quality and rhythms of life that her characters experience. Celie's dialect also reflects her lack of formal education. Nettie, who was formally educated, writes her letters in standard English. They are full of information that becomes a source of knowledge for Celie outside the world of her own small community.

Structure

The structure of *The Color Purple* is the series of letters Celie writes to God and to her sister Nettie. Some of the letters in the book are written by Nettie to Celie. This literary form is called the epistolary novel, a form developed in eighteenth-century England by novelists like Samuel Richardson. A major advantage of this structure is that the reader becomes intimate with the character of the letter writer. With the epistolary form, Walker was able to focus on the inner life of her main character and create a sense of intimacy that may be partly responsible for the success of the book. This technique creates a confidential reading experience. The reader has a chance to read over the character's shoulder and look inside her. Nettie, to a great extent, escaped the cruelty that Celie experienced because she was able to leave home early. The tone of her letters to Celie contrasts sharply with Celie's letters to God. In Nettie's letters, there is much less intimacy. They do not contain the suffering that Celie has expressed in her letters to God. By introducing Nettie's letters, Walker is able to shift her story from Celie's life of despair to a life that begins to have hope. It is through the help of Shug Avery that Celie finds her hope—the letters from Nettie that Albert had hidden from her.

Basically there are four time frames of the novel. In the first period of her life, Celie experiences the misery of poverty and cruelty at the hands of her stepfather. In the second closely-related period, Celie experiences continued cruelty from her husband Albert. In the third period, she awakens to the possibility of self-realization through her relationship with Shug and her renewed contact with her sister Nettie. Finally, Celie has realized herself and has established a life where she has control; she has found the happiness and contentment that come from self-realization. Another period, not directly a part of Celie's life, is Nettie's time spent in Africa. The letters from Nettie serve as a contrast to Celie's life. They also enlarge Celie's perspective and help to universalize her life.

Symbolism

The primary symbol of *The Color Purple* is found in the title, *The Color Purple*. The significance of the color purple is that it stands for human hope. It is a miraculous color, when found in

Jim Crow laws in the South legally segregated blacks from whites, even at drinking fountains, as illustrated in this picture.

nature, and one which indicates that the feeling of hope, despite misery, is a miracle of the human spirit.

Historical Context

Black-White Relations in the Rural South

After slavery, the social and economic relations for African Americans remained much the same. While no longer slaves, many blacks remained on the land as sharecroppers. They tilled the soil, but the land was owned by their former slave masters. After 1915, economic opportunities in cities of the industrial North encouraged many blacks to leave the South. Those that remained continued to live isolated from white society. Schools and churches were segregated, as well as housing. There were few opportunities for blacks to establish themselves outside of sharecropping. During the period of the novel, segregation between blacks and whites was enforced legally to the point that blacks had to sit in separate parts of movie houses and drink out of separate fountains, and were forbidden from eating at white lunch counters. The laws that were passed to enforce this segregation

were called Jim Crow laws, named after a pre-Civil War minstrel character. In *The Color Purple* Sofia is victimized by this social policy. When she shows defiance to the white mayor's wife who insults her, she is arrested and given a stiff jail sentence for her actions. The difficulty in relations between black men and women had its source in white male-dominated society. Within white society, men were expected to control the family and had status over women. This attitude filtered into black culture, but the black male, unlike his white counterpart, was humiliated daily for the color of his skin. In frustration, many black males turned their anger towards women. Black women then experienced the double oppression that Alice Walker explores in the novel.

Lynching, murder by a mob, was prevalent in the South from the 1880s to the 1930s. Celie's real father had been lynched in the 1900s because he had established a business that competed with white businesses. White southern businessmen felt economically threatened when a black business took black customers from them. Retaliation by lynching went unchallenged until the United States Congress tried to pass an anti-lynching law in 1937. Southern senators killed the bill by not letting it come to a vote in the Senate.

Compare & Contrast

- **1930s:** The relationship between men and women is clearly defined. Men are the breadwinners and the heads of the families. Women stay at home to take care of the children and the housework.

  Today: Men and women share the economic burden of the household. Many married women with children are in the workplace. Preschool children are cared for in daycare centers or at home with paid baby-sitters.

- **1930s:** Racism is condoned throughout the country, and laws in the South enforce segregation. African Americans are kept out of many industries.

  Today: Discrimination on the basis of race, gender, ethnicity, or disability in the workplace is illegal.

- **1930s:** Violence against women is widespread and ignored by the police.

  Today: Violence against women is illegal, and perpetrators are being vigorously prosecuted in both civilian and military life.

- **1930s:** Most religious African Americans belong to either a Baptist or Methodist congregation.

  Today: Many African Americans have turned away from Christianity to the Muslim religion. Strong leadership has developed within the Black Muslim movement to keep it a viable religious alternative for African Americans.

- **1930s:** Colonialism dominates the African continent. It is carved up among the major nations of Europe who exploit it for its rich resources.

  Today: All nations in Africa are self-governed, but the remnants of colonial mismanagement have led to unrest in a number of African countries.

African-American Religion

In their letters, Celie and Nettie talk about God. Celie confesses that she sees God as white, but Nettie replies that being in Africa has made her see God differently. Her African experience has made her see God spiritually rather than in the physical form that is represented in Western Christianity. While most African Americans were either Baptist or Methodist during the first half of the twentieth century, the way they expressed their religion in church was much different from white congregations. Infused into the services were elements from their African roots, particularly a distinct musical style and delivery of the sermon in a moving manner. The congregation answered the preacher at key points in the service, and singing was accompanied with expressive physical movements, like clapping and swaying. The main reason that African Americans were drawn to the Baptists and Methodist churches was that these two denominations had opposed slavery early in American history. By the late eighteenth century, blacks were forming congregations within these Protestant sects. In 1816 religious leaders from the black community met in Philadelphia and established the African Methodist Episcopal Church (AME), which still has sizable congregations throughout the United States.

Critical Overview

Since its publication, *The Color Purple* has aroused critics to both praise and to sharply criticize elements in the book. Trudier Harris in *Black American Literature Forum* criticizes the media for dictating the tastes of the reading public. The book "has been canonized," she states. It has "become *the* classic novel by a black woman," because "the pendulum determining focus on black writers had swung in their favor ... and Alice Walker had been waiting in the wings of the feminist movement...."

Harris contends that the popularity of the book has been harmful because it has created "spectator readers," and it "reinforces racist stereotypes." Because of the book's popularity, Harris maintains that black women critics are particularly reluctant to find fault with the book, even when they find elements in it disturbing. She also questions the novel's morality, which other critics praise. "What kind of morality is it that espouses that all human degradation is justified if the individual somehow survives all the tortures and ugliness heaped upon her?" The morality other critics find in *The Color Purple,* Harris feels "resurrect[s] old myths about black women." This critic cites Celie's response to her abuse as an example of the myth of submissiveness of black women. She also criticizes the sections dealing with Nettie and Africa because she feels they "were really extraneous to the central concerns of the novel" and accuses Walker of including them "more for the exhibition of a certain kind of knowledge than for the good of the work." The relationship between Celie and Shug, Harris also felt, was silly. Another criticism Harris has of the book is what she considered its fairy tale element. "Celie becomes the ugly duckling who will eventually be redeemed through suffering," says Harris. The book, she feels, "affirms passivity ... affirms silence ... affirms secrecy concerning violence and violation ... affirms ... the myth of the American Dream...." Anyone can achieve "a piece of that great American pie." Harris accuses the author of preparing "a political shopping list of all the IOUs Walker felt that it was time to repay." In spite of her sharp criticism of *The Color Purple,* Harris confesses that she is "caught in a love/hate relationship with" it.

Surprisingly, one of the most positive reviewers of the book was Richard Wesley. Writing in *Ms.* magazine, Wesley says "As an African-American male, I found little that was offensive as far as the images of black men," as they were portrayed in the book and the film. In his review, Wesley sees the character of Mr. emblematic of "male privilege. As long as black men seek to imitate the power structure that crushes them ... and as long as black women submit ... then the morbid relationship of Celie, the oppressed, and Mr., the oppressed oppressor, will continue to be played out in homes all across America." In his article, Wesley criticizes those who fault *The Color Purple* for painting a negative image of black males. "Walker is airing dirty linen in public. She is reminding many of us men of our own failures. She is reminding women of *their* failures as well.... A lot of people do not

want to hear that." His strong support of the novel concludes his review. "No one in America—and black America, especially—should be telling writers what they may or may not say. Writers are the antennae of any society. They have to speak when others dare not." Another male writer, J. Charles Washington, writes in *Obsidian* that Walker is justified in concentrating on female characters, who have been neglected by male writers. It "does not mean that she is anti-male," he says, "but that she has less time and energy to devote to exploring more fully the problems of men or the common causes of the oppression of both...."

Also writing in *Ms.,* Gloria Steinem finds much to praise and little to criticize in Walker's novel. " ... white women, and women of diverse ethnic backgrounds, also feel tied to Alice Walker. The struggle to have work and minds of our own, vulnerability, our debt to our mothers, the price of childbirth, friendships among women, the problem of loving men who regard us as less than themselves ... are major themes" of Walker's writings. "She speaks the female experience more powerfully for being able to pursue it across boundaries of race and class," Steinem maintains. She finds the author's storytelling style "irresistible to read." Countering Trudier Harris's criticism, Steinem feels pleasure in "watching people redeem themselves and grow." Its symbolism of purple, Steinem notes, represents "the miracle of human possibilities."

Criticism

Margara Averbach
In the following essay, Averbach, a writer and translator with a doctorate from the University of Buenos Aires, talks about Celie's growth as a person and her evolving perception of God as a consequence of this growth.

In *The Color Purple,* the story is told through letters. It is a novel about an oppressed woman, and the letters are important. Letters have been one of the few means of expression of oppressed women for many years. The author's choice of letters as a form of presentation has a number of consequences. In the first place, the story will be told by the author or authors of the letters: in this case, Celie and, in a small part of the novel, her sister, Nettie. This means the language of the story will be the one used by the person who writes the letter. In *The*

What Do I Read Next?

- Maya Angelou's autobiographical *I Know Why the Caged Bird Sings,* published in 1970, describes her childhood in segregated Arkansas. The book paints a vivid picture of life in the rural South during the 1930s. When Maya moves to St. Louis with her mother, she is raped and remains mute for a number of years. Like Celie in *The Color Purple,* she eventually develops self-esteem.

- Jane Hamilton's 1988 novel *The Book of Ruth* is the story of a poor, white, small-town girl, who comes of age through great trauma. Like Celie, she too finds self-realization in spite of the despair of her life circumstances.

- In 1959, playwright Lorraine Hansberry became the first black woman writer to have a play produced on Broadway. *A Raisin in the Sun* is about the aspirations of a black family to attain a better life in racist America. Hansberry won the New York Drama Critics Circle Award for the play, and it was made into a film in 1961.

- Jamaica Kincaid was born in St. John's, Antigua. Her 1983 book *At the Bottom of the River* explores the mother-daughter relationship in the setting of British colonial rule. In this novel, as well as her other works, Kincaid explores themes of racial domination, poverty, and coming of age.

- Nobel Prize and Pulitzer Prize winner Toni Morrison has produced a number of novels that deal with the complexities of black life in America. She depicts how African Americans are threatened from within by their own culture and history, and repressed from without by the white world. *The Bluest Eye* was published in 1969, *Sula* in 1973, *Tar Baby* in 1981, and *Jazz* in 1992.

- The renowned southern author Eudora Welty is known mostly as a short story writer, but she has written a number of novels that deal with the complex relationships in families. In *Delta Wedding,* published in 1946, Welty explores the intricacies of the close ties within the family. She is noted for her portrayal of powerful and engaging women.

Color Purple, Celie's letters are in the language of a black girl who has left school very early in life while Nettie's are in perfect, standard English.

Secondly, a letter is a document with a specific form and, in *The Color Purple,* the openings of the letters mark the changes in the character. There are only four openings: "Dear God," "Dear Nettie," "Dear Celie," and the long opening of the last letter, which is a variation of "Dear God." We will study the novel taking these openings into account. Before that, though, let's analyze the two sentences which are outside the letters. They appear at the beginning of the book in italics: "You better not never tell nobody but God. It'd kill your mammy." They are a strong prohibition to speak (notice the words "not never nobody") given by a powerful man (the father) to a weak child (Celie, the daughter).

From that sentence onwards, Celie understands that she must not communicate her desires, fears and terrors to anybody. She starts writing to God because He is the only thing she has left. The letters will not be read by anyone. They are only a means of self-analysis. God is obviously not there: Celie asks him for signals all the time and does not receive them. In this first period, her life is marked by infinite loneliness. There is no use of the word *we.* The only small group Celie manages to form is with her sister, Nettie, and when she leaves, Celie is left totally alone. She feels she is buried alive. The most important character around her is her oppressor and he has no name. *Mr.* is only a role.

Yet, Celie manages to throw a number of bottles into the sea. She tries to communicate certain things, and she succeeds, though she does not realize. For instance, she embroiders the name of her child in her clothes: Olivia. The clothes help the child to keep her name, that is to say, to keep her identity, to be herself. This type of communication is not linguistic. It has to do with the activities a woman is allowed to perform in a house (sewing, cooking, cleaning). Celie turns them into a means of expression.

Celie is so immersed in oppression, she accepts the point of view of Mr.: she advises Harpo to beat Sofia. Thus, she agrees with her oppressor in the idea that a woman should only obey, work, and be silent. After this moment of deep humiliation, Celie has the first serious conversation in the book. Sofia comes to see her, furious, and Celie has to explain her attitude. She discovers she is jealous of Sofia's capacity to fight. This conversation is a new beginning for Celie. Both women find a moment of community, they *do* something together. The pronoun "us" is finally used: "I laugh. She laugh. Then us both laugh so hard us flop down on the step."

When Shug comes to Celie's life (she has seen the singer before in a photograph and has turned her into another God to contemplate from far away), Celie is prepared. Shug does not help her, as Sofia did. Celie has to conquer her with the only tools she has: the feminine activities. She cooks for her, helps her to take a bath, combs her. No words are spoken, Celie cannot face language communication (the order forbids it) but even in silence, she communicates. She gives life. And Shug does what men did not do: she thanks Celie. She dedicates her new song to her, shows her she is important.

In this second period, Celie changes radically. For instance, instead of telling a man he must beat a woman, she starts advising women to defend themselves. She tells Squeak she must make Harpo call her by her real name, Mary Agnes. She even begins to see Mr. in a new light. When Mr.'s father comes to the house and attacks Shug, Mr. and Celie feel united for the first time, and that scene will be developed at the end of the novel when they start talking to each other. Celie is beginning to communicate, but at this moment of her development, she can do so only with women. She has not broken the silence about her father and children yet, but she is beginning to combine nonlinguistic communication with words: "Me and Shug cook, talk, clean the house, talk, fix up the tree, talk, wake up in the morning, talk."

The last period of Celie's education starts when she discovers Nettie had not deserted her. She finds out the first small "we" she had with her sister was a reality. At the beginning of the novel,

when Sofia told her she should be furious, Celie could not feel rage. Now, with Nettie's letters in her hands, she is so angry only a creative activity (sewing pants) can keep her from killing Mr. This rage is healthy for her. It makes her stop writing to a God that does not answer: "I don't write to God no more, I write to you," she says. "You" is a real person, who will answer her. The God she was writing to before was a man, and a white man, she realizes suddenly. He was the oppressor: "The God I been praying and writing to is a man. And act just like all the other mens I know. Trifling, forgitful and lowdown."

Yet, Celie does not abandon the idea of God. She needs to replace it by a less oppressive figure. The new God, provided by Shug, is completely different from the "white old man": "God ain't a he or a she, but a It…. I believe God is everything…. Everything that is or ever was or ever will be…. one day when I was sitting quiet and feeling like a motherless child, which I was, it come to me: that feeling of being part of everything, not separate at all. I knew that if I cut a tree, my arm would bleed…. I think it pisses God off if you walk by the color purple in a field somewhere and don't notice it." What is important in this presentation of God is the radical contrast of this idea with the American Dream. Celie is discovering something she had already seen in the groups women formed around her, in the solidarity between Squeak and Sofia, between she herself and Shug. She is discovering the interdependence of the world around her ("not separate at all," says Shug), the need to "belong." This discovery explains her words to her husband: "Anything you do to me, already done to you." Until Mr. starts looking around and belonging to the world and caring for it, he is condemned to be Mr. and not Albert. The same can be said of his father, and Harpo and Pa. The legacy of what feminists call patriarchal education (the American Dream) is loneliness.

Now that she can communicate, Celie gets what she needed: company, community, a "we." She gets answers, not only from people, but from God also (unlike the first one, this God speaks). In a very important scene in which she is sitting in the house smoking with Harpo and Sofia to communicate with God, they hear a sound:

… UMMMMMMMM.

I think I know what it is, I say.

They say, What?

I say, Everything.

Yeah, they say. That make a lots of sense."

Once Celie learns to listen to this God—Everything—she can help others do the same. She helps Mary Agnes, she helps Shug, and what is even more impressive, she helps Mr. Mr. has been a role, a puppet of his father's patriarchal ideas. These ideas stopped him from marrying Shug, the woman he loved. He has repeated his father all his life but at the end of the novel, he discovers himself again. He had always loved sewing, but as everyone laughed at him when he said so (a man does not sew), he had to stop. Patriarchal society forbids him to sew and love, and turns him into Mr. the Man. He needs Celie to become Albert again.

When they become themselves, Celie, Mr., and Squeak become visible to others as they really are. They fight stereotype. Not just one stereotype but many: the stereotype of what a man should be, of what a woman should do, of what a black person is entitled to. This fight has to start with oneself: "Well, we all have to start somewhere if us want to do better and our own self is what us have to hand."

This fight for the self appears in many texts by minority authors. Native, Asian, Latin and Black Americans have felt the pressure of stereotype in their lives and have talked about it in art. In this novel, the pressure of stereotypes is enormous. The episode of Sofia and the mayor's wife describes one of the fronts of this battle. Nettie's letters about missionaries in Africa describe another. In all these fronts, the battle is in favor of the need to accept the difference in Others and in oneself.

In *The Color Purple,* this fight is presented through a myth, the African version of the biblical Adam and Eve story. According to this version, black people were the first human beings, and their sin was to hate the Other, the different. They killed all albino children because they were different. Adam and Eve were the first whites they threw out of town, instead of killing. The rejected whites were furious and started destroying black peoples. After crushing colored peoples as if they were serpents, it was predicted, "they [whites] gon kill each other off, they still so mad bout being unwanted. Gon kill off a lot of other folk too who got some color. In fact, they go kill off so much of the earth and the colored that everybody gon hate them just like they hate us today. Then they will become the new serpent. And wherever a white person is found he'll be crush by somebody not white, just like they do us today."

According to the African myth, there is a way to cut this horror, and that is to stop inventing serpents and "accept everybody else as a child of God, or one mother's children, no matter what they look like or how they act." That is why Olinkas worship serpents in Africa. This is the novel's central idea about prejudice and stereotype and difference, three important themes in twentieth century literature. And the only way to bring about the change is to communicate. *The Color Purple*'s conclusion is that first we must communicate with ourselves (our real "I"), then with the rest of the human beings (with whom we will achieve a "we," a community), and then with God (It)—this different God who appears in the opening of the last letter: "Dear God. Dear stars, dear trees, dear sky, dear peoples. Dear Everything, Dear God." The travel towards communication is dangerous, especially if one starts it as a prisoner of eternal silence, as Celie does. Nettie's travel is parallel but less complex. The final scene, that of the meeting of the two sisters, represents the recovery of Celie's and Nettie's "we," their *home.* In *The Color Purple, home* is something one must fight to find. Celie does not move from her birthplace but she has traveled as much as her sister.

Source: Margara Averbach, in an essay for *Novels for Students,* Gale, 1999.

Trudier Harris

In the following excerpt, Harris denies that the passive Celie is a progressive character and contends that The Color Purple *contains faults in logic which strain credibility.*

Alice Walker's *The Color Purple* depicts a black woman who is sexually abused, verbally dominated, and physically beaten for almost thirty years. As an adolescent, Celie is repeatedly raped and twice impregnated by the man she believes to be her father. That unscrupulous violator sells her children, destroys her reputation while keeping his own untarnished, and barters her off to an older man who uses her as a surrogate mother for his four horrible children and as a receptacle for his passion. After twenty years of enduring abuse after marriage, Celie finds the strength to engage in a lesbian relationship with her husband's former lover, to leave the church and her home, and to start a pant-making business. This brief scenario of the novel traces a remarkable transformation from victimization to entrepreneurship, and it all seems wonderfully affirming. Yet the novel raises many questions about Walker's [portrayal] of black female character and about where it fits in the schema of development she had outlined for her works early in her career. Walker maintained in a 1973 interview that some of her earlier victimized women characters were at a sort of "cave woman" level of a process that would take them beyond destruction and into positive images of themselves. Her characters in future works, she said, would no longer go crazy, as Myrna does in "Really, Doesn't Crime Pay?" or burn themselves up, as Mrs. Jerome Washington, III, does in "Her Sweet Jerome"; rather, they would become the black-eyed Susans who would have found the soil most suitable not only to their survival but to their active nurturing.

A look at some of the women in Walker's earlier works, who, like Celie, are victims of sexual and communal abuse, and who are sometimes victims of their own minds, reveals that Celie is not substantially different from them and that the culmination may be the reaffirmation of many old stereotypes rather than the assertion of a new identity. In Walker's early fiction, to be a victim is to give one's labor for the benefit of others, often to the detriment of one's self. To be a victim is to be the quintessential caring mother, self-effacing under all circumstances where the welfare of children is concerned....

The world of Walker's early fiction is one in which black people make victims of other black people *because* of white people. Grange cannot see an end to the life he is forced to lead under the sharecropping system in Georgia, so he destroys his marriage and indirectly destroys Margaret and her child. Brownfield bows and scrapes to the white men for whom he works, but he beats his wife unmercifully. The progression in Walker's world is from external to internal, from male control of female lives to women controlling their own lives. Such a progression, however, is at the expense of realistic portrayal of black female character, a change that culminates in the character of Celie in *The Color Purple....*

Celie may evolve within the scheme Walker has set up for her black women characters, but she does so at the price of reliving many portions of the lives of women in Walker's earlier fiction. She is sexually brutalized by her stepfather and exploited as a commodity by him and the man she marries. She becomes more of a sexual object than Mem or Margaret [in *The Third Life of Grange Copeland*], and she responds to her environment as an object would. Numbed into allowing her stepfather to take her body, she rather feebly rejects the act in her mind. She takes his advice and tells "no-

body but God" by writing the letters that provide the form for the novel.

Her initial victimization at fourteen is only the beginning of a series of uglinesses that characterize Celie's life and that show that she shares much with the women who have gone before her. Her status as a sexual object is initially problematic. Celie's sexual passivity, even if it could be stretched into a form of defiance, *may* suggest some iota of resistance to her situation, but the fact remains that she shares with Mem the sexual violation of her body, which amounts to an obvious lack of control over the most personal, private parts of herself. And she shares with many of the other Walker women the subservience to men. To her stepfather, who might as well be a descendant of plantation owners and other historical and literary males who view women as "chattel," Celie has little value as a human being and, beyond the sexual, none as a woman. She is like the one-eyed mule who is traded off to the buyer who believes that he has at least purchased sound flesh. The attitudes of others toward her, and the attitude of Celie toward herself, suggest that her place in the evolutionary development is not far beyond the level of Margaret and may, in some ways, be below Mem Copeland.

Walker emphasized in her comments on the future progression of black women characters that they would learn to make room for themselves, that they would carve out "a new place to move." That is perhaps the only thing about Celie that seems to fit with Walker's blueprint. Celie, by her own estimation and that of others, is a survivor. *How* she overcomes victimization to survive is the problem. Anyone can use her, or say anything to her, or commit violence against her, and she will placidly say something to the effect that she is still here. One vivid example of this occurs at the point where Celie's sister Nettie, having run away from home, visits the newly married Celie. To Nettie's insistence that Celie resist the mean children, that she fight back, Celie can only respond: "But I don't know how to fight. All I know how to do is stay alive." There is a contradiction in a survival that permits these kinds of suppressions of the self as well as a contradiction in how this kind of survival represents a remotely healthy progression for the fictional black woman character.

Celie survives by being a victim, by recognizing that fighting back causes one more problems than not. After Nettie has been forced to leave and Celie thinks she is dead, one of Albert's sisters suggests that Celie fight him as well as his children. In response, Celie thinks: "I don't say nothing. I think bout Nettie, dead. She fight, she run away. What good it do? I don't fight, I stay where I'm told. But I'm alive." Her passivity rivals that of many slave women. She will take any abuse to her body and mind as long as she is *allowed* to stay alive. The emphasis is on allowed because Celie continues to believe that others are responsible for her destiny, that she can have only as much space as they will grant.

Celie's self-effacing stance is given ironic reinforcement in the novel in the character of her daughter-in-law, Sofia, a black woman who does fight back. For cursing the mayor's wife and fighting back when slapped, Sofia is carted off to jail, then to prison for *twelve* years; released after eleven and a half years with six months off for good behavior, she has lost her husband, her children, and a portion of her sanity. When the family had visited her in the prison laundry and asked how she was doing, she had said: "Every time they ast me to do something, Miss Celie, I act like I'm you. I jump up and do just what they say." Sofia must eventually suppress most of the traits that make her an interesting character, turning from vibrancy to somnambulism, and Celie's formula for survival is mirrored back to her with a vengeance. Still, it is not enough to make her change her behavior.

Celie's notion of woman's place is as old as the history of black women in America. She stays in the home, no matter how ugly and unlivable it may be for her, and she finds comfort in the church and in the preparations, such as sweeping and washing the wine glasses, that she performs for church services. Albert brought her into his home to be wife and mother in the tradition of the mail-order bride—she should take care of his house and his children, be available to him sexually, and be seen but not heard. Although he chases Shug, he does not want Celie to appear in the local juke-joint because wives are not supposed to be seen in such places. Celie accepts her place and submits to the beatings that go along with it; she even tells Albert's son, Harpo, that he should beat his wife Sofia. Somewhere in her feelings, she knows she has given ill advice, but her experience prompts her in that moment to give the advice. When Sofia thinks of leaving Harpo because he will not accept the fact that she refuses to be beaten, Celie says, "He your husband... Got to stay with him. Else, what you gon do?" Celie knows that Sofia is a good wife, just as she knows that Harpo is happier with her (when he did not try to beat her) than he has

ever been, yet she advises Sofia to stay even after the attempted beatings. At this stage, the place in the home is all that Celie can envision for women like herself and Sofia.

The only permissible diversion from the home is God and the church. Celie's situation with Albert is so bad that Nettie describes it as a burial. "It's worse than that," Celie thinks. "If I was buried, I wouldn't have to work. But I just say, Never mine, never mine, long as I can spell G-o-d I got somebody along." Celie has grown up in the church and has attended during both of her pregnancies, so she continues that tradition during the years she is with Albert. In a conversation with Sofia, Celie makes her religious position clear; in the face of her stepfather's abuse, she forces herself beyond anger to feel "nothing at all" because the Bible teaches that one should "honor father and mother no matter what." She does not dwell on Albert's misuse of her because "he my husband. I shrug my shoulders. This life soon be over, I say. Heaven last all ways." It is all very familiar. When the life here gets too difficult and one lacks the strength to change it, one turns to Jesus and heaven. Celie tries to effect a transcendence of her earthly situation that dissolves each time she must undergo another beating from Albert.

Of her role in the church, where the women who have seen her twice pregnant before marriage are sometimes nice to her and sometimes not, Celie comments:

> I keep my head up, best I can. I do a right smart for the preacher. Clean the floor and the windows, make the wine, wash the alter linen. Make sure there's wood for the stove in wintertime. He call me Sister Celie. Sister Celie, he say, You faithful as the day is long. Then he talk to the other ladies and they mens. I scurry bout, doing this, doing that. Mr. ____ sit back by the door gazing here and there. The womens smile in his direction every chance they git. He never look at me or even notice.

In the institution that has traditionally allowed even the most rejected and victimized in the black community an opportunity to serve, Celie is a model of Christian behavior. She accepts those spaces in which she can operate without offending and without calling undue attention to herself.

The most vivid instance of the place to which Celie has been assigned and which she accepts without outright complaint occurs upon Shug's arrival at their house. Shug, an entertainer who was in love with Albert years before, and who has three children by him, is brought to their house to recover from a lingering illness. Her mean and condescending treatment of Celie during the nursing she provides is only matched by her behavior once she is well enough to move around. She and Albert go about as if they are courting, leaving Celie to think whatever she pleases. The two become lovers again under Celie's own roof. Ridiculous in its conception, the situation becomes more so when Shug asks and is granted permission from Celie to continue sleeping with Albert. The visual layout is itself preposterous. On one side of a wall, Celie lies regretting the fact that she has had no proper sexual initiation and is hardly aroused even by caressing the clitoris Shug has newly pointed out to her. On the other side of the wall, Albert makes passionate love to a woman he has been in love with all his life. The situation is only mildly regrettable to Celie. She does not object to the violation of her home (at times, it seems as if she is pleased that Shug can take care of Albert in ways she cannot). She holds no malice toward Shug for being a luscious slut (one with whom Celie will also fall in love), and she seems to have little sense of the usual decorum involved in human relationships.

Walker can certainly be developing the case that the usual does not apply to Celie and the environment in which she lives, but there must be some kind of logic at work in the novel, no matter how vehemently the reader may disapprove of it. When the characters themselves do not seem to respond to that internal logic, then serious questions arise about the meaning of the work as a whole. For Celie is not merely an animal; she thinks, whether or not she is able to articulate those thoughts, and, though her ability to feel may sometimes appear incongruous, there are certainly things that make her angry, happy, or sad.

So often treated as an object, Celie is put into the position of responding favorably to the first person other than her sister who treats her with the humanity she deserves. That person is Shug Avery. After treating Celie so harshly, and being forced to admire the quiet resignation Celie has in responding to such treatment, Shug's bad treatment turns to good. She comes to view Celie as the survivor she is—in spite of Albert and the rest of the world—and she comes to believe that there must be something special about Celie (Miss Celie, she respectfully calls her).

It is a testament to the good things that Shug evokes in Celie that she is able to enter the lesbian relationship so easily. She thinks only that here is someone who cares about her, not that she is doing something that might be objectionable. She has shown evidence of a traditional moral sense; after all, she had objected, in a way, to the "unnatural" relationship her stepfather had with her. No such value judgment is allowed to enter the relationship with Shug. Celie is allowed to bask in the discovery of the good feelings emotionally and the pleasure of the body she experiences with Shug, for this woman is able to bring out things in her that neither her stepfather nor Albert could. Walker embues the relationship with a forgiving aura of innocence; there can be nothing wrong with this wide-eyed discovery of what it means not only to be human, but to be a woman.

The beauty of this relationship stands in sharp contrast to the ugliness present in Celie's early life and the ugliness she felt was hers. The issue of physical beauty, in fact, is another problem in consideration of the presumably progressive character Walker has created. Black women throughout their history in the United States have been victimized by a standard of beauty alien and inapplicable to them. Gwendolyn Brooks, Maya Angelou, Toni Morrison, Paule Marshall, and others have all written of the consequences for the dark-skinned black woman, the one who was not light and did not have "good" hair. That woman suffered from color prejudices originating within the black community as well as from without. Many contemporary writers have written of the need to find identity and value in sources other than a narrow-minded conception of physical beauty. It is somewhat anachronistic, therefore, that Celie judges herself so harshly, by the standards of those around her, for her lack of physical attractiveness. She does not object to her stepfather's evaluation of her because she *believes* she is ugly. Objective analysis of one's physical features is one thing, but belief that one is ugly is quite another. Celie sees nothing in her environment to contradict her basic feeling of ugliness; she therefore accepts it as gospel. Her response is that ugly people should be seen and not heard; they should work and keep silent and try to make an inconspicuous space for themselves in the grimy little worlds they must inhabit.

From the time that they are children, Celie believes that she is neither as pretty nor as smart as Nettie. Although Nettie encourages Celie toward a more positive self-conception, Nettie soon leaves, and Celie is left with those whose harsh judgments of her looks mirror her own beliefs. Shug's initial reaction to Celie is perhaps what Celie feels is the world's reaction to her. "She look me over from head to foot. Then she cackle. Sound like a death rattle. You sure *is* ugly, she say, like she ain't believed it." What Shug verbalizes is what Celie has felt about her general appearance a few minutes before when she saw the wagon approaching. She puts on, then takes off, a new dress because it "won't help none with my notty head and dusty headrag, my old everyday shoes and the way I smell." Her effort to change is inspired in part by the fact that she knows Shug Avery is a glamorous woman (Celie has worshipped her photograph for years), but it also grows out of a basic inferiority complex about looks. On another occasion when company comes, Celie says she stands "in front the glass trying to make something out my hair. It too short to be long, too long to be short. Too nappy to be kinky, too kinky to be nappy. No set color to it either. I give up, tie on a headrag." Her looks are used to keep her in her place, to keep her from dreaming of being anything other than a mule. Albert learns of her desire to go to Memphis with Shug and is brutal in his comparison of the two women:

> Shug got talent, he say. She can sing. She got spunk, he say, She can talk to anybody. Shug got looks, he say. She can stand up and be notice. But what you got? You ugly. You skinny. You shape funny. You too scared to open your mouth to people. All you fit to do in Memphis is be Shug's maid. Take out her slop-jar and maybe cook her food. You not that good a cook neither. And this house ain't been clean good since my first wife died. And nobody crazy or backward enough to want to marry you, neither. What you gon do? Hire yourself out to farm? He laugh. Maybe somebody let you work on they railroad.

Partly inspired by jealousy, Albert's outburst shows his regret that it is Celie, not himself, who is going to Memphis with Shug; still, the ugliness directed at Celie overshadows everything else. Even in a calmer mood later in the novel, when he and Celie are somewhat reconciled, he offers essentially the same evaluation of her looks. Celie's whole life is a negation of Albert's evaluation of her domestic talents, yet her response to all of his comments is a lapsing into her usual rationale: "I'm pore, I'm black, I may be ugly and can't cook, a voice say to everything listening. But I'm here." Even the trip to Memphis does not change her evaluation of her looks. After the wonderful times with Shug, after she sees that things can be different for a woman like herself, she is still overly critical of herself when Shug is unfaithful to her:

> Sometimes I think Shug never love me. I stand looking at my naked self in the looking glass. What would she love? I ast myself. My hair is short and kinky because I don't straighten it anymore. Once Shug say

she love it no need to. My skin dark. My nose just a nose. My lips just lips. My body just any woman's body going through the changes of age. Nothing special here for nobody to love. No honey colored curly hair, no cuteness. Nothing young and fresh.

Celie's catalog reads as if she had adopted all the stereotyped notions of looks that black women have been unwarranted heir to for centuries in America. She will eventually reach contentment, but that contentment will represent no softening of her attitude toward her physical features. In this area of her life so very vital to self-conception, Celie reflects no evolved state of mind, no substantial change from the majority of her dark-skinned black sisters of the 1930s and 1940s and perhaps a few of those who still devalued themselves early in the 1980s, when Walker published the novel.

Through Shug, Celie does gain a confidence that moves her toward independence. Her confidence increases once she discovers that Nettie, believed to be dead, is still alive. She changes her attitude toward God when she realizes that He has allowed Albert to keep Nettie's letters from her. Resolving to leave Albert, Celie's stance becomes a refusal to be victimized by God or Albert. Her declaration of independence achieves great stature when it is measured against her former, passive existence. That this thing, this object that could be shunted around by almost everyone, finds the strength to extricate herself from her circumstances is truly remarkable. Not only has she been mentally bound, but she has probably never before been more than twenty-five miles away from home. Contemplating a new life, and moving geographically to achieve it, adds a new dimension to the consideration of Celie as stifled character. One of her last conversations with Albert shows the extent to which she has changed and illustrates the effect of that change upon the people who have been closest to Celie; their shock emphasizes how initially incredible Celie's new stance really is. This usually inarticulate woman (verbally, that is) is able to command words that undercut Albert in ways comparable to that of Janie with Jody Starks in Zora Neale Hurston's *Their Eyes Were Watching God.* Shug maintains that Celie is going to Memphis with her:

> Over my dead body, Mr. _____ say.

> You satisfied that what you want, Shug say, cool as clabber.

> Mr. _____ start up from his seat, look at Shug, plop back down again. He look over at me. I thought you was finally happy, he say, What wrong now?

You a lowdown dog is what's wrong, I say. It's time to leave you and enter into the Creation. And your dead body just the welcome mat I need.

Say what? he ast. Shock.

All round the table folkses mouths be dropping open.

You took my sister Nettie away from me, I say. And she was the only person love me in the world.

Mr. ____ start to sputter ButButButButBut. Sound like some kind of motor.

But Nettie and my children coming home soon, I say. And when she do, all us together gon whup your ass.

Nettie and your children! say Mr. ____. You talking crazy.

I got children, I say. Being brought up in Africa. Good schools, lots of fresh air and exercise. Turning out a heap better than the fools you didn't even try to raise.

Hold on, say Harpo.

Oh, hold on hell, I say. If you hadn't tried to rule over Sofia the white folks never would have caught her.

Sofia so surprise to hear me speak up she ain't chewed for ten minutes....

You was all rotten children, I say. You made my life a hell on earth. And your daddy here ain't dead horse's shit.

Mr. ____ reach over to slap me. I jab my case knife in his hand.

Adding a physical articulateness to the longest and the most significant conversation she has had with Albert, Celie goes another step in shedding off the authority that has been placed over her (she still is unable to call Albert by his name). She rejects the role of wife when Albert asks what people will say about her leaving and laughs when Grady, Shug's husband, responds that "a woman can't git a man if peoples talk." It is clearly not a man that Celie wants, a factor that further strengthens her decision to leave.

Surprisingly, Celie's home-bound sojourn in Memphis as companion and lover to Shug seems unliberating, but, taken in its context, it gives Celie a new lease on life. The tasks she has performed for so many years simply because she was expected and forced to do them now become a measure of her love for Shug. Through making pants for Shug, Celie discovers her final declaration of independence. She turns pant-making into a full time occupation and rather quickly becomes a competent, highly patronized seamstress. She establishes Folkspants, Unlimited, and hires a couple of helpers in the business. She even makes pants for the folks back down home, and they in turn spread

the word of her good work. The ultimate transformation is complete; she has effaced herself into free enterprise.

Within the context of a consideration of growth and liberation, Celie's pants making is an appropriate and effective symbol. When she wore the first pair of pants, it was a sign that she was breaking out of the role the men in her life had assigned to her. Albert thought it scandalous for his wife to wear pants; Celie defied him and destroyed the power of his attitude over her. Since men have been her most cruel oppressors, it is ironically appropriate that she take something traditionally assigned to them in shaking off the power they have over her. And not only does she shake off that power; she turns it against them by getting them to like the pants she sews. Therefore, they can no longer object to what she wears or how she makes her living.

Celie's survival, without the blare of trumpets, is presented as the progression in the novel. From a used and abused woman, Celie emerges as an independent, creative businesswoman. She moves from being ugly duckling to a figuratively beautiful swan. She moves from being Hurston's mule, the beast of burden, to physical and mental declarations of independence, to a reunion with her children and her sister. She moves from seeing God as the center of her universe to redefining the concept of the supernatural as an "It" that dwells in everyone. She moves from being beaten and used by others to establishing her own business. She moves from being a strait-laced church woman to being a reefer smoker. She moves from the back room of the house in which her stepfather has violated her to sharing a huge house in Memphis with her lover to returning to a house, property, and a store she has inherited. She moves from being Albert's footstool to demanding his respect and teaching him how to sew

Celie is almost archetypal in the transformations she undergoes. In her, black women are visible at various stages in their history and in their representations in literature. As a representative character, Celie presents fewer problems than those that arise in considering her individual case. As a character in evolution, some of the things that happen to her tax credibility; to go from being object to being self-determined is certainly not impossible, but Celie's case raises questions about that process as well as about the evolved state of black womanhood she is portrayed as representing. Despite the fact that Celie "is based on Walker's great-grandmother, a slave who was raped at 12 by the man who owned her," Walker's assertion that she "liberated" Celie "from her own history" because she "wanted her to be happy" crystallizes the conflicts at work in portraying Celie as a progressive character.

While it was never suggested that black women had to be dignified in their struggles, it was also never suggested that survival demanded the harshest struggles the imagination can conceive. Celie survives, unlike Mrs. Jerome Washington, III, and Mem, but other Walker characters, such as Myrna, Imani, and the unnamed lawyer killer, also survive.... Celie's path of extrication might be more dramatic than the other three, but ultimately all the women find a new sense of self and act upon that discovery—no matter how unrealistic it may seem.

What makes Celie different is the sensational quality surrounding her life. Walker uses the subjects of incest and lesbianism to add an aura to a story that might otherwise have been rather ordinary. And she uses the rather strained device of Nettie's trip to and letters from Africa to point out African connections between behavior in the Olinka village and behavior among African-Americans in Celie's home town. Incest does perhaps serve to explain why Celie prefers women lovers to men, but the reader must infer that purpose. Celie goes through the somnambulism of her days without consideration of it in any special way; her emotional state is such that few things draw her far out of her passive existence. Her state might just as well have been caused by a lover who was especially brutal to her at an early age. The issue of incest, therefore, is really not as convincingly relevant to the formation of Celie's personality or to the understanding of her situation as it might initially seem. And Walker apparently agrees to an extent with that position by having the "incest" be revealed in a "father" figure rather than a biological father; she inadvertently suggests that this is somehow less startling or that Celie is more prone to transcend the abuse of a stepfather.

The epistolary form of the novel also contributes to what makes Celie different from the other Walker women. As one reviewer of the novel suggests [Gloria Steinem in *Ms.*], Celie can affirm herself through the act of writing; while others would deny her humanity, she can assert it through the process of creation in the letters. The actual language of the letters, which are written in Celie's folk speech without any attempt at editorializing on Walker's part, is similarly reaffirming; something essential to her personality is given shape on the page. Unfortunately, these very things that make the novel so affirming, from such a perspective, are also in part what make it problematic. Writing may save in the abstract, but it does not prevent Albert from going upside Celie's head. It is a personal, quiet comfort that reiterates isolation and Celie's inability to act in more tangible ways to extricate herself from or change her situation.

While the reader is inclined to feel good that Celie does survive, and to appreciate the good qualities she has, she or he is still equally skeptical about accepting the logic of a novel that posits so many changes as a credible progression for a character. Such a total change of lifestyle, attitudes, and beliefs for a character well settled in her ways as she approaches fifty and the last third of her life asks more of the reader than can be reasonably expected. Readers are constantly torn between their desire to believe and the experience and history that suggest that even a single individual like Celie (even if her representative qualities are ignored) would have more difficulty and more serious wrestling with the spirit to effect the kinds of changes Walker presents, just as they have difficulty accepting the extremity of the abuses in her life. Celie, though interesting, provocative, and unlike many other black women characters in black literature and in Walker's fiction, is nonetheless so like many of them that that kinship overshadows other statements Walker may wish to make in *The Color Purple.*

Source: Trudier Harris, "From Victimization to Free Enterprise: Alice Walker's *The Color Purple*," in *Studies in American Fiction,* Vol. 14, No. 1, Spring, 1986, pp. 1–17.

Dinitia Smith

In the following review, Smith praises Walker for the pungency and tenderness of The Color Purple *as well as for its strong characterizations.*

As admirers of *The Third Life of Grange Copeland* and *Meridian* already know, to read an Alice Walker novel is to enter the country of surprise. It is to be admitted to the world of rural black women, a world long neglected by most whites, perhaps out of ignorance, perhaps out of willed indifference. The loss is ours, for the lives of these women are so extraordinary in their tragedy, their culture, their humor and their courage that we are immediately gripped by them.

Witness the opening passage of *The Color Purple,* a tale of violence, incest and redemption that starts out in Georgia in the 1900s and goes on for about thirty years. Beginning when her mother is laid up in childbirth, skinny, "ugly" 14-year-old Celie is repeatedly raped by the man she believes to be her father:

> Dear God, I am fourteen years old. I am I have always been a good girl. Maybe you can give me a sign letting me know what is happening to me.

Celie, who retreats into an emotional numbness that will last for years, has two babies by her "father"; he gives them away. They end up in Africa with Celie's sister Nettie, who works for the missionary family that adopted them. (The novel is a series of letters, first from Celie to God, and then back and forth between Celie and Nettie.)

Celie is married off to Mr. ____, a downtrodden farmer who beats her. At night, she parts her legs for him and forces all thought and feeling from her body: "I make myself wood. I say to myself, Celie, you a tree. That's how come I know trees fear man."

Along comes Shug Avery, a blues singer of legendary beauty. Mr. ____ has been in love with her for years, and when she falls sick, he brings her home to Celie to nurse. Celie and Shug become friends and then lovers. Through Shug, Celie discovers that Mr. ____ has been intercepting Nettie's letters for several years. And from the letters, which Shug helps her obtain, she learns that the man who raped her wasn't her real father. Her real father had been lynched. With the stigma of incest removed, Celie finally stands up to Mr. ____:

> You lowdown dog…. It's time to leave you and enter into Creation. And your dead body just the welcome mat I need.

I wanted to cheer.

Celie goes with Shug to Memphis, and there she learns to live and love. When her "father" dies, she inherits his farm and returns to Georgia, where she sleeps in a room painted purple for Walker, the color of radiance and majesty (and also the emblematic color of lesbianism). She is reunited with her children and Nettie, and, surprisingly, she befriends Mr. ____, who has been broken and humbled by Shug and Celie's joint departure. The end of the book finds Celie and her erstwhile tormentor sitting companionably on the front porch smoking their pipes, "two old fools left over from love, keeping each other company under the stars."

Walker can be a pungent writer. When Celie's father-in-law, Old Mr. ____, criticizes Shug, Celie, who has been sent to get the man a glass of water, overhears him:

> I drop little spit in Old Mr. ____ water…. I twirl the spit round with my finger…. Next time he come I put a little Shug Avery pee in his glass. See how he like that.

And sometimes she can break our hearts. When the aging Shug wants to have one last fling with a young man, Celie is so devastated she cannot speak. She can only talk to Shug in writing:

> He's nineteen. A baby. How long can it last? [Shug says.]
>
> He's a man. I write on the paper.
>
> Yeah, she say … but some mens can be lots of fun.
>
> Spare me, I write.

No writer has made the intimate hurt of racism more palpable than Walker. In one of the novel's most rending scenes, Celie's step-daughter-in-law, Sofia, is sentenced to work as a maid in the white mayor's house for "sassing" the mayor's wife. In a fit of magnanimity, the mayor's wife offers to drive Sofia home to see her children, whom she hasn't laid eyes on in five years. The reunion lasts only fifteen minutes—then the mayor's wife insists that Sofia drive her home.

The Color Purple is about the struggle between redemption and revenge. And the chief agency of redemption, Walker is saying, is the strength of the relationships between women: their friendships, their love, their shared oppression. Even the white mayor's family is redeemed when his daughter cares for Sofia's sick daughter.

There is a note of tendentiousness here, though. The men in this book change *only* when their women join together and rebel—and then, the change is so complete as to be unrealistic. It was hard for me to believe that a person as violent, brooding and just plain nasty as Mr. ____ could ever become that sweet, quiet man smoking and chatting on the porch.

Walker's didacticism is especially evident in Nettie's letters from Africa, which make up a large portion of the book. Nettie relates the story of the Olinka tribe, particularly of one girl, Tashi, as a kind of feminist fable:

> The Olinka do not believe girls should be educated. When I asked a mother what she thought of this, she said: A girl is nothing to herself; only to her husband can she become something.
>
> What can she become? I asked.
>
> Why, she said, the mother of his children.
>
> But I am not the mother of anybody's children, I said, and I am something.

Later, Nettie tells Tashi's parents that "the world is changing.... It is no longer a world just for boys and men," and we wince at the ponderousness, the obviousness of the message. At times the message is confusing, too. The white rubber planters who disrupt Olinka society also destroy the old (and presumably bad) tribal patriarchy. Does this mean the white man's coming is a good thing? I doubt it, but I was puzzled.

Walker's politics are not the problem—*of course* sexism and racism are terrible, *of course* women should band together to help each other. But the politics have to be incarnated in complex, contradictory characters—characters to whom the novelist grants the freedom to act, as it were, on their own.

I wish Walker had let herself be carried along more by her language, with all its vivid figures of speech, Biblical cadences, distinctive grammar and true-to-life starts and stops. The pithy, direct black folk idiom of *The Color Purple* is in the end its greatest strength, reminding us that if Walker is sometimes an ideologue, she is also a poet.

Despite its occasional preachiness, *The Color Purple* marks a major advance for Walker's art. At its best, and at least half the book is superb, it places her in the company of Faulkner, from whom she appears to have learned a great deal: the use of a shifting first-person narrator, for instance, and the presentation of a complex story from a naïve point of view, like that of 14-year-old Celie. Walker has not turned her back on the southern fictional tradition. She has absorbed it and made it her own. By infusing the black experience into the southern novel, she enriches both it and us.

Source: Dinitia Smith, "Celie, You a Tree," in *The Nation*, Vol. 235, No. 6, September 4, 1982, pp. 181–83.

Sources

Trudier Harris, "On *The Color Purple*, Stereotypes, and Silence," in *Black American Literature Forum*, vol. 18, no. 4, 1984, pp. 155-61.

Gloria Steinem, "Do You Know This Woman? She Knows You: A Profile of Alice Walker," in *Ms.*, June, 1982, pp. 35, 37, 89-94.

J. Charles Washington, "Positive Black Male Images in Alice Walker's Fiction," in *Obsidian*, Spring, 1988, pp. 23-48.

Richard Wesley, "*The Color Purple* Debate: Reading between the Lines," in *Ms.*, September, 1986, pp. 62, 90-2.

For Further Study

Richard Abcarian, *Negro American Literature*, Wadworth, California, 1970.

An early but fundamental commentary on African American literature, its roots and importance. There is a deep discussion of Richard Wright's novel.

Gordon W. Allport, *The Nature of Prejudice*, Cambridge, 1954.

An early, fundamental source to understand the problem of prejudice, and racism in general, and to help define concepts such as visibility and difference.

Barbara Christian, editor, *Black Feminist Criticism*, Pergamon Texto, University of California Press, 1985.

A number of essays about black literature from the feminist criticism perspective.

Arthur Davis and Michael W. Peplow, *Anthology of Negro American Literature*, Holt, New York, 1975.

A collection of critical essays on early African American literature.

Leslie Fiedler, "Negro and Jew: Encounter in America", in *No! In Thunder*, Stein and Day, New York, 1972.

An interesting article by a very well-known critic about the relationships between Jews and African Americans in the United States.

Paula Giddings, *When and Where I Enter: The Impact of Black Women on Race and Power in America*, Bantam, 1985, p. 186.

Giddings, a historian, discusses the role of color and its impact on achievement. She offers supporting evidence that African Americans of mixed race (with lighter skin color) had better educational and economic opportunities than those with dark skin color.

Nathan Glazer and Daniel P. Moynihan, editors. *Ethnicity: Theory and Experience*, Harvard University Press, Cambridge, MA, 1975.

A study of the relationships between "Self" and "Other," written after some important observations of the sixties.

Jacquelyn Grant, "Womanist Theology: Black Woman's Experience as a Source for Doing Theology," in *Encyclopedia of African American Religions*, Garland, 1993, p. 1.

Grant explains the concept of *womanist* as opposed to *feminist*. A distinction in terminology is made for black women because their struggle for expression has been different from white women.

Bell Hooks, *Ain't I Woman: Black Women and Feminism*, South End, 1981.

Hooks discusses the sexual assault black women endured after the end of slavery and the passive role of black women after World War II.

Charles Frederick Marden and Gladys Meyer, *Minorities in American Society*, Van Nostrand, New York, 1973.

An early study of ethnic relationships in the United States. The most detailed section of the book is devoted to the problems faced by African Americans in the United States.

S. Dale McLemore, *Racial and Ethnic Relations in America,* Allyn and Bacon, Boston, 1980.

A much more advanced study of the subject of ethnic relations in the United States with a big section devoted to African Americans and a deep discussion of cultural versus racial differences and visibility.

Toni Morrison, *Playing in the Dark, Whiteness and the Literary Imagination,* Picador, 1992.

The essential, interesting ideas of Nobel Prize winner Toni Morrison about African American literature, its roots, purposes and future.

Carol Pearson and Katherine Pope, *The Female Hero in American and British Literature,* Bowker, New York, 1981.

An essential study of women in literature that is very interesting for understanding the position of Celie as heroine in *The Color Purple.*

Annis Pratt, *Archetypal Patterns in Women's Fiction,* Indiana University Press, Indiana, 1981.

This study can be applied to the use of archetypes and myth in *The Color Purple.*

Elaine Showalter, *Towards a Feminist Poetics,* Oxford, 1979.

A study about feminist poetic theory, with interesting ideas that are applicable to *The Color Purple.*

Claudia Tate, *Black Women Writers at Work,* Continuum, New York, 1983.

A series of interviews with black female authors, including one with Alice Walker. The interviews have a distinctively feminist focus, making them especially interesting to anyone studying *The Color Purple.*

Fannie Barrier Williams, in Paula Giddings's book, *When and Where I Enter: The Impact of Black Women on Race and Power in America,* Bantam, 1985, p. 114.

Williams discusses the historical attitude of black men toward black women, an attitude that devalued black women and assumed they were not virtuous.

Do Androids Dream of Electric Sheep?

Philip K. Dick

1968

The importance of Philip Kindred Dick may never be fully assessed or accepted by mainstream analysts of English literature. The reason is simply that Dick's chosen genre, science fiction, has little standing with academic critics. In addition, Dick's fiction can be incredibly difficult to grapple with. As Robert Scholes and Eric S. Rabkin noted in their *Science Fiction: History, Science, Vision,* "His work is not easy to discuss, since it does not fall neatly into a few books of exceptional achievement and a larger body of lesser works. All his books offer ideas, situations, and passages of considerable interest. None quite achieves that seamless perfection of form that constitutes one form of literary excellence." Nevertheless, Dick is widely regarded as a master of his chosen medium and through more than one hundred short stories, some fifty novels (mostly science fiction), many essays, and lectures, he has created a cult following around the world. Most people know him as the writer behind the epoch setting 1982 film *Blade Runner.* Sadly, few outside the science fiction community have read the more complex original work that formed the basis for the film, *Do Androids Dream of Electric Sheep?*

In this novel, Dick furthers his exploration of his staple obsessions: What is reality? What does it mean to be human in a digital, mechanized world? Where, if anywhere, does one draw a line between the value of real and artificial life? *Do Androids Dream of Electric Sheep?* takes place on a post-nuclear apocalyptic Earth, where eight an-

droids—artificially constructed humanoid robots—have recently arrived after killing their human masters on Mars. Androids are not allowed on Earth and Mercer, the religious cult figure of the book, has declared that killers must be killed. The increasing difficulty of distinguishing androids from humans disturbs Rick Deckard, a bounty hunter called in to "retire" the fugitives. In a world where animal life is prized so highly that people buy artificial sheep to tend, why should androids be treated any differently? In examining these questions, the novel provides a brilliant pause for reflection on the meaning of human life and humanity's responsibility for the environment it is so determined to destroy.

Author Biography

Son of Joseph Edgar Dick, a government employee, and his wife Dorothy Kindred, Philip K. Dick was born in Chicago in 1928. He lived most of his life in California, however, and spent his life commenting on America and encouraging Americans to break through to a better, less strife-filled reality. A music lover, Dick worked as an announcer on a classical music station, KSMO, in 1947, and worked in a record store from 1948 to 1952. In 1950 he attended the University of California at Berkeley, but dropped out because the University's required ROTC courses conflicted with his antiwar convictions. Meanwhile, he had begun writing, and in 1952 sold his first story, "Roog," to the *Magazine of Fantasy and Science Fiction.* In the same year, *Planet Stories* published his more well-known short story "Beyond Lies the Wub."

In 1953, Dick published twenty-eight short stories, and another twenty-eight followed in 1954. After the success of *Solar Lottery* in 1955, he focused mainly on science fiction novels. In 1962, he won the Hugo Award for *The Man in the High Castle,* an "alternate reality" novel in which the United States has lost World War II and has been split by the Germans and Japanese. He was most prolific during the years 1964 to 1969, when he published sixteen volumes; *Do Androids Dream of Electric Sheep?* was part of this peak. In 1974, the author claimed to have had a mystical experience during which a "transcendentally rational mind" inhabited his consciousness and straightened out his life. This led him to explore religious themes in the novels *VALIS* (1981), *The Divine Invasion* (1981), and *The Transmigration of Timothy Archer* (1982).

During his lifetime, Dick was active in the antiwar, anti-abortion, and animal rights movements. He was also involved with drug rehabilitation programs, both out of concern for others and from personal experience. Like many artists of his generation, Dick viewed drug use as a tool for breaking through the reality of the everyday world and freeing the creative spirit. Drug use, Dick said, allowed him to experience as different a reality as possible and, therefore, to believe not only in alternate dystopic worlds but that a better world could be created. His 1965 novel *The Three Stigmata of Palmer Eldritch* explored issues of drug use and reality in its focus on a hallucinogen that never seems to wear off. Dick recognized, however, the toll that drug use had taken on him and others. He suffered pancreatic damage and the use of amphetamines resulted in high blood pressure, which eventually led to the stroke which killed him.

Dick died from heart failure after a stroke in March of 1982, soon after the release of *Blade Runner.* He was survived by five ex-wives and three children: Laura, Isolde, and Christopher. While Dick also wrote mainstream fiction—two novels of 1950s America, *Mary and the Giant* (1987) and *The Broken Bubble* (1988), were published posthumously—his greatest successes were within the genre that permitted him to explore questions of reality to the fullest. "My major preoccupation," Dick said, "is to question, 'What is reality?'" As the author wrote in an afterword to *The Golden Man:* "SF is a field of rebellion, against accepted ideas, institutions, against all that is. In my writing I even question the universe; wonder out loud if it is real, and wonder out loud if all of us are real."

Plot Summary

The Situation

Do Androids Dream of Electric Sheep? takes place in the year 1992, after World War Terminus has spread a cloud of radioactive dust across the globe. Many plant and animal species are extinct, and many of the surviving humans have emigrated to colonies on Mars. The remaining humans are divided between regulars and "specials," people who are either too stupid or too affected by radiation to be allowed to reproduce. As a result of these combined factors, cities are underpopulated and ownership of animals is considered both a status symbol and a sign of righteous empathy. Both real and imitation animals are expensive, with price lists updated monthly. In demand by Martian colonists are androids, manufactured to be as much like humans as possible, both in flesh and in emotion. Colonists are offered custom designed androids when they emigrate, and the androids serve as slaves. Discontented androids can escape from servitude by killing their masters and then returning to Earth to hide. Bounty hunters from Earth's various police forces are sent to locate these escapees and "retire" them. As the androids have become more human-like, retiring them has become more and more like killing.

The novel opens in the apartment of bounty hunter Rick Deckard and his wife, Iran. As he leaves for work, she tries to decide what mood to "dial up" for herself with their Penfield mood enhancing machine. Going to his car on the roof, Deckard stops to feed his electronic sheep. He takes a moment to admire his neighbor's real, living, horse. Upon hearing that the horse is pregnant, Rick's frustration surfaces and he admits to his neighbor that his sheep is false.

At work, his superior explains Deckard's new mission to him: eight androids have escaped from Mars, and San Francisco's lead bounty hunter, Dave Holden, has been shot down after retiring two. Deckard's first step is to go the androids' manufacturer, Rosen Association, to learn about this newest, most realistic model, the Nexus-6. The company's president, Eldon Rosen, doubts the accuracy of the "Voigt-Kampff" empathy test that the police use to distinguish androids from humans. His niece, Rachael, takes the test, and when it concludes that she is not human they assume that the test is flawed. The Rosens then attempt to bribe Deckard by offering him a real owl. Following a hunch, Deckard asks one last question that proves that his test results were accurate: Rachael Rosen is indeed an android.

Alternating with Deckard's story, the novel follows the day of John "J. R." Isidore, a "special" laborer with a low I.Q. who works for a veterinary clinic that cares for artificial animals. Isidore is a devotee of Wilbur Mercer, the religious figure that most people, including the Deckards, believe in. They relate to Mercer via "empathy boxes": they watch video images of him climbing a mountain, pelted with stones by skeptics, and when a stone hits Mercer the viewers who have real empathy for him will also bruise or bleed. Isidore is also a fan of Buster Friendly, the cheerful show business personality who somehow hosts talk shows on both radio and television simultaneously for twenty-

three hours a day. On this morning, Isidore comes across a strange woman, Pris Stratton, in one of the empty apartments in his building. She is mysteriously cold and factual, but the idea that she is an android does not occur to Isidore, both because he is desperately lonely and because of his limited mental capacity. Later that day, Isidore picks up a cat for repair and it expires in his van. Only later does he discover it was actually a living creature.

The Hunt

Deckard is assigned to work with a Soviet bounty hunter named Kadalyi while hunting the android named Max Polokov, who ambushed Dave Holden and put him in the hospital. Almost immediately after they meet, Deckard realizes that Kadalyi is Polokov, and retires him. The next android on his list is an opera singer, Luba Luft; he listens to her and is surprised at the quality of her voice. "Perhaps the better she functions, the better singer she is, the more I am needed," he muses. When Deckard interviews her at the opera house, she accuses him of being a sex criminal, and he is amused when she calls the police, certain that they will support him. The policeman who answers her call, though, is unfamiliar, and he takes Deckard to a police station that is not the Hall of Justice that he knows.

The investigating officer at this station, Inspector Garland, is the next name on Deckard's list of androids to retire. He tells Deckard that the bounty hunter in this parallel police force, Phil Resch, is also an android, but that he does not know it. When tests prove that Polokov was an android, Resch leaves to get equipment to test Garland. Garland pulls a laser when Resch returns, and Resch retires Garland in turn. He then goes with Deckard to the art museum, where they apprehend Luba Luft and retire her. The coolness with which Resch destroys androids seems to support Garland's claim that Resch is an android himself, but the test Deckard gives him proves that he is not. Deckard is disgusted with Resch's emotionless killing and how it reflects his own lack of empathy in dealing with androids. To affirm his humanity, he stops at the store and puts a down payment on an expensive live animal, a goat.

Deckard wants time to rest, and at home he uses the empathy machine on impulse. While using it, Mercer tells him "there is no salvation" and that he will always be "required to do wrong." Called by his office to find the remaining androids, Deckard takes up Rachael Rosen's offer of help. They meet at a San Francisco hotel room, drink, and become romantically involved. Rachael tells Deckard that she has fallen in love with him; later she admits that seducing him is a standard maneuver used to make bounty hunters feel uncomfortable about killing androids. On a lead from his department, Deckard goes to John Isidore's apartment building to find Pris Stratton. The remaining androids, Roy Baty and his wife Irmgard, are living at the building too, sheltered by the innocent Isidore.

While Deckard is on his way to the building, Isidore finds out two discouraging facts. The first comes when Buster Friendly announces on the television that Mercer is a fraud, and supports his claim with expert analysis of the artificiality of Mercer's ascent up the mountain and evidence that Mercer is played by an old, unemployed, alcoholic character actor. Isidore's second revelation is that his android friends are not simply, like him, misunderstood, persecuted humans. When Isidore finds a rare spider, a living thing which he treasures, Irmgard Baty proceeds to snip its legs off out of curiosity, offering to pay Isidore the catalog price of the spider, ignorant to the inherent value of life. Roy Baty tells Isidore that "Mercerism is a swindle. The whole experience of empathy is a swindle."

When Deckard arrives, he runs into Isidore, who tells him that he is looking after the three androids and that he will not help Deckard capture them. Inside of the building Deckard is aided by an apparition of Mercer, the religious figure, who assures him that retiring androids is not contrary to the teachings of Mercerism:

> Mercer said, "Mr. Isidore spoke for himself, not for me. What you are doing has to be done. I said that already." Raising his arm he pointed at the stairs behind Rick. "I came to tell you that one of them is behind you and below, not in the apartment. It will be the hard one of the three and you must retire it first." The rustling, ancient voice gained abrupt fervor. "Quick, Mr. Deckard. *On the steps.*

The first android, Pris, is most difficult because she is the same model as Rachael Rosen and resembles her exactly. After retiring her, Deckard goes to the apartment and retires Irmgard Baty. Just before shooting Roy Baty, Deckard has a realization: that Baty loved his wife, Isidore loved Pris, and he himself loved Rachael, but that none of it mattered because they were all androids.

The Aftermath

Retiring six Nexus-6 androids in one day is a record-breaking achievement, and the bounty Deckard receives for it makes him wealthy. Nevertheless, the emotions stirred up by the day's events leave him depressed. His depression worsens when he returns home to find that Rachael Rosen, showing emotions that androids are not supposed to feel, has killed his goat. He flies off in a hovercar to a desolate area near Oregon, and climbs a hill in an imitation of Mercer. While analyzing the source of his depression, he makes an amazing discovery: in the dust at his feet is a toad, although toads are supposed to be extinct. With renewed faith, Deckard returns home to his wife Iran and shows this marvelous creature to her. While examining it she opens a panel in the toad's back, revealing that it is really just another mechanical animal. Deckard goes to bed feeling more depressed than ever, while Iran phones the pet store to find out what supplies are needed to take care of Deckard's mechanical toad in the best way possible.

Characters

Bill Barbour

The neighbor in the Deckards' apartment building who is wealthy enough to own a real live horse. Deckard and Barbour's interaction is mainly one of competition, and provides an interesting commentary on interpersonal relations in their society. When Barbour reveals his horse is pregnant, Deckard asks if he can buy the colt from him. After Barbour refuses, Deckard's desperation leads him to reveal that his sheep is a fake. Barbour can afford to feel sorry for Deckard—"you poor guy," he sympathizes—because he has a live animal, after all. His empathy does not extend to helping Deckard with his problem, however. Only after Deckard brings home a live goat does Barbour consider dealing his future colt to his neighbor.

Irmgard Baty

Wife of Roy, Irmgard is a "small woman, lovely in the manner of [1940s film star] Greta Garbo, with blue eyes and yellow-blonde hair." Of all the fugitive androids, she seems nearest to understanding human attributes—if only from a cold, objective standpoint. She appreciates Isidore's peaches as Pris cannot, and she is able to recognize how Isidore has emotionally accepted them. But while she seems to be sympathetic to Isidore, she cannot comprehend what the spider means to him, and she is the one who suggests they cut off its legs to see what will happen.

Media Adaptations

- The novel was adapted to film as *Blade Runner* in 1982. Directed by Ridley Scott, the movie starred Harrison Ford as retired bounty hunter, or Blade Runner, Rick Deckard, called back for a final job. The film is true to the feel but different from the plot of the original novel—in this version, the hero gets the girl. The film has become a phenomenal cult classic.

- *Do Androids Dream of Electric Sheep?* was made into an Audio Cassette Cassettes edition in August of 1994 by Time Warner Audio Books.

Roy Baty

Leader of the renegade android troop, Roy is the android who proposes flight to Earth for the eight "friends." Roy is the most intelligent and most dangerous of the eight illegal androids. Deckard's report tells him how Baty framed the escape attempt within the context of a new religion. The basis of this ideology, says the report, is the "fiction" that android "life" is sacred. Baty attempts to instill an ideology within the group that would somehow mimic human Mercerism. That is, he attempts to fake the very emotional empathy that the eight androids are unable to experience. To further his plan and improve the fakery, he experimented with various drugs.

Despite his efforts, the cooperation of the androids lasts only as long as it takes to make their escape. After that, they break up. In the end, one reason the Batys are the last to be retired is that they understand that they are different from humans. The others, particularly Garland, Polokov, and Luft, tried to masquerade as human, and failed. Roy Baty recognizes that the androids can never duplicate the human sense of empathy, and hopes they will be accepted once Buster Friendly reveals the "truth" behind Mercerism. After the announcement, he proclaims proudly that now everyone will know that "the whole experience of empathy is a swindle." He does not understand, as Mercer tells Isidore, that the revelations will change nothing because humans *need* to share with each other. Instead, Baty easily falls victim to Deckard's laser tube.

Milt Borogrove

Borogrove is the repairman at the Van Ness "Pet Hospital." He sympathizes with Isidore after he discovers that the wheezing cat he has just picked up from the Pilsens' was real. He tries to diffuse the tension between Sloat and Isidore when the former forces Isidore to call the owner and report the cat's death. He has the best manner on the phone and cuts in on the call to help convince Mrs. Pilsen to replace the cat with an electric duplicate.

Harry Bryant

Inspector Harry Bryant, "jug-eared and red-headed, sloppily dressed but wise-eyed," gives Deckard the assignment Holden could not finish. He is worried about this assignment, particularly by the possibility that the Voigt-Kampff empathy scale may no longer be an accurate method of distinguishing androids from humans. Only after Deckard successfully assesses androids at the Rosen offices does Bryant turn over Holden's notes to assist him in his hunt. Even after Deckard retires three of the androids during one day, Bryant pressures him into resuming the chase that same evening.

Iran Deckard

Wife of Rick, she is the very image of the stereotypical bored housewife. While technology has provided her with a mood machine that enables a toleration of her tedious life, its very artificiality depresses her. This upsets Rick, who, after talking to her during one of her dialled "depressions," thinks that "most androids I've know have more vitality and desire to live than my wife." Rick feels responsible for Iran, however, and so she inspires him to continue on with his job, with the electric sheep, and everything else that seems hopeless. In many ways, she is the only one in the novel to have a practical epiphany. She realizes she loves Rick: when he returns from his assignments, she thinks "I don't need to dial, now; I already have it—if it is Rick." This leads her to cover up the panel on the electric frog and take on its care—she orders some electric flies.

Rick Deckard

The lead character of the novel is having doubts about himself, his professional abilities, and the morality of his job. His doubts are embodied in his relationship with his electric sheep. He is tired of pretending that his electric sheep is real; "owning and maintaining a fraud had a way of gradually demoralizing one." He is trying to deal with these emotions when he is called on to "retire" six Nexus-6 androids who have escaped to Earth. Although he recognizes that "the empathic gift blurred the boundaries between hunter and victim," he is able to rationalize his duty: "A humanoid robot is like any other machine," Deckard tells Rachael Rosen; "it can fluctuate between being a benefit and a hazard very rapidly. As a benefit it's not our problem." Yet though he tells himself clearly that he is justified in killing killers who have "no ability to feel emphatic joy for another life form's success or grief at its defeat," he begins to have doubts. "This is insane," he says after killing Luba Luft, whose singing could have been a joy to humans.

His experience with Phil Resch creates more doubts. As he later tells Iran, "For the first time, after being with him, I looked at them differently. I mean, in my own way I had been viewing them as he did.... I've begun to empathize with androids." This only makes his task more difficult, not impossible. To get over his doubt, he takes Resch's advice and sleeps with Rachael. The act does not affect him as Rachael had planned, however. She reveals that she has seduced several other bounty hunters, and all except Phil Resch have been unable to continue killing androids. She believes that Deckard has been rendered harmless as well, for he cannot bring himself to kill her. For Deckard, however, her coldly calculated confession gives him new inspiration. His regret, finally, is that he didn't kill her when he had the chance. If he had, the goat would still be alive.

After he is done retiring androids and discovers his dead goat, he flies off for some time alone. He contemplates the day's events: "What I've done, he thought; that's become alien to me. In fact everything about me has become unnatural; I've become an unnatural self." He has a spiritual experience akin to the Mercer story. He finds himself climbing up a hill as rocks are thrown at him. He thinks he has somehow merged with Mercer. Instead, he gives up on the climb and the toad he finds is a fake. He may now be known as the greatest bounty

Harrison Ford in Blade Runner.

hunter, but in reality he is just another man, feeling confused and defeated.

Buster Friendly

Buster Friendly is on television and radio practically all the time. Unknown to most of his audience, however, everyone's favorite talk show host is an android. He aims to keep the housewives, and anyone else who watches, entertained and happy. He and Eldon Rosen are at the forefront in the struggle of android's rights. Part of his work involves the unmasking of Mercer as a fraud. The thinking is that if Mercer, who originated the rule that only life is sacred, is a fake, then perhaps his rules can be rewritten. As Isidore recognizes, "Buster Friendly and Mercerism are fighting for control of our psychic souls."

Garland

Garland is an officer in an alternative police force summoned by Luba Luft after Deckard's attempts to question her. His police headquarters is unknown to the real police headquarters, and he similarly professes to have no knowledge of Deckard or his superiors. When he finds his name on Deckard's list, Garland tries to confuse the issue by claiming that Deckard is the android. When his own bounty hunter, Phil Resch, seems to support Deckard, Garland admits to Deckard that they are all part of the escaped android group. Garland's police are attempting to create a safe haven for androids by imitating real police security. Resch becomes convinced of Deckard's story, however, and kills Garland before Garland can kill him.

Dave Holden

The senior bounty hunter in the San Francisco police department is Dave Holden. He has been tracking eight illegal androids recently arrived in the district. He successfully tests and retires two androids before the third injures him. He has notes on the remaining six which are passed on to Rick Deckard.

J. R. Isidore

See John R. Isidore

John R. Isidore

"My name's J. R. Isidore and I work for the well-known animal vet Mr. Hannibal Sloat; you've heard of him. I'm reputable; I have a job. I drive Mr. Sloat's truck." So Isidore would like to believe about himself, and so he wants his newly discovered neighbor, Pris Stratton, to believe about him. In reality, at least in the legal terms of the novel's universe, Isidore is "special" or, in slang, a chickenhead. This status is given to those individuals so affected by the radioactive dust that they fail a standard IQ test. Thus labeled, they are given the grunt tasks of earth's remaining society; they cannot emigrate off the planet; they cannot procreate. Isidore is not completely nonfunctional; but he is classified as such and is easily intimidated by his superiors. "I'm hairy, ugly, dirty, stooped, snaggle-toothed, and grey.... I feel sick from the radiation; I think I'm going to die," he protests when Sloat forces him to tell an owner her pet has died.

Nevertheless, Isidore has a highly developed sense of empathy. As Milt Borogrove observes, "To him they're all alive, false animals included." Thus Isidore befriends the renegade android band even after he discovers their secret. He knows they are using him but given his caste-like status as a special, he enjoys the trust and society the androids seem to be giving him. Irmgard recognizes this: "They don't treat him very well either, as he said.... He knows us and he likes us and an emotional acceptance like that—it's everything to him." He vows to be loyal to them and protect Pris from the Bounty Hunter. But when Pris begins to amputate the legs of a spider he found, Isidore is enraged. He rescues the spider and puts it out of its distress.

His hopes seem to die then. Buster Friendly has announced that Mercer is a fraud, and the cruelty of his "friends" bewilders him.

Isidore's tale is similar to Deckard's, however. The humanity that had been sacrificed to his chickenhead label begins to assert itself again. Out of his depression comes renewed contact with Mercer, who reassures him that "nothing has changed" and gives him a healed spider. While he reveals the androids' presence to Deckard, he refuses to help him hunt them down. He cries at their deaths, just as bewildered over their executions as he was at the spider's torture. He yearns for society once more and tells Deckard he is moving in to town.

Sandor Kadalyi

See Max Polokov

Luba Luft

Luba Luft is an escaped android trying to pass as a human opera singer. She disturbs Deckard because of the way she handles the test—confusing his reading and insisting on questioning his own humanity. Cleverly, she says he must be an android because he does not care about androids. She is retired by Phil Resch, but not until Deckard proves himself human (and possessing a growing empathy for androids) by granting her last request. He purchases a copy of Munch's *Puberty* for her—something that Phil would be incapable of doing. Her death upsets Deckard greatly, for he wonders why someone with such talent should be considered a liability to society.

Wilbur Mercer

Mercer is the central figure of a religion that is supported by the government. Mercer's legend recalls how he had the gift of reversing time, which he used to bring dead animals back to life until the government stopped him. He was then "plunged into a different world," and began to ascend from the pits of this world onto a mountain, where he is attacked by "Killers." Mercer's followers can join him on this ascent by use of an "empathy machine," which links their consciousness together. They feel his struggle and those of others linked to them, and they also experience the wounds he receives. The sole tenant of Mercerism is empathy for all living things: *You shall kill only the killers,* Mercer announced from the beginning. Just who may be defined as "killers" is left up to the individual, however.

Adhering to Mercerism, or having empathy, clearly marks humans as separate from the constructs they have made. The androids believe that proving Mercerism a fraud will aid them in gaining status as "living" beings. Buster Friendly, in a Wizard of Oz move, does reveal Mercer as a drunken actor named Al Jarry, pretending to climb a mountain on a poorly constructed set. But because the shared experience of Mercerism has relevance for humans, the revelation will not change anything, despite Roy Baty's euphoria. Deckard's final encounters with Mercer, which seem to happen without the use of an empathy box, seem to reinforce this notion.

Mrs. Pilsen

Mrs. Pilsen is the owner of a real cat, and her husband has mistakenly called the Van Ness "Pet Hospital" after it became ill. When Isidore informs her of the cat's death, she is unsure what to do. Ironically, although her husband loved the cat "more than any other cat he ever had," he never got "physically close" to the cat. As a result, Mrs. Pilsen would rather attempt to fool her husband with a mechanical replica than inform him of its death.

Max Polokov

The android who injured Dave Holden, senior bounty hunter, has taken on the identity of a chickenhead garbage collector. Now discovered, he poses as a soviet officer from the WPO coming to help and observe Deckard. Deckard retires him.

Phil Resch

One of the bounty hunters working for the false policeman Garland is Phil Resch. After revealing his own identity, Garland tells Deckard that Resch is an android because he hopes that Deckard will kill Resch—thus making him guilty of murder and putting him out of commission. The problem with Resch, according to Deckard, is that he enjoys killing too much. Disturbed by Garland's real identity, Resch starts to wonder if he too might be an android, despite the fact that he loves his pet squirrel. Resch demands that Deckard test him—and he passes. The contrast between Resch and himself leads Deckard to reconsider his line of work.

Resch kills two of the androids on the list but Deckard will take the credit since Resch is now a fraudulent bounty hunter who just killed his boss. Deckard then confides his doubts about the job. Resch proposes an easy solution which he himself used—sleep with Rachael. Deckard follows this advice, but it has different effects on him than he expects.

Eldon Rosen

Eldon Rosen is chairman of the Rosen Association and is Rachael's "uncle." He is nervous about Deckard's pursuit of the escaped eight androids. If the bounty hunter's test is unable to distinguish humans from androids, his corporation will have to cease production of the androids until a replacement test is developed. Thus, Deckard, "a little police department employee," is in the incredible position of being able to stop production of all Nexus-6 androids. One direct result of this would be a system-wide business failure, because Rosen's output is one of the essential pivots for the working of the economic system. The colonization effort depends on the allure of the settler being given an android. If the androids are not available, colonization ceases. The economic system of the planets would then collapse.

Eldon faces the problem by attempting to call the Voigt-Kampff Test into question. If Deckard is convinced Rachael is a schizoid girl who grew up on a colonization ship then her positive result on the Voigt-Kampff means that the test is no longer valid. "Your police department," Eldon says to Deckard, " … may have retired, very probably have retired, authentic humans with underdeveloped empathic ability…. Your position … is extremely bad morally. Ours isn't." The manufacturing of androids is an essential component of systemic operation. If retiring androids is suspect due to the inherent risk Eldon sites, then it may be done away with. Eldon can then buy Deckard's allegiance and continue to perfect his androids and dominate the market. Still not quite convinced, Deckard is offered a bribe. Fortunately, he comes up with one more question when he hears Rachael repeatedly refer to the Rosens' owl as "it," and proves she is an android. The Voigt-Kampff test still works and production can continue—but so can the retiring of escaped androids.

Rachael Rosen

Rachael Rosen is a Nexus-6 android made available to Deckard by the manufacturers to see if the police tests will work on this new model. Although his test indicates she is an android, the Rosens claim she is human. Deckard is not sure, but a final question solves his dilemma and proves her origin. This near misidentification causes him to begin feeling empathy for the nearly human androids. The doubt this causes him leads him to take Rachael up on her offer to help him catch the remaining fugitives. This leads the two into bed, and Rachael confesses that she loves him and will give him an instrument to render the fugitive androids helpless. Rick begins to wonder if he might love her in return. He considers that she only has two years of life remaining—androids live for four years because technology has failed to master cell replacement. However, the revelation that her agenda is to curtail bounty hunting efforts causes him to reject her. She takes revenge by murdering his Nubian goat.

Hannibal Sloat

The famous (in Isidore's mind) Hannibal Sloat owns a fake animal repair shop called the Van Ness Pet Hospital "—that carefully misnamed little enterprise which barely existed in the tough, competitive field of false-animal repair." Sloat is too old to emigrate and, therefore, is "doomed to creep out his remaining life on Earth." Though he has a fully functioning brain, he is as susceptible to the radioactive dust as anyone else. He sight is obscured—but he never cleans his glasses anyway—and his other senses are also deteriorating. Still, he is not a special and though he likes Isidore he is not above making himself feel better at his employee's expense.

Sloat's greatest fear is that one day a real animal will be picked up by mistake and brought to the shop. Isidore, innocently, makes this mistake and they have a dead cat on their hands. Remarkably, Isidore handles it—though he is helped by Milt—and tenders them an order for a replacement as well as a new confidential customer in Mrs. Pilsen.

Pris Stratton

Pris hides out in what she thinks is an abandoned apartment building in the suburbs. But it is Isidore's building. He senses another person in the building and comes to make friends. She accepts him grudgingly, even though he senses there is something strange and cold about her: "it was not what she did or said but what she did *not* do and say." Although she treats Isidore disdainfully, calling him a "chickenhead," she does cast the deciding vote to remain with him in his apartment, rather than kill him, as Roy Baty suggests.

Pris is the same Nexus-6 model as Rachael Rosen—in fact, that is the first name she gives Isidore, until she figures out it might give away her android origin. Deckard believes that he will be unable to kill Pris because of her resemblance to Rachael. Following Resch's advice of having sex with Rachael has not helped. He worries that he might be in love with Rachael. But he realizes it

was an infatuation, that she was deceiving him. He further realizes that Rachael is a type of machine and Pris is another version, just slightly different. Disgusted by the idea of "legions" of Rachaels, he retires Pris with no difficulty.

Themes

Science and Technology

One of the goals of Dick's fiction is to show that the idea of technology as passive helpmate, slave, or fantastic mistress is unrealistic. Similarly, the opposite notion—that humanity can somehow return to a pastoral way of life and live in an agriculturally based paradise—is naive. These two beliefs, according to Dick, actually endanger the evolution of humankind: so long as humans are uneasy about their own tools, or regard them as in some way mysterious, those tools will be seen as having some innate power over mankind. In other words, regardless of technology's fallibility, if humans regard themselves as less smart or less able than their tools, then they will be at the mercy of their tools. Technology will advance, regardless of what the majority of humanity feels about that technology. Any struggle to remain the ruler or owner of new technology will surely fail. Dick believes the only solution to human uneasiness with technology is a wholesale acceptance of it.

Do Androids Dream of Electric Sheep? expresses Dick's ideas about technology in ways very similar to the story of Mary Shelley's *Frankenstein*. That creature, animated from lifeless flesh, was its creator's scientific success. But the good doctor was so horrified by his creature's grotesque appearance that he ended up destroying it. In Dick's version, the trouble with scientifically created androids is that they resemble their masters too closely. Yet that is what the market has created and that is "what the colonists wanted," says Eldon Rosen. "If our firm hadn't made these progressively more human types, other firms in the field would have." So the problem is not whether androids can approximate humans, but continuing the classification of androids as non-life. It becomes harder to justify the slavery and "retiring" of androids if there is little difference between them and humans. As Isidore tries to teach the group of illegal androids, all life is sacred: all of it, even spiders—whose lack of empathy at one point is compared to the androids' lack. The question then becomes, why can't androids and technology, in all its glorious animation, be defined as a type of life and, therefore, sacred?

Human Condition

Throughout the novel, humans are defined as constructs capable of empathy and "empathetic, role-taking ability." Human empathy is what the Voigt-Kampff test looks for; whether the test subject responds to a described situation as if it were real for them. Even without the test, humans reveal themselves through their need for other living creatures and their being needed in return. "You have to be with other people … in order to live at all," says Isidore. To be human, to be alive, is to depend on other people. Pris, Roy, and Irmgard have accomplished this to some extent, and they decide to accept Isidore. That is all he needs as verification that though "not alive" and illegal, the three are people. Through the ability of the three androids to work as a team and Isidore's acceptance of them, Dick leaves open the possibility of a harmonious future. At present, however, the definition of human is constantly challenged and then reconfirmed by human relations with androids—humans remain humans by eliminating the almost human. Dick is reflecting on man's inhumanity to man by putting humans in the position of defending their identity through the elimination of their imitators. It is a tense condition, and similar to the tension between the chickenhead and his employer, which is full of anger and resentment. The laws separating "human" from "special" from "android" are parallel to the Jim Crow laws in America, Apartheid in South Africa, or ethnic cleansing.

Phil Resch is an example of an exception to this general theory of the human condition as put forth in the novel. (One can make a similar case for Iran, who, until the very end, is absorbed only with her own individual problems.) Resch is a human who shows concern for Deckard, and he takes good care of his real squirrel. Yet his callous disregard for his android victims leads Deckard to doubt his humanity. Resch feels that artificial constructs have no value. He dehumanizes them, similar to the way that the Nazis viewed Jews during the Holocaust. Such a breakdown of empathy in one area of an individual's psyche enables violence. The question then becomes, why single out androids as the ones to be retired? How do you confine the exertion of violence to illegal androids? This worries everyone, especially if the Voigt-Kampff test is no longer valid. What if some schizophrenics are not locked up and one is retired by mistake? What happens when Sloat really goes af-

Topics for Further Study

- Do some research into the pieces of art and music mentioned in the novel. What is the significance of the paintings of Edvard Munch or Mozart's *The Magic Flute* to the themes or plot of the novel?

- Based on the evidence provided by the novel, what moral distinctions do you think can be made between life and simulated-life? Make sure to cite examples from the text.

- Pretend you are a Martian colonist or an Earth native in Dick's world. Write an essay arguing for or against the abolition of androids.

- Consider the depiction of sexuality and sex roles in the novel: compare Rachael to Pris or Iran or Irmgard. Argue whether Dick is misogynist (a woman-hater) or exaggerating inequality to make an effective commentary. Consider the idea of having sex with the enemy—and then killing "her"? What does this say about our society, about violence, about sexual attitudes?

- Draw parallels between *Do Androids Dream of Electric Sheep* and other abolitionist novels. Imagine the speech of Shylock in Shakespeare's *The Merchant of Venice* ("If you prick us, do we not bleed?") as spoken by an android. Or make direct comparisons with the civil rights movement of the 1960s and discuss how Dick was reflecting on the secondary status of blacks in America in the 1960s. Or compare Dick's bounty hunter to portrayals of southern fugitive slave trackers of the antebellum period.

ter Isidore? Deckard comes to realize that humanity can and must extend itself to empathy toward artificial constructs. For the environment, it is the only way to return the owls to the skies.

In terms of Deckard's personal growth, he has realized that his interaction with his Electric Sheep is wearing down his self-respect. Every day he pretends to care for an object as if it were real. He feels oppressed by his need to keep up the appearance that he owns a real animal. "The tyranny of an object ... [is that] it doesn't know I exist. Like the androids, it had no ability to appreciate the existence of another." That is why Deckard needs a real animal, so that something not only knows he exists, but needs him in return. Gradually, he finds empathy for artificial life and is even prepared to accept the toad. But, ultimately, peace comes to Deckard as his wife fulfills the role of making him feel needed.

American Dream

The "American Dream" is often defined as the freedom to pursue material success, as symbolized by owning one's own home in a cozy suburb. In a perverse rendering of the suburban dream, Dick presents a society where a home on a space colony is the goal of most people. In his vision, the healthy people of earth are exported to other planets and given a slave robot to work their own homestead. (Ironically, the term "robot" comes from an Czech play about a nobleman who replaces his serfs with manlike machines.) On Earth, home of those not intelligent or healthy enough to emigrate, the dream of most people is to own a real animal. The darker side of this suburban reality is that the wife stays securely at home. She, like her 1950s counterpart, spends her time watching television. In Dick's view of the future, she has a machine for dialing up moods. There is even a number to dial for the mood to watch television—and Dick does not envision the programming getting better. Fantastically, Iran can even dial up her own depression. To ward off loneliness, she can bond with unhappy people everywhere through an empathy machine. These perverse twists on the "American Dream" present a view of suburbia as an inherently alienating society that speeds the decay of human community.

Morals and Morality

Decades ahead of his time, Dick foresaw the moral issues which would develop from a capitalist, technological society. In the world of *Do Androids Dream of Electric Sheep?,* good moral codes are those which support the economic system and keep people happy. Mercerism teaches people an empathy that is coincidentally profitable; every living being is sacred because of the nuclear war, therefore, the ownership of a living animal marks status. Caring for a living creature is important for Mercerists, but ironically, this responsibility is also market driven. Similarly, Eldon Rosen has no need to consider whether it is ethical to create androids that are indistinguishable

from humans, because he is just producing what the customers want. "We followed the time-honored principle underlying every commercial venture," he tells Deckard. "If our firm hadn't made these progressively more human types, other firms in the field would have." Eldon Rosen claims his moral standing is better than the dubious position of the police and their faulty empathy test. The system's security rests on whether the bounty hunter is able to verify and destroy illegal androids—but the growth of the same system rests on whether the Rosen Association can produce androids so lifelike as to make the bounty hunter's job impossible. When the Rosens succeed, industry will take over the job of natural evolution; industry will put perfect animals back in the wild and gradually make a perfect human/android race. But everyone will be happy for there will be no bounty hunters to fret over identity questions.

Style

Narrative/Point of View

Do Androids Dream of Electric Sheep? is narrated in third person, with the characters described as "he" or "she." The narrator is reliable, but is not omniscient ("all-knowing"). Unless a character speaks his thoughts, they remain unknown. The narrator limits the point of view to the characters of Rick Deckard and J. R. Isidore, with a brief exception for Iran at the end of the novel. The narrator knows the world of this future society well enough to explain Isidore's condition, as well the importance of the Rosen Association. The narrator is not perfect, however, and at times the reader has to just go along with the story. For example, the narrator portrays Deckard's job as very difficult, particularly the challenge posed by the new Nexus-6 androids. Nevertheless, he finds it rather easy to retire Pris, and the "worst" android, Roy, is no problem either. The appearance of Mercer to assist Deckard with Pris is a clumsy type of "deus ex machina" (literally, "god out of a machine"), in which the gratuitous assistance of an outside force saves the hero.

Science Fiction

The most fundamental requirement of this genre is that it make use of science in some way. Secondly, and perhaps as important, this genre is concerned with the impact of real or imagined science upon an individual or society. Beyond those two principles, the genre is quite open to everything from the most fantastic (e.g. "Star Wars" or *Dune*) to the most pedestrian (e.g. "Honey, I Shrunk the Kids").

Another frequent, but not necessary, component of science fiction is social criticism. Science fiction inherits this trait from earlier writers, who satirized their own time by displacing and exaggerating their society as a real society somewhere else. Perhaps the most famous version with some remaining currency is Jonathan's Swift's *Gulliver's Travels.* Were Swift writing two hundred years later, it is easy to see that Gulliver's boat would have been a space ship. In other words, storytellers often have an easier time pointing out foibles and complaining about their own times by placing them to a fantasy world or to other worlds entirely.

Dick is obviously a science fiction writer because he employs hovercrafts, space colonies, androids, lasers, sine wave disrupters, and so on. He also uses the familiar science fiction formula of an post-nuclear holocaust Earth. The idea of Earth after an all-out war is an old one, but the intricacies of possible survival after a nuclear war has offered much cause for speculation. Dick wants the reader to believe life would continue, although society would have to impose caste-like marks on its people for the good of the whole. Further, evolution would depend on the further development of biotechnologies and the acceptance of its byproducts as real.

Detective Story

Detective stories first began with Edgar Allan Poe's "The Murders in the Rue Morgue" (1841) and became a mature genre with Sir Arthur Conan Doyle's Sherlock Holmes mysteries. Normally, a detective story presents a crime that the inspector has to solve. *Do Androids Dream of Electric Sheep?* is a detective story with a twist. A crime (murder) has been committed by the androids, and Deckard is assigned to track them down and "retire" them in turn, as dictated by the law. As the novel progresses, however, Deckard comes to question the morality of carrying out the law. The test used to determine the android's death sentence eliminates that android's right to be a productive being. She may fail the test, but Luba Luft was capable of enjoying and participating in a very human activity—art.

From the start, the reader knows who the unlawful constructs are and it is readily apparent that the purveyor of justice is Rick Deckard, bounty hunter. But this is not a usual assignment. These androids are working together and in league with their manufacturers to win acknowledgement that these new constructs merit legal standing. Deckard's job becomes a potentially immoral act, by unmasking them as escapees and then denying them their rights. In fact, he doesn't even test the most progressive androids because they attack him first. So Deckard solves the "case," but not the problem of whether the androids were advanced enough to warrant a change in their legal standing.

Anti-hero

An anti-hero is a protagonist of a narrative distinctly lacking in heroic qualities. That is, he does not possess outstanding courage, strength, or morals; frequently he is an outsider who has difficulty accepting conventional values. Rick Deckard is an average sort of man who does not have exception skills or strength. He is only a backup bounty hunter, and he has an unsatisfied wife, an electric sheep, and a great deal of doubt about whether he is fit for his profession. Yet all these failings enable the reader to identify with him, root for him, and sympathize with his predicament. In addition, Deckard's doubts about his work, in contrast to Phil Resch's callous manner, highlight an empathy which approaches the heroic. Nevertheless, Deckard's "heroic" final confrontation with Roy Baty—which ought to be the book's climax—is described as a rather boring action. A true hero would be rewarded with his greatest dream, but in the end Deckard's goat is dead and the toad he discovers is false. He also thinks he has merged with Mercer; instead, it is an illusion brought on by exhaustion. By portraying Deckard's achievements and rewards as less than heroic, Dick seems to suggest that perhaps this is the best anyone can do in such anti-heroic times.

Historical Context

The Cold War and Vietnam

Do Androids Dream of Electric Sheep? portrays a world that has survived a nuclear holocaust, a possibility that did not seem too far-fetched in the 1960s. Since the end of World War II, when the United States dropped two atomic bombs on Japan, the Soviet Union had been developing their own nuclear arsenal. Many Americans saw the spread of Soviet Communism as the country's greatest threat, and they engaged the Soviets in a "Cold

Harrison Ford atop a Metrocab in Blade Runner.

War" throughout the 1950s and 1960s. The two sides never directly engaged each other in combat, although they came close in 1962, when the U.S. challenged the Soviets over their placement of missiles in Cuba. By the late 1960s, both sides had enough nuclear missiles to destroy each other—and the entire world—several times over. The Cuban Missile Crisis, however, had shown both sides that a nuclear confrontation was something to be avoided at all costs: the only thing that it could achieve was Mutual Assured Destruction. By 1968, U.S.-Soviet relations had warmed to the point where several treaties had been signed, including a 1967 treaty that prohibited the military use of space. Pessimists, however, still worried that total nuclear destruction could come with just one press of a button.

America's involvement in the Vietnam War, although involving no nuclear weapons, was another front of the Cold War against communism. The United States had been providing military advisors to the government of South Vietnam since the 1950s. The South Vietnamese were struggling against communist insurgents, and the U.S. feared that if Vietnam fell to the communists, the rest of Southeast Asia would follow. By 1968, U.S. military involvement had grown to include over half a

million American troops in Vietnam. Nevertheless, the war effort was not particularly successful in driving out the communists. The Tet offensive by the North Vietnamese began at the end of January, 1968, surprising the South Vietnamese and their U.S. allies. These events further embarrassed the U.S., and the war grew more unpopular as people doubted whether it was winnable. In March of that year, although it would be unknown to the American public for twenty months, American soldiers committed what has come to be known as the My Lai massacre. Searching for enemy soldiers, U.S. troops entered a village and rounded up hundreds of inhabitants—men, women, children, old and young—and shot them all.

A World of Political Unrest

As U.S. involvement in Vietnam escalated, so did public opposition to it. People questioned both the effectiveness and the morality of sending American soldiers to fight in another country's civil war. Thousands of Americans, particularly students, protested the war, sometimes clashing with police. The 1968 presidential election provided many opportunities for such confrontations. In August, the Democratic Party convention was held in Chicago, and antiwar protesters found it the perfect forum for

Compare & Contrast

- **1968:** The Americans are caught in a space race with the Soviets to reach the moon. Many predict moon colonies and interplanetary travel.

  Late 1990s: The Americans and the Russians are working together on an international space station. There is talk about returning to the moon because ice crystals were discovered at the lunar poles. A return to the moon, some hope, will be a first step to the colonization of Mars.

- **1968:** The Pacific Rim economies are humming. Japan leads the way by passing West Germany to become second to the United States in terms of Gross Domestic Product.

  Late 1990s: The Pacific Rim is in financial crisis, if not collapse. Japanese financial companies are frantically warding off bankruptcy after having overextended themselves over the previous decade. The "Asian Contagion" sets off fears of a worldwide financial crisis.

- **1968:** Amphibians seem fine although increasing numbers of fish are dying from the effects of industrial pollution.

  Late 1990s: Amphibians are disappearing at an alarming rate. Whether high altitude frogs or desert toads, amphibians are showing up deformed and dead in record numbers. The causes are many: increases in ultraviolet light, fungal attacks, polluted water, or new predators. Meanwhile, "fish kills" now describe commonplace occurrences where miles of streams become depopulated due to accidental or intentional chemical dumping. Fish are also threatened by over-fishing, so that the North Sea is "fished out."

- **1968:** Reproductive rights become a hotter topic when the British legalize abortion and Pope Paul VI condemns any artificial means of birth control in his encyclical *Humanae Vitae.*

  Late 1990s: Reproductive rights are still a hot issue, but the cloning of a Scottish sheep named "Dolly" has raised the level of debate. Bans have been imposed on human cloning but renegade scientists promise it will only be a matter of time. Clones, not androids, threaten some people's notion of human grace.

---

expressing their opposition. Some ten thousand protesters responded to calls from antiwar activists David Dellinger, Rennie Davis, and Thomas E. Hayden and radical "Yippies" Abbie Hoffman and Jerry Rubin. Determined to maintain order, Chicago mayor Richard J. Daley called up 16,000 city police officers, 4,000 state police, and 4,000 National Guardsmen armed with tear gas, grenades, night sticks, and firearms. The police clubbed and gassed demonstrators and observes alike in attempting to prevent the demonstrators from marching, giving speeches, and sleeping overnight in the city's parks. The "Chicago Seven"—including Dellinger, Davis, Hayden, Hoffman, Rubin, and Black Panther Leader Bobby Seale—were convicted of violating a federal anti-riot law during a boisterous trial, but later had their convictions overturned.

The late 1960s were a time of conflict, confusion, and moral uncertainty, and demonstrations were not limited to antiwar causes or even America. People all over the world peaceably demonstrated for a better world. 1968 was a particularly violent year worldwide, as the efforts of leaders to motivate people for equal rights, justice, and peace began to pay off. Thousands of people were on the streets marching. From San Francisco to Mexico City, Chicago to Memphis, and all the way to France and Czechoslovakia, people were demonstrating for peace, change, and a better life. People were beginning to protest the inequitable distribution of wealth and governments were answering with force. Thus there is a particular irony in a statement by Dick's character J. R. Isidore, who will not believe that bounty hunters exist, "B-b-because things like that don't happen. The g-g-government never kills anyone, for any crime."

In April of 1968, several months after FBI Director J. Edgar Hoover's order to shut down "Black

Nationalist hate-Groups," civil rights leader Martin Luther King, Jr., was assassinated in Memphis, Tennessee. Racial rioting broke out nationwide as a result, and Chicago's Mayor Daley gave a "shoot to kill" order in that city to stop the rioters. Nationwide, 46 died and 21,270 were arrested. Columbia University students shut down their campus to protest gymnasium construction because it eliminated affordable housing in the area; they were stormed by police and 628 people were arrested. In France, student protests led to a revolution in the University system, events which continue to be discussed in French academia. Meanwhile, the Soviets thwarted a revolution in Czechoslovakia with an occupation army of 650,000 and a system of censorship. In the fall of 1968, Mexico City police fired on student demonstrators in Tlatelolco Square. Officials reported forty dead; other observers put the figure at seven hundred.

The Growth of Environmentalism

In the 1960s, people became more aware of the environment and the need to protect it. Rachel Carson had published her groundbreaking work *Silent Spring* in 1962, alerting Americans to the potential dangers of industrial contamination of the environment. This work motivated environmentally concerned Americans to create the Environmental Defense Fund, which lobbied for the creation of a federal agency to protect America's environment. Although the Environmental Protection Agency was not created until 1970, Congress still took action on many environmental issues in 1968. They approved two new national parks: North Cascades National Park set aside 505,000 acres, while Redwood National Park contained 58,000 acres along forty miles of the Pacific Coast and included the world's tallest tree. The Congress also issued a report in 1968 which officially declared Lake Erie, one of the five Great Lakes, dead from the effects of pollution. Similarly discouraging reports emerged in that same year. Enzyme detergents made by several companies were reported to create problems in American water and sewage systems. The Coast Guard reported 714 major oil spills for the year, almost double the number from previous years. Not surprisingly, fish kills (a term normally associated with spring thaw, when pollutants are most concentrated) are estimated to have increased to fifteen million fish. Many people warned of coming environmental disaster, similar to the one portrayed in Dick's novel.

Medicine and Health in the 1960s

In *Do Androids Dream of Electric Sheep?*, a class of physically and mentally inferior humans develops as a result of nuclear fallout. In the world of 1968, a similar subclass of humans seemed to be in the making, as the result of inequitable resource distribution. Many people, especially children, were suffering from inadequate nutrition, despite huge increases in food production levels worldwide. For example, India's food minister, Chidambara Subramaniam, estimated that in his nation between 35 and 40 percent of children had suffered brain damage because of a lack of protein in their diets. In the United States, nutrition investigator Arnold E. Schaefer was appalled at the vitamin A deficiency which he discovered in certain schools. This led him to comment that the low-income children he studied might go blind "five minutes from now or a year from now." Meanwhile, a Citizens Board discovered that federal food aid programs only reached 18 percent of the nation's poor.

Medical advances, on the other hand, seemed to promise longer and healthier lives for humanity. In late 1967, the first successful human heart transplant was performed by Dr. Christiaan Barnard in Cape Town, South Africa. Dr. Denton A. Cooley echoed this success in the United States a few months later. This development increased the anxious discussion about organ replacement and the sanctity of the human body. It also made juicy fodder for science fiction writers, who specialized in androids, cybernetic prostheses, and the loss of identity which comes with the mechanization of the body.

Critical Overview

The first problem with assessing the critical reputation of *Do Androids Dream of Sheep?* is distinguishing the novel from the film it inspired, 1982's *Blade Runner*. There are film reviews, there are book reviews, and there are reviews which confuse the two; anything written before the movie's release in 1982 is probably a safe bet, however. Therefore, before engaging with the criticism of the novel in any form, be sure that the critic is discussing the novel by checking its title and its references to the plot line. Reviews of the novel alone are few, and there are many that confuse it with the film. Telling signs of this confusion are references to Rachael (varying last names) as love interest and end of story girlfriend; lack of discussion on Dick's thoughts about real and fake animals; and no interest in Dick's statements about human nature as revealed in his portrayal of Mercerism. Not that this confusion would have bothered Dick, however, who outlined some of these changes in suggestions on making the novel into a film.

Nevertheless, critics have analyzed *Do Androids Dream of Electric Sheep?* and compared it to the works of several distinguished writers. One such resemblance is to the fiction of Franz Kafka, a Czech writer who wrote in German; the general theme of metamorphosis is explored by both writers, and Rick Deckard can be compared to Joseph K. from Kafka's novel *The Trial*. Parallels can also be drawn to the work of nineteenth-century novelist Charles Dickens, for the honesty of "ordinary" people is crucial to both authors: Isidore is reminiscent of Jo in *Bleak House,* for example. Similarly, Mercer's continuous struggle up a hill, beset by enemies, recalls the principles outlined in French author Albert Camus's essay "The Myth of Sisyphus."

In general, Dick's work is difficult to evaluate because, despite the crudeness of his art, his story is riveting. The visions he offers are earth-shattering and unique but relayed with a careless style. That style delivers a narrative structure that is sometimes incredibly difficult to decipher. As Philip Strick described it in *Sight and Sound,* "his phrasing is often clumsy, bathetic, despairing, a tangle of moods and impressions hurled like warnings of imminent catastrophe…. What renders his work so absorbing is its inventiveness and its humor, dizzyingly based on a lunatic logic." Some partisan reviewers say these failings simply testify to the author's profundity. More objective critics admit that despite his crudeness, Dick has an amazing ability to portray humanity's condition. Dick is further credited for having sympathy with his own characters and, thereby, making them admirable and believable. He accomplishes this by making his characters anti-heroic and letting them survive only when they are able to care for others.

Throughout his career, Dick played with several themes. One of these themes is the difference between the real and the simulated; for Dick, authentic life and the mechanical are not easily separated or distinguished. Another favorite concept is that of the android, or artificially constructed human. As the android is made into a perfect replica of man, the authentic human becomes more and more mechanical. Eventually the human withdraws into schizophrenic madness until the human, like the android, must be programmed with personality. Given these major themes, it is surprising that so few critics have dealt with *Do Androids dream of Electric Sheep?* as a serious enterprise. A few have understood, however, that "his novels are linked by obsessively recurring motifs and details, each of which is itself a key or a cue to the nature of reality in the Dick universe," as Ursula K. Le Guin wrote in the *New Republic.* And *Do Androids Dream of Electric Sheep?,* while it may be a kind of *Dickian* parable, renders those "recurring motifs and details" in clear and simple terms.

For example, a close examination of Mercer, said Angus Taylor in *Philip K. Dick and the Umbrella of Light,* gives fast insight into Dick's theory of the transcendent. As outlined before the author's 1974 religious experience, this theory described people merging into a single empathy field or collective human consciousness (what has been called the *noosphere* by French philosopher Pierre Teilhard de Chardin). Taylor writes that Dick's metaphysical comment is that a world without a vision of a goal or of a "divine animation" is mechanical. But when that same world becomes informed with a goal that humankind sets for itself (whatever that may be), then that world has life and meaning at every level—even the mechanical. "The concept of God is not to be confused with that of a transcendent deity; it denotes instead the realization of the human potential through the creation of a better world—a dialectical movement whereby man remakes himself and his environment in the process of becoming reconciled to that environment." Taylor's essay is rather typical of critical engagement with Dick's work, exploring the philosophical insights that can be learned from less-than-perfect fiction.

In his 1982 essay, Strick performed a similar analysis. He is moved by the translation of humanity's obsession with status and wealth into the awesome need that Rick Deckard has for a real animal. It is a short way of condemning humanity's awful environmental record and goes straight to the heart. But even more disturbing, for Strick, is the subtle mechanization of the body. "The erosion of authentic humanity by undetectable android imitations has all the plausibility of a new and lethal plague whereby evolution would become substitution and nobody would notice the difference. The notion is rich with political and metaphysical implications, but Dick pins it firmly on the obvious target of technology through which, should man wish to lift a finger, future prosthetics will do it for him. And in his view, defeat is already in sight."

Patricia S. Warrick, however, is delighted with Dick's narrative for the development of its form as well as its philosophy. Her article in the 1983 anthology *Philip K. Dick* traces the development of Dick's notion of the android as a way to embody human foibles. In this way, Dick is not unlike the early novelists John Bunyan (author of *Pilgrim's Progress,* 1678) or Henry Fielding (author of *Tom Jones,* 1749). For Warrick, the android motif expresses the idea that due to pursuit of money or some other fetish, people have become mechanical. They are "humans who have lost their humanness [like Resch] and become mere mechanical constructs unable to respond with creativity and feeling." But Warrick, despite her love of Dick's narrative process, cannot resist an answer to the title question, *Do Androids dream of Electric Sheep?:* "Yes, as each form contains within itself the shadow image of the potential forms that seed its inevitable transformation, so do androids dream."

Criticism

David J. Kelly

David J. Kelly is a an English instructor at several colleges in Illinois, as well as a novelist and playwright. In the following essay, he compares Do Androids Dream of Electric Sheep? *to* Blade Runner, *the popular movie that was adapted from it.*

It is awkward to tell friends that you are reading *Do Androids Dream of Electric Sheep?* The title is long and complex, and besides, few people outside of the small, particular community of science fiction fans are familiar with it. Much easier is to tell friends that you are reading the book that *Blade Runner* is based on. Why not? The publisher even uses this shorter title on the paperback reissue editions, remembering to include Philip Dick's original title only in parentheses. The 1982 movie *Blade Runner* was a critical success upon its release, and its reputation has grown since then. Special effects technicians point to this movie as a turning point in cinematic design. The Library of Congress has listed it with the "culturally, historically or aesthetically significant" films on the National Film Registry. Fifteen years after the movie's release, a video game based on it has become a best seller, introducing a new generation to the *Blade Runner* idea.

The problem is that the *Blade Runner* idea is not the same thing as the complex examination of humanity's goals and weaknesses found in *Do Androids Dream of Electric Sheep?* The film does have its virtues, but, as is almost always the case with cinematic adaptations, the book is better.

The emphasis of the movie can be found in its title, which uses a phrase for bounty hunters that never appears in the novel. The words "blade" and "runner" suggest weapons, action, fighting, hunting, and, by extension, survival. Rick Deckard is played by Harrison Ford as a familiar movie type, a man of few words, the lonesome, weary private eye slogging through the filth and hopelessness of a corrupt society. Rather than taking place in a deserted San Francisco, the film moves the action to jam-packed Los Angeles, where the street scenes are dominated by twin influences of advertising and Asian design: aspects of today's Los Angeles projected to an extreme. This setting keeps the viewers' eyes busy and realistically projects the social changes that Southern California is expected to undergo in the decades to come. It has less to do with Dick's novel, though, than with the detective movies of the 1940s and 1950s that spun off of Raymond Chandler's fiction. In the film version Deckard struggles against the dehumanizing effect of the corrupt culture that he lives in, which actually is a different thing than the book—Deckard's struggle to retain his humanity. Only his growing respect for android life is presented in the film, dramatized by Rachael Rosen's simplified role as a traditional love interest and by Roy Baty's touching sacrifice of his own life at the end.

While the film is able to insinuate the ways in which humans and androids are similar (very convincingly, since the androids in the film are played by humans), it is unable to come near the book's intricate understanding of the many ways we humans relate to the world around us. Focusing our concentration on hunting and killing the androids invites the viewer to think of them as objects, to focus on the ways that they deserve to be found and destroyed, and this draws viewers away from the empathy that is at the core of *Do Androids Dream of Electric Sheep?* and that is found throughout most of Philip K. Dick's works.

The quasi-religion Mercerism, based on empathy with the struggles of Wilbur Mercer, is just too complex to convey to a motion picture audience with sounds and images. Introduced in Dick's 1964 short story "The Little Black Box," Mercerism is a well-conceived religion for modern times, offering a touch of the spiritualism that has been pushed aside by technology throughout the twentieth century. Dick shrewdly gave Mercerism the structure that a post-apocalyptic society will require only slightly more than our own: its focus is away from moral laws and toward unity, but it achieves unity, as our society increasingly does, via the shared experience of an image on a screen. Mercerism is a believable practice in the novel because it represents the struggle against the forces that try to isolate us from each other. So convincing is it at fulfilling a human desire that readers tend to empathize with Deckard and ignore the evidence that Mercer is a fraud, a character played by an old drunkard, and to accept Mercer as being more real than ever when he mysteriously, supernaturally, appears to Deckard.

Unfortunately, the only way to include the practice of Mercerism in the movie would be to waste precious screen seconds showing Deckard, Iran, or Isidore staring at a video tube. Dick did suggest a cinematic quality to Mercerism by having the empathy that is felt by its practitioners show up as physical bruises and welts, which is at least a step closer to the visual language of film than simple emotional bonding would be. In a quieter film, it would give viewers chills to see a character on screen who is so entwined with a distant figure that their empathy could draw blood, but *Blade Runner* is too active, too predatory, to slow down for this kind of abstract point.

The fact that this movie has no way to include animals in its futuristic scenario represents a true loss. In the novel, Deckard's electric sheep, his goat, and the toad that he finds in his moment of despair at the end all are important. They indicate how individuals in this society relate to those they come in contact with, and to society in general.

The electric sheep helps define just how badly people in Deckard's world long for something to care for, to look after and love. The mention of lead codpieces in the first chapter indicates that radiation has made people in this society sterile, unable to bear the children that might otherwise be the objects of their affection. Deckard's electric sheep also functions to give readers a sense of his humanity by showing him as a failed, vulnerable human being: not the chisel-jawed tough guy of the film but a poor schnook, looking at his neighbor's horse with envy.

When Deckard buys his goat, his good fortune is as balanced as it is for real humans struggling in modern society. The fact that he can at last afford a live animal is a mark of his growing success, but the fact that he feels a need to immediately squander his windfall, that he has to get an animal *right away,* indicates a desperate, slightly pathetic need for something warm and alive. A goat is not the most loveable of creatures—as the android Rachael notes, "Goats smell terrible"—but that is what the shop had available at the time, and Deckard is so in need that he appreciates what he can get. The goat is also significant because, while representing Deckard's attempt to forget society's faults by establishing a one-to-one relationship with an animal, it also traps him in a job that he has come to despise: his mortgage on the goat ensures that he will have to work for years to pay it off. At the end of the film *Blade Runner,* Deckard escapes with Rachael Rosen to a new, happy life, but the novel's Deckard stays true to his responsibilities.

In the end of the novel, after all of his struggles, his raised and shattered hopes, it all comes down to the toad that Deckard finds. This final touch is so important to the story that one of Dick's earlier titles was "The Electric Toad," to give readers a hint at what really matters. In the final chapters, Deckard finds a life form that is supposed to be extinct, raising his hopes not just for the future of toads, but for life on this planet. He finds out that it is fake, indicating that reality is slipping away, becoming irrelevant in his world. After he has gone to sleep, Iran makes provisions to care for Deckard's toad, indicating that whether a thing is real or unreal is irrelevant; it is caring about it that counts. Compared with this web of despair and hope, the film's ultimate point that Deckard can love a beautiful android as if she were human seems crass and primitive.

Other animals are mentioned in the story, and although they are not as prominent, they help the reader refine a sense of what Deckard's world is like. In the first chapter he recalls a sheep he once owned that Iran's father had left to the Deckards upon emigrating to Mars. From this little fact we gain a perspective on how valuable real animals are, that a policeman's salary would not be able to buy one on the open market. The film gives no such realistic detail. Later, when the owl owned by the Rosen Association is introduced, readers have some idea of how phenomenally expensive such a rare animal must be: we understand the magnitude of Rosens' power, and of the bribe Deckard is offered and rejects. The cat that dies while J. R. Isidore is taking it to the hospital informs readers of Isidore's inability to distinguish real from imitation, a particular manifestation of

What Do I Read Next?

- Dick presents some insight into his fictional cosmology in his essay "Man, Android, and Machine," published in the anthology *Science Fiction at Large* (1976), edited by Peter Nicholls. There he describes the complexity of a dream universe wherein there are beings aware of man's plight but offering no help. There are also entities existing outside the dreams of humans which are helping.

- Dick's Hugo Award-winning novel *The Man in the High Castle* (1962) explores notions of authority and political oligarchy by supposing that the United States had lost World War II. Japan and Germany divide the U.S. and Dick shows how easily Americans adopt their respective rulers.

- Perhaps the best insight into the very enigmatic figure that was Philip K. Dick is the one offered by Paul Williams, close friend and literary executor. Using his access to all of Dick's papers and tapes as well as his own experience with his friend, Williams' portrait of Dick, *Only Apparently Real: The World of Philip K. Dick* (1997), is a must read for any fan.

- Scientific and technological progress has always been accompanied by the fear that a creation or discovery would somehow turn on its creator—an idea as old as Adam. But this story was not classically defined (in English) until Mary Shelley won a contest, amongst vacationing friends in Switzerland, with her story, *Frankenstein; or The Modern Prometheus* (1818). Since then, *Frankenstein* has become a byword for any situation in which a created being (android, computer, or clone) turns on its master. A fictional rule has hence arisen that such a thankless being must be, in Dickian terminology, retired.

- Arthur C. Clarke, though he is very dissimilar, was a contemporary with Dick. Clarke is honored as having given a great deal of respectability to Science Fiction as a genre. One of his great contributions was *2001: A Space Odyssey* (also 1968) which grew out of a short story, "The Sentinel" (1951). In terms of computer fiction, this story's main computer, the HAL 9000, has best merited the "Frankenstein" label.

- The science fiction giant Isaac Asimov first set forth the laws of robotics in his story collection *I, Robot* (1950). There he creates the archetype of the helpful robot to which Dick reacts. Most notable in the basic programming of Asimov's machines are the laws of robotics. The foremost of these is that a robot cannot harm a human.

- An early Isaac Asimov novel, *The Caves of Steel* (1954), deals with many of the same issues confronting Rick Deckard. In Asimov's crime story, detective Lije Baley is a New York cop who must swallow his hatred for robots when an android is assigned to help him investigate the murder of a colonialist on earth.

- *A Philosophical Investigation,* by Philip Kerr (1992), is in many ways very close to Dick's work. Instead of testing out androids and retiring them, Jake Jakowicz works for Scotland Yard in a world where a small minority of men are "VMN-negatives"—they lack a certain brain structure and are, therefore, unable to control their murderous impulses. In this world, the testing is for this condition, not for being an android. In Kerr's story, somebody is using the confidential test results as a list of victims and Jakowicz must stop the killer of the killers.

- Another huge cult, known as cyberpunks, took their inspiration from the novels of William Gibson. Beginning with *Neuromancer* (1984), Gibson places the struggle for universal dominance not over planets or systems but information. His world of high intrigue depends to a large extent on virtual reality and cyberspace as the site of action. Thus, rather than killing real androids, space cowboys must infiltrate security systems or kill other virtual characters. In a similar fashion to Dick's detective's test-giving ability, the fate of the universe depends on the cowboy's ability to hack into a secure system and retrieve information.

his radiation-induced weakness that becomes significant in his later dealings with Pris and the Batys. Though Isidore accepts the androids as being enough like himself for friendship and maybe even love, he does realize, when Irmgard mutilates the spider—an insect that most of the novel's readers would destroy without a second thought—what the difference between a false human and a true human is.

The omissions made when translating this novel for the screen may thin out the story's substance, but it would be wrong to imply that this is one of those cases where the author had to suffer the indignity of watching his work watered down. Philip K. Dick suggested most of these changes. In 1968 he wrote notes on different ways the novel could be handled as a film script. Some of his suggestions seem quaint from a perspective of modern time—Gregory Peck seemed to him a good choice to play Deckard, and his idea of a good contemporary film script shows an obsession with the newly released film *The Graduate,* which was indeed cutting-edge artistry in its time but seems raw and clumsy compared to the film that became *Blade Runner.* Dick's main concern for the film was that it raise the question of what reality is, which might be why he related it to a coming-of-age movie like *The Graduate.* He was quite willing to sacrifice much of the novel. "We can have a many-sided film …" he wrote, "or, I would think, some of the moods (and plot, etc.) can be eliminated entirely, however important they are to the novel." His notes specifically recommend keeping "the search and destroy androids theme" and the sexual relationship between Deckard and Rachael, which, probably not by coincidence, would have been the elements to most interest prospective movie makers. Dick was still a fairly obscure and underpaid science fiction writer when he prepared these notes, and he may well have been simply doing what he could to sell the screen rights and make a buck, but there can be no question about whether Hollywood surprised him by changing his story. The filmmakers probably were not following his directions, but the simplification they did in 1982 ended up following the changes he anticipated in 1968.

Source: David J. Kelly, in an essay for *Novels for Students,* Gale, 1999.

Nigel Wheale

In the following excerpt, Wheale examines "the conflict between 'authentic' and 'artificial' personality".

It really is time to take science fiction seriously. The genre now forms about ten per cent of paperback fiction sales, and with the continuing success of comics such as *2000 AD* and graphic-novel fiction such as *Watchmen* there's every reason to think that the readership will continue to grow. Literary syllabuses in schools and colleges have traditionally been slow to catch on to the study of contemporary forms of popular narrative, whether they are soaps, pulp romances, detective novels, or science fiction. But the growing number of self-constructed course work options does offer the possibility of bringing new kinds of contemporary writing and reading-experience onto the syllabus. I want to suggest some ways of approaching the writing of one of the most celebrated SF authors, Philip K. Dick, through a discussion of his novel *Do Androids Dream of Electric Sheep?* (1968) and its acclaimed film realisation as Ridley Scott's *Blade Runner* (1982). I concentrate on the central theme of both novel and film: the conflict between 'authentic' and 'artificial' personality, that is between people and robots.…

A common reason often given for not paying attention to science fiction is the supposed lack of 'human interest' in the genre: technology dominates to the exclusion of developed personalities or relationships. Philip K. Dick's *Do Androids Dream?* is a special case for this kind of objection because it explicitly plays with confusions between human personality and artificial or machine-derived intelligence: what *would* be the difference between a physically perfect android kitted out with memories and emotions passably like our own, and a person nurtured through the usual channels? The question can stimulate good discussion: name as many robots as you can think of; do we believe artificial intelligence will ever equal human resources; and if all robots look like the Ford automated-assembly line then why are we even beginning to take the idea of androids seriously?

One answer to the last question is that in all periods 'human-Things' have been imagined as entities which test or define the contemporary sense of human value: the incubus or succubus in Christian tradition, the Golem in Jewish folklore, Prospero's Ariel and Caliban (and perhaps even Miranda too?), E. T. A. Hoffmann's Sandman, and of course Mary Shelley's Frankenstein. Philip K. Dick's androids are no exception; they belong to their period, the late 1960s, in the way that they are defined in relation to authentic human emotionality and sanity. But as soon as we have written the glib phrase, we are brought up short, in exactly the manner which the novel provokes: what *is* an authentic human psyche?

Do Androids Dream? is set in the decaying megalopolis of Los Angeles, AD 2020, a post-holocaust society where the human population has been decimated by the effects of radiation sickness. So far, so conventional; the scenario is one major cliché of pulp SF. This novel's originality is created by the compelling logic to be found in the details of the North Californian world which it evokes. The effects of 'World War Terminus' have induced progressive species death, beginning with birds, then 'foxes one morning, badgers the next, until people had stopped reading the perpetual animal obits.' This species-scarcity induces a kind of religion of animal-ownership in the surviving human population, where everyone aspires to possess and care for one of the beast creation. Curating animals is also partly a replacement for child-rearing, because the fear of genetic damage has discouraged human reproduction. The bounty-hunter hero of the novel, Rick Deckard, keeps a black-faced Suffolk ewe on the roof of the apartment block where he lives with his wife Iran. But the sheep is not ideal, in fact it's electric; Deckard can't afford a real one, and he continually checks the list-price of animals in 'his creased, much-studied copy of Sidney's Animal & Fowl Catalogue.'

At the verge of its extinction, the natural world becomes a valuable commodity; the process of collecting and buying the living merchandise itself accelerates the destruction, increasing scarcity, raising prices. Here the often-praised predictive aspect of good science fiction is very evident. But the keeping of animals in the future world of the novel is an element of a larger belief system: everyone views their own life as part of 'the Ascent', a progress up an increasingly steep incline which they share with the god-like figure of Wilbur Mercer. This religious empathy, or feeling-with, is generated and experienced through technology. By tuning in to an 'empathy box' each individual shares in the Ascent of Mercer, and shares the antagonism directed to their god-figure by some unknown enemies, 'the old antagonists': 'He had crossed over in the usual perplexing fashion; physical merging—accompanied by mental and spiritual identification … As it did for everyone who at this moment clutched the handles, either here on Earth or on one of the colony planets.'

'Empathy' joins believers with Mercer, either through use of the black box, or through the empathy which they extend towards the animals they keep or, more rarely, to other individuals. And at the centre of the novel's increasingly tortured attempts to locate absolute differences between androids and human beings, we find the linked ideas of *empathy* and *affect*. The *Oxford English Dictionary* defines 'empathy' as 'The power of entering into the experience of or understanding objects or emotions outside ourselves.' It is a relatively recent word in English, first recorded by the *OED* in 1912, and imported from the vocabulary of German philosophical aesthetics. Through empathy we know and feel what it is that other people know and feel; it is an experience of (literal) fellow-feeling. 'Compassion' is the medieval word used to designate this sort of emotion (from 1340), and 'sympathy' the Renaissance term (1596).

'Affect' is a much older word that has taken on a new lease of life again in the early twentieth century. It is first recorded by the *OED* from about 1400, conveying a group of related meanings: 'Inward disposition, feeling, as contrasted with external manifestation or action; intent, intention, earnest', and 'Feeling towards or in favour of; kind feeling, affection'. So even in the medieval period 'affect' was already a word with psychological resonances, and it is used for this reason in our own period by Freudian psychoanalysts to describe emotional value within the psyche. *Do Androids Dream?* employs this idea of 'affect' to distinguish between a 'person-Thing' and a human entity: humanity experiences affect (and affect-ion), robots don't. But again there is a problem: some people suffer from a 'flattening of affect', and in the test situation could be mistaken for robots, on this criterion.

The androids of AD 2020 are organic beings— soft robots—designed by scientific-industrial corporations for use on the planetary colonies to which people from earth are emigrating because of all-pervasive radioactive contamination—'The saying currently blabbed by posters, TV ads, and government junk mail, ran: "Emigrate or degenerate! The choice is yours!"' The robots act as slaves for the off-earth colonies where they labour or work as servants. They are modelled as mature individuals who never age but, tragically, they only have a shelf-life of four years: this also gives them a certain desperation. Periodically androids run wild in the colonies and return to earth, hoping not to be recognised.

Because they don't possess empathy, the androids represent a potential threat to the human population; they are physically powerful but completely lacking in conscience, moral sense, guilt, and human sympathy: 'Now that her initial fear had diminished, something else had begun to emerge from her. Something more strange. And, he thought, deplorable. A coldness. Like, he thought, a breath from the vacuum between inhabited worlds, in fact from nowhere....' The androids are, potentially, manufactured psychotic killers. And it is only by identifying them through their lack of empathetic response that they can be located and destroyed. Rick Deckard is a bounty hunter, a twenty-first-century version of Raymond Chandler's Philip Marlowe; he traces androids which illegally return to earth, administers the empathy test, and 'retires' them with a laser gun.

This sounds like a no-nonsense kind of job, but Deckard becomes more and more anguished as the boundaries between android response and human response are systematically blurred by the action of the novel. Deckard administers the Voigt-Kampff Empathy Test to suspect androids; this consists of a series of questions which stimulate minute but measurable reflex responses in the subject being tested. The questions are framed to provoke emotional reaction in the 'suspect', the logic being that there is an innate, automatic response within the human psyche which is triggered by particularly emotive descriptions. Ironically, many of the Voigt-Kampff questions describe cruelties which we presently accept as routine, and which presumably would not unduly trouble many people today: lobsters boiled alive, bull-fighting, hunting trophies. In AD 2020 these are crimes against animals which universally horrify humanity, and supposedly leave androids unaffected. But the latest generation of Nexus-6 'andys' approaches nearer and nearer to human empathetic ability, and these robots cause Deckard particular difficulty.

The first Nexus-6 which (who?) Deckard meets is Rachael Rosen, and she very nearly passes the empathy-test ordeal; more difficult still, she ceases to be an inanimate object for Deckard, because he finds himself attracted to 'her'. Rachael also turns the tables on Deckard, accusing him of being *in*human because of the instrumental, cold way in which he tries to deal with her. But Deckard does not destroy her, because she is 'the property' of the corporation that made her, 'used as a sales device for prospective emigrant.' Luba Luft is the next person-Thing whom Deckard has to hunt and destroy, and who has become a fine opera singer: 'The Rosen Association built her well, he had to admit. And again he perceived himself "sub specie aeternitatis", the form-destroyer called forth by what he heard and saw here. Perhaps the better she functions, the better a singer she is, the more I am

needed.' Luba Luft is a cultured andy: Deckard finds her at an exhibition of Edvard Munch's work, and as a last request before being 'retired' she asks Deckard to buy her a reproduction of Munch's painting *Puberty*. (Why this painting? Is it because it represents a developmental stage which the android never had, and wishes to experience?) He spends $25.00 on a book containing the print, and after he has destroyed Luft, 'systematically burned into blurred ash the book of pictures which he had just a few minutes ago bought Luba'. Who exactly is exhibiting android behaviour in this situation? 'Luba Luft had seemed genuinely alive; it had not worn the aspect of a simulation.'...

The debates which this novel stimulates by creating 'artificial' people who are effectively indistinguishable from 'authentic' people reproduce in fictional form some elaborate arguments from philosophy. For example, I've taken the phrase 'person-Thing' from Martin Heidegger's *Being and Time,* an influential but now increasingly controversial work, written in Germany during the 1920s. Heidegger's subsequent relations with Hitler and National Socialism cast a long shadow across his philosophical work, but *Being and Time* remains a unique contribution to many questions. What is the quality of our knowledge of other people? How should we avoid treating other people instrumentally, exactly as person-Things? What kinds of criticism can be made of empathy, as a means of understanding others? Are we condemned to treat the world only as an object, and so progressively degrade it?...

Blade Runner radically simplifies the plot-line and 'metaphysics' of *Do Androids Dream?*, but constructs a different logic through visual coding, as all films do. This emphasis on appearance can be said to intensify one of the problems of science fiction as a genre, and this has to do with the representation of gender. Is science fiction inescapably a genre written by men, for boys/men? The loving attention paid to technology, and the flattened portrayal of human character, particularly women's roles, might indicate as much. Authors such as Ursula Le Guin and Doris Lessing have taken up the genre with the explicit intention of creating new kinds of SF narrative and value. *Do Androids Dream?* and *Blade Runner* are not tender-hearted works, they display the routine brutalities and masculinist attitudes of the popular genres to which they owe so many of their conventions. (e.g. *Do Androids Dream?*, p. 145: 'He began hunting through the purse. Like a human woman, Rachael had every class of object conceivable filched and hidden away in her purse; he found himself rooting interminably.') Rick Deckard's infatuation with Rachael is the most troubling instance of this problem. In the novel, bounty hunter and android sleep together, prior to the final shoot-out with the remaining three Nexus-6 robots. Rachael articulates the dilemma: 'You're not going to bed with a woman … Remember, though: don't think about it, just do it. Don't pause and be philosophical, because from a philosophical standpoint it's dreary. For us both.'

That the problem is 'philosophically dreary' is a drole way of putting it, and this goes some way to rescuing the situation. But not all the way. *Blade Runner* opts for a softer option. The closing sequence shows Deckard and Rachael flying at speed to the good green country in the north, and Deckard reveals that Rachael has no 'termination date'. He has an ageless companion for the duration. Is this also tacky? Or is it a witty rewriting of the Greek myth of the dawn goddess Eos and her mortal lover Tithonus? Eos begged Zeus to grant Tithonus immortality, but forgot also to ask for perpetual youth on his behalf.

Source: Nigel Wheale, "Recognising a 'human-Thing': cyborgs, robots and replicants in Philip K. Dick's *Do Androids Dream of Electric Sheep?* and Ridley Scott's *Blade Runner*," Critical Survey, Vol. 3, No. 3, 1991, pp. 297–304.

Marilyn Gwaltney

Gwaltney outlines the issues of humanity, personhood, and the idealogical problems technology creates in Do Androids Dream of Electric Sheep?

Both the movie *Blade Runner* and the book *Do Androids Dream of Electric Sheep?* are centrally concerned about the definition of humanness in the context of modern technology. The irony present in both works is that through its technology, humanity has diminished its own capacity to survive, necessitating the invention and mass production of a new life form (the android) which is capable of challenging humanity. This situation gives rise to the central dilemma of both movie and book: if the creature is virtually identical in kind to the creator, should not the creature have virtually all the same rights and privileges as the creator? (The theological theme here is obvious, but I leave others to deal with it.)

Thinking about the moral status of androids gives us a test case, a model, that we are emotionally removed from, for thinking about the moral status of different stages of human life and the relationship of those stages to each other. Reflection on the moral status of the android helps us to think more dispassionately about just what qualities of human life are required for the presence of personhood. In thinking about these qualities and when they are acquired or lost in relation to the android, we are not confused by the images of, for example, infants and the feelings that attend such images. It is not the purpose of this paper to resolve difficult and inflammatory moral issues such as, for example, abortion and euthanasia; its purpose is merely to point out how reflection on the androids presented in *Blade Runner* and *Do Androids Dream of Electric Sheep?* might facilitate resolution of such issues.

The action in both works centers on the progressive feeling of moral wrongness that the protagonist has in "retiring" androids. The more Deckard gets to know them, the less he is able to distinguish between androids and human persons. Rachael is the "clincher" for him in the film. When he first meets her, she does not know that she is an android. It is difficult not to think of Rachael as a person and to sympathize with her as she goes through one of the most painful of human experiences: an identity crisis. In Rachael's case the crisis involves the discovery that she is an android, thus raising the question for herself of her humanity and her personhood. In the novel, Deckard's colleague Phil Resch goes through an identity crisis that is even more poignant given that he is in the business of "retiring" androids. Deckard can ask himself the question "If Rachael and Resch are not human, what am I?"

In the movie, Roy Batty develops into a sympathetic character. Our understanding of his cruelty changes as we come to understand it as a very human reaction to his existential situation: the imminence of his death and that of those he loves; the feeling of betrayal by the beings that brought him into existence.

Roy Batty and his friends are hunted and killed as non-persons, as though they were rabid dogs. The only "official" problem is that the hunters, even after long acquaintance with the androids, cannot tell if the androids are persons or not, except by a clumsy test of questionable validity. However, the moral problem perceived by the protagonist broadens this to the question of whether the androids are indeed the moral equivalent of rabid dogs or defective equipment, in which there is no issue of moral or legal rights and no question of restraint in the use of deadly force.

Generally it is accepted that only persons or collectives of persons have legal and moral rights.

Examples of collectives of persons would include corporations (which are legal persons), families, churches, schools, social clubs and perhaps friendships. It is difficult to ascribe a "right to live" to any collective. But persons cannot justifiably be pursued and killed without due process no matter what hideous crimes they are accused of committing. The book and the movie both raise the question of what it means to be a person and thus to be protected by rights.

To be a person certainly means not to be merely a thing or object. That is, a person is a different kind of thing than stones, tables, or cars are. I am only appealing to ordinary experience when referring to these differences but it may not be possible to avoid metaphysical assumptions altogether, because the notion of personhood takes us to the heart of one of the most difficult philosophical problems: the nature of the self.

Under most circumstances the terms "a human being" (i.e., a particular individual human), "person," and "self" can be used interchangeably because they are denotatively synonymous. But that synonymity does not necessarily hold if androids like those in the film and the novel exist. Since these androids are biologically human, even if they are not sexually reproduced, they must be considered human beings in the sense of being *homo sapiens*. When we think of androids as beings "crafted" from human tissue to have human form and functions, we would not assume that such a being is necessarily a person or "has" a self. We would want such a being to meet certain functional criteria before being declared to be a person or to have a self.

The android is in the same theoretical position as the fetus in the abortion debate. Is being live, growing human tissue sufficient for being considered a person with all the protection of a moral and legal society? Human cancer cells growing in a petrie dish are not persons; neither are cloned human thyroid cells. No moral dilemma arises if we throw them into the garbage when they turn "bad" or we have no more use for them. But if the cells in the petrie dish are a human zygote, we may have moral qualms about discarding them or ever having started them.

The reason for these qualms is presumably that a zygote is a potentially "complete" human being and thus a potential person. The androids are presumably assemblies of cloned cells. We are not given any clues about either the techniques or the principles whereby assembly takes place, integrating specialized cells from diverse sources into a single functioning organism. We can assume that it must be the reverse of the cell differentiation by which the zygote becomes an embryo, a cluster of identical cells differentiating into many specialized cells functioning together. If we decide that the end of these two processes, human cell differentiation and human specialized cell integration, results in beings with the same moral status, then why should not the beginnings have the same moral status? That is, human zygotes and cloned human cells would have comparable value. However, this is *not* to say that the human zygote has the same moral value as a human infant nor that the clusters of cloned cells have the same moral value as the android.

If we can imagine that it is morally permissible to throw away cloned cells intended for inclusion in an android and if we have decided that androids are the moral equivalent of persons, then we should be able to imagine that it is morally permissible to throw away zygotes and perhaps even embryos.

The androids are clearly human beings, but are they persons? Do they have "selves"? We cannot answer that question until we decide what a self is, and what it means to be a person. This brings us to the philosophical problem of the nature of the self, which has a very long history....

The qualities usually associated with personhood are rationality and self-consciousness. Persons are able to give purposes to themselves and to act on those purposes. The androids must have these qualities if they are to fulfill the functions for which they are needed: to take the place of "conventional" humans in situations in which there are not enough humans or which are dangerous or distasteful to humans. To act in such situations, the androids must be able to think like human beings, not like today's computers with all possible decisions programmed but as self-regulating, self-correcting beings. In the language of moral philosophy, they must be able to act autonomously.

Computers may be thought to act rationally, in the sense of acting logically, but they do not act to any purpose of their own, only to the purposes of others. To act with purpose requires consciousness of self. It means having an awareness of being an identity over time, an identity that can act to achieve a variety of ends or goals, and that, furthermore, can *choose* among that variety of goals. The androids are portrayed as having these qualities in a variety of ways in both book and movie. Rachael, of course, exhibits the greatest sense of self and the greatest freedom of choice in both texts. In the book, the other androids are portrayed as acting in much the way any group of hunted persons forced to go underground might act; in the movie, they are portrayed as somewhat "unfinished" persons as suggested by striking moments of child-like or animal-like behavior, with the drama of emerging self-consciousness focused on Roy Batty. The drama of the movie really derives from Batty asserting his freedom by asserting his right to a meaningful length of life not only for himself, but for those he loves.

The androids are clearly persons, but with the exception of Rachael, all are felt to be somewhat defective, not quite right. The book locates the defect in the lack of empathy; the movie more cogently locates the defect in the lack of maturity or developmental experiences which remain with us through memory. Rachael was "given" memories and treated like a natural human person, which accounts for her sense of personhood and our "reading" her as a real or normal person. Leon clinging to his photographs symbolizes his awareness of his self as enduring through time; the photos remind him of that duration, i.e., his own identity.

The androids are an interesting thought experiment: what kind of person would you produce if you eliminated the unproductive periods of infancy, childhood and adolescence, and produced a fully grown adult from the start. It might be a tempting scientific and commercial goal, or even a survival goal if faced with a drastic drop in human fertility. Society invests much of its energy in economically unproductive persons. Non-adults in industrial societies are economically non-productive. Why not find ways to reproduce the species that produce useful adults in a shorter period of time? What kind of being would one have? One with all the intellectual, emotional, and physical capacities of an adult human being but with no experience in learning how to use those capacities. Such a being would, of course, be potentially self-reflective, and would, in a relatively short period of time, become aware of the absence of useful necessary knowledge and experience, just as the human child does. Imagine the frustrated rage of a child expressed in the body of an adult! The android in *Blade Runner* is such a being. No one expects a toddler to have empathy. He is too socially inexperienced. Neither does one expect a toddler to have control over murderous emotions. But as the child grows in experience, she gains in empathy and self-control.

Perhaps personhood is developmental and children and androids are in the process of becoming persons, depending on their degree of experience. Children, however, can be "comforted" in the knowledge that their immaturity is natural, i.e., it is not within the power of anyone except themselves to change it, over the course of a fairly long period of time. The androids do not have such comfort: they know they were manufactured, and thus someone could have made them different from what they are or need not have made them at all. *And* they do not have very much time in which to perfect themselves as persons. The android lives just long enough to become aware of his potentiality as a person before he dies. Both his immaturity and his retirement are determined by others. The genius of the movie, as opposed to the book, is that it makes us feel the pain Roy Batty feels when faced with the knowledge of his approaching death in conjunction with his consciousness of his potentiality for knowledge and accomplishment. We are aware with him of all the valuable things he will never know or do. This is the same pain we feel when confronted with the death of a child or adolescent: it is a profound sense of loss of potentiality.

While death itself may not always be an evil, the suffering that attends death is, and the suffering that attends the death of a child is an undoubtable evil. There is something evil about manufacturing or in *any* way producing a being who will become conscious of his early death. It would not be surprising if such a being developed a warped and dangerous personality.

A dilemma appears to be present with respect to who is morally responsible for the murders the androids commit, the manufacturers or the androids themselves. We generally hold the manufacturers of products responsible for their products' defects. However the androids are not mechanical objects, but possess "wills" of their own. To the degree to which androids are persons, to that degree we would say they are morally responsible for their actions. Even so, we might say that they are persons suffering from diminished responsibility: anyone created to exist under the circumstances which obtain in the androids case would almost certainly go mad upon becoming fully conscious of the situation. Thus the manufacturers of the androids are morally responsible for the deaths caused by the androids. In any case, to kill an android as the blade runner does is clearly murder. As persons, the androids should be entitled to the same moral and legal rights as a "normal" human being of comparable maturity.

Well, one might say, androids of this sort might be theoretically possible, but who would want to bother? Natural reproduction will always be a cheaper, surer and more satisfactory way of increasing human capacities in the universe. If human fertility drops so low as to make such androids desirable, the question "why bother?" is even more relevant. So what kind of light does all the heat in *Blade Runner* generate? I think it is, at least in part, a parable about the morally responsible use of scientific creativity. The misuses of the discoveries of science led to the need for the androids in the first place. The scientific processes and products used to create the androids resulted in conscious beings of the sort that are clearly persons, and persons demand moral consideration.

One of the newest frontiers of science is the realm of consciousness. Science is exploring the physical basis for consciousness, ways of manipulating consciousness, exploring similarities between human and non-human consciousness. But consciousness is a necessary, but not a sufficient condition for personhood, and it is to personhood that we attach moral rights and responsibilities.

Regardless of whether we conceive of personhood as something spiritual or something rooted in the natural world, we mean by the concept of "person" something which should lead us to constrain our behavior. That is, we feel obligations in the presence of persons. We feel that at least we should not kill or even cause unnecessary pain to persons. Most of us would say we also should not lie to or steal from another person, and that, in general, we should accord every person the same rights that we expect to have extended to us in so far as that person can exercise that right.

Immanuel Kant taught that we should always treat persons as ends in themselves and never as means only. In other words, it is morally wrong to use persons as *mere* means; we must always treat them as having intrinsic value. In Western capitalist culture we are accustomed to believing that the creator or discoverer of something is its owner and thus has the authority to use it or dispose of it. *Blade Runner* and *Do Androids Dream of Electric Sheep?* carry that belief to its logical conclusion in the context not only of the modern world but of the future. This belief that ownership gives an absolute right of disposal of and authority over the owned has defined the relationships of father and child, husband and wife, master and slave in the past; in our times we have denied this belief in relation to those kinds of persons.

The belief that we have the right to use and dispose of what we own in any way we like, and

that we own whatever we make, is still lurking to trap us in a morally untenable situation, because we still have not adequately reflected upon what it means to be a person nor appropriately extended the status of personhood. The abortion rights debate is really over whether personhood can appropriately be extended to fetuses. *Blade Runner* prompts us to wonder if the concept should not be extended beyond *the conventional* human and even to the non-human.

Science fiction has long operated on the premise that personhood cannot be confined to the human species, because science fiction writers have long understood that intelligence is to be respected wherever it is found. Intelligent beings, of course, are the rational, self-conscious, purposive beings we have described as persons.

But extending personhood to the non-human or the unconventionally human is no longer an activity that should be confined to the art of the science fiction writer; it must be seriously contemplated by scientists and lay persons in respect to any endeavor dealing with consciousness. If chimpanzees, gorillas, dolphins, whales, etc., meet the criteria of personness to the same degree as some humans, why should they not be extended the same moral and legal rights? Or conversely, if we deny such moral and legal rights to highly intelligent animals, why should we not deny them to some types of humans? Both questions have far reaching implications for the way we view ourselves and how we engage in much scientific and commercial enterprise. Animal behaviorists and medical researchers using animals must consider whether their subjects might meet the criteria for personhood. If they think they might meet those criteria, then they must either stop their research or proceed as though they were dealing with human subjects. Medical scientists and the public must consider the implications for personhood of their life-saving, life-altering or live-creating technology.

Sources

Philip K. Dick, afterword to *The Golden Man,* Berkley Publishing, 1980.

Ursula K. Le Guin, "Science Fiction as Prophesy," in *The New Republic,* Vol. 175, No. 18, October 30, 1976, pp. 33-34.

Robert Scholes and Eric S. Rabkin, *Science Fiction: History, Science, Vision,* Oxford University Press, 1977, pp. 71-75, 180.

Philip Strick, "The Age of the Replicant," in *Sight & Sound,* Vol. 5, No. 3, Summer, 1982, pp. 168-172.

Angus Taylor, *Philip K. Dick and the Umbrella of Light,* T-K Graphics, 1975, p. 52.

Patricia S. Warrick, "The Labyrinthian Process of the Artificial: Philip K. Dick's Androids and Mechanical Constructs," in *Philip K. Dick,* edited by Joseph D. Olander and Martin Harry Greenberg, Taplinger Publishing Company, 1983, pp. 189-214.

For Further Study

Philip K. Dick, "Notes on *Do Androids Dream of Electric Sheep?* (1968)," in *The Shifting Realities of Philip K. Dick,* Pantheon Books, 1995, pp. 155-161.
   These are the ideas Dick had early after the book was published regarding how to adapt it for a movie.

Kenneth M. Ford, Clark Glymour, and Patrick J. Hayes, editors, *Android Epistemology,* MIT Press, 1995.
   A good introduction to the state of android technology today and where it is headed.

Carl Freedman, "Towards a Theory of Paranoia: The Science Fiction of Philip K. Dick," in *Science-Fiction Studies,* Volume 11, No. 1, March, 1984, pp. 15-22.
   This scholarly work looks at characters from several of Dick's novels, including *Do Androids Dream of Electric Sheep?,* to put together a theory of the human condition that is constant throughout Dick's works.

John Huntington, "Philip K. Dick: Authenticity and Insincerity," in *Science-Fiction Studies,* Volume 15, No. 2, July, 1988, pp. 152-60.
   One of the central questions in Dick's works, certainly one of the central questions explored in *Do Androids Dream of Electric Sheep?,* is: what constitutes reality? Huntington surveys Dick's works and at least examines the question, although the answer is still left open.

Hazel Pierce, "Philip K. Dick's Political Dreams," in *Philip K. Dick,* edited by Martin Harry Greenberg and Joseph D. Olander, Taplinger Publishing Co., 1983, pp. 105-135.
   This essay, notable in a good collection of essays about the author, examines the reasons readers like or dislike Dick.

Lawrence Sutin, *Divine Invasion: A Life of Philip K. Dick,* Harmony Books, 1989.
   A biography of the author that gives real-life sources that inspired characters and events from the novel.

Patricia S. Warrick, *Mind in Motion: The Fiction of Philip K. Dick,* Southern Illinois University Press, 1987.
   This source examines the morality present in Dick's works, especially his special use of the concept of "empathy."

Ender's Game

Orson Scott Card
1985

Orson Scott Card first wrote *Ender's Game* as a short story in 1975. He submitted the work to a leading science fiction magazine, *Analog,* hoping to make some money to help pay his school debts. Not only did *Analog* publish the story, the 1977 World Science Fiction Convention nominated it for a Hugo Award and gave Card the John W. Campbell Award for best new writer. In 1985, the author developed *Ender's Game* into a novel, and it became the work which established his reputation as one of science fiction's most prominent new writers. This longer version swept both the Hugo and Nebula Awards, the most prestigious accolades given to science fiction and fantasy works. A favorite with readers, the novel has inspired three additional works featuring Ender Wiggin and his struggles to understand the universe.

Ender's Game follows the training of Andrew "Ender" Wiggin, a six-year-old genius who may be Earth's only hope for victory against an invasion of insectoid aliens. While most critics consider the plot elements of human-against-alien and the child-soldier to be science-fiction cliché, Card renders them new with his stress on the underlying themes of empathy, compassion, and moral intent. It is only Ender's ability to empathize with the "buggers" that enables him to overcome them, and the reader experiences his solitude, anguish, and remorse over his various "victories." As a result, Michael Collings noted in the *Fantasy Review,* the novel "succeed[s] equally as straightforward SF adventure and as [an] allegorical, analogical disquisi-

tion … on humanity, morality, salvation, and re-demption."

Author Biography

Born to Willard and Peggy Card on August 24, 1951, Card grew up in Utah, where he was raised in the Mormon faith. When he was sixteen, he read Isaac Asimov's *Foundation* trilogy, which had a profound effect on his thinking about the future. The plot of *Foundation* implies that history repeats itself, regardless of the people involved or the specific situations that they encounter. Asimov softens this message through his idea that humans can learn these patterns and work to minimize the most harmful effects of change. Since Card's Mormon beliefs hold that people are basically good, he liked Asimov's notion that human beings are capable of overcoming adversity through self-improvement and cooperation. As a result of his thinking about Asimov's message, Card decided he wanted to write stories that would affect others in the positive way that Asimov's writing had affected him.

At the time, he focused on military topics. His brother served in the army, and Card had read Bruce Catton's three-volume *Army of the Potomac*. He learned from his reading that leadership makes the difference in an army's success. This led him to think about how future leaders would successfully train their armies, particularly for battles in space. His thinking led to his creation of the Battle Room in *Ender's Game,* where the children-warriors practice for three-dimensional warfare with three-dimensional games. The young Card had little experience writing, however, and the idea would remain undeveloped for almost ten years.

Card graduated from high school as a junior in 1968 and went on to study archaeology at Brigham Young University. He soon found he preferred writing plays to digging for artifacts and studied theater instead. After returning from a stint as a Mormon missionary in Brazil, Card graduated with distinction from Brigham Young University in 1975. The "Battle Room" had lived in the back of Card's mind since he first imagined it as a boy of sixteen. In debt for his college education, he decided to try to incorporate the Battle Room idea into a story. He began the short-story version of *Ender's Game* on an afternoon outing with a friend and her children. The short-story version won Card the 1977 John W. Campbell Award for best new writer, which launched his career. That same year

Orson Scott Card

Card married his wife, Kristine. The couple are the parents of five children.

Card had published five novels to little notice when he began reworking the story "Ender's Game" into a novel. He intended the work to set up his second novel featuring Ender Wiggin, *Speaker for the Dead.* The success of the novel version surprised Card, winning both the Nebula (1985) and Hugo (1986) awards. The author achieved an unprecedented "double-double" when *Speaker for the Dead* duplicated the sweep the following year. Since then, Card has continued to write science fiction, while also branching out into fantasy, horror, and mainstream fiction. He has also penned an award-winning guide to writing science fiction and fantasy, and frequently contributes columns to various writing, genre, and computing magazines.

Plot Summary

Earth

Each chapter of *Ender's Game* opens with a conversation between the government officials who are responsible for finding a military genius to lead Earth to victory against the alien "bugger" fleet. From these conversations, the reader learns that

Andrew "Ender" Wiggin is considered humanity's best hope for such a leader. It is also made clear that these officials will isolate and test Ender as much as possible to mold him into the effective military leader they so desperately need.

Ender's story opens as he is finally losing the monitor implanted in the base of his neck, a device which allows government officials to see and hear whatever he experiences. He is later than most in having the device removed—six years old—thus separating him from his peers. He is also the third child of his family, in a futuristic society that seldom allows more than two children. Although Ender is a legal "Third," he is still an object of scorn and derision. After the monitor is removed, an older, bigger boy, Stilson, leads a group of bullies against Ender. Ender fights him viciously, attempting to discourage further attacks in the future. (The fact that Stilson dies in the process is not revealed until the book's later chapters.)

At home, Ender's older sister Valentine sympathizes with him, but his sadistic brother Peter brutalizes him and says that someday he will kill Ender and Valentine. The following day, Colonial Hyrum Graff of the International Fleet comes to the house and convinces Ender to accompany him to Battle School. There he will train to fight the Buggers, a race of insect-like aliens that has invaded Earth twice already and nearly destroyed humankind. Ender agrees to go, due to a combination of three things: love for his sister; fear of his brother; and the knowledge that his conception as a Third was only allowed because it might produce a qualified candidate for the school. In the spaceship that takes new cadets to the orbiting Battle School, Graff shows preferential treatment to Ender. An older boy bullies Ender because of this, and Ender responds too hard for the weightlessness of space, breaking the other boy's arm. Even before entering the school, Ender has once again been set apart from the other children.

Battle School

From the first, Ender is the object of bullying at Battle School, in part because the school's leaders intend for him to be isolated and feared. He wins some respect by devising clever new strategies in battle simulation games and for cracking the security codes on his tormentors' computer files. He and his fellow beginners, called "Launchies," are finally introduced to the null-gravity battleroom, where the older recruits learn strategy by conducting battles against each other's armies. Just as Ender begins making friends, he is promoted from the Launchies into a student army, the Salamanders. Not quite seven, he is at least a year early for the promotion. He becomes an outcast once again; his commander, Bonzo Madrid, forbids him to participate in battles and vows to trade him away at the earliest opportunity.

A fellow soldier in his army, Petra Arkanian, helps Ender learn some of the basics of fighting in the battleroom. Forbidden to work with the Salamander Army, Ender begins practicing with his old Launchy comrades. Ender later wins a crucial battle by disregarding Bonzo's orders. From then on, Ender's imaginative strategies draw attention to him as he is transferred from one army to another, absorbing effective and ineffective military techniques by observing his commanders. Some of the older children resent him, however, and try to break up his Launchy session. He is once again forced into violence to protect himself. The frustration he feels spills over into the fantasy computer game he plays, and Ender fears he is becoming a cold-blooded killer like his brother Peter.

When Ender is given command of his own army it is not, as usual, manned with soldiers from other armies, but is filled with new recruits; they are inexperienced but intelligent and inventive, and not held down by outdated strategies. The maneuvers Ender devises are imaginative and complex, and his Dragon Army maintains a perfect record. The Battle School rules change to keep pressure on Ender's army: instead of getting three months to prepare for their first battle, they are given a few weeks; instead of fighting every second week they face other armies daily; finally, they have to face two opposing armies at once. Ender resents the way the game changes to challenge him, but he adapts new strategies and wins. The other commanders resent his success, and a group of boys, led by Bonzo Madrid, confront Ender in the shower. Ender defends himself, and, as with Stilson on Earth, he is not told that he has left the other boy dead.

Earth

While Ender has been growing up at Battle School, his twelve-year-old brother Peter has been concocting a plot to gain political power. Peter has noticed that, despite international cooperation in the war against the aliens, the Russians seem to be maneuvering troops for a war. He and ten-year-old Valentine devise fictitious personalities, Locke and Demosthenes, to publish political essays on the internet. Valentine's character, Demosthenes, is more radical and favors war, which is the opposite of what she really believes. Locke, on the other hand, is tolerant in a way Peter is not. Their essays are so persuasive that soon major news organizations are carrying columns by them both. Their views are cited in political speeches, their thoughts are affecting policy decisions, and no one suspects that the writers are children.

Ender, his spirit broken by the increasingly meaningless battle games and by his own surprising cruelty in the fight with Bonzo Madrid, graduates from Battle School. He returns to Earth and is allowed to rest for a few months, but he refuses to cooperate with the military any more. Colonial Graff brings Valentine, now twelve, to see him at the lake cabin where he is kept. They have a discussion while Ender agonizes over all that is being asked of him. Out of concern for all mankind, especially his sister, and for the natural beauty of planet Earth, he agrees to continue with his training.

Eros

Ender is taken to the International Fleet's command post on Eros, where top secret plans are explained to him. He is told of the First and Second Invasions. In the First Invasion the enemy was defeated because they were surprised to find humans capable of intelligence. The hero of the Second Invasion, Mazer Rackham, teaches Ender that he won the war because of a lucky hunch. Guessing that the Buggers would behave like insects, he destroyed the invasion's central ship, killing the queen and thereby shutting down the mental abilities of their entire fleet. Currently, Ender is told, the Earth is invading the Buggers' home planet, with ships that left five years earlier. They will be within attacking distance very soon, which is why Ender's training has been at such an accelerated pace.

For over a year, Ender studies alone, tutored by individuals and tested by more realistic computer simulations. He trains with Mazer Rackham, and learns more about his Bugger opponents. Eventually, he is reunited with his closest and most respected colleagues from the Battle School. Together they compete against what seems to be a series of computer simulations. While Ender's forces always win, his dreams are tormented by visions of the buggers. He stumbles through his training until he is posed with a "final exam." After winning this last, particularly difficult battle, Ender is told that he has not been playing against the computer for months. Instead, he has been leading the invading fleet, and he has just destroyed the Buggers' home planet, wiping their race into extinction. He is eleven.

The Colony

After the war, Ender stays on Eros, but he receives word of wars on Earth, where he is known worldwide as the hero who saved the human race. Ender is promoted to admiral, and so the truth cannot be kept from him any more. He watches Colonel Graff on trial for war crimes and child abuse, and sees broadcast footage of himself killing Stilson and Bonzo. He learns about a worldwide peace treaty engineered by Locke, whom he knows is his brother Peter. He knows he can never return home, as Peter will attempt to make him a political pawn. He is also uncomfortable with the admiration he is receiving for having murdered an entire sentient race.

Valentine comes to him, however, and suggests that he join her as part of the first colonial expedition to occupy one of the Buggers' planets. At the new colony, Valentine becomes an historian and Ender becomes the colony's governor. Years pass, until Ender comes across a familiar structure while looking for land for a new colony: it is an abandoned city, built inside the decayed skeleton of a giant. It is an exact duplicate of a scene that haunted him from the video game he played in Battle School. He realizes that the Buggers were able to monitor his game, that they knew he would come to destroy them, and so they built this imitation as a sign to him.

At a symbolic place in the city he finds a Bugger queen egg, and it communicates with him telepathically. He takes the egg with him, promising to let it hatch when he can find some place safe for it. To atone for his crime, he writes a book telling the Hive Queen's story, signing it "Speaker for the Dead." After Ender's brother Peter dies, having ruled Earth as the Hegemon, Ender writes a similar book, again signing it anonymously. A religion forms around the writings, even though nobody knows who wrote them. Speakers for the Dead arise to interpret the lives, in all their goodness and cruelty, of people who have passed. Seeking a new home for the Queen, Ender takes Valentine, now a historian, into space. There they travel the galaxy, learning and interpreting the stories of the living and the dead.

Characters

Alai

A member of Ender's Launchy group, Alai is originally Bernard's best friend. Alai comes to appreciate Ender's many talents and becomes leader of a group that includes both Bernard's in-group and Ender's outcasts. When Ender gets assigned to Salamander Army, Alai reveals his true friendship in a hug and a whispered "Salaam": "Whatever it meant to Alai, Ender knew that it was sacred; that he had uncovered himself for Ender, as Ender's mother had done, when he was very young." Alai's voice is the first Ender hears when he is finally allowed to work with others at Command School.

Major Anderson

Major Anderson assists Colonel Graff in commanding the Battle School. Anderson runs the "games," and is upset when Graff disturbs their rules in order to develop Ender's potential. After Ender's fight with Bonzo, Major Anderson is promoted to colonel and takes over command of the Battle School. After the war, it is implied he will become commissioner of a football league.

Petra Arkanian

The only girl and the best shooter in Salamander Army, Petra possesses enough courage to stand up to Bonzo. She befriends Ender and teaches him her sharpshooting skills. She later commands Phoenix Army while Ender is a member. She is a very good soldier, but cracks under the pressure of the Command School battles anyway. Her collapse reminds Ender he must remember the limitations of his commanders: "As he eased the pressure on them, he increased the pressure on himself."

Bean

Bean, the smallest soldier in Ender's Dragon Army, gets Ender's attention immediately by demonstrating his quick adaptation to instructions in the Battle Room. Not only is Bean smart, he is cocky and rebellious. Recognizing Bean's leadership potential, Ender treats Bean the same way Graff treated Ender—to toughen Bean and force him to separate from the others. Ender recognizes this, however, and thinks of Bean, "When the time is right you'll find that I'm your friend, and you are the soldier you want to be." Bean becomes one of Ender's best soldiers and leads one of his best platoons. Ender later reveals some of his worries to Bean and entrusts him with a special squad of Dragon Army. Bean joins Ender in the final game.

Bernard

Ender first meets Bernard, a fellow Battle School candidate from France, on the shuttle transport. Bernard targets Ender for punishment because

Media Adaptations

- Mark Rolston narrates *Ender's Game* in an abridged three-hour audiotaped version adapted by Audio Renaissance Tapes, Inc., in 1991.

- Card has authored a screenplay based on *Ender's Game;* as of 1998 he was working with Chartoff Productions and Fresco Pictures to produce the film.

Graff has spoken so highly of him. Bernard attacks Ender on the shuttle, but Ender has adjusted more quickly to the null gravity conditions. As a result, Ender accidentally breaks Bernard's arm in reaction to Bernard's blows. Bernard and his sadistic friends quickly become Ender's enemies at Battle School. Ender fights back using the computer, and later Bernard becomes one of Alai's group. His resentment continues, however, and he is present during the confrontation with Bonzo in the showers.

Buggers

"Buggers" is the name humans have given to the insect-like organisms who have twice attacked the Earth. While they evolved on another planet, they could easily have developed on Earth, having a genetic makeup similar to that of Earth insects. They look like Earth insects but have internal skeletons. During the Second Invasion, Mazer Rackham discovered the key to defeating them was to destroy their queen. Their starships represent great technological know-how, but there is no evidence that they use any communication devices. They seem to be able to communicate with each other telepathically. Ender discovers this is true when he discovers the queen egg they left behind for him. He cannot reawaken her yet, however, for everyone fears their capabilities. Instead, he writes her story for all to understand.

Carn Carby

Carn Carby commands Rabbit Army, the first one Ender's Dragon Army faces in battle. Ender is impressed with how honorably Carn accepts his defeat at Ender's hands. Carn helps command in the final battle.

Dap

Dap is the "mom" assigned to Ender's Launch group. He introduces the Launchies to how things work at the Battle School, and comforts some of the boys on their first night. Ender makes sure not to show any sign of weakness before him.

Colonel Hyrum Graff

Colonel Graff directs primary training at the Battle School. Ender thinks of him as the principal of the Battle School and likes him right away. He believes that because Graff is honest with him, he will be Ender's friend. Colonel Graff, however, soon shows Ender that he should trust no one. Graff praises Ender so much on the shuttle to Battle School that he turns all the other boys against Ender. He also engineers Ender's isolation at the school. Even though Colonel Graff does consider himself the students' friend and truly worries about their mental welfare, he has to keep his mission in mind. As a result, he is gruff with the students and demanding of them, trying to teach them to be tough. Colonel Graff faces a court-martial after Bonzo's death in Battle School, but is acquitted.

Hot Soup

See Han Tzu

Locke

See Peter Wiggin

Bonzo Madrid

Commander of the Salamander Army, Bonzo Madrid stands tall and slender, with black eyes and delicate lips. His beauty hides his cruel nature. He resents Ender's being assigned to him from the beginning and forbids him to participate in the group's battles. He rules Salamander by fear, not respect, and Ender observes that his desire for total control makes him a less effective leader. Bonzo particularly hates it when Ender rescues Salamander from total defeat during a battle; afterwards, he trades Ender to Rat Army. His resentment grows after Ender's Dragon Army humiliates him. He meets Ender again in a deadly battle in the showers.

Dink Meeker

Dink runs the platoon to which Rose the Nose assigns Ender in Rat Army. Dink respects Ender's abilities and has asked that Ender be assigned to him. Dink has turned down command of an army twice before because he fears what it will do to him. Dink knows there is more to life than the Game; he has recognized that the School "doesn't create *anything*. It just destroys." He also tells Ender of his belief that the I.F. has blown the Bugger menace out of proportion in order to retain power. Nevertheless, Dink leads his platoon well, and he and Ender become friends. Not only does Dink support Ender when Bonzo attacks him in the shower, he assists him in the final battle.

Fly Molo

Fly Molo leads Dragon Army's A platoon. He reappears in the final battle to help Ender fight.

Mazer Rackham

Mazer Rackham commanded the Strike Force, which shattered and destroyed the buggers during the Second Invasion. A half-Maori New Zealander who seemed to come from nowhere, Rackham succeeded in saving the world from destruction. Ender watches the censored films of hero Rackham's battles, continually frustrated that the events of the final battle are kept secret. After the I.F. promotes Ender to commander and Ender masters all the simulator games, the I.F. assigns him a teacher: Mazer Rackham. Rackham shares the secret behind his defeat of the buggers that Ender has already inferred.

Rose the Nose

Rose the Nose is commander of the Rat Army when Ender joins it. Rose is proud of his Jewish heritage and lets everyone know it by mocking himself—partly to forestall anti-Semitic remarks and partly to remind people that all the former military leaders of the International Fleet have been Jewish. His army has little discipline, but it stands in second place when Ender joins it. Nevertheless, he too provides Ender with valuable lessons about how *not* to command. As Dink says, "He's winning, but that scares him worst of all, because he doesn't know *why* he's winning."

Shen

One of Ender's first real friends in Battle School, Shen gets tormented because he is "small, ambitious, and easily needled." Bernard and his group make fun of the way Shen walks, saying he wriggles like a worm. Ender helps Shen retaliate by using the computer, and later he and Ender join Alai's group and take away Bernard's followers. Shen also joins Ender in the final battle.

Stilson

The first school bully Ender faces, Stilson teases Ender because he is a Third. After Ender's monitor is removed, Stilson leads a group of boys against Ender. Ender fights him, and beats him severely in order to forestall future retaliation. He does not learn until much later that Stilson died from the assault.

Crazy Tom

Crazy Tom leads Dragon Army's C platoon. Ender is pleased to have his assistance once again in the final battle.

Han Tzu

Hot Soup leads Dragon Army's D platoon. Hot Soup fights along with Ender in the final battle.

Andrew Wiggin

Even from an early age, Andrew "Ender" Wiggin knows he is different from all the children around him. He is the third child in his family, something rarely permitted in his overpopulated country. At six years old, he still wears the monitor the government has implanted to assess whether he is a good candidate for the International Fleet's Battle School. Only children whom the Fleet considers geniuses are so monitored. Because Ender is not just different but also smarter than his peers, he inspires their jealousy and harassment. To survive, he must learn to deal with a series of bullies, beginning with his older brother Peter and continuing with his schoolmate Stilson, his fellow Launchy Bernard, and finally the Battle School commander Bonzo. While he can outwit them one-on-one, when faced with a group he has to resort to physical force. To not just win but to prevent future attacks, Ender ruthlessly assaults and defeats these enemies. It is a lesson the military wants him to learn. As Ender thinks after fighting Bonzo: "Peter might be scum, but Peter had been right, always right; the power to cause pain is the only power that matters, the power to kill and destroy, because if you can't kill then you are always subject to those who can, and nothing and no one will ever save you."

Ender is not like Peter, however, although this is his constant fear. Peter had been too merciless and cruel to enter Battle School, while his sister Valentine had been too sensitive. Ender is like a combination of the two: ruthless enough to earn total victory, but compassionate enough to hate the methods needed to gain it. He is also different from Peter in that he does not always feel the need to win. He only fights when forced to, and takes little pleasure in his victories. When Valentine explains to him how he can defeat his oldest neme-

sis, Ender replies: "You don't understand.... I don't want to beat Peter.... I want him to love me." Ender continually experiences emotional conflict between his need to protect himself by winning and his fear of becoming a killer. This conflict often manifests itself in Ender's fantasy computer game, an intelligent program that responds to the player's feelings.

Ironically, it is Ender's ability to understand and empathize with other people which makes him such a brilliant strategist. From his first days in Battle School, he observes the other children. He studies the commanders, learns their strengths and weaknesses, and uses this knowledge to defeat them. This ability does not comfort him, however. As he tells Valentine: "In the moment when I truly understand my enemy, understand my enemy well enough to defeat him, then in that very moment I also love him.... And then, in that very moment when I *love* them ... I *destroy* them." After he discovers his final "game" was actually the battle that exterminated the bugger species, Ender is not sure how to live with himself. It is his empathy which shows him a way: he will join Valentine on a colony ship to a bugger planet. "Maybe if I go there I can understand them better," he tells Valentine. "I stole their future from them; I can only begin to repay by seeing what I can learn from their past." He does so by finding the Hive Queen egg and telling her story. His dual nature allows him to relate "all the good and all the evil" he finds in her story and the stories of those he will understand as a Speaker for the Dead.

Ender Wiggin

See Andrew Wiggin

Peter Wiggin

Ender's older brother, Peter, scares him to death. He is sneaky and manipulative and delights in threatening his younger siblings. Peter is particularly hostile towards Ender, jealous that the I.F. considers Ender superior after his own intelligence was unrecognized. (The Fleet eliminated Peter from their roster of Battle School candidates because of his sadistic nature.) At school, Peter torments other children by finding "what they most feared and [making] sure they faced it often." Peter's cruelty is disguised by his dark and handsome appearance and his ability to hide his actions. After Ender leaves home, Peter learns to act like adults expect him to. Valentine knows he has not really changed, however, for she sees evidence he has been torturing small animals. As he matures, how-

ever, Peter learns to be in total control of himself;
he only acts out of self-interest, not anger or passion.

Peter understands how to use people's fears to
get them to do what he wants. At first he uses this
power to bully others, but then he learns to use it
to influence people. Although manipulative, Peter
is highly intelligent and ambitious. He tells Valentine that having control is "the most important thing
to me, it's my greatest gift, I can see where the
weak points are, I can see how to get in and use
them." At twelve years old he knows that he wants
to have control of "something worth ruling," and
envisions himself as the person who can save
mankind from self-destruction. He forms a plan
where he and his sister will influence political opinion through their writings. Ironically, the identity
Peter adopts, the pseudonym "Locke," is more understanding than he really is. The subterfuge eventually mellows Peter, and later in life he does become ruler of Earth.

Worm

See Shen

Themes

Alienation and Loneliness

From the beginning of the story, Ender feels
alienated from almost everyone around him. First,
he is a "Third"—an extra child that under ordinary
circumstances would not be allowed in school. In
addition, the International Fleet has branded him as
different by implanting a device that monitors his
every move. Other children, including Ender's
brother Peter, understand that the gifted Ender is
being considered for selection to the Battle School.
This creates jealousy, making him a target for bullies. They delight in tormenting Ender, especially
when the monitor is removed and they think that
Ender is a failure. Not only does Ender have to endure ridicule at school, he also faces it at home
from Peter. Although his sister Valentine comforts
him and commiserates with him, she does not receive the same treatment from their brother as Ender does.

Ender's solitude is crucial to his development
as a military leader. "His isolation can't be broken," one of the school supervisors says. "He can
never come to believe that anybody will ever help
him out, *ever*. If he once thinks there's an easy way

out, he's wrecked." As a result, the International
Fleet deliberately isolates Ender at the Battle
School. Even before Ender's arrival, Colonel Graff
deliberately praises him so that the other boys on
the transport will resent him. As soon as Ender begins to make friends within one group, he is transferred to another. All the other students recognize
that Ender has a genius that they do not possess;
even when they do not resent him for it, they still
hold him in awe. When Ender is given command
of an army, he is further isolated by his inability to
share the burdens of command. Even Ender's success against the buggers alienates him; the celebrity
and guilt it bestows on him ensures he will always
be different from everyone else around him.

Good and Evil

Throughout *Ender's Game,* the line between
good and evil acts is continually blurred. Is it acceptable to commit an evil act in order to protect
oneself? To find a military commander who will
save humanity from the buggers, the International
Fleet separates children from their families, while
their "teachers" manipulate the emotions of children. These despicable acts seem acceptable, however, because they occur to bring about an eventual good for all mankind. Ender himself embodies
these contradictory impulses. In order to protect
himself from harm, he kills two other children. He
also ends up destroying an entire species of beings.
Ender remains a sympathetic character, however,
because he both recognizes and fears his own potential for evil. After his first confrontation with
older boys ends in violence, he sees Peter's face in
his computer game. He tells himself that he is not
like Peter, that he does not enjoy the power of violence as Peter does, but he still doubts: "Then a
worse fear, that he *was* a killer, only better at it
than Peter ever was; that it was this very trait that
pleased the teachers."

Punishment

The blurred lines between good and evil also
make judgments of guilt and innocence very difficult to make. As a result, punishment is often with-
held for acts that might otherwise require some
penalty. In *Ender's Game,* adults do not hold Ender responsible for his actions, hoping to create the
perfect military leader. While they do not protect
Ender from his enemies, they do protect him from
the negative consequences of his battles against
them. When Ender fights Stilson, and unknowingly
kills him, the adults in charge do nothing—in fact,
they keep the knowledge of his crime from him.

Topics For Further Study

- In her review of *Ender's Game* in *Fantasy Review,* Elaine Radford criticizes Card, claiming that he fashioned Ender's character after Adolf Hitler's persona. Card refutes Radford's analysis in a response published in the same issue of the magazine. Read both articles. Then write an essay agreeing with either Radford or Card. Your defense should provide solid evidence from the reviews and from the novel itself.

- Research project: Read the book, *The Psychopathic God: Adolf Hitler,* by Robert G. L. Waite, to which Elaine Radford refers in her review of *Ender's Game* in *Fantasy Review.* Locate information related to the psychology of mass murderers. How does Ender Wiggin compare to Hitler and other mass murderers identified in history? Include a chart or other visual presentation describing the results of your research.

- You are a news broadcaster living in the time after Ender's victorious battle (assuming that news broadcasters would exist); choose a partner to play Ender. You will role play an interview with him. Prior to the interview, prepare your questions and let your partner know the kinds of questions you will ask without giving him the specific details. Your partner should

also prepare for the interview so that he can play a credible Ender. Videotape your interview and share it with the class.

- *Ender's Game* creates an image of gifted children as being social outcasts. Research the term "gifted" and write a paper that answers the following questions. Who are gifted children? What are their characteristics? Are gifted children outcasts? Why or why not? What are gifted children like as adults? Does the Ender character give a true picture of a gifted child? Why or why not? Give examples from your novel and from your research.

- What does a "bugger" look like? Consider the description in the novel, as well as research on insect anatomy. Draw or create a model of your vision of a bugger.

- Are you familiar with a video game that seems to compare to the "game" Ender was playing when he destroyed the buggers? Do one of the following: (1) write a comparison of Ender's game and the game with which you are familiar, or (2) demonstrate the game and draw the comparison through your demonstration.

This happens to Ender on three other occasions: during the flight to the Battle School when he breaks Bernard's arm; when a group of older boys attempt to break up his Launchy training sessions; and finally when he kills Bonzo. Graff feels he is justified in suspending punishment, for a military leader cannot think about the human cost of his victories. (The public seems to agree, for Graff is acquitted when he is prosecuted for criminal negligence for his role in the deaths.) Nevertheless, Ender himself feels guilty for what he has done: "I'm your tool, and what difference does it make if I hate the part of me that you most need? What difference does it make that when the little serpents killed me in the game, I agreed with them, and was glad."

Intelligence

The value of intelligence is thoroughly examined in *Ender's Game.* The children whom the International Fleet selects to attend Battle School have high IQs and rank the highest in their classes and schools. Yet, intellectual ability does not always ensure a child's success in Battle School. Children must also possess an ability to adapt quickly to new situations; empathy, or the ability to understand and care for others, is also a valuable character trait. Peter, for example, has the intellect the I.F. requires, and understands people well enough to control them by exploiting their fears. But he condemns those who think differently from him, and his lack of compassion for others prevents him from being selected for the prestigious Battle School. The children who succeed in Battle School, who become the commanders, possess the knowledge, flexibility, and people skills necessary to lead. Ender not only conquers all of the games he plays, he also quickly adjusts to changes in battle schedules and appreciates other students' skills and abilities. By understanding how others think and interact, he becomes a better strategist and a better motivator.

Ethics

Besides the obvious questions related to murder without punishment, moral and ethical questions related to the manipulation of children and the significance of compassion arise throughout *Ender's Game*. Even though Ender commits murder and receives no punishment, he does feel remorse. It is Ender's ability to empathize, however, that targets him for the role of a mass murderer. The Battle School leaders know that if Ender can feel compassion for the buggers, he will better understand how they exist and operate. Thus, he will be better able to take advantage of their weaknesses and thus destroy them. As a child, Ender does not fully understand how the adults are using him for their own purposes. As Graff tells him, "We might both do despicable things, Ender, but if humankind survives, then we were good tools." Ender senses this is a half-truth, but Graff adds that "you can worry about the other half after we win this war." The adults' seemingly cold manipulation of Ender and his feelings and their apparent lack of concern for its effects on him comprise controversial themes. Card's attention to these themes separates the novel from many other science fiction offerings.

Heritage and Ancestry

While Ender and his schoolmates are members of an "International Fleet," the heritage of individual characters is still an important factor for many of them. Cooperation between people of different backgrounds is essential for Earth to fight the buggers, and racial strife seems to be a thing of the past, as Alai and Ender exchange slurs as a joke. Ironically, however, in this age of cooperation people still make a point to separate themselves by ancestry. Bernard, for instance, is from a French separatist group who "insisted that the teaching of Standard not begin until the age of four, when the French language patterns were already set. His accent made him exotic and interesting." Rose the Nose makes sure that everyone knows of his Jewish ancestry in an attempt to place himself within

a long tradition of successful generals. Similarly, Bonzo Madrid insists on exaggerating his Spanish heritage by following a "macho" code that isolates his one female soldier and permits no shows of weakness. Ender turns this against him when Bonzo brings a gang to confront him in the shower, using Bonzo's pride to make him face him alone.

While others are not so public about their backgrounds, they still play an important role in their lives. Dink Meeker, for instance, is from the Netherlands, a country which has been under Russian control for several generations. As a result, he worries over a potential civil war involving the I.F., which is largely run by American allies. When Ender is promoted from the Launchies, his friend Alai shares a kiss and a whispered "Salaam." Ender senses these are part of a "suppressed religion," and thus the gesture becomes "a gift so sacred that even Ender could not be allowed to understand what it meant." Even Ender's own background plays a factor in the novel, as Graff uses it to convince him to come to Battle School. Ender's father was a Polish Catholic and his mother was a Mormon; they both had to renounce their religion in order to comply with the Population laws. They are secretly proud of having a Third, but are still ashamed of not being able to follow their beliefs more openly. All these details form an ironic commentary on race, religion, and other differences in background, suggesting that no matter how great the need to cooperate together, humanity will still find differences to separate themselves from each other.

Style

Narration/Point of View

Card believes that a breakthrough occurred for him when he discovered that fiction allows the writer to reveal a character's thoughts, whereas play writing does not. Card tells *Ender's Game* primarily from a third-person ("he/she") point of view, where the narrator can describe scenes involving different characters. Nevertheless, the story most often uses a "limited" point of view, focusing solely on Ender's character. This is useful in creating a greater identification with his character. At times, the narrative very easily slips into a first-person viewpoint by dropping into Ender's thoughts. For example, when Ender first arrives at the Battle School, there is a scene where he is eating with an older boy. The scene begins in the third-person narrative, then switches to reveal Ender's thoughts. "Ender shut up and ate. He didn't like Mick. And he knew there was no chance he would end up like that. Maybe that was what the teachers were planning, but Ender didn't intend to fit in with their plans. I will not be the bugger of my group, Ender thought. I didn't leave Valentine and Mother and Father to come here just to be iced."

Setting

Setting is vitally important in the genre of science fiction—not just because it might involve the future or another galaxy, but because it usually involves great social changes. *Ender's Game* begins on Earth sometime in the future. There are several social changes that are important to Ender's story: the Population laws that restrict the number of children in a family; the technological developments that permit space travel; and, of course, the existence of an alien civilization which has attempted to conquer Earth. These changes form the social setting for Ender's story.

The physical settings spring from these changes as well. Although the story starts on Earth, it continues on space stations both inside and out of Earth's solar system. When the International Fleet comes for Ender, they take him via space shuttle to the Battle School, located in the Asteroid Belt. Next, Ender attends Command School on the planetoid Eros. Eros is a spindle-shaped planet with a smooth surface that absorbs sunlight and converts it to energy; the gravity is one-half that of Earth's. The planetoid was originally developed into a space station by the Buggers during one of their invasions. The final physical setting that has significance is on the bugger planet that Ender and Valentine have helped to colonize. There, Ender finds a landscape that resembles the dead giant from his computer fantasy game. This resemblance leads him to discover the queen egg that will communicate the history of her people to humanity.

Structure

The structure of *Ender's Game* is fairly straightforward, relating events in a fairly linear fashion. Although told in third person, most of these events are portrayed from Ender's perspective so that the reader does not know more than he does. An interesting complement to Ender's story is the conversations between Colonel Graff and his associates that preface each chapter. These conversations provide additional perspective, providing more information to the reader than can be found from Ender's limited point of view. The chapters on Valentine and Peter's efforts bring additional background to the eventual conclusion, involving the adult Ender's new career as a Speaker for the Dead. Some critics, however, have faulted the structure of the novel, in particular the rapid finale. Michael Lassell even goes so far as to say in his *Los Angeles Times Book Review* that Card "has not mastered structure. His tale is too expansive and detailed throughout—too fascinated by his own hardware—but foreshortened in its conclusion."

Climax

The climax of a novel is the point at which the major conflict is resolved. *Ender's Game* has a particularly dramatic turning point, as Ender not only wins his final "battle" in Command School, but learns that it is actually the victorious conclusion of the Third Invasion. Up until this point Ender, like the reader, believes that he has been playing yet another battle game. While some critics have faulted this climax as a "trick," others find it a logical resolution to the ethical dilemma of the novel. All throughout, Ender has questioned whether his nature is good or evil; his empathy most likely would not have permitted him to annihilate an entire species. Only by remaining ignorant can he perform the task that has been set before him. In revealing the truth at the moment of victory, *Ender's Game* addresses both the physical and moral conflicts of the story at the same time.

Dialogue

Card feels that his ability to write believable dialogue, developed during his years as a playwright, is another skill that strengthens his writing. Not only does the dialogue allow Card to take different points of view, but it creates tension in scenes and provides the reader with a strong sense of character. For example, in the scene where Ender first meets Bonzo, Bonzo's vicious nature emerges through his speech. The dialogue between Ender and Bonzo sets the stage for their impending battle. Petra's contributions to the conversation establish her character and also add to the tension between Ender and Bonzo.

Historical Context

The Cold War in the 1980s

Ender's Game takes place in Earth's future, one in which all countries are cooperating together to save the planet from alien invasion. Nevertheless, the novel does suggest that the international conflicts of the twentieth century will not be forgotten, as an American hegemony (a group of nations dominated by one) will be pitted against a Second Warsaw Pact, led by the Russians. In this world, Russia rules Eurasia from the Netherlands to Pakistan. Peter believes that Russia is preparing for a "fundamental shift in world order." Once the bugger wars are over, the North American alliances will dissolve, and Russia will take over. This conflict may have seemed inevitable in the early and mid-1980s, when the novel was written. Since the end of World War II, the United States and the Soviet Union had engaged in a "cold war" which involved military buildups but no direct military confrontations. Almost forty years later, this conflict showed few signs of being resolved peacefully.

The two sides of the cold war were led by the democratic United States and the communist Soviet Union. The Warsaw Pact, signed in 1955, established an alliance among the Soviet Union, Albania, Bulgaria, Czechoslovakia, East Germany, Hungary, Poland, and Romania. It served to defend the group against any potential military or economic threats from the West. It also strengthened the Soviet Union's hold over its Eastern European satellites and prevented them from making close ties with the West. On the other side was the North Atlantic Treaty Organization (NATO), which bound Western Europe and the United States together in defense against the communists. From the end of World War II, both the Americans and the Soviets increased their nuclear arsenals, each trying to prevent the other from gaining a military advantage.

The tenseness of the 1950s and 1960s had given way in the 1970s to a limited "detente," or lessening of friction between the two sides. By the 1980s, however, the Cold War began heating up once again. The Soviet Union had invaded neighboring Afghanistan in 1979, leading to increased U.S. fears of spreading communism. Ronald Reagan was elected president in 1980 on a platform that included promises of a tougher stance against the Soviets. Reagan referred to the Soviet Union as an "evil empire," and his administration planned for 1.2 trillion dollars in new military spending. The government also proposed a "Strategic Defense Initiative," commonly called "Star Wars," a space-based defensive system that would intercept incoming nuclear missiles. These actions were in contrast to public reassurances from the Americans that they wanted to procede with arms reduction treaties, so the Soviets remained nervous of American intentions. It was not until after Soviet leader Mikhail Gorbachev came to power in 1985 that ten-

sions eased between the two nations. The Warsaw Pact was dissolved, along with the Soviet Union itself, in 1991.

Science and Technology in the 1980s

One of the most startling technological revolutions of the 1980s was the growth of the personal computer. While large mainframe computers had been in use for many years, they were mainly limited to large research facilities. Advances in design made computers smaller and more affordable, and computers became available to a broad spectrum of businesses and individuals. Apple Computer introduced the Apple II, a system designed for home use, in 1977, while IBM countered with the PC (personal computer) in 1981. "Computer literacy"—a familiarity with how computers worked—became a coveted skill among workers, and schools began offering classes in programming. In 1980 there were only 100,000 computers in schools throughout the United States; by 1987, that number had increased to more than two million. In addition, the internet of the 1980s was just a loosely organized system that helped academics and researchers send messages to each other; it was only in the mid-1990s that it became a powerful media available to any home with a computer and a modem. The use of computer games, simulations, school programs, and "nets" in *Ender's Game* reflects the growing influence that computers were coming to have in the 1980s.

A technological revolution was also happening on the biological frontier during the 1980s. Technical advances in the 1970s had led researchers to better understand how an organism's DNA (deoxyribonucleic acid) influences its development. In the 1980s, scientists began applying that knowledge to manipulate the genetic makeup of organisms to create new and improved strains of plants and animals. While this "genetic engineering" led to more productive, disease-resistant crops, people worried about its possible application to humans. The world's first "test-tube baby"—a baby conceived outside its mother's womb—had been born in 1978, and the first U.S. clinic opened two years later. If people could now use science to aid conception, critics wondered, might they not also use it to create babies with "designer genes"? Moral issues surrounding the birth of children also figure in *Ender's Game,* as Ender's character seems to be a deliberate combination of his two older siblings, ordered by the government to produce the military genius they need.

Religion in the 1980s

The 1980s saw people searching for ways to re-establish traditions in their homes and lives. The 1960s and 1970s had been a time of experimentation and free-style living, and church attendance declined as people began exploring spirituality outside the bounds of organized religion. In the 1980s, however, many individuals wanted a return to a simpler existence, one in which there were fewer surprises. They wanted to be able to believe in something that was never-changing, something dependable around which to structure their lives. Religious conservatives, who became prominent in the 1980s, offered one route toward accomplishing that goal. Increase in fundamentalist faiths increased in the 1980s: a Gallup poll in 1986 showed thirty-one percent of respondents classified themselves as evangelical or "born-again" Christians. This increase was reflected in a growing conservative Christian political movement, which sought to bring moral issues more into the political mainstream. For many people, however, religion became more of a personal expression, and this was reflected in the growth of the "New Age" movement. Interestingly enough, the world of *Ender's Game* is a world where one's religion has become a matter for embarrassment or even persecution. Both of Ender's parents have had to renounce their faith in order to conform; Alai's whispered "Salaam" similarly seems something outlawed. Ironically, however, this persecution seems to have made their faith even more precious to the characters.

The background of Card's own faith, Mormonism, includes its own bouts of persecution. The Church of Jesus Christ of Latter-Day Saints was founded in New York in 1830 by Joseph Smith, who published the divine revelations he claimed to have received in *The Book of Mormon*. The most controversial of Smith's precepts was the practice of polygamy, and Smith and his followers were driven out of communities in New York, Ohio, Illinois, and Missouri. A large Mormon settlement was established in Utah in 1847 by Smith's successor, Brigham Young, but they continued to be feared and mistrusted by outsiders, including the federal government. The Edmunds-Tucker Act of 1887 dissolved the Mormon Church as a corporate entity, and their leaders had to renounce polygamy before Utah could gain its statehood in 1896. Since then, the Mormon Church has increased ties with more mainstream faiths and has grown considerably; by the end of the 1980s, membership within the church had risen to over seven million members. Nevertheless, Mormons still sometimes suffer prejudice from outsiders who stereotype them or misunderstand their beliefs. Understanding this background can provide an interesting insight into the way religion is portrayed in *Ender's Game*.

Critical Overview

Ender's Game presents the age-old science-fiction conflict of human against alien. While the plot is time-worn, many critics have observed that Card's storytelling ability, as well as the story's details and characterization, are vivid enough to maintain the reader's interest. Reviewer Roland Green, for example, stated in *Booklist* that *Ender's Game* is "a seamless story of compelling power." Card's peers and fans concurred, as the novel won both the Nebula (given by science fiction writers) and Hugo (given by science fiction readers) Awards.

Card originally wrote *Ender's Game* as a short story that he submitted to the leading science fiction magazine, *Analog,* after having had one story rejected by the publication. Not only did the editor like *Ender's Game* enough to publish it, others took notice. The short-story version won for Card the World Science Fiction Convention's John W. Campbell Award for best new writer in 1977. Encouraged by his success, Card continued to write and to further develop his skills. He began working on the novel *Speaker for the Dead* and realized that the main character should be Ender Wiggin from *Ender's Game*. This inspiration led to Card's writing the full version of the short story *Ender's Game*. When Tor Books published *Ender's Game* as a full-length novel in 1985, reviewers especially applauded Card's compelling portrayal of Ender as an innocent child being manipulated by controlling adults. A *Kirkus Reviews* critic noted that "long passages focusing on Ender are nearly always enthralling—the details are handled with flair and assurance."

Card depicts Ender as an "abused" child in the sense that adults use him for their own purpose— to save the world for the good of mankind. This manipulation, and the resulting sympathy readers feel for Ender, underlie the "compelling power" about which reviewer Green spoke. Readers can identify with Ender throughout the story, even though he eventually annihilates an entire species of beings. Ender is very much the typical kid— loving and hating his siblings, playing video games, and missing his family when he is separated from them. Yet he possesses a genius and mature assuredness that makes him a target for abuse by peer-group bullies and adults who are in control. Readers feel compelled to side with Ender because he is a child, and because they understand and relate to the problems Ender encounters as a child who is different. In the *New York Times Book Review*, Gerald Jonas noted the complexity of Ender's character, stating that "alternately likable and insufferable, he is a convincing little Napoleon in short pants." Tom Easton, in a review in *Analog Science Fiction*, agreed that Ender is believable if readers withhold their skepticism and remember that "the kid's a genius."

Other critics, however, offer more negative viewpoints. While admirers praised Card's characterization skills and his storytelling ability, his most severe critics denounced his use of violence and standard science-fiction elements. In a segment of *Los Angeles Times Book Review*, Michael Lassell stated bluntly, "Orson Scott Card is not a great writer, nor does *Ender's Game* break any new ground." In particular, the critic faulted the climax of *Ender's Game* as "a trick (on the reader as well as on Ender) for which there is no adequate preparation." Other reviewers have criticized Card's use of violence. Elaine Radford, for instance, views Ender as another brute of history; in her *Fantasy Review* article, she likened his character to that of Adolf Hitler. She asserted that Ender "goes Hitler one better" because he not only kills an entire race, he also robs them of their heritage. Other reviewers, however, have recognized that *Ender's Game* does not advocate or apologize for violence, but rather explores the moral issues surrounding its use. *Analog's* Easton observed that by stressing Ender's empathy, Card saves the novel from becoming a story about a truly ruthless villain. The violence is seen as "evil for the sake of good.... [Card] goes to great pains to shield Ender's childish innocence from truth, to keep us from calling him one more brute of history."

Other reviewers have taken issue with the believability of Ender's character. Some critics felt that although he is gifted, young Ender is still not credible as a child. Lassell noted that while "likeable," the novel's protagonist "is utterly unbelievable as a child his age, genius or no." In contrast, many young readers who have written to Card have applauded him for his realism. Card says in the Introduction to *Ender's Game:* "They didn't love Ender, or pity Ender (a frequent adult response); they *were* Ender, all of them. Ender's experience was not foreign or strange to them; in their minds, En-

der's life echoed their own lives. The truth of the story was not truth in general, but *their* truth." Calling the work "the best novel I've read in a long time," Dan K. Moran echoed this assessment in the *West Coast Review of Books:* "Ender Wiggin is a unique creation. Orson Scott Card has created a character who deserves to be remembered with the likes of Huckleberry Finn. *Ender's Game* is *that* good."

Criticism

David J. Kelly

David J. Kelly is a an English instructor at several colleges in Illinois, as well as a novelist and playwright. In the following essay, he examines why referring to characters as "children" does not necessarily make them well-rendered child characters.

There can be no question that Orson Scott Card's novel *Ender's Game* is a graceful and useful piece of fiction, with a convincing sense of time and place that only comes from a writer in complete control of his or her material. To certain fans, *Ender's Game* is one novel brave enough to really look at children without making them childish. They are relieved that somebody finally got it right, and they praise Card for his unflinching honesty about the cunning and cruelty, the wisdom and humanity, of children. But is it really about children? They are called kids, but they don't act or talk like kids. Card seems to take pride in this, considering it an innovation, as if the only alternative would be having the cadets in the Battle School play marbles and talk baby talk. I suspect that the children in *Ender's Game* are written as adults and then called kids—like stunt doubles in the movies, fresh-faced, diminutive adults playing the parts of kids, snubbing out their cigars to go out and lick lollipops before the cameras.

Let there be no mistake: I don't object to his characters because I foolishly think they are not any more vicious than kids are in real life, or could be. I can tell the difference between childhood innocence and sweetness, and the first does not necessary lead to the second. In the book, the nastiness that Peter, Stilson, and Bonzo show toward Ender is unprovoked, but it still makes sense as their characters are drawn. It makes sense that children become defensive and cliquish when their place in the world is uncertain. Insecurity is unavoidable in new

What Do I Read Next?

- Card's *Speaker for the Dead,* published by Tor Books in 1986, follows *Ender's Game* as its sequel. Ender, still dealing with evil and empathy, tries to find a suitable home for the surviving eggs from the queen of the species he destroyed while trying to prevent the extermination of another intelligent race. This novel also won the Nebula and Hugo Awards.

- Tor Books published *Xenocide,* the third novel in Card's Ender series, in 1991. Ender works to save his adopted world from a deadly virus.

- The final novel in Card's Ender series, *Children of the Mind,* finds Ender taking a minor role. Published by Tor Books in 1996, the story revolves around a mission to stop a deadly virus from destroying Earth. Two beings built from Ender's consciousness and memory, named after his brother and sister, play the lead characters.

- Card demonstrates his use of symbolism and allegory in his "Tales of Alvin Maker" series, a fantasy series set in a magical America. The first novel in the series, *Seventh Son* (1987), tells the story of the seventh son of a seventh son, who possesses the potential to be the defender of evil through his magical powers. This first novel of the series deals with the issue of religion in America.

- Further volumes in Card's "Tales of Alvin Maker" series include: *Red Prophet* (1988), which novel focuses on the treatment of Indians; *Prentice Alvin* (1989), which deals with is-

sues of black slavery; *Alvin Journeyman* (1995), in which Alvin returns to his birthplace to face a girl's accusations of improprieties; and *Heartfire* (1998), which again delves into the issues of ignorance and racism.

- Isaac Asimov's *Foundation* (1951) is the first novel in the first Foundation trilogy—which includes *Foundation and Empire* and *Second Foundation.* This story takes place in a Galactic Empire where Earth is all but forgotten. The administrative planet is on the verge of a complete breakdown. Only one person sees the problem and is willing to confront it.

- One of Card's inspirations, Bruce Catton's *Mr. Lincoln's Army* (1962; "Army of the Potomac Trilogy," Vol. 1) chronicles the early years of the Civil War and the struggle between the Armies of Virginia and the Potomac. The Army of the Potomac undergoes a hard-earned transformation from a group of novices to an army of pros.

- Frank Herbert's complex science-fiction classic *Dune* (1965) deals with a young man who becomes the leader of a desert people because they believe he fulfills their prophecy of a messiah.

- *The Child Buyer* (1960), by Pulitzer Prize-winner John Hersey, concerns a stranger from a corporation who comes to a small American town and proposes to buy a child genius from his family, so that he can be cultivated for intellectual work.

---

situations, and in childhood everything is a new situation—maturity is just a matter of recognizing repeating patterns, and without comforting recognition, all these kids have to protect themselves with is violence. Stilson and Bonzo, in particular, lash out for reasons that they themselves would probably not recognize, in response to their insecurity. I accept this as a depiction of children and their behavior, as much as I don't like it.

Ender's response to the other boys' bullying is more intelligent and calculating, as everything Ender does is, and Card uses it to show another aspect of childhood, the struggle between intellect and fear. Ender kills Stilson and Bonzo without realizing that he has done it—in all other things, his behavior is precise and he gets the results he intends, but in physical struggles he lashes out with a fear-driven response that is beyond his control, a cyclone so violent that he does not even see the results and only suspects them. Fear pushing intellect into the back seat is a reasonable characterization of childhood.

Peter's continual sadism is more serious than the other hostilities in the novel because it is intentional, not spontaneous. He may feel threatened by the success of his younger brother, as is implied in the early chapters, but then why is he torturing animals years after Ender has left the Earth? And what does that have to do with the statesman he becomes? The message is either that Peter somehow outgrew the sadist he was, only to later fake it so that Valentine would aid him, or that he was faking all along. Or else we are to believe that Peter is psychotic from start to finish. As much as sadistic children remind us of power-mad adults, it is almost impossible that a child, even one with the intellect Peter is supposed to have, would have the emotional control to fake, correct, or mask his psychosis this thoroughly. The character seems patterned on such evil geniuses as Hitler and Ted Bundy, but never does he show a hint of a child's mental formation. He is fully grown from the start—an adult.

All of the children in Ender's family are more intelligent than children commonly are. That is the premise of the novel, and it is as much Card's right to explore it, as it is the right of any sci-fi writer to stretch the bounds of the known world, free of the bystanders who would complain, "But that's not the way things are."

Ender comes from a long-standing tradition of inquiry about what would happen if intellect could somehow exist separately from the psychological baggage that comes from growing up in society. From the works of Jean-Jacques Rousseau, whose novel *Emile* first gave serious consideration to child psychology, to Barry Rudd, the child genius who a corporation bids on in John Hersey's 1960 novel *The Child Buyer* (which makes a splendid companion piece to *Ender's Game*), writers have watched the struggle between genius and personality. The military system Ender is placed in encourages only his intellect, and he has to fight the system for room to develop his personality.

In the embarrassing Demosthenes/Locke plot line, on the other hand, everything comes easily to the genius children: Peter sets his mind on world domination, Valentine agrees to aid him, and, by golly, a few years later the world is in his control. Again, no distinction is made between a child's insatiable ego and the evil genius's power-hunger, crossed this time with a dated speculation that the anonymity of the internet would allow propaganda from any illegitimate source to dominate. The only thing separating Peter and Valentine from adulthood here is the fact that the world can see that they are children and therefore discriminates against them for it. Card plasters over the holes in his character development by designating these particular children as super-geniuses.

In the book's Definitive Introduction, added for the 1991 edition, Card defends his treatment of child characters. He describes a letter from a guidance counselor who worked with gifted children, a label definitely appropriate for Ender and his kin. According to Card, she "loathed" the book (probably his word, not hers: later in the Introduction his critics are said to have "*really* hated" his book and to consider it "despicable"). He writes, "It was important to her, and to others, to believe that children don't actually think or speak the way the children in *Ender's Game* think and speak." To him, the guidance counselor's training and experience count as nothing: he seems to believe that her judgment is based on some hidden motive, a defense of tradition or a fear that her career will be unmasked as hollow. His response to her, he says, would be this: "The only reason you don't think gifted children talk this way is because they know better than to talk this way in front of *you*." It is not clear why children "know better," what punishment he fears a guidance counselor might bring down on the head of a particularly sophisticated child. It is unlikely that Card thinks *all* gifted children have plans for world domination, although that would give them good reason to hide their talents. Using this defense of his characters, Card brings the paranoia from his science fiction novel into the real world.

At its root, Card's problem with handling children as characters is not an inability to see how they think and behave differently than adults, but, worse, a refusal to admit that they do. He holds to a self-sufficient posture, trusting only his own observations and the conclusions that he reached from them. "[N]ever in my entire childhood did I feel like a child," he says in an extended defense against the skeptical guidance counselor. "I never felt that I spoke childishly. I never felt that my emotions and desires were somehow less real than adult emotions and desires." He seems to have taken his defense against writing in baby talk a few yards too far. Card's refusal to compromise his principles is admirable, but what kind of compromise is he actually resisting? Does he really believe that there is an outcry to see children's experiences as "less real" than adults'? If this actually were the case—if guidance counselors and psychologists and writers were all part of a vast conspiracy to belittle the young people they spend their lives studying—then Card would be as heroic as the posture he takes. More likely, it just looks like a conspiracy to him because he doesn't see his memories of childhood reflected in print. Could it be that his memory is lacking? I myself do not remember thinking childish thoughts while developing an adult personality, but if the people who study such things can give me a good explanation for it, I'm willing to listen. I have never seen my colon or liver, either, but that doesn't mean I would scoff at anyone who tries to tell me how they work.

"If everybody came to agree that stories should be told this clearly," Card says of his own work in the Introduction, "the professors of literature would be out of a job, and the writers of obscure, encoded fiction would be, not honored, but pitied for their impenetrability." Is he saying that obscurity itself is bad? Who is the judge? Am I allowed to dismiss his writing as pitiable and obscure if I don't know the word "impenetrability"? His problem with other writers mirrors his problem with the entire field of child psychology. In both cases, Card seems to feel that people who see things that he doesn't are fools, conspirators, or con artists. A good healthy dose of skepticism about established beliefs is necessary—it's what pushes human thought ahead—but Card shouldn't let the popularity of his book blind him to the fact that its characterizations may be flawed. It's true, there are a lot of bad writers who have the idea that the way to create children in fiction is to just write stupid adults, but one does not correct this simply by portraying children as smart adults. James Joyce, J. D. Salinger, and Roald Dahl are among the hundreds who have written about children, giving them the specific concerns of children without making them talk or behave like idiots. But maybe Card would judge these artists "too obscure." Maybe there is something to be said for complexity when trying to understand a complex world.

Source: David J. Kelly, in an essay for *Novels for Students*, Gale, 1999.

Tim Blackmore

In the following excerpt, Blackmore discusses the military paradigm in which Ender must operate to survive.

Ender lives in a military paradigm which assumes humans are malleable, controllable objects.

Control resides in large institutions, not individuals or parochial units. The military paradigm abides by a strict utilitarian philosophy in which ends overcome any and all means; human costs are unimportant. Within the paradigm is an accepted paradox that the individual must be sacrificed in order to maintain the rights of other individuals. Because it accepts its own built-in flaws, the military paradigm is extremely robust. Graff lectures Ender: "The Earth is deep, and right to the heart it's alive, Ender. We people only live on the top, like the bugs that live on the scum of the still water near the shore." Graff's aerial view distances him from the unpleasant decisions he must make if the war is to be won. There is no room for doubt that all wars, or contests, must be won—especially when these "bugs" cling so tenaciously to life (the word "bugs" is loaded with meaning; Card uses it to refer both to humans and "buggers"). Graff is proud of, rather than ashamed of, the power that allows the military to "requisition" Ender. At the core of the military paradigm is a mechanistic view of humans, who are to be shaped to the purposes of the machine. Anderson expresses the utilitarian military code tersely: "All right. We're saving the world, after all. Take him"; he picks up Ender as one might choose a tool from a tool kit.

Much of the paradigm's invulnerability comes from the fact that the characters are aware of their roles in the machine. The reader feels sympathy for them because they have thought through their beliefs; they don't blindly follow a creed. Yet their humane qualities—emotion and heart—never interfere with their decision to sacrifice anything necessary to keep the mechanism functioning. Graff directs us to practicalities—"We're trying to save the world, not heal the wounded heart"—and provokes a further exchange:

"General Levy has no pity for anyone. All the videos say so. But don't hurt this boy."

"Are you joking?"

"I mean, don't hurt him more than you have to."

In a utilitarian world a plea to leave Ender untouched is not only irrelevant, it is potentially treasonous. Physical and psychological pain are necessary if Ender is to be deformed for the machine's uses. The amount of pain indicates the degree of injustice the individual meets at the hands of the system; and in Ender's case, both the pain and injustice are severe. The military is purposefully structured to be unjust, breaking those who cannot rise above injustice fast enough. Those who survive the injustices will become commanders—they will be given the power to inflict pain. The children in the Battle Room raise "a tumult of complaint that it wasn't fair how Bernard and Alai had shot them all when they weren't ready." The military world has no patience for those who demand fairness; Graff notes bluntly, "Fairness is a wonderful attribute, Major Anderson. It has nothing to do with war."

Card prevents the reader from making quick judgements about Graff and Anderson. At first the two men seem dangerously smug about their roles ("We promise gingerbread, but we eat the little bastards alive.") The utilitarian *seems* to forget he is dealing with humans, cold-bloodedly informing Ender that "maybe you're not going to work out for us, and maybe you are. Maybe you'll break down under pressure, maybe it'll ruin your life, maybe you'll hate me for coming here to your house today." Graff's ability to speak such truths impresses Ender, who otherwise would not be lured away. Graff's honesty is not a sham; in private he notes ominously that "this time if we lose there won't be any criticism of us at all." Accustomed to serving the machine, Graff and Anderson slide unhesitatingly into the worst Machiavellian tactics to achieve their goals. Petra warns Ender to "remember this.... They never tell you any more truth than they have to," a fact all the children promptly forget. Graff and Anderson, the two Machiavels, prepare to trap Ender:

> "So what are you going to do?"
>
> "Persuade him that he wants to come with us more than he wants to stay with her."
>
> "How will you do that?"
>
> "I'll lie to him."
>
> "And if that doesn't work?"
>
> "Then I'll tell him the truth. We're allowed to do that in emergencies. We can't plan for everything, you know."

There is gleeful madness in this speech; the two most "practical" characters are quick to accept the interchangeability of lies and truth. It is impossible, apparently, to detect Graff's and Anderson's true feelings. The latter notes grimly, "Sometimes I think you enjoy breaking these little geniuses," recognizing that Graff, like Anderson, has a favorite game. Anderson's concern—"what kind of man would heal a broken child ... just so he could throw him back into battle again"—maintains our faith in the two commanders. Card forces the reader to move between two viewpoints: that of the suspicious, manipulated child and that of the paranoid, utilitarian machine worker.

The phrase "the good of the whole" sanctions military atrocities. Ender's relationship with Valentine is like one of "billions of ... connections between human beings. That's what [he's] fighting to keep alive." The reader is one such unit, for the audience may be forced to approve of—even as it dislikes—Graff. Each individual must surrender the self completely. The post of officer, or supreme commander, does not make Ender an individual; it simply gives him a higher function in the machine. Graff has made peace with the possibility that "we might both do despicable things, Ender," because "if humankind survives, then we were good tools." Ender begins to realize the magnitude of his sacrifice, asking, "Is that all? Just tools?" And he elicits the utilitarian answer from Graff, "Individual human beings are all tools, that the others use to help us all survive." Here is the paradox of one stripped of his individuality in order to protect the ideal of individuality.

Games, game theory, and simulation are an integral part of the mechanistic Machiavellian world; surprises or spontaneity are dangerous because they are organic. Graff notes brusquely, "as for toys—there's only one game." The supremacy of the game and the Battle Room is total; those who believe in endless rehearsal refuse to draw the line between simulation and reality for the child-warriors. The principal danger of game theory is that reality becomes blurred, making human costs appear inconsequential. Anderson is angry that Graff has played one of his games "betting [Anderson's] life on it." It comes as an unwelcome—and ironic—shock for a gamer to discover that he too is on the playing board.

The military paradigm consisting of a utilitarian stance, belief in the good of the whole, subordination of the individual, and simulation of reality takes great pleasure in its rituals and makes a religion out of war. It is extremely dangerous that "status, identity, purpose, name; all that makes these children who they are comes out of this game." The children have become ciphers. It follows that if the ritual of the game is not upheld, the identities of whole groups may be erased. Particularly striking is Card's revision of Golding's *Lord of the Flies*. Bonzo accepts Ender into his army and begins a ritual war chant:

> "We are still—"
>
> "Salamander!" cried the soldiers in one voice ...

"We are the fire that will consume them, belly and bowel, head and heart, many flames of us, but one fire."

"Salamander!" they cried again.

"Even this one will not weaken us."

The ritual call-and-response nature of this chorus is an example of the unity Anderson strives to instill in all his recruits: alone they are flames, but together they are a fire that overwhelms others. The philosophy may be rooted in the past, but the military is firmly webbed to the future—specifically technology. The military sees technology as a mystical force allowing basic laws of nature to be revoked, such as gravity and time. It also relies on machines to explore human minds. Ender charges the two commanders, "You're the ones with the computer games that play with people's minds. You tell *me*." Dink is simultaneously correct and incorrect when he claims that "the Battle Room doesn't create *anything*. It just destroys." The Battle Room destroys individuality while it creates a unitary killing machine.

Of the tools the military paradigm uses to manipulate individuals, isolation is the most powerful. Ender must be prevented from being "at home" or able to "adopt the system we have here," because as soon as Ender finds a surrogate family the military will lose their leverage on him. Isolation makes dependence on others impossible; Ender is forced to fall back on and develop his own resources. Graff argues defensively that "isolation is—the optimum environment for creativity. It was *his* ideas we wanted, not the—never mind." Graff cuts off the admission that isolation may well bring madness and alienation, not creativity. Ender sees the machine at work and knows instinctively that "this wasn't the way the show was supposed to go. Graff was supposed to pick on him, not set him up.... They were supposed to be against each other at first, so they could become friends later." Neither Ender nor Graff realizes that isolation will, simultaneously, ostracize Ender from the human race and create an unbreakable bond with an alien one. Graff panics when Ender's isolation excludes the commanders and the military. Upset with Major Imbu, Graff notes that there is nothing in the manuals "about the End of the World. We don't have any experience with it." Card's irony underlines just how much the military is fixated on simulation. Here is one scenario they cannot countenance, nor can they go to Ender and display their ignorance. Panic turns to anger as Graff barks, "I don't want Ender being comfortable with the end of the world." Graff's comment indicates how much he has underestimated Ender.

Truth and trust are also useful tools. Graff uses Machiavellian means to further utilitarian ends. Ender consistently swallows Graff's lies regarding Stilson and Bonzo. Doubt nags at Ender because he has equated trust and friendship with the fact that the Colonel "didn't lie." Graff answers, "I won't lie to you now, either.... My job isn't to be friends. My job is to produce the best soldiers in the world." What Graff never fully explains are the enormous personal costs Ender faces. Graff understands the risk of being able "to decide the fate of Ender Wiggin," but the utilitarian in him triumphs as he lashes out at Major Anderson: "Of course I mind [the interference], you meddlesome ass. This is something to be decided by people who know what they're doing, not these frightened politicians." Military belief in specialization and expertise overrides Anderson's concerns. The military organizes the pieces of events it needs to provide useful truths. Ender has internalized the commander's law: no soldier can rise above the others because "it spoils the symmetry. You must get him in line, break him down, isolate him, beat him until he gets in line with everyone else."

In the service of manipulation of the individual, the military abolishes parents. Friends can only provide *part* of the reassurance a parent offers the child. Dink sees pieces of truth: "The game is everything. Win win win. It amounts to nothing." The military has declared what is and is not to be important in these children's lives. Dink notes caustically, "*They* decided I was right for the program, but nobody ever asked if the program was right for me." Parental authority is replaced by dependence on the self; Ender "must believe that no matter what happens, no adult will ever, ever step in to help him in any way. He must believe, to the core of his soul, that he can only do what he and the other children work out for themselves."

Manipulation of truth continues when the military takes charge of the media. Free speech is an acceptable concept, as long as the true bastions of power are not attacked. Ender cannot figure out why, if "students in the Battle School had much to learn from Mazer Rackham ... [everything] was concealed from view." Due to military caginess (or vanity), the truth—that nobody understands Rackham's victory, except perhaps Rackham himself—does not come out until it is almost too late. Ender feels the full impact of media handling when he receives Valentine's letter but must force himself to discount it: "Even if she wrote it in her own blood, it isn't the real thing because they made her write it. She'd written before, and they didn't let any of those letters through. Those might have been real, but this was asked for, this was part of their manipulation." The manipulation of Valentine by the military teaches Ender more than Dink can ever tell him about their "skills" with communication. Ender notes succinctly, "So the whole war is because we can't talk to each other." This exchange between Ender and Graff recalls one of the most striking scenes in Joe Haldeman's *The Forever War:* "The 1143-year-long war had begun on false pretenses and only continued because the two races were unable to communicate. Once they could talk, the first question was 'Why did you start this thing?' and the answer was 'Me?'" Both Card and Haldeman stress that energy would be better spent on communication than on war games. The military *appears* to be using force out of desperation, just as Ender does when fighting Stilson and Bonzo, but it may simply prefer the role of aggressor. Even if the latter is the correct motive, it is cloaked by the former.

The military regularly pawns off horrible responsibilities to generals in the front line. For example, when Ender asks whether the Molecular Detachment Device (M.D. Device, a.k.a. the Little Doctor) works on a planet and "Mazer's face [goes] rigid. 'Ender, the buggers never attacked a civilian population in either invasion. You decide whether it would be wise to adopt a strategy that would invite reprisals.'" Like those who flew the *Enola Gay*, Ender becomes much more than an accomplice to the military's most unconscionable acts. There is no hypocrisy from the military; Graff and Rackham believe Ender had saved them all. Typically, Mazer Rackham pushes both victory and genocide on Ender: "You made the hard choice, boy. All or nothing." In Haldeman's *The Forever War*, Potter and Mandella sum up the feeling of being abandoned by the military:

"It's so dirty."

I shrugged. "It's so army."

The military paradigm withstands severe attacks without fracturing. The pressure forces Graff to comment sourly that his "eagerness to sacrifice little children in order to save mankind is wearing thin." The incredible speed with which Ender becomes a commander leads Bean to guess that "the system is breaking up. No doubt about it. Either somebody at the top is going crazy, or something's gone wrong with the war, the real war, the bugger war." None of these pressures divert Graff, Anderson, or Rackham from their course. With victory, the paradigm snaps back into shape. Graff recounts that after Ender's "rights" had been explained "it was simple. The exigencies of war" explain everything. If anything, there is increased faith in game theory—the system *has* worked. Anderson notes wistfully, "Now that the wars are over, it's time to play games again." The military would rather not handle shades of grey. The Major notes, "It's too deep for me, Graff. Give me the game. Nice neat rules. Referees. Beginnings and ending. Winners and losers and then everybody goes home to their wives." During the lifetime of Ender's tyrant brother Peter, the military paradigm continues to exist. Only later, when Ender has grown in power, does he provide an answer in the form of a religious paradigm which is constructed around the concept of the Speaker for the Dead. The Speaker is a figure who gives an account of an individual's ethical role in life and society. Before he can achieve that stage, Ender's own paradigm must be tested and purified. It is ironic that the military's most successful creation will also bring the eventual downfall of the paradigm.

Source: Tim Blackmore, "Ender's Beginning: Battling the Military in Orson Scott Card's *Ender's Game,*" in Extrapolation, Vol. 32, No. 2, Summer, 1991, pp. 125–140.

Tim Blackmore

This excerpt explores Ender's role as a reluctant warrior who "fights in order to prevent further battles."

Card endows each of the three Wiggin children with a particular strength: Peter is a conqueror, another Alexander; Valentine is an empath; and Ender is a warrior who hates fighting but must win.

Given this trinity it is not hard to separate the three and then join them into one. Ender functions as a cross between the head and the heart, with Peter as the head and Valentine as the heart.... As Ender absorbs each of these he eventually becomes the wise old man. Even further afield is the possibility that the three form a religious Trinity. Rather than push any of these readings on the characters, attempting to make them into one, the author accepts the fact that Card saw fit to write three separate characters, where each listens to, and learns from, the others. It seems wiser and more useful, in terms of opening the text, to consider them as three discrete individuals, each representing a separate paradigm.

Ender's pacifism separates him from the other soldiers, the military, and his society. His apparently fatalistic attitude toward beating others is remarkably similar to what Eastern philosophy would call *Bushido*, or the Way of the Warrior (Samurai). Ender represents an elite, powerful warrior class which is at heart pacific but often fights in order to prevent further battles. Ender is a triple outcast. On Earth he is an "outcaste," wanting "to scream at [his father], I know I'm a Third. I know it." Ender is a *persona non grata* who "has no rights"; and at the Battle School his excellence and isolation ensure his outcast status. For a long time even Ender rejects himself: "[Ender] didn't like Peter's kind, the strong against the weak, and he didn't like his own kind either, the smart against the stupid." Balancing his alien status is Ender's possession of something unique for a soldier, a name. After a victory he thinks, "[I] may be short, but they know [my] name." Mick, a fellow student, notices the implications right away: "Not a bad name. Ender. Finisher. Hey." Finishing things is Ender's way of attempting to gain peace: "Knocking him down won the first fight. I wanted to win all the next ones, too, right then, so they'd leave me alone." He wins not for the sake of winning, but so he needn't "fight every day [until] it... gets worse and worse." Anderson comes to the realization that "Ender Wiggin isn't a killer. He just wins—thoroughly." Ender admits ashamedly, "I didn't fight with honor...I fought to win." For Ender finishing *is* winning. Learning to rely only on "his own head and hands," Ender embodies the archetype of the individual who maintains his identity in the face of a hostile society and environment.

Card uses the Battle Room as a metaphor for life. Winning does not mean peace; it simply means one is allowed to play again. Ender catches on late that what he plays are no longer games; "It stopped being a game when they threw away the rules." The events in and outside the Battle Room are "sometimes games, sometimes—not games." Ender has been aged by the constant threat of annihilation: he must be able to end each game, otherwise his life is worthless. He notes desperately that losing is "'the worst that could happen. I can't lose *any*.... Because if I lose *any*'—He didn't explain himself." Ender is more strategist than aggressor. While the children are "all wondering if [Stilson] was dead.... [Ender] was trying to figure out a way to forestall vengeance." Discussing similar strategy, Yamamoto comments, "In the 'Notes on Martial Laws' it is written that: The phrase, 'Win first, fight later,' can be summed up in the two words 'Win beforehand.'"

Ender's perpetual attempts to co-opt the system, to "use the system, and even excel," are symptomatic of his lifelong obsession with preparedness. In order to work free of the commanders' power, Ender must prepare more than he ever has. Obedience is not a Manichean issue, as Dink suggests it is. Ender is vulnerable, as the military knows, to pressure exerted on Valentine. In his Earth school he's left alone because "he always knew the answer, even when [the teacher] thought he wasn't paying attention." Preparation and risk-taking give Ender an ability to adapt to and master any given situation. The result is that he never makes the same mistake twice. Faced by the challenging Battle Room, he plunges in: "Better get started." But even here he is prepared. During the shuttle flight to Battle School, Ender has observed that "Gravity could go any which way. However [he] want[s] it to go." All things are a prelude to battle: "If one makes a distinction between public places and one's sleeping quarters, or between being on the battlefield and on the *tatami*, when the moment comes there will not be time for making amends. There is only the matter of constant awareness. If it were not for men who demonstrate valor on the *tatami*, one could not find them on the battlefield either" [observes Tsunetomo Yamamoto in *Hagakure: The Book of the Samurai*]. Ender scrutinizes his environment, noticing on the shuttle "how Graff and the other officers were watching them. Analyzing. Everything we do means something, Ender realized. Them laughing. Me not laughing." Ender's mind automatically produces strategic analyses. Traded from Salamander, "Ender listed things in his mind as he undressed.... The enemy's gate is down. Use my legs as a shield.... And soldiers can sometimes make decisions that are smarter than the orders they've been given." Such dispassionate analysis gives Ender the necessary information he needs to win his coming battles. The more he understands how he works, the more he sees that emotions, particularly anger, interfere with decision making. Ender instructs his class, "If you ever want to make your enemy crazy, shout that kind of stuff at them. It makes them do dumb things.... But *we* don't get mad." Ender's ability to calculate probabilities makes him appear as canny as the adults around him. They treat him so well he wonders, "How important am I.... And like a whisper of Peter's voice inside his mind, he heard the question, How can I use this?"

Part of the warrior's way is to *use,* not *be* used. Valentine's letter makes him lose hope because "he had no control over his own life. They ran everything. They made all the choices." Despite his wish to deny his human fragility, Ender eventually incorporates his flaws, reassuring himself that "although he had never sought power, he had always had it. But he decided that it was power born of excellence, not manipulation." He accepts that he has power over others, just as others have power over him; however, he can control a great deal of power. Ender "could see Bonzo's anger growing hot. Ender's anger was cold, and he could use it. Bonzo's anger was hot, and so it used him." Ender cannot afford to lose control once. He uses a meditation trick to distract himself, and when he returns to his thoughts "the pain was gone. The tears were gone. He would not cry." Things that affect him after this make "him sorrowful, but Ender did not weep. He was done with that," and using his anger "he decided he was strong enough to defeat them [all]." Ender relinquishes his trust in adults, learning to show them "the lying face he presented to Mother and Father." Ender's isolation goes beyond anything Graff could have dreamed of. Confronted by Petra's plea for forgiveness ("Sometimes we make mistakes"), it is the warrior in Ender who answers coldly, "And sometimes we don't." Meditation, cold anger, hidden emotion, lack of forgiveness, and utter solitude are superb defenses against a deadly world as well as trademarks of a blind form of Puritanism. The Puritan vein in Ender explains why and how he manages to live without love, loyalty, and companionship. Through the bars of his cell, Ender sees that "they knew about everything and to them Val was just one more tool to use to control him, just one more trick to play." The biggest mistake he can make is to show emotion and reveal a desire. As a commander, Ender does not fool himself that his soldiers are loyal to him; they are in awe of him, revere him, but he won't (perhaps with the exception of Bean) allow them to be loyal to him. Love and loyalty are vulnerabilities that neither the Samurai nor the Puritan warrior can afford.

Nor can the warrior conceive of spontaneous acts of affection. When Graff touches Ender's hand, Ender decides "Graff was creating a commander out of a little boy. No doubt Unit 17 in the course of studies included an affectionate gesture from the teacher." Similarly, he cannot trust Valentine's childish affection any longer. Loyalty is replaced by obedience; Ender notes calmly in the face of his peers' disbelief, "I obey orders." When his army "attempt[s] to start a chant of Dragon, Dragon," Ender puts a stop to it. Tribal rituals suggest tribal loyalty, and Ender knows that he may face any member of his army in the Battle Room one day. Loyalty, like all emotion, clouds strategy and preparedness; but obedience does not.

It is also necessary that the warrior cultivate empathy, particularly the ability to empathize with the enemy. Peter notes proleptically, "They meant you to be human, little Third, but you're really a bugger." [Michael R.] Collings notes [in his article "The Rational and Revelatory in the Science Fiction of Orson Scott Card," *Sunstone,* May, 1987] that "Ender cannot become fully human" because "he is constantly manipulated by others." Ender points out to Valentine, the empath, that "every time, I've won because I could understand the way my enemy thought. From what they *did....* I'm very good at that. Understanding how other people think." Empathy allows Ender to exchange his worldview for the enemy's, see the internal vulnerabilities, and attack in precisely the right spot.

The final and most important part of the warrior's paradigm is the complete acceptance of death. Learning to fight each battle as if it were the last, the warrior must face "lots of deaths.... That was OK, games were like that, you died a lot until you got the hang of it." And in getting "the hang of it," the individual becomes accustomed to dying (not an unfamiliar theme for Card). Death means a release from the battles of life and is, therefore, much desired by Ender. The combination of readiness and relaxation prepares Ender's troops to "win beforehand." They are relaxed because they are ready to die. As Yamamoto states: "There is something to be learned from a rainstorm. When meeting with a sudden shower, you try not to get wet and run quickly along the road. But doing such things as passing under the eaves of houses, you still get wet. When you are resolved from the beginning, you will not be perplexed, though you still get the same soaking. This understanding extends to everything." Stoicism and resolution of this nature are crucial to the Puritan warrior who is self-sufficient; he is not a fighter, but he wins battles when and where he must; he is not a joiner, but he is ready to lead; he is not anxious, but he is always prepared; most of all, he hates power, but he is supremely capable of handling it. Such self-reliance gives the warrior the strength to deny love and loyalty, understand the enemy, and accept death unhesitatingly. The rugged individualist who lives his own life and relies on his neighbors to do the same is caught in a terrible vice when his community demands his help.

Source: Tim Blackmore, "Ender's Beginning: Battling the Military in Orson Scott Card's *Ender's Game*," in Extrapolation, Vol. 32, No. 2, Summer, 1991, pp. 125–140.

Sources

Orson Scott Card, Introduction to *Ender's Game,* Tor Books, 1991.

Michael Collings, review of *Speaker for the Dead, Fantasy Review,* April, 1986, p. 20.

Tom Easton, review of *Ender's Game,* in *Analog Science Fiction/Science Fact,* Vol. CV, No. 7, July, 1985, pp. 180-81.

Review of *Ender's Game,* in *Kirkus Reviews,* Vol. LII, No. 21, November 1, 1984, p. 1021.

Roland Green, review of *Ender's Game,* in *Booklist,* Vol. 81, No. 7, December 1, 1984, p. 458.

Gerald Jonas, review of *Ender's Game,* in *New York Times Book Review,* June 16, 1985, p. 18.

Dan K. Moran, review of *Ender's Game,* in *West Coast Review of Books,* Vol. 12, No. 2, July/August, 1986, p. 20.

Michael Lassell, "A Youngster Saves the Planet," in *Los Angeles Times Book Review,* February 3, 1985, p. 11.

Elaine Radford, "Ender and Hitler: Sympathy for the Superman," in *Fantasy Review,* Vol. 10, No. 5, June, 1987, pp. 11-12, 48-9.

For Further Study

Orson Scott Card, "Rebuttal," *Fantasy Review,* Volume 10, No. 5, June, 1987, pp. 13-14, 49-52.

In this response to Radford's negative assessment of *Ender's Game,* Card takes issue with the critic's comparison of Ender with Hitler. He suggests the critic

has misinterpreted the novel by overlooking the complex way in which it addresses issues of empathy and violence.

Orson Scott Card, *Characters and Viewpoint,* Writers Digest Books, 1988.

Taking a general approach to writing instruction, Card details the creation, introduction, and development of characters in long and short fiction, and explains the various points of view available to the fiction writer.

Orson Scott Card, *How to Write Science Fiction and Fantasy,* Writers Digest Books, 1990.

Card provides the aspiring science-fiction writer with tips on creatively devising other worlds, peoples, and magical occurrences.

Orson Scott Card, "Hatrack River: The Official Website of Orson Scott Card," http://www.hatrack.com.

This website contains a wealth of material on Card and his work. It includes an area for student research as well as a question-and-answer section on writing with the author himself.

Contemporary Literary Criticism, Vol. 44, Gale, 1987.

This entry collects criticism focusing on *Ender's Game.*

Graceanne A. and Keith R. A. Decandido, "PW Interviews: Orson Scott Card," *Publishers Weekly,* November 30, 1990, pp. 54-55.

An interview with the author in which he discusses the belief system behind his work, his explorations of moral issues, and his use of violence.

Janrae Frank, "War of the Worlds," *Washington Post Book World,* February 23, 1986, p. 10.

This author questions the religious imagery at the climax of *Ender's Game* and its sequel, *Speaker For the Dead,* and she wonders whether this recurring motif might be a sign of some personal conflict.

Jean-Jacques Rousseau, *Emile,* Dutton, 1974.

Originally published in 1762, this work is credited with being one of the first to explore how a child's mind differs from that of an adult. The author is one of the world's great social philosophers, whose ideas directly influenced the Declaration of Independence.

Ethan Frome

Edith Wharton
1911

Critics have called *Ethan Frome* the most carefully constructed of Edith Wharton's novels, and have praised the economy of its language and its intensity. The novel is a naturalistic—that is, unsentimental—portrait of emotional frigidity set in the New England winter. Young Mattie Silver arrives in the mountain village of Starkfield to help with housekeeping for her cousin Zeena, the sickly, cantankerous wife of Ethan Frome. Ethan, who has long been resigned to the care of his ailing wife and farm, is drawn to Mattie's youthful beauty and good humor. When Zeena realizes their mutual attraction, she arranges to engage a less attractive companion and to have Mattie sent away. Unable to bear the idea of parting, the lovers attempt to kill themselves by sledding into a tree. The attempt is a failure, and it leaves Mattie and Ethan crippled for life and condemned to Zeena's care. Early reviewers praised Wharton's style but were dismayed by the novel's bleakness and the inability of her characters to find a way out of their situation. Later critics were even harsher in their evaluations, citing numerous inconsistencies and debating whether Ethan Frome himself is truly tragic or simply morally inert. All the same, this study in frustration, loneliness, and moral responsibility became a popular favorite, somewhat to the surprise of its author, and is frequently taught at the high school and college level.

Author Biography

Edith Wharton was born January 24, 1862, to a wealthy New York family. She showed an interest in writing and literature from an early age. Despite the attempts of her family to discourage her, Edith regularly wrote poems and short stories, some of which were published in magazines such as *Scribner's* and *Harper's*. Walter Berry, a family friend, encouraged her ambitions and would remain her lifelong confidante. Although she recognized that the culture of New York's established gentry was anemic and repressive, Edith was just as repulsed by the philistinism of the newly rich who replaced it. She preferred traveling with her parents to Europe, where she met Henry James, who became her mentor and critic. In 1885 Edith married a Boston banker named Edward Wharton. Although her parents approved the choice, Edward was ten years older than Edith was, and physically and emotionally fragile. Edith's aversion to society life and her disappointment over her marriage drove her to devote more time to her writing.

Wharton's first book, which discussed house decor, was published in 1897 and launched her career as a writer. From 1902 until the end of her life, Wharton would publish a book a year. *The House of Mirth,* the story of a girl who cannot reconcile her position in society with moral respect, appeared in 1905 and became a best seller. *Ethan Frome,* the most often read of Wharton's novels, was published in 1911.

The years from 1905 to 1913 were tumultuous ones for Wharton. Edward's diagnosis as a manic-depressive and his increasing instability led to the couple's divorce in 1913. In 1907 Wharton began a deeply satisfying three-year love affair with Morton Fullerton, a friend of Henry James. Although she would maintain an estate in Lenox, Massachusetts, after 1913 Wharton made Europe her permanent home. During and after the First World War she worked tirelessly to raise funds for a variety of causes in France and Belgium. She wrote several novels based on these experiences, but they are not considered among her best. Wharton's literary triumph was *The Age of Innocence* (1921), which won her a Pulitzer Prize.

Wharton is known especially as a novelist of manners, but she also composed poetry, criticism, short stories, and travel pieces. Her themes include the corrupting power of wealth, social pressure among the poor, and the essential rightness of moral action. Her work was sometimes lost in the

Edith Wharton

shadow of that of Henry James, and her later writing never matched the quality of her earlier efforts. Some critics objected to her negative portrayals of men. But the complex psychology of her characters and her keen satiric sense are unparalleled in American literature. In 1921 Wharton became the first woman to receive an honorary degree from Yale. She died of a heart attack on August 11, 1937, in St. Brice-sous-Fort, France.

Plot Summary

Ethan Frome is the story of a man who, following the death of his father, gives up his education and other opportunities to return to the family farm in Starkfield, Massachusetts, to support his ailing mother. When his mother dies, Ethan, overcome by loneliness, impulsively marries Zeena Pierce, an older cousin who helped nurse his dying mother. Within a year of their marriage, Zeena becomes ill and Ethan must again assume the role of caregiver and give up his dreams of moving to a large town and becoming an engineer. Ethan's outlook changes, however, when Zeena's cousin, Mattie Silver, comes to live with them as Zeena's aid. She shares Ethan's sense of wonder and sensitivity to the appeal of natural beauty. Mattie is everything that Zeena is not. She restores Ethan's ability to imagine happiness and, before long, a mutual but unexpressed passion develops.

The story is told by an unnamed narrator who is sent to Starkfield on business. He first meets Ethan in the town's post office and, finding the fifty-two-year-old "ruin of a man" the "most striking figure in Starkfield," becomes fascinated by his life story. He learns from a local resident that Ethan has looked this way ever since his "smash-up" twenty-four years ago. Bit by bit, the narrator hears fragments of Ethan's story and constructs a narrative based on the paradoxical accounts of his life. His task is facilitated when, one stormy winter night, he is given a rare invitation to spend the night at Frome's farm. It is there, after hearing a woman's voice drone querulously as he approached the house, that the narrator claims to have found the "clue to Ethan Frome." The chapters that follow constitute the narrator's "vision" of the story.

This "vision" goes back twenty-four years to the days leading up to Ethan's smash-up and begins on the night of a church dance. Ethan, arrived to accompany Mattie back to the farm, waits outside while the musicians play a final tune. As they are walking home Mattie mentions that, earlier in the evening, some of her friends had gone coasting down the hill behind the church. Ethan asks if she too would like to go coasting and proposes that they go tomorrow if there is a moon. Their path leads them by the Frome gravestones, a place that, in the past, has made Ethan feel as though his restlessness and desire to get away were being mocked. But, on this night, he is filled with a "sense of continuance and stability" and finds pleasure in the thought that Mattie will one day be lying there beside him.

When they arrive home, Ethan discovers that the kitchen door is locked. He and Mattie are trying to account for this unprecedented occurrence when Zeena suddenly opens the door and says: "I just felt so mean I couldn't sleep." Although Zeena has never shown any signs of jealousy, there have, of late, been disquieting "signs of her disfavour." As a result, this incident, combined with complaints about Mattie's inefficiency as a housekeeper and suggestions that a hired girl may become necessary, instill in Ethan a "vague dread." This dread is relieved, however, when Zeena announces the next morning that she is going to stay with her Aunt to see a new doctor. The news convinces Ethan that the previous night's explanation was merely a sign that Zeena is absorbed in her own health and that

his "vague apprehensions" of troubles with his wife are unfounded.

To mark their first-ever evening alone together, Mattie prepares a special dinner and wears a ribbon in her hair as a "tribute to the unusual." Although the mood of the evening is threatened when Zeena's beloved pickle dish—a never-used wedding gift—is accidentally broken, the cozy after-dinner scene by the stove produces in Ethan the "illusion of long-established intimacy." Without knowing what he is doing, Ethan stoops and kisses the end of the "stuff [Mattie is] hemming." In response, Mattie gets up, puts away her work and retires to her room.

When Zeena returns the next day, she informs Ethan that she is a great deal sicker than he thinks and that she has hired a girl to take care of her. Ethan objects on financial grounds but Zeena, explaining that they will no longer need to worry about Mattie's board, effectively tells him that her cousin will be leaving tomorrow. A few moments later, Ethan is alone with Mattie in the kitchen. Sensing that something is wrong, Mattie melts against him in terror and asks him what it is. Instead of answering, Ethan kisses her and cries out: "You can't go, Matt! I'll never let you!" It is on this night that Zeena discovers the broken pieces of her pickle dish and accuses Mattie of taking from her the thing she cared for most of all.

That night, alone in his private study, Ethan recalls the case of a man who escaped from a similar life of misery by going West with the girl he loved. Believing for a moment that he and Mattie could do the same, he begins to write a letter to Zeena. However, economic realities thwart his plans and oblige him to concede that he is a "prisoner for life." Rebellious passions resurface the following morning, but again his plan is aborted when he realizes he would have to deceive someone.

When the time of Mattie's departure finally arrives, Ethan delays their separation by bringing her to Shadow Pond, the location of a church picnic they attended together. They reminisce about the event and Ethan imagines that he is a "free man, wooing the girl he meant to marry." He begins to tell Mattie that he would do anything, would even go away with her if he could, when Mattie pulls out the letter he had started to write the night before and forgot to destroy. She reveals that she too has dreamed of going away with him but Ethan still feels unable to prevent their separation.

As they approach the church, they are reminded that they were to have gone sledding the night before. Ethan finds a sled and, finally, the two get to enjoy their long-awaited coast. On their way back up the hill, Mattie flings her arms around Ethan's neck and kisses him. Then, in despair over their lack of options, she leads Ethan back to the sled and instructs him to steer them directly into the big elm at the bottom of the hill so they will "never have to leave each other any more." Tragically, Mattie's plan proves imperfect: while it does prevent the lovers' separation, both Ethan and Mattie survive the crash and are left lying in the snow, crippled and in pain.

The novel ends with the resumption of the narrator's account of his overnight stay at Frome's farm. As he enters the kitchen, the "querulous drone" stops and he is unable to determine which of the two old women before him had been the speaker. One of the women gets up to prepare Ethan's meal while the other, whose hair is just as gray and whose face just as bloodless and shriveled as her companion's, remains seated and limp by the stove. Ethan introduces the first woman as his wife, and the other as Miss Mattie Silver. Upon hearing their voices, the narrator concludes that it was Mattie's voice he heard as he approached the house. He learns the next day that Zeena has been caring for Mattie and Ethan ever since the accident twenty-four years ago.

Characters

Dennis Eady

The son of Michael Eady, an ambitious Irish grocer. Dennis has a reputation for applying the same techniques his father used so successfully in business in pursuit of the young women of Starkfiled.

Ethan Frome

Ethan Frome is twenty-eight years old and physically impressive at the time the events in the novel take place. A series of family crises put a premature end to his engineering studies and force him into agriculture, for which he has no inclination, and now he must also care for Zeena, his cranky, hypochondriacal wife of seven years. Ethan's brief studies made him "aware of the huge cloudy meanings behind the daily face of things," and because he is "by nature grave and inarticulate," he is "warmed to the marrow by friendly human intercourse." He cannot expect this from Zeena, who basically stopped speaking a year into their marriage. So when Mattie Silver comes to live

Media Adaptations

- A dramatization of *Ethan Frome* by Owen and Donald Davis was produced in New York in 1936.

- A 1993 screen version directed by John Madden starred Liam Neeson as Ethan, Joan Allen as Zeena, and Patricia Arquette as Mattie. It was coproduced by American Playhouse, Companion Productions, and BBC Films and released by Miramax.

- Richard Krausnick adapted and directed the novel as a full-length stage play for Shakespeare and Company, who first performed it in 1995 in Lenox, Massachusetts, where Wharton had a home.

- An unabridged audio recording read by C. M. Herbert is available from Blackstone Audiobooks.

with the Fromes as a companion to Zeena, Ethan takes to her immediately. "Always … more sensitive than the people about him to the appeal of natural beauty," Ethan delights in showing Mattie the stars in the sky and rock formations, and in accompanying her to and from her social outings. He is "never gay but in her presence." His generosity is evident in his taking time from his own chores to cover for her inadequate housekeeping by creeping down late on Saturday nights to scrub the kitchen floor.

Though he has longed despairingly for years for change and freedom, his sole desire now is to have things remain the way they are, with Mattie near him. In fact, as Kenneth Bernard wrote, "Throughout the book, Frome recognizes his futility and accepts it rather than trying to fight his way out of it." An example of this kind of acceptance is Ethan's penchant for daydreaming about Mattie. When Zeena's overnight trip to the doctor leaves Ethan and Mattie alone for an evening, instead of trying to touch her, he "set his imagination adrift on the fiction that they had always spent their

Liam Neeson and Patricia Arquette in Ethan Frome.

evenings thus and would always go on doing so." The next morning, he is "glad ... that he had done nothing to trouble the sweetness of the picture." Although Ethan's first reaction to Zeena's sudden decision to send Mattie away is that he is "too young, too strong, too full of the sap of living, to submit so easily to the destruction of his hopes," he cannot bring himself to lie to the Hales to get the money he would need to run away with Mattie. Many critics see Ethan as a weak and negative person. At the end of the novel, it is Mattie who suggests the suicide pact. Blake Nevius maintains that Wharton intended "to invest her rather unpromising human material with a tragic dignity," but ac-

cording to Bernard "his character never changes. Both before and after the accident he is the same." "No hero of fantastic legend," wrote *The Nation* on publication of the novel, "was ever more literally hag-ridden than was Ethan Frome."

Zeena Frome

See Zenobia Frome

Zenobia Frome

Zenobia (Zeena) is Ethan Frome's unhappy, malady-plagued wife. She is thirty-five at the time the events of the novel take place, and "already an old woman." Her hair is gray, her clothing is described as "slatternly," and she makes a "familiar gesture of adjusting her false teeth" before eating. Zeena first came to the Frome farmhouse to help Ethan nurse his ailing, deranged mother, and he was "shamed and dazzled" by her efficiency. The couple's plan on marrying was to sell the farm and sawmill and to move to a large town. But although Zeena had no desire to live on an isolated farm, neither could she tolerate the loss of identity that moving to the sort of city Ethan had in mind would mean. Within a year of the marriage she turned peevish and sickly, then silent, just like his mother. Her sole pleasure, as Ethan sees it, is to make him miserable.

It is Zeena who suggests that her cousin Mattie Silver come to live with them as her aid. But once the attraction between Ethan and Mattie becomes apparent, Zeena begins to find fault with the girl. Zeena is hard to figure, in fact; she appears hardly human. As Mrs. Ned Hale remarks, no one knows her thoughts. To Ethan, her silence seems "deliberately assumed to conceal far-reaching intentions, mysterious conclusions drawn from suspicions and resentments impossible to guess." Indeed, Zeena arranges both Mattie's departure and her replacement without consulting Ethan. The only emotional outburst Zeena gives into happens when she discovers the broken pickle dish and breaks into sobs. But once she has prevailed in her decision to be rid of Mattie, she reverts to her self-absorption. When Ethan comes into the house to take Mattie to the station, he finds Zeena with her head wrapped in her shawl, "reading a book called 'Kidney Troubles and Their Cure.'" After the accident, Zeena has both Ethan and Mattie brought back to the farm. In what many critics cite as a supreme irony of the story, Zeena ends up having to take care of her rival.

Harmon Gow

The narrator of the story calls Harmon Gow the "village oracle." He drove the stage from Bettsbridge to Starkfield in pre-trolley days, and knows the history of all the families along his route. It is from Gow that the narrator first begins to piece together the enigma of Ethan Frome.

Andrew Hale

Andrew is a builder, Ned Hale's father, and an old friend of Ethan's family. To avoid having to drive Zeena to the Flats, Ethan pleads that he has to collect cash for lumber from Hale. The lie forces him to go to see Hale and ask for an advance, which "the builder refused genially, as he did everything

else." In a desperate attempt to procure money so he can run away with Mattie, Ethan considers approaching Hale a second time. But he cannot bring himself to deceive Hale and his wife, "two kindly people who had pitied him."

Mrs. Ned Hale

Ruth is Andrew Hale's daughter-in-law. She is a middle-aged widow with whom the narrator stays while he is in Starkfield. Twenty-four years earlier, she had been a friend of Mattie Silver's, and Mattie was to have been her bridesmaid. Like Harmon Gow, Mrs. Ned Hale helps the narrator to piece together the story. Normally voluble, on the subject of Ethan Frome the narrator finds her "unexpectedly reticent." However, she is a kindly soul who looks in on the Frome household twice a year, "when Ethan's off somewhere. It's bad enough to see the two women sitting there—but *his* face, when he looks round that bare place, just kills me."

Narrator

The entire story of *Ethan Frome* is told from the point of view of an unnamed narrator. Sent to the area in connection with an engineering project at Corbury Junction, he is obliged to stay most of the winter in Starkfield on account of unexpected delays. When he encounters Ethan Frome at the post office, he is so intrigued by this "ruin of man" that he begins to ask around and eventually "[has] the story, bit by bit, from various people." The narrator feels sympathy for Ethan, and tends to think of him in heroic terms, as when he is driving in the buggy with him and sees Ethan's "brown seamed profile, under the helmet-like peak of the cap, relieved against the banks of snow like the bronze image of a hero." An indication of the extent of the narrator's fantasizing is that when Harmon Gow remarks that "Most of the smart ones get away," the narrator wonders how "any combination of obstacles [could] have hindered the flight of a man like Ethan Frome." But a single winter in the mountains is sufficient for the narrator to begin to imagine what "life there—or rather its negation—must have been in Ethan Frome's young manhood." And when a blizzard forces the narrator to take shelter at Ethan's farmhouse for the night, he finds "the clue to Ethan Frome, and [begins] to put together this vision of the story." The narrator's use of the word "vision" here is significant. According to critic Cynthia Griffin Wolff, "the 'story' of Ethan Frome is nothing more than a dream vision.... The overriding question becomes then—not who is Ethan Frome, but who in the world is this ghastly guide to whom we must submit as we read the tale."

Some critics make the point that in this kind of storytelling, there is inevitably a confusion of sensibilities. Indeed, Wolff perceives the questions the narrator asks the locals about Ethan Frome "projections of his own morbid imagination." His romanticism, most evident in his associating Mattie with delicate things in nature such as field mice and small birds, and Zeena with predators such as cats and owls, lessen the credibility of his account. Ultimately, wrote Allen F. Stein, it is possible to conclude that *Ethan Frome* "is irresolvably ambiguous."

Jotham Powell

The Fromes's hired man.

Mattie Silver

Mattie Silver is a beautiful young relative of Zeena Frome's who is sent to provide help for Zeena after her father dies, leaving her penniless. She is ill-prepared to seek economic independence, and in the past, attempts at stenography and bookkeeping threatened her health. As the story opens, Mattie has been with the Fromes for a year. When Ethan first goes to meet her, he thinks, "She don't look much on housework, but she ain't a fretter, anyhow." Mattie is "quick to learn, but forgetful and dreamy," and her friendship with Ethan evolves from their shared laughter at her initial efforts. Mattie's sweetness is contrasted with Zeena's sourness, and her strength with Ethan's helplessness. For example, the first time Ethan proposes that they go sledding and asks her whether she would be afraid, Mattie responds, "I told you I ain't the kind to be afraid." When Zeena confronts Ethan and Mattie with the broken pickle dish, and Ethan tries to cover for her, Mattie says, "It wasn't Ethan's fault, Zeena! The cat *did* break the dish; but I got it down from the china-closet, and I'm the one to blame for its getting broken." Mattie is self-possessed as Ethan takes her to the train to leave Starkfield, although she has no idea where she is going. "You mustn't think but what I'll do all right," she comforts him. The suicide attempt is Mattie's idea, and when Ethan changes places with her on the sled at the last minute "because I want to feel you holding me," she agrees. Critics cite as one of several ironies in the novel the fact that after the accident, Mattie turns as querulous as Zeena.

Ruth Varnum

See Mrs. Ned Hale

Themes

Frustration

The theme of frustration is central to *Ethan Frome*. Sometimes the frustration is a product of the oppressive environment, and sometimes it stems from their personalities. Ethan's early plans to become an engineer are frustrated by the need to care for his father and mother as well as for the farm. He had always wanted to "live in towns, where there were lectures and big libraries and 'fellows doing things.'" His marriage to Zeena is a study in frustration, not only because of her hypochondria and the fact that they are childless, but because their interests are so different. "Other possibilities had been in him, possibilities sacrificed, one by one, to Zeena's narrow-mindedness and ignorance. And what good had come of it?"

Mattie, in turn, is limited by her poverty and lack of skills. Even Zeena is frustrated. As the narrator of the story tells it, "She had let her husband see from the first that life on an isolated farm was not what she had expected when she married." But though Zeena is contemptuous of Starkfield, she would never have been able to live in a new town that looked down on her, and as a result the couple never moves. The theme of frustration is reinforced by the inarticulateness of all of the characters in *Ethan Frome*. None of these people are very good at expressing themselves. In fact, Wharton referred to the characters in the novel as her "granite outcroppings." Walking Mattie back to the farm, deliriously happy in her company, Ethan gropes for a "dazzling phrase" to impress her with, but can only growl "Come along." Frustration is evident also in Ethan and Mattie's longing for each other. Their physical contact is passionate but mostly limited to furtive handholding. When Ethan surprises Ned Hale and Ruth Varnum kissing under the Varnum spruces, he feels "a pang at the thought that these two need not hide their happiness."

Individual Responsibility

Related to the theme of frustration is that of individual responsibility, insofar as it is Ethan's sense of duty that chains him to his circumstances. Critic Blake Nevius defined the "great question posed by Ethan Frome" as "What is the extent of one's moral obligation to those individuals who, legally or within the framework of manners, conventions, taboos, apparently have the strictest claim on one's loyalty?" Responsibility interrupts Ethan's studies and brings him home to the farm to care for his parents, and self-sacrifice characterizes his marriage to Zeena, whose "one pleasure … was to inflict pain on him." Toward the end of the novel, it is duty that prevents Ethan from asking the Hales for money so he can run away with Mattie. The reality, he tells himself, is that he is a poor man, "the husband of a sickly woman, whom his desertion would leave alone and destitute." Critics have disputed whether Ethan's choices constitute moral decisions, that is, decisions that are guided by moral principles, as opposed to need or expedience. Lionel Trilling wrote, "Choice is incompatible with [Ethan's] idea of his existence; he can only elect to die," whereas according to K. R. Shrinivasa Iyengar, "It would be an oversimplification to say that the chief characters in Ethan Frome are only moved by blind necessity." Marius Bewley saw Ethan's decision to die with Mattie as a clear moral decision that "entails tragic consequences because it is the *wrong* decision."

Loneliness

The theme of loneliness pervades the novel. At the outset, the narrator remarks of Ethan Frome, "I simply felt that he lived in a depth of moral isolation too remote for casual access, and I had the sense that his loneliness was not merely the result of his personal plight, tragic as I guessed that to be, but had in it, as Harmon Gow had hinted, the profound accumulated cold of many Starkfield winters." Ethan's home is "one of those lonely New England farm-houses that make the landscape lonelier." After the coming of the railroad, local traffic diminished, a change Ethan's mother was never able to comprehend. "It preyed on her right along till she died," he tells the narrator. As Ethan's mother's dementia increases, she grows so silent that Ethan begs her to "say something." And in fact, it is Ethan's dread of being left alone on the farm after his mother's death that drives him to marry Zeena. When Mattie first comes to stay with the Fromes, Zeena encourages her to find diversion because "it was thought best … not to let her feel too sharp a contrast between the life she had left and the isolation of a Starkfield farm."

Style

Point of View

Critics hail *Ethan Frome* as the most carefully constructed of Wharton's novels. The story relates events that occurred twenty-four years previously within a narrative frame of the present, similar to

Topics for Further Study

- Explore the various options young people have today for getting an education and making their own way in the world, and explain how the lives of the characters in *Ethan Frome* might have been different if these options had been open to them.

- Investigate the trend to urbanization of the 1920s and explain how it would have affected towns like Starkfield.

- How has the worldwide lumber industry changed since the late 19th century, and is there any role in it for small operators like Ethan Frome?

- Research the technology available to today's amateur astronomers for exploring the night sky, and describe the kinds of things Ethan would have been able to show Mattie if he had had access to that same technology.

Emily Brönte's *Wuthering Heights*. Of the story-within-a-story structure, the *Nation* wrote in 1911, "Such an approach could not be improved." A single, unnamed narrator tells the entire tale. Wharton frankly acknowledged that she borrowed the technique of the narrator as omniscient author from Honoré de Balzac's *La Grande Bretche*. The pieces of the story the narrator is able to glean from the inhabitants of Starkfield are presented within this narrative frame. Critics emphasize that the story the reader reads is at best the narrator's vision of events. As biographer Cynthia Wolff writes, "Everything that the reader can accept as reliably true can be found in the narrative frame; everything else bears the imprint of the narrator's own interpretation." The difficulty inherent in a complex structure of this sort is that it makes the story ambiguous. As Allen F. Stein maintains: "One cannot be sure that the real Ethan Frome ever felt anything akin to what the narrator attributes to him or did the things he did for the reasons the narrator either consciously or inadvertently offers."

Imagery

A universally acclaimed strength of the novel is Wharton's use of imagery and symbolism. According to critic Kenneth Bernard, these elements, particularly the compatibility of setting and character, reveal the novel's "true dimensions." Like the frozen landscape around him, Ethan is cold and unapproachable. The narrator observes that Ethan "seemed a part of the mute melancholy landscape, an incarnation of its frozen woe, with all that was warm and sentient in him fast bound below the surface." There are many references to darkness, and darkness is Ethan's element. For example, when he goes to fetch Mattie from a dance, he hangs back in the shadows, watching her through a window. Later, he wishes he could "stand there with her all night in the blackness." When they return to the farmhouse, the windows are dark, and they strain to see each other "through the icy darkness." On the night of the accident, Mattie confesses to Ethan that she first dreamed of going away with him at a picnic they both attended at Shadow Pond. Images of warmth and brightness in the novel are associated with Mattie, and are contrasted with Ethan's frozen self and Zeena's soullessness. Even her name, Mattie Silver, connotes something bright. Her "fresh lips and cheeks" and "slim young throat" are contrasted with Zeena's "gaunt countenance," "puckered throat," and "flat breast."

Mattie is also associated with images of birds. Wharton makes repeated references to voices. At first, in comparison to his mother's silence, Zeena's gregarious nature was music in Ethan's ears. But her voice has become a "flat whine," unlike Mattie's "sweet treble," though at the end of the novel Mattie's voice, too, becomes a querulous drone. Even the kitchen reflects the contrasts between the two women. It is a "poor place, not 'spruce' and shining as his mother had kept it in his boyhood; but it was surprising what a homelike look the mere fact of Zeena's absence gave it." Images of death are evident in the "black wraith of a deciduous creeper flagged on the porch," the missing "L" in Ethan's farmhouse, and a "dead cucumber-vine" dangling from the porch.

Symbolism

Critic R. Baird Shuman writes that "there is probably no more pervasive single element in *Ethan Frome* than the symbolism." The landscape and farmhouse are closely related to elements of the story's action. For example, the missing "L" in Ethan's farmhouse gives the house a "forlorn and stunted" aspect and symbolizes the lack of life within. An obvious symbol is the name of the town, Starkfield, which Shuman calls "a cemetery for those who are still physically living."

Many critics point to the sexual symbols in the novel. "Barrenness, infertility, is at the heart of Frome's frozen woe," asserts dramatist and critic Kenneth Bernard. The red pickle dish, for instance, unbroken and unused, symbolizes the Fromes's marriage. Once it is broken, it represents Mattie and Ethan's disloyalty. Shuman notes the "Freudian overtones of the shutterless windows and of the dead cucumber-vine." And biographer Cynthia Griffin Wolff refers to Frome and the narrator entering the kitchen through a small, dark back hallway at the end of the novel as "a perverse and grotesque inversion of the terms of birth." The elm tree is seen as both plant and symbol. Shuman frankly sees it as a phallic symbol, "a representation of sexual temptation." The sled Mattie and Ethan are riding when they collide into the elm is borrowed, one that, like their passion, "technically they have no right to."

Setting

The setting for *Ethan Frome* is the fictional town of Starkfield, located in the mountains of western Massachusetts. In the words of Edith Wharton: "Insanity, incest and slow mental and moral starvation were hidden away behind the paintless wooden housefronts of the long village street, or in the isolated farm-houses on the neighbouring hills." The cold and snow in particular had a wearying effect on the inhabitants. One of the first things the narrator hears about Ethan Frome is a remark made by Harmon Gow: "Guess he's been in Starkfield too many winters." The narrator at first fails to understand the burden of winter in these parts. When the snows of December are followed by "crystal clearness," he notices the "vitality of the climate and the deadness of the community." But once he has passed a winter there, and has "seen this phase of crystal clearness followed by long stretches of sunless cold; when the storms of February had pitched their white tents about the devoted village and the wild cavalry of March winds had charged down to their support; I began to understand why Starkfield emerged from its six months' siege like a starved garrison capitulating without quarter."

The Frome farm itself is "kinder side-tracked." Traffic that used to pass by ceased once the railroad was carried through to an area beyond called Corbury Flats, a distance of three miles that took an hour by horse and carriage. The Frome farmhouse is a building of "plaintive ugliness." The building has lost its "L," a deep-roofed section that normally connects the main house with the wood-shed and cow barn, enabling the inhabitants to avoid having to go outside to get to their work. So integral is the setting to the action of the novel, that a review published in the *Nation* in 1911 credited Wharton with having chronicled "a consciousness of depleted resources, a reticence and self-contained endurance that even the houses know how to express, retired from the public way, or turned sideways to preserve a secluded entrance."

Irony

Irony is an incongruity between the actual result of a sequence of events and what we might normally expect that result to be. Margaret B. McDowell cites the many ironies in *Ethan Frome:* "The dish that is treasured is the one that is broken; the pleasure of the one solitary meal that Ethan and Mattie share ends in distress; the ecstasy of the coasting ends in suffering; the moment of dramatic renunciation when Ethan and Mattie choose suicide rather than elopement ends not in glorious death but in years of pain." At the time of publication, the *Nation* reported that "the profound irony of [Ethan's] case is that it required his own goodness to complete [Zeena's] parasitic power over him." When Ethan goes to the widow Homan's store to buy glue to repair the broken pickle dish, the widow tells him, "I hope Zeena ain't broken anything she sets store by." There are other such ironies. Beautiful Mattie becomes ugly and peevish. Zeena ends up having to care for her rival. Critics have noted irony in the narrator's account of Mattie's attempts to support herself. And Kenneth Bernard cites Ethan's fantasy that he and Mattie would spend their evenings together as they had the night Zeena was away from home. "Ironically, this is just about what he achieves by crippling instead of killing himself and Mattie."

Historical Context

Expansion and Reform in the 1910s

The decade of the 1910s in which Edith Wharton wrote *Ethan Frome* was characterized by economic prosperity in the United States and increasing political influence in the world, especially as it endured and triumphed in the First World War. It was a time in which the country's freedom became

a principal feature of America's identity, but also a time in which these values were questioned by the unfinished business of women's suffrage. Competing values of labor and capitalism also continued to work themselves out, sometimes violently through riots and strikes, like the "long-drawn carpenters' strike" that is the reason for the narrator's stay in Starkfield.

Tensions between conservative and liberal ideals became more apparent from the 1890s, and they came to a head during the decade of the 1910s. The progressive movement was not confined to a single party. It was advanced by the Republican former president Theodore Roosevelt; Woodrow Wilson, the Democrat president elected in 1912; and the Socialist party presidential candidate in that election, Eugene V. Debs. Wilson's term of office advanced the progressive movement through a series of landmark legislative accomplishments. These included setting up the Federal Reserve System, regulating trusts, providing credit to farmers, restricting child labor, and establishing a graduated income tax. In addition, constitutional amendments were adopted governing direct election of senators, the federal income tax, woman suffrage, and Prohibition. These laid the foundation for the New Deal of the 1930s and the Great Society of the 1960s.

Innovation in Industry and the Arts

Industrial growth and the use of new technologies were two of the reasons for the explosive economic expansion of the 1910s. The first direct telephone link between New York and Denver was opened in 1911, the year *Ethan Frome* was published. Examples of these developments are evident in the narrator's remarks about having come to Starkfield in the "degenerate day of trolley, bicycle and rural delivery" and easy communication between the mountain villages," which he contrasts with conditions twenty-four years earlier. Although Ethan Frome is still driving a horse-drawn buggy, Ford Motor Company's moving assembly line was typical of the kinds of innovations in the automobile industry that made the United States the decade's world leader in producing cars. Productivity in this and other industries was further enhanced by application of scientific management theory and new manufacturing techniques. The "personnel management" of the 1910s was incorporated into the welfare capitalism of the 1920s, which used measures such as profit-sharing plans and grievance procedures to improve relations between workers and employers. This period of pros-

New England in winter.

perity mostly benefited a new middle class of professionals and managers. The poor remained poor, particularly rural Southerners, urban immigrants, and African Americans.

A prosperous middle class was a boon to the arts, which enjoyed a period of great vitality during the 1910s. Inspired by European modernists such as Vaslav Nijinsky, Igor Stravinsky, Marc Chagall, Gabriele D'Annunzio, and Walter Adolf Gropius, American painters, photographers, poets, dramatists, writers, and dancers broke free of tradition and experimented with both form and subject. Magazines such as *The Masses* and *The New Republic* reflected the radical vision of this generation of artists. In *Ethan Frome,* the narrator's ironic recitation of Mattie's cultural accomplishments illustrates the disdain of the rebels of the 1910s for the tastes of their parents.

The First World War (1914-1918)

America's attempts at neutrality became irrelevant as the efforts of American manufacturers to capture world markets drew the United States into the affairs of other nations. U.S. economic interests were particularly strong in Latin America and the Caribbean, exemplified by Bethlehem Steel's purchase of Chile's Tofo Iron Mines in 1911, and the completion of the Panama Canal in 1914. The

policies of interventionist presidents like Roosevelt and Taft contrasted with those of Woodrow Wilson. But Wilson was not blind to international realities and the need of U.S. industries for open markets. American economic ties were behind U.S. intervention in the Mexican Revolution of 1911 and the landing of U.S. Marines in Honduras, Cuba, and Nicaragua the same year. They were also what ultimately drew the United States into the First World War.

The war created tensions among a nation of immigrants, who in 1911 constituted a quarter of the U.S. population in every area of the country except the south. But the war also spelled opportunities for American bankers and businessmen. In addition, the commitment of millions of men called into service opened the doors to jobs for women and African Americans. Four hundred thousand blacks left the south for jobs in the north, beginning the "Great Migration" that was to affect not only African American life but American culture as a whole. In a move that would also have profound economic repercussions, close to a million American women joined the labor force for the first time. The government became an increasing presence in the lives of Americans, most notably in matters related to economic policy, production decisions, and labor disputes. Govern-

Compare & Contrast

- **1880s:** People in New England farming communities led a difficult, culturally void existence.

  1911: Innovations in transportation made communication easier between the villages and gave residents access to recreational activities in the bigger towns.

  Today: Videocassettes, radio, cable television, and the Internet have made the world a global village.

- **1880s:** The era of railroad building made earlier methods of transportation in the United States largely obsolete.

  1911: Automobiles (and later buses and trucks) came to exceed the railroad in importance.

  Today: Jet travel makes it possible to travel almost anywhere in the world in a day, and supersonic transport reduces long-distance air travel by half.

- **1880s:** Although Thomas Edison patented an incandescent lamp in 1879, most lighting was still by candlelight, oil lamp, or gas jet.

  1911: Electricity was increasingly available in homes, which used incandescent lighting. French physicist Georges Claude developed the neon lamp, which was used in commercial signs.

  Today: Variations of Thomas Edison's incandescent lamp (light bulbs) are used to light homes, whereas factories, offices, stores, and public buildings generally use fluorescent lighting; street and highway lighting is still an evolving technology.

- **1880s:** Techniques based on photography and spectroscopy (a method of measuring the wavelength and intensity of spectral lines) revolutionized astronomy.

  1911: The main ideas about the evolution, that is, the life history, of stars become clear.

  Today: Since its launch from the shuttle Atlantis in 1990, the Hubble Space Telescope has provided a flood of new images of the universe. For example, it shows star clusters 2.2 million light years away, springtime dust storms at the Martian north pole, and (for the first time) the surface of Pluto.

ment-fostered xenophobia, backed by the Espionage and Sedition Acts of 1917 and 1918, resulted in the abusive treatment of German Americans and of anarchists, communists, and socialists, particularly following the Bolshevik Revolution in Russia in November 1917.

The conclusion of the war brought not the long hoped for serenity but widespread disorder. President Wilson's design for the League of Nations foundered. Workers and employers were at loggerheads. The Red Scare resulted in the deportation of alien radicals and the expulsion of radical labor organizers from the New York State legislature. Conflicts between returning African American soldiers and other migrant southern workers, and their white counterparts in the North, led to race riots in several major northern cities.

Critical Overview

Critics generally regard *Ethan Frome* as a departure from Wharton's usual subject matter. Wharton herself remarked that "it was frequently criticized as 'painful,' and at first had much less success than my previous books." The enduring popularity of the novel has somewhat cynically been attributed to its brevity and its place in the high school and college curriculum. Yet, wrote the critic R. Baird Shuman, it "remains a monument in the Edith Wharton canon." According to Allen F. Stein, the novel represents "the fullest treatment of the disasters that can occur when one attempts to leave even a repellent marriage." And biographer Cynthia Griffin Wolff calls *Ethan Frome* "a tantalizingly literary work."

At the time of the novel's publication in 1911, a review in the *Nation* praised the style as "assured and entirely individual." In a review titled "Three Lives in Supreme Torture," the *New York Times Book Review* reported that "Wharton has ... chosen to build of small, crude things and a rude and violent event a structure whose purpose is the infinite refinement of torture." The *Saturday Review* called the writing "singularly beautiful," but asserted that Wharton had gratuitously marred the work by allowing Mattie and Ethan to live. The review also made a point that other critics, particularly Lionel Trilling, would take up: "The end of Ethan Frome is something at which we cover the eyes. We do not cover the eyes at the spectacle of a really great tragedy."

Later critics found the novel too contrived and its characters unmotivated. Margaret B. McDowell was a dissenting voice, calling the characterization "subtle, strong, and masterful," and Richard H. Lawson called the characters Wharton's "best yet." To Blake Nevius, the novel counted for no more than a minor classic. J. D. Thomas took issue with the story's inconsistencies and what he called Wharton's fundamental ignorance of rural life and "uncertainty ... about the occupational concerns of men." He wrote, "It is regrettable that she felt obliged to narrate her story from the masculine point of view." R. Baird Shuman admitted that there were inconsistencies, as well as "digressive" passages, but wrote that "they have not been so great as to reduce the popularity of the work."

Lionel Trilling declared the novel morally bankrupt, and claimed that if it had anything at all to say, it was "this: that moral inertia, the *not* making of moral decisions, constitutes a very large part of the moral life of humanity." Gerald Walton agreed: "It is not difficult to criticize Ethan Frome," he wrote, citing the bleakness of the setting and the grotesqueness of the characters. He called the end "unrelievedly wretched." Marius Bewley, on the other hand, saw moral choices both in Ethan's plan to ask the Hales for money so he could run away with Mattie, and to die with her rather than to be parted from her. K. R. Shrinivasa Iyengar also saw moral intention in Wharton's message that "to fail in love ... is to set up evil currents." Critic David Eggenschwiler concurred: "Ethan's refusal to cheat Andrew Hale is his last decisive act in the novel."

Critics have praised the use of symbolism and irony in the novel, the development of characters, and the economy of language. Bernard called the use of imagery and symbolism to get around the problem of the characters' inarticulateness "mas-

terful." In what sounds like a backhanded compliment, R. Baird Shuman found the book to be "such a mixture of good and bad writing technique that it is a valuable book to use for discussions of writing." Bernard repeats an early criticism that Ethan lacks a tragic dimension in the Greek sense: "His tragedy is entirely of his own making." But others disagreed. Edwin Bjoerkman argued that Ethan lives "between those two spectres of his lost hopes: the woman he needed and the woman he loved. All other tragedies that I can think of seem mild and bearable beside this one."

Criticism

Jeffrey M. Lilburn

Jeffrey M. Lilburn, M.A. (The University of Western Ontario) is the author of a study guide on Margaret Atwood's The Edible Woman *and of numerous educational essays. In the following essay, he discusses the narrative and moral ambiguity in* Ethan Frome.

First published in 1911, *Ethan Frome* is now considered a classic of twentieth-century American literature. A tale of lost opportunity, failed romance and disappointed dreams ending with a botched suicide attempt that leaves two people crippled and dooms another to a life of servitude, *Ethan Frome* immerses its readers in a world of unrelenting pain and misery. To some, the suffering endured by Wharton's characters is excessive and unjustified; to others, the novel addresses difficult moral questions and provides insightful commentary on the American economic and cultural realities that produced and allowed such suffering. Others still look to the novel for clues about the author's own life. However, no explanation is completely satisfying because regardless of the meaning one chooses to find in the novel, this meaning, like the vision put together by the narrator, will inevitably be shrouded in mystery and ambiguity.

Much of the discussion about *Ethan Frome* involves the frame story with which the novel begins. Although the framing narrative and the story embedded within it are told by the same unnamed narrator, the reliability of the latter is made problematic by the various and varying sources used to construct it. Also, by introducing his story as a "vision," the narrator makes very clear the fact that what we are about to read is not a factual record of the occurrences leading up to Ethan's accident, but his own impressions of what those occurrences may have been. As several critics have pointed out, the only "facts" of Ethan's story are to be found in the narrative frame; the information contained within the frame cannot be considered reliable because, as Cynthia Griffin Wolff explains, it "bears the imprint of the narrator's own interpretation." His vision is a "hypothesis," one vision among many possible others. Wolff argues that Wharton's novel is not about Ethan Frome, but about the narrator and his reaction to the story he tells. Pointing to the "disconcerting similarities" between Ethan and the narrator, she suggests that the narrator's vision depicts his own "shadow self, the man he might become if the reassuring appurtenances of busy, active, professional, adult mobility were taken from him."

Jean Franz Blackall offers another possibility. Blackall agrees that the narrator's knowledge is based on inference but believes there is evidence in the text to support his story. He finds this evidence in the final pages of the novel, arguing that Mrs. Hale, who was with Mattie on the morning after the accident, corroborates the narrator's intuitive discovery. According to Blackall, the ellipses representing Mrs. Hale's unfinished report of what Mattie told her signifies that she knows about the love affair between Mattie and Ethan and their subsequent suicide attempt. However, it is important to remember that Mrs. Hale never actually tells the narrator what it is she heard Mattie say; a sense of shared secret knowledge between her and the narrator is suggested but never confirmed.

Complicating the debate over the novel's narrative structure even further is Orlene Murad who, believing that a biographical tie exists between Edith Wharton and Ethan Frome, argues that it is the author herself who narrates the "vision." Murad believes there is nothing in the narrator's character that would make him capable of so lyrically articulating Ethan's thoughts and actions. Instead, she believes that Wharton abandons the "engineer-narrator" of the first part of the novel and "continues her story as its omniscient narrator." Murad even suggests that Wharton "becomes" Ethan Frome, explaining that the author can so well enter into Ethan's point of view because she is experiencing Ethan's dilemma herself. By creating a character "who painfully takes on the burdensome care of those for whom he is responsible," Murad claims that Wharton "has fashioned a scapegoat" and has pushed onto Ethan the grueling life that her own marital circumstances might easily have pushed onto her.

Despite the biographical similarities between the author and her fictional character, readers and

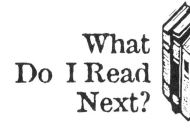

What Do I Read Next?

- A spinster romance writer exiled to a stately hotel in Switzerland ponders love, work, and the lives of her fellow residents in Anita Brookner's *Hotel du Lac* (1984).

- In *The Ring and the Book* (1868-1869), Robert Browning's tale in blank verse based on a 1698 Roman murder trial, a beautiful young woman's attempt to escape an unhappy marriage ends in tragedy.

- Nathaniel Hawthorne's *The Scarlet Letter* (1850) is a classic moral study of adultery and revenge set in Puritan New England.

- *The Age of Innocence* (1920) is Edith Wharton's Pulitzer Prize-winning novel of frustrated passion set in 19th-century New York high society.

- *Edith Wharton Abroad: Selected Travel Writings, 1888-1920* is a collection of Wharton's observations over a thirty-year period from her journeys through Europe, Morocco, and the Mediterranean, edited by Sara Bird Wright.

critics continue to seek additional justification for the interminable suffering depicted in the novel. Biography may provide insight into the inspiration for the characters and their particular dilemmas, but it cannot reveal all of a text's meaning. Consequently, the novel's conclusion leads many readers to ask: Do Ethan, Mattie and Zeena deserve their horrible fate? For many, the answer to this question is no. Lionel Trilling, for example, argues that Wharton is unable to lay claim to any justification for the suffering her characters experience. Moreover, he contends that in *Ethan Frome,* Wharton presents "no moral issue at all." He thinks the ending "terrible to contemplate," but says that "the mind can do nothing with it, can only endure it."

Other readers find much to do with Wharton's ending. Marlene Springer believes that *Ethan Frome* explores the possibility that life can offer equally strong conflicting choices. Among the moral choices she identifies are: "perceived duty versus genuine love; personal happiness for two versus righteous loneliness and penury for one; and the pressure of social structures versus the particularly American desire to 'light out for the territory.'" Springer also contends that *Ethan Frome* offers a "stark realization of what life can be like if you accept circumstances with resignation—refusing ... to look at the variety of moral options to its dilemmas." Read in this fashion, the narrator's vision becomes a cautionary tale about the dangers of inaction and moral paralysis.

Recalling that Wharton was careful to label *Ethan Frome* a "tale" instead of a "novel," Elizabeth Ammons searches for meaning by comparing the work to the archetypes of fairy tales. What she finds is a "modern fairy story" that is "as moral as the classic fairy tale" and which functions as "realistic social criticism." Specifically, she believes that a network of imagery in the novel "calls up the fairy tale *Snow White*": the frozen landscape, Mattie's physical appearance, her role as housekeeper, and her persecution by witchlike Zeena all have "obvious parallels in the traditional fairy tale about a little girl whose jealous step-mother tries to keep her from maturing into a healthy, marriageable young woman." The difference is that in Wharton's "inverted fairy tale," it is the witch who wins. This victory is then amplified by the failed suicide attempt that transforms Mattie into "a mirror image of Zeena." According to Ammons, in Wharton's modern fairy story, witches not only win, they multiply.

Whereas Trilling and other critics have found *Ethan Frome* to be without moral content, Ammons argues that Wharton's moral "emerges cold and grim as her Starkfield setting." She explains this moral as follows: "as long as women are kept isolated and dependent ... Mattie Silvers will become Zeena Fromes: frigid crippled wrecks of human beings...." To her, the fact that Wharton cripples Mattie but does not let her die reflects not the author's cruelty, but the culture's. Without a family or skills she can utilize in the workplace, Ammons believes that Mattie's fate is unalterable—she will live in poverty, will become prematurely old, and her dreams will be shattered no matter what she does. The sledding accident merely accelerates the process, sparing Mattie the "gradual disintegration into queerness that Ethan has witnessed in Zeena and his mother."

Ammons's reading of the novel suggests that witches are made, not born. In Zeena's case, the transition appears to have begun soon after her marriage to Ethan. Like her beloved but never-used pickle dish, Zeena's life was also put on a shelf the day she was married. The lack of communication between husband and wife, the absence of intimacy, and the isolation of life on a farm in a rural community make Zeena's a very lonely existence. To her husband, preoccupied by dreams of Mattie, Zeena has "faded into an insubstantial shade." Blake Nevius draws attention to the scene in which Zeena, face streaming with tears, confronts Ethan and Mattie with the shattered remains of her pickle dish. In this scene, Nevius argues, "we get a terrible glimpse of the starved emotional life that has made her what she is." We also get a glimpse, a vision, of the life Mattie would have known had she replaced Zeena as Ethan's wife.

What makes Ethan's and Mattie's fate so frustrating for so many readers are the many wasted opportunities to invent for themselves a new one. Over and over, Ethan is stormed by feelings of rebellion, words of resistance rise to his lips, instincts of self-defense intensify, but each time, the feelings wane, the words remain unspoken, and the instincts fade away. Ethan's decision not to ask Andrew Hale for the money that would give him and Mattie the opportunity to begin a new life together is particularly troubling. Nevius views this scene as the turning point of the novel: Ethan has been and continues to be "hemmed in by circumstances," but here, it is his own "sense of responsibility that blocks the last avenue of escape and condemns him to a life of sterile expiation." Why does Ethan choose not to ask Hale for the money? The answer to this question might have more to do with Ethan's reluctance to actualize his dreams and visions than it does with a sudden attack of conscience.

Throughout the novel, Ethan continually shifts his attention from his immediate surroundings to another moment, another space existing in his imagination. We are told, early in the novel, that it is when abandoning himself to these dreams that Ethan is most happy. At various times before the accident, Ethan imagines that he and Mattie will one day in the future lie side by side in the Frome graveyard, that they have and will continue to enjoy a long-standing intimacy and, just moments before their impending separation, that he is "a free man, wooing the girl he meant to marry." He even imagines the means through which he might once again become a free man. A cucumber vine dangling from his porch "like the crape streamer tied to the door for a death" leads him to imagine that it is Zeena who has died. The news that she is "a great deal sicker" than he thinks has a similar effect, causing him to wonder if at last her words are true.

Cynthia Griffin Wolff argues that Ethan retreats "from life into a 'vision'" because, to him, the "uncompromized richness of the dream is more alluring than the harsher limitations of actual, realized satisfactions." And indeed, to Ethan, nothing can compete with his own visions of what life with Mattie would be like. On the morning after his evening alone with Mattie, he is glad that he "had done nothing to trouble the sweetness of the picture" he had created in his mind. Consequently, when circumstances force upon him a situation in which he must act and make a decision, he is unable to do so, leaving to Mattie the final decision to sled down the hill into the big elm. According to Wolff, Ethan is "like a man who has become addicted to some strong narcotic, [savouring] emotional indolence as if it were a sensual experience."

Perhaps the most difficult moment for readers to understand is Ethan's lack of reaction when he discovers that Mattie has long shared his feelings and desires. The news gives Ethan a "fierce thrill of joy" but does not incite action. Mattie's love represents the renewal of opportunity, a second chance to become one of "the smart ones [who] get away." But because of the novel's structure, we know that Ethan does not get away. We know there will be a "smash-up," that Ethan will suffer crippling injuries, and that he will spend "too many winters" in Starkfield. Perhaps it is this predictability which reveals the novel's ultimate meaning. Perhaps Wharton reveals Ethan's fate early in the novel so her readers may share the sense of helpless resignation that her characters feel with respect to their miserable fates. Then again, Ethan's unrealized visions of a new life with Mattie—themselves the visions of a man who reminds Ethan of the life he could have had—may be the true source of the novel's tragedy.

Source: Jeffrey M. Lilburn, in an essay for *Novels for Students,* Gale, 1999.

Elizabeth   Ammons

Addressing the opposing viewpoints of fellow critics, Ammons gives evidence supporting Ethan Frome *as a modern but inverted fairy tale of substance, moral content, and theme.*

In her Introduction Wharton is careful to label her piece a "tale" as distinct from a "novel." The haunting fiction draws on archetypes of the fairy tale—the witch, the silvery maiden, the honest woodcutter—and brings them to life in the landscape and social structure of rural New England.... *Ethan Frome* is as moral as the classic fairy tale,

and as rich. First it works as a modern fairy story, a deliberately inverted one; second it functions as realistic social criticism; third, by virtue of its narrative frame, it dramatizes a particular, and deeply rooted, male fear of woman....

As in most fairy stories, plot in Wharton's tale is simple. After seven miserable years married to sickly Zeena, a woman seven years his senior, Ethan Frome (who is twenty-eight) falls in love with twenty-one-year-old Mattie Silver. She is the daughter of Zeena's cousin and works as the childless couple's live-in "girl." When Zeena banishes Mattie because she knows that Ethan and the girl have fallen in love, the young lovers resolve to kill themselves by sledding down a treacherous incline into an ancient elm. The suicide attempt fails, leaving Ethan lame and Mattie a helpless invalid. The narrator reconstructs this story when he visits Starkfield twenty-four years after the event; Ethan is fifty-two and the three principals have been living together for almost two and a half decades, Zeena taking care of Mattie and Ethan supporting them both.

The numbers that accumulate in Wharton's story suggest natural cycles: fifty-two (the weeks of the year); twenty-four (the hours of the day and a multiple of the months of the year); seven (the days of the week) which echoes in the multiples twenty-one, twenty-eight, thirty-five; three (among other things, morning, afternoon, night). This numerical pattern, though subtly established, is carefully worked out; and its implication of generation and natural order ironically underlines Wharton's awful *donnee.* Expressed figuratively: in the frozen unyielding world of Ethan Frome, there is no generative natural order; there is no mother earth. There is only her nightmare reverse image, the witch, figured in Zeena Frome.

Specifically, a network of imagery and event in *Ethan Frome* calls up the fairy tale *Snow White.* The frozen landscape, the emphasis on sevens, the physical appearance of Mattie Silver (black hair, red cheeks, white skin), her persecution by witch-like Zeena (an older woman who takes the girl in when her mother dies and thus serves as a step-mother to her), Mattie's role as housekeeper: all have obvious parallels in the traditional fairy tale about a little girl whose jealous step-mother tries to keep her from maturing into a healthy, marriageable young woman. Although Wharton is not imitating this well-known fairy tale—rather, she draws on familiar elements of *Snow White* as touchstones for a new, original fairy tale—still, the implicit contrast between Zeena's victory in *Ethan*

A scene from the movie Ethan Frome.

Frome and the step-mother's defeat in *Snow-White* subtly contributes to the terror of Wharton's story. Customarily fairy tales reassure by teaching that witches lose in the end. Children and heroines ("Snow Whites") do not remain the victims of ogres. Someone saves them. Here is part of the horror of *Ethan Frome:* Wharton's modern fairy tale for adults, while true to traditional models in the way it teaches a moral about "real" life at the same time that it addresses elemental fears (e.g., the fear of death, the fear of being abandoned), does not conform to the genre's typical denouement. The lovers do not live happily ever after. The witch wins.

Zeena's face alone would type her as a witch. Sallow-complexioned and old at thirty-five, her bloodless countenance is composed of high protruding cheekbones, lashless lids over piercing eyes, thin colorless hair, and a mesh of minute vertical lines between her gaunt nose and granite chin. Black calico, with a brown shawl in winter, makes up her ordinary daytime wear, and her muffled body is as fleshless as her face....

In contrast, Mattie Silver seems a fairy maiden, a princess of nature in Ethan's eyes. Her expressive face changes "like a wheat-field under a summer breeze," and her voice reminds him of "a rustling covert leading to enchanted glades." When she sews, her hands flutter like birds building a nest; when she cries, her eyelashes feel like butterflies. Especially intoxicating is her luxuriant dark hair, which curls like the tendrils on a wildflower and is "soft yet springy, like certain mosses on warm slopes."...

Hurting young people and depriving them of hope and joy is the fairy-tale witch's job, and Zeena does not shirk the task. She constantly finds fault with Mattie, and for seven years she has tortured her youthful husband with whining complaints about her various ailments....

The horror of the story is that the suicide attempt transforms Mattie into a mirror-image of Zeena....

The end of *Ethan Frome* images Zeena Frome and Mattie Silver not as two individual and entirely opposite female figures but as two virtually indistinguishable examples of one type of woman: in fairy-tale terms, the witch; in social mythology, the shrew. Mattie, in effect, has become Zeena. Shocking as that replicate image may at first seem, it has been prepared for throughout the story. Mattie and Zeena are related by blood. They live in the same house and wait on the same man, and they came to that man's house for the same purpose: to take the place of an infirm old woman (Zeena takes over for Ethan's mother, Mattie for his wife). The two women, viewed symbolically, do not contrast with each other....

As a fairy story, *Ethan Frome* terrifies because it is inverted. Incredibly, the witch triumphs. Mattie Silver becomes Zeena's double rather than Ethan's complement.

Wharton's moral, her social criticism, emerges logically from this fairy tale. *Ethan Frome* maintains that witches are real. There are women whose occupation in life consists of making other people unhappy. *Ethan Frome* includes three. Ethan's mother, housebound and isolated for years on a failing farm, lived out her life an insane, wizened creature peering out her window for passersby who never came and listening for voices that only she could hear. Her frightening silence oppressed Ethan until Zeena joined the household to care for her. But then Zeena too fell silent.... Zeena's hypochondria, her frigidity, her taciturnity broken only by querulous nagging, her drab appearance—these make her an unsympathetic character. They also make her a typically "queer" woman of the region, a twisted human being produced by poverty and isolation and deadening routine....

In reality, Mattie had no future to lose. Ethan asks for assurance that she does not want to leave the farm, and "he had to stoop his head to catch her stifled whisper: 'Where'd I go, if I did?'" There is nowhere for her to go. She has no immediate family and no saleable skills;... Ethan thinks of Mattie "setting out alone to renew the weary quest for work.... What chance had she, inexperienced and untrained, among the million breadseekers of the cities? There came back to him miserable tales he had heard at Worcester, and the faces of girls whose lives had begun as hopefully as Mattie's ..." (final ellipsis Wharton's). Mattie's prospects are grim. She can work in a factory and lose her health; she can become a prostitute and lose her dignity as well; she can marry a farmer and lose her mind. Or she can be crushed in a sledding accident and lose all three at once. It makes no difference. Poverty, premature old age, and shattered dreams comprise her inevitable reward no matter what she does. The fact that Wharton cripples Mattie, but does not let her die, reflects not the author's but the culture's cruelty.... Mattie Silver has been prepared for no economically independent life. The system is designed to keep her a parasite.

Ethan himself is only slightly less trapped.... "He was a prisoner for life." The prison, Edith Wharton makes clear by setting the story at the simplest and therefore most obvious level of society, was the American economic system itself, which laid on most men a killing load of work and responsibility and on most women barely enough variety and adult human contact to keep one's spirit alive.... At least Ethan meets fellow workers when he carts his timber to sale or goes in to town for supplies and mail. Farmers' womenfolk normally went nowhere and did nothing but repeat identical tasks in unvaried monotony. To make that isolation of women stark and to emphasize the sterility of life at the level of *Ethan Frome,* Wharton gives the couple no children; and the woman's name she chooses for bold-faced inscription on the only tombstone described in the Frome family-plot is also instructive: "ENDURANCE." If Ethan's life is hard, and it is, woman's is harder yet; and it is sad but not surprising that isolated, housebound women make man feel the full burden of their misery. He is their only connection with the outer world, the vast economic and social system that consigns them to solitary, monotonous domestic lives from which their only escape is madness or death.

Ethan Frome departs from traditional fairy tales by showing that life does not contain happy endings. Good girls do not grow up into happy wives; and good-hearted, worthy lovers do not ride off into the western sun with the maiden of their dreams. For, in Wharton's fairy tale, witches do not get vanquished and disappear. They multiply. First there is Ethan's mother, then Zeena, then Mattie; and they represent only three of the many women gone "queer" in this wintry American landscape. Wharton's moral emerges cold and grim as her Starkfield setting. *Ethan Frome* mocks the fantasy that witches will disappear and romance with a woods-nymph will liberate man into a miraculous world of masterful love and erotic fulfillment. As long as women are kept isolated and dependent, *Ethan Frome* implies, Mattie Silvers will become Zeena Fromes: frigid crippled wrecks of human beings whose pleasure in life derives from depriving others of theirs....

The narrator exists to unlock the deepest, the psycho/sexual, level of *Ethan Frome.* Empathically, he projects himself into young Ethan's situation and sees in it the realization of a specific male fear: the fear that Woman will turn into Witch. The fear that Mother will turn into Witch (love into hate, day into night, life into death) everyone has known.... Precisely this inversion occurs in *Ethan Frome,* and because the terror is man's it makes emotional and intellectual sense to have a man, and one temperamentally close to Ethan, visualize the sinister fairy tale in which man, in this case Ethan, can be caught.

Women's nightmare shift from a positive to a negative force in man's life is the theme of *Ethan Frome*. In part Wharton treats fear of maternal rejection. First Ethan's mother abandons his needs and then Zeena, his mother's replacement, does the same. But airy Mattie Silver is not a mother-figure and her transformation moves the pattern beyond fear of maternal betrayal to fear of female betrayal in general. Male fear of woman and perpetuation of the social system that makes that fear well-founded—Mattie Silvers *do* turn into Zeena Fromes—are the combined focus of *Ethan Frome*. The tale looks at man's romantic dream of feminine solace and transport and, with a hideous twist, allows Ethan's fantasy to materialize. Mattie Silver does become "his" but with, rather than without, Zeena; and the two witchlike women hold him prisoner for life in the severely limited economy and social landscape which traps all three of them....

Ethan Frome—as a fairy tale, as social criticism, as fictive psychohistory—expresses a coherent moral. In her French draft Edith Wharton explicitly states that Mattie "exemplified all the dull anguish of the long line of women who, for two hundred years, had been buffeted by life and who had eaten out their hearts in the constricted and gloomy existence of the American countryside." In the finished version of *Ethan Frome* Wharton is more subtle but no less clear. Witchlike Zenobia Frome, a terrifying and repulsive figure archetypally, is in social terms not at all mysterious. It is a commonplace of scholarship about the persecution of witches that many of them were ordinary women bent and twisted by the conditions of their lives as women, their isolation and powerlessness. Stated simply, Zeena Frome is the witch that conservative New England will make of unskilled young Mattie; and Wharton's inverted fairy tale about the multiplication of witches in Ethan's life, a story appropriately told by a horrified young man whose job is to build the future, finally serves as a lesson from the past. Witches do exist, Wharton's tale says, and the culture creates them.

Source: Elizabeth Ammons, "Edith Wharton's Ethan Frome and the Question of Meaning," in *Studies in American Fiction*, Vol. 7, No. 2, 1979, pp. 127–40.

Kenneth Bernard

In the following excerpt, Bernard cites Wharton's substantial use of imagery and symbolism in Ethan Frome *as a successful method to establish depth in a tale inhabited by reticent and inarticulate characters.*

A common criticism of Edith Wharton's *Ethan Frome* is that it is too contrived. In the last analysis, the characters seem peculiarly unmotivated, put through their paces in a clever, but mechanical, way. Such an opinion can only be the result of a cursory reading. It is true that the book has a kind of stylistic and organizational brilliance. But it is not merely a display; it is invariably at the service of plot and character. The nature of her subject imposed certain difficulties on Wharton, particularly her characters' lack of articulation. How could she, without over-narrating, get at a deep problem involving such characters when they do not speak enough to reveal that problem? Frome's character and his marital relationship are at the heart of the novel, but they are revealed only indirectly. Wharton solved her difficulty in a masterful way by her use of imagery and symbolism. It is in her use of imagery and symbolism that the depths of the story are to be found. Without an understanding of them, a reader *would* find the characters unmotivated and the tragedy contrived. For easy discussion, the imagery and symbolism may be divided into three parts: the compatibility of setting and character, the uses of light and dark, and the sexual symbolism. A survey of these three parts in the novel will, it is hoped, clarify the real story in *Ethan Frome* by adding a new dimension of meaning.

The beginning of this new dimension of meaning is the first mention of the New England village—Starkfield. On many levels the *locus* of the story is a stark field. The village lies under "a sky of iron," points of the dipper over it hang "like icicles," and Orion flashes "cold fires." The countryside is "gray and lonely." Each farmhouse is "mute and cold as a grave-stone." This characterization of Starkfield is consistent throughout the book. Frome, in all ways, fits into this setting. On several occasions his integration with it is described. The narrator, upon first seeing him, sees him as "bleak and unapproachable." Later he says of Frome, "He seemed a part of the mute melancholy landscape, an incarnation of its frozen woe, with all that was warm and sentient in him bound fast below the surface ... he lived in a depth of moral isolation too remote for casual access." Frome, unhappily married to Zeena, and pining for her cousin Mattie, is indeed parallel to the Starkfield setting. Everything on the surface is hard and frozen. His feeling, his love, for Mattie cannot break loose, just as spring and summer are fast bound by winter's cold...." Finally there is Frome's inarticulateness. Not only are his feelings locked, frozen; his very speech is also, beyond the natural reticence of the local people. Neither he nor the landscape can express its warm and tender part…. "Again he struggled for the all expressive word, and again, his arm in hers, found only a deep 'Come along.'" He is truly a man of "dumb melancholy."

The separation of feeling from its expression, the idea of emotion being locked away, separated, or frozen, just as Starkfield is bound by ice and snow, is demonstrated also by the Frome farm. The house seems to "shiver in the wind," has a "broken down gate," and has an "unusually forlorn and stunted look." More important, though, is the "L.pond"… Frome casually mentions to the narrator that he had had to take down the "L." Thus Frome's home is disjointed, separated from its vital functions, even as he is…. Just as Frome is emotionally trapped, just as Starkfield is frozen in the winter landscape, just as Frome's home is cut off from its vitals, so too is he cut off physically from his former strength, trapped in his crippled frame. Images of being caught, bound, trapped are frequent. "He was a prisoner for life." "It seemed to Ethan that his heart was bound with cords which an unseen hand was tightening with every tick of the clock."… Thus the setting of the novel, the landscape and the farm, is parallel to Frome's condition and serves to illuminate it. But Wharton does not stop at this point.

There is hardly a page throughout the book that does not have some reference to light and dark. Wharton uses all of them with effect. The supreme light image is Mattie Silver, as her name implies. She is in contrast to everything in Starkfield; her feelings bubble near the surface. Frome, on the other hand, is all dark. He lives in the dark, especially emotionally. At the beginning of the novel, when he has come to meet Mattie, she is dancing gaily in a church filled with "broad bands of yellow light." Frome keeps "out of the range of the revealing rays from within." "Hugging the shadow," he stands in the "frosty darkness" and looks in. Later he catches up to her "in the black shade of the Varnum spruces," the spot from where they finally begin the attempted suicide that cripples them. He stands with her in "the gloom of the spruces," where it is "so dark … he could barely see the shape of her head," or walks with her "in silence through the blackness of the hemlock-shaded lane." Blackness is his element. As they walk back to the farm he revels in their closeness. "It was during their night walks back to the farm that he felt most intensely the sweetness of this communion." Their love is a bloom of night. "He would have liked to stand there with her all night

in the blackness." He does not see Mattie so much as sense her: " … he felt in the darkness, that her face was lifted quickly to his." "They strained their eyes to each other through the icy darkness." Frome's favorite spot is a secluded place in the woods called Shadow Pond. On their last visit there "the darkness descended with them, dropping down like a black veil from the heavy hemlock boughs." Frome cannot seem to get out of the dark. And often, as in quotations above, the dark is pregnant with suggestions of death and cold. Frome's kitchen, on their return from the village, has "the deadly chill of a vault after the dry cold of night." As Ethan settles in his tomblike house, Mattie's effect on him dies away. He lies in bed and watches the light from her candle, which

> sending its small ray across the landing, drew a scarcely perceptible line of light under his door. He kept his eyes fixed on the light till it vanished. Then the room grew perfectly black, and not a sound was audible but Zeena's asthmatic breathing.

Without Mattie's "light" he is left with the ugly reality of his wife. In numerous small ways also Wharton makes the light and dark images work for her. When Mattie relieves Ethan's jealousy at one point, "The blackness lifted and light flooded Ethan's brain." When Mattie is told by Zeena she must go, and she repeats the words to Ethan, "The words went on sounding between them as though a torch of warning flew from hand to hand through a dark landscape." Before their suicide plunge, "The spruces swatched them in blackness and silence." A bitter argument between Ethan and Zeena is "as senseless and savage as a physical fight between two enemies in the darkness." After, Zeena's face "stood grimly out against the uncurtained pane, which had turned from grey to black." The cumulative effect of all these images is to tell us a great deal about Frome and his tortured psyche.

The most important thing the images of light and dark reveal about Frome is that he is a negative person. Frome is a heroic figure: nothing less than the entire landscape can suffice to describe him effectively; his agony is as broad and deep as that of the winter scene. But he is not tragic because he is a man of great potential subdued and trapped by forces beyond his capacity. His tragedy is entirely of his own making. He is weak. His character never changes. Both before and after the accident he is the same. Like his environment he has a kind of dumb endurance for harsh conditions. There are several indications of his weakness besides his identity with darkness. Frome married Zeena because she had nursed his mother through her final illness. He was twenty-one and she twenty-eight. He married her less because he loved her than because he needed a replacement for his mother. Certainly it is Zeena who cracks the whip in the household, and Ethan who jumps. What Zeena says, goes. Frome "had often thought since that it would not have happened if his mother had died in spring instead of winter ... " When he and Mattie are about to attempt suicide, Mattie sitting in front of Ethan on the sled, he asks her to change places with him. She asks why. Quite sincerely he answers, "Because I want to feel you holding me." He wants to die being cuddled and comforted, leaving to Mattie the role of protector and shelterer.

Throughout the book, Frome recognizes his futility and accepts it rather than trying to fight his way out of it. He does not ever realistically reach for a solution. His love inspires little more than dreams. He thinks of another man who left his wife for another woman and invests the event with fairy tale qualities: "They had a little girl with fair curls, who wore a gold locket and was dressed like a princess." Once he imagines Zeena might be dead: "What if tramps had been there—what if ... " When he spends his one night alone with Mattie, instead of thinking of a way to achieve permanence for their relationship he "set his imagination adrift on the fiction that they had always spent their evenings thus and would always go on doing so..." Ironically, this is just about what he achieves by crippling instead of killing himself and Mattie. He did not, however, envision that Zeena would be a necessary part of the arrangement, as a nurse to Mattie.

The negation, the blackness, in his character is revealed also in his funereal satisfactions. When Mattie says she is not thinking of leaving because she has no place to go, "The answer sent a pang through him but the tone suffused him with joy." He rejoices in her helplessness; he is pained and thrilled at the same time because she has nowhere to go, because she too is trapped.... Frome's aspirations do not finally go beyond darkness. His final acceptance of suicide is the culmination of his negative instincts: death is the blackest blackness.

Although the meaningful use of light and dark is pervasive in the book and is illuminating, it is the sexual symbolism that cuts deepest. The sexual symbolism is more dramatic than the two elements already discussed because it revolves around the key scenes in the book, Ethan and Mattie's night together and Zeena's return. It is also more significant because without an understanding of it the source of Zeena and Ethan's estrangement and antagonism re-

mains unknown. After all, what *is* the deep gulf that lies between them? There is no explicit revelation in the book. In part, Wharton's use of symbolism to clarify the book's central problem is compatible with the inarticulateness of the characters. But perhaps also it represents a reticence or modesty of the author's. Ethan and Mattie's night together is ostensibly a mild affair. Wharton might well have revealed then the true relationship between Frome and his wife and demonstrated overtly Mattie and Ethan's transgression. But was it really necessary for her to do so? Even as it is, the evening progresses with the greatest of intensity. Every action, every word, even every silence quivers. It is because these apparently innocent actions and words exist in such intensity that they must be scrutinized. There are disproportions of feeling, particularly centering around the pickle dish, that are revealing. A proper understanding of the events of that evening sheds light throughout the book, and particularly makes the light and dark imagery more meaningful.

Barrenness, infertility, is at the heart of Frome's frozen woe. Not only is his farm crippled, and finally his body too; his sexuality is crippled also. Zeena, already hypochondriac when he married her, has had the effect of burying his manhood as deeply as everything else in him. In seven years of marriage there have been no children. Within a year of their marriage, Zeena developed her "sickliness." Medicine, sickness, and death are, in fact, rarely out of sight in the book. The farm itself, with its separation of its vital center, its regenerative center, suggests of course the sexual repression. The name Starkfield also connotes barrenness. However, Ethan and Zeena's sexual relationship is suggested most by the incident of the pickle dish, a dish which, unless understood, lies rather unaccountably at the very center of the book.

The red pickle dish is Zeena's most prized possession. She received it as a wedding gift. But she never uses it. Instead she keeps it on a shelf, hidden away. She takes it down only during spring cleaning, "and then I always lifted it with my own hands, so's 't shouldn't get broke." The dish has only ceremonial, not functional, use. The sexual connotations here are obvious. The fact that the wedding dish, which was meant to contain pickles, in fact never does, explains a lot of the heaviness of atmosphere, the chill, the frigidity. The most intense scenes of the book, the most revealing, center around this dish. For example, Zeena never does discover an affair in the making between Ethan and Mattie, nor does she ever say anything, except for one hint not followed up, that reveals such knowledge. Her only discovery (and it is *the* discovery of the book) is of her broken (and used) pickle dish. It is this which brings the only tears to her eyes in the entire book. When Zeena is gone for a day, Mattie, significantly, brings down and uses the pickle dish in serving Ethan supper. Only if the dish is properly understood can it be seen how her violation is a sacrilege, as Zeena's emotions amply testify. The dish is broken, and Ethan plans to glue it together. Of course the dish can never be the same. This kind of violation is irrevocable. Zeena does not discover that the dish is broken until she gets, again significantly, heartburn, the powders for which she keeps on the same private shelf as the pickle dish. The scene following is a symbolic recognition of the fact that Mattie has usurped her place, broken her marriage, and become one with Ethan, though in fact it was the cat (Zeena) who actually broke the dish. The fact that Zeena never truly filled her place, acted the role of wife, and is herself responsible for the failure of the marriage does not bother her. Ethan is hers, however ceremonially, and she resents what has happened.... The evening that Mattie and Ethan spend together, then, is not as innocent as it seems on the surface. That Mattie and Ethan's infidelity is so indirectly presented, whether because of Wharton's sense of propriety or her desire to maintain a minimum of direct statement, does not at all lessen the reality of that fact. If the overt act of infidelity is not present, the emotional and symbolic act is. The passage is full of passion; the moment, for example, when Frome kisses the piece of material Mattie is holding has climatic intensity.

The sterility of their marriage, Frome's emasculation, is represented elsewhere. For example, just before Zeena leaves for the overnight trip to a doctor, she finishes a bottle of medicine and pushes it to Mattie: "It ain't done me a speck of good, but I guess I might as well use it up… If you can get the taste out it'll do for pickles." This is the only other mention of pickles in the book. Significantly, it is the last word in the chapter before the one devoted to Ethan and Mattie's night together. The action might be interpreted as follows: after Zeena has exhausted the possibilities of her medicine for her "trouble," she turns to sex—but she passes on that alternative to Mattie. Mattie may use the jar for pickles if she wishes. The action is a foreshadowing of Mattie's use of the pickle dish. In a sense, Zeena has urged her to that act, for she is abdicating the position of sexual initiative.

Again, in *Ethan Frome* each word counts. But there are some descriptions, obviously very partic-

ular, that do not fit in with any generalizations already presented. However, in the light of an understanding of the pickle dish incident, they are clarified. When Frome first points out his home, the narrator notes "the black wraith of a deciduous creeper" flapping on the porch. Deciduous means shedding leaves, or antlers, or horns, or teeth, at a particular season or stage of growth. Frome has indeed shed his manhood. Sexually he is in his winter season. Later, another vegetation is described on the porch: "A dead cucumber vine dangled from the porch like the crape streamer tied to the door for a death…" A cucumber is no more than a pickle. The pickle dish is not used; the cucumber vine is dead. That it should be connected with crape (black) and death is perfectly logical in the light of what has already been discussed about Frome. Frome's sexuality is dead. There is, of course, in all this the suggestion that Frome could revive if he could but reach spring, escape the winter of his soul. Mattie is his new season.... Mattie, as Zeena never does, makes Ethan feel the springs of his masculinity. But he never overcomes the ice of accumulated Starkfield winters. His final solution is to merge himself with winter forever.

Thus Ethan Frome, when he plunges towards what he considers certain death, is a failure but not a mystery. His behavior is not unmotivated; the tragedy is not contrived. The very heart of the novel is Frome's weakness of character, his negation of life. Behind that is his true, unfulfilled, relationship with Zeena. Wharton's economy of language in the novel is superb. There is hardly a word unnecessary to the total effect. Her final economy is the very brevity of the book. It fits the scene and character. There were depths to plumb; her people were not simple. To overcome the deficiencies of their natural reticence (and perhaps her own), to retain the strength of the severe and rugged setting, particularly the "outcropping granite," she resorted to a brilliant pattern of interlocking imagery and symbolism, three facets of which have been outlined here, to create a memorable work.

Source: Kenneth Bernard, "Imagery and Symbolism in Ethan Frome," in *College English*, Vol. 23, No. 1, October, 1961, pp. 178–84.

Sources

Kenneth Bernard, "Imagery and Symbolism in 'Ethan Frome,'" in *College English*, Vol. 23, No. 3, December, 1961, pp. 182-84.

Marius Bewley, "Mrs. Wharton's Mask," in the *New York Review of Books*, Vol. 3, No. 3, September 24, 1964, pp. 7-9.

David Eggenschwiler, "The Ordered Disorder of 'Ethan Frome,'" in *Studies in the Novel,* Vol. 9, No. 3, Fall, 1977, pp. 237-45.

K. R. Srinivisa Iyengar, "A Note on 'Ethan Frome,'" in *Literary Criterion,* Vol. 5, No. 3, Winter, 1962, pp. 168-78.

Margaret B. McDowell, in *Edith Wharton,* Twayne Publishers, 1976, pp. 67-9.

The Nation, Vol. 93, No. 2147, October 26, 1911, pp. 67-9.

Blake Nevius, "'Ethan Frome' and the Themes of Edith Warton's Fiction," in *The New England Quarterly,* Vol. 24, No. 2, June, 1951, pp. 197-207.

"Three Lives in Supreme Torture," in *New York Times Book Review,* Vol. 16, No. 40, October 8, 1911, p. 603.

The Saturday Review, Vol. 112, No. 2925, November 18, 1911, p. 650.

R. Baird Shuman, "The Continued Popularity of 'Ethan Frome,'" in *Revue des langues vivantes,* Vol. 37, No. 3, 1971, pp. 257-63.

Allen F. Stein, "Edith Wharton: The Marriage of Entrapment," in *After the Vows Were Spoken: Marriage in American Literary Realism,* Ohio State University Press, 1984, pp. 209-30.

J. D. Thomas, "Marginalia or 'Ethan Frome,'" in *American Literature,* Vol. 27, No. 3, November, 1955, pp. 405-09.

Lionel Trilling, "The Morality of Inertia," in *A Gathering of Fugitives,* Harcourt Brace Jovanovich, 1977, pp. 34-44.

Geoffrey Walton, in *Edith Wharton: A Critical Interpretation,* Farleigh Dickinson University Press, 1971, pp. 78-83.

Edith Wharton, in *A Backward Glance,* D. Appleton-Century, 1934, pp. 295-96.

Edith Wharton, in *Ethan Frome,* Penguin, 1987, p. xviii.

Cynthia Griffin Wolff, in *A Feast of Words: The Triumph of Edith Wharton,* Oxford University Press, 1977, pp. 183-84.

For Further Study

Elizabeth Ammons, "Edith Wharton's 'Ethan Frome' and the Question of Meaning," in *Studies in American Fiction,* Vol. 7, 1979, pp. 127-40.
    Ammons discusses *Ethan Frome* in relation to the classic fairytale, arguing that the novel works as modern fairy story, as social criticism, and that it dramatizes male fear of woman.

Shari Benstock and Barbara Grossman, in *No Gifts from Chance: A Biography of Edith Wharton,* Scribner's, 1994.
    An investigation into Wharton's work and personal relationships from a feminist perspective, drawing on many previously unavailable sources.

Jean Frantz Blackall, "Edith Wharton's Art of Ellipsis," in *'Ethan Frome': Authoritative Text, Backgrounds and Contexts, Criticism,* edited by Kristin O. Lauer and Cynthia Griffin Wolff, Norton, 1995, pp. 170-74.
    Blackall discusses Wharton's use of the ellipsis, showing how they may represent (among other things) the inexpressible or that which a character is unwilling to express. They might also be used to entice the reader into imaginative collaboration with the writer.

Anthony Burgess, "Austere in Whalebone," in *Spectator,* No. 7171, December 3, 1965, p. 745.
    A review of three of Wharton's works, including *Ethan Frome,* which novelist and critic Burgess calls too pessimistic to be true.

Dorothy Yost Deegan, "What Does the Reader Find?: The Synthesis-Portrait in Miniature," in *The Stereotype of the Single Woman in American Novels,* King's Crown Press, 1951, pp. 40-126.
    Examines Mattie Silver as a literary type, that is, the young single woman who ends up in an unfortunate position owing to her inability to make her own way in the world economically.

R. W. B. Lewis, "Ethan Frome and Other Dramas," in *Edith Wharton: A Biography,* Harper and Row, 1975, pp. 294-313.
    Argues that *Ethan Frome* reflects features of Wharton's own experience, exaggerated and transplanted to a hopeless rural setting.

Orlene Murad, "Edith Wharton and Ethan Frome," in *Modern Language Studies,* Vol. 13, No. 3, Summer, 1983, pp. 90-103.
    Murad explores the biographical ties between Edith Wharton and Ethan Frome.

Blake Nevius, "On 'Ethan Frome,'" in *Edith Wharton: A Collection of Critical Essays,* edited by Irving Howe, Prentice-Hall, 1962, pp. 130-36.
    An excerpt from Nevius's *Edith Wharton* in which he discusses, among other things, Ethan's heroic possibilities and Wharton's handling of point of view.

Alan Price, in *The End of the Age of Innocence: Edith Wharton and the First World War,* St. Martin's Press, 1998.
    A book-length chronicle of Wharton's wartime relief and charity activities and her wartime writings.

Marlene Springer, in *Ethan Frome: A Nightmare of Need,* Twayne, 1993.
    A book-length study of *Ethan Frome* that includes discussions on the literary and historical context of the novel, characterization, style and symbolism.

Lionel Trilling, "The Morality of Inertia," in *Edith Wharton: A Collection of Critical Essays,* edited by Irving Howe, Prentice-Hall, 1962, pp. 137-46.
    Trilling argues that the one idea of considerable importance to be found in Wharton's novel is that moral inertia, the not making of moral decisions, constitutes a large part of the moral life of humanity.

Cynthia Griffin Wolff, "The Narrator's Vision," in *'Ethan Frome': Authoritative Text, Backgrounds and Contexts, Criticism,* edited by Kristin O. Lauer and Cynthia Griffin Wolff, Norton, 1995, pp. 130-44.
    Arguing that *Ethan Frome* is about its narrator, Cynthia Griffin Wolff discusses the novel's narrative structure and the implications of the narrator's vision.

Giants in the Earth

O. E. Rölvaag
1927

Giants in the Earth was O. E. Rölvaag's most influential novel. It chronicles the story of a group of Norwegian pioneers who make the long trek from a fishing village in Norway through Canada to Spring Creek, in Dakota Territory. Although the westward migration means opportunity, the settlers must contend with the isolation and monotony of prairie life; primitive housing; long, frigid winters; and crop-destroying infestations in summer. These conditions are hard enough for people of robust nature, eager for a new life, but for people of delicate sensibility, like Per Hansa's wife Beret, life on the prairie becomes unbearable. *Giants in the Earth* deals with timeless themes of immigration, fear and loneliness, myth, and religion. The novel does not end happily but it is, nonetheless, an exuberant sprawling work that has won consistent praise for its unsparing account of the spiritual as well as the physical experience of its characters.

Author Biography

O. E. Rölvaag was born April 2, 1876, on Dønna Island off the coast of Norway, where he lived until he was twenty. Despite an early and voracious appetite for literature, both Norwegian classics and writers such as Charles Dickens and James Fenimore Cooper, Rölvaag seemed destined to be a fisherman. A violent storm at sea in which several of his friends lost their lives was a defining ex-

O.E. Rölvaag

perience for him. Unwilling to face the prospect of the hazards and desolation of life on the North Atlantic, Rölvaag opted instead to emigrate to America, asking his uncle in Elk Point, Minnesota, to lend him money for the passage.

His first two years in America he worked as a farmhand. But farming was scarcely more appealing to Rölvaag than fishing, and he decided to further his education. He studied first at Augustana Academy in Sioux Falls, South Dakota, then at St. Olaf College in Northfield, Minnesota, where he graduated in 1905. At St. Olaf, Rölvaag studied the works of Norwegian novelists and discovered Norwegian folklore. The work of Henrik Ibsen was a powerful influence on him, and it was while at St. Olaf that Rölvaag recognized his desire to become a writer. After graduating, Rölvaag returned to Norway for advanced study at the University of Kristiana in Oslo. This sojourn in his own country drove home to him the importance of preserving one's cultural identity in an alien land, and in fact Rölvaag would be adamantly opposed to the idea of a melting pot his whole life.

Once back in America, Rölvaag took up a position at St. Olaf teaching Norwegian language and literature. He introduced Norwegian immigrant history as a subject at the college and helped to found several organizations for the preservation of Nor-wegian culture. Rölvaag's first fictional work, titled *Amerika-breve* (Letters from America), was published in Norwegian in 1912 under the pseudonym Paal Mörck. It was an account in epistolary form, that is, told through a series of letters, of a young immigrant's dubious exchange of the perilous life of a fisherman in Norway for the servile life of a farmhand in America. He published two more novels, also in Norwegian, before taking a sabbatical from St. Olaf to work on a trilogy titled *I de dage* (In Those Days), the first volume of which was published in Norway in 1924, and in the United States in English in 1927 as *Giants in the Earth.*

Rölvaag's saga of the settling of South Dakota by a group of intrepid Norwegian immigrants was an immediate success and sold more than 80,000 copies by year's end. Critics praised the true-to-life thoughts and feelings of the characters and Rölvaag's powerful descriptions of nature. Over the next four years, despite a series of heart attacks, he completed the second and third volumes in the trilogy. *Peder Victorious* (1929) and *Their Fathers' God* (1931), however, lacked the universal import of *Giants in the Earth*, which stands as Rölvaag's singular contribution to American pioneer literature. Rölvaag died in 1931.

Plot Summary

O. E. Rölvaag's *Giants in the Earth* narrates the story of a Norwegian immigrant family's struggles on the American plains from 1873 to 1881. The novel details the triumphs, hardships, and ultimate tragedies of South Dakota farmers as they try to wrest a livelihood from a land that, while fertile, often proves actively hostile to human habitation.

Book I: "The Land-Taking"

As the novel opens, Per Hansa leads his family with their meager possessions over the vast emptiness of the Dakotas' grassy plains. With him are his pregnant wife Beret, his sons Ole and Store-Hans, and his young daughter, And-Ongen. The family is searching for their traveling party, whom they had to leave when their rickety wagon was damaged. The family, especially Beret, fears that they are lost and may never locate their settlement, a predicament that could prove fatal. Unable to sleep, Per Hansa travels out at night and discovers evidence of a campsite, proof that they have the right trail.

At the settlement itself (called Spring Creek), Per Hansa's friends fear for him. They are soon reunited, however, and realize that Per Hansa had traveled too far west. Per Hansa and the other settlers, Hans Olsa and his wife Sörine, Syvert Tönseten and his wife Kjertsi, and the Solum brothers, Henry and Sam, all gather and speak enthusiastically of their opportunities as the first farmers on this land. Only Beret feels a sense of foreboding.

Per Hansa goes to see his quarter-section of land and realizes that it contains an Indian burial mound. He does not fear the possible implications of building on such a sacred place. After registering his land in Sioux Falls, Per Hansa plows energetically and builds a mud house that contains the house and barn in one structure. A traveling Indian band appears, scaring everyone in the settlement. Per Hansa heals one Indian man's infected hand wound, however, and receives a pony in return.

A panic overtakes the settlement when their cows, which are necessary for their survival, run away. Over Beret's frightened protests, Per Hansa leaves to retrieve them. He brings them back, along with a borrowed bull and some chickens.

While walking over the fields, Per Hansa discovers someone else's land markers on Tönseten's and Hans Olsa's lands. He secretly takes and burns the stakes, though this act is considered a grievous transgression. When she discovers his deed, Beret is deeply ashamed and afraid, for their religious traditions prohibit such actions. The Irish settlers who planted the stakes (but did not register their claim in Sioux Falls) soon come. When they cannot find their markers, a physical conflict ensues, which the large, gentle Hans Olsa ends by soundly defeating one man. The Irish families move a little further west, and the Spring Creek residents are delighted when they find how Per Hansa protected their claims. Beret, however, fears they are all turning into savages and upbraids them for celebrating an obvious sin.

When Norwegian travelers arrive, Tönseten convinces twenty of them to stay in the region, expanding the settlement. The Spring Creek men travel to town for winter supplies. On the trip, Per Hansa trades potatoes for a number of items that baffle his companions, including net twine. Always inventive, he plans to use the net to catch ducks that his sons had discovered in the swamps. At one stop, he learns how to whitewash the inside of a mud house, an accomplishment which astonishes his friends.

Winter arrives and the snow traps everyone indoors for extended periods. The lonely Solum boys intend to leave for Minnesota, but the others convince them to stay. The settlers appoint Henry, who speaks English, the settlement schoolteacher.

Beret begins to see this harsh life as retribution for her passionate love for Per Hansa, which led to their conceiving their first child out of wedlock and her leaving her family to come to America. She becomes convinced that she will die giving birth to their fourth child and wants to be buried in her only family heirloom: a large trunk. The birth is strenuous and Per Hansa is frantic. Beret and the child almost die, but fortunately Sörine and Kjertsi save them, and the baby is born on Christmas. Per Hansa has a reluctant Hans Olsa baptize the child, and, to honor Sörine, he names his son Peder Seier, which means Peder Victorious.

Book II: "Founding the Kingdom"

Two factors help the settlers withstand the winter: the new child and the school they all attend, both of which bring everyone together.

The men must journey again for more supplies. Per Hansa, though he has only oxen rather than horses, goes along. A blizzard strikes, and Per Hansa is separated from the others. He and the oxen forge their way through snowdrifts, almost freezing to death. Eventually, the oxen run into the wall of a Sioux River house, in which Per Hansa finds his companions. The men stay at the village for two days, chopping wood and attending a dance, before returning home.

Back in Spring Creek, the families discuss the future of this territory and the possibility of taking new, more American names. Per Hansa decides on Holm for a last name. Everyone except Beret applauds his choice. She thinks it wicked to abandon one's baptized name, and she silently fears that their new ways are stripping them of their civility and belief in the sacred.

In March, Per Hansa undertakes a trading expedition to the Indian settlements. He buys Indian furs and travels to Minnesota to sell them, making a large profit. He cannot understand Beret's lingering depression or her lack of excitement over his venture. He hopes the coming spring will revive her spirits.

The time for planting comes. Since Per Hansa's property sits highest in the settlement, the land dries quickly and he begins planting early. Soon, an unexpected snow comes, leading Per Hansa to believe that his impatience has destroyed the crop and, thus, his family's future. A week later, though, the wheat unexpectedly begins to sprout from the ground. Per Hansa is overcome with joy.

A disturbing episode occurs when a wandering, poverty-stricken family arrives at the settlement. The father, Jakob, must tie his wife, Kari, into their cart so she will not try to return to the grave of their youngest son, who fell ill and died on the plains. Per Hansa goes with Hans Olsa to place the dead boy in a coffin, but they cannot find his grave. The family leaves to locate their traveling party. Beret sympathizes with the woman and contemplates the misery that she has suffered and that Beret, in part, shares. She begins covering the windows to block out the evil she sees on the prairie.

After Per Hansa's wheat is harvested, a locust plague strikes the region, destroying everyone's crops. Returning home, a horrified Per Hansa finds Beret, And-Ongen, and Peder Victorious in the family chest, which was blocking the door. Beret says they must all climb inside to protect themselves from the devil. The locust plagues last from 1873 to 1878, leaving destitution in their wake. Many in the settlement hang on, however, because they have nowhere else to go.

In June of 1877, a traveling minister stops in the settlement, to everyone's delight. He holds a service at Per Hansa's, since his home is the largest. Per Hansa has done well in the intervening years, now owning three quarter-sections of land. The minister preaches about the entrance of the Israelites into the land of Canaan. He baptizes many children. When he begins baptizing Peder Victorious, however, Beret violently protests fixing her son with such a sinful name. The minister later consults with Per Hansa, who tells him of Beret's growing insanity. She talks with her dead mother, and he even fears she will try to kill her children. Per Hansa blames himself for bringing her to the prairie. Still, he cannot see any sin in this way of life and often protests against the minister's religious admonitions. The minister consults with Beret and puts her mind at ease about her son's name.

That fall, the minister returns for a communion service. He makes Beret's trunk into his altar. Though the minister has begun to doubt his own faith and feels he delivers an incomprehensible sermon, he successfully speaks to the villagers by referring to the common features of their lives. Soon after, Beret experiences a reawakened happiness and returns to her old self, much to everyone's surprise.

In the final chapter, "The Great Plain Drinks the Blood of Christian Men and Is Satisfied," the winter of 1880-81 comes with an eighty-day snowstorm, bringing great privation to the village. Hans Olsa, in an attempt to save his cattle during a blizzard, comes down with a fatal illness. A now vocally religious Beret attends him on his sick bed and makes him realize his need for a minister since he is dying. Both Hans Olsa and Beret want Per Hansa to travel to find the minister, though the snowed-in prairie is impassable. Because of his previous feats, however, Hans Olsa and Sörine believe he can accomplish the task, and Beret believes it would be a sin not to try. Finally, angry at Beret, Per Hansa takes skis and makes the journey into the swirling snow.

That May, two boys discover a frozen, dead Per Hansa sitting by a haystack. The book ends, "His face was ashen and drawn. His eyes were set toward the west."

Characters

Crazy Bridget

An old Irish woman the settlers turn to for help when they are sick. The Norwegians think she is a fraud but concede that she has "a remarkable way with sick folks."

And-Ongen Hansa

See Anna Marie Hansa

Anna Marie Hansa

Anna Marie is Per and Beret's daughter.

Beret Hansa

Beret symbolizes the moral foundation of the pioneer experience, and critics call her the most completely drawn of Rölvaag's characters. She is pregnant when the party sets off from Lofoten and is skeptical of the westward journey from the start. The product of a rigid, moralistic upbringing that considered God as the incarnation of law, Beret is ill-equipped for life as a pioneer. Fear is her motivating emotion. "Oh, Per!" she says as they make their way across the prairie. "Not another human being from here to the end of the world!" Beret is so lonely that when Per builds a sod house and barn under one roof, Beret thinks that at least the cow will be a "comfortable companion" on long winter nights. She is appalled by Per's removal of the Irish

Nineteenth-century emigrant camp.

settlers' landmarks, even though he has done it to protect his friends' rightful claims, because she recognizes it as the worst sin a person can commit against a fellow human. Thus it adds to her nameless fears of the prairie "a new terror—the terror of consequences!"

Beret also fears the consequences of having her first child Ole out of wedlock, marrying Per Hansa against the wishes of her parents, and delighting in Per's desire for her. "The sweet desires of the flesh," she thinks, "are the nets of Satan." Beret is temporarily at peace after the birth on Christmas Day of Peder Victorious. But Per's choice of the child's second name seems sacrilegious to her. When the other settlers begin discussing name changes, Beret worries that, having "discarded the names of their fathers, soon they would be discarding other sacred things." Beret's isolation is spiritual as well as environmental, and it sets her apart from everyone else, including her husband. The other settlers want to be sympathetic to her, but her deepening derangement and her moralizing exasperates them. Yet, wrote critic George Leroy White, Jr., "She is not a chronic fault-finder.... She first of all does not love pioneering. She has torn the home-ties from her heart solely because she loved Per more than anything else."

Hans Kristian Hansa

Known as Store-Hans, he is the second son of Per and Beret Hansa. He is frequently enlisted to watch over his mother and sister. He is never so happy as when he is alongside his father, and he shares Per's enthusiasms. Store-Hans is given to frequent tears and nightmares. He is terrified by what is happening to his mother, and at one point he is afraid that she will kill Permand.

Ole Hansa

See Olemand Hansa

Olemand Hansa

Ole is Per Hansa's elder son. He considers himself the master of the house in his father's absence. He is impatient to be an adult, and frustrated when his father's trust in him results in his being asked to stay home to care for his mother and sister while the men make trips into town. Like his younger brother Store-Hans, Ole is frightened by his mother's increasing strangeness, but he is compelled to protect her. When, in frustration, Beret takes a willow switch to the boys, they lie to their father about how they got their bruises. Ole is too young to be burdened by the ties from home that still bind his mother. "Did you ever see anything so beautiful!" he whispers at the fall of evening when the family first reaches the Spring Creek settlement.

Peder Victorious Hansa

The youngest son of Per and Beret, Peder's arrival is loaded with portent. First, he is born on Christmas Day. He is also born with a caul, a part of the fetal membrane covering his head, and Norwegians folklore suggests that such children are destined for extraordinary things. At first, Beret considers the choice of his second name—Victorious—to be a sacrilege. "This sin shall not happen! How can a man be *victorious* out here, where the evil one gets us all!" she cries out at his christening. But when the minister blesses the child and prays that he, too, will answer the call of the ministry, Beret's worries are temporarily put to rest. Even Per is aware that his youngest son has a special destiny. As Per sets out on a snowy errand from which he will never return, he thinks, "Oh, Permand, Permand! Something great must come of you—you who are so tenderly watched over!"

Per Hansa

Per Hansa is the epitome of the immigrant spirit. Unlike his wife Beret, whose nature is delicate, Per is built to "wrestle with fortune." For him, the westward journey from the island of Lofoten, Norway represents the ultimate opportunity. Per is deeply devoted to his wife, whom he thinks of as "a woman of tender kindness, of deep fine fancie—one whom you could not treat like an ordinary clod." But Beret's "scruples and misgivings" about the journey fail to change his plans. "Is a man to refuse to go where his whole future calls, only because his wife doesn't like it?" Per asks the minister after Beret becomes deranged from life on the prairie.

Per's indomitable spirit and fierce individualism distinguish him from his neighbors. His best friend, Hans Olsa, recalls that Per "never would take help from any man." He takes a major risk in deciding on his own to pull up stakes planted by Irish settlers—something he would never have done at home—to avoid their usurping Hans Olsa's and Syvert Tönseten's claims to their properties. Per is impetuous and impelled by fantasies. He builds a sod hut and barn under one roof, a structure Syvert Tönseten warns him will collapse, and he is so eager to get the jump on the other settlers that he plants his wheat before the ground is dry. Sometimes his determination to survive pioneering borders on the insane, as when he attempts to disperse the invasion of locusts by shooting at them.

But in Per his neighbors see what is possible. He is painfully aware of what is happening to his wife, but he cannot help her. "I have lived with her all these years," he tells the minister, "yet I must confess that I don't know her." Per is delighted by Beret's initial recovery under the guidance of the minister, but perplexed by her increasing piety. It is to fulfill a request of Beret's that Per heads out on his fatal mission at the end of the novel.

Permand Hansa

See Peder Victorious Hansa

Store-Hans Hansa

See Hans Kristian Hansa

Minister

The minister first shows up at the Spring Creek settlement in June, to the overwhelming joy of the inhabitants. His humanity is immediately evident in his response to Tönseten's confession that, as a layperson, he may have blasphemed by performing a marriage: "This probably is not the worst sin you have committed," the minister tells him. In response to Per's troubled question whether the name Peder Victorious is a "human" name, the minister says, "It is the handsomest name I can ever remember giving to any child." The minister is instrumental in bringing Beret out of her insanity. Moreover, faced with the reality of life on the prairie, he worries about his own faith and his ability to preach to the settlers meaningfully: "How can they understand [a sermon about] the things that happened to an alien people, living ages ago, in a distant land? The Israelites were an Oriental race; they didn't know anything about the Dakota Territory, either."

Hans Olsa

Per Hansa's best friend from their fishing days in the Lofoten Islands. Per depends on him "for everything," and Hans Olsa thinks he will "never tire of gazing into the bearded, roguish face of Per Hansa's." Their dream since formulating their plans for coming to America has been to be "nearest neighbours." Hans Olsa is so big that strangers stop to look, and so strong that "things that he took hold of often got crushed in his grip." Slow to react, he is steadfast in his decisions; "on this account he always found it difficult to turn back, once he had chosen his path."

Hans Olsa does not abuse his physical advantage. When the Irish settlers dispute Hans Olsa's and Syvert Tönseten's claims to their land, Hans

Olsa's first impulse is to "convince them that we are here with the full sanction of law and justice," and he is remorseful when one of the settlers manages to goad him into a fight. He is a fatalist. When Per Hansa wants to shoot at the locusts to frighten them, Hans Olsa tells him, "Don't do that, Per Hansa! If the Lord has sent this affliction on us, then…." Hans Olsa's generosity is as big as the rest of him. As he is dying, Hans Olsa reviews with Per Hansa the debts other settlers still owe him. "It transpired later that in every case he had stated less than what was owing to him."

Sofie Olsa

Hans Olsa's ten-year-old daughter.

Sörine Olsa

Sörine is Hans Olsa's wife. Per Hansa admires her lack of fear, and is repeatedly impressed by the "goodness and intelligence" in her face. Sörine helps Beret through the birth of Peder Victorious, and the child's second name is chosen out of gratitude to her. As Hans Olsa lays dying, Sörine asks Per Hansa whether he would be willing to venture out into the blizzard to find the doctor, explaining, "We all have a feeling that nothing is ever impossible for you."

Henry Solum

One of the two Solum boys. Henry and his brother Sam are the only ones of the group who know both American and Indian languages. At Syvert Tönseten's suggestion, Henry and Sam start a school for the settlers.

Sam Solum

The second of the two Solum boys.

Torkel Tallaksen

A member of the Sognings and a wealthy braggart. Store-Hans and Tallaksen's son become friends.

Kjersti Tönseten

Kjersti is Syvert Tönsetens' wife. She indulges his enthusiasms, but often compares him unfavorably with Per Hansa. When Per Hansa explains how he destroyed the Irish settlers' stakes in order to protect Hans Olsa's and Syvert's rightful claims to their land, Kjersti is "moved almost to tears over such a man. What a difference from that spineless jellyfish of a husband of hers!" Kjersti and Syvert are childless, and Kjersti finds frequent occasion to remind Syvert of that fact.

Syvert Tönseten

Another of the Lofoten group of settlers to Spring Creek. Tönseten is notorious among his neighbors for having something to say about everything. Though a hard worker, he lacks Per Hansa's spirit of enterprise. He compensates his feelings of inadequacy by criticizing Per's plans. For example, when Per whitewashes the walls of his sod hut in an effort to cheer Beret up, Tönseten tells him sourly, "It's getting to be so damned swell in here that pretty soon a fellow can't even spit!" Tönseten's own plans for building a decent house never seem to materialize. He does work tirelessly, though, to draw new members to the settlement, a mission that gives him a sense of purpose. It is his idea to start the school, which solves the dual problem of the Solum boys' sinking morale and the need of the settlers to occupy themselves during the long winter days. Tönseten blames Beret for what he calls Per Hansa's "stuck-up airs," and his dislike of her grows worse after she recovers from her nervous breakdown.

Themes

Immigration and the Westward Movement

Critics have praised Rölvaag's synthesis of the themes of immigration and the westward migration in *Giants in the Earth*. Per Hansa is the perfect embodiment of the immigrant spirit. "Good God!" he pants at the opening of the novel, "This kingdom is going to be mine!" Per sees economic opportunity everywhere, and he fantasizes endlessly about a fancy house and a bounty of farm animals. But the price the immigrant pays is high in terms of lost supports, prejudice, the need to remake social networks and to reformulate cultural values, and intergenerational conflicts. Beret is the supreme example of the immigrant's dilemma. As Per tells the minister, "She has never felt at home here in America…. There are some people, I know now who never should emigrate, because, you see, they can't take pleasure in that which is to come."

The paucity of culture on the frontier is such that when the Solum boys organize a school to teach the children to read, all the adults attend it as well. The settlers' inability to speak English makes communications difficult for them. For example, in settling a dispute with Irish settlers over land claims, Per must enlist the Solum boys to act as spokesman and interpreter. In the novel, the themes

Topics for Further Study

- Research the Indian Reorganization Act of 1934 and explain how the provisions of the act might have affected the land claims of the settlers at Spring Creek.

- Explore modern methods of farming and crop protection and explain how the characters in *Giants in the Earth* could have been helped by them.

- Investigate current U.S. immigration patterns and policies, and compare the various experiences and concerns of today's immigrants with those of the characters in the novel.

- Research the architecture and structure of a sod house and barn like the one Per Hansa built for his family, and make some hypotheses about its advantages and disadvantages.

of immigration and westward movement are inseparable. Per's party sets off from Lofoten traveling "farther and farther onward … always west." Their original destination is Fillmore County, Minnesota. But no sooner do they reach America than they are "intoxicated by bewildering visions; they spoke dazedly, as though under the force of spell…. Go west! … Go west, folks! … The farther west, the better the land!" When Per Hansa is lost in a snowstorm, he fears that the oxen are headed east, and the name of the Rocky Mountains keeps running through his mind. "Rocky-ocky Moun-tains, Rocky-ocky Moun-tains! … Directly behind those mountains lay the Pacific Ocean…. They had no winter on that coast…. God! no winter!"

Perhaps the most poignant statement of the theme of westward movement comes at the end of the novel. Per Hansa perishes in a snowstorm, and the following spring some boys discover his body seated on the west side of a haystack, his eyes "set toward the west."

Fear and Loneliness

Fear and loneliness are the constant companions of the pioneers. The isolation Rölvaag's char-

acters feel is both a reflection of and a reaction to the environment. They are desolate souls in a desolate place. No one experiences this isolation more keenly than Beret Hansa. From the outset she notices the "deep silence" of the prairie, the "endless blue-green solitude that had neither heart nor soul." She cannot imagine that other people had ever dwelt there or would ever come. "Never could they find home in this vast, wind-swept void." Fear is a byproduct of loneliness, and it takes many forms. It strikes the men as well as the women, "but the women were the worst off; Kjersti feared the Indians, Sörine the storms; and Beret, poor thing, feared both—feared the very air." Beret feels exposed on the prairie, where there is "nothing to hide behind," and she covers the windows with clothes to shut out the night. In the same way that Beret embodies the theme of loneliness, she incarnates that of fear as well. Critic George Leroy White, Jr., wrote that she "is a victim of the small things of life that prey upon her: the loneliness of their place; the taking of new name; the naming of the boy Peder Victorious; the stake incident; the fear of Indians, and the fear of the stars."

Myth

Rölvaag makes liberal use of mythic themes. This emphasis is immediately apparent from the novel's title. When Beret first sees Hans Olsa's sod house, she compares its center pole with the "giants she had read about as a child." She sees the plain as a monster. The settlers easily incorporate beliefs about trolls from Norse fairy tales into their explanations for various events that take place in the story. When the cows disappear, the little group sent to look for them worry that the cows might have been spirited away by trolls. Per Hansa refers to the decision over Hans Olsa's and Syvert Tönseten's land claims as being in the "grip of the trolls." The trolls are also associated with visible phenomena. The blizzard that the men run into on their way to the Trönder settlement is described as "a giant troll [that] had risen up in the west, ripped open his great sack of woolly fleece, and emptied the whole contents of it above their heads."

Other elements of Norse mythology crop up in the novel. Per Hansa makes repeated references to his "kingdom" and to Beret as the "princess" of Norse fairy tales, "a romance in which he was both prince and king, the sole possessor of countless treasures." He refers to the kernels of wheat he is about to plant as "good fairies that had the power to create a new life over this Endless Wilderness, and transform it into a habitable land for human beings." The plague of locusts descending from the north brings to the minds of the settlers the Norse adage that "all evil dwells below and springs from the north." Mythic themes are reinforced by the title of the final chapter: "The Great Plain Drinks the Blood of Christian Men and Is Satisfied." As scholars Theodore Jorgenson and Nora O. Solum point out, "In the Norwegian fairy tale, the troll drinks the blood of Christian men."

Religion

Another important theme in the novel is religion. Sometimes the themes of myth and religion are intermingled, as in the reference to the trolls drinking the blood of Christian men. There are many biblical references in the novel. For example, Per Hansa compares the prairie to "the pastures of Goshen in the Land of Egypt." And when Per asks Syvert Tönseten whether he has seen signs of life, Tönseten answers, "Neither Israelites nor Canaanites!" The settlers regard the invasion of locusts as one of the plagues mentioned in the bible. The arrival of the minister and the birth of Peder Victorious on Christmas Day are significant events. Before the child is born, Store-Hans dreams that "he had seen both Joseph and Benjamin playing just beyond the house, and with them had been a tiny little fellow, who wasn't mentioned in the Bible story!" In the same way that Beret feels the loss of culture, she also fears the loss of the Lutheran religion. When the Spring Creek settlers start discussing name changes, Beret wonders whether they will abandon all sacred things. In the depths of her derangement, she imagines that Peder Victorious's name is one that "Satan has tricked Per into giving him."

According to literary critic Harold P. Simonson, "To Beret, the psychological cost in leaving their fathers' homeland is nothing when compared with the spiritual cost in forsaking their fathers' God." The minister's evaluation of Beret's condition is that she needs "above everything else ... the gladness of salvation." In fact, at the end of the novel, it is an argument over religion—whether the doctor or the minister should be fetched to attend to the dying Hans Olsa—that drives Per out into the snow to his doom.

Style

Setting

Giants in the Earth is set in the so-called east-river region of what is now South Dakota,

that is, along the Big Sioux River at the Iowa border, southeast of Sioux Falls. It is a place of both astounding beauty and stark wilderness. The area is subject to extremes of weather, and these extremes have a profound effect on the characters in the novel. Winters are so cold and the snow so deep that the settlers can safely store the dead in snow banks for burial in the spring. In the summer, storms blow up with "appalling violence." The risks of living on the prairie are many: madness, pestilence, storms, and prairie fire. After weeks and months of winter, "the courage of the men was slowly ebbing away." Their relief at the passing of winter is short-lived; no sooner is the wheat up than a plague of locusts causes massive crop destruction, an event that will be repeated year after year. Eventually, Beret goes insane from the accumulated insults of prairie life. At the time the story takes place, the railroad has not yet come to the settlement, and trips to the nearest town for supplies take several days. In trying to persuade a new group of Norwegians to settle at Spring Creek, Syvert tells them that "the railroad had already reached Worthington—soon it would be at Sioux Falls! Then they would have only a twenty-five-mile journey to town—did they realize that?"

Structure

Giants in the Earth comprises two books, or parts, each of which ends with death or near-death. The novel is unique in its emphasis on psychology and character development, as opposed to plot and incident. Patrick D. Morrow is one of many critics who see the novel as a tragedy. He explains its form as "ten chapters of five well-defined acts, adhering to the tragic rhythm of exposition, conflict, crisis, and catastrophe." Other elements that confirm the work as a tragedy are its emphasis on free will and individual responsibility, a chain of events leading to catastrophe (Per Hansa's death), and its tragic rhythm. But the structure of the novel can also be considered from other points of view. Critic Steve Hahn notes the "tense dichotomy of structure: the physical world of the Great Plains, and a reality which is envisioned in terms of Norwegian religious and cultural structures." Paul A. Olson likens the structure of the book to "early Germanic epics in that the hero begins with a conquest over a series of physical threats and ends with defeat before some spiritual ones." Other scholars see a deliberate association between Book I of the novel, "The Land-Taking," and the traditional account of Norse colonization in Iceland.

Snow-covered mountains reflecting off water in Norway, Rölvaag's native country.

Imagery

The imagery of *Giants in the Earth* is rich and varied. Per Hansa was a fisherman before leaving for America, and there are many images of boats and the sea. The fact that the wagons crossing the plains actually were called prairie schooners adds to the power of this image. As Beret's insanity deepens, Per himself behaves "like a good boat in a heavy sea." And on the afternoon of the locust invasion, his sod hut looks to him "like a quay thrust out into a turbulent current."

Nature and the elements are often given night-mare-like qualities. In her distress, Beret fixes on a "cloud that had taken on the shape of a face, awful of mien and giantlike in proportions." At first, Per sees the locust invasion as the work of a giant's hand "shaking an immense tablecloth of iridescent colours." The night that follows Per's discovery of Beret and the smallest children hiding in the big chest, "the Great Prairie stretched herself voluptuously; giantlike." Images of light are used to varying effect. For example, the day after the birth of Peder Victorious, "The sun shone brightly through the window, spreading a golden lustre over the white walls." But after months of winter, the daylight inside the Hansas' hut casts a "pale, sickly gleam."

Compare & Contrast

- **1870s**: Prior to the 1880s, the majority of immigrants to the United States came from the British Isles and northwestern Europe.

  1927: A quota law passed in 1924, fixing the number of immigrants from each nation of origin, favored Europeans and effectively barred most Asians.

  Today: Since 1965 national quotas have been replaced with hemispheric limitations, and provisions exist for acceptance of political refugees. The United States grapples with the issue of illegal immigration, particularly from Latin America, and its social, economic, and political effects.

- **1870s:** The Indian Removal Act of 1830 and western migration of whites following the discovery of gold in California in 1848 signaled the beginning of a grisly struggle for territory between the European immigrants and Native Americans.

  1927: By 1887 most Native Americans had been forced onto reservations, where life was marked by poverty, poor education, and unemployment that would persist throughout the century.

  Today: Restoration of original treaty lands and land won in legal battles has increased Native American property within U.S. boundaries to 53 million acres, much of which is valuable either for its natural beauty or for its mineral reserves. Native American communities struggle to find the best way to tap the economic and political potential of these lands.

- **1870s**: The railroads grew rapidly after 1830, and on May 10, 1869, the eastern and western tracks of the first transcontinental railroad in the United States met at Promontory Point, Utah.

  1927: By 1916 the railroads were handling 77% of all intercity freight traffic, but after 1920, they faced increasing competition from automobiles, buses, long-distance trucking, oil pipelines, and airplanes.

  Today: The amount of freight moved by the railroads had declined to 33% in 1990 but has since remained stable; passenger traffic, however, never recovered, except for a brief period during the Second World War, and although intercity trains continue to operate, generally revenues do not cover costs.

- **1870s:** Between 1878 and 1886, South Dakota experienced a land boom, initially stimulated by the discovery of gold in the Black Hills but subsequently fueled by cattle ranching and railroad building.

  1927: A combination of droughts and the Great Depression caused widespread destruction to the area in the late 1920s, and over the following decade the population of the State of South Dakota declined by 50,000.

  Today: After the Second World War, improvements in farming methods increased agricultural and livestock production in South Dakota but also resulted in the consolidation of small farms into large units and the displacement of many small farmers. Since 1981, however, a shift to service, finance, and trade industries has been accompanied by significant economic growth.

Historical Context

The Postwar Boom

The much ballyhooed prosperity of the 1920s, the so-called Jazz Age, was largely confined to the upper-middle class. Although quick fortunes were made in the stock market and in real-estate speculation, most Americans did not see their economic situation improve in the postwar years. In *Giants in the Earth,* Rölvaag describes the formation of farm settlements on the southeastern Dakota prairies in the late 1870s, and over the next half a century, many of these farms would do well. The

First World War permanently reversed the fortunes of farmers, and during the 1920s, 4 million farmers left their farms. Nonetheless, these were important years for business, which a succession of American presidents from Warren G. Harding to Herbert Hoover believed would banish poverty in the United States. Sinclair Lewis incarnated this belief in business as the ultimate panacea in the main character of his novel *Babbitt* (1922).

Postwar Isolationism and Social Change

When post-First World War peace did not bring long-hoped-for prosperity, Americans reacted by avoiding foreign entanglements. They rejected the League of Nations, and viewed the Russian Revolution with suspicion. Idealism in general was not highly valued. Although the United States received about 60% of the world's immigrants from 1820 to 1930, a quota law passed in 1924 reduced the total number of immigrants and established fixed numbers for each nation, and had the practical effect of barring most Asians.

But the 1920s turned out to be an era of important social changes. Women in particular achieved significant gains, including increased access to education. Sexual mores were less restrained. In 1928 women were granted equal voting rights. The disciplines of medicine, architecture, science, and social reform all produced achievements of enduring worth. In business, entrepreneurs such as Walter P. Chrysler, Alfred P. Sloan, William C. Durant, and Henry Ford profited from the favorable political climate to make big business bigger. For a small segment of the population, these were years of optimism, symbolized by Charles Lindbergh's flight across the Atlantic in *The Spirit of St. Louis* and Ford's Model-T automotive technology, which made cars affordable for many people. Throughout the decade, the United States remained a segregated country, although there were some exceptions. For example, during this time Jews organized the movie industry, and black jazz, made popular by Louis Armstrong and Duke Ellington, had a permanent influence on world culture. Sports remained closed, however, and except for some of the writers of the Harlem Renaissance and a handful of Jewish publishers, the publishing industry remained white and Protestant.

Growing Urbanization

In *Giants in the Earth,* the settlers dream of the coming of the railroad to lessen the length of trips to town for supplies. The development of communications in the 1920s was an even more dramatic leap forward. By the end of the decade, 18.5 million telephones and 10.2 million radios were in service in the United States. A network of paved roads connected towns with major cities. By 1929, 20 million cars were on these roads. These changes helped to break down regional divisions in the country, but a by-product of the link with the cities was the death of the small towns. In the time Rölvaag's novel is set, there is no school at Spring Creek, and two of the younger settlers are pressed into service to teach the others. In contrast, between 1919 and 1928 access to education increased across the United States. College enrollment tripled, and women made up a third of the student population. Collegiate lifestyle made itself felt throughout the culture. Overall, the decade was one of real achievement in many areas, especially the arts and media. The speculative excesses of the 1920s were later blamed for the Depression, and in the decade that followed, the carefree lifestyle and values symbolic of the Jazz Age were considered frivolous.

Critical Overview

Early reviews of *Giants in the Earth* were highly favorable. Writing in the *Chicago Daily News,* Carl Sandburg called the story "so terrible and panoramic, piling up its facts with incessantly subtle intimations, that it belongs among the books to be kept and cherished." Walter Vogdes wrote in *The Nation* that "We may wish desperately that Rölvaag could have ended his tale in triumph and satisfaction…. But no, Rölvaag had to stand close to the facts and the truth." In his introduction to the novel, Lincoln Colcord, Rölvaag's co-translator, called the work unique for being "so palpably European in its art and atmosphere, so distinctly American in everything it deals with."

Other contemporary evaluations were equally positive. Historian Henry Commager called the novel "a milestone on American literature" and "the most penetrating and mature depictment of the westward movement in our literature." Scandinavian studies scholar Julius E. Olson was impressed that the book (which was first published in Norwegian) had "passed muster with Norwegian critics and Norwegian readers in the homeland." Clifton P. Fadiman had praise for Rölvaag's ethnic sensitivity, "as delicate as a seismograph."

Giants in the Earth has maintained its value over time. Critics often note the influence of

Lutheranism and the writings of Henrik Ibsen and Kierkegaard on Rölvaag's characterization. According to Harold P. Simonson, "In spite of Beret's indomitable effort to preserve her Norwegian ways, her greater strivings concern a transcendent faith." Theodore Jorgenson and Nora O. Solum pointed out that "the robust conscience [such as Per Hansa's] is an element of character that Ibsen used time and again. The Vikings are said to be blessed with it.... They never seemed to regret their deeds, were never inclined to be morbid."

Other frequently cited literary influences are Old Norse sagas, Norwegian fairy tales, and Nordland dialect and folk memories. Particularly the Askeladd—a Norse tale in which the hero triumphs over adversity and wins the hand of a princess—is invoked in discussing the novel. Joseph E. Baker compared Rölvaag's respect for man to Homer's, and he calls the novel "a modern epic of Western man." Einer Haugen agreed. "By themselves, the events are simple and everyday, such as might have occurred to anyone. But the framework into which he has placed them deserves to be called epic." George Leroy White, Jr., praised Rölvaag's description of nature and his "Scandinavian" ability to evoke atmosphere. "It becomes oppressive; you feel that you must put the book down, you are so tired." Baker considered the passage where the minister brings Beret out of "utter darkness" to be "the greatest yet written in American fiction."

A universally acknowledged strength is Rölvaag's psychological realism, that is, his unromantic portrayal of the internal state of his characters. Though other writers such as Hamlin Garland, Edward W. Howe, and Willa Cather also dealt with psychological aspects of the westward movement, none had done it on the same scale as Rölvaag. "For the first time," wrote Commager, "a novelist has measured the westward movement with a psychological yardstick and found it wanting."

There is little disagreement that the work is tragic on several levels. According to Commager, "The westward movement ... becomes the tragedy of earth's humbling of man." But this would not have been news to Rölvaag. He knew that "immigration is always tragic," wrote Julius E. Olson. "It is the price the pioneer pays for the future welfare of his children." Kristoffer Paulson recognized a tragic pattern typical of Rölvaag's novels, "inevitably ending in catastrophe," and he ranked the book among other great American tragedies such as *A Farewell to Arms, The Sound and the Fury,* and *The Red Badge of Courage.*

Critics dispute whether Per or Beret is the true hero of the story. Harold P. Simonson saw Per Hansa as "heroic in his choosing ... fallen in his choice. This is the paradox informing great tragedy. Choice and the dreadful possibility of damnation are inseparable." But for Paul A. Olson, it is Beret's heroism that "is the tragic heroism of Lear, or Kierkegaard's Abraham or Job."

Critics do not stress the work's weaknesses. Charles Boewe found *Giants in the Earth* the most "aesthetically satisfying" of the books in Rölvaag's trilogy, "but at the same time the poorest history," because it is based on secondhand knowledge.

Criticism

Darren Felty

Darren Felty is a Visiting Instructor at the College of Charleston. In the following essay, he explores O. E. Rölvaag's characterization of the Dakota plains settlers and the internal and external conflicts that ultimately determine their fate.

After publishing the English version of *Giants in the Earth* in 1927, O. E. Rölvaag was praised by many critics for helping to redefine the novel of the American frontier. Originally written in Norwegian and translated by Rölvaag and Lincoln Colcord, the novel dramatizes the vast opportunity the Western plains offered to those daring enough to settle it, but, unlike former plains novels, it does not overromanticize this settlement. Instead, Rölvaag details the harshness of life on the frontier and the destructive effects it had on both the weak and the hearty. Revolving around the conflict between Per Hansa and his wife Beret, who hold widely divergent views on American farm life, the novel contrasts the power of Per Hansa's vital ambition with Beret's fatalistic conviction that frontier pursuits will destroy her family's civility and jeopardize their religious salvation. An omnipresent factor in both their lives, however, is the prairie itself, which Rölvaag alternately personifies as indifferent to human beings and as intensely bent on preventing farmers' encroachments. Rölvaag's characterizations of the plains help the reader comprehend the forces arrayed against immigrant settlers. Even more important, though, Rölvaag's portrayals of Per Hansa and Beret reveal the emotional and psychological consequences of settlement, wherein

What Do I Read Next?

- *Bury My Heart at Wounded Knee,* is Dee Brown's critically acclaimed 1970 account of the methodical annihilation of Native Americans by whites during the nineteenth century.

- In Willa Cather's *My Antonia* (1918), a family of Bohemian immigrants confronts the hardships of pioneer life, including poverty and suicide, on the Nebraska plains.

- *The Last of the Mohicans* (1826) is James Fenimore Cooper's classic tale of nobility and frontier adventure during the French and Indian War.

- In *A Doll's House* (1879), one of the realistic plays for which Henrik Ibsen is best known, Nora Helmer courageously cuts herself loose from her degrading marriage of eight years to seek an independent life.

- Mark Twain humorously recalls his escapades during a stagecoach journey through the American Midwest in *Roughing It* (1872).

- *Kristin Lavransdatter* (1920-22) is Nobel Prize-winner Sigrid Unset's trilogy of love and religion set in medieval Norway.

---

one's material gains are always offset by tragedy and loss.

Rölvaag's early descriptions of the plain establish both its centrality to his work and the degree to which it dwarfs human endeavors. He opens the novel, "Bright, clear sky over a plain so wide that the rim of the heavens cut down on it around the entire horizon.... Bright, clear sky, to-day, to-morrow, and for all time to come.... A gust of wind, sweeping across the plain, threw into life waves of yellow and blue and green. Now and then a dead black wave would race over the scene ... a cloud's gliding shadow ... now and then...." As in the rest of the book, the immensity of the frontier pervades these descriptions, as do impressions of eternity, beauty, and foreboding. Rölvaag explicitly contrasts the sense of vastness with Per Hansa's small

family crossing the grassy fields. Immediately, the reader grasps one of the central questions of the novel and of plains experience: how can people survive in an environment that perpetually highlights their own insignificance and vulnerability? Rölvaag answers this question through the lives of his central characters, revealing that, in numerous cases, settlers do not survive, and those who do often suffer profound emotional and psychological afflictions because of their surroundings.

Rölvaag further emphasizes the intimidating difficulties of plains life by coupling characterizations of a vast, indifferent prairie with personified representations of an actively hostile natural world. Rölvaag presents the plain as alive, conscious, and frequently malevolent. For instance, in the beginning of Book II he describes the plain as "Monsterlike.... Man she scorned; his works she would not brook.... She would know, when the time came, how to guard herself and her own against him!" In such passages, Rölvaag's prairie jealously protects itself against settlers' attempts to tame it and exploit its fertility. The small humans who occupy the land have ambition and industry on their side, but the prairie can muster blizzards, violent storms, rampaging fires, and locust plagues. Thus, the plain wins even against the stout Hans Olsa and Per Hansa in the final chapter, chillingly entitled "The Great Plain Drinks the Blood of Christian Men and Is Satisfied." According to Theodore Jorgenson and Nora O. Solum, Rölvaag derives this title from the Norwegian fairy tale in which the troll, satisfied by nothing else, drinks man's blood, and the characterization of the land as a troll runs through much of the book. These references to bloodthirsty retribution evoke an image of a beast both zealous and merciless as it attacks its foe and satiates itself upon his destruction. For Rölvaag, such is the life for many frontier dwellers.

In Per Hansa, Rölvaag best embodies his views of the failed conquest of the early plains settlers. Per Hansa tames a small patch of land and even begins to gain some measure of material prosperity, but his grand visions are never realized because of both external and internal antagonistic forces. First, of course, he must confront his immediate environment. Though he recognizes the brutalities of the prairie, Per Hansa feels his own strength too profoundly to fear this adversary. For him, the vast stretches of the plains evoke not loneliness or oppressiveness but a fit arena for his ambitions. Here, indeed, is a worthy opponent for him, a creature of great beauty, fecundity, and cruelty. Full of his own vibrancy, he often sings the praises of the land and revels in the work required to tame it. He dreams of building a kingdom and being the lord of his own destiny, and it is the life-giving soil that will enable him to fashion his dream into reality. Much of the book glories in Per Hansa's ingenuity, energy, and optimism. He is like the Norwegian mythological Askeladd, the hero who rises from meager beginnings to defeat, through goodness, perseverance, and strength, the forces arrayed against him, in this case the land as a vicious troll. But Rölvaag is far too realistic about human limitations to push this mythological allusion past the point of believability. If Per Hansa is a triumphant hero, it is only in isolated moments, and his ability to overcome seemingly any obstacle ultimately leads to his death while trying to navigate a blizzard. He cannot overcome the forces of nature, however much he conceives them as a conquerable enemy.

Perhaps more significant than his confrontations with the plains, however, are his conflicts with his own ambition and pride, both of which blind him to his wife's character. He is not an overbearing man, yet because he glories in the life he has chosen, he cannot believe that Beret will remain burdened by it. He puzzles over her depressions but asserts that a change in weather or their immediate living conditions will revive her spirit. That Beret is by nature unfit for such a life does not occur to him until she moves rapidly toward psychological ruin. Though he finally blames himself for Beret's condition, he still does not abandon the tenets of his dream of frontier conquest, nor does he embrace a religious faith of humility. For him, human vitality and ambition are not sins. To reject these elements in the human character would be to reject two of his most fundamental attributes. In fact, he plants these characteristics in his youngest son by naming him Peder Victorious. True to form, though, he does not consider the effect of such a name on his wife. She is deeply offended and terrified by it, because she maintains that no one can be victorious on the prairie and any belief otherwise proves one is in Satan's grip. He later realizes his mistake, but, even so, when the kindly minister criticizes him for his complaints by saying, "'You are not willing to beat your cross with humility!'" Per Hansa replies defiantly, "'No, I am not…. We find other things to do out here than to carry crosses!'" Despite his guilt and self-recriminations, he does not alter his way of viewing the world or his place in it in order to understand his wife better. He is a man who directly confronts physical challenges, but the subtleties of

the emotional realm remain beyond his reach, much to the detriment of himself and his family.

Beret, too, suffers from an inability to alter her perception of the world, leading to her own debilitating unhappiness. Like her husband, Beret sees plains life as an opportunity. But for her it is an opportunity for people to sink to the level of animals, violating all that is sacred. She cannot see the prairie as beautiful or fecund; it is only terrible, the devil's instrument to lure people into baseness. She views the entire Western Movement as a destructive unleashing of human appetite: "Now she saw it clearly: here on the trackless plains, the thousand-year-old hunger of the poor after human happiness had been unloosed!" While to Per Hansa and the other settlers such an event is cause for celebration, for Beret it is cause for distress. Throughout the book, Beret is the epitome of a traditionalist, believing completely in the religious tenets of her upbringing and the superiority of Norwegian life. Giving in to human passions and rejecting one's familial obligations in order to chase after elusive treasure, as she has done with Per Hansa, invite God's wrath. Indeed, she views their lives on the plains as a punishment for her own sins of sexual passion, filial betrayal, and excessive pride, and the intensity of her convictions prevents her from critically confronting her own responses and feelings of impending doom. As a result, she cannot truly see the good in others or in herself.

The plain, Per Hansa's reputation for amazing exploits, and his and Beret's irreconcilable perceptions all help lead to the final tragedy in the book: Per Hansa's death. He sees the proposed journey to find the minister as the height of folly because no man could survive in such a blizzard. In addition, he does not think Hans Olsa, a good man, needs a minister. Beret, on the other hand, believes that the dangers to Hans Olsa's soul far outweigh the dangers to her husband's life. In her mind, one cannot stand idly by and watch a man be condemned to damnation. To do so would be committing a grievous sin that could bring damnation upon oneself. Added to the pressures from his wife, Per Hansa must contend with Hans Olsa and Sörine's fearful pleadings and belief in his near invincibility. When Per Hansa acquiesces, he is not convinced about the rightness of his errand, unlike his other dangerous ventures. Instead, he is angry at Beret and resigned to do his best, though he seems to know he is walking to his death. His last thoughts, fittingly, are of his home and family as he bids himself to "Move on!—Move on!", driving himself forward, as he always does. In the end, Per

Hansa is killed by a combination of his anger, pride, and sympathy; his wife's singular convictions; his friends' fears and unqualified belief in him; and the vicious might of the plain. Yet, despite his defeat, he dies still adhering to his visions, as the reader sees in his Westward death gaze.

While the novel contains a number of tones, it ultimately strikes more of a naturalistic than a romantic chord. If one sees the book as romantic, then the "Giants" in the title reflect the heroic stature of the Dakota settlers, thereby glorifying Western expansion. Yet the romantic tones in the book derive mainly from Per Hansa's praises and condemnations of the plains, as well as his sense of his own vibrant individuality. This sensibility comes through in Rölvaag's prose, but he counters it with darker, more enduring perceptions of frontier life. Individuals in the book are always at the mercy of their environment. Thus, Rölvaag implies, the "Giants" of the title refer to the natural forces (or trolls) working to prevent the success of the settlers' endeavors. Rölvaag's strongest message may be, though, that the characters suffer because of their own flawed characters. Per Hansa, for instance, is so caught by his visions that he allows his wife to suffer greatly. Even after recognizing his failings, he does not forsake his ambitions, showing the implacable grip of one's nature and dreams. Therefore, as critic Paul Reigstad asserts, the "Giants" could include the traits of the settlers themselves that, whether caused by inclination or upbringing, blind them to others' needs and to their own destructive shortcomings. Through this approach to his subject, Rölvaag identifies the settling of the plains as a widespread hunger for autonomy, adventure, and material prosperity whose silent costs often outweighed its loudly celebrated gains.

Source: Darren Felty, in an essay for *Novels for Students*, Gale, 1999.

Patrick D. Morrow

In the following excerpt, Morrow discusses Rölvaag's use of and departure from tragic conventions in Giants in the Earth, *a novel the critic ranks along with the great American tragedies* A Farewell to Arms, The Sound and the Fury, *and* The Red Badge of Courage.

> It's nothing but a common, ordinary romantic lie that we are 'captains of our own souls'! Nothing but one of those damned poetic phrases. Just look back over your own life and see how much you have captained!

This statement by Ole Rölvaag, less about fate than the human error of false pride, points us in a rewarding direction for an interpretation of *Giants in the Earth.* Concerned with *hamartia,* irreconcilable values, and dramatically rising to state man's universal predicament, Rölvaag's masterpiece is fundamentally a tragedy. Henry Steele Commager [in "The Literature of the Pioneer West," *Minnesota History,* VIII (December, 1927)] and Vernon Louis Parrington [in *Main Currents in American Thought,* III (New York, 1930)] suggested this possibility in 1927, shortly after the book's publication. But neither Commager nor Parrington shed much light on Rölvaag's methods for establishing *Giants* as a tragedy. Since those early days, the considerable scholarship on this important writer has pretty much moved to do battle on other fronts. Yet, by understanding *Giants* as a tragedy, I believe we can resolve much critical debate over the novel, especially about Beret and Per Hansa; perceive the book's real form, motivations, and complex thematic unity; and finally, appreciate Rölvaag's intention and considerable accomplishments as an artist.

Rölvaag develops *Giants in the Earth* as a tragedy by several methods, to be noted now and developed throughout this paper. In terms of genre, tragedy becomes established with a process of definition by negation. Rölvaag includes many aspects and conventions of both saga and epic, but then undercuts both by parodying them, and by having the tragic aspects increasingly dominate as his novel progresses. In terms of form, *Giants* has ten chapters of five well-defined acts, adhering to the tragic rhythm of exposition, conflict, crisis, and catastrophe. Unities of time and place appear with the predictable seasons, tragic winter being dominant, and almost all action takes place within the Norwegian prairie settlements. Imitations of Ibsen's dramas and Shakespearian tragedy abound, hardly surprising since from early youth Ole Rölvaag had been an avid reader of great literature. (He went on, of course, to become a literature professor at St. Olaf College from 1906 to 1931.) Finally, for the key issue of tragic recognition, Rölvaag fashions out of his Norwegian milieu and literary consciousness, a particularly American awareness....

It seems widely agreed that tragedy emphasizes free will and individual responsibility, rather than inevitability and an external determinism, so happy in the saga or epic, but so dismal in naturalism. A tragic work typically presents a chain of events leading to catastrophe, often depicting a fall from high or successful station because of the hero's pride or *hybris,* an apt description of Per

Hansa's life journey and fate. Some kind of chorus or community voice may function as spokesman for society's viewpoint and values. In *Giants in the Earth* the chorus not only advises but judges. As a community, they support Per; but later, as a congregation, they start to rally behind Beret.

Giants also has a tragic rhythm—nothing so episodic as scenes constructed and then struck, but a thematic movement of wax and wane. The exposition, the establishment of this Norwegian colony on the far edge of the prairie, is long, almost three and a half chapters. About midway in Chapter IV, "What the Waving Grass Revealed," Beret's disaffiliation and conflict with Per begins to become the book's dominant issue. Beret's withdrawal and conflict become deeper, even shocking, until a crisis is reached in Chapter VIII, "The Power of Evil in High Places." After a chapter of reprieve or counter-action, the catastrophe is consumated in the final chapter with its outrageous title. Before we can understand the recognition phase, the final tragic aspect in this book, we must see the terms of this tragedy.

Professor Harold Simonson [in "The Tenacity of History: Rolvaag's *Giants in the Earth*," paper presented at the Twelfth Annual Meeting, Western Literature Association, October 7, 1977, Sioux Falls, South Dakota.] has suggested that *Giants in the Earth* presents two intersecting but irreconcilable dimensions, Time (Beret) and Space (Per). Simonson is concerned with the opposition between traditional Lutheran faith and the frontier ethic in *Giants*, but if expanded, this notion can also clarify the tragic character conflict in this novel. Forceful, physically powerful and handsome, skillful and even lucky, Per Hansa is a great natural leader. He loves the frontier because it is so expansive, a fitting, infinite surface on which to move his will, enact his own destiny and that of his people. Per attempts to change the prairie, or conquer time, by establishing a kind of immortality with his pioneer kingdom. Per's will and ego fill all space. Morally, he is a pragmatic teleologist who first ignores then hates the past. In the tradition of American Romanticism, he sees himself motivated by a dream of absolute good and right. Per fears rejection by those whom he leads far more than he fears impending failure because of the overwhelmingly hostile Dakota environment with its blizzards, floods, wind, clay soil, and grasshopper plagues. Per Hansa has confused his dream with reality.

As Per acts in terms of his vision, Beret acts in terms of consequences. Beret is the party of time; she wants to find her place in history, not escape it. Beret is defined and informed by what has already been created, and thus she is drawn to the old Norwegian culture, the Lutheran religion, and such other institutions as education, motherhood, and being a wife. Within an established community, institutions have been developed to deal with time, ritualizing the cycle of birth, growth, and death. But the prairie is infinity, as Rölvaag relentlessly reminds us throughout *Giants,* the zone where space cancels time, making the individual reach an absolutely Kierkegaardian state of being forever alone.

> Bright, clear sky over a plain so wide that the rim of the heavens cut down on it around the entire horizon.... Bright, clear sky, to-day, to-morrow, and for all time to come.... "Tish-ah!" said the grass.... "Tish-ah, tish-ah!".... Never had it said anything else—never would it say anything else.

From this beginning, then, Beret is literally and figuratively "spaced-out."

Nevertheless, as critic Barbara Meldrum has established [in "Fate, Sex, and Naturalism in Rölvaag's Trilogy" in *Ole Rölvaag: Artist and Cultural Leader,* ed. Gerald Thorson (Northfield, Minn., 1975), 41–49.] Beret can control her disorientation and depression until she comes to feel that Per Hansa has rejected her. Like Hester in *The Scarlet Letter,* Beret is no witch, but a passionate woman. She does feel guilt for her productive passion with Per, but her love for him continues to increase. Out on the prairie, she loses all sense of purpose with the realization that it is his dream, not Beret, which Per loves more than life. Beret comes to see Per as a person without fear, totally, blindly committed to his vision through his all-consuming pride. Per is thus daemonic, and the consequences for following this evil course shall most certainly be destruction. Beret must bear this burden alone. She has reached a Cassandra-like impasse—doomed to knowledge, but never to be believed because he who hears her cries heeds only his own voice.

In terms of Per's dream and the ideal goals of the community, Beret does indeed lose her sanity. But in Beret's terms, her bizarre behavior—having tea with her absent mother, sleeping in her hope chest, ceasing her household chores, and attacking Per for godless megalomania—ritualizes punishment for worshiping Per, the false god, her punishment for sins against time. Beret is not, as Lloyd Hustvedt [in discussion following this paper, "The Johnson Rölvaag Correspondence," at the above noted Western Literature Association meeting] once half-seriously proffered, "a party pooper out on the prairie." Nor is she a pietistic, guilt-ridden fanatic bent on precipitating Per Hansa's early death. Nor is she the opposing view, Kierkegaard's "Knight of Faith" following God's divine imperative. However critically misunderstood, Beret remains a very human character, very hurt, and very much alone, pursuing a direction out of her moral and emotional wilderness by the only way she trusts....

That *Giants in the Earth* is a tragedy of two characters frozen in their irreconcilable dimensions may now seem evident, but where is that tragic recognition scene that changes and enlightens the protagonist? Since, as Maynard Mack [in "The Jacobean Shakespeare: Some Observations on the Construction of the Tragedies," in *Stratford Upon Avon Studies,* I (London, 1960)] reminds us, "tragic drama is in one way or other, a record of man's affair with transcendence," where might this transcendence be found? Nowhere in the novel. Playing his trump card of dramatic irony, of making his characters realize less about themselves than the audience understands, Rölvaag throws not only the burden of interpretation but the responsibility of awareness squarely on his readers. Far from undercutting tragic conventions, by this strategy Rölvaag expands *Giants* into relevance, into our own dimension and consciousness.

Four key scenes in *Giants,* all revealing to the audience rather than to the characters, establish our participatory role in this tragic novel. The first is that opening scene of the prairie as mystical infinity, a landscape more formidable and incomprehensible than any of the characters. The second scene is the visitation of the grief-stricken and insane Kari, her husband Jakob, and their children. This episode forms a kind of play-within-a-play, a dumbshow or mirroring device for the relationship between Per and Beret. Kari's hysteria is Beret's largely self-contained depression put into action, and Jakob surely must be enacting a Per Hansa fantasy by roping Kari down in the wagon and saying: "Physically she seems as well as ever.... She certainly hasn't overworked since we've been travelling." The third scene is the christening of Peder Victorius, where the Per-Beret schism becomes public, but here too, actions are taken and positions are stated without any understanding by the characters. This pattern continues into the last scene. Per departs for his death with an almost spitefully disconnected calm, while Beret broods, paralyzed by guilt and doubt, wondering how history and the community will judge her.

Dramatically, then, Rölvaag opposes his audience's recognition against his characters' actions. But beyond dramaturgy, Rölvaag limits his characters' awareness by significantly limiting their language. Typically a tragic hero defines himself by overstatement, using hyperbole and metaphor to establish a momentum towards change and understanding. But Beret moves in circles inside the soddie, while Per Hansa moves in circles outside the house. Never soliloquizing, Beret conducts a long series of spinning monologues, usually in the form of unanswered questions in the conditional voice. Per Hansa, as suspicious of words as he is of emotions, wanders a path around the community, seeking tasks and deeds that will establish his goodness. Per and Beret are not fools blindly driven by some all-powerful malignant force. Perhaps the novel's greatest tragedy is that it centers on two very human characters who cannot understand their own tragedy. We can.

In the establishment of *Giants in the Earth* as a tragedy, Rölvaag owes a particular debt to two sources, Ibsen and Shakespeare. From Ibsen, whom Rölvaag intensely studied and taught for many years, he adopts a tone of pervasive overcast along with the thematic emphasis of self-deception as a psychological prison. Thus, Per Hansa is a synthesis of Brand and Peer Gynt, Brand predominating. Surely Beret's character has been filtered through the apprehension of Nora and Hedda Gabler. Ibsen's celebrated and tragically overwhelming momentum of cause and effect gives the pattern for the plot of *Giants.* As Rölvaag once concluded in a potent lecture on Ibsen: "... the free exercise of will in the dramas results in disaster.... Life is tragic."

Shakespeare's *Macbeth* provides an analogue if not a source for the characterization and context in *Giants.* Both Lady Macbeth and Beret act with a sane and visionary madness, reflecting on all that has happened before and its consequences. Like Macbeth, Per Hansa just gives up. Certainly the eerie atmosphere of *Macbeth* exists out on the prairie, but, like the knocking at the gate in *Macbeth, Giants* also has its moments of saving humor. Maynard Mack notes an aspect of Shakespeare's later tragedies particularly appropriate to the tragic movement of *Giants in the Earth:*

> Whatever the themes of individual plays ... the one pervasive Jacobean theme tends to be the undertaking and working out of acts of will, and especially (in that strongly Calvinistic age) of acts of self-will.

Tragedy provides neither eternal answers nor temporal game plans, but heightens our awareness, our realization of the human condition. This is Rölvaag's mission with *Giants in the Earth.*

Giants in the Earth, then, is not a saga or epic about Norwegian settlements and triumphs in the Land of Goshen. This tragic novel is an amalgamation of Norwegian culture and concerns turned to a pioneer experience, set on the most extreme American frontier. As John R. Milton [in "The Dakota Image," *The South Dakota Review,* 8 (Autumn, 1970)] has noted, *Giants* is the premier account of "how people remember the Dakotas or learn about them." As such, especially with Rölvaag forcing the tragic realization upon his audience, *Giants* is squarely in the tradition of American tragic realism, in the company of such works as *The Red Badge of Courage, A Farewell to Arms, The Sound and the Fury,* and even *One Flew Over the Cuckoo's Nest.* In the manner of Ibsen and Shakespeare, Rölvaag's masterpiece transcends time and space to make a dramatic and universal statement about the meaning of life.

Source: Patrick D. Morrow, "Rölvaag's Giants in the Earth as Tragedy," in *North Dakota Quarterly,* Vol. 28, No. 4, Autumn, 1980, pp. 83–90.

Joseph E. Baker

In the following review, Baker notes, particularly in the character of Per Hansa, an affirmation of the Western ideas of humans possessing free will as opposed to the Eastern, deterministic outlook held by American romantic writers such as Henry David Thoreau and Ralph Waldo Emerson.

Rölvaag's *Giants in the Earth* is a vision of human life rich in its implications. Here the pioneer struggle with the untamed universe may serve as a symbol for the condition of man himself against inhuman Destiny. The hero, Per Hansa, is a typical man of the West, both in the regional sense that he represents our pioneer background and in the universal human sense that he embodies the independent spirit, the rationalism, and what has often been condemned as the utilitarianism of Western civilization—European mankind's determination to cherish human values against the brute force of Fate. Under the influence of German philosophy and Romantic pantheism, many modern writers have bent the knee to the gods of nature and worshiped a fatal Destiny. On the other side, we turn to French literature and its greatest thinker, Pascal, for the classic statement of the Western attitude: "Man is but a reed, the feeblest thing in Na-

ture; but he is a thinking reed.... If the universe were to crush him, man would still be more noble than that which killed him, because he *knows* that he dies."

This conception is developed most fully in the great tragic dramas of European literatures, but we find a similar respect for man at the very dawn of our civilization in the first Western author, Homer. His men are "like gods"; indeed, sometimes they are better and wiser than the supernatural forces and divine giants they come in contact with. Before the Heroic Age, mankind was sunk in an Age of Terror, given over to the superstition that the world is ruled by forces which can be dealt with only by magical rites—a view that still survives in Per Hansa's wife Beret. But with Homer, man emerges into the epic stage of human consciousness, with its great admiration for men of ability. Rölvaag's *Giants in the Earth* is a modern epic of Western man.

In this novel, as in Homer, or, for that matter, in *Beowulf,* there is the heartiest gusto and admiration for human achievement—sophisticates would say a naïve delight in the simplest things: "Wonder of wonders!" What had Per Hansa brought back with him? "It was a bird cage, made of thin slats; and inside lay a rooster and two hens!" Nobody but Homer and Rölvaag can get us so excited over merely economic prosperity, man's achievement in acquiring fine things for his own use. One of the high dramatic points in the novel is the discovery that, after all, the wheat has come up! This sort of thing means life or death; and the preservation of human life, or the evaluation of things according to the pleasure they can give to individual men, is the very opposite of submission to material forces.

> Hans Olsa was cutting hay; his new machine hummed lustily over the prairie, shearing the grass so evenly and so close to the ground that his heart leaped with joy to behold the sight. What a difference, this, from pounding away with an old scythe, on steep, stony hillsides! All the men had gathered round to see him start.

That sounds like a passage from the *Odyssey.* And the central figure in the novel is an epic hero. Like Odysseus, Per Hansa is "never at a loss." Hans Olsa says to him, "No matter how hard you're put to it, you always give a good account of yourself!" This might be used to translate one of Athena's remarks to Odysseus. Or one may think of Virgil. Here are some of the phrases that make the novel seem epic: "[They talked] of land and crops, and of the new kingdom which they were about to found.... Now they had gone back to the very beginning of things." This comes in the earliest pages of the book; while the last chapter states their attitude thus: "There was no such thing as the Impossible any more. The human race has not known such faith and such self-confidence since history began"—one ought to say, since the Homeric Greeks. But in the translation of this novel from Norwegian into English, made by a New Englander, there has been added, out of respect for our Atlantic seaboard, "so had been the Spirit since the day the first settlers landed on the eastern shores." Thus the novel, especially in the English translation, brings out what America meant to mankind. "He felt profoundly that the greatest moment of his life had come. Now he was about to sow wheat on his own ground!" This is exactly what Jefferson wanted America to be. And as the Middle West became the most complete type of democratic civilization that the world has ever known, our leaders have fought many battles, in politics and war, to enable the ordinary hard-working farmer to sow his wheat on his own ground.

America at its most American, this is embodied in Per Hansa, who "never liked to follow an old path while there was still unexplored land left around him." That is the spirit of the West against the East, of America against Europe, of Europe against Asia. It is not that the amenities of life are undervalued; even Per Hansa is working to achieve a civilized life. But the amenities are less exciting than the achieving. Much of the dramatic tension between the characters turns upon this choice. It is the pioneer faith that "a good barn may perhaps pay for a decent house, but no one has ever heard of a fine dwelling that paid for a decent barn." But the opposite view is expressed by one of the men: "One doesn't need to live in a gopher hole, in order to get ahead." There speaks the conservative culture of a more Eastern or more European mind. The conquest of material nature has been superciliously criticized by comfortable New Englanders from Emerson to Irving Babbitt (both guilty of an undue respect for oriental passivity) as a case of forgetting the distinction between the "law for man and law for thing," meaning by the "law for thing" not material force but human mastery. It "builds town and fleet," says Emerson; by it the forest is felled, the orchard planted, the prairie tilled, the steamer built. But it seems to me that human triumph over matter is a genuine practical humanism, and that this is the true spirit of the West; that in Bacon's phrase, knowledge may well be used for "the relief of man's estate." Emerson was closer to the

spirit of the pioneers when he said, in "The Young American":

> Any relation to the land, the habit of tilling it, or mining it, or even hunting on it, generates the feeling of patriotism. He who keeps shop on it, or he who merely uses it as a support to his desk ... or ... manufactory, values it less.... We in the Atlantic states, by position, have been commercial, and have ... imbibed easily an European culture. Luckily for us ... the nervous, rocky West is intruding a new and continental element into the national mind, and we shall yet have an American genius.

And he calls it a "false state of things" that "our people have their intellectual culture from one country and their duties from another." But happily "America is beginning to assert herself to the senses and to the imagination of her children." If this be true—and I must confess that it seems rather extreme doctrine even to a middle western regionalist like myself—then Rölvaag, born in Europe, is more American than some of our authors of old New England stock. All Emerson's "Representative Men" were Europeans. It was not until the Middle West came into literature that we get an epic and broadly democratic spirit in works never to be mistaken for the products of modern Europe. Emerson recognized this in Lincoln; at last he admired a representative man who came from the West. And middle western leadership in American literature, begun with Lincoln's prose, established beyond a doubt by Mark Twain, was confirmed in our day by Rölvaag....

In "The Method of Nature" Emerson says, "When man curses, nature still testifies to truth and love. We may therefore safely study the mind in nature, because we cannot steadily gaze on it in mind"; and he proposes that "we should piously celebrate this hour: [August 11, 1841] by exploring the *method of nature*." We may take this to represent the attitude toward Nature that we find in the Romantic period of American literature: that is to say, the New England masters and their followers continuing up through Whitman. But romanticism came late to America. Already in England Tennyson was recognizing that the method of nature is red with blood in tooth and claw. It was this later view that came to prevail in literature toward the end of the nineteenth century, even in America, doubtless because of the increased knowledge of nature. I refer not only to the progress of science, but to the fact that later authors had struggled with Nature, more than the Romantics, whose Nature had been tamed by centuries of conquest. Thoreau said: "I love the wild not less than the good," but his Walden was within suburban distance of the cultural center and the financial center of the New World. Rölvaag had known Nature as the sea from which, as a Norwegian fisherman, he must wring his living. In 1893 a storm at sea drowned many of his companions; and this, he says, caused him "to question the romantic notion of nature's purposeful benevolence." So in this novel there are giants in the earth. On the prairie, "Man's strength availed but little out here."

> That night the Great Prairie stretched herself voluptuously; giantlike and full of cunning, she laughed softly into the reddish moon. "Now we will see what human might may avail against us!... Now we'll see!" And now had begun a seemingly endless struggle between man's fortitude in adversity, on the one hand, and power of evil in high places.

"The Power of Evil in High Places" is the title of the chapter, which includes a plague of locusts and also the terrible insanity of Per Hansa's wife. That is what we really find to be the method of Nature. For by this term Rölvaag, of course, does not merely mean scenery. He means the whole created universe that man is up against and the blind inhuman force or might that moves it. Sometimes he calls it Destiny, as in speaking of the murderous storm of 1893: "That storm changed my nature. As the seas broke over us and I believed that death was inescapable, I felt a resentment against Destiny." Twenty-seven years later another even more bitter tragedy occurred to impress Rölvaag with the murderousness of Nature: His five-year-old son Gunnar was drowned, under terrible circumstances. He writes that this tragedy changed his view of life. Previously he "had looked upon God as a logical mind in Whom the least happening" was planned and willed. Now he saw that much is "due to chance and to lawbound nature." In this novel, written later, it should be noticed that Per Hansa's wife Beret, especially when she is insane, continues Rölvaag's older view, blaming God for all miseries as if he had planned all. She broods that "beyond a doubt, it was Destiny that had brought her thither. Destiny, the inexorable law of life, which the Lord God from eternity had laid down for every human being, according to the path He knew would be taken.... Destiny had so arranged everything." Another poor miserable woman in this novel, her husband receiving his death blow from a cruel Nature, has this same dark pagan view: "Now the worst had happened and there was nothing to do about it, for Fate is inexorable." This is a continuation of the deadliest oriental fatalism, always current in misconceptions of Christianity, though actually it is just this which it

has been the function of Christian philosophy and Western humanism to cast out, to exorcise in rationalizing man's relation to the universe. Emerson put his finger on the difference between West and East when he wrote in his *Journals* in 1847:

> The Americans are free-willers, fussy, self-asserting, buzzing all round creation. But the Asiatics believe it is writ on the iron leaf, and will not turn on their heel to save them from famine, plague, or the sword. That is great, gives a great air to the people.... Orientalism is Fatalism, resignation; Occidentalism is Freedom and Will.

So, Beret does not believe they should try to conquer the prairie; she feels that it is sinful to undergo the conditions of pioneer life; she is "ashamed" that they have to put up with poor food. "Couldn't he understand that if the Lord God had intended these infinities to be peopled, He would not have left them desolate down through the ages?"

But her husband, Per Hansa, is a man of the West; he glories in the fact that he is an American free-willer, self-asserting. He rebels against Destiny and tries to master Nature. Carlyle says that the struggle between human free will and material necessity "is the sole Poetry possible," and certainly this makes the poetic content of Rölvaag's masterpiece. During the plague of locusts one of the other characters gives vent to an expression of Asiatic abnegation:

> "Now the Lord is taking back what he has given.... I might have guessed that I would never be permitted to harvest such wheat." ... "Stop your silly gabble!" snarled Per Hansa. "Do you really suppose *He* needs to take the bread out of your mouth?" There was a certain consolation in Per Hansa's outbursts of angry rationalism. [But when Per tries to scare the locusts away, Hans Olsa says, "Don't do that, Per Hansa! If the Lord has sent this affliction on us...."]

It should be noticed that Per Hansa, though a rationalist, is also a Christian; so the author designates him in the title of the last chapter, "The Great Plain Drinks the Blood of Christian Men." Per is defending a higher conception of God. When Hans Olsa, dying, quotes "It is terrible to fall into the hands of the living God," Per says, "Hush, now, man! Don't talk blasphemy!" Rölvaag is aware of the divine gentleness of Christianity; the words of the minister "flowed on ... softly and sweetly, like the warm rain of a summer evening" in a tender scene which suggests "Suffer little children to come unto me." This is in a chapter entitled "The Glory of the Lord"—for it is a clergyman who ministers to the "mind disease" of Beret and brings her out of her "utter darkness" in a passage that may be considered the greatest yet written in American fiction. What is implied in this novel becomes explicit in the sequel, *Peder Victorious,* where the first chapter is concerned with the religious musing of Per's fatherless son Peder. At one point he feels a difference between a Western as opposed to an Eastern or Old World conception of God and concludes that "no one could make him believe that a really American God would go about killing people with snowstorms and the like." But more significant is the account, in this sequel, of what the minister said to Beret after she had driven her husband out into the fatal snowstorm to satisfy her superstitious reverence for rites:

> You have permitted a great sin to blind your sight; you have forgotten that it is God who muses all life to flower and who has put both good and evil into the hearts of men. I don't think I have known two better men than your husband and the friend he gave his life for ... your worst sin ... lies in your discontent with ... your fellow men.

Surely, whatever Rölvaag's religious affiliations may have been, this is the expression of a Christian humanism. From this point of view it is far from true to say that American literature has sunk down in two or three generations from the high wisdom of Emerson to the degradation of the "naturalistic" novel. *Giants in the Earth* is a step in the right direction, abandoning the romantic idolatry that worshiped a Destiny in Nature and believed "the central intention of Nature to be harmony and joy." "Let us build altars to the Beautiful Necessity"—as Emerson puts it in his "Fate"— "Why should we be afraid of Nature, which is no other than 'philosophy and theology embodied?'" This sentiment can be found repeated in many forms throughout the rhapsodies of the "prophets" of our "Golden Day." I, for one, am rather tired of the glorification of these false prophets, and I am glad that American literature has outgrown their enthusiasms, so lacking in a sense for the genuine dignity of man. Wisdom was not monopolized by the stretch of earth's surface from a little north of Boston to a little south of Brooklyn Ferry. Another passage from "The Young American" could bring home to us the repulsive inhumanity of Emerson's conception of God. Enumerating the suffering and miseries of man's lot, how individuals are crushed and "find it so hard to live," Emerson blandly tells us this is the

> sublime and friendly Destiny by which the human race is guided ... the individual[s] never spared.... Genius or Destiny ... is not discovered in their calculated and voluntary activity, but in what befalls, with or without their design.... That Genius has infused itself into nature.... For Nature is the noblest engineer.

In opposition to this deadly submission to cruel natural force, I contend that Western civilization was built by innumerable details of calculated and voluntary activity, that the Christian God is a God concerned not with race but with individuals according to their moral worth, and that in the tragic event which befalls Per Hansa in this novel, without his design, we do *not* witness a God infused into Nature.

Source: Joseph E. Baker, "Western Man Against Nature: Giants in the Earth," in *College English,* Vol. 4, October, 1942–May, 1943, pp. 19–26.

Sources

Joseph E. Baker, "Western Man against Nature: 'Giants in the Earth'," in *College English,* Vol. 4, No. 1, October, 1941, pp. 19-26.

Charles Boewe, "Rölvaag's America: An Immigrant Novelist's Views," in *Western Humanities Review,* Vol. 11, No. 1, Winter, 1957, pp. 3-12.

Percy H. Boynton, "O. E. Rölvaag and the Conquest of the Pioneer," in *English Journal,* Vol. 18, No. 7, September, 1929, pp. 535-42.

Lincoln Colcord, in an introduction to *Giants in the Earth: A Saga of the Prairie* by O. E. Rölvaag, translated by Lincoln Colcord and O. E. Rölvaag, Harper and Row, 1927, pp. xi-xxii.

Henry Commager, "The Literature of the Pioneer West," in *Minnesota History,* Vol. 8, No. 4, December, 1927, pp. 319-28.

Clifton P. Fadiman, "Diminished Giants," in *Forum,* Vol. 81, No. 3, March, 1929, pp. xx, xxii.

Steve Hahn, "Vision and Reality in 'Giants in the Earth'," in *The South Dakota Review,* Vol. 17, No. 1, Spring, 1979, pp. 85-100.

Einar Haugen, in *Ole Edvart Rölvaag,* Twayne, 1983, pp. 80-1.

Theodore Jorgenson and Nora O. Solum, *Ole Edvart Rölvaag: A Biography,* Harper and Brothers, 1939, pp. 344-46.

Patrick D. Morrow, "Rölvaag's 'Giants in the Earth' as Tragedy," in *North Dakota Quarterly,* Vol. 48, No. 4, Autumn, 1980, pp. 83-90.

Julius E. Olsen, "Rölvaag's Novels of Norwegian Pioneer Life in the Dakotas," in *Scandinavian Studies and Notes,* Vol. 9, No. 3, August, 1926, pp. 45-55.

Paul A. Olson, "The Epic and Great Plains Literature: Rölvaag, Cather, and Neidhardt," in *Prairie Schooner,* Vol. 55, No. 182, Spring-Summer, 1981, pp. 263-85.

Kristoffer Paulson, "What Was Lost: Ole Rölvaag's 'The Boat of Longing'," in *MELUS,* Vol. 7, No. 1, Spring, 1980, pp. 51-60.

Carl Sandburg, "Review of *Giants in the Earth,* by Ole Rölvaag," in *The Chicago Daily News,* February 11, 1928, p. 9.

Harold P. Simonson, "Rölvaag and Kierkegaard," in *Scandinavian Studies,* Vol. 49, No. 1, Winter, 1977, pp. 67-80.

Walter Vogdes, "Hamsun's Rival," in *The Nation,* Vol. 125, No. 3236, July 13, 1927, pp. 41-2.

George Leroy White, Jr., "The Scandinavian Settlement in American Fiction," in *Scandinavian Themes in American Fiction,* University of Pennsylvania Press, 1937, pp. 69-108.

For Further Study

American Prefaces, Vol. 1, No. 7, April, 1936, pp. 98-112.
An issue devoted to Rölvaag that includes a commemorative poem written by Paul Engle, an excerpt of Rölvaag's unfinished autobiography, and recollections by his daughter.

Joseph E. Baker, "Western Man Against Nature: 'Giants in the Earth'," in *College English* Vol. 4, No. 1, October, 1942, pp. 19-26.
Baker views Per Hansa as a typically rational, independent Western man concerned with achievement, contrasting him with a more Eastern, submissive, and romantic figure one would find in the work of Ralph Waldo Emerson.

Charles Boewe, "Rölvaag's America: An Immigrant Novelist's Views," in *Western Humanities Review,* Vol. 11, No. 1, Winter, 1957, pp. 3-12.
Boewe discusses Rölvaag's focus on the Norwegian-American immigrant experience and his philosophy of culture.

Lincoln Colcord, "Rölvaag the Fisherman Shook His Fist at Fate," in *The American Magazine,* Vol. 105, No. 3, March, 1928, pp. 36-7, 188-9, 192.
Conversations between Rölvaag and his translator, Colcord, about emigrating to America and the writing of *Giants in the Earth.*

Henry Commager, "The Literature of the Pioneer West," in *Minnesota History,* Vol. 8, No. 4, December, 1927, pp. 319-28.
Commager connects Rölvaag's exploration of the suffering and futility of plains settlement with similar strains in historical studies. He discusses Rölvaag's contrast between the romantic ideal of the West and the harsh reality of pioneer life.

Sylvia Grider, "Madness and Personification in Giants in the Earth," in *Women, Women Writers, and the West,* edited by L. L. Lee and Merrill Lewis, Whitson, 1979, pp. 111-17.
A study of Beret Hansa's struggles with the forces of nature on the prairie, her mental breakdown, and her recovery.

Steve Hahn, "Vision and Reality in 'Giants in the Earth'," in *South Dakota Review,* Vol. 17, No. 1, Spring, 1979, pp. 85-100.
Hahn explores the impact of Norwegian heritage on Rölvaag's characters and their search for selfhood. He contends that Norse, folk, and especially Christian traditions dominate the narrative.

Theodore Jorgenson and Nora O. Solum, in *Ole Edvart Rölvaag: A Biography,* Harper, 1939.
In the first extensive English biography of Rölvaag, Jorgenson and Solum analyze the influence of Henrik Ibsen and Norwegian saga and folk tale culture on Rölvaag's prairie novels.

Barbara Howard Meldrum, "Agrarian versus Frontiersman in Midwestern Fiction," in *Vision and Refuge: Essays on the Literature of the Great Plains,* edited by Virginia Faulkner and Frederick C. Luebke, University of Nebraska Press, 1982, pp. 44-63.
In one section of her essay, Meldrum explores Per Hansa's dual nature as a frontiersman and an agrarian. She also discusses Beret's role as a truth-teller in the book.

Patrick D. Morrow, "Rölvaag's 'Giants in the Earth' as Tragedy," in *North Dakota Quarterly,* Vol. 48, No. 4, Autumn, 1980, pp. 83-90.
Though he recognizes Rölvaag's use of saga and epic, Morrow contends that tragic conventions define the progress of Rölvaag's narrative and characters, placing the novel firmly in the tradition of American tragic realism.

Paul A. Olson, "The Epic and Great Plains Literature: Rölvaag, Cather, and Neidhardt," in *Prairie Schooner,* Vol. 55, No. 182, Spring-Summer, 1981, pp. 263-85.
Olson asserts that Beret is Rölvaag's true hero because of her God-centered heroic vision, while Per Hansa is a failed epic hero because of his disconnection to his community and God.

Paul Reigstad, "Mythical Aspects of *Giants in the Earth,*" in *Vision and Refuge: Essays on the Literature of the Great Plains,* edited by Virginia Faulkner and Frederick C. Luebke, University of Nebraska Press, 1982, pp. 64-70.
Reigstad briefly examines Per Hansa's connections with Faust, the multiple connotations of the book's title, and Rölvaag's use of trolls in the novel.

Paul Reigstad, in *Rölvaag: His Life and Art,* University of Nebraska Press, 1972.
Reigstad explores the development of Rölvaag's art and, in the chapter on *Giants in the Earth,* cites Rölvaag's letters to recount the composition history of the novel.

Harold P. Simonson, "Rölvaag and Kierkegaard," in *Scandinavian Studies,* Vol. 49, No. 1, Winter, 1977, pp. 67-80.
Simonson examines Kierkegaard's influence on Rölvaag's prairie novels and their characters' religious sensibilities. From this perspective, Beret becomes the true hero of the novels.

How the García Girls Lost Their Accents

Julia Alvarez

1991

Julia Alvarez's first novel, the semi-autobiographical *How the García Girls Lost Their Accents,* gained generally favorable reviews and brought her work to the attention of a wide group of critics and readers. Most reviewers praise the novel's exploration of a Dominican-American family's struggle with assimilation and the resulting clash between Hispanic and American cultures. The novel's collection of fifteen short stories relates, in reverse chronological order, the experiences of the de la Torre-García family: patriarch Carlos (Papi), mother Laura (Mami), and their four daughters—Carla, Sandra, Yolanda, and Sofía. The stories begin in 1989 with Yolanda's visit to her native country, the Dominican Republic, and work backward to 1956, before the family immigrated to New York City. The years in between are filled with the difficult process of acculturation for all members of the family. Donna Rifkind, in the *New York Times Book Review,* writes that Alvarez has "beautifully captured the threshold experiences of the new immigrant, where the past is not yet a memory and the future remains an anxious dream." Jason Zappe similarly notes in *The American Review* that "Alvarez speaks for many families and brings to light the challenges faced by many immigrants. She shows how the tensions of successes and failures don't have to tear families apart."

Author Biography

Julia Alvarez admits that her critically acclaimed novel *How the García Girls Lost Their Accents* is a semi-autobiographical account of her family as they struggled to adjust to American culture. Alvarez was born in New York City on March 27, 1950, but soon relocated to the Dominican Republic, where she lived until she was ten. While there, her father, like the novel's patriarch, was forced to flee with his family after he led a failed attempt to oust Dominican dictator Rafael Trujillo. The family returned to the Bronx, in New York City, where her father started a successful medical practice. Like Yolanda, the main character in *How the García Girls Lost Their Accents*, Alvarez turned to books and writing as an escape from her frustrating acculturation experiences. In an interview with Catherine Wiley in *Bloomsbury Review*, Alvarez explains, "I think when I write, I write out of who I am and the questions I need to figure out. A lot of what I have worked through has got to do with coming to this country and losing a homeland and a culture, as a way of making sense."

Alvarez graduated summa cum laude from Middlebury College in Vermont, where she presently teaches, and earned a Masters degree from Syracuse University. She has also taught at the University of Vermont at Burlington, George Washington University in Washington, D.C., and the University of Illinois. Her work includes two more novels, *In the Time of the Butterflies* (1994) and *Yo!* (1997), and several collections of poetry: *The Housekeeping Book*, *Homecoming*, and *The Other Side/El Otro Lado*. She has also published a collection of essays, 1998's *Something to Declare*. She has earned several awards and grants, including a National Endowment for the Arts grant, an Ingram Merrill Foundation grant, and the PEN Oakland/Josephine Miles Award for excellence in multicultural literature. This last award was given for her achievement in her first novel, *How the García Girls Lost Their Accents*.

Plot Summary

Part I: 1989-1972

Julia Alvarez's *How the García Girls Lost Their Accents* is a collection of stories that recounts experiences in the lives of four Dominican-American sisters—Carla, Sandra, Yolanda, and Sofía—and their parents. Alvarez divides the novel into

Julia Alvarez

three sections that she presents in reverse chronological order, beginning with a story from 1989 and ending with one from 1956. Collectively, the stories chronicle the difficulties each member of the family faces as he or she tries to adjust to life in America without losing a sense of tradition and heritage.

The first story, "Antojos," focuses on the third daughter, Yolanda, who returns after five years to the Dominican Republic, where she was born, to visit her aunts and cousins. When asked what she wants to do there, she says she has a craving—an *antojo*—for guavas. Ignoring her aunt's warning about how dangerous it is for women traveling alone, Yolanda drives north to a small village where José, a young boy, takes her to find some guavas on the hillside. When she gets a flat tire, Jose goes to search for help. Two men soon approach who offer help, but appear menacing. Remembering her aunt's fears, she blurts out the name of relatives who live nearby. They become respectful after hearing the name and help her change her tire. Jose returns, upset after being hit by a guard who did not believe his story. Yolanda gives him several dollars for his trouble.

In "The Kiss," Sofía, the youngest daughter, carefully plans their father's seventieth birthday party. "For the first time since she had run off with her husband six years ago, she and her father were on speaking terms." Her father is generally pleased with the party, but becomes gradually more withdrawn until they play a guessing game. He is blindfolded as each woman present gives him a kiss and he tries to guess who it is. During the game Sofía gets angry that her father never guesses her name, and so she plants a sensuous kiss on his ear and tells him to guess who it is. His physical pleasure from the kiss angers him and he ends the game.

"Four Girls" explains that while growing up Mami dressed all her daughters alike in different colored versions of what she wore. On special occasions she told a favorite story about each one "as a way of celebrating that daughter." Mami tells a story about Carla wanting red sneakers but not being able to afford them. When a neighbor gives them white ones, her father helps her paint them red. Next she tells a story about Yolanda getting lost in New York City, where they made their new home, and reciting poetry to strangers on a bus. Their mother explains that she does not have a favorite story about Sandra anymore, because she is trying to forget her troubled past, which includes a breakdown in a mental hospital. Finally, while visiting Sofía's new son in the hospital, she tells a stranger how Sofía met the man she married. The entire family comes together for Christmas a week after the baby's birth and the sisters reminisce, especially about their mother telling stories. Their mother concludes with a new story about the latest member of the family.

"Joe" and "The Rudy Elmenhurst Story" both focus on Yolanda, or "Joe" as she is often called in America. The first story opens with Joe in the mental hospital, thinking about her ex-husband John. She had left him and gone back to live with her parents, but started acting strangely, continually quoting famous lines from literary classics. As a result, they put her in the hospital, where she thinks she is falling in love with her therapist, Dr. Payne. She then tells a story about Rudy Elmenhurst, her first love. She met him in college, and soon after they started dating, he wanted to have sexual relations with her. She kept putting him off until he got so angry he left her. Five years later, while in grad school, he drops by her apartment and again wants to have sex. This time she throws him out. In both stories Yolanda relates how she has problems communicating with these men, how words often serve to separate rather than unite them.

Part II: 1970-1960

"A Regular Revolution" explains that after another revolution breaks out on the Island, Papi decides the family will stay in America for good. At first, the four girls are disappointed, since they were poor in America and ostracized at school. Soon, however, when they became Americanized, their parents worry they will lose their heritage and so send them back home to Santo Domingo for the summers. After Mami finds a bag of marijuana in Sofía's room, she decides to keep her back home for a year. While there, Sofía turns into a "Spanish-American princess," according to her sisters, and falls in love with her cousin, Manuel Gustavo, who takes control of her life. The sisters execute a successful plan to have Sofía caught with him and thus sent back to America.

"Daughter of Invention" details Mami's attempts at invention. She comes up with good ideas sometimes, like wheels on suitcases, but does not have the means to realize them. One day Yoyo (Yolanda) is chosen to give a speech at school. She works hard at it until she feels "she finally sounded like herself in English." Her father, however, objects to what he considers a disrespectful tone and tears it up. Mami intervenes and helps her write a new, unremarkable one. The next day Papi brings home her own typewriter.

In "Trespass," on the evening that the family celebrates being in America for one year, Carla is homesick. Boys in school have called her names and the unfamiliarity of her maturing body makes her uncomfortable. While walking home from school one day, a man calls her over to his car and exposes himself. When the police arrive at her home, Carla is mortified that she has to explain what happened. "Snow" notes that the year before, when they lived in the city, Yolanda was the "only immigrant" in her class and thus sat apart from the other students so she could be tutored. In school they learned about the Cuban Missile Crisis and practiced air-raid drills. One day Yolanda saw dots in the air that she thought were nuclear fallout. She screamed "bomb," and then was told that the dots were snow, something she had never seen before.

"Floor Show" describes a night three months after the family arrived in America, when the family goes out to dinner with Dr. Fanning—the man who helped them escape their homeland—and his wife. At the restaurant, Mrs. Fanning gets drunk and flirts with Papi and dances with the entertainers in the floorshow. Later she and her husband buy the girls dolls along with paying for the dinner, which embarrasses Papi.

Part III: 1960-1956

"The Blood of the Conquistadores" begins the section of stories that take place before the family emigrates from the Dominican Republic. One day the secret police come to question Carlos (Papi), but he hides in a secret cubicle in the house. Victor Hubbard, a CIA operative posing as an American consul, arrives and gets rid of the police, promising the family will be out of the country in forty-eight hours. While packing, Sandi recognizes a hole that was opening inside of her, a need "nothing would quite fill," even years after their escape.

"The Human Body" explains that when the sisters were children, they all lived in adjoining houses on property that belonged to their grandparents. After returning from another visit to America, their grandmother gives their cousin Mundín a transparent human body doll, which displays all the body parts, and a ball of clay. When Yoyo asks to trade for the clay, Mundín tells her she can have it if she will show him she is "a girl." After she and Sofía show him, he declares, "you're just like dolls." Later they get caught being in the shed, but avoid punishment by saying they were only hiding from the secret police.

In "Still Lives" Sandi takes art classes, along with her other cousins, from Doña Charito. When she turned eight, her parents decided she had artistic abilities. Sandi, however, is "not ready yet to pose as one of the model children of the world" and so is banished from the Doña Charito's house. While outside, she peers into Doña Charito's shed and sees Don José, Doña Charito's husband, whom everyone says has gone crazy. He is chained to the wall, sculpting large figures. When he catches her spying on him, she screams and falls, breaking her arm, which gains her a lot of attention. She has lost her ability to draw, however. Later, at the nativity pageant, Sandi sees the figures Don José was carving, and is thrilled to discover that the face of the Virgin is hers.

"An American Surprise" opens with Papi's return from one of his trips to New York City. The girls listen "with wonder" to his stories about snow and a toy store called "F.A.O. Schwartz" and are delighted with the mechanical toy banks he brings them. After Carla loses interest in hers, Gladys, the family's servant, asks if she can buy it. After thinking about the right thing to do, Carla decides to give it to her. Later when Mami finds the bank in Gladys' room, she fires her, even though Carla admits she gave it to her.

The final story, "The Drum," begins with a focus on a toy Yoyo's grandmother, Mamita, brings her from New York. Yoyo plays it constantly until both sticks break. She then bangs it with other things, but the sound is never the same. During this time, Pila comes to work at the house as a laundry maid and tells Yoyo of voodoo spirits and "devil stories." After a few months, Pila runs away with things she has stolen from the house. One day Yoyo finds kittens in the shed but is afraid to take one of them for fear that the mother will come after her. A stranger she sees crossing their yard tells her not to separate the kitten from its mother for a week. When she hears him shooting birds in the orchard, she feels justified in taking the kitten, but its mother appears after hearing its cries. Yoyo grabs the kitten and runs inside, but soon, unable to quiet it, she throws it out the window. She never finds out what happened to it, but the mother keeps reappearing in her dreams, crying for her lost kitten. Jumping into the future, Yoyo admits that she now and then still hears "a black furred thing lurking in the corners of my life … wailing over some violation that lies at the center of my art."

Characters

La Bruja

"La Bruja" ("The Witch"), as the girls call her, is the racist woman who lives in the apartment underneath the family in New York City. She calls them "spics" and tells them to "go back to where you came from."

Carlos

Child of Sofía and Otto. His birth—the first boy in two generations—helps reunite Papi and Sofía.

Doña Charito

A German woman who lives in the same neighborhood as the family in the Dominican Republic. "She was an islander only by her marriage to Don José," having met him in Madrid on a tour of the Prado, the national museum. Doña Charito is an artist who requires strict obedience to her teaching methods when she conducts art classes for the cousins. She did not want to take students at first, but payment in American dollars changed her mind. Many consider her husband Don José to be crazy, a judgment that appears to be confirmed when Sandi discovers him chained to the wall, carving statues.

Chucha

Chucha, the family's devoted Haitian cook, practices Voodoo and often casts spells to ward off evil spirits. She was taken in by Laura's parents during the massacre of black Haitians engineered by the Dominican dictator Trujillo. Her dark skin and spells cause the other maids to avoid her and look down on her. Nevertheless, she has been with the family so long that she gets her way as often as not. She narrates the very last portion of "The Blood of the Conquistadores."

Edmundo Alejandro de la Torre Rodríguez

See Mundín de la Torre

Carmen de la Torre

The girls' aunt, who married Tío Mundo. Tía Carmen is the "reigning head of the family." Hers is the largest house in the family compound since she is the widow of the head of the clan. When the girls come back to visit the island, they stay with her. After Fifi's escapade with Manuel Gustavo threatens the girls' visits, it is "Tía Carmen's love [that] revives our old homesickness."

Edmundo Antonio de la Torre

Don Edmundo Antonio de la Torre, the girls' maternal grandfather, is a "kindly, educated" man who "entertained no political ambitions." Yet Trujillo forced him to accept a "bogus" diplomatic post, which Papito reluctantly accepted in order to appease his hypochondriac wife. The family referred to him as a saint, due largely to his patience with his wife.

Flor de la Torre

The cousins refer to Tía Flor, the wife of Tío Arturo, as "the politician" because she flashes a broad smile "no matter the circumstances." Flor wants no part of the sisters' consciousness-raising, telling them, "Look at me, I'm a queen…. I can sleep until noon, if I want. I'm going to protest for my *rights?*"

Lucinda de la Torre

The eldest child of Tío Mundo and Tía Carmen, Lucinda is the cousin "who has never minced her words." She helps the older sisters help thwart the romance of Sofía and Manuel Gustavo, know-

ing that the once-independent Sofía could end up stuck on the island. Nevertheless, as an adult Lucinda adopts the island taste and "looks like a Dominican magazine model."

Mimi de la Torre

Tía Mimi is the unmarried daughter of Papito and Mamita, and is known as "the genius in the family." She spent two years at an American college, and the family fears she has been spoiled for marriage because she is still single at twenty-eight. She has a great love of reading which inspires Yolanda.

Mundín de la Torre

When the sisters are living on the island with their cousins, Mundín is most often paired with Yolanda. The two get in trouble for being in the gardener's shed, where Yolanda has promised to "show him [she's] a girl" in exchange for his modeling clay. When the sisters are older and they come back to visit Santo Domingo, Mundín takes them out and shows them the motel where lovers go. When he is in college in America, the sisters insist, "he's one of us … but back on the Island, he struts and turns macho."

Yolanda Laura María Rochet de la Torre

Doña Yolanda Laura María Rochet de la Torre, the girls' grandmother, is known for her willfulness and "tyrannical constitution." She convinces her husband to accept the "bogus" foreign post because she likes to make shopping trips to New York City. Her inability to deal with her fading beauty causes her to become ill in later years.

Rudy Elmenhurst

Rudolf Brodermann Elmenhurst, the third, is the shallow, insensitive college boy who becomes Yolanda's first love. She admires his "ironic self-assured face" and his quick thinking when he tries to ask her out. They see each other constantly for a whole term, while Rudy tries to take advantage of the "hot-blooded" woman he believes Yolanda should be. Yolanda is a shy virgin, however, and he leaves her when she won't have sex with him, which fills her with self doubt. When he returns five years later demanding the same thing, Yolanda happily throws him out.

Dr. Fanning

Dr. Fanning is Papi's generous American benefactor. He found the medical fellowship for Papi so he could leave the Dominican Republic and tries to help him find work in New York. He has little patience, though, with his wife when she drinks too much. The Garcías relationship with the Fannings illustrates their drastic change in social status: while in Santo Domingo, the Fannings stayed in the family compound and the Garcías "treated them like royalty." In the States, however, Dr. García is embarrassed by his new beholden relationship with the Fannings.

Sylvia Fanning

Sylvia is the boisterous and hard-drinking wife of Dr. Fanning. Sandi is not sure why the handsome Dr. Fanning has married this "plain, bucktoothed woman." When she drinks, she gets flirtatious and uninhibited. At dinner, she flirts with Papi and gets up on stage to dance with the entertainers. She is also very generous, offering to buy the girls dolls, although she is blind to the discomfort this causes Mami and Papi.

Dr. Carlos García

Youngest of his father's thirty-five children, Papi becomes a successful doctor in America after he narrowly escapes persecution in his homeland. However, his daughters consider him to be "heavy duty old world." Even when his girls are successful adults, he feels the need to protect and look after them, giving them cash on his birthday. Although his dreams are filled with his fears of being harassed by the secret police as he was back in the Dominican Republic, he is still homesick for his homeland. He "stubbornly clings to the memories and accents of the old world." When the situation on the island calms down, he wants to move back, even though "for the rest of his life, he would be haunted by blood in the streets and late night disappearances."

Laura de la Torre García

When Mami comes to America, she has "her own little revolution brewing" against traditional Latino concepts of a woman's place. As she takes adult courses in real estate and international economics and business management, she dreams "of a bigger-than-family-size life for herself." She "still did lip service to the old ways," but at the same time, she nibbled "away at forbidden fruit." Mami does not want to move back "to the old country where … she was only a wife and a mother…. Better an independent nobody than a high-class house-slave." She is also a very proud woman, who continually scribbles her inventions on notepads, insisting, "she would show them. She would prove to these Americans what a smart woman could do with a pencil and pad." Yet Mami sometimes embarrasses her daughters with her "old world" ways. She often speaks in malaprops ("It takes two to tangle, you know") and her matching shoes and bag disqualify her as a "girlfriend parent" and so is considered a "real failure of a Mom." In her article in the *American Book Review,* Elizabeth Starcevic writes, "she merges the self-confidence of her wealthy background with a receptivity toward the new challenges. Energetic and intelligent, she is always thinking of new inventions. Her creativity is stymied, yet she finds other outlets in the activities of her children and her husband. She is a vivid, alive character whose contributions to the necessary adjustments of her new life are both critiqued and appreciated by her daughters."

Manuel Gustavo García

Manuel Gustavo is the traditionally macho, illegitimate child of Papi's brother, Tío Orlando. When Sofía falls in love with him after she is sent to live with her aunt in Santo Domingo, he tries to take complete control of her life. Sofía's sisters consider him "a tyrant, a mini Papi and Mami rolled into one" and so hatch a plot to save Sofía from him.

Carla García de la Torre

Carla, the oldest sister, is thirty-one and a child psychologist when the novel opens. She feels the need to continually analyze those around her in order to make sense of her world. She insists her mother did not give her enough attention when she was a child, as explained in her autobiographical paper, "I Was There Too." She claims that the color system her mother used to clothe her daughters "weakened [their] identity differentiation abilities and made them forever unclear about personality boundaries." She also "intimated that [Mami] was a mild anal retentive personality." After moving to America, Carla has difficulty adjusting to her new school. Her discomfort over her maturing body adds to her sense of displacement. Even after Mami accompanies her to school because of the pervert who exposed himself to her, Carla is haunted by the taunts of classmates.

Fifi García de la Torre

See Sofía García de la Torre

Joe García de la Torre

See Yolanda García de la Torre

Lolo García

See Dr. Carlos García

Sandi García de la Torre

See Sandra García de la Torre

Sandra García de la Torre

Sandra is considered to be "the pretty one," with "blue eyes, peaches and ice cream skin, everything going for her!" Although her lighter skin confers prestige, she wants to be darker like her sisters. While at graduate school, she becomes anorexic and suffers a breakdown. She thinks she is turning into a monkey and so she reads a lot of books to try and retain her humanness. When she is eight, her parents decide she has artistic abilities and so send her for instruction. Sandi's independent spirit surfaces, however, and she rebels against the strict art teacher. She is "not ready yet to pose as one of the model children of the world." Looking back on the time she had broken her arm, she notes, "months of pampering and the ridicule of my cousins had turned me inward.... I was sullen and dependent on my mother's sole attention, tender-hearted, and whiney." Sandi no longer draws, but she is still spirited: she is the one who requests Cokes and Barbies from the Fannings during their dinner, despite her mother's warnings not to.

Sofía García de la Torre

Sofía, the youngest daughter, is twenty-six when the novel opens. She was always considered the maverick out of all the sisters, although her mother considers her to be lucky. Unlike her sisters, she drops out of college. Her Americanization, especially her lack of sexual restraint, angers her father and causes tension between them. Her hasty and impulsive marriage to a German she met while on vacation causes a further rift between them, and Papi refuses to speak to her for several years. Her need for her father's attention, though, is evident when she works hard to plan a special party for his seventieth birthday. Yet, she retains "old antagonism toward her father." She also proves herself to be impressionable, at least when she is young. After her mother finds some marijuana stashed in her room, she is sent to live with her relatives in Santo Domingo where she becomes a "Spanish-American princess," according to her sisters, as many of her cousins had done. She also falls in love with a traditionally macho man whom she lets run her life, until she is "rescued" by her sisters.

Yolanda García de la Torre

When the novel opens, Yolanda García de la Torre is confused about where she belongs. When she returns to the Dominican Republic for a visit, her cousins consider her to be "like one of those Peace Corps girls who have let themselves go so as to do dubious good in the world." She refuses to be a "Spanish-American princess" like her cousins, yet she has not yet been able to find an alternate definition for herself. Deciding that "she has never felt at home in the States," she returns to her homeland for a visit, wondering if she can find a place there, but the land seems strange to her. She had hoped to be a poet, but she has not been able to write much lately. Like her sisters, Yolanda felt alienated from her classmates while she was growing up. The narrator describes her as "caught between the woman's libber and the Catholic señorita." She feels that she is a "peculiar mix of Catholicism and agnosticism, Hispanic and American styles." In college she curses her immigrant origins because she feels she doesn't fit in with everyone else in the experimental 1960s— she refuses drugs and sex. At the end of the novel, she admits that taking a kitten away from its mother when she was young haunts her still, and that a similar violation "lies at the center of my art."

Yoyo García de la Torre

See Yolanda García de la Torre

Gladys

The family's outgoing pantry maid in Santo Domingo. Gladys wants to go to New York to become an actress, but Mami looks down on her as "only a country girl." Carla enjoys her singing and her company. After Carla gives Gladys her toy bank, Mami and Papi find out and fire her.

Victor Hubbard

A Yale classmate of Tío Mundo's, Victor Hubbard poses as an American consul at the American Embassy, but he is really working for the CIA. He was sent to the Dominican Republic to groom "every firebrand among the upper-class fellas" for revolution and has been trying to protect the men in the de la Torre family. He helps the family escape to New York. In his spare time, he has sex with young island women.

John

Yolanda's first husband. He seemed to be in love with her but continually tried to categorize her.

Mami

See Laura de la Torre García

Mamita

See Yolanda Laura María Rochet de la Torre

Nivea

Nivea is one of the family's maids, a "black-black" whose mother named her after the American face cream she used in hope of lightening her baby's skin. Nivea's complaints "were bitter and snuck up on you even during the nicest conversations."

Otto

Sofía's husband, considered the "jolly, good-natured one among the brothers-in-law." The sisters call him "the camp counselor." Mami's favorite story about Sofía involves how she met Otto, a German chemist, at a market in South America. Ironically, it was his involvement with Fifi that led to her falling out with Papi.

Papi

See Dr. Carlos García

Papito

See Edmundo Antonio de la Torre

Dr. Payne

Yolanda's therapist. She thinks she is falling in love with him.

Pila

Pila, the family's Haitian laundry maid in Santo Domingo, fascinates the sisters because she has one eye, mottled skin, and brings spirits and "story devils" to the house. She steals from the family and soon after leaves.

Themes

Culture Clash

The themes of culture clash, custom and tradition, and change and transformation together form the novel's major conflict. All the members of the de la Torre-García family experience a clash between the fast-paced American way of life and the more conservative Latin culture of the Dominican Republic. The clash stems from the conflict between their desire to retain the customs and traditions of their homeland and their need to affect some change in order to adapt to their new surroundings in New York City. When they first move to America, each family member feels strong links to the traditions of their homeland. The girls especially have a hard time adapting to life in America, at least at first. Before they immigrated, their only sense of America came from Papi's presents, which prompted them to think that it must be a wondrous place where all the children played with expensive toys. After they immigrated, however, they discovered a place where language and skin color could prevent a smooth assimilation. As recalled in Carla's story "Trespass," the changes they undergo to fit in are not always comfortable: "[The boys] were disclosing her secret shame: her body was changing. The girl she had been back home in Spanish was being shed. In her place—almost as if the boys' ugly words and taunts had the power of spells—was a hairy, breast-budding grownup no one would ever love."

American Dream

Closely linked to the central conflict revolving around the clash of cultures the family experiences is Papi's and Mami's pursuit of the American dream of success. This pursuit is one of the reasons why both understand the need to adapt to their new home. The family enjoyed the benefits of their upper-class status in Santo Domingo, but when they relocated to the United States, they lived in relative poverty in a poor section of New York City. Their poverty in their early years in America especially embarrasses Papi. His self-confidence and insistence on being treated as head of the family returns, however, when he establishes a successful medical practice in New York. As the novel progresses, it is interesting to observe the similarities and differences in class conflicts as the Garcías experience them in the United States and in the Dominican Republic. The recollection of their previous socioeconomic standing makes their American transition especially hard. As Sandi recalls, her mother says that without their grandfather's help, "'we would have to go on welfare.' Welfare, they knew, was what people in this country got so they wouldn't turn into beggars like those outside La Catedral back home."

Limitations and Opportunities

The family discovers the opportunity in America to move from one social class to another—something that was much more difficult in Santo Domingo. Yet the de la Torre-García family is limited by the color of their skin, which ironically enabled them to achieve a higher status in their home-

Topics for Further Study

- Research the regime of Rafael Trujillo and describe what it was like to live under his dictatorship.

- Investigate the culture of the late 1960s, especially as it appeared on college campuses. Explain how this culture could create added pressures for the García sisters.

- Research the status of women in Latin culture and American culture in the 1970s and 1980s. How do these differences affect the women in the novel?

- Read another work on the immigrant experience, written by an author from another culture, and compare it to the experiences related in *How the García Girls Lost Their Accents.*

land. Their skin was lighter than the neighboring Haitians, who were relegated to servant positions. As children, the García girls find themselves picked upon, insulted, and stereotyped because of their accent, their names, and their appearance. Yet their father knows that America can provide more opportunity for his children than the Dominican Republic could, and he is "so ambitious for presidents and geniuses in the family." Indeed, three of his daughters are professional, college-educated women.

Race and Racism

The racism inherent in American society creates one of the main limitations the family faces when they first arrive in the United States. The woman who lives below them in the city calls them "spics" and insists they "go back to where [they] came from." Yolanda's first boyfriend, Rudy, stereotypes her as "hot-blooded, being Spanish and all," and then dumps her when she refuses to sleep with him. Racism, of course, had previously provided an opportunity to be part of the upper class in Santo Domingo. The family also engages in its own subtle form of racism when the mem-

bers often praise the lighter skin of offspring they claim have acquired their Swedish great-great-grandmother's genes.

Difference

Feelings of difference, especially within the girls, result from the culture clash and racism experienced by the family. At school, Carla and Yolanda feel isolated from their classmates, who tease them about the color of their skin and their faulty English. After losing Rudy Elmenhurst's affections, Yolanda worries that she will always be different and alone: "I would never find someone who would understand my peculiar mix of Catholicism and agnosticism, Hispanic and American styles."

Search for Self

As a result of their feelings of difference and alienation, the girls embark on a search for self. As they slowly adapt to their surroundings, they become "Americanized," which angers their father, who wants them to retain their ties to the "old world." Yet, they do not completely feel at home in America, and this lack of a strong sense of self and place causes future problems in relationships with others. Carla, the eldest, believes that by dressing the sisters alike, their mother "had weakened the four girls' identity differentiation abilities and made them forever unclear about personality boundaries." Determining the self is a neverending process, however, as Dr. Payne reminds Yolanda: "We constantly have to redefine the things that are important to us. It's okay not to know." The maturation process each girl must go through complicates the search for self. Changes in their bodies and experiences with the opposite sex often leave them feeling confused.

Sex Roles

Part of this development process involves determining sex roles, which becomes complicated by the vastly different definitions Latin and American societies impose on men and women. An example of cultural differences in this area occurs when Sofía falls in love with a traditionally macho man in Santo Domingo. He believes it is his role to supervise his women, and Sofía allows him to control her every move almost without question. Her sisters, who have at this point become modern American women, rescue her from what they consider to be unacceptable sexism. Their mother also appreciates the freedom women enjoy in America. She admits that she does not want to move back "to the old country where … she was only a wife and a mother…. Better an independent nobody than a high-class houseslave."

Style

Point of View

The point of view of a piece of fiction is the perspective from which the story is told. A third-person narrator relates most of the stories in *How the García Girls Lost Their Accents,* referring to characters as "he" or "she." For the most part, this narrator is omniscient, or "all-knowing," able to reveal the thoughts of all the characters in the story. There are stories or portions of stories, however, when one or another of the sisters takes over the narration, making it first person ("I"). Yolanda, the poet and writer, is the sister who most often takes the role of narrator.

Setting

The setting of a novel is the time, place, and society in which the story takes place. The novel's dual settings—the Bronx in New York City and Santo Domingo in the Dominican Republic—provide the perfect setting for a study on the problems associated with immigration, assimilation, and acculturation. Each place represents a unique culture that strongly influences all the members of the de la Torre-García family. The most influential historical details include the rebellion against the tyrannical regime of Rafael Trujillo Molina and the American age of experimentation in the 1960s. Both events symbolize the struggle between tradition and change, and dominance and rebellion that figure so prominently in the novel.

Structure

Alvarez's unique structure in *How the García Girls Lost Their Accents* illustrates the struggle the girls endure in their search for identity. The novel consists of fifteen short stories that sometimes center on one family member and sometimes on several. The shifting perspectives provide only fragments of each character's life, never presenting a clear portrait of any one of them. In an interview with Catherine Wiley in the *Bloomsbury Review,* Alvarez says she was thinking "relationally" when she structured the novel. "I was talking about the plot as a quilt, which is a way that I think a lot of women experience plot, as opposed to the hero directed on his adventures and conquering things and getting a prize, at all odds doing what he needs to do."

Symbols/Imagery

A symbol is an object, character, or image that stands for something else while still retaining its original meaning. The title of the novel contains a symbol that figures prominently in the novel's main theme. The García girls are continually facing the conflict between losing their Latin heritage and gaining acceptance in America. Their accents are symbolic of that heritage, and losing them would be the first sure sign of acculturation. Some characters also act as symbols. Mrs. Fanning becomes a symbol of the unrestrained American lifestyle when she drinks too much, flirts with Papi, and then dances with the entertainers at a supper club. Manuel Gustavo becomes a symbol of the Latin conception of a woman's place. He takes full control of Sofía's life, determining that she is unable to make decisions for herself.

Bildungsroman

Bildungsroman is a German term meaning "novel of development" and is also known as a "Coming of Age" or "Apprenticeship" novel. *How the García Girls Lost Their Accents* can be considered a female *Bildungsroman* since it traces the maturation process of all the de la Torre-García daughters. Cecilia Rodriquez Milanes, in her article in the *Women's Review of Books,* notes that the novel "is not simply about adjustment and acculturation. It is about its protagonists' precarious coming of age as Latinas in the United States and *gringas* in Santo Domingo."

Historical Context

The Dominican Republic and Trujillo's Regime

The Dominican Republic is a Caribbean nation that occupies the eastern two-thirds of the island Hispaniola, located between the islands of Cuba and Puerto Rico. Christopher Columbus landed on the island in 1492, and Hispaniola was the site of the first Spanish settlement in the New World. The western part of the island was settled by the French and the entire island was conquered by 1795. The French imported large numbers of African slaves to work their sugar plantations, until a rebellion led

Raphael Trujillo, president of the Dominican Republic from 1930–61.

to independence for the island, now known as Haiti. The Spanish-speaking inhabitants declared their own independence in 1844, and called their new nation the Dominican Republic. Because the country was rich in agricultural products such as sugar cane, cocoa, and coffee, many American companies had economic interests in the Dominican Republic. As a result, the United States often wielded great influence over the country; they established partial control of the Dominican economy in 1905, and sent the U.S. Marines to quell unrest in 1916. This occupation lasted until 1924.

A general in the Dominican Army, Rafael Trujillo Molina was a leader in the military coup against Dominican President Horacio Vasquez in 1930. He ran for president unopposed later that year, and established a dictatorship. Border clashes with Haiti continued during the early years of his regime and in response, in 1937, Trujillo ordered Dominican troops to massacre thousands of immigrant Haitians. Although his government was cruel and civil liberties were severely curtailed, Trujillo suppressed domestic revolt by implementing improvements in roads, agriculture, sanitation, and education. In 1959 exiled Dominicans based in Cuba made an unsuccessful attempt to overthrow Trujillo. In 1960, the Organization of American States (OAS) found Trujillo guilty of planning the assassination of the President of Venezuela and so imposed diplomatic and economic sanctions on his regime. Trujillo was assassinated in 1961. The first free elections in nearly forty years brought leftist Juan Bosch the presidency in 1962. The military opposed his reforms, however, and overthrew his government in 1963. A civil war broke out in 1965, and U.S. troops once again intervened to restore the status quo. A new constitution was ratified in 1966, and since then presidential elections have been held every four years. The turmoil of the early 1960s, including visits by Trujillo's secret police, are often referred to in *How the García Girls Lost Their Accents.*

The ethnic makeup of the Dominican Republic also provides an interesting insight into the novel. Since the original native inhabitants were either driven off or absorbed within the first hundred years of European occupation, most Dominicans are of European, African, or mixed ancestry. While almost three-quarters of the population come from a mixed background, those of European ancestry are more likely to belong to the economic upperclass. The all-black Haitian minority, conversely, are more likely to live below the poverty line. The importance of family background, including name and color, to social standing can be seen in various sections of *How the García Girls Lost Their Accents.*

The Cold War

Soon after World War II, Russian leader Joseph Stalin set up satellite communist states in Eastern Europe and Asia. The "cold war" had begun, ushering in a new age of warfare and fear triggered by several circumstances: the United States' and the Soviet Union's emergence as superpowers; each country's ability to use the atomic bomb; and communist expansion and American determination to check it. The Cold War induced anxiety among Americans, who feared both annihilation by the Russians and the spread of communism at home. Panic reached the inner city and suburbia as children practiced air raid drills in school and many families built bomb shelters. Americans were encouraged to stereotype all Russians as barbarians and atheists who were plotting to overthrow the U.S. government. This paranoid atmosphere encouraged Americans to conform to the traditional values of church, home, and country. Yet, during this time voices of protest began to emerge. Some refused to succumb to the anti-Communist hysteria. Others began to rebel against a system that encouraged discrimination and social and economic inequality. All these various concerns are experienced by the García family during the course of the novel.

The Women's Movement

In the 1960s the Women's Movement reemerged and gained most of its strength in the United States. The National Organization for Women (NOW), formed in 1966, and other groups like the National Women's Political Caucus gained support for abortion reform, federally supported child care centers, equal pay for women, and the removal of educational, political, and social barriers to women. Bella Abzug, Shirley Chisolm, Betty Friedan, Gloria Steinem, and others helped influence Congress to pass the Equal Rights Amendment bill in 1972 that banned sex discrimination at the national level (the amendment failed to be ratified by the states, however, and never became law). The increasing consciousness of women's roles, both at home and in Santo Domingo, are reflected in the various actions of the García women, including Mami.

The Backlash against Multiculturalism

As women and blacks made political gains in the 1960s, Hispanics, gays, and other cultural groups fought to bring their own concerns to the fore in the 1970s. Ethnic roots, while always a matter of individual pride, became fashionable as the success of the 1977 television miniseries *Roots* drove scores of Americans to research their own genealogical and cultural heritage. Various departments devoted to ethnic studies emerged as major universities looked to expand history and literature studies beyond the canon of "dead white males" that had dominated academia until that point. The 1980s, however, were a much more conservative era, and a backlash sprang up against what critics called "special treatment" of minority groups. Immigrant groups were often singled out as receiving special treatment, as conservatives lobbied against affirmative action programs, bilingual education, and government benefits for legal immigrants and worked to establish English as the single "official" language of the United States. This climate persisted into the early 1990s, when *How the García Girls Lost Their Accents* was published. As a work showing the struggles and successes of an immigrant family in the United States, it provides an interesting response to the backlash against multiculturalism of the time.

Critical Overview

Since its publication in 1991, most critics have responded positively to Julia Alvarez's novel *How the García Girls Lost Their Accents.* This first novel received the PEN/Oakland Josephine Miles Award and was named by both the American Library Association and the *New York Times Book Review* as a Notable Book of 1991. Many have praised Alvarez's insightful and sympathetic portrait of family life amidst the pressures of adapting to a new culture. Ilan Stavans considers the novel "a brilliant debut," and claims in his *Commonweal* review that "Alvarez has an acute eye for the secret complexities that permeate family life.... [The García de la Torre family's] rejection of the native background ... is told with humor and has a sense of unrecoverable loss because, for as much as the García sisters want to become American, they remain conscious of the advantages of their Dominican selves. Hence, Alvarez's is a chronicle of the ambivalence with which Hispanics adapt to Anglo-Saxon idiosyncrasies." Donna Rifkind writes in the *New York Times Book Review* that the author has, "to her great credit, beautifully captured the threshold experience of the new immigrant, where the past is not yet a memory and the future remains an anxious dream." Cecilia Rodriquez Milanes, in her article in the *Women's Review of Books,* finds a second important theme in the novel. She notes that it "is not simply about adjustment and acculturation. It is about its protagonists' precarious coming of age as Latinas in the United States and *gringas* in Santo Domingo."

In the same *Commonweal* article, Stavans argues that the novel "holds a unique place in the context of the ethnic literature from which it emerges." He notes that the novel does not contain ethnic stereotypes caught up in drug addiction and poverty. The García de la Torre family has its roots in the Spanish *conquistadores* and becomes financially successful in their new homeland. Stavans also praises the novel's breadth: "Through the García family's sorrow and happiness, through the spiritual and quotidian search that leads to their voluntary exile in the United States, the dramatic changes of an entire era are recorded."

Some critics, however, have found fault with Alvarez's narrative structure and characterizations. Stavans describes the novel as "imperfect and at times unbalanced." In her mixed review, Rifkind insists Alvarez's "goal ... of translating her characters' voices into an unhackneyed American idiom has gone unrealized. The García girls may indeed have lost their accents, but in her first book of fiction Julia Alvarez has not yet quite found a voice." Elizabeth Starcevic concurs with this assessment in the *American Book Review,* finding the book "uneven," and determines that "its organization into individual stories highlights this. The author has not really found consistently developed voices."

Others, though, have praised Alvarez's construction. Stephen Henighan notes in the Toronto *Globe and Mail* that *How the García Girls Lost Their Accents* is a "humane, gracefully written novel." Juan D. Bruce-Novoa sees "maturity and technical polish" in the novel and concludes in his *World Literature Today* review that it is "a most entertaining, significant contribution to U.S. Latino literature."

Alvarez has also gained critical praise for her poetry collections: *The Housekeeping Book* (1984), *Homecoming* (1984; revised edition, 1995), and *The Other Side/El Otro Lado* (1995). Her second novel, *In the Time of the Butterflies,* (1994) focuses on the true story of the Mirabel sisters and the tragic consequences of their denunciation of Trujillo's dictatorship in the Dominican Republic. Her third novel *Yo!,* is a continuation of the story of Yolanda García, central character of *How the García Girls Lost Their Accents. Butterflies* was nominated for the 1995 National Book Critics Circle Award.

Criticism

Wendy Perkins

Wendy Perkins, an Associate Professor of English at Prince George's Community College in Maryland, has published articles on several twentieth-century authors. In this essay she argues that Alvarez's effective structuring of the stories in How the García Girls Lost Their Accents *reinforces the novel's focus on the problems inherent in the immigrant experience.*

Many critics have praised Julia Alvarez's sensitive and adept portrait of a family's struggle with assimilation in *How the García Girls Lost Their Accents.* Donna Rifkind, in the *New York Times Book Review,* wrote that Alvarez "beautifully captured the threshold experiences of the new immigrant, where the past is not yet a memory and the future remains an anxious dream." Jason Zappe noted in the *American Review* that "Alvarez speaks

for many families and brings to light the challenges faced by many immigrants. She shows how the tensions of successes and failures don't have to tear families apart." Some critics, however, find fault with the novel's narrative structure. In an article published in *Commonweal,* Ilan Stavan considered the novel "imperfect and at times unbalanced." Elizabeth Starcevic, in the *American Book Review,* determined the book to be "uneven," arguing that "its organization into individual stories highlights this. The author has not really found consistently developed voices." Alvarez in fact does present only fragmented voices in *How the García Girls Lost Their Accents.* This structural fragmentation, however, skillfully reinforces the novel's main point—that the difficult process of acculturation can result in feelings of dislocation and a fragmented sense of self.

How the García Girls Lost Their Accents consists of fifteen short stories that focus on different members of the Dominican-American de la Torre-García family, especially on the four daughters, as they leave their native Santo Domingo and resettle in New York City. The narrative's shifting perspective provides only fragments of the girls' experiences as each struggles to assimilate to a new home while being caught up in the resulting clash between Hispanic and American culture. This structure highlights the García girls' inability to discover and maintain a strong identity in either place.

The reverse chronological order of the narrative also helps to further deconstruct any sense of self. The stories begin in 1989 with Yolanda's return visit to Santo Domingo and work backward to 1956, before the family immigrates to New York City. The novel ends with a story told by Yolanda about her experiences as a young girl in Santo Domingo. These two stories serve as an effective narrative frame for the family's experiences in both locations. The first story relates Yolanda's present sense of displacement both in America and in Santo Domingo. Her immigration experience has left her, as with the other members of her family, with a sense of not fitting in to either culture. By ending the novel with Yolanda's story of her life back in Santo Domingo, where she felt a surer sense of who she was, Alvarez effectively illuminates how Yolanda's identity, as well as that of each member of her family, deconstructs as a result of the acculturation process she experiences in America.

The title of the opening chapter, "Antojos," serves as a symbol of Yolanda's and her sister's feelings of displacement. When Yolanda returns to

Santa Domingo for a visit, she is not sure she wants to return to America. While there, she feels a craving—an *antojo*—for guavas. She eventually finds the guavas, but the experience is far from satisfying. During her search for the fruit, she encounters a more pronounced sense of class conflict and sexism than she has found in America. Thus Yolanda is in effect caught between two cultures: she looks to her homeland to provide her with a more complete sense of herself, but at the same time, recognizes that she has been Americanized enough to be unable to return to a more traditional way of life.

In the final chapter, "The Drum," Yolanda relates a story from 1956, when she was a young self-assured girl in Santo Domingo. When Yolanda, or Yoyo as her family calls her, is given a toy drum by her grandmother, she bangs furiously and confidently on it. She soon, however, breaks the drumsticks and is unable to find anything to replace them that will provide the exact same sound she enjoyed. The narrative then shifts to Yoyo's admission that during that time, she took a newborn kitten away from its mother. Afterwards, the mother keeps reappearing in her dreams, crying for her lost kitten. The two experiences related in this story symbolize in a condensed form the difficult progression the girls have made from the Dominican Republic to America. Like her sisters, Yoyo, in her homeland, felt a sure sense of identity and place as she announced herself to the world with her confident drumbeats. Yet, like the kitten, Yolanda and her sisters have been wrenched from the security of their home. Jumping into the future in that final story, Yoyo, now a writer, admits that she now and then still hears "a black furred thing lurking in the corners of my life … wailing over some violation that lies at the center of my art." That "violation," the separation of the girls from their culture and thus their identity, becomes the heart of the novel.

In the Dominican Republic, the girls grew up in a communal atmosphere. They lived and played in a family compound made up of aunts, uncles, and cousins. This sense of community, of being part of a group, provided them with a strong sense of identity. Part of that identity came from their feelings of superiority over the Haitians who are relegated to the lower class in the Dominican Republic. In an article in *Essence*, Alvarez admitted, "Growing up in the Dominican Republic, my cousins and I were always encouraged to stay out of the sun so we wouldn't 'look like Haitians.'" When the girls immigrate to America, however, the situation is ironically reversed when they are ostracized, in large part, for the color of their skin.

What Do I Read Next?

- Alvarez's *Yo!* (1997) is a continuation of the story of Yolanda García, the poetic sister of *How the García Girls Lost Their Accents.*

- *Something to Declare* (1998) is Alvarez's collection of essays on her struggles to integrate two cultures.

- *The Joy Luck Club,* published in 1989, is Amy Tan's chronicle of the lives of four Chinese-American women and their families, who pass down the stories of their heritage.

- *The House on Mango Street* (1983), by Sandra Cisneros, is a collection of episodes in a young Mexican American girl's life as she is caught between two cultures.

- Mexican writer Laura Esquivel's *Like Water for Chocolate* (1989) chronicles the tensions between a Latin woman and her family.

- Maxine Hong Kingston's memoir *The Woman Warrior* (1976) explores the Asian immigrant experience in America.

Donna Rifkind, in her review of the novel in the *New York Times Book Review,* explained that the girls lose a sense of communal identity when they leave Santo Domingo for New York City. She wrote: "With the García girls' new-world individuality comes the pain of discrimination, the greenhorn's terror. Their characters are forged amid the taunts of schoolmates, who raise questions about identity in a language they barely understand."

Alvarez's stories present glimpses of the family's often painful assimilation experiences. Their first encounter with discrimination occurs when they move into an apartment in the city. The woman who lives beneath the family calls them "spics" and insists they "go back to where [they] came from." Later, schoolmates attack the girls with racist epithets and critiques of their faulty English. Their reduced economic status in America adds to their sense of inferiority. Even as the girls become

"Americanized," their old-world parents remain an embarrassment to them. Their mother's frequent malaprops ("It takes two to tangle, you know") and her matching shoes and bag disqualify her as an "American Mom" and thus help frustrate the girls' efforts to fit in.

The stories also chronicle the clash between the traditional Latin culture and American culture, notably during the experimental 1960s, and how that clash contributes to the girls' sense of confusion and dislocation. Yolanda especially feels "caught between the woman's libber and the Catholic señorita." While at college she refuses to experiment with drugs and sex, yet at the same time, strives to become accepted by the group. She decides that she is a "peculiar mix of Catholicism and agnosticism, Hispanic and American styles," and as a result has no clear identity.

When the girls return to Santo Domingo on visits, their partial Americanization prevents them from feeling a part of their old community. The youthful Sofía falls in love with a cousin while spending a year back home and begins to fall into a traditional relationship with him, but sometimes balks at his dominant position. When her sisters arrive, they swiftly engineer a plan to "rescue" their sister from such a conventional fate. Yet in America, the sisters often seem unable to maintain successful relationships, due, for the most part, to their inability to gain a clear vision of themselves.

In an interview with Catherine Wiley in the *Bloomsbury Review*, Alvarez said she was thinking "relationally" when she structured the novel. "I was talking about the plot as a quilt, which is a way that I think a lot of women experience plot, as opposed to the hero directed on his adventures and conquering things and getting a prize, at all odds doing what he needs to do." Alvarez's "quilting" in *How the García Girls Lost Their Accents* effectively portrays the García girls struggle to stitch together the fragmented pieces of their lives and to try and rediscover a true sense of self and place.

Source: Wendy Perkins, in an essay for *Novels for Students,* Gale, 1999.

Jonathan Ring

In this article, Alvarez discusses her career as a Latino writer.

In 1991, Julia Alvarez made a resounding splash on the literary scene with her first novel, *How the Garcia Girls Lost Their Accents,* whose narrators, the four vibrant and distinctive Garcia siblings, captivated readers and critics. Like their author, the characters emigrated to middle-class Queens, N.Y., from the Dominican Republic, and the novel provided a keen look at the island social structure they wistfully remember and the political turmoil they escaped.

The second-oldest sister, Yolanda, now a well-known author, is the protagonist of Alvarez's third novel, *¡Yo!,* out next month from Algonquin. Alvarez brings to Yo's portrait an empathy of shared experiences, anxieties and hopes.

In 1960 at the age of 10, Alvarez fled the Dominican Republic with her parents and three sisters (her father was involved in the underground against the dictator Raphael Trujillo). She has since roamed this country, teaching writing in far-flung schools and communities, before finally putting down roots in Middlebury, Vt., and writing two books of poetry and three novels, including 1994's *In the Time of the Butterflies* (Algonquin).

A current exhibit at the New York Public Library, "The Hand of the Poet from John Donne to Julia Alvarez," displays snapshots of the author in the Dominican Republic (she travels there at least once a year), riding horseback, dancing the merengue and obstreperously bartering for plantains. When *PW* catches up with Alvarez, it is in the rare-book room of the Middlebury College library, where a standing-room-only audience has gathered to hear her read from the new novel. Brushing unruly, dark bangs from her lively face, her voice inflected by a faint Latin twang, she shows few signs of the butterflies fluttering in her stomach, induced by the prospect of reciting her work on her own turf.

"I couldn't sleep last night before this reading," she confesses, later ushering *PW* into the living room of her secluded ranch house, which is brimming with plants, cacti and photographs of her extended family. Alvarez, who first came to Middlebury to attend the Breadloaf Writers' Conference as an undergraduate in the late 1960s and is now a tenured professor of English, has lived here permanently since 1988, and it is here that she met her husband, an ophthalmologist. Yet she expresses ambivalence at the thought of becoming something of a local fixture.

"I see myself marginally in the academic community, which I think in part is good for a writer, because it keeps you on your toes," she says. "When I first moved here, people would come up to me and say things that I hadn't told them. Or remark upon things that I didn't know they knew. I didn't realize that everything's connected. There's no anonymity. The good part of that is, as a friend said, 'Julia, you've always wanted roots. But now you realize that once there are roots, there are worms in the soil.'"

In conversation, Alvarez is an ebullient blend of insecurities, tart anecdotes and spitfire judgments, often punctuated by a deep, chesty laugh. Scooping up an obese marmalade cat named Lucia, she babbles half in English and half in Spanish into its fur, then offers us a glass of wine and sits cross-legged on a leather ottoman, recalling the tumult of a childhood bifurcated by conflicting cultural milieus.

"I grew up in that generation of women thinking I would keep house. Especially with my Latino background, I wasn't even expected to go to college," she says. "I had never been raised to have a public voice."

Herself the second-oldest, Alvarez was sent to boarding school in her early teens under the protective wing of her older sister. "My parents were afraid of public school. I think they were just afraid in general of this country. So I went away to school and was on the move and not living at home since I was 13 years old."

Like many political refugees, Alvarez soon found the displacements of language and geography to be the stuff of art. As an adolescent, she says, the act of writing helped to allay the pain of acculturation and the stigma of being an outsider. "I came late into the language but I came early into the profession. In high school, I fell in love with how words can make you feel complete in a way that I hadn't felt complete since leaving the island. Early on, I fell in love with books, which I didn't have at all growing up. In the Dominican Republic, I was a nonreader in what was basically an oral culture and I hated books, school, anything that had to do with work."

Alvarez went to Connecticut College, but after winning the school's poetry prize, she departed for Breadloaf and Middlebury, where she earned her B.A. in 1971. After an M.F.A at Syracuse University, she lit out for the heartland, taking a job with the Kentucky Arts Commission as a traveling poet-in-residence. For two years, Alvarez traversed the back roads of the Bluegrass State, with *Leaves of Grass* as her Baedeker. "I would just pack up my car. I had a little Volkswagen. My whole car was a file system. Everything I owned was in there.

"In some communities I'd give workshops or talk at night in the local church. I loved it. I felt like the Whitman poem where he travels through-

out the country and now will do nothing but listen. I was listening. I was seeing the inside of so many places and so many people, from the Mennonites of Southern Kentucky to the people of Appalachia who thought I had come to do something with poultry."

When that job ended, other teaching jobs beckoned, and Alvarez careened around the country for more than a decade. "I was a migrant poet," she laughs. "I would go anywhere."

With no fixed address, Alvarez gradually assembled her first collection of poetry, which Breadloaf director Bob Pack placed with Grove. Aptly called *Homecomings,* it featured a 33-sonnet sequence called "33," which portrays the emotional vertigo Alvarez suffered on her 33rd birthday, facing middle age without a secure job, a family of her own or a career blueprint to sustain her. Alvarez nevertheless greeted the book's publication, in 1984, with great trepidation. "It was scary," she says. "I thought 'Oh, my God, what if my parents read this? There are love affairs in here. Maybe I can go out and buy all the copies.'"

She has since reprinted *Homecomings* and issued another book of verse with Dutton (*The Other Side,* 1995). Now, however, she writes poetry less frequently than fiction. "I think what's hard for me about writing poetry is that it is so naked," Alvarez explains. In retrospect, it's not surprising that her emergence as a novelist coincided with her first tenure-track job at Middlebury. *How the Garcia Girls Lost Their Accents,* a novel displaying a historical sweep and mobility of voice not found in her poetry, was a natural next step after years of rootlessness.

"It used to turn me off, the idea of writing something bigger than a poem," she reflects. "But you grow as a writer and you start to imagine other possibilities."

Susan Bergholz, certainly the most influential agent of Latino fiction, whose clients include Ana Castillo, Sandra Cisneros and Denise Chávez, has represented Alvarez since placing *Garcia Girls* with Shannon Ravenel at Algonquin. As Alvarez remembers, Bergholz approached her at a reading she gave in New York after winning a 1986 G.E. Foundation Award for Younger Writers. "She was interested in my work, so I sent her a bunch of things. She really plugged away at that stuff, sending it around and talking to people and finally she landed Shannon. I'm very grateful to Susan as the person who really fought that battle for me, which—because of my background and because of my self-doubt—I probably would not have fought for myself."

Yet when *Garcia Girls* first reached Ravenel, "there was no book there," Alvarez says. "I sent portions of it to Shannon and she said: 'There's a bigger story here you're trying to tell.'"

Today Alvarez can't imagine publishing with a larger house at any price, provided that Ravenel stays put. "Shannon helped form me as a writer. She often helps me to think of how to put my books together. Sometimes, I'll say, 'our book' and she'll say, 'Julia, it's your book.' Maybe a place could initially offer you more money or more razzmatazz. But I was 41 when *Garcia Girls* came out. If I were writing to make a whole lot of money, I would have given this craft up a long time ago. I'm doing the writing because it's the way I understand my life. It's what I do and I want a place that is sympatico to that."

Alvarez's trajectory as a novelist has hardly followed a predictable scheme. Her second novel revisits the last days of the Trujillo regime and retells the story of the three Mirabal sisters, Patricia, Minerva and Maria Teresa—actual political dissidents called Las Mariposas (the Butterflies)—who in 1960 were murdered by Trujillo's henchmen. The event galvanized the political insurrection that led to Trujillo's assassination in 1961. "It's always been a story I wanted to tell. But I didn't know how to do it. They seemed to me such enormous, mythical figures. I didn't know how to touch them and make them real. I thought it would be a sacrilege even to do that in some people's eyes. But I knew it was a story I wanted to tell."

Alvarez had previously tackled the subject in an essay in a small press book on heroic women, but in returning to the island to research the novel, she made an astonishing discovery: there were, in fact, four sisters, and the eldest, Dédé, had survived and was still living in the Dominican Republic. Alvarez interviewed Dédé and began to piece together the minutiae of the sisters' lives. "I understand the politics of a four-daughter family with no boys in a Latino culture," she notes.

All of Alvarez's novels are constructed from multiple viewpoints, ranging freely from sassy gossip to animated autobiography, but always concealing a forceful political undercurrent. She attributes her interest in voice to the storytelling traditions of Dominican life. "We didn't have TV, we didn't have books. It was just what people did. That was our newspaper."

Yo, of course, means "I" in Spanish, but Alvarez has shrewdly left the self at the center of the novel absent. Yolanda isn't granted a voice in the novel. Instead, Alvarez builds the book around the memories of those who have suffered the manipulations of the budding author. The liberty a writer takes with her family and background is a subject of increasing importance to Alvarez as her books grow more popular. "My sisters had a hard time with *Garcia Girls*. But I think they're proud of me, and I think the books have helped them understand their lives better. Sometimes they will remember something that I think I invented. Now it's almost like the stories in that book are part of the memory pool."

In 1993, *Vanity Fair* ran a splashy profile of Alvarez, Castillo, Cisneros and Chávez (all are indeed friends) under the rubric "Los Girlfriends," portraying a cliquish set of Latina writers sharing the same literary concerns and themes. It's precisely such hype and labeling that *¡Yo!* set out to interrogate. "One thing I didn't like about it from the beginning, which didn't have to do with the people involved, is I thought how I would feel if I was a Latino writer and I saw *the* Girlfriends and these are the [only] Latino writers. I felt there should have been 100 writers on either side of us. Not that I think it was a terrible thing. I just wonder and worry about what all of this publicity and labeling comes to."

Discussing the extravagant antics of book marketing, the 22-city tour she is about to embark on and the persistent film interest in her work (*Butterflies* has been optioned to Phoenix Pictures), Alvarez grows antsy. "As you talk, I realize I am always that immigrant. This, too, I am experiencing and watching. But I don't put faith in it. In a minute, it can be swept away." She needn't worry. Once an author without an address, a language or a homeland to call her own, Alvarez now has a loyal readership that in years to come will undoubtedly only grow larger.

Source: Jonathan Ring, "Julia Alvarez: Books That Cross Borders," in *Publishers Weekly,* December 16, 1996, pp. 38–9.

Ilan Stavans

The following review praises How the García Girls Lost Their Accents, *alternately describing the novel as "a tour de force," "delightful," and "brilliant."*

In the mood for a Dominican author writing in English? You are likely to find only one: Julia Alvarez, who left her country at ten and now lives and teaches at Middlebury College. Besides a book of poetry published in 1986 (intriguingly titled *Home-coming*), she is the writer of this delightful novel, a tour de force that holds a unique place in the context of the ethnic literature from which it emerges. In the age of affirmative action in life and literature, those looking for themes like drug addiction, poverty, and Hispanic stereotypes are in for a surprise. Much in the tradition of nineteenth-century Russian realism, and in the line of the genuine "porcelain" narrative creations of Nina Berberova, *How the García Girls Lost Their Accents* has as its protagonist the García de la Torre, a rich family in Santo Domingo and its surroundings whose genealogical tree reaches back to the Spanish *conquistadores.* Through the García family's sorrow and happiness, through the spiritual and quotidian search that leads to their voluntary exile in the United States, the dramatic changes of an entire era are recorded. Energetic, curious, and bellicose, their collective plight is a struggle to keep up with the times, and also, an adjustment to a culture that isn't theirs.

The plot focuses on the relationship of four sisters: Carla, Sandra (Sandi), Yolanda (Yo, Yoyo, or Joe), and Sofia (Fifi). Their aristocratic upbringing as S.A.P.s—Spanish American Princesses—takes them from their "savage Caribbean island" to prestigious schools in New England and from there to an existence as middle-class citizens in the Bronx. They undergo discrimination and suffer from linguistic misunderstandings. They iron their hair according to the latest fashion and buy bell-bottom pants with fringe. As women in difficult marriages and troubled breakups, theirs is the customary rite of passage of immigrants assimilating into another reality. Their rejection of the native background, nevertheless, is told with humor and has a sense of unrecoverable loss because, for as much as the García sisters want to become American, they remain conscious of the advantages of their Dominican selves. Hence, Alvarez's is a chronicle of the ambivalence with which Hispanics adapt to Anglo-Saxon idiosyncracies.

Made of fifteen self-contained chapters collected in three symmetrical parts, more than a novel the volume ought to be read as a collection of interrelated stories. Each segment reads as an independent unit, with the same set of characters recurring time and again in different epochs and places. As a whole, the narrative spans three decades, the first chapter beginning in 1988 and the last reaching as far back as 1956. Similar to some plots by the Cuban musicologist Alejo Carpentier and the British playwright Harold Pinter, the García girls, as if on a journey back to the source, navigate from matu-

rity to adolescence, from knowledge to naïveté, from light to darkness—that is, their lives are perceived in reverse. In the process, the characters slowly deconstruct their personalities and reflect upon their Catholic education at home in the hands of a "respectable," highly schematic father. In his 1982 autobiography *Hunger for Memory,* Richard Rodriguez, while attacking bilingual education, discussed the impairment of the native tongue and the acquisition of the "father" tongue, English. Because Alvarez is uninterested in such meditations, her book, in spite of the title, isn't about language. Here and there the narrative does offer insightful reflections on the transition from an ancestral vehicle of communication to an active, convenient one. Yet the idea of "losing" one's accent is nothing but a metaphor: a symbol of cultural abandonment.

A secondary leitmotif also colors the plot—that of the coming of age of a candid female writer and her indomitable need to describe, in literary terms, her feelings and immediate milieu. Yoyo, the author's alter ego, is a sensible, extroverted adolescent who loves to write poetry. In "Daughter of Invention," perhaps the volume's best story and one recalling Ralph Ellison's first chapter of *Invisible Man,* she is asked to deliver a commencement speech. Her mother helps her out. In search of inspiration, Yoyo finds Whitman's *Leaves of Grass,* in particular "Song of Myself," and writes a speech celebrating her egotism, her excessive self-interest. The theme infuriates her father. In a rage of anger, he tears up the manuscript. But the mother's support encourages the girl to deliver the speech, which she does quite successfully. She is praised by her own repentant father with a gift of a personal typewriter.

Obviously, as a whole *How the García Girls Lost Their Accent* is Yoyo's product. Although its content is told by shifting narrators, she is the soul inside the text. She contrasts and ponders. She is puzzled and flabbergasted by the circumstances around her. The world gains and loses its coherence in her mind. In an illuminating segment about Pila, a bizarre maid with voodoo powers who inspired nightmares, Yoyo writes about her first discovery of things Dominican. Hers is a story of wonder and disbelief. Accustomed to a certain climate of order and to the rules set forth by her parents, she is disoriented by the behavior of the maid. After a series of mishaps that involve a cat and strange tales by a grandmother, the section concludes:

> [After those experiences] we moved to the United States.... I saw snow. I solved the riddle of an outdoors made mostly of concrete in New York. My

grandmother grew so old she could not remember who she was. I went away to school. I read books. You understand I am collapsing all time now so that it fits what's left in the hollow of my story? I began to write, the story of Pila, the story of my grandmother.... I grew up, a curious woman, a woman of story ghosts and story devils, a woman prone to bad dreams and bad insomnia. There are still times I wake up at three o'clock in the morning and peer into the darkness. At that hour and in that loneliness, I hear [Pila], a black furred thing lurking in the corners of my life, her magenta mouth opening, wailing over some violation that lies at the center of my art.

The entire volume is a gathering of memories, a literary attempt to make sense of the past. Alvarez has an acute eye for the secret complexities that permeate family life. Although once in a while she steps into melodrama, her descriptions are full of pathos. The political reality in the Dominican Republic, although never at center stage, marks the background. The repressive thirty-year-long Trujillo dictatorship, which culminated with the leader's assassination in 1961, makes the Garcías happy but complicates their lives. The democratic elections that brought Juan Bosch into power bring a period of tranquillity, interrupted by the 1965 civil war that brought the U.S. intervention and ended in the election, supervised by the Organization of American States, of Joaquín Balaguer. The family is pushed to an exile that makes its religious faith stumble and its traditions collapse. Yet *How the García Girls Lost Their Accents,* unlike scores of narratives from south of the Rio Grande, is free from an anti-American message: in Tennessee Williams's terms, its primary concern is a minuscule glass menagerie, the fragile life of a group of individuals swept by epic events they constantly fight to ignore.

While imperfect and at times unbalanced, this is a brilliant debut—an important addition to the canon of Hispanic letters in the U.S. By choosing to write for an English-speaking audience, Alvarez is confessing her own loyalty: albeit reluctantly, she is in the process of losing her accent. Still, the accent refuses to die.

Source: Ilan Stavans, a review of How the García Girls Lost Their Accents, in *Commonweal,* Vol. CXIX, No. 7, April 10, 1992, pp. 23–5.

Elizabeth Starcevic

The following excerpt offers a mixed review of How the García Girls Lost Their Accents, *ultimately concluding that "we feel included in their lively, passionate world, and we want more."*

It is the voices of the García girls, the four lovely daughters of Mami and Papi García, who singly and in chorus offer the shifting choral poem that recounts their life as "strangers in a strange land." (Julia Alvarez left the Domincan Republic when she was ten years old. She published *Homecoming,* her first book of poetry, in 1986.) Privileged children of a privileged Dominican upper-class family, they are forced to leave their idyllic family compound to come and live in New York. Their father, Carlos García, one of thirty-three children, is a well-established professional in his country. Their mother, Laura de la Torre, traces her heritage back to the conquistadors and never forgets to mention a Swedish grandmother among her ancestors. Her father, a representative from the Dominican Republic to the United Nations, is involved in national politics, but with a difficult and complex relationship to the reigning dictator Rafael Trujillo. Carlos García and many of his relatives and friends become involved in an attempt to overthrow Trujillo that is at first supported and then abandoned by the United States. García is aided in his flight from his homeland by one of the Americans who implement this policy of fluctuating imperialism.

The threads of politics, race, and class surface often in this circular depiction of the García family's life in the United States. Beginning and ending in the Dominican Republic, in a quest to perhaps go home again, the stories unfurl from the present to the past, from 1989 to 1959. They are grouped in three sections with five stories each. Weaving together the life "before" and the life "after," these histories of immigrant experience are filled with humor, love, and intimate detail.

The shock felt by the girls when they abruptly change their life circumstances seems unbearable at first. Initially in limbo and wishing to return to their home, the girls experience racism, sexism, perversion, and a poverty that they were totally unused to. Isolated by language, they bond together within their already clannish patriarchal family, which is also being bombarded by the demands of the new world. Traditional roles are challenged, and upheaval permeates their interactions.

Although Carlos García is drawn as the patriarch and all the girls seek his approval, it is Laura de la Torre who plays the significant role as a mediator between two cultures. Educated in the United States, she merges the self-confidence of her wealthy background with a receptivity toward the new challenges. Energetic and intelligent, she is always thinking of new inventions. Her creativity is stymied, yet she finds other outlets in the activities of her children and her husband. She is a vivid, alive character whose contributions to the necessary adjustments of her new life are both critiqued and appreciated by her daughters. Through her stories about them we discover their accomplishments and their defeats, their adventures and professional advances. When Mami tells their story, each girl feels herself to be the favorite.

Carla, Yolanda, Sandra, and Sofía García grow up in a tumultuous period in the United States. This is the time of the Vietnam War, the sexual revolution, drugs, and feminism. While trying to negotiate the strict limits imposed on them by their parents, the sisters develop as a group and individually. "The four girls," as they are called, constantly see themselves as part of a similarly dressed collective, understanding only later that this made their mother's life easier while making them miserable. Their parents, while appreciated and loved, were not really able to guide them in their new tasks. Indeed, the cultures often seem to war against each other as the girls are told to be good, Catholic, respectful, unsullied virgins in an atmosphere that pushes for new mores and individualistic attitudes. They are sent to prep school in Boston and later go on to college. Marriages, divorces, breakdowns, and careers all form part of the adjustment. At least one, Yolanda, the poet, the writer whose voice is perhaps the strongest throughout the novel, decides as an adult to consider spending some time in the Dominican Republic and perhaps discovering at last her real home. There is overlay, however, in the cultural clashes. On one of their visits, these "American" sisters, who no longer fit as Dominicans, unite to rescue Sofía, the youngest. Having fallen in love and become emptyheaded almost simultaneously, she is ready to go off to a motel with her macho cousin, who believes that using condoms is an offense to his manhood.

In these visits and in their memories of their birthplace, we learn of the prejudices toward Haitians and darker-skinned country girls who are both needed and looked down upon. The portrayal of Chucha, the ancient Haitian servant, who is feared for her temper, her voodoo spells, and her practice of sleeping in a coffin, offers a glimpse into the historical complexity of the relationships of the two countries that share the island of Hispaniola. Comfort and ease that are taken for granted are provided by a series of servants who may spend their entire lives in the compound. Their livelihood depends on the whims of the employer, and one of the Garcías' maids is abruptly dismissed for having one of the children's toys in her possession even though Carla had given it to her as a gift.

The class privilege that was abruptly disturbed by the failed coup attempt does not disappear completely in the new world. Carlos García obtains a job immediately through his American benefactor Dr. Fanning. Little by little he is able to establish a practice and to provide ever greater comfort for his family. The Garcías are helped as well by Mrs. García's father. It is on a special evening out with the Fannings that we see the problematic relationship of U.S. neocolonialism replayed and that Sandi learns the power of emotional blackmail.

Scenes of pain and hardship but also of great humor are found throughout the novel. We listen to Laura García describe finding her husband and Carla in the bathroom painting white sneakers red with nail polish. Or, shades of magical realism, we watch Sandi discover one of the island's famous sculptors, naked and chained, in a shed strewn with giant figures in wood. Eventually she sees that he has sculpted her face on the statue of the virgin for the annual nativity crèche. Banding together, the sisters play on the names of their family in Santo Domingo, translating them literally so that they sound silly in English.

Language is a central feature of the book, beginning with the title. From Mrs. García's "mixed-up idioms that showed she was green behind the ears," to Yolanda's poetry, to the author, the girls, the mother and the father, all the aunts who want them to speak Spanish, the nuns and the police who want them to speak English, all the characters talk about language.

These are stories about relationships. Women are at the center, and we see the world through their eyes but also hear of it through their mouths. These are people of an oral tradition, and even though they have moved on to a writing stage, the power of the voice is what carries them. The book is uneven, and its organization into individual stories highlights this. The author has not really found consistently developed voices. Nevertheless, as we are pulled backward toward the moment when these Dominicans will become immigrants, we are pulled into the world of this family, we are drawn into their hopes and their dreams and their strategies for living, and we are glad. We enjoy what we learn, we enjoy the music of this chorus, we feel included in their lively, passionate world, and we want more.

Source: Elizabeth Starcevic, a review of *How the García Girls Lost Their Accents,* in *American Book Review,* Vol. 14, No. 3, August-September, 1992, pg. 15.

Sources

Juan D. Bruce-Novoa, review of *How the García Girls Lost Their Accents,* in *World Literature Today,* Vol. 66, No. 3, Summer, 1992, p. 516.

Stephen Henighan, review of *How the García Girls Lost Their Accents,* in *Globe and Mail* (Toronto), August 31, 1991, p. C6.

Cecilia Rodriquez Milanes, "No Place Like Home," in *Women's Review of Books,* Vol. 8, Nos. 10-11, July, 1991, p. 39.

Donna Rifkind, "Speaking American," in *New York Times Book Review,* October 6, 1991, p. 14.

Elizabeth Starcevic, "Talking about Language," in *American Book Review,* Vol. 14, No. 3, August-September, 1992, p. 15.

Ilan Stavans, "Daughters of Invention," in *Commonweal,* Vol. CXIX, No. 7, April 10, 1992, pp. 23-25.

Catherine Wiley, interview with Julia Alvarez in *Bloomsbury Review,* Vol. 12, No. 2, March, 1992, pp. 9-10.

Jason Zappe, review of *How the García Girls Lost Their Accents,* in *Americas Review,* Vol. XIX, Nos. 3-4, Winter, 1991, pp. 150-52.

For Further Study

Julia Alvarez, "Black behind the Ears," in *Essence,* Vol. 23, No. 10, February, 1993, p. 42, 129, 132.
    Alvarez talks about her Latin heritage and growing up in the Dominican Republic.

Contemporary Literary Criticism, Volume 93, Gale, 1996, pp. 1-20.
    A collection of critical excerpts on Alvarez's work, including *How the García Girls Lost Their Accents.*

Like Water for Chocolate

First published in 1989, Laura Esquivel's first novel, *Como agua para chocolate: novela de entregas mensuales con recetas, amores, y remedios caseros,* became a best seller in the author's native Mexico. It has been translated into numerous languages, and the English version, *Like Water for Chocolate: A Novel in Monthly Installments, with Recipes, Romances and Home Remedies,* enjoyed similar success in the United States. The film version, scripted by the author and directed by her husband, Alfonso Arau, has become one of the most popular foreign films of the past few decades. In a *New York Times* interview, Laura Esquivel told Marialisa Calta that her ideas for the novel came out of her own experiences in the kitchen: "When I cook certain dishes, I smell my grandmother's kitchen, my grandmother's smells. I thought: what a wonderful way to tell a story." The story Esquivel tells is that of Tita De la Garza, a young Mexican woman whose family's kitchen becomes her world after her mother forbids her to marry the man she loves. Esquivel chronicles Tita's life from her teenage to middle-age years, as she submits to and eventually rebels against her mother's domination. Readers have praised the novel's imaginative mix of recipes, home remedies, and love story set in Mexico in the early part of the century. Employing the technique of magic realism, Esquivel has created a bittersweet tale of love and loss and a compelling exploration of a woman's search for identity and fulfillment.

Laura Esquivel

1989

Laura Esquivel

Author Biography

Esquivel was born in 1951 in Mexico, the third of four children of Julio Caesar Esquivel, a telegraph operator, and his wife, Josephina. In an interview with Molly O'Neill in the *New York Times,* Esquivel explained, "I grew up in a modern home, but my grandmother lived across the street in an old house that was built when churches were illegal in Mexico. She had a chapel in the home, right between the kitchen and dining room. The smell of nuts and chilies and garlic got all mixed up with the smells from the chapel, my grandmother's carnations, the liniments and healing herbs." These experiences in her family's kitchen provided the inspiration for Esquivel's first novel.

Esquivel grew up in Mexico City and attended the Escuela Normal de Maestros, the national teachers' college. After teaching school for eight years, Esquivel began writing and directing for children's theater. In the early 1980s she wrote the screenplay for the Mexican film *Chido One,* directed by her husband, Alfonso Arau, and released in 1985. Arau also directed her screenplay for *Like Water for Chocolate,* released in Mexico in 1989 and in the United States in 1993. First published in 1989, the novel version of *Like Water for Chocolate* became a best seller in Mexico and the United

States and has been translated into numerous languages. The film version has become one of the most popular foreign films of the past few decades. In her second, less successful novel, *Ley del amor,* published in English in 1996 as *The Law of Love,* Esquivel again creates a magical world where love becomes the dominant force of life. The novel includes illustrations and music on compact disc to accompany it. Esquivel continues to write, working on screenplays and fiction from her home in Mexico City.

Plot Summary

Chapters 1-4: Under Mama Elena's Rule

In Laura Esquivel's *Like Water for Chocolate,* the narrator chronicles the life of her great-aunt, Tita De la Garza, who lives in northern Mexico during the early 1900s. The novel's twelve chapters, written one per month in diary/installment form, relate details from over two decades of Tita's life, beginning in 1910, when she is fifteen years old, and ending with her death at thirty-nine. Each chapter also includes a recipe that Tita prepares for her family during this period. After her mother refuses to allow her to marry the man she loves, Tita channels her frustrated desires into the creation of delicious meals that often have strange effects on her family. Through the expression of her culinary art, Tita learns to cope with and ultimately break free from her mother's domination.

Tita is born on her family's kitchen table, amid the fragrant and pungent odors of cooking. Since Tita's mother, Mama Elena, is unable to nurse her, Nacha, the family's cook, takes over the task of feeding her. "From that day on, Tita's domain was the kitchen" and "the joy of living [for her] was wrapped up in the delights of food."

When Tita is a teenager, Pedro Muzquiz comes to the family's ranch and asks for her hand in marriage, but Mama Elena refuses his request. Ignoring Tita's protestations, Mama Elena forbids her to marry, insisting that she abide by the family tradition that forces the youngest daughter to stay home and care for her widowed mother until her mother dies. Mama Elena suggests that Pedro marry Tita's sister Rosaura instead and Pedro agrees, deciding that a marriage to her sister is the only way he can stay close to Tita.

Mama Elena orders Tita to cook the wedding feast. As she prepares the cake, her sorrow over the impending marriage causes her tears to fall into the batter and icing. Nacha later tastes the icing and immediately is "overcome with an intense longing" as she thinks about her fiancé, driven away by Mama Elena's mother. The next morning Tita finds the elderly Nacha lying dead, "a picture of her fiancé clutched in her hands."

Tita now becomes the official cook for the ranch. Soon after the wedding, Pedro gives Tita a bouquet of roses to ease her depression over Nacha's death. She clasps them to her so tightly that the thorns cut her and she bleeds on them. When her mother forbids her to keep them, Tita mixes the petals in a dish that acts as an aphrodisiac for all who eat it, except Rosaura. Her eldest sister, Gertrudis, becomes so aroused by the meal that she runs to the outside shower, but the heat emanating from her body causes the wooden shower walls to burst into flames. Her body also exudes the scent of roses, which attracts a passing revolutionary. He sweeps her up still naked, on his horse, and rides away with her. When Mama Elena discovers that Gertrudis started to work at a brothel soon after her disappearance from the ranch, she disowns her.

The following year, Tita prepares the celebration feast for the baptism of her nephew Roberto, son of Pedro and Rosaura. Tita had been the only one present at Roberto's birth, which left Rosaura precariously ill. Since Rosaura had no milk after the birth, Tita tried to feed Roberto tea, but he refused it. One day, frustrated by his crying, Tita offers him her breast and is surprised to discover that she can nurse him. When Pedro observes Tita nursing his son, their secret moment together further bonds them. Tita's celebration feast generates a sense of euphoria in everyone who shares it—except Mama Elena, who suspects a secret relationship between Tita and Pedro. Her suspicions lead her to send Rosaura, Pedro, and Roberto to her cousin's home in San Antonio, Texas.

Chapters 5-8: Tita's Rebellion

After they leave, Tita loses "all interest in life," missing the nephew that was almost like her own child. One day rebels ride up to the ranch and ask for food. Mama Elena tells them they can have what they find outdoors, but they are not permitted in the house. Finding little, a sergeant decides to search inside. Mama Elena threatens him with her shotgun, and the captain, respecting her show of strength, stops the sergeant. Tita becomes even more depressed when she realizes that the men took the doves that she had enjoyed caring for. Later that day, as Tita prepares the family's meal, a servant appears and announces that Roberto has died because "whatever he ate, it didn't agree with him and he died." When Tita collapses in tears, her mother tells her to go back to work. Tita rebels, saying she is sick of obeying her mother's orders. Mama Elena smacks her across the face with a wooden spoon and breaks her nose. Tita then blames Mama Elena for Roberto's death and escapes to the pigeon house. The next morning, Tita refuses to leave the pigeon house and acts strangely. Mama Elena brings Dr. John Brown to remove her to an insane asylum, but, feeling sorry for her, he takes her to his home instead.

Tita is badly shaken and refuses to speak. As she sits in her room at John's home, she sees an old Native American woman making tea on the patio. They establish a silent communication with each other. Later she discovers that the old woman is the spirit of John's dead grandmother, a Kikapu Indian who had healing powers. John tells Tita stories about how his family had ostracized his grandmother and about her theory that all people need love to nourish their souls. When John asks her why she does not speak, she writes, "because I don't want to," which becomes her first step toward freedom.

One day Chencha, the De la Garza family's servant, brings some soup for Tita, and the food and Chencha's visit return Tita to her senses. Chencha then tells Tita that Mama Elena has disowned her. She also gives Tita a letter from Gertrudis, who writes that she is leaving the brothel because "I know that I have to find the right place for myself somewhere." Later, Tita accepts John's marriage proposal. When Chencha returns to the ranch, bandits break in, rape her, and attack Mama Elena, who is left paralyzed. Tita returns to care for her mother, who feels humiliated because of her need for Tita's help. Tita carefully prepares meals for her, but they taste bitter to Mama Elena, who refuses to eat them. She accuses Tita of trying to poison her so that she will be free to marry John.

Within a month Mama Elena dies, probably due to the medicine she was secretly taking to try to counter the effect of the poison she thought she was being given. Sorting through her mother's things, Tita finds letters hidden in her closet that tell of a secret love affair with a man of black ancestry, and of the birth of their child, Gertrudis. At her funeral Tita weeps for her mother's lost love.

Pedro and Rosaura return for the funeral and Pedro is angry that Tita and John are engaged. While at the ranch, Rosaura gives birth to Esperanza who like Roberto, must be cared for by Tita, since Rosaura has no milk. Rosaura determines that her daughter, like Tita, will care for her and never marry, which angers Tita. When John leaves to bring his aunt to meet Tita, she and Pedro consummate their love.

Chapters 9-12: Tita's Fulfillment

Later, when Tita suspects that she is pregnant, Mama Elena's spirit appears, warning her to stay away from Pedro. Gertrudis, now married and a general in the revolutionary army, returns for a visit. After Tita relates her fears for her future, Gertrudis insists she must follow her heart and thus find a way to be with Pedro. One night Pedro gets drunk and sings love songs outside Tita's window. A furious Mama Elena soon appears to Tita and threatens her. When Tita tells her mother she hates her, her mother's spirit shrinks to a tiny light. The apparent reduction of Mama Elena's control relieves Tita, which brings on menstruation and her realization that she is not pregnant. However, the tiny light begins to spin feverishly, causing an oil lamp to explode and engulf Pedro in flames. As Tita tends to his burns, Rosaura and John note the strong bond that still exists between them. Upset, Rosaura locks herself in her bedroom for a week.

John has returned with his aunt, wanting to introduce her to his fiancée. Tita prepares a meal for them, knowing she will have to disappoint them by calling off the wedding. When Pedro argues with her because she is taking such care with John's feelings, Tita is angered that he doubts her love. "Pedro had turned into a monster of selfishness and suspicion," she muses. That same morning Rosaura finally emerges from her room, having lost sixty-five pounds, and warns Tita not to make Rosaura look like a fool by carrying on with her husband in public. That afternoon Tita receives John and his Aunt Mary, and confesses that she has lost her virginity and cannot marry him. She also tells him that she does not know which man she loves best, as it changes depending on which man is nearer. John tells Tita that he still wants to marry her, and that she would live a happy life if she agreed to be his wife.

The narrative then jumps to twenty years in the future as Tita is preparing a wedding feast. However, it is to celebrate the union of Esperanza and Alex, John's son. The death of Rosaura a year ago had freed Esperanza and Tita, making it possible for both to openly express their love. Tita's wedding meal again stirs the passions of all who enjoy it. Pedro's feelings for her, however, have been repressed too long; when he is finally able to acknowledge his passion freely, it overwhelms him and he dies. Devastated by his death, Tita eats candles so she can light the same kind of fire within her, and soon joins him in death. The sparks the lovers give off burn down the ranch. When Esperanza returns from her wedding trip, she finds Tita's cookbook and passes it down to her daughter, the narrator of the story, who insists that Tita "will go on living as long as there is someone who cooks her recipes."

Characters

Juan Alejandrez

Juan is a captain in the revolutionary army when he first sees Gertrudis. He is known for his bravery, but when he smells the scent of roses emanating from Gertrudis's body after she eats one of Tita's magical dishes, he leaves the battlefield for the ranch. Juan sweeps Gertrudis up on his horse and carries her away from her home and her mother's tyranny. The two later marry and return for a visit to the ranch as generals.

Alex Brown

He is the son of Dr. John Brown; his mother died during his birth. He marries Esperanza Muzquiz, daughter of Pedro Muzquiz and Rosaura De la Garza, at the novel's end.

Dr. John Brown

The family doctor who lives in Eagle Pass. When he comes to attend Rosaura after Roberto's birth, he is astounded by Tita's beauty as well as her ability to assist her nephew's difficult birth. He returns to the ranch when Mama Elena De la Garza calls him to take Tita to an insane asylum. He instead takes Tita to his home and nurses her back to health. Tita responds to his kindness and patience and agrees to marry him. His understanding of her dilemma after she confesses her infidelity with Pedro leads her to reconsider her decision to call off the wedding: "What a fine man he was. How he had grown in her eyes! And how the doubts had grown in her head!" At the last minute, however, she realizes that her love for Pedro is stronger than her affection for John.

Gertrudis De la Garza

Gertrudis De la Garza is Tita's strong-willed, free-spirited sister. The eldest of the sisters, she is a passionate woman who takes sensual pleasure in life. Tita's cooking arouses such strong emotions in her that she runs off with a soldier in the revolutionary army and thus away from her mother's oppression. When Mama Elena discovers that Gertrudis is working at a brothel soon after her disappearance from the ranch, she disowns her. Only after Mama Elena's death does Tita ironically discover that Gertrudis was the product of their mother's illicit affair with a half-black man. Gertrudis returns to the ranch after Mama Elena's death, now married and a general in the revolutionary army. She advises Tita to follow her heart as she has done.

Mama Elena De la Garza

Mama Elena De la Garza is the tyrannical, authoritarian, middle-class matron who runs her daughters' lives along with the family ranch. Not only does she enforce the tradition that compels the youngest daughter to care for her widowed mother for the remainder of her life, but she compounds Tita's suffering by forcing her to prepare the wedding feast for Pedro and her sister. Suspecting a secret relationship between Pedro and Tita, she sends Rosaura, Pedro, and Roberto to her cousin's in San Antonio. When Roberto subsequently dies, Tita blames her mother because she separated the child from Tita, who fed and nurtured him. Mama Elena doles out severe beatings and/or banishment from the family in response to any acts of rebellion. She beats Tita after the wedding guests eat Tita's meal and become ill, and breaks her nose with a wooden spoon when Tita blames her for Roberto's death. She banishes Tita from the ranch after Tita shows signs of madness and disowns Gertrudis for working in a brothel. Her need for control over her daughters is so strong that it does not end with her death. Her spirit appears to Tita to warn her to stay away from Pedro. When Tita refuses, Mama Elena becomes so angry that she causes Pedro to be severely burned. Her proud and stubborn nature also emerges after the bandits who raid the ranch injure her health. She feels humiliated by her need for Tita's assistance and thus cannot accept her daughter's offer of food and comfort—a rejection that ultimately leads to her death. Mama Elena does appear more human, though, when Tita discovers letters in her closet that reveal a secret passionate love affair from her past. After her lover and her

husband died, Mama Elena suppressed her sorrow and never again was able to accept love.

Rosaura De la Garza

The middle of the three sisters, Rosaura De la Garza marries the man Tita loves. She causes Tita further pain when she determines that her only daughter will care for her and never marry, according to family tradition. Maria Elena de Valdes, in her article in *World Literature Today*, notes that Rosaura tries to model herself after Mama Elena in her treatment of Tita and Esperanza. She becomes, however, "an insignificant imitation of her mother. She lacks the strength, skill, and determination of Mama Elena." She also lacks her mother's passion. Tita discovers that Mama Elena has suffered from the loss of her true love and suppressed her emotions. Rosaura, on the other hand, never seems to display any capacity for love. Rosaura does, however, share some similarities with her mother. Like Mama Elena, she is unable to provide nurturance for her children. Tita must provide sustenance for both of Rosaura's children, just as Nacha had done for Tita. Also, Rosaura dies as her mother did, because of her inability to accept nurturance in the form of food from Tita.

Tita De la Garza

Tita De la Garza is the obedient but strong-willed youngest daughter of Mama Elena. On the surface she accepts her mother's dictates, even when they cause her to suffer the loss of the man she loves. Yet, she subtly rebels by rechannelling her feelings for him into the creation of delicious meals that express her passionate and giving nature. She obeys her mother's order to throw away

Media Adaptations

- Based on Esquivel's own screenplay, *Like Water for Chocolate* was adapted as a film in Spanish by Alfonso Arau, starring Lumi Cavazos, Regina Torne, and Marco Leonardi, Arau Films, 1992; with English subtitles, New Republic, 1993.

Lumi Cavazos in a scene from Like Water for Chocolate.

the roses Pedro has given her, but not before she creates an exquisite sauce from the petals. Through her cooking, she successfully communicates her love to Pedro. Tita's caring and forgiving nature emerges as she takes over the feeding of Rosaura's two children when their mother is unable to nurse them and as she tends to her mother after being banished from the ranch. Even after Mama Elena accuses Tita of trying to poison her so she will be free to marry John, Tita patiently prepares her meals. When Rosaura suffers from severe digestive problems, Tita also comes to her aid. Even while Rosaura rails against Tita about her feelings for Pedro and threatens to send Esperanza away to school, Tita serves a special diet to help her sister lose weight and ease her suffering. Tita does, however, have a breaking point. Her strength crumbles when Mama Elena sends Pedro, Roberto, and Rosaura away, and later she hears the news of Roberto's death, which pushes her into madness. After she regains her sanity, she seems to redouble her will. She stands up to Mama Elena's spirit and thus refuses to be influenced by her. She also holds her own with Rosaura, and works out an arrangement where she can continue to have a relationship with Pedro and Esperanza. Her passion, however, is her most apparent characteristic. For over two decades, her intense feelings for Pedro never fade. Tita ultimately sacrifices her life for him when she lights

herself on fire after his death so that their souls can forever be united.

Paquita Lobo

The De la Garzas' neighbor, who has unusually sharp senses. She is able to tell something is wrong with Tita when she is overcome by Pedro's presence at their first meeting. She also suggests that Tita appears pregnant at the very time when Tita suspects the same thing.

Chencha Martinez

A servant in the De la Garza household, Chencha becomes Tita's confidante. She takes pity on Tita after Mama Elena banishes her from the ranch and pays her a secret visit at John Brown's home. The soup she brings restores Tita's sanity. When she returns to the ranch, she is brutally raped, but is strong enough to survive the ordeal. Tita allows her to leave the ranch after this trauma, knowing that "if Chencha stayed on the ranch near her mother, she would never be saved." Chencha eventually marries her first love, Jesús Martinez, and returns to the ranch.

Morning Light

John Brown's grandmother, a Kikapu Indian, whom his grandfather had captured and brought back to live with him. Rejected by his grandfather's proud, intensely Yankee family, Morning Light spent most of her time studying the curative properties of plants. After her medicines saved John's great-grandfather's life, the family and the community accepted her as a miracle healer. While at John's home, Tita sees her, or her spirit, making tea on the patio. As Tita spends time with her, they establish a silent communication with each other. Her spirit helps calm Tita. Later John tells Tita about his grandmother's theory that we all need love to nourish our souls: "Each of us is born with a box of matches inside us but we can't strike them all by ourselves.... Each person has to discover what will set off those explosions in order to live." Tita comes to accept and live by this theory.

Esperanza Muzquiz

Pedro's and Rosaura's daughter. Tita insists that they name her Esperanza instead of Josefita, because she does not want to "influence her destiny." Nevertheless, Rosaura tries to impose on Esperanza the same kind of fate that Mama Elena imposed on Tita, but Rosaura's death frees Esperanza to marry Alex Brown, the man she loves.

Pedro Muzquiz

Pedro Muzquiz marries Tita's sister Rosaura only so he can stay close to Tita. He loves Tita, but shows little strength of character. He allows Mama Elena to run his life and separate him from the woman he loves. He also observes Tita's suffering under Mama Elena's domination and does little to intervene on her behalf. At one point Tita berates him for not having the courage to run off with her instead of marrying Rosaura. Marisa Januzzi, in her article in *The Review of Contemporary Fiction,* claims that "Pedro sometimes seems so unimaginative that only in fantasy ... could such an underdeveloped male character and magical ending satisfy Tita."

Roberto Muzquiz

First child of Pedro and Rosaura. Tita establishes a mother-child bond with him when his mother is too ill to feed him. When Pedro observes Tita nursing his son, their relationship is further strengthened. After Roberto's death, Tita is unable to cope with the sorrow and descends into madness.

Nacha

Nacha cooks for the De La Garza family and their ranch. Soon after she is born, Tita establishes a close relationship with Nacha. Since Tita's mother is unable to nurse her, Nacha takes over the task of feeding her and exposes her to the magical world of the kitchen. During her childhood, Tita often escapes her mother's overbearing presence and finds comfort in Nacha's company. Nacha becomes Tita's surrogate mother and the kitchen her playground and schoolhouse as Nacha passes down traditional Mexican recipes to her. Unfortunately, Tita loses Nacha's support when, after tasting the icing Tita has prepared for Rosaura's wedding cake, Nacha is "overcome with an intense longing" for her lost love, and she dies of a broken heart. Her spirit continues to aid Tita after her death, however, coming to her aid when she is delivering Rosaura's first baby.

Narrator

Esperanza's daughter and Tita's grandniece. The narrator explains that her mother found Tita's cookbook in the ruins of the De la Garza ranch. Esperanza told her daughter the story of Tita's life as she prepared the cookbook's recipes. The narrator has combined those recipes and the stories her mother told her about Tita, explaining that Tita "will go on living as long as there is someone who cooks her recipes."

José Treviño

José Treviño was the love of Mama Elena's life. Because he was mulatto—half-black—her parents forbid her to see him and forced her to marry Juan De la Garza instead. Mama Elena continued a relationship with him, however, and Gertrudis is his daughter. Tita only discovers this secret relationship after her mother's death.

Themes

Duty and Responsibility

The first chapter begins the novel's exploration of duty, responsibility, and tradition as they present Tita's main conflict. Family tradition requires that she reject Pedro's marriage proposal so she can stay at home and take care of her widowed mother for the rest of her life. If she turns her back on this tradition, she will not fulfill what society considers her responsibility to her mother. Rosaura decides that she also will impose this tradition upon her daughter Esperanza and so prevent her from marrying Alex Brown. Tita recognizes, however, that the tradition is unfair; if she cannot marry and have children, who will support her in her old age? She

Topics for Further Study

- Research the rebellion against the Mexican government led by Francisco "Pancho" Villa and Emiliano Zapata. Explain how this rebellion provides an effective backdrop for the tensions in the De la Garza family.

- Explore Freud's psychological theory on the process of sublimation. Write an essay determining whether or not it can be applied to any situations in the novel. Use examples from the text.

- Investigate the term "magic realism." Read another work that employs this technique and compare it to *Like Water for Chocolate*.

- Research the position of women in Mexican society in the early part of the twentieth century. How can your findings help define the novel's female characters?

tells Rosaura that she will go against tradition as long as she has to, "as long as this cursed tradition doesn't take me into account." Nevertheless, she and Pedro respect his duty toward his wife and child, for they remain discreet in their love as long as she lives.

Obedience

In order to fulfill her responsibilities toward her mother, Tita must obey her—a difficult task, given Mama Elena's authoritative nature. Mama Elena makes harsh demands on Tita throughout her life and expects her to obey without question. Mama Elena feels that Tita has never had the "proper deference" towards her mother, and so she is particularly harsh on her youngest daughter. Even when Tita sews "perfect creation" for the wedding, Mama Elena makes her rip out the seam and do it over because she did not baste it first, as Mama instructed. After Mama Elena decides that Pedro will marry Rosaura, she insists that Tita cook the wedding feast, knowing how difficult that task will be for her. When Nacha dies, Mama Elena decides Tita must take full responsibility for the meals

on the ranch, which leaves Tita little time for anything else. Tita's struggle to determine what is the proper degree of obedience due to her mother is a major conflict in the novel.

Cruelty and Violence

Mama Elena often resorts to cruelty and violence as she forces Tita to obey her. Many of the responsibilities she imposes on Tita, especially those relating to Pedro and Rosaura's wedding, are blatant acts of cruelty, given Tita's pain over losing Pedro. Mama Elena meets Tita's slightest protest with angry tirades and beatings. If she even suspects that Tita has not fulfilled her duties, as when she thought that Tita intentionally ruined the wedding cake, she beats her. When Tita dares to stand up to her mother and to blame her for Roberto's death, Mama Elena smacks her across the face with a wooden spoon and breaks her nose. This everyday cruelty does not seem so unusual, however, in a land where a widow must protect herself and her family from bandits and revolutionaries.

Victim and Victimization

When Mama Elena coerces Tita into obeying her cruel dictates, she victimizes her. Tita becomes a victim of Mama Elena's obsessive need for power and control. Mama Elena confines Tita to the kitchen, where her life consists of providing for the needs of others. She rejects Tita's individuality and tries to force her to suppress her sense of selfhood. Tita's growth as an individual depends on her ability to free herself from the role of victim.

Sex Roles

The novel closely relates Tita's victimization to the issue of sex roles. When Tita's mother confines her to the kitchen, she relegates her to a limited domestic sphere. There Tita's role becomes a traditionally female one—that of selfless nurturer, placing the needs of others before her own. In this limited role, Tita struggles to find a sense of identity. When Tita is taken to Dr. Brown's house, she marvels at her hands, for she discovers "she could move them however she pleased." At the ranch, "what she had to do with her hands was strictly determined." She learns of Dr. Brown's grandmother, Morning Light, who experimented with herbs and became a respected healer.

Love and Passion

The forces of love and passion conflict with Tita's desire to fulfill her responsibilities toward her mother. In obeying her mother, Tita must suppress her feelings for Pedro. Her sister Gertrudis, on the other hand, allows herself to freely express her passion when she runs off with Juan and soon begins work at a brothel. Tita's and Gertrudis's passionate natures also emerge through their enjoyment of food. Both relish good meals, although Tita is the only one who knows how to prepare one. At one point, Gertrudis brings the revolutionary army to the De la Garza ranch so she can sample her sister's hot chocolate, cream fritters, and other recipes. The food analogy also applies to the love of John Brown for Tita. Although he is captivated by her beauty, he feels no passionate jealousy over her relationship with Pedro. He comes from a North American family where the food, as Tita finds, "is bland and didn't appeal."

Sanity and Insanity

As the need to obey her mother clashes with her own desires, Tita begins to lose her sanity. When Mama Elena sends Rosaura, Pedro, and Roberto away, Tita loses all interest in life. The news of Roberto's death pushes her over the edge and she escapes to the pigeon house, refusing to come out. When John removes her from the oppressive atmosphere her mother has created, and he and Chencha offer her comfort and love, her sanity returns. Mama Elena never questions her own state of mind, although she is obsessive in her need to dominate her daughters. When Tita is found in the pigeon house, Mama Elena ironically states that "there's no place in this house for maniacs!"

Creativity and Imagination

Through Tita's creativity in the kitchen, she finds an outlet for her suppressed emotions. Thus, ironically, while Mama Elena tries to control Tita by confining her to the kitchen and forcing her to prepare all of the family's meals, Tita is also able to strengthen her relationship with others and to gain a clearer sense of herself. She pours all of her passion for Pedro into her meals, which helps to further bond the two. Her cooking also creates a bond with Pedro's two children, easing her pain over not being able to have children of her own with him. Tita's imaginative cooking is also a way for her to rebel against her mother; she recalls that whenever she failed to follow a recipe exactly, "she was always sure ... that Mama Elena would find out and, instead of congratulating her on her creativity, give her a terrible tongue-lashing for disobeying the rules."

Supernatural

The final important element of the novel is Esquivel's use of the supernatural. Tita's magical dishes, which produce waves of longing and uncontrollable desire, become a metaphor for creativity and self-expression. Like an artist, Tita pours herself into her cooking and produces works of art that evoke strong emotions in others. Her careful preparation of her family's food also reveals her loving nature. Another supernatural aspect, the spirits of the dead that appear to Tita throughout the novel, suggest that one's influence does not disappear after death. Nacha's spirit gives Tita confidence when she needs it, much like Nacha had done while she was alive. Mama Elena's spirit tries to control Tita from the grave, making her feel guilty about her passion for Pedro.

Style

Point of View

In fiction, the point of view is the perspective from which the story is presented. The unique point of view in *Like Water for Chocolate* helps convey the significance of the narrative. Esperanza, Tita De la Garza's niece, finds her aunt's cookbook in the ruins of the De la Garza ranch. As she recreates the recipes in her own home, she passes down the family stories to her daughter. Her daughter becomes the novel's narrator as she incorporates her great-aunt's recipes, remedies, and experiences into one book. She justifies her unique narrative when she explains that Tita "will go on living as long as there is someone who cooks her recipes."

Setting

The turbulent age of rebellion in Mexico provides an appropriate setting for the novel's focus on tyranny and resistance. Soldiers, bandits, and rebels are regularly mentioned in the novel, and often make appearances important to the narrative. It is a bandit's attack, for instance, that compels Tita's return home after her mother has disowned her. As Pancho Villa's revolutionary forces clash with the oppressive Mexican regime, Tita wages her own battle against her mother's dictates.

Structure

The narrative structure, or form, of the novel intersperses Tita's story with the recipes and remedies that figure so prominently in her life. By placing an actual recipe at the beginning of each chapter, the author is reinforcing the importance of food to the narrative. This structure thus attests to the female bonding and creativity that can emerge within a focus on the domestic arts.

Symbolism

A symbol is an object or image that suggests or stands for another object or image. Food is the dominant symbol in the novel, especially as expressed in the title. "Like water for (hot) chocolate" is a Mexican expression that literally means water at the boiling point and figuratively means intense emotions on the verge of exploding into expression. Throughout the novel, Tita's passion for Pedro is "like water for chocolate" but is constantly repressed by her dictatorial mother. An incident that symbolizes Mama Elena's oppression occurs when Tita is preparing two hundred roosters for the wedding feast. As she castrates live roosters to insure that they will be fat and tender enough for the guests, the violent and gruesome process makes her swoon and shake with anger. She admits "when they had chosen something to be neutered, they'd made a mistake, they should have chosen her. At least then there would be some justification for not allowing her to marry and giving Rosaura her place beside the man she loved." Food becomes a symbol of Tita's love for Pedro as she uses it to communicate her feelings. Even though Tita remains confined to the kitchen, her creative preparation of the family's meals continues to serve as a vehicle for her love for Pedro and his children, and thus as an expression of her rebellion against her mother's efforts to separate them.

Style

Magic realism is a fictional style, popularized by Colombian author Gabriel García Márquez, that appears most often in Latin American literature. Authors who use this technique mingle the fantastic or bizarre with the realistic. Magic realism often involves time shifts, dreams, myths, fairy tales, surrealistic descriptions, the element of surprise and shock, and the inexplicable. Examples of magic realism in *Like Water for Chocolate* occur when Tita's recipes have strange effects on those who eat them, when spirits appear to her, and when she cries actual rivers of tears. The fantastic element in Tita's cooking is that it produces such strong emotions in her family. The art of cooking, however, does reflect the patience and talent of the cook—qualities that are appreciated by those who enjoy the results. The spirits who appear to Tita symbolize the long

lasting effects of those who impact our lives and our own feelings of responsibility and guilt.

Foreshadowing

Foreshadowing is a literary device used to create an expectation of future events. In *Like Water for Chocolate,* foreshadowing occurs when John tells Tita about his grandmother's theory of love and life. She said that "each of us is born with a box of matches inside us but we can't strike them all by ourselves." We need the breath of the person we love to light them and thus nourish our souls. She warns, however, that lighting the matches all at once would be fatal. This process occurs at the end of the novel when Pedro's suppressed passion for Tita is finally "lit," and the intense flame is too much for him to bear.

Paradox

A paradox is a statement or situation that seems contradictory or absurd, but is actually true. The kitchen becomes a paradoxical symbol in the novel. On the one hand, it is a place where Tita is confined exclusively to domestic tasks, a place that threatens to deny her a sense of identity. Yet it is also a nurturing and creative domain, providing Tita with an outlet for her passions and providing others with sustenance and pleasure.

Historical Context

The Mexican Revolution

Although Mexico had been independent from Spain since the early nineteenth century, their governments were continually beset by internal and external conflicts. In the early part of the twentieth century, revolution tore the country apart. In November 1910, liberal leader Francisco Madero led a successful revolt against Mexican President Porfirio Díaz after having lost a rigged election. Díaz soon resigned and Madero replaced him as president in November 1911. Considered ineffectual by both conservatives and liberals, Madero was soon overthrown and executed by his general, Victoriano Huerta. Soon after the tyrannical Huerta became president, his oppressive regime came under attack. Venustiano Carranza, Francisco "Pancho" Villa, and Emiliano Zapata led revolts against the government. In 1914 Carranza became president as civil war erupted. By the end of 1915, the war ended, but Villa and Zapata continued to oppose the new government and maintained rebel groups for several years.

A Woman's Place

Richard Corliss, in his *Time* review of *Like Water for Chocolate,* writes that "Laura Esquivel brought Gabriel García Márquez's brand of magic realism into the kitchen and the bedroom, the Latin woman's traditional castle and dungeon." Traditionally, a Latin woman's place is in the home. In the patriarchal society of the early part of the twentieth century, Mexican women were expected to serve their fathers and brothers and then when married, their husbands, sons, and daughters. These women often turned to the domestic arts—cooking, sewing, and interior decoration—for creative outlets, along with storytelling, gossip, and advice. As a result, they created their own female culture within the social prison of married life.

Maria Elena de Valdes, in her article on *Like Water for Chocolate* in *World Literature Today,* notes that little has changed for the Mexican woman. She defines the model Mexican rural, middle-class woman: "She must be strong and far more clever that the men who supposedly protect her. She must be pious, observing all the religious requirements of a virtuous daughter, wife, and mother. She must exercise great care to keep her sentimental relations as private as possible, and, most important of all, she must be in control of life in her house, which means essentially the kitchen and bedroom or food and sex."

Reading women's magazines became a popular pastime for many married Mexican women. These magazines often contained fiction published in monthly installments, poetry, recipes, home remedies, sewing and decoration tips, advice, and a calendar of religious observances. Valdes finds similarities between the structure of *Like Water for Chocolate* and these magazines. She explains that "since home and church were the private and public sites of all educated young ladies, these publications represented the written counterpart to women's socialization, and as such, they are documents that conserve and transmit a Mexican female culture in which the social context and cultural space are particularly for women by women."

Critical Overview

When *Como agua para chocolate: novela de entregas mensuales con recetas, arores, y remedios*

Pancho Villa on his horse.

caseros by Laura Esquivel was published by Editorial Planeta Mexicana in Mexico in 1989, it quickly became a best seller. The 1991 English version, *Like Water for Chocolate: A Novel in Monthly Installments, with Recipes, Romances and Home Remedies,* translated by Carol and Thomas Christensen, also gained commercial success. The novel has been translated into several other languages.

Critical reception has been generally positive, especially when noting Esquivel's imaginative narrative structure. Karen Stabiner states in the *Los Angeles Times Book Review* that the novel is a "wondrous, romantic tale, fueled by mystery and superstition, as well as by the recipes that introduce each chapter." James Polk, in his review in the *Chicago Tribune,* describes the work as an "inventive and mischievous romp—part cookbook, part novel." Marisa Januzzi similarly notes in her assessment in the *Review of Contemporary Fiction* that "this short novel's got more heat and light and imaginative spice than the American literary diet usually provides."

Few scholarly articles, however, have been published on the novel. Molly O'Neill, in her interview with Esquivel in the *New York Times,* notes that American critics often consign the novel to the "'charming but aren't we moderns above it' ghetto of magical realism." Scholars also may have avoided the novel because of what some consider its melodramatic tone. In a mixed review for the *Nation,* Ilan Stavans finds a "convoluted sentimentality" in the novel.

The articles that have been published praise the novel's cultural focus. Ilan Stavans, in the same *Nation* review, observes that the novel accurately "map[s] the trajectory of feminist history in Mexican society." Maria Elena de Valdes, in her article in *World Literature Today,* argues that the novel contains an intricate structure that serves as an effective parody of Mexican women's fiction. She also praises its main theme: "a woman's creation of space that is hers in a hostile world." Victor Zamudio-Taylor insists the work is one of those that "reactualize tradition, make different women's voices heard, and revitalize identity—both personal and collective—as a social and national cultural construction."

Esquivel's screenplay of *Like Water for Chocolate,* along with her husband Alfonso Arau's direction, helped the film become one of the most successful foreign films of the past few decades. Esquivel has also written the screenplay for the popular Mexican film *Chido One.* Her most recent novel, *The Law of Love,* again focuses on the importance of love and incorporates the technique of magic realism. Reviews of the novel have been mixed. Barbara Hoffert argues in her *Library Journal* review that the novel "is at once wildly inventive and slightly silly, energetic and cliched." Lilian Pizzichini, however, writes in her review in the *Times Literary Supplement:* "Esquivel dresses her ancient story in a collision of literary styles that confirm her wit and ingenuity. She sets herself a mission to explore the redemptive powers of love and art and displays boundless enthusiasm for parody."

Criticism

Wendy Perkins

Perkins, Associate Professor of English at Prince George's Community College in Maryland, explores how Esquivel's use of magic realism in Like Water for Chocolate *reinforces the novel's celebration and condemnation of domesticity.*

In an interview with Laura Esquivel, published in the *New York Times Book Review,* Molly O'Neill notes that *Like Water for Chocolate* has not re-ceived a great deal of critical attention because it is "often consigned to the 'charming but aren't we moderns above it' ghetto of magical realism." Some critics, however, recognize the importance of the novel's themes: Ilan Stavans, in his review of the novel for *The Nation,* praises its mapping of "the trajectory of feminist history in Mexican society." In an article in *World Literature Today,* Maria Elena de Valdes argues that the novel reveals how a woman's culture can be created and maintained "within the social prison of marriage." Esquivel's unique narrative design is also worthy of critical attention. Her employment of magic realism, with its mingling of the fantastic and the real, provides an apt vehicle for the exploration of the forces of rebellion, submission, and retribution, and of the domestic sphere that can both limit and encourage self-expression.

Tita De la Garza, the novel's central character, makes her entrance into the world in her mother's kitchen, and this female realm becomes both a creative retreat and a prison for her. As a site for the crucial link between food and life, the kitchen becomes the center of Tita's world. Here she gains physical and emotional sustenance as Nacha, the family's servant and Tita's surrogate mother, teaches her the art of cooking. The kitchen also, however, becomes a site of oppression when Tita's mother forbids her to marry the man she loves and forces her into the role of family cook. The novel's public and private realms merge under the symbol of rebellion. As Pancho Villa's revolutionary forces clash with the oppressive Mexican regime, Tita wages her own battle against her mother's dictates. As Tita prepares magical dishes that stir strong emotions in all who enjoy them, the kitchen becomes an outlet for her thwarted passion. Thus the kitchen becomes a site for hunger and fulfillment. Yet Tita's cooking does not nourish all who sample it. In some instances her meals exact a certain retribution for her confinement to this domestic arena.

Throughout Tita's childhood, "the joy of living was wrapped up in the delights of food." The kitchen was her domain, the place where Nacha taught her the domestic and communal rituals of food preparation and encouraged her creative input. Here she lovingly prepares meals for her family, including her sister's children, who thrive under her care. The narrative structure of the novel attests to the female bonding and creativity that can emerge within this domestic realm. The narrator, Tita's grandniece, intersperses Tita's story with the recipes that figure so prominently in her life.

The kitchen, however, soon becomes a site of repression for Tita when her mother, Mama Elena, refuses to allow her to marry. Here the mother/daughter relationship enacts a structure of political authority and submission when Mama Elena enforces the family tradition that compels the youngest daughter to care for her widowed mother for the remainder of her life. Thus the walls of the kitchen restrict Tita's life as she resigns herself to the role of cook for her mother as well as the other members of her family. An incident that symbolizes Mama Elena's oppression occurs when Tita is preparing two hundred roosters for the wedding feast. Mama Elena has compounded Tita's despair over losing Pedro by announcing that her sister, Rosaura, will marry Pedro instead, and that Tita will cook for the wedding party. One task Tita must complete is the castration of live roosters to ensure that they will be fat and tender enough for the guests. The violent and gruesome process makes Tita swoon and shake with anger, as she thinks "when they had chosen something to be neutered, they'd made a mistake, they should have chosen her. At least then there would be some justification for not allowing her to marry and giving Rosaura her place beside the man she loved."

Yet ironically, Tita's passion for Pedro, her lost love, and her independent spirit find a creative and rebellious outlet in this same domestic realm. While Mama Elena successfully represses Tita's public voice, she cannot quell the private expression of her emotion. Tita subconsciously redefines her domestic space, transforming it from a site of repression into one of expression when she is forced to prepare her sister's wedding dinner. This time her creativity results in an act of retribution. As she completes the wedding cake, her sorrow over Rosaura's impending marriage to Pedro causes her tears to spill into the icing. This alchemic mixture affects the entire wedding party: "The moment they took their first bite of the cake, everyone was flooded with a great wave of longing.... Mama Elena, who hadn't shed a single tear over her husband's death, was sobbing silently. But the weeping was just the first symptom of a strange intoxication—an acute attack of pain and frustration—that seized the guests and scattered them across the patio and the grounds and in the bathrooms, all of them wailing over lost love." Thus Tita effectively, if not purposely, ruins her sister's wedding.

The kitchen also becomes an outlet for Tita's repressed passion for Pedro. After Pedro gives Tita a bouquet of pink roses, Tita clutches them to her

What Do I Read Next?

- Esquivel's second novel, 1996's *The Law of Love,* opens with the sixteenth-century Spanish conquest of Tenochtitlan, the future site of Mexico City. Many centuries later the reincarnated actors of this earlier drama confront each other as an astroanalyst, her missing soulmate, and a planetary presidential candidate.

- *The House of the Spirits* (1982) by Chilean Isabel Allende is a magical story about a Latin American family that survives internal and external pressures.

- Whitney Otto's 1991 novel, *How to Make an American Quilt,* focuses on women sharing the stories of their lives as they sit together and sew a quilt.

- *One Hundred Years of Solitude,* written by Colombian Nobel laureate Gabriel García Márquez in 1967, is considered the classic example of magic realism. This novel explores several generations of a Latin American family set against the age of revolution.

- The recipes in Ntozake Shange's 1982 novel, *Sassafras, Cypress & Indigo,* become part of the plot which focuses on the lives of three sisters.

- Shirlene Ann Soto's 1990 study, *Emergence of the Modern Mexican Woman: Her Participation in Revolution and Struggle for Equality, 1910-1940,* provides a good look at the varied roles of Mexican women during the time period of the novel.

chest so tightly, "that when she got to the kitchen, the roses, which had been mostly pink, had turned quite red from the blood that was flowing from [her] hands and breasts." She then creates a sauce from these stained petals that she serves over quail. The dish elicits a unique response from each member of her family that reflects and intensifies hidden desires or the lack thereof: Pedro "couldn't help closing his eyes in voluptuous delight," while

Lumi Cavazos and Marco Leonardi in Like Water for Chocolate.

Rosaura, a woman who does not appear to have the capacity for love, becomes nauseous.

The most startling response comes from Tita's other sister, Gertrudis, who responds to the food as an aphrodisiac. Unable to bear the heat emanating from her body, Gertrudis runs from the table, tears off her clothes, and attempts to cool herself in the shower. Her body radiates so much heat, however, that the wooden walls of the shower "split and burst into flame." Her perfumed scent carries across the plain and attracts a revolutionary soldier, who swoops her up, naked, onto his horse and rides off with her, freeing her, if not her sister, from Mama Elena's oppression. Private and public worlds merge as Gertrudis escapes the confinements of her life on the farm and begins a journey of self-discovery that results in her success as a revolutionary general. The meal of rose petals and quail also intensifies the passion between Tita and Pedro and initiates a new system of communication between them that will help sustain their love while they are physically separated. Even though Tita remains confined to the kitchen, her creative preparation of the family's meals continues to serve as a vehicle for her love for Pedro, and thus as an expression of her rebellion against her mother's efforts to separate the two. Her cooking also contin-

ues to exact retribution against those who have contributed to her suffering.

When Rosaura and Pedro move away from the ranch, Tita's confinement to the kitchen drives her mad, and she leaves in an effort to regain her sanity. She later returns to the ranch and to the domestic realm, willingly, to care for Mama Elena, who has become an invalid. This willingness to return to the kitchen, coupled with her mother's need for her, empowers her, yet her mother continues her battle for authority. Even though Tita prepares her mother's meals carefully, Mama Elena cannot stand the taste and refuses to eat. Convinced that Tita intends to poison her slowly in order to be free to marry, she continues to refuse all nourishment and soon conveniently dies—suggesting the cause to be either her refusal to accept Tita's offer of love and nourishment, or the food itself. Esquivel leaves this question unanswered.

When Rosaura and Pedro return to the ranch after Mama Elena's death, Tita again resumes her role as family cook. Even though she has decided to stay in the kitchen and not run off with Pedro so as not to hurt her sister, she ultimately, albeit unwittingly, causes her sister's death. Tita confronts her sister over her part in aiding Mama Elena's efforts to separate Tita from the man she loves.

Rosaura, however, refuses to acknowledge her role in her sister's oppression and threatens to leave with Pedro and her daughter, whom Tita has grown to love as her own. As a result, Tita wishes "with all her heart that her sister would be swallowed up by the earth. That was the least she deserved." As Tita continues to cook for the family, Rosaura begins to have severe digestive problems. Tita shows concern over her sister's health and tries to alter her diet to ease her suffering. But Rosaura's severe flatulence and bad breath continue unabated, to the point where her husband and child cannot stand to be in the same room with her. Rosaura's suffering increases until one evening Pedro finds "her lips purple, body deflated, eyes wild, with a distant look, sighing out her last flatulent breath." The doctor determines the cause of death as "an acute congestion of the stomach."

Here Esquivel again, as she did after Mama Elena's death, leaves the question of cause open. Rosaura could have died from a diseased system, compounded by her inability to receive and provide love and comfort. Or she could have died as a direct result of Tita's subconscious efforts to poison her. Either way, Rosaura's death releases Tita from the oppressive nature of her domestic realm and allows her to continue to express herself through her cooking.

In *Like Water for Chocolate,* magic realism becomes an appropriate vehicle for the expression of the paradoxical nature of the kitchen as domestic space. This novel reveals how the kitchen can become a nurturing and creative domain, providing sustenance and pleasure for others; a site for repression, where one can be confined exclusively to domestic tasks and lose or be denied a sense of self; and a site for rebellion against traditional boundaries.

Source: Wendy Perkins, in an essay for *Novels for Students,* Gale, 1999.

Ksenija Bilbija

In this excerpt, Bilbija examines traditional feminine and masculine roles as they are presented in Like Water for Chocolate.

When Virginia Woolf argues in *A Room of One's Own* for an appropriate and pertinent place for a woman, she never mentions the kitchen as a possible space in which her intellectual liberation from the patriarchal system could be enacted. At first glance, this area had always been assigned to a wife, servant, daughter, slave, mother, grandmother, sister or an aunt. For feminists, the kitchen

has come to symbolize the world that traditionally marginalized and limited a woman. It represents a space associated with repetitive work, lacking any "real" creativity, and having no possibility for the fulfillment of women's existential needs, individualization or self-expression....

A different, quite parodic and critical gender perspective has been presented in several recently published (cook)books by Latin American women writers. Laura Esquivel's *Como agua para chocolate: Novela de entregas mensuales con recetas, amores y remedios caseros* (1989) (*Like Water for Chocolate: A Novel in Monthly Installments with Recipes, Romances and Home Remedies*) and Silvia Plager's *Como papas para varenikes: Novela contraentregas mensuales, en tarjeta o efectivo. Romances apasionados, recetas judías con poder afrodisíaco y chimentos (Like Potatoes for Varenike: A Novel in Monthly Installments, Cash or Charge. Passionate Romances, Jewish Recipes With Aphrodisiac Power and Gossips*) (1994) have tried to revise stereotypical power relations and interpretations of male and female identity symbols. After all, alchemy and cooking probably did not always have rooms of their own, but may have shared the same transformative space.

In these novels the mythical, homogenized wholeness of Latin American identity posited by García Márquez, along with the exploration of its origins *vis-a-vis* Europe, becomes fragmented. The power of medieval alchemy, introduced by a vagabond tribe of gypsies who paradoxically bring the spirit of Western modernity, is parodically replaced by different ethnic cuisines: Aztec in the case of the Mexican writer and Jewish in the Argentine example. Both gastrotexts can be labeled as postmodern in the sense that they mimic mass-mediated explorations of gender identities. Their surprisingly similar subtitles replicate the format of a monthly magazine whose readers are housewives, or to use a more expressive, literal translation from the Spanish term *amas de casa,* mistresses of the home. *Like Water for Chocolate* is composed of twelve parts clearly identified by months and their corresponding dishes, with the list of ingredients heading the "Preparation" section.... By amalgamating the novelistic genre with cookbook recipes, Esquivel and Plager actualize a postmodern blurring of distinctions between high and low cultural values. Both writers insist on the cover that their respective books are actually novels, but they also subvert this code of reference by adding a lengthy subtitle that recalls and imitates the particular realms of popular culture that are associated with women. Although both of the books under consideration here are authored by women, I am not making the claim that recipe-writing is an archetypically female activity. As a matter of fact, by making a connection with alchemy, I would like to suggest that both activities have a common androginous origin in the past.

Esquivel's book was originally published in Mexico in 1989, became a national bestseller in 1990, continued its success with a movie version that garnered many international film awards, and in 1992 swept across the English speaking world—primarily the North American market—as a New York Times bestseller for several weeks. Plager's book came out in Argentina in April of 1994 and the public is still digesting it. Critics too. The editors' blurb on the jacket suggests that in *Like potatoes for varenike* the writer... 'shows us her culinary and humorous talents through an entertaining parody of the successful *Like Water for Chocolate*.' This statement is very significant for several reasons: first of all it represents the female writer *primarily* as a talented cook; second, it invokes the model, recognizes its success and appeals to the rights of cultural reproduction; and third, it claims that the book that the reader has in hand is actually a parody of that model.

Invoking the culinary expertise of the fiction writer, specially if the writer is a woman, fits all too well into the current, end of the century, wave of neo-conservativism. It also feeds into the postmodern confusion between reality and its simulation. Fiction is required to have the qualities of reality and reality is defined as what we see on television or read about in the newspaper; that "reality," however, is physically and psychologically fragmented and can only offer an illusion of wholeness. The avant garde insistence on the power of the imagination is giving way to research, "objectivity" and "expertise." Personal confession and "true stories" are valued higher than "imagined" ones and experience—in this case the culinary one—becomes the basis of identity and the source of discursive production. No wonder that the genre of the nineties is testimonial writing!...

The gastrotexts that I am discussing deal with gendered identities in a truly postmodern fashion: by situating the female protagonist in the kitchen and by literally allowing her to produce only a "kitchen table talk" spiced with melodrama instead of grandiose philosophical contraptions, their authors "install and destabilize convention in parodic ways, self-consciously pointing both to their own

inherent paradoxes and . . . to their critical or ironic rereading of the art of the past [according to Linda Hutcheon in her book *A Poetics of Modernism*]." In that sense the feminist discourse becomes paradoxical: instead of insisting on the liberational dimension of feminism which wants to get woman out of the kitchen, the postmodernist return to the discourses of power leads Esquivel and Plager to reclaim the kitchen as a not necessarily gender exclusive space of "one's own." Both writers rely heavily on traditional cultural practices and subvert the patriarchal values associated with masculinity and femininity....

Esquivel and Plager construct texts that do not fit into the traditional discourse of maternity. *Like Water for Chocolate* is constructed around the mother, who by invoking social rules, requires her youngest daughter Tita to reject any prospects of independent life, and take care of her until death. After Tita's premature birth on the kitchen table,...'amid the smells of simmering noodle soup, thyme, bayleaves, and cilantro, steamed milk, garlic, and, of course, onion,' Mamá Elena does not satisfy the baby's need for food, and Tita has to turn to Nacha, the cook, with whom she establishes the successful object relation. The proto object—the breast—determines the relationship that the individual will have with other objects in the course of life, is the foundation upon which the construction of individual subjectivity takes place. In this carnavalesque farce, the mother becomes a fairy-tale-like stepmother, while Tita, who will never feed her own child, becomes the nurturer for all in need. She appropriates the space of the kitchen, transforming it into the center of her power which alters the dominant patriarchal family structure. Hence, her emotions and well being determine the course of other's lives and she literally shares herself with the outside world: when she makes the cake for her sister's wedding to Pedro—with whom she was planning to get married—her tears of desperation mix with sugar, flour, eggs and lime peel. This later provokes melancholy, sadness and finally uncontrollable vomiting among the guests:...

> The moment they took their first bite of the cake, everyone was flooded with a great wave of longing. Even Pedro, usually so proper, was having trouble holding back his tears. Mama Elena, who hadn't shed a single tear over her husband's death, was sobbing silently. But the weeping was just the first symptom of a strange intoxication—an acute attack of pain and frustration—that seized the guests and scattered them across the patio and the grounds and in the bathrooms, all of them wailing over lost love. Everyone there, every last person, fell under this spell, and not

very many of them made it to the bathrooms in time—those who didn't joined the collective vomiting that was going on all over the patio.

The somatic reaction provoked by Tita's bodily fluids actually shows how the daughter undermines the mother's authority and prohibition. Something similar happens with "Quail in Rose Petal Sauce": Tita decides to use the rose that Pedro gave her as a sign of his eternal love, and prepares a meal that will awake Gertrudis' uncontrollable sexual appetite. By introducing the discourse of sexuality without necessarily relating it to marriage and by nurturing without procreating, Esquivel opens for discussion the ever present topics of feminine self-sacrifice and subordination that have traditionally been promoted by patriarchal literature....

By breaking the boundaries between body and soul and by showing that they are actually one, both Esquivel and Plager successfully undermine the duality so embedded in Western culture. They—latter day apprentices of Sor Juana Inés de la Cruz—go against Plato and his all too well known argument that the soul can best reflect if there are no distractions from the body. They dismantle that same duality that puts masculinity on one side and femininity on the other. *Like Water for Chocolate* and *Like Potatoes for Varenike* unlock the kitchen door and present us its most common inhabitants—women. Then, they leave this door wide open and invite man to share. In Esquivel's version sergeant Treviño is the one who helps Gertrudis decipher the recipe for cream fritters and in Plager's book Saul and Kathy work together from the beginning in meal preparation. By going against the rigid patriarchal binary thinking they, in Derridean fashion, reveal that there is no "transcendental signified." There is no original recipe either, nor original cook. It is all about transcending ego boundaries through dialogic, polyphonic texts, emphasizing the importance of nurturing, both for man and women, going against sexual oppression and connecting those "honey-tongued" people who are not only making their cake, but are ready to eat it too.

Source: Ksenija Bilbija, "Spanish American Women Writers: Simmering Identity Over a Low Fire," in *Studies in 20th Century Literature,* Vol. 20, No. 1, Winter 1996, pg. 147–61.

María Elena de Valdés

In the excerpt below, de Valdés explores "the interplay between the verbal and visual representation of women" in Like Water for Chocolate.

Como agua para chocolate is the first novel by Laura Esquivel (b. 1950). Published in Spanish in 1989 and in English translation in 1992, followed by the release of the feature film that same year, the novel has thrust this Mexican woman writer into the world of international critical acclaim as well as best-seller popularity. Since Esquivel also wrote the screenplay for director Alfonso Arau, the novel and the film together offer us an excellent opportunity to examine the interplay between the verbal and visual representation of women. Esquivel's previous work had all been as a screenwriter. Her script for *Chido Guan, el Tacos de Oro* (1985) was nominated for the Ariel in Mexico, an award she won eight years later for *Como agua para chocolate.*

The study of verbal and visual imagery must begin with the understanding that both the novel and, to a lesser extent, the film work as a parody of a genre. The genre in question is the Mexican version of women's fiction published in monthly installments together with recipes, home remedies, dressmaking patterns, short poems, moral exhortations, ideas on home decoration, and the calendar of church observances. In brief, this genre is the nineteenth-century forerunner of what is known throughout Europe and America as a woman's magazine. Around 1850 these publications in Mexico were called "calendars for young ladies." Since home and church were the private and public sites of all educated young ladies, these publications represented the written counterpart to women's socialization, and as such, they are documents that conserve and transmit a Mexican female culture in which the social context and cultural space are particularly for women by women.

It was in the 1850s that fiction began to take a prominent role. At first the writings were descriptions of places for family excursions, moralizing tales, or detailed narratives on cooking. By 1860 the installment novel grew out of the monthly recipe or recommended excursion. More elaborate love stories by women began to appear regularly by the 1880s. The genre was never considered literature by the literary establishment because of its episodic plots, overt sentimentality, and highly stylized characterization. Nevertheless, by the turn of the century every literate woman in Mexico was or had been an avid reader of the genre. But what has been completely overlooked by the male-dominated literary culture of Mexico is that these novels were highly coded in an authentic women's language of inference and reference to the commonplaces of the kitchen and the home which were completely unknown by any man.

Behind the purportedly simple episodic plots there was an infrahistory of life as it was lived, with all its multiple restrictions for women of this social class. The characterization followed the forms of life of these women rather than their unique individuality; thus the heroines were the survivors, those who were able to live out a full life in spite of the institution of marriage, which in theory, if not in practice, was a form of indentured slavery for life in which a woman served father and brothers then moved on to serve husband and sons together with her daughters and, of course, the women from the servant class. The women's fiction of this woman's world concentrated on one overwhelming fact of life: how to transcend the conditions of existence and express oneself in love and in creativity.

Cooking, sewing, embroidery, and decoration were the usual creative outlets for these women, and of course conversation, storytelling, gossip, and advice, which engulfed every waking day of the Mexican lady of the home. Writing for other women was quite naturally an extension of this infrahistorical conversation and gossip. Therefore, if one has the social codes of these women, one can read these novels as a way of life in nineteenth-century Mexico. Laura Esquivel's recognition of this world and its language comes from her Mexican heritage of fiercely independent women, who created a woman's culture within the social prison of marriage.

Como agua para chocolate is a parody of nineteenth-century women's periodical fiction in the same way that *Don Quijote* is a parody of the novel of chivalry. Both genres were expressions of popular culture that created a unique space for a segment of the population....

Obviously, for the parody to work at its highest level of dual representation, both the parody and the parodic model must be present in the reading experience. Esquivel creates the duality in several ways. First, she begins with the title of the novel, *Like Water for Chocolate,* a locution which translates as "water at the boiling point" and is used as a simile in Mexico to describe any event or relationship that is so tense, hot, and extraordinary that it can only be compared to scalding water on the verge of boiling, as called for in the preparation of that most Mexican of all beverages, dating from at least the thirteenth century: hot chocolate. Second, the subtitle is taken directly from the model: "A

Novel in Monthly Installments, with Recipes, Romances, and Home Remedies." Together the title and subtitle therefore cover both the parody and the model. Third, the reader finds upon opening the book, in place of an epigraph, a traditional Mexican proverb: "A la mesa y a la cama / Una sola vez se llama" (To the table or to bed / You must come when you are bid). The woodcut that decorates the page is the typical nineteenth-century cooking stove. The fourth and most explicit dualistic technique is Esquivel's reproduction of the format of her model.

Each chapter is prefaced by the title, the subtitle, the month, and the recipe for that month. The narration that follows is a combination of direct address on how to prepare the recipe of the month and interspersed stories about the loves and times of the narrator's great-aunt Tita. The narration moves effortlessly from the first person to the third-person omniscient narrative voice of all storytellers. Each chapter ends with the information that the story will be continued and an announcement of what the next month's—that is, the next chapter's—recipe will be. These elements, taken from the model, are never mere embellishments. The recipes and their preparation, as well as the home remedies and their application, are an intrinsic part of the story. There is therefore an intricate symbiotic relationship between the novel and its model in the reading experience. Each is feeding on the other.

In this study I am concerned with the model of the human subject, specifically the female subject, as it is developed in and through language and visual signification in a situated context of time and place. The verbal imaging of the novel makes use of the elaborate signifying system of language as a dwelling place. The visual imagery that at first expands the narrative in the film soon exacts its own place as a nonlinguistic signifying system drawing upon its own repertoire of referentiality and establishing a different model of the human subject than that elucidated by the verbal imagery alone. I intend to examine the novelistic signifying system and the model thus established and then follow with the cinematic signifying system and its model.

The speaking subject or narrative voice in the novel is characterized, as Emile Benveniste has shown, as a living presence by speaking. That voice begins in the first person, speaking the conversational Mexican Spanish of a woman from Mexico's north, near the U.S. border. Like all Mexican speech, it is clearly marked with register and socio-cultural indicators, in this case of the land-owning middle class, mixing colloquial local usage with standard Spanish. The entry point is always the same: the direct address of one woman telling another how to prepare the recipe she is recommending. As one does the cooking, it is quite natural for the cook to liven the session with some storytelling, prompted by the previous preparation of the food. As she effortlessly moves from first-person culinary instructor to storyteller, she shifts to the third person and gradually appropriates a time and place and refigures a social world.

A verbal image emerges of the model Mexican rural, middle-class woman. She must be strong and far more clever than the men who supposedly protect her. She must be pious, observing all the religious requirements of a virtuous daughter, wife, and mother. She must exercise great care to keep her sentimental relations as private as possible, and, most important of all, she must be in control of life in her house, which means essentially the kitchen and bedroom or food and sex. In Esquivel's novel there are four women who must respond to the model: the mother Elena and the three daughters Rosaura, Gertrudis, and Josefita, known as Tita.

The ways of living within the limits of the model are demonstrated first by the mother, who thinks of herself as its very incarnation. She interprets the model in terms of control and domination of her entire household. She is represented through a filter of awe and fear, for the ostensible source is Tita's diary-cookbook, written beginning in 1910, when she was fifteen years old, and now transmitted by her grandniece. Therefore the verbal images that characterize Mamá Elena must be understood as those of her youngest daughter, who has been made into a personal servant from the time the little girl was able to work.

Mamá Elena is depicted as strong, self-reliant, absolutely tyrannical with her daughters and servants, but especially so with Tita, who from birth has been designated as the one who will not marry because she must care for her mother until she dies. Mamá Elena believes in order, *her* order. Although she observes the strictures of church and society, she has secretly had an adulterous love affair with an African American, and her second daughter, Gertrudis, is the offspring of that relationship. This transgression of the norms of proper behavior remains hidden from public view, although there is gossip, but only after her mother's death does Tita discover that Gertrudis is her half-sister. The tyranny imposed on the three sisters is therefore the

rigid, self-designed model of a woman's life pitilessly enforced by Mamá Elena, and each of the three responds in her own way to the model.

Rosaura never questions her mother's authority and follows her dictates submissively; after she is married she becomes an insignificant imitation of her mother. She lacks the strength, skill, and determination of Mamá Elena and tries to compensate by appealing to the mother's model as absolute. She therefore tries to live the model, invoking her mother's authority because she has none of her own. Gertrudis does not challenge her mother but instead responds to her emotions and passions in a direct manner unbecoming a lady. This physical directness leads her to adopt an androgynous life-style: she leaves home and her mother's authority, escapes from the brothel where she subsequently landed, and becomes a general of the revolutionary army, taking a subordinate as her lover and, later, husband. When she returns to the family hacienda, she dresses like a man, gives orders like a man, and is the dominant sexual partner.

Tita, the youngest of the three daughters, speaks out against her mother's arbitrary rule but cannot escape until she temporarily loses her mind. She is able to survive her mother's harsh rule by transferring her love, joy, sadness, and anger into her cooking. Tita's emotions and passions are the impetus for expression and action, not through the normal means of communication but through the food she prepares. She is therefore able to consummate her love with Pedro through the food she serves....

> It was as if a strange alchemical process had dissolved her entire being in the rose petal sauce, in the tender flesh of the quails, in the wine, in every one of the meal's aromas. That was the way she entered Pedro's body, hot, voluptuous, perfumed, totally sensuous.

This clearly is much more than communication through food or a mere aphrodisiac; this is a form of sexual transubstantiation whereby the rose petal sauce and the quail have been turned into the body of Tita.

Thus it is that the reader gets to know these women as persons but, above all, becomes involved with the embodied speaking subject from the past, Tita, represented by her grandniece (who transmits her story) and her cooking. The reader receives verbal food for the imaginative refiguration of one woman's response to the model that was imposed on her by accident of birth. The body of these women is the place of living. It is the dwelling place of the human subject. The essential questions of health, illness, pregnancy, childbirth, and sexuality are tied very directly in this novel to the physical and emotional needs of the body. The preparation and eating of food is thus a symbolic representation of living, and Tita's cookbook bequeaths to Esperanza and to Esperanza's daughter, her grand-niece, a woman's creation of space that is hers in a hostile world.

Source: María Elena de Valdés, "Verbal and Visual Representation of Women: *Como agua para chocolate / Like Water for Chocolate*," in *World Literature Today,* Vol. 69, No. 1, Winter 1995, pp. 78–82.

Sources

Marialisa Calta, "The Art of the Novel as Cookbook," in the *New York Times Book Review,* February 17, 1993.

Richard Corliss, review of *Like Water for Chocolate,* in *Time,* Vol. 141, No. 14, April 5, 1993, p. 61.

María Elena de Valdés, "Verbal and Visual Representation of Women: 'Like Water for Chocolate,'" in *World Literature Today,* Vol. 69, No. 1, Winter 1995, pp. 78-82.

Barbara Hoffert, review of *The Law of Love,* in *Library Journal,* July, 1996, p. 156.

Marisa Januzzi, review of *Like Water for Chocolate,* in *Review of Contemporary Fiction,* Vol. 13, No. 2, Summer, 1993, pp. 245-46.

Molly O'Neill, "At Dinner with Laura Esquivel: Sensing the Spirit in All Things, Seen and Unseen," in the *New York Times,* March 31, 1993, pp. C1, C8.

Lilian Pizzichini, review of *The Law of Love,* in *Times Literary Supplement,* October 18, 1996, p. 23.

James Polk, review of *Like Water for Chocolate,* in *Tribune Books* (Chicago), October 8, 1992, p. 8.

Karen Stabiner, review of *Like Water for Chocolate,* in the *Los Angeles Times Book Review,* November 1, 1992, p. 6.

Ilan Stavans, review of *Like Water for Chocolate,* in *Nation,* Vol. 256, No. 23, June 14, 1993, p. 846.

Victor Zamudio-Taylor and Inma Gulu, "Criss-Crossing Texts: Reading Images in 'Like Water for Chocolate,'" in *The Mexican Cinema Project: Studies in History, Criticism, and Theory,* edited by Chon Noriega and Steven Ricci, The UCLA Film and TV Archive, 1994, pp. 45-52.

For Further Study

Mary Batts Estrada, review of *Like Water for Chocolate,* in the *Washington Post,* September 25, 1993, p. B2.
This review praises the novel for its mixture of culinary knowledge, sensuality, and magic as "the secrets of love and life [are] revealed by the kitchen."

Stanley Kauffmann, review of *Like Water for Chocolate,* in *New Republic,* Vol. 208, No. 9, March 1, 1993, pp. 24-25.
Kauffmann reviews the movie version of the novel and finds it "drawn-out" and "lacking in focus."

Love Medicine

Louise Erdrich
1983

When Louise Erdrich and her husband, Michael Dorris, first sent *Love Medicine* to publishers, they received nothing but polite rejections. Finally, Dorris decided to promote the book himself and was successful. Holt published the book in 1983, and it became an immediate best seller. Critics applaud Erdrich's wit, tenderness, and powerful style of writing. They particularly like the manner in which Erdrich creates the Native American voice through the form of a traditional Chippewa story cycle. Her characters tell their own stories. In *Love Medicine,* seven characters from two families present fourteen stories about themselves and their relationships. Readers, especially Native Americans, appreciate her realistic portrayal of Native American life. The book has translations in eighteen languages and has received enthusiastic readerships through the Book-of-the-Month and Quality Paperback Book Clubs. In addition, television producers have discussed the possibilities of made-for-television serials as well as movies.

Love Medicine has won many awards for Erdrich's ability to demonstrate the differences among individuals within the sameness of their culture. While each of the characters reveals his or her personality, the distinct ties between the characters and their culture are obvious. For example, Nector, the iconic Indian whose portrait has hung in the state capitol, leads the same personal life led by men of lesser stature. He carries on an affair, has a failed marriage, and lives out his final days in a state of near oblivion. The theme of generational connections holds strongly throughout the novel.

Author Biography

Erdrich was born on July 6, 1954, in Little Falls, Minnesota. One of seven children, Erdrich and her family later lived in Wahpeton, North Dakota, close to the Turtle Mountain Chippewa Reservation. Her parents, Rita Joanne Gourneau Erdrich and Ralph Louis Erdrich, both taught at the Bureau of Indian Affairs boarding school. Erdrich's mother was born on the reservation, and Erdrich's grandfather, Patrick Gourneau, served as tribal chairman. Erdrich thinks highly of her grandfather, who keeps the old traditions alive within the context of modern culture and is respected in both cultures. While Erdrich says that none of her fiction is autobiographical, she does admit to picturing her grandfather's best traits through Nector Kashpaw in *Love Medicine.*

Erdrich entered Dartmouth College in 1972. That same year, Dartmouth established its Native American Studies department. Anthropologist Michael Dorris, Erdrich's future husband, chaired the department. As a student in his classes, she began to explore her Native American heritage. She and Dorris collaborated on a children's story which was published in an Indian magazine. At the same time, one of her other teachers encouraged her poetry writing. While she had several publications in Dartmouth literary magazines, Erdrich felt she had achieved true success when *Ms.* published one of her poems. Then, in 1975, the American Academy of Poets awarded her a prize. Feeling validated as a poet, Erdrich worked after graduation for the State Arts Council of North Dakota, teaching poetry in schools, prisons, and rehabilitation centers.

In addition to being a poetry teacher, Erdrich worked various jobs that have provided her with experiences she uses in her writing: as a waitress, lifeguard, construction worker, etc. As a specific example, Erdrich once weighed trucks on the interstate. In *Love Medicine,* Albertine and Dot weigh trucks for the state highway system. Through working at these jobs, Erdrich gained an understanding of and compassion for people of mixed blood. She felt compelled to write about them. In an interview with Michael Schumacher for *Writer's Digest* she says, "There were lots of people with mixed blood, lots of people who had their own confusions. I realized that this was part of my life—it wasn't something that I was making up—and that it was something I *wanted* to write about."

Motivated to focus on her writing, Erdrich began her Master's program at Johns Hopkins Uni-

Louise Erdrich

versity. When she graduated, Dartmouth College hired her as a writer-in-residence. While at Dartmouth, she and Dorris renewed their acquaintance. Then, she left for Boston to work on a textbook, and Dorris went to New Zealand to do research. They kept in touch by sharing their work with one another. When their story, "The World's Greatest Fisherman" won five thousand dollars in the Nelson Algren fiction competition, the two decided to expand it into the novel, *Love Medicine.* Since the publication of her debut novel, she has published several other novels, poetry, and her memoir.

Plot Summary

The World's Greatest Fishermen (1981)

The novel opens with June Kashpaw walking down the main street of Williston, North Dakota, killing time until she can board the bus home to the reservation. Instead of boarding that bus, however, she meets a man in a bar, and after several drinks they drive out of town and have sex in the front seat of his car. When he falls into a drunken sleep on top of her, she squeezes out and begins to walk home, but an Easter snow storm surprises her and she dies before she reaches the reservation.

The memories of family members fill in June's background. Raised by her bachelor uncle, Eli, she had married her cousin, Gordie, and had a son, King. The marriage had ended unhappily, however, and June ran off. Now King, her son, has used the insurance money from her death to buy a new car. June also had an illegitimate son, Lipsha, who was raised by Marie Kashpaw, but Lipsha does not know that June was his mother.

Saint Marie (1934)

At fourteen Marie goes to the convent to become a nun. In an effort to fight off the devil and tame Marie's proud spirit, Sister Leopolda pours scalding hot water on the girl's back, and pierces her hand with a fork. Marie passes out from the pain of this last wound, and wakes to find the nuns all kneeling before her, awaiting her blessing, as Leopolda has told them that it is a holy wound which magically appeared on the girl's hand.

Wild Geese (1934)

Nector Kashpaw is thinking about Lulu while walking to town to sell some geese. He sees Marie Lazarre running down the hill from the convent with a convent pillowcase. Thinking that she has stolen it, he tries to stop her. He wrestles her to the ground and then cannot stop himself from touching her under her skirt. Only when he pulls back, shocked at what he has done, does he realize that the pillowcase is bandaging a wound on her hand. They sit holding hands as the sun goes down.

The Island

When Nector turns to Marie, Lulu begins to think of Moses Pillager, a strange, ghostlike man who lives as a hermit on an island. She goes to his home, and they fall in love. When they are expecting their child she realizes that she cannot stay there forever, but that Moses will never be able to leave.

The Beads (1948)

Marie takes in her niece, June Kashpaw, even though she has too many mouths to feed already. Though Marie loves June, June decides to go live with her Uncle Eli. Nector leaves Marie and she must struggle to support the children herself.

Rushes Bear, Nector's mother, comes to stay with Marie. When Marie is ready to give birth again, Nector returns. After the child is born, Nector tries to pay his mother, but she refuses the money saying that she no longer has a son, only a daughter, Marie.

Lulu's Boys (1957)

Lulu is visited by her late husband's brother, Beverly Lamartine. Beverly believes that the boy born nine months after his brother's funeral is in fact Beverly's son, conceived on the day of Henry's wake. He has come with the hope of retrieving that son, but Lulu reminds him of his old passion for her. Finally he slips into Lulu's bed, and becomes her next husband.

The Plunge of the Brave (1957)

Nector tells how everything has always come easily to him. He receives many job offers, and he can have any woman he wants. The one he wants is Lulu, and they seem to be moving easily towards each other, until he meets Marie. He marries Marie and soon feels overwhelmed by their many children and the demands of his job. One hot summer day some butter is delivered to the town, and Nector asks Lulu to help deliver the butter. When they are alone Nector asks for her forgiveness, and they make love. After that he sneaks into her bedroom regularly. This continues until he begins to fear that she will marry her brother-in-law. He writes two notes, one to Marie, telling her that he is in love with Lulu, and the other to Lulu, telling her that he is leaving Marie. He leaves the note for Marie under the sugar jar on their table, and he takes the other note to Lulu's house. She is not home, so he waits in her backyard, but his cigarette starts a fire and burns the house down.

Flesh and Blood (1957)

Zelda finds the note her father has left on the table. Frightened, she brings it to Marie. Hours later Marie hears Zelda and Nector returning, and she wonders how to face him. She decides to put the note back on the table, but she puts it under the salt shaker, not the sugar jar, so that Nector will always wonder whether she has read it or not.

A Bridge (1973)

Albertine runs away from home and takes the bus to Fargo. She meets Henry Lamartine Jr., recently returned from a POW camp in Vietnam, and they spend the night together in a motel.

The Red Convertible (1974)

When Henry returns from Vietnam he is not interested in anything. Lyman breaks the car they had bought together in an attempt to get Henry interested in fixing it. Henry does fix it and takes a trip with Lyman, but then Henry jumps in the river and drowns. Lyman drives the car into the water and lets it sink.

Scales (1980)

Gerry Nanapush is constantly breaking out of prison and being caught again. Dot is pregnant with a child they managed to conceive in a prison visiting room. When Dot is very close to delivering the baby, Gerry breaks out so he can be with her. Weeks later Gerry is arrested again, this time for shooting and killing a state trooper.

Crown of Thorns (1981)

Gordie, June's ex-husband, begins to drink heavily after her death. Driving drunk one night, he hits a deer and puts the body in his back seat. He continues to drive, but then the deer, merely stunned, wakes up. Gordie grabs a crow bar and kills it, but then he becomes convinced that it is June he has just killed. He drives to a convent and confesses to a nun that he has killed his wife. She tries to explain to him that it is a deer he has killed, but he runs crying into the woods.

Love Medicine (1982)

Marie asks Lipsha to get her love medicine so that Nector will return the love she has always felt for him. Lipsha decides to shoot two geese, birds that mate for life, and have his grandparents eat the hearts. But when he is not able to shoot the geese, he buys two turkey hearts, reasoning that the faith is what is important. Nector, however, chokes on the heart and dies.

Resurrection (1982)

Gordie shows up at his mother's house and begs for some alcohol. She has none, but when she is not looking he drinks Lysol and dies.

The Good Tears (1983)

Lulu has surgery on her eyes, which are failing her, and she needs someone to put drops in them for her. Marie Kashpaw comes to do it, and, after a life-long animosity, the two women become allies.

The Tomahawk Factory (1983)

Lyman builds a factory that will make souvenirs. The products do not sell quickly, and the workers become disgruntled at the continual layoffs. Finally there is a revolt and the factory is destroyed.

Lyman's Luck (1983)

Lyman decides to start running Bingo games. He hopes to eventually open casinos.

Crossing the Water (1984)

Lulu tells Lipsha that he is the son of June and Gerry. Lipsha goes to King's house looking for Gerry. Gerry appears and reveals that when he and King were in prison together, King told officials of Gerry's plans to escape. The three men play poker, with the car bought with June's insurance money as the stakes. Lipsha wins and offers to drive Gerry anywhere he wants to go. Just then the police show up, and Gerry disappears. Lipsha begins driving the car home, but he hears a knocking in the trunk. He pulls over and discovers Gerry in the trunk. He drives Gerry to Canada and then heads home.

Characters

Uncle Eli
See Eli Kashpaw

Uncle Gordie
See Gordie Kashpaw

Henry Junior
See Henry Lamartine, Jr.

Henry Senior
See Henry Lamartine

Albertine Johnson

At the beginning of the story in 1981, Albertine Johnson—daughter of Zelda and granddaughter of Marie—is away from the reservation studying to be a nurse. She returns home upon hearing of her Aunt June's death. Once home, she tries to get Grandpa Kashpaw to recall his years as an Indian revolutionary.

Albertine has always been independent. In 1973, the fifteen-year-old runs away from home to Fargo, where she meets and sleeps with Henry Lamartine, Jr. In 1980, trying to decide what to do with her life, Albertine meets Gerry Nanapush and his girlfriend, Dot Adare. Albertine works on the construction sight with Dot until Dot delivers Gerry's baby.

Zelda Johnson

Zelda, sister to Aurelia and daughter of Marie, is Albertine's mother. Zelda was raised as June's sister. Zelda thinks Albertine should be married. She also criticizes June's son, King, for marrying a white girl when Zelda, herself, had been married to a Swede.

Aurelia Kashpaw

Aurelia, Albertine's aunt, is Marie's other daughter and Zelda's sister. She lives in the old homeplace on the reservation.

Eli Kashpaw

Eli Kashpaw, one of the youngest of Rushes Bear's twelve children, was raised in Indian ways while his brother, Nector, attended the white man's boarding school. Eli is Albertine's great uncle. Eli raises June after she leaves Marie's house. He remains a bachelor. While his brother Nector's mind has deteriorated, Eli's remains clear and sharp.

Gordie Kashpaw

First-born son of Marie and Nector, Gordie is the brother of Zelda and Aurelia, and was raised as June's brother. He marries June, however, angering Marie. He and June have one son, King. Gordie truly loves June and is never able to deal with her death. He begins drinking one month after her death. In 1982, he dies from heartbreak and alcoholism in his mother's home.

Grandma Kashpaw

See Marie Kashpaw

Grandpa Kashpaw

See Nector Kashpaw

June Kashpaw

The story begins in 1981 with the final episode of June Morrissey Kashpaw's life. A long-legged, hardened Chippewa woman, June appears young to the casual observer. A close look, however, reveals her broken nails, ragged hair, and clothes held together by safety pins. June is the daughter of Lucille Lazarre Morrissey, the dead sister of Marie Lazarre Kashpaw (Grandma Kashpaw). June resides with Marie until she decides to go live with Eli. June marries Marie's son, Gordie, much to Marie's displeasure.

On one of her many leaves from Gordie, June meets a mud engineer, Andy, in a bar in Williston, North Dakota. She has drinks with him, knowing that he will want to sleep with her afterwards. Tired of the routine she knows so well, June plays along until Andy passes out in his truck. June, drunk, de-

Media Adaptations

- *Love Medicine* is read by Erdrich and her husband/collaborator, Michael Dorris on this audiotaped, 180-minute abridged version of the book; available from Audiobooks.com.

- An audiocassette version of *Love Medicine*, along with *The Beet Queen* is available from Amazon.com. Entitled *The Beet Queen: Love Medicine (Excerpt E)*, the cost of this audiotape is $13.95.

cides to walk back to the reservation but never makes it. She dies in a snow-covered field.

King Kashpaw

King is the son of June and Gordie. King is married to Lynette, a white girl, and they have a son named King, Jr. (Howard). King wants to believe he is the only true son of June and torments Lipsha for most of his life. At the end of the story, Lipsha and Gerry both visit King and his family—reminding King of his acts against them and putting him in his place.

Marie Kashpaw

Marie grew up as Marie Lazarre, the daughter of drunken horse thieves, a Catholic girl who believed that Satan talked to her. One of the sisters who taught at Marie's school convinced Marie that Satan lived in her, and that the only way to be rid of him was to join the convent. Marie lived in the convent from 1931 until 1934, enduring physical and mental abuse from the sister, Leopolda, who had cajoled her into coming to the convent. When Leopolda stabs Marie with a fork and knocks her out with a poker, Marie finally finds a way to escape her abuse. She allows the other sisters to believe Leopolda's story that the injury in Marie's palm is actually the mark of Christ—the evidence of a miracle that has occurred in the face of Satan's work. With this lie, Marie holds a power over Leopolda that enables Marie to leave the convent.

Marie meets Nector Kashpaw on the day she leaves the convent. Nector is a handsome Indian who is returning from shooting geese that he sells to the convent sisters. He throws Marie to the ground without thinking, and with one sexual act, seals his fate with Marie forever. While Nector really loves Lulu Nanapush, he marries Marie in 1934 and fathers her children—Gordie, Zelda, Aurelia—and raises the children they take in—Lipsha Morrissey and June Kashpaw.

Nector Kashpaw

Nector Kashpaw—son of Rushes Bear (Margaret Kashpaw), brother of Eli, and husband of Marie—attended boarding school as a young man, where he learned to read and write as well as the white man's ways. He represented his tribe well in his younger days, testifying in Washington for Indians' rights, getting a school and factory built, and saving his tribe's land. When the story opens in 1981, however, Nector Kashpaw has little memory of anything that has happened in the past.

In his lucid moments, Nector remembers his first meeting with Marie and wonders at the fact that he was unable to let her go. At that time in his life, he loved Lulu Nanapush, whom his own mother had raised. Yet he married Marie Lazarre, for which Lulu never forgave him. Nector, himself, could never forget Lulu. In 1952, realizing that he had to follow his heart, Nector begins a five-year affair with Lulu. The affair ends when Beverly Lamartine, Lulu's late husband's brother, arrives and becomes her lover. Nector gets Lulu kicked off her land, and as a result, Lulu ends the affair. He tries to forget her but ends up writing a letter to Marie telling her that he is leaving her. When he returns to Lulu's house and finds her gone, he burns her house down.

Beverly Lamartine

Henry Senior's brother, Beverly appears at Henry's funeral and then again, seven years after Henry dies. His secret motive for returning is to claim Henry Junior as his own so that he can "use" Henry Junior in his book-selling tactics. He succeeds in seducing Lulu and is the cause of the end of Lulu's affair with Nector Kashpaw.

Henry Lamartine

The man Lulu married out of "fondness," Henry dies in 1950 when a train crashes into his car.

Henry Lamartine, Jr.

Henry Junior, son of Lulu (and probably Henry Senior), is not the same person when he returns from Vietnam. Having been a happy-go-lucky kind of guy, the Henry who returns from three years overseas is very different. He suffers from depression, but there is no help available for him on the reservation. He seems happier after he begins working on the red car that he loves. One night, however, he and Lyman get drunk and Henry jumps into the river. When he doesn't reappear, Lyman tries to save him. Realizing that Henry has drowned, Lyman pushes the car into the river—leaving it there for his brother who loved it.

Lulu Lamartine

Lulu Lamartine loved Nector Kashpaw from the time that she was a young girl. When Nector married Marie instead, Lulu tried to put him out of her mind. She went to live with Moses Pillager, the crazy island man whose family had sent him to live in the land of the spirits. She bore him a son, Gerry, and returned to town to live. When Pillager did not follow her, she married a Morrissey out of spite. Later, she married Henry Lamartine because she was fond of him. Lulu had eight sons, none of whom were Henry's and one daughter, Bonita, whose father was Mexican. The last of the eight boys was Nector's son, Lyman Kashpaw.

After Nector signed Lulu's land away, Lulu married Beverly Lamartine, Henry's brother, but did not live with him. She spent a few months living in a shack on her burned-out property, until the tribe built a government house for her on a piece of land bought from a white farmer. After she had turned sixty-five and with eyesight failing, Lulu moves to the Senior Citizen's Center where she and Nector have their last encounter with one another.

Lyman Lamartine

It is 1983. Lyman Lamartine, son of Lulu and brother to Henry Junior, has difficulty dealing with his brother's death. An astute businessman, Lyman begins to lose money, unable to bring himself out of his depression. A notice from the IRS prompts him to action, though. He goes to work for the Bureau of Indian Affairs and opens a factory. When the factory is destroyed as the result of rioting among its employees, he begins planning a Chippewa casino.

Marie Lazarre

See Marie Kashpaw

St. Marie

See Marie Kashpaw

June Morrissey

See June Kashpaw

Lipsha Morrissey

Lipsha was raised by Grandma Kashpaw, but he was June's son by Gerry Nanapush during one of June's separations from Gordie. Lipsha, however, goes through most of his life not knowing that June is his mother. Lipsha has special talents—an Indian medicine with which he was born. He decides to practice his medicine on his grandparents by concocting a love charm for them. When he "cheats" on the concoction, he believes he is the cause of his grandfather's death. His grandmother reassures him and gives him the beads that had belonged to his mother. He does not really understand the significance of the beads until Lulu Lamartine tells the nineteen-year-old that he is June's son. Lipsha decides to find and meet his father.

Lulu Morrissey

See Lulu Lamartine

Gerry Nanapush

Gerry Nanapush—the result of Lulu Nanapush's time with Moses Pillager—is a renegade, nearly as wild as his father is. Known for his numerous breaks from prison and his dedication to the American Indian Movement, Gerry keeps on the run from the authorities. He feels his true place in life is with his family, in the bosom of his tribe. He finds it difficult to live the white man's life. On his last break from prison, he seeks out King to punish him for turning him in to the authorities.

Lulu Nanapush

See Lulu Lamartine

Topics for Further Study

- Part of Erdrich's unique style is her narration by different speakers. She asserts that she writes in the traditional storytelling form of the Chippewa. Research storytelling techniques to learn more about this Chippewa tradition. Explain in your own words what Erdrich means by this. Think about other authors who use this technique in similar ways. List at least one, and give examples that will show the comparison between the authors' styles.

- There are distinct similarities between Erdrich's style in *Love Medicine* and Gloria Naylor's style in *The Women of Brewster Place*. List and explain the similarities using specific examples from both novels.

- While Erdrich's writing in *Love Medicine* is said to be non-autobiographical, there are many aspects of the story that Erdrich has taken from her own experiences. Locate and read a biographical sketch of Erdrich and compare it to *Love Medicine*.

- Trace the history of the Bureau of Indian Affairs. Describe its original intent and purpose. Discuss its place in contemporary America.

- Fetal Alcohol Syndrome (FAS) is said to be prevalent among Native Americans. Research this disease. Describe the symptoms and causes as well as the treatments and current studies that are being done. Locate and discuss references to the relationship between the disease and Native American culture.

Themes

Family Ties

The characters in *Love Medicine* exhibit distinct personality traits and live their lives accordingly. Yet, very strong ties exist among all the characters—the ties to their common families and heritage. For example, while Albertine has chosen to leave the reservation to study nursing, she is drawn back home upon hearing about her Aunt June's death. Back on the reservation, Albertine wants to connect with her grandfather, hoping to understand more of her heritage. She asks him questions about his days as an advocate for Indian rights, hoping that something she says will rekindle his memory. The other characters also tell their stories through their relationships to June. Thus, the familial bonds provide a common thread throughout *Love Medicine,* offering a universal theme to which everyone can relate.

Individual vs. Society

In addition to their ties to family, the characters in *Love Medicine* hold their cultural heritage close to their hearts. They try to live in contemporary society while keeping their Chippewa traditions alive. Lipsha Morrissey presents a good example. The family recognizes that Lipsha has the "touch," that he possesses the ability to heal with his hands as many of his ancestors could. He tries to use his ability to make his grandfather love his grandmother again. Feeling at loose ends when he cheats on his potion for love medicine and his grandfather dies, and having the newfound knowledge that Gerry Nanapush is his father, Lipsha allows the white man's world to lure him into joining the Army.

Culture Clash

Gerry Nanapush's self-identity has always been at odds with the society in which he lives. Like his son, Lipsha, Gerry has a strong sense of his heritage and feels wronged by the white man, who will not give him a fair chance. When he fights a white man by "reservation rules" (Erdrich) in a bar one night, he loses and gets a prison sentence. He escapes from prison because he believes that his rightful place is with his family. Because white man's law dictates that he be returned to prison, Gerry must hide from everyone—unable to live the honest and peaceful life that is his heritage.

Race and Racism

Gerry Nanapush's barroom fight resulted from his trying to defend his heritage. A "cowboy" had asked him whether a Chippewa was also a "nigger." Gerry fought him by "reservation rules"; he kicked the man in the groin. That ended the fight, and Gerry thought the issue was settled. Yet he had to go to court, where the white witnesses and the white doctor stacked the evidence against him. His Indian friends provided him with no help as witnesses; they did not believe in the United States judicial system. Gerry received a sentence that was stiff for a first offense but "not bad for an Indian."

Identity

Lipsha Morrissey grew up in Grandma Kashpaw's home. He never really knew who his parents were until he was nineteen years old, when Lulu Lamartine told him. All of those years, though, the family treated him well. He thought that it was be-

cause he had his special "touch." Yet, he discovers that he is June's son by Gerry Nanapush during one of June's separations from Gordie. When Lulu tells him the news, she says that she thinks he should know because she feels that he has always been troubled, not knowing where he really belonged. He decides shortly after this that he wants to meet his father. When Lipsha and Gerry meet, and Lipsha helps him escape, he finds his true identity in Gerry's words: "You're a Nanapush man. We all have this odd thing with our hearts."

God and Religion

Erdrich's Catholic upbringing is reflected in Marie's stories. As a young girl, Marie (Saint Marie) aspires to rise to the stature of the nuns who live in the convent on the hill. She feels that she is as good as they are. "They were not any lighter than me. I was going up there to pray as good as they could. Because I don't have that much Indian blood." Sister Leopolda, Marie's teacher, constantly warned the children that to disobey her was to let Satan take over their lives. When Marie's attention once strayed from her schoolwork, Leopolda convinced Marie that Satan had chosen her. As a result, Marie sought salvation through Leopolda. To rid herself of Satan, she would conquer Leopolda; she would get to heaven before Leopolda. Marie joined the convent. For three years, she endured the emotional and physical abuse Leopolda inflicted on her, believing that the harder she prayed and praised God, the sooner she would be free of Leopolda and Satan's grasp. Then, Leopolda nearly killed her with a poker. Regaining consciousness, she realized that Leopolda was telling the other sisters that Marie had undergone a spiritual transformation and received the mark of Christ in her hand. When Marie understood that she had been living a faithless lie and that Leopolda was a sick woman, Marie no longer believed that she needed the faith that the nuns offered.

Style

Point of View

The point of view varies with the speakers. Sometimes they speak in the first person; at other times, they speak in third person. While there are actually fourteen stories in *Love Medicine,* seven members of five families—the Kashpaws, Lazarres, Lamartines, Nanapushes, and Morrisseys—tell their views of many of the same incidents. For example, both Nector and Marie tell about their encounter on the hill below the convent. Many critics view this technique as a strength, because the reader gets to hear both sides of a story. Other critics think that the use of so many voices makes the novel too confusing; readers must reread to find relationships among the characters and the stories they tell.

Structure

Above all else, critics discuss the manner in which Erdrich presents her story through the separate voices of seven characters. Some say that Erdrich's use of this technique provides a rich portrait of not only the events in the lives of the characters, but also a realistic illustration of Native Americans trying to cope in modern culture. For example, Harriett Gilbert says in *New Statesman,* "Largely using her characters' own voices, she washes their stories backward and forward in rollers of powerful, concentrated prose through half a century (1930s to now) of loving, hating, adapting, surviving and tragically failing to survive." Others criticize her style. Gene Lyons, in *Newsweek* says that *Love Medicine* is not a novel but a book of short stories. "No central action unifies the narrative, and the voices all sound pretty much the same—making it difficult to recall sometimes who's talking and what they're talking about."

Setting

Most of *Love Medicine* takes place on the Turtle Mountain Chippewa Reservation in North Dakota, or in the area close to it. The story spans a period of 50 years, from 1934 to 1984. The setting lends credence to the story; white readers get a glimpse of life in a culture that is foreign to most of them. The details Erdrich provides emphasize the lives of many contemporary Indians on reservations. According to Robert Towers in *The New York Review of Books,* "... impoverished, feckless lives far gone in alcoholism and promiscuity ... an irrefutable indictment against an official policy that tried to make farmers out of the hunting and fishing Chippewas, moving them from the Great Lakes to the hilly tracts west of the wheat-growing plains of North Dakota."

Poetic License

Literary experts say that writers who deviate from the conventional form are taking "poetic license." Many think that Erdrich does this with *Love Medicine.* Not only does she use separate charac-

ters to tell their versions of the events in the book in a nonlinear fashion, but also she adds a lyric quality to her writing that is more typically seen in poetry. Because she is a poet, Erdrich has a practiced mastery of words; she is able to write concisely without losing meaning. This is especially evident in the way her characters talk. According to D. J. R. Bruckner in a review in *The New York Times,* "... many of their tales have the structure and lyric voice of ballads."

Dialogue

Native American readers appreciate Erdrich's artistry with dialogue. They have written to her saying that she was the first writer who knew how Indians really talked. The language the characters speak has evolved from several other languages blended together to result in a unique voice that is now an established part of the culture. The verbs used come from Chippewa, while most nouns are French. Also heard are traces of other Native American and European languages.

Historical Context

The Chippewa (Ojibwa) Tribe

Seventeenth-century French explorers found the Chippewa Indians, or Ojibwa, in Canada. They lived there in small villages around the Upper Great Lakes near Sault Sainte Marie. At the time, they lacked tribal organization, and the village people governed themselves. They worked as fur traders, used birchbark canoes, and were skilled woodcraftsmen. As they prospered, however, their population grew, and they acquired more territory. In addition, they began focusing more on developing tribal customs and rituals. They established one organization in particular: the Midewiwin, or Grand Medicine Society. In *Love Medicine,* Lipsha Morrissey, known for his inherited "touch," practices the ways of the old medicine. *Love Medicine* is named for the love-potion ritual Lipsha tries to recreate for his grandparents.

As the tribe grew, they drove out other tribes. For example, they expanded to take over the entire Ontario peninsula by the late 1700s, forcing the Iroquois to leave. This expansion reached into western Wisconsin and northeastern Minnesota. In the United States, the Ojibwa became known as the Chippewa. By the early 19th century, Chippewa lived in Ontario, Manitoba, and Saskatchewan in Canada—where they were still called Ojibwa—and

A Chippewa Indian home on Turtle Mountain Reservation, North Dakota, the same setting Erdrich used in her book Love Medicine.

in North Dakota, Minnesota, Michigan, Wisconsin, Indiana, and Ohio in the United States. They lived away from the white man's settlements and continued to practice their tribal customs. The Kashpaws and Lamartines are fictional descendants of the Chippewa who settled in North Dakota. As of 1990, there are more than 100,000 Chippewa living in the United States.

Indian Territory

In the late 1700s and early 1800s, the large areas of land in the western United States that were originally settled by Indians were known as Indian Territory. As white settlers moved westward, however, the United States government passed laws that removed the Indians from Indian Territory. Two such laws were the Indian Removal Act (1930) and the Indian Intercourse Act (1834). These laws made Indian Territory the areas including Oklahoma, Kansas, Nebraska, and the Dakotas. The government forced Indians to move to these new lands. As a result, many Indians had to learn new ways to support themselves. The Chippewa, for example, existed as hunters and fishermen when they lived on their original homelands. After being forced to the Great Plains regions, they had to become farmers if they were to survive.

Indian Reservations

The lands to which Indians were forced to move were known as Indian reservations, designated by the Bureau of Indian Affairs. Between 1830 and 1840, more than 70,000 members of the "Five Civilized Tribes" had to move to reservations. In *Love Medicine,* the Kashpaws and Lamartines lived on one such reservation, Turtle Mountain. Many Indians fought this forced resettlement, in battles known as the Indian Wars.

The Bureau of Indian Affairs

Established in 1824 as part of the War Department, the Bureau of Indian Affairs still exists as the governmental agency through which Indian affairs are handled. Earlier names for the agency include the Office of Indian Affairs, the Indian Department, and the Indian Service. The agency now resides in the Department of the Interior rather than the War Department, and is directed by the Interior Department's Assistant Secretary of Indian Affairs. The twelve offices of the agency oversee reservation and Indian-community programs and, on some reservations, manage education, social services, law enforcement, mineral and water rights, and land leasing. Erdrich's parents both worked as teachers for the Bureau of Indian Affairs.

Compare & Contrast

- **1830s:** Through the Indian Removal Act (1830) and the Indian Intercourse Act (1834), Indian tribes were forced to move onto reservations into territory now known as Oklahoma, Kansas, Nebraska, and the Dakotas.

- **1850s:** Indians were further confined to present day Oklahoma through the Kansas-Nebraska Act.

- **1860s:** The Indians living in Oklahoma were forced to give up the western half of their territory.

- **Late 1800s and early 1900s:** The Dawes Act, or General Allotment Act, allowed tribal lands to be parceled out to individual Indians, resulting in widespread sale of the land to white settlers.

- **1930s:** Tribal ownership of reservation lands was restored through the Wheeler-Howard Indian Reorganization Act, overturning the 1887 General Allotment (Dawes) Act. Indians also re-

ceived limited self-governing privileges and help with development and management of land and resources.

- **1950s:** Policies ended special federal programs and trust agreements with Indians.

- **1960s:** The termination policy of the 1950s was abandoned.

- **1970s:** Native American groups become more aggressive in reestablishing their rights. The Narragansett, Dakota, Oneida, and other Indians' claims were upheld in the Supreme Court, gaining them fishing, water, and mining rights, among others.

- **1990s:** Native Americans continue to regain their rights. Legislation passed in 1990 protects Indian gravesites and allows return of remains. In 1991, Chippewa Indians gained the right to hunt, fish, and gather plants from reservations in Wisconsin.

The Dawes Act or General Allotment Act

The Dawes Act enabled individual Indians to claim parts of tribal lands for themselves. The Act meant to encourage the Indians to become farmers but resulted in loss of tribal lands to white settlers. To halt this tribal loss of land, the government enacted the 1934 Wheeler-Howard Indian Reorganization Act. Not only did the Indians reclaim ownership of the reservation lands, they also became self-governing in a partnership with the Bureau of Indian Affairs. In addition, the partnership provided assistance in developing the land, managing resources, and establishing other programs.

Tribal Rights

The 1950s saw the termination of special federal programs and trust relationships with Indians, legislation enacted to force Indians to more quickly become a part of white society. This resulted in economic disaster for many tribes. There was so

much opposition to the policy, the government withdrew it by the mid-1960s. Since the Bureau of Indian Affairs was established, many Native Americans have protested the lack of Native American input into the agency. They have felt that no one speaks for their rights. In the 1970s, members of the American Indian Movement, an Indian-rights group, demanded that the agency pay more attention to Native American needs and interests.

Modern-Day Social Ills

Forced assimilation into white society has, in part, been responsible for the many problems Indians face today. Those who live on reservations lack education, have few jobs, suffer early deaths, and have a higher tendency to commit suicide. Those who leave the reservations to live in cities, assisted by a relocation program sponsored by the Bureau of Indian Affairs, are often unable to adjust. Without skills that would enable them to be successful away from the reservations, they either return to

the reservations or face failure in the cities. Unhappy and at loose ends, many Indians resort to
crime and alcoholism.

Improved Outlook

While many problems still exist for Indians living in modern-day society, more and more Native
Americans are overcoming the odds. The Bureau
of Indian Affairs works harder today within the
government to protect Native American interests.
The Office of Tribal Justice, created in 1995 within
the U.S. Department of Justice, now assists with
questions of state-tribal jurisdiction. Reservations
themselves support education through tribal colleges and employment endeavors such as radio stations and gambling casinos.

Critical Overview

In view of the overwhelmingly positive reviews that *Love Medicine* continually receives, it
is difficult to believe that publishers at first rejected the book. Only after Dorris promoted *Love
Medicine* himself did Holt publish it in 1983. It immediately became a huge success. Reviewers believed that Erdrich's writing was comparable to
Faulkner's and O'Connor's. They predicted a successful career for her. For example, Marco Portales
said in the *New York Times Book Review,* "With
this impressive debut Louis Erdrich enters the company of America's best novelists, and I'm certain
readers will want to see more from this imaginative and accomplished young writer." Jascha
Kessler said in a radio broadcast, "I am glad to report that in 1984 a really first-rate novel by a young
woman named Louise Erdrich appeared, and I think
it is a book that everyone on the lookout for good,
imaginative, rewarding writing will enjoy and
admire."

The fact that reviewers think that the book can
appeal to everyone represents one of its best qualities: the universal nature of its themes. *Love Medicine* tells stories of enduring truths such as love
and survival. Like all Americans, the Native Americans in the story struggle with problems on a daily
basis. These families must cope with alcoholism,
economic deprivation, and marital problems. Like
all people, they seek solutions to these dilemmas
while attempting to live normal lives. Cynthia Kooi
says in *Booklist,* "Erdrich creates characters who
... reveal the differences between individuals by
the similarities of their society...." Because the

families in *Love Medicine* act so much like families everywhere, readers relate to them and their situations.

Reviewers also appreciate the skill with which
Erdrich realistically portrays the lives of two
Chippewa families who are attempting to foster
their heritage while living in contemporary society.
Jeanne Kinney notes in *Best Sellers,* "By showing
their world impinging on the white world that sur-
rounds them and by showing the white world impinging on them, the author leads us into another
culture, her own." Through a period of 50 years,
readers become acquainted with seven members of
the Kashpaw and Lamartine extended families. All
characters hold Chippewa tradition close to their
hearts in some way, while having to constantly
fight poverty and racism. Even though the Native
American culture and beliefs very subtly underlie
the stories common to all people, Erdrich manages
to provide a vivid picture of Native American society. Kooi says, "The book poignantly reflects the
plight of contemporary Indians and at the same time
depicts people the reader wants to be with a little
longer."

Erdrich presents her realistic characters living
universal lives through prose that critics praise for
its lyric quality. Even while the characters suffer,
the joy and beauty that they experience emerges
with a poetic sense. To accomplish this, Erdrich
uses not only the characters' multiple voices but
also language that, according to Bruckner in *The
New York Times,* "convinces you you have heard
them speaking all your life...." The characters' stories resemble ballads. The characters, themselves,
live through the vivid events, details, and attitudes
offered by the individual speakers. Erdrich manages to use the combination of the characters' stories and their personal narration to create a community voice that, according to Kessler, "...
conveys the magic, the ancient mysteries and lore,
the inner heart of the religious and of the traditional
ways of thought and feeling of groups who
have never been part of the European cultural experience."

While most critics appreciate Erdrich's multi-
voice style and the richness of her characters' language, some view these aspects of Erdrich's writing to be distracting. Gene Lyons says in
Newsweek, "The first thing readers ought to be told
about Louise Erdrich's novel *Love Medicine* ... is
that no matter what the dust jacket says, it's not
a novel. It's a book of short stories ... so self-
consciously literary that they are a whole lot eas-

ier to admire than to read…. No central action unifies the narrative, and the voices all sound pretty much the same—making it difficult to recall sometimes who's talking and what they're talking about." Robert Towers also criticizes Erdrich's style. He says in *The New York Review of Books,* "*Love Medicine* … is very much a poet's novel. By that I mean that the book achieves its effect through moments of almost searing intensity rather than through the rise, climax, and closing of a sustained action, and that its stylistic virtuosity has become almost an end in itself." He, too, thinks the relationships among characters confuse the reader. Yet he credits Erdrich's ability to write dramatic, graphic scenes.

Most literary experts agree that Erdrich writes powerfully, chronicling events in the lives of a society about which most people know nothing. She is able to remain loyal to her heritage while maintaining her art; her writing appeals to everyone. Marco Portales says it best in *The New York Times Book Review,* "Ethnic writing—works that focus on the lives and particular concerns of America's minorities—labors under a peculiar burden: only certain types of people are supposed to be interested. Louise Erdrich's first novel, *Love Medicine,*… dispels these spurious notions."

In summary, *Love Medicine* continues to receive high marks, even though a few critics disagree with all the accolades. The book has won numerous awards including: the Sue Kaufman Prize for Best First Fiction (1983); the National Book Critics Circle award for year's best novelist (1984); the Virginia Scully Award for Best Book Dealing with Western Indians (1984); the American Book Award from the Before Columbus Foundation (1985); and the Great Lakes Colleges Association prize for Best First Work of Fiction (1984).

Criticism

Donna Woodford

Donna Woodford is a doctoral candidate at Washington University and has written for a wide variety of academic journals and educational publishers. In the following essay she discusses the story as a form of love medicine.

Louise Erdrich's *Love Medicine* is a novel made up of several stories about the people that reside on a Chippewa reservation in North Dakota.

The stories cover three generations, fifty years, and several families, and there are eight distinct narrators. Because the stories seem so loosely related, some critics have questioned whether the novel is truly a novel. Alan Velie suggests that it is, rather, a "collection of short stories, all of which deal with the same set of characters." Furthermore, Catherine Rainwater asserts that the novel is full of conflicting codes which lead the reader to expect one type of novel, and then frustrate that expectation by producing a very different sort of narrative. She claims, in fact, that "Erdrich's novels conspicuously lack plot in this traditional sense of the term. One need only ask oneself for a plot summary of *Love Medicine* to substantiate this claim. The novel seems rife with narrators (eight, to be exact, bereft of a focal narrative point of view, and replete with characters whose lives are equally emphasized."

But what unites these seemingly disconnected stories is the common theme of characters in search of love and in need of stories. Throughout the many stories that make up the novel, characters search for a "love medicine," a trick or a potion that will bring them the love they so desperately need. In the end, however, it is the stories themselves that prove to be the love medicine. As Margaret J. Downes notes, "Love and stories are both imaginative creations essentially aware of the presence of The Other, who responds as if this offered figment were real—who observes, judges, and participates, who willingly suspends disbelief and meets halfway." In *Love Medicine* it is the imaginative creation of stories which allow for the imaginative creation of love.

The first overt mention of a "love medicine" is from Lulu Nanapush. As a child she comes to live with her uncle Nanapush and his wife, Rushes Bear, a woman so renowned for her temper that she is said to have scared off a bear by rushing at it head on, with no weapon. Even the wild animal was afraid to face her, but old Nanapush seems to possess a strange power over her. Noting this, Lulu asks him, "What's your love medicine?…. She hates you but you drive her crazy." Nanapush replies that his secret is, "No clocks. These young boys who went to the Bureau school, they run their love life on white time. Now me, I go on Indian time. Stop in the middle for a bowl of soup. Go right back to it when I've got my strength. I got nothing else to do, after all." But Lulu has already received the first clues that the real love medicine is not just Indian time, but Indian language and stories. As a young child bereft of her mother, Lulu has only the memory of her mother's voice to con-

What Do I Read Next?

- *The Beet Queen,* published by Holt in 1986, continues the story of the Chippewa, but Erdrich focuses on people connected to the Lamartines and Kashpaws through the community beyond the reservation. This story is about the family of Dot, the woman with whom Gerry Nanapush is involved in *Love Medicine.*

- While *Tracks* was published after *The Beet Queen* (by Harper in 1988), the story centers around the events that occurred and the people who lived before those in *Love Medicine.* In *Tracks,* the evil medicine woman, Fleur Pillager, works her magic. She is the ancestor of several of the people in *Love Medicine,* including Moses Pillager.

- Erdrich interrupted her work on *Tales of Burning Love* to write *The Bingo Palace,* published by HarperCollins in 1994. *The Bingo Palace* provides readers not only with the continuation of the story of Lyman Lamartine and his bingo palace, but also with the tale of the reconciliation between Lipsha and Lyman and a renewal of Chippewa ways.

- HarperCollins published *Tales of Burning Love,* Erdrich's sixth novel, in 1996. Going back to the story of June Kashpaw, this book relates the events in the life of Jack Mauser, the man whom June has sex with on the night of her death. Af-

ter June's death, Mauser has four wives. His life is both comedic and tragic; Jack dies in a house fire.

- Erdrich's first work of nonfiction, *The Blue Jay's Dance,* was published by HarperCollins in 1995. In this book, Erdrich chronicles her child's birth and first year of life. It examines the balancing act that working parents experience on a daily basis.

- *Grandmother's Pigeon,* published by Hyperion in 1996, is Erdrich's first children's book. It is about an adventurous grandmother who travels to Greenland on the back of a porpoise, and her children who get messages to her by way of carrier pigeons.

- Gloria Naylor's *The Women of Brewster Place* offers a style of writing comparable to Erdrich's. Naylor tells her story through the distinct voices of seven women struggling to survive ghetto life. *The Women of Brewster Place* was published by Viking in 1982.

- Critics have compared Erdrich's nonchronological storytelling through characters voices to William Faulkner's *As I Lay Dying.* Published in 1930 by Jonathan Cape and Harrison Smith, *As I Lay Dying* is a dying woman's story told in a stream-of-consciousness fashion.

---

sole her. She dislikes the "flat voices, rough English" which she hears spoken at the government school, and she longs for the old language and her mother's voice:

> Sometimes, I heard her, N'dawnis, n'dawnis. My daughter, she consoled me. Her voice came from all directions, mysteriously keeping me from inner harm. Her voice was the struck match. Her voice was the steady flame. But it was my old uncle Nanapush who wrote the letters that brought be home.

The memory of her mother's spoken words provides Lulu with the love medicine which keeps

her from inner harm, which allows her to continue loving her mother, even though she is gone, and to love herself, though she is motherless and without anyone to teach her love. Likewise it is her Uncle's command of the written language that brings her love a second time by bringing her to a loving home. The words of her mother and uncle are what allow Lulu to change from the child who "stumbled in [the] shoes of desire," longing for her mother and someone to guide her, into a woman who can say, "I was in love with the whole world and all that lived in its rainy arms." Their words give her the ability to love the world and herself. When she goes to live with Moses Pillager, she will again discover the power of stories. His life has already been dramatically affected by the story with which his mother fooled the spirits and kept him from sickness. But while this story kept him alive, it also made him into a ghost. When Lulu goes to the Island, however, she is able to reverse the spell of this old story by retelling it. She restores his voice to him, allowing him to finally speak his thought aloud to another person, and she undoes his mother's spell by finally speaking the name no one had been allowed to say: "He told me his real name. I whispered it, once. Not the name that fooled the dead, but the word that harbored his life…. I hold his name close as my own blood and I will never let it out. I only spoke it that once so that he would know he was alive." The same word which had to be hidden to keep him from death is now the name that harbors his life, and by knowing his story and speaking his name, Lulu can restore him to life. Her speech is the love medicine she brings to the island with her. The most obvious story about love medicine, of course, is the chapter entitled "Love Medicine," and once again this chapter is not just about love medicine but also about stories. When Marie Kashpaw asks her grandson Lipsha to find her a love medicine so that Nector will return her love and forget Lulu, Lipsha initially tries to think of traditional love medicines such as special seeds, frogs caught in the act of mating, or nail clippings. But the love medicine he finally settles on is pure fiction, as all love medicines must be. First he invents the idea for the love medicine: he sees a pair of geese and thinks that if he feeds the hearts of birds that mate for life to his grandparents that will surely be a powerful love medicine. When he fails to shoot the geese, he decides to buy two turkey hearts instead, and he convinces himself that the medicine will still work since it is faith that really matters:

> I thought of faith. I thought to myself that faith could be called belief against the odds and whether or not there's any proof. How does that sound? I thought how we might have to yell to be heard by Higher Power, but that's not saying it's not there. And that is faith for you. It's belief even when the goods don't deliver…. Faith might be stupid, but it gets us through. So what I'm heading at is this. I finally convinced myself that the real actual power to the love medicine was not the goose heart itself but the faith in the cure.

He is, in essence, saying that a myth to believe in, something to "get us through" is more important and more powerful and traditional love medi-

cine. And indeed, in this chapter, it is the story that proves to be the true love medicine. When Marie is convinced that Nector's ghost is returning because of the love medicine, Lipsha tells her the truth about the turkey hearts:

> Love medicine ain't what brings him back to you, Grandma. No, it's something else. He loved you over time and distance, but he went off so quick he never got the chance to tell you how he loves you, how he doesn't blame you, how he understands. It's true feeling, not no magic. No supermarket heart could have brung him back.
>
> She looked at me. She was seeing the years and days I had no way of knowing, and she didn't believe me. I could tell this. Yet a look came on her face. It was like the look of mothers drinking sweetness from their children's eyes. It was tenderness.
>
> Lipsha, she said, you was always my favorite.

Though his stories cannot cause his grandfather to fall in love with his grandmother, his words do work medicine between Lipsha and his grandmother. She feels the depth of his love for her in the words he speaks to ease her pain and in the stories and lies he creates to help her, and his words evoke from her a mother's love for him, the love he has longed for always. The story of Lipsha's mother is perhaps the most powerful example of the story as love medicine. All of his life he is told that his mother tried to drown him in the slough and that Grandma Kashpaw rescued him, although everyone else knows that June was his real mother and that Grandmother Kashpaw took him in because June was already married to Gordie when she became pregnant with Gerry's child. When Lulu tells him that he is the son of June and Gerry he is shocked. He does not, at first, know what to do with this powerful new story of his life. He "couldn't take it in." Lulu has given him "knowledge that could make or break" him, and he does not at first know which it will do. But as he pieces together the story of his life, the love medicine of the story begins to work its magic. He gets to know his father, and learns about his mother. He sees how miserable and bitter King, June's acknowledged son has become, and he makes peace with the story of his life. When Gerry says, "Enough about me anyhows … What's your story?" he is able to answer without bitterness. He can tell his story now, and his only "problem" is that he is running from the army police. In this instance, too, a story saves him, for Gerry is able to tell him that he, like all men in his family, will fail the army physical because of an irregular heart rhythm. Knowing the story of his past allows him to avoid a future of running need-lessly. And finally, knowing the true story of his life, he is able to forgive and love the mother who gave him up and the grandmother who took him in:

> I thought of June…. How weakly I remembered her. If it made any sense at all, she was part of the great loneliness being carried up the driving current. I tell you, there was good in what she did for me, I know now. The son that she acknowledged suffered more that Lipsha Morrissey did. The thought of June grabbed my heart so, but I was lucky she turned me over the Grandma Kashpaw.

Knowing his story allows him to be reborn. The story functions as a love medicine, allowing him to love his mother, his grandmother, his father, and most importantly, himself. Speaking of Chippewa beliefs and myths, Victoria Brehm states, "They considered all stores to be true, whether they classified them as daebaudjimowin (chronicles from personal experience) or Auwaetchigum (what Western cultures describe as myths)." So, in love medicine, the personal stories and the cultural myths of these people are woven together and intermixed, but they are all "true" stories, and all can function as love medicines.

Source: Donna Woodford, in an essay for *Novels for Students*, Gale, 1999.

Lissa Schneider

In the following excerpt, Schneider examines the unifying role that storytelling plays within Erdrich's novel and between characters in the novel.

Louise Erdrich's *Love Medicine* has been regarded as simply a collection of short stories, lacking in novelistic unity and overriding structure. Yet despite shifts in narrative style and a virtual cacophony of often individually unreliable narrative voices, Erdrich successfully weds structure and theme, style and content. For the novel is as much about the act of storytelling as it is about the individual narratives and the symbols and interrelationships which weave them together thematically. In *Love Medicine,* storytelling constitutes both theme and style. Erdrich repeatedly shows how storytelling—characters sharing their troubles or their "stories" with one another—becomes a spiritual act, a means of achieving transformation, transcendence, forgiveness. And in this often comic novel, forgiveness is the true "love medicine," bringing a sense of wholeness, despite circumstances of loss or broken connections, to those who reach for it. Moreover, the novel is in itself the stylistic embodiment of Erdrich's theme; as a series of narratives or chapters/stories shared with the reader, the work as a whole becomes a kind of "love medicine" of forgiveness and healing in its own right.…

[T]he means by which Erdrich's characters learn to internalize and integrate past with present is through the transformative power of storytelling. A non-Native reader, or any reader, is not the sole audience to these stories, for it is the characters themselves who, within the course of the narratives, begin this recovery of stories as they move beyond gossip to share with one another intimate revelations of highly personal desires, guilts, and troubles. It is in the personal stories that the characters *tell each other* that the real spiritual force of the novel can be felt.

Stories as "love medicine," moreover, provide the alternative in the novel to the characters' struggles with experiences of alcohol abuse, religious fanaticism, or compulsive sex relations, as well as the spiritual havoc that these kinds of seductive but hollow "love medicines" wreak on human relations. But although Erdrich focuses on the Chippewa experience, the troubles her characters experience are not exclusively "Indian problems." Erdrich herself sees the novel in terms of its articulation of "the universal human struggle," and her characters, as Bo Schöler has said of other Native literary depictions of alcohol-related themes, are motivated by "complex and ultimately profoundly human causes." These are problems common to every society, and the solution she posits is relevant for both Native and non-Native cultures alike. Forgiveness in *Love Medicine* is thus of the everyday variety, that which is extended from a child to a parent, a wife to a husband, brother to brother. Moreover, for Erdrich, forgiveness is not explanation, not unconditional, not forgetting. It is the transformation that comes through the sharing and recovery of stories, and the giving up of the notion of oneself as victim.…

The novel opens on Easter in 1981 with June Morrissey Kashpaw's thoughts and feelings, related in third person, as she commences upon the alcoholic binge which will lead to her death. June's death will affect all the other characters. In a radical revision of Christ's Easter resurrection, the death of this alcoholic Indian woman becomes the impetus which propels many of the other characters toward healing. In this scene, June is clearly reaching for something spiritual, something to hold on to in a life broken by divorce and disappointment. But she looks for her answers in a bar, and comes up empty. Intending to catch a noon bus for the reservation where she was raised, she stops at the invitation of a man to "tip down one or two." When she enters the barroom, the narrator tells us, "What she walked toward more than anything else was that blue egg in the white hand, a beacon in the murky air." Blue is the color of sky, of spirit and transcendence, signaling to her like a "beacon." But instead of the blue egg the man in the red vest peels her a pink one, thwarting her impulse and replacing it with the faded color of earth, of blood, of sexuality. When she drinks, it is "Blue Ribbon" beer and "Angel Wings," again symbolizing a frustrated spiritual instinct, and she says to the man, "Ahhhhh, you got to be. You got to be different." June seeks transformation through sex and alcohol, but the only metamorphosis they are able to bring is degradation and death.

The balance of chapter one shifts to the first person narrative of June's niece, Albertine Kashpaw, who introduces the theme of the recovery and sharing of stories. Albertine has been attending nursing school off-reservation, but returns several months after June's demise seeking a sense of completion with a death she cannot understand.

Albertine's denial of June's alcoholism may relate to her own psychic connection with June, a connection which becomes clearer in the central chapter entitled "A Bridge," where the narrative spins back to 1973. There we learn that Albertine takes a journey remarkably similar to June's own, one that, but for small differences, could have resulted in equally tragic consequences. The two journeys are contrasted in almost every detail. Albertine has taken the bus to run away from the reservation. It is another "harsh spring," if not Easter then close to it, for we learn it is "not yet May." Albertine also sees something which she compares to a "beacon," but unlike June, interprets this to be a "warning beacon." Where the man June meets only looks familiar to her, the man Albertine sees in the bus station turns out to be Henry Lamartine Junior, another Chippewa whose family is known to her from the reservation. June wears white, the color of death in Chippewa culture, and Albertine wears black. June drinks "Angel Wings" with a man who doesn't listen to her, while Henry romantically whispers to Albertine, "Angel, where's your wings." When June enters the ladies room, "All of a sudden she seemed to drift out of her clothes and skin with no help from anyone"; Albertine, on the other hand, feels her body "shrink and contract" while alone in the bathroom, and feels herself becoming "bitterly small." Perhaps the greatest difference between the two is that while

June intends to stop drinking after "a few" but cannot, the younger Albertine still retains some control: "She had stopped after a few and let him go on drinking, talking, until he spilled too many and knew it was time to taper off."

But in the opening chapter, Albertine only alludes to these links. She says:

> I had gone through a long phase of wickedness and run away. Yet now that I was on the straight and narrow, things were even worse between [my mother and me].

> After two months were gone and my classes were done, and although I still had not forgiven my mother, I decided to go home.

What Erdrich shows here is that simply getting on "the straight and narrow" is not enough; that alone does not fill the spiritual void that leaves Albertine full of resentment. It is in fact only the beginning, just as Albertine's return to the reservation is only the beginning of the novel. And just as the car she drives has "a windshield wiper only on the passenger side" and "the dust [hangs] thick," her vision is still obscured. But once she arrives home, she initiates the recovery of stories that begins a transformation process....

Throughout the novel, the narratives balance and play off of one another, forming a crystalline structure with smoothly interwoven themes and symbols. And although each chapter is its own story, able to stand alone, taken all together the novel becomes a synergetic whole of chapters/stories about telling stories. The theme of storytelling as healing, as resolution, as spiritual, thus becomes incorporated into the structure of the novel itself. In contrast to the dust that obscures vision, and the water that drowns, in the final chapter the characters are humorously drinking 7-Up, and Lipsha says, "The sun flared"; with many stories told, nothing is forgotten, yet there is the strong sense of forgiveness and transformation.

Source: Lissa Schneider, "*Love Medicine:* A Metaphor for Forgiveness," in *Studies in American Literature,* Vol. 4, No. 1, Spring, 1992, pp. 1–13.

Thomas Matchie

In the following excerpt, Matchie compares Love Medicine, *which has been criticized for its lack of unity, to Herman Melville's* Moby-Dick, *asserting that Erdrich's work functions as a complete novel.*

Published in 1984, *Love Medicine* is about a tribe of Indians living in North Dakota. Its author, Louise Erdrich, is part Chippewa and in the book returns to her prairie roots for her literary materials. Recently, Erdrich published another work entitled *Beet Queen,* also about the Red River Valley, and some of the same characters appear in both novels. *Love Medicine* is different from so much of Native American literature in that it is not polemic—there is no ax to grind, no major indictment of white society. It is simply a story about Indian life—its politics, humor, emptiness, and occasional triumphs. If Erdrich has a gift, it is the ability to capture the inner life and language of her people.

Since its publication, *Love Medicine* has won several national awards. Still, critics see in it a serious lack of unity—it was originally published as a series of short stories or vignettes. Also, some think it has little connection to authentic Indian values; students at the White Earth Indian Reservation in Minnesota identified more with *Giants in the Earth,* Rölvaag's epic novel about white immigrants on the Dakota prairie. My contention is just the opposite, that the book does function as a whole, though this may not be immediately evident, and that the author is highly aware of Indian history and tradition, which emerge in subtle ways, helping us to understand the mystery of existence, whatever our color or ethnic origin.

While reading the novel it may help, strangely enough, to keep in mind another novel, Herman Melville's *Moby-Dick.* These two works may seem far apart, one about the sea—"in landlessness alone lies the highest truth"—and the other about the Dakota prairie, the geographic center of North America. But one of Erdrich's characters, Nector Kashpah, sees himself as Ishmael—"call me Ishmael," he says, after escaping a particularly difficult situation. If one looks further into the matter, it becomes evident that there are many ways these two books are alike. First, they have similar episodic or disjointed structures. Then, the major characters in one story seem to draw upon those in the other. And through it all, the same motifs (e.g., water and fishing, wildness—particularly among the males, preoccupation with power as well as the importance of the heart, the alternating realities of life and death, concern with colors, especially white and red) appear again and again. Indeed, it may be that the truest unity and deepest values of *Love Medicine* come clear when juxtaposed with Melville's classic novel of the sea.

In regard to structure, *Love Medicine* begins with a short account, told in third person, of the death of June Kashpah in 1981 in the boomtown of Williston, North Dakota. Then the novel proceeds with many short, seemingly unrelated episodes—some descriptive/narrative, some dramatic—told from multiple perspectives, but all about life on and off the reservation over a period of fifty years (1934–1984). Each vignette centers on shattered family life and the alienation of individuals. The parts may indeed seem dissimilar, unless one views them in an organic way, much as *Moby-Dick* in 1850 represented a departure from the classic or three-part structure so common at that time. *Moby-Dick,* of course, is about the disintegration of a ship, not only physically, but spiritually, for the purpose of the voyage and the unity of the crew collapse, all because of Ahab's preoccupation with one white whale. It begins with Ishmael's narrative, but then switches to everything from descriptions of the whaling industry, to poetic monologues, to dramatic episodes both comic and tragic. The parts, though different, are interposed erratically and often unexpectedly, but in the end they work together toward the whole. And that is how one must view *Love Medicine.*

In both cases the circle, so indigenous to Indian life, governs all, though in the case of the structure of *Love Medicine,* it takes fifty years to see it. *Moby Dick* starts with Ishmael's leaving New Bedford, contemplating many kinds of images of death (e.g., in the chapel, through Fr. Maple's sermon, in the Sprouter-Inn, in the prophecies of Elijah). Then, after the wreck of the *Pequod* (named after an extinct tribe of Indians), he surfaces in a circular vortex as he rises out of the chaos before coming home. In Erdrich's novel the action starts with June's death and then, after going back in time through a series of chaotic scenes dealing with Indian family life, circles back to the beginning when June's lost son Lipsha surfaces—rises psychologically and spiritually, not only to discover his real mother and family, but in his words to "cross the water, and bring her home."

Undoubtedly, Erdrich did not set out to write a book like *Moby-Dick,* but like Melville she writes about what she knows best—Indian life in this century—and like him she seeks through her characters the answers to some profound questions about human existence. It is in this context that she parallels in broad and general ways Melville's pattern of development, themes, characterizations, and motifs to create a virtual allegory of his work. In many ways her novel mirrors his, for her Dakota prairie can be as wild as his ocean typhoons, just as his sea can be as calm and dreamy as the midwestern prairie. Indeed, as we shall see, the motif of wildness runs through the novel, but the character most directly exhibiting this quality is Nector Kashpah, who sees himself as reliving *Moby-Dick*. Nector literally connects the various Indian families on the reservation; himself a Kashpah, he marries Marie Lazarre Morrissey, but never loses his passion for Lulu Lamartine, a promiscuous mother of a girl and at least nineteen boys, one of whom is Nector's.

Midway in the book Nector, a type of figure not uncommon in Melville because he is both comic and tragic, says:

> I kept thinking about the one book I read in high school … *Moby Dick,* the story of the great white whale. I knew that book inside and out. I'd even stolen a copy from school and taken it home in my suitcase.…
>
> "You're always reading that book," my mother said once. "What's in it?"
>
> "The story of the great white whale."
>
> She could not believe it. After a while, she said, "What do they got to wail about, those whites?"
>
> I told her the whale was a fish as big as the church. She did not believe this either. Who would?
>
> "Call me Ismael," I said sometimes, only to myself. For he survived the great white monster like I got out of the rich lady's picture [he'd been paid by a rich lady to disrobe for a painting she called "Plunge of the Brave"]. He let the water bounce his coffin to the top. In my life so far, I'd gone easy and come out on top, like him. But the river wasn't done with me yet. I floated through the calm sweet spots, but somewhere the river branched.

Here is where he falls headlong again for Lulu.

One of the ironies of the novel is that Nector is not really Ishmael at all, but more like Ahab, in that he is an irrational figure who thinks he can control all worlds—the Kashpahs and the Lamartines, his wife's and his lover's. A member of a most respected family and the chairman of the tribe, Nector becomes the victim of his sexual passions, falling for Marie as she escapes from the Sacred Heart Convent, but equally possessed with the beautiful and lascivious Lulu, into whose waters he continually sails to satisfy his fantasies. He finally concludes:

> I try to think of anything but Lulu or Marie or my children. I think back to the mad captain in *Moby Dick* and how his leg was bit off. Perhaps I was wrong, about Ishmael I mean, for now I see signs of the captain in myself.

In trying to burn a letter he's written to Lulu saying he is leaving Marie, he actually sets fire to Lulu's house—an event reminiscent of Ahab's burning masts in *Moby-Dick*—before returning sheepishly to Marie. In the end he dies a pathetic old man, one who has literally lost his mind and has "to have his candy." He chokes to death on turkey hearts, the ironic symbol of his erotic needs and manipulative ways.

The Ishmael who discovers the real "love medicine" is Lipsha Morrissey, the bastard son of June Kashpah—the one who brings Nector the hearts. Like Melville's narrator, he is a wanderer who has to discover in painful ways the meaning of his universe and how he fits. He has to find that his true mother is June, who dies on her way home crossing the prairie. He has to find that his brother is King, his boyhood tormentor, disrupted by the Vietnam War and as wild and torn as Nector.…

But most of all Lipsha has to find that his father is the perennial criminal Gerry Nanapush, one of the older sons of Lulu Lamertine.… With this discovery late in the novel, Lipsha combines in his own person the larger symbolic family of the Chippewas. He does all this as a kind of innocent observer, like Ishmael, who only occasionally takes part in the action. But out of the death and destruction of his people he, unlike Nector-Ahab and his male counterparts, accepts the responsibility for his life and worth as he rises to the surface in the end. He is the one who truly "connects" all, for he completes the cycle begun by his mother whose spirit he now brings home.

If there is a parallel to Moby-Dick in *Love Medicine,* it is June Kashpah. She dies early in the novel, but like the great white whale, her presence pervades the entire story and gives it depth. She is not there and yet there. Sometimes she even "comes alive," as when Gordie thinks the deer in his back seat, stunned and yet moving, is June herself. Initially having run away from Gordie, June is hungry and picked up in Williston by a stranger, whom she thinks is "different," but after falling from his truck, perishes walking across the cold white prairie as she "came home." In this early vignette, Erdrich captures the bleakness and boredom at the center of so much Indian life in this century. It is that dark side of life, the side which preoccupies Ahab in *Moby-Dick,* something he equates through the white whale with an "inscrutable malice" behind the universe—a mask he wants to penetrate. Erdrich does not philosophize as much as Melville, but this concept of evil is a legitimate way of viewing the source of so many of the destructive aspects of Indian life depicted in *Love Medicine.* It is interesting that when June's inlaws—Gordie and Zelda and Aurelian—recall her life, one of the dominant incidents they remember is their trying to hang her, and her egging them on, like some kind of evil mind. *Love Medicine,* like *Moby-Dick,* is a type of journey to penetrate the enticing but illusive mask that conceals the mystery of evil.

As the story unfolds, however, we discover a beautiful side to June, much as Ishmael sees a mystifying and uplifting aspect to the white whale to counter Ahab's view. June has been raised by Eli, Nector's brother, the moral center of the novel, who lives in the woods and represents the old Indian past. At one point in the novel the irascible King insists that Eli have his hat, on which are the words the "World's Greatest Fisherman," for all agree Eli deserves it most. June is inevitably associated with Eli, with water, with fishing, with the good in the Kashpah history. All the Kashpah women admire June, as do her husband Gordie and son King, to whom she leaves money for a car. Like so many of the males, however, King's destructive wildness keeps him from being the responsible human being his mother wanted; this is left for Lipsha to achieve. June, then, is a driving force behind the Chippewa world, but the reader must pick between the beautiful and humanizing aspects of such a presence, and what Ishmael calls when reflecting upon the whiteness of the whale, "the all-color of atheism"—the possibility that behind the Indians' life patterns (which are now white patterns) is not much of anything at all....

[T]he characters—the Kashpahs, the Morrisseys, the Lamartines—whose stories stretch from 1934 to 1984, much as the characters on the *Pequod* evolve on the voyage to capture Moby-Dick....

Good human relationships are important to both authors, and if Ishmael crosses cultures in making friends with the pagan harpooner Queequeg (who like Eli in *Love Medicine* is a kind of noble savage), Albertine is herself a half-breed, red and white, the daughter of Zelda and the "Swede." She suffers because of her double-nature, but her return, like Ishmael's setting out, comes from her uneasiness and is an effort to escape loneliness and build human bridges. Curiously enough, Albertine has her own chaotic history, and just as Ishmael may be an innocent observer, but is taken in by Ahab's powerful dark influence, so is Albertine taken in. As Erdrich's story circles back in time we find that Albertine in 1973 at fifteen tries to run away from the reservation. She goes to Fargo, only

to end up sleeping with Henry Lamartine Jr., one of Lulu's sons, on N. P. Avenue in the cheap Round Up Hotel. After making love, Albertine feels empty and wants to separate herself from him, whereupon he senses that she has "crossed a deep river and disappeared." In short, he needs her, and her horror pales beside his nightmare explosion. Like King, he has been damaged by the Vietnam War, and when he touches her the next day "weeping," she is now touched emotionally by the depth of their mutual loneliness.

In the beginning of the novel, however, Albertine returns to the reservation. Like Ishmael, she is not pure, but she has more distance than the others, having lived in a white woman's basement for some time away from home. Through her we meet Zelda and Aurelia. On the *Pequod* the chief mates, like Stubb and Flask, are skillful whalers, but not thinkers, and soon become extensions of Ahab's mind. The women of the reservation are also servants, but they are more free and happy people—like the harpooners in *Moby-Dick* who dine in an atmosphere of merriment following their humorless captain's meal. These women don't fight the system, run by the males, but they are basic to its existence—giving birth to the children, planting and growing the food, cooking and baking for the men—like Gordie and King and Lipsha, who unconsciously quarrel over and destroy the newly baked pies. Among the Nanapushes, Gerry leaves prison temporarily to impregnate Dot, who is then left to raise and feed the child. These women may be treated like dogs, as Ahab treats Stubb, but they keep the whole operation afloat. They maintain the land, encourage their men, survive catastrophe. The *Pequod* is a commercial enterprise where under contract the mates and harpooners follow their mad leader without question. The women in *Love Medicine* are not paid, but they keep the family itself intact, in spite of the alcohol, the violence, the abuse and misuse of one another.

Albertine identifies with these women—their fun, their hopes, but also their fears and worry about the men. In one of the most powerful scenes in *Moby-Dick,* Ishmael almost loses control of the ship as he gazes into the Try-Works (the red-hot pots of sperm oil), contemplating how intertwined are both the magnificent as well as the most hellish moments of life, even as the Catskill eagle flies high and yet at times swoops very low. Albertine-Ishmael, amid all the fighting and confusion, is worried about Lipsha and takes him for a walk in the fields, and gazing at the northern lights, she muses:

I thought of June. She would be dancing if there was a dance hall in space. She would be dancing a two-step for wandering souls [like Lipsha]. Her long legs lifting and falling. Her laugh an ace. Her sweet perfume the way all grown-up women were supposed to smell. Her amusement at both the bad and the good. Her defeat. Her reckless victory. Her sons.

So June, amid the high moments and the low, the bad and the good, gives substance to the Indians' quest for meaning. Lipsha will find himself in the end, but it is too early to know that now, and Albertine, his alter ego, can only hold his hand, and like Ishmael, try to keep the ship on course....

There are other major incidents in *Love Medicine* that pick up key threads in *Moby-Dick*, like the close relationship between madness and wisdom. Both King Jr. and Henry Jr. are affected mentally by the Vietnam War to the point they become violent souls. Henry Jr., after a long drive with his brother Lyman, who cannot save him, drowns himself in his red convertible. In Melville's story, the castaway Pip loses his mind when Stubb will not save him from the sea, but he returns in his madness to offer sharp, bitter wisdom to Captain Ahab, and from him the captain accepts it. In Erdrich's world where one generation fails, the next seems to succeed, as when King Howard Kashpah Jr. (King and Lynette's young son), after all his father's rage, learns to write his name, Howard Kashpah, in school on a red paper heart. The marker label says "PERMANENT," and the teacher tells him "that means forever." So Howard in his Pip-like childish wisdom undercuts the adult world around him to establish his own identity as a human being. In this way Howard parallels the growth in Lipsha Morrisey, the other son of June.

Colors, especially red and white, are also crucial in both novels, for they are a part of the very texture. White and red seem to go back and forth in *Moby-Dick,* as the red heat of the tri-pots lights up the *Pequod,* just as do the tapering white candles or mastheads struck by lightning. In one case Ishmael philosophizes on life, while in the other Ahab commits himself to death. In *Love Medicine* the Indian is, of course, the redman living in a white world. June in the beginning has on a red nylon vest when the stranger in a white jacket "plunged down against her" with a "great wide mouth," as though she were entering the whale itself. Then there is the red convertible in which Henry Jr. drowns; the mark of white society, this is the machine that spells freedom, but it cannot solve basic human problems where so many are held psychologically captive.

Finally, there is the red of the heart itself—a powerful symbol in both novels. On the *Pequod* Ahab, just before the fatal chase, talks to Starbuck about the importance of the heart, family, love. His words are touching, coming from a man bent on destruction: "I ... do what in my own ... natural heart, I durst not ... dare," he says. In *Love Medicine* both Lipsha and Howard come to know the meaning of the heart—Lipsha through the turkey hearts which kill his Ahab-like grandfather, and Howard through the paper heart on which he writes his name. Lipsha says that love means forgiveness, that it is not magic, but a "true feeling." Later, when he discovers in a card game his true father and sees himself as part of the larger family, he says, "The jack of hearts is me." These awakenings give a kind of tragic joy to a story pervaded by so many deaths.

Love Medicine, then, is a book about the prairie that examines the wild, chaotic lives of several Indian families whose lives on the reservation have immersed them in a dark and often violent existence, one that the author seems to equate with Ahab. It is a world created by a white—shall we say malicious—intelligence, except that behind the scenes hovers an amazing human being, June Kashpah, whose life and recent death still give meaning and hope to its members. Albertine-Ishmael goes back to that world to experience again the rage dramatized by her grandfather Nector-Ahab, as well as other violent males. But she also discovers the values sustained by women like her mother, Zelda, and Aurelia and Dot Adare, but especially by Marie and Lulu, who in spite of the men and the systems and the power, give dignity and spirit to an otherwise hollow and violent world.

Out of the chaos emerges, through Howard and Lipsha, possible new worlds, just as June would have wished. Indeed, Lipsha-Ishmael begins to see the importance of love within all the families and in this way "brings June home" as he (to use Nector's words) lets "the water bounce his coffin to the top" in the end. *Love Medicine* is a novel about the land, but one which has so many parallels to *Moby-Dick* that it draws tremendous power when placed beside Melville's classic novel about the sea.

Source: Thomas Matchie, *"Love Medicine:* A Female *Moby-Dick,"* in *Midwest Quarterly,* Vol. 30, No. 4, Summer, 1989, pp. 478–91.

Sources

D. J. R. Bruckner, a review in *The New York Times,* December 20, 1984, p. C21.

Louise Erdrich, "Scales," in *Love Medicine,* New York: HarperFlamingo, 1998, pp. 43, 201-202, 366.

Harriett Gilbert, "Mixed Feelings," in *New Statesman,* Vol. 109, No. 2812, February 8, 1985, p. 31.

Jascha Kessler, "Louise Erdrich: *Love Medicine,*" in a radio broadcast on KUSC-FM—Los Angeles, CA, January, 1985.

Jeanne Kinney, in a review of *Love Medicine,* in *Best Sellers,* Vol. 44, No. 9, December, 1984, pp. 324-25.

Cynthia Kooi, in a review of *Love Medicine,* in *Booklist,* Vol. 81, No. 1, September 1, 1984, p. 24.

Gene Lyons, "In Indian Territory," in *Newsweek,* Vol. CV, No. 6, February 11, 1985, pp. 70-1.

Marco Portales, "People with Holes in Their Lives," in *The New York Times Book Review,* December 23, 1984, p. 6.

Michael Schumacher, in an interview in *Writer's Digest,* June, 1991, pp. 28-31.

Robert Towers, "Uprooted," in *The New York Review of Books,* Vol. XXXII, No. 6, April 11, 1985, pp. 36-7.

For Further Study

Miriam Berkley, in an interview in *Publishers Weekly,* August 15, 1986, pp. 58-9.
    Erdrich describes to Berkley how her many jobs have provided rich experiences from which to draw to create believable characters and their lives.

Robert Bly, in a review in *New York Times Book Review,* August 31, 1982, p. 2.
    Poet Bly describes Erdrich's unique approach to telling a story through characters who speak at any time and in any place.

Victoria Brehm, "The Metamorphoses of an Ojibwa Manido," *American Literature: A Journal of Literary History, Criticism, and Bibliography,* Vol. 68, No. 4, December, 1996, pp. 677-706.
    Brehm discusses Erdrich's use of Native American mythology, specifically the figure of the water god, Micipijiu.

D. J. R. Bruckner, in a review in *The New York Times,* December 20, 1984, p. C21.
    Bruckner applauds the lyrical quality of *Love Medicine* and Erdrich's rich characters.

Allan and Nancy Feyl Chavkin, eds., in *Conversations with Louise Erdrich and Michael Dorris,* University Press of Mississippi, 1993.
    A collection of 25 interviews with Erdrich and Dorris, this book includes a description of the unusual collaborative relationship the two share.

Mary B. Davis, ed., in *Native America in the Twentieth Century: An Encyclopedia,* Garland Publishing, 1994.
    An alphabetized reference that includes works by Native Americans and other experts dealing with Native American life in the twentieth century.

Margaret J. Downes, "Narrativity, Myth, and Metaphor: Louise Erdrich and Raymond Carver Talk about Love," in *MELUS: The Journal of the Society for the Study of Multi-Ethnic Literature of the United States,* Vol. 21, No. 2, Summer, 1996, pp. 49-61.
    A comparison of two novels about love, Louise Erdrich's *Love Medicine* and Raymond Carver's *What We Talk About When We Talk About Love.* Downes says that she finds Erdrich's novel more satisfying because of the characters' belief in and use of myth and storytelling.

Louise Erdrich, in *The Blue Jay's Dance,* HarperCollins, 1995.
    In this book, Erdrich chronicles her child's birth and first year of life. It examines the balancing act that working parents experience on a daily basis.

Paul Pasquaretta, "Sacred Chance: Gambling and the Contemporary Native American Indian Novel," in *MELUS: The Journal of the Society for the Study of the Multi-Ethnic Literature of the United States,* Vol. 21, No. 2, Summer, 1996, pp. 21-33.
    An analysis of the gambling stories in novels by three Native American authors. Pasquaretta says that these gambling stories serve as a ritual site on which to contest the forces of corruption and assimilation.

Barbara L. Pittman, "Cross-Cultural Reading and Generic Transformations: The Chronotope of the Road in Erdrich's *Love Medicine,*" in *American Literature: A Journal of Literary History, Criticism, and Bibliography,* Vol. 67, No. 4, December, 1995, pp. 777-92.
    An analysis of the road motif in *Love Medicine.* Pittman sees the motif as mediating between the Euro-American and Native-American traditions in which the novel participates.

Catherine Rainwater, "Reading Between Worlds: Narrativity in the Fiction of Louise Erdrich," in *American Literature: A Journal of Literary History, Criticism, and Bibliography,* Vol. 62, No. 3, September, 1990, pp. 405-22.
    Rainwater discusses the many sets of conflicting codes in *Love Medicine.* Rainwater claims that these codes frustrate the reader's expectations, but in so doing they also make the narrative more powerful.

Michael Schumacher, in an interview in *Writer's Digest,* June, 1991, pp. 28-31.
    In this interview, Erdrich tells how her childhood experiences and heritage have influenced her writing.

Alan Velie, "The Trickster Novel," in *Narrative Chance: Postmodern Discourse on Native American Indian Literatures,* edited by Gerald Vizenor, University of New Mexico Press, 1989, pp. 55-6.
    An analysis of the novel in terms of the picaresque, or trickster genre.

Les Misérables

Victor Hugo
1862

When Victor Hugo's novel *Les Misérables* first came out in 1862, people in Paris and elsewhere lined up to buy it. Although critics were less receptive, the novel was an instant popular success. The French word "misérables" means both poor wretches and scoundrels or villains. The novel offers a huge cast that includes both kinds of "misérables." A product of France's most prominent Romantic writer, *Les Misérables* ranges far and wide. It paints a vivid picture of Paris's seamier side, discusses the causes and results of revolution, and includes discourses on topics ranging from the Battle of Waterloo to Parisian street slang. But the two central themes that dominate the novel are the moral redemption of its main character, Jean Valjean, an ex-convict, and the moral redemption of a nation through revolution. Victor Hugo said: "I condemn slavery, I banish poverty, I teach ignorance, I treat disease, I lighten the night, and I hate hatred. That is what I am, and that is why I have written *Les Misérables.*" The novel is a critical statement against human suffering, poverty, and ignorance. Its purpose is as much political as it is artistic.

Author Biography

As a novelist, poet, political activist, and painter, Victor Hugo was a central figure in the Romantic movement of nineteenth-century France. Both his family and his times influenced Hugo's

Victor Hugo

social views and politics, which included a deep concern with human rights, social injustice, and poverty as the root of evil. Born in Besançon, France, in 1802, Hugo grew up in the years of Napoleon Bonaparte's empire. In 1815, the empire collapsed at the Battle of Waterloo, which Hugo describes in detail in *Les Misérables,* and a constitutional monarchy was established. His father was a general in the Napoleonic army with republican sympathies while his middle-class mother had royalist leanings. The young Hugo spent a large part of his childhood in Paris with his mother. He also traveled through Europe in his father's wake and glimpsed the Napoleonic campaigns. After attending school in Paris, he married his childhood love, Adèle Foucher, in 1822.

In that same year, Hugo published his first volume of poetry, beginning a long and diverse literary career that also included drama and novels. He was acquainted with many major figures on the intellectual and artistic scene. His political convictions changed over time as various French governments rose and fell, but his belief in human rights was consistent. In a letter to a friend describing why he wrote *Les Misérables,* Hugo said: "If the radical is the ideal, yes, I am a radical.... A society which admits poverty, a religion which admits hell, a humanity which sanctions war, seem to me an in-

ferior society, an inferior religion and humanity, and it is towards the higher society, the higher humanity and religion that I turn: society without a king, humanity without frontiers, religion without a book.... I condemn slavery, I banish poverty, I teach ignorance, I treat disease, I lighten the night, and I hate hatred. That is what I am, and that is why I have written *Les Misérables.*"

The 1840s to the 1860s were an active time for the writer. He was elected to the Académie Française in 1841 and to the peerage in 1845 in recognition of his literary achievements. The late 1840s marked a period of serious political involvement for Hugo. He spoke up in the Chamber of Peers, criticizing the legal system and the treatment of the poor, themes to which he returned in *Les Misérables.* Disillusioned with monarchism, he publicly espoused republicanism and participated in the revolution of 1848. These experiences gave him firsthand knowledge of what barricade fighting was like, which he used in the novel. Louis Napoleon, the elected president of the newly established republic, seized power in a coup d'état in 1851. Hugo criticized the new ruler and ended up in exile, first in Belgium, then later on the Isle of Guernsey in the English Channel, where he remained until 1870. It was during this exile that he wrote most of *Les Misérables.*

Les Misérables was first published in 1862, appearing simultaneously in cities across Europe. In spite of a mixed critical reaction, the novel, with its championing of the poor and disenfranchised, was an immediate popular success in France and abroad. It sealed Hugo's reputation as a legend.

Upon his return to France in 1870, he received a hero's welcome. He continued to write for the rest of his life, but abstained from politics. After his death in 1885, Victor Hugo lay in state under the Arc de Triomphe and was buried in the Pantheon, in the heart of his beloved city, Paris.

Plot Summary

Les Misérables is the story of four people, Bishop Myriel, Jean Valjean, Fantine, and Marius Pontmercy, who meet, part, then meet again during the most agitated decades of nineteenth-century France. It also tells the story of the 1832 revolution and describes the unpleasant side of Paris. The novel is in essence a plea for humane treatment of the poor and for equality among all citizens.

Part I—Fantine

The year is 1815 and Napoleon has just been defeated at Waterloo. Bishop Myriel lives a quiet life as a just man, who is especially sympathetic toward the poor, bandits, and convicts. One day a strange man asks for shelter at his home and, with his usual compassion, the bishop gives him room and board. This man is Jean Valjean, who has just been released from prison after serving a lengthy, unjust sentence, during which he tried to escape numerous times. Valjean is angry, hurt, and vengeful. His soul has "withered" and all but died. The bishop urges him to replace anger with goodwill in order to be worthy of respect: "You have left a place of suffering. But listen, there will be more joy in heaven over the tears of a repentant sinner, than over the white robes of a hundred good men. If you are leaving that sorrowful place with hate and anger against men, you are worthy of compassion; if you leave it with goodwill, gentleness, and peace, you are better than any of us."

Valjean listens. Nevertheless, he decides to rob the good bishop. During the night, he runs away with the bishop's silver. He is caught and brought back to the bishop, who tells the police that he himself gave Valjean these precious objects. Later Bishop Myriel tells Valjean, "you belong no longer to evil, but to good. It is your soul I am buying for you. I withdraw it from dark thoughts and from the spirit of perdition and I give it to God!" Valjean is stunned. After he steals a coin from a little boy, he has an epiphany: "he could see his life, and it seemed horrible; his soul, and it seemed frightful. There was, however, a gentler light shining on that life and soul."

Fantine is a seamstress unjustly fired once her employer learns about her scandalous past. Abandoned by her lover, she is hungry, destitute, and unable to care for her daughter, Cosette. First she sells her hair, then her teeth, before finally prostituting herself. At this stage of the story, Fantine has "endured all, borne all, experienced all, suffered all, lost all, wept for all. She is resigned, with that resignation that resembles indifference as death resembles sleep." She leaves two-year-old Cosette to the care of the Thénardiers, who run a tavern in the outskirts of Paris. Cosette is poorly treated by the couple and their two daughters. The Thénardiers view Cosette as their domestic slave, all the while demanding more and more money for Cosette's care. Fantine must continue selling her body to pay for Cosette's keep.

Valjean assumes a new identity as Monsieur Madeleine, and becomes a good citizen, a rich industrialist, and ultimately mayor. Valjean saves Fantine from the police (headed by Inspector Javert) once he discovers she was fired from the very factory under his care. He wants to redeem her, but it is too late. Fantine is sick and soon dies.

At the same time, Champmathieu is falsely accused of being Valjean by Inspector Javert, whose lifelong goal has been to find the escaped convict Valjean. Javert was a "formidable man" whose mother was a fortune-teller and whose father was in the galleys. "His stare was cold and as piercing as a gimlet. His whole life was contained in these two words: waking and watching." After a long night of hesitation—to accuse Champmathieu would save him from Javert, to keep silent would send an innocent man to death—Valjean decides to confess his true identity to save the wrongly accused man:

> He declared that his life, in truth, did have an object. But what object? to conceal his name? to deceive the police? was it for so petty a thing that he had done all that he had done? had he no other object, which was the great one, which was the true one? To save, not his body, but his soul. To become honest and good again. To be an upright man! was it not that, above all, that alone, which he had always wished, and which the bishop had enjoined upon him!... To deliver himself up, to save this man stricken by so ghastly a mistake, to reassume his name, to become again from duty the convict Jean Valjean; that was really to achieve his resurrection, and to close for ever the hell from whence he had emerged! to fall into it in appearance, was to emerge in reality! he must do that! all he had done was nothing, if he did not do that! all his life was useless, all his suffering was lost. He had only to ask the question: "What is the use?"

When the unyielding Javert arrests him, Valjean escapes, and a long hunt begins.

Part II—Cosette

Valjean does not run far. Fantine has told him about Cosette, so he goes to the Thénardiers' and saves the little girl from her terrible life. They settle in Paris, where they constantly have to hide from Javert's eye. They finally find shelter in a convent, the Petit-Picpus, where they spend five happy years of redemption: "Everything around him, this quiet garden, these balmy flowers, these children, shouting with joy, these meek and simple women, this silent cloister, gradually entered into all his being, and his soul subsided into silence.... His whole heart melted in gratitude and he loved more and more."

Part III—Marius

Marius is a young student, and like many other young men of his generation, he is passionately interested in Napoleon: "Napoleon had become to him the people-man as Jesus was the God-man." In Paris he meets a group a young radical students, the Friends of the ABC, who are very much like him and who convert him to republicanism: "my mother is the republic." One day, he spots in a park a young girl, walking with her father. "She was a marvelous beauty. The only remark which could be made ... is that the contradiction between her look, which was sad, and her smile, which was joyous, gave to her countenance something a little wild." He sees her again the next day, and the next, until six months later, he falls in love with her. It is the fifteen-year-old Cosette.

Part IV—Saint Denis

Cosette has noticed Marius and falls in love with him, but she does not want Valjean to know about it. One day Marius writes to her and they secretly meet: "these two hearts poured themselves into each other, so that at the end of an hour, it was the young man who had the young girl's soul and the young girl who had the soul of the young man." Valjean suspects nothing until he accidentally intercepts one of Marius's letters.

Part V—Jean Valjean

Workers and republican students are on the barricades, opposing the police and the army of the monarchy. Many of the revolutionaries are killed in the struggle. Valjean discovers Marius and Cosette's love, but still saves Marius's life on the barricades. He carries the wounded and unconscious young man through the Paris sewers. He has one last confrontation with Javert, his old nemesis, who is at his mercy. He decides to let him go. Moved by this gesture and appalled at himself, Javert kills himself: "Terrible situation! to be moved! To be granite, and to doubt! to be ice and to melt! to feel your fingers suddenly open! to lose your hold, appalling thing!... The projectile man no longer knowing his road, and recoiling!" Still, many died, including Gavroche, a little Parisian boy whose courage inspired the fighters of the barricades.

Cosette restores Marius to health, and they decide to get married. On the wedding day, Marius meets Valjean, who tells him who he really is, a convict still hunted by the police, and that Cosette does not know anything about his unsavory past. However, Valjean does not tell Marius that he

saved his life during the insurrections. Marius wants to help him win his pardon, but Valjean refuses: "I need pardon of none but one, that is my conscience." Marius decides to stay silent, but he is horrified by the revelations. Valjean stops visiting the young couple. Soon, Marius learns that he was saved by him and, accompanied by Cosette, rushes to Valjean's home, but it is too late: Valjean is dying. Uttering his last words, Valjean advises them, "There is scarcely anything else in the world but that: to love one another." He is buried under a blank stone.

Characters

Bahorel

Bahorel is a student and a member of the ABC Society, a secret revolutionary group of students and workers. But he has no respect for authority and is a real troublemaker, liking nothing better than a good fight.

Mademoiselle Baptistine

The unmarried sister of the Bishop of Digne, she lives with him and runs his household. She is a gentle, respectable woman who does good works.

Bishop of Digne

See Charles Myriel

Bossuet

A member of the ABC Society, Bossuet is a law student. He is cheerful but unlucky; everything he undertakes seems to go wrong.

Combeferre

Combeferre is a member of the ABC Society, a student, and a philosopher of revolution. He has a scientific mind and dreams of the inventions of the future and how they will benefit the human race.

Cosette

Cosette is the illegitimate daughter of Fantine, a Parisian "grisette" (working woman) whose lover, Félix Tholomyès, abandons her when she is pregnant. Valjean rescues Cosette from the Thénardiers, and she becomes the love of his life and the motivation for his goodness. She is raised and educated in a convent. When she and Valjean move out into the real Paris, she turns into a beautiful young Parisian woman and falls in love with Marius Pontmercy.

Media Adaptations

- Recorded in 1988, *Les Misérables* is available from Dove Books on Tape in an abridged version read by Christopher Cazenove.

- *Les Misérables* was adapted for the stage as a musical by Alain Boublil and Claude-Michel Schonberg, with the lyrics composed by Herbert Kretzmer. In 1995, the tenth anniversary concert in Royal Albert Hall, London, was released as a movie by Columbia Tristar Home Video. The musical is also available as a sound recording from Geffen produced in 1987. This version features the original Broadway cast.

- *Les Misérables* was made into a film in 1935, starring Fredric March, Charles Laughton, Cedric Hardwicke, Rochelle Hudson, and John Beal. Directed by Richard Boleslawski, this adaptation is detailed and faithful to the novel, except for a changed ending. Considered a classic, the film received Academy Award nominations for Best Cinematography and Best Picture.

- There are many French film adaptations of the novel. A version released in 1957 stars Jean Gabin, Daniele Delorme, Bernard Blier, Bourvil, Gianni Esposito, and Serge Reggiani. Directed by Jean-Paul LeChanois, the film is in French with English subtitles.

- A version directed by Glenn Jordan was made for television in 1978, starring Richard Jordan, Anthony Perkins, John Gielgud, Cyril Cusack, Flora Robson, Celia Johnson, and Claude Dauphin.

- An animated version of *Les Misérables* appeared in 1979, produced by Toei Animation Company.

- A 1994 film version of the novel transferred its setting to early twentieth-century France. Directed, produced, and adapted by Claude Lelouch, the movie, starring Jean-Paul Belmondo, Michel Boujenah, Alessandrea Martines, and Annie Girador, received a Golden Globe award for Best Foreign Film.

Courfeyrac

A member of the ABC Society, Courfeyrac becomes Marius's friend and takes him in.

Enjolras

Enjolras is a leader of the ABC Society. Marius first meets him there and ends up fighting with him on the barricade. The only son of rich parents, Enjolras is a student of the Revolution and has "a nature at once scholarly and warlike." He is indifferent to women and pleasure, but passionate about justice. Enjolras defines what he is fighting for in a speech on the barricade: "Citizens, no matter what happens today, in defeat no less than in victory, we shall be making a revolution. [... Equality] means, in civic terms, an equal outlet for all talents; in political terms, that all votes will carry the same weight; and in religious terms that all beliefs will enjoy equal rights. Equality has a means at its disposal—compulsory free education. The right to learn the alphabet, that is where we must start."

Fantine

Fantine is a Parisian "grisette," or working woman, who falls in love with a student, Félix Tholomyès. Just after Félix breaks off their relationship, she gives birth to their daughter, Cosette. From that point forward her life is a downward spiral. She gives up her child to the mercenary Thénardiers and finds a job in her home town, but is dismissed when her supervisor finds out about her past. She struggles to make ends meet, selling everything she has: her hair, her teeth, and herself (becoming a prostitute). Fantine represents society's cruelty to the poor and its degradation of poor women in particular. Only Valjean shows her any kindness.

Still from the 1935 movie Les Misérables, *starring Fredric March as Jean Valjean.*

Père Fauchelevent

When Fauchelevent, an elderly carrier, gets caught beneath the wheels of his own cart, Valjean rescues him and afterward finds work for him as a gardener in a Paris convent. In doing so, Valjean risks giving away his identity to Javert, who is already suspicious, by showing his great strength. But Fauchelevent repays Valjean by taking him and Cosette in when they are on the run from the police. Fauchelevent, an educated peasant, is both shrewd and good-willed. He recognizes his debt and finds the means to repay it.

Feuilly

A member of the ABC Society of revolutionaries, Feuilly earns his living as a fan-maker and is self-educated.

Mademoiselle Gillenormand

Monsieur Gillenormand's eldest daughter is a prudish, narrow-minded old woman who runs her father's household.

Monsieur Gillenormand

Monsieur Gillenormand, Marius Pontmercy's grandfather and caretaker, is a relic of the past. He had his heyday in the decadent Ancien Régime, the pre-Revolutionary monarchy, in which the nobility dominated France. He still looks back to those days with nostalgia and regret. Gillenormand believes that in modern times people lack the gift of living life to the fullest and enjoying all of its pleasures. He raises Marius to believe that the Revolution "was a load of scoundrels." When Marius discovers that his father was a Revolutionary hero, it causes a bitter break between them.

Théodule Gillenormand

Théodule is Monsieur Gillenormand's great-nephew and a lieutenant in the army. He is a vain young man and a favorite of his Aunt Gillenormand. He tries to become Gillenormand's favorite when Marius is out of the picture, but he can't replace Marius in the old man's affections.

Grantaire

Although Grantaire belongs to the ABC Society, he is a cynic and a hedonist and does not believe in the ideals of revolution. But he does believe in one ideal: Enjolras, whom he regards with love and admiration.

Inspector Javert

Inspector Javert is nearly as renowned a character as Jean Valjean, perhaps due to the dramatized versions of *Les Misérables,* which have tended to present the novel as more of a detective story than a morality tale. Javert serves as Valjean's nemesis throughout the novel, continually threatening to expose his past and bring him under the control of the law. In his exaggerated, nearly fanatical devotion to duty and his lack of compassion, Javert represents a punitive, vengeful form of justice.

Hugo suggests that Javert's "respect for authority and hatred of revolt" are rooted in his past, for he was born in a prison. As if to compensate for this fact, he has spent his life in faithful service to law enforcement. When Valjean saves Javert by helping him escape from the revolutionaries, Javert's rigid system of behavior is upset, for he realizes that Valjean, a criminal who has not yet been officially punished, has performed an act of great kindness and courage. Javert previously would have overlooked such an act and arrested the criminal, but his realization proves more than he can bear. Unable to resolve his inner conflict, Javert drowns himself in the Seine River.

Joly

A member of the ABC Society, Joly is studying medicine. He is something of a hypochondriac.

Monsieur Mabeuf

An elderly churchwarden, Mabeuf befriends Marius's father, Colonel Pontmercy, and Marius becomes friends with Mabeuf after his father dies. He is a gentle man whose main interests in life are his garden and his books, but he becomes very poor and has to sell all of his books. Impoverished and without hope in life, Mabeuf joins the rebels, courageously climbs to the top of the barricade to plant a flag, and is shot by the militia. His age and gentleness make his courage even more remarkable, showing that revolution can come in any form.

Madame Magloire

Madame Magloire is the personal maid of Mademoiselle Baptistine and the Bishop of Digne's housekeeper.

Charles Myriel

Myriel is a kind and generous bishop who gives Jean Valjean aid when everyone else refuses him. Searching for a place to spend the night, the ex-convict finds that he is a branded man and no inn will let him stay. His last resort is the home of the bishop, who takes him in and treats him as an honored guest. After Valjean steals the Bishop's silver and is caught by the police, the bishop protects him by insisting that the silver was actually a gift. Afterward, he says to Valjean, "[You] no longer belong to what is evil but to what is good. I have bought your soul to save it from black thoughts and the spirit of perdition, and I give it to God." The bishop's selfless act inspires Valjean to change his life.

Colonel Georges Pontmercy

A hero of the Napoleonic wars, Pontmercy marries Gillenormand's youngest daughter and has a son, Marius. The villainous innkeeper, Thénardier, drags Pontmercy to safety from the battlefield of Waterloo. Although Marius does not meet his father, Pontmercy watches him from afar in church and loves his son. He leaves Marius a note telling him to adopt the title of Baron (Napoleon gave it to Pontmercy on the field of battle), and to do Thénardier every good in his power. Marius worships his father as a hero and is strongly influenced by his political beliefs.

Marius Pontmercy

Marius is a young law student who falls in love with Cosette. He also saves Valjean from a plot against his life by the innkeeper-turned-criminal, Thénardier. In turn, Marius is saved by Valjean while fighting on the barricade. He is the son of Georges Pontmercy, a colonel and war hero under Napoleon. But Marius's grandfather, Monsieur Gillenormand, despises Georges and takes Marius into his own home to raise him.

Marius is at a stage of life where he doesn't know yet what he believes. His image of the world keeps opening up as he encounters new points of view. When Marius discovers his father's identity, he worships him as a war hero and adopts a pro-Napoleon stance opposed to his grandfather's royalism. He gets into a quarrel with Gillenormand and storms out of the house to make his way through Paris as a starving student. Marius falls in with a group of students, the ABC Society led by Enjolras, who share his republican beliefs. At first he is reluctant to give up his belief that conquest and war are the greatest ideals of a nation. But he begins to have doubts when the students present him with a new ideal, freedom: "Having so lately found a faith, must he renounce it? He told himself that he need not; he resolved not to doubt, and began despite himself to do so." When unrest stirs Paris in 1832 and his friends take up arms, he joins them on the barricades. But it is more out of desperation, because he fears he has lost Cosette, than out of political conviction. He is lured there by the voice of the street girl Eponine Thénardier telling him that his friends await him.

Jean Prouvaire

Prouvaire is a member of the ABC Society of students and workers. A wealthy student, he is interested in social questions, but is also a poet and lover with a romantic side.

Eponine Thénardier

The poor daughter of the Thénardiers, Eponine falls in love with Marius and becomes jealous of his love for Cosette. She is torn between wanting to help him and wanting to keep him away from Cosette. She courageously saves his life on the barricade by stepping between him and a bullet, and dies in his arms. Her life is an example of poverty's degradation: "What it came to was that in the heart of our society, as at present constituted, two unhappy mortals [Eponine and her sister] had been turned by extreme poverty into monsters at once depraved and innocent, drab creatures without name or age or sex, no longer capable of good or evil, deprived of all freedom, virtue, and responsibility; souls born yesterday and shrivelled today like flowers dropped in the street which lie fading in the mud until a cartwheel comes to crush them."

Gavroche Thénardier

Gavroche is a Parisian urchin (street child), the son of the villainous Thénardiers. Lively and clever, he lives by his wits. He dies by them as well and proves his courage, getting shot by soldiers when he teases them on the barricade. His fate is interwoven with that of Marius, Cosette, and the Thénardiers. The novel presents him as an essential representative of Paris: "He had neither hearth nor home, nor any regular source of food; yet he was happy because he was free. By the time the poor have grown to man's estate they have nearly always been caught in the wheels of the social order and become shaped to its requirements; but while they are children their smallness saves them."

Madame Thénardier

The coarse wife of the innkeeper Thénardier, she takes in Fantine's daughter, Cosette. But she treats her like a Cinderella, feeding and clothing her poorly and making her do the worst work in the household. She helps hatch a plot to entrap Valjean and steal his fortune, but instead ends up in prison. The narrator states that she is naturally cruel and scheming and offers her as an example of those who commit crimes not because they are driven to it, but because it suits them.

Monsieur Thénardier

The unscrupulous innkeeper and his wife take care of Cosette, but treat her poorly. He embarks on a life of crime, getting involved with the worst criminals in Paris, and attempts to entrap and rob Valjean. Although he ends up in prison, he escapes. He helps Valjean escape from the sewers when Valjean is trapped there with Marius. Thénardier plays a central part in the plot. He does good in spite of his evil intentions, not knowing what the consequences of his own actions will be.

Felix Tholomyès

A wealthy, rakish student, Tholomyès is Fantine's lover for a while and then abandons her. Their affair ruins Fantine. She becomes pregnant and cannot earn enough to save herself and her child. The narrator says of the relationship: "For him it was a passing affair, for her the love of her life."

Jean Valjean

The chief protagonist, Jean Valjean, is an ex-convict who struggles to redeem himself morally and to find acceptance in a society that rejects him as a former criminal. Valjean's redemption through his many trials is the central plot of *Les Misérables*.

The child of a poor peasant family, he loses both his parents as a young child and moves in with an older sister. When her husband dies, Valjean supports her and her seven children by working as a tree pruner. Unable to feed the family on his earnings, he steals a loaf of bread from a baker and ends up serving nineteen years in prison for his crime. Finally free, he finds that he cannot find lodging, work, or acceptance in the outside world. As an ex-convict he is at the bottom of the social order.

But Valjean has a transforming experience when he meets the Bishop of Digne, who accepts and shelters him regardless of his past, even after Valjean tries to steal from his household. Here Valjean learns the lesson of unconditional love, a reason for living that sustains him through all of his trials. And they are many. He lives on the run from two forces: the justice of the law, represented by Javert, a police detective who doggedly pursues him, and his own conscience, which leads him to make difficult choices between what is right and what is easiest.

Valjean starts a new life as the mayor of Montreuil sur Mer. He is the savior of this manufacturing town, rebuilding its industries and economy and sustaining the population with new jobs. But he lives on the run from his dogged pursuer, Javert, and in his first moral trial he has to give himself up to keep an innocent man from going to prison in his place. He escapes again and lives the rest of his life as a fugitive.

The harshness of the society in which he lives presents great obstacles to Valjean's moral redemption. Only the transforming power of love lets him overcome them. He loves a young girl, Cosette, daughter of the prostitute Fantine, and raises her as his daughter. Most of his good acts center on her welfare: saving the life of her lover, Marius; protecting her, whatever the cost to himself; even giving up Cosette after she marries, so that she will not be sullied by connection to an ex-convict. His love for her teaches him how to act in the world at large. In all of his actions he strives to be honorable and generous.

Themes

Change and Transformation

The most important theme the novel examines is that of transformation, in the individual and in society. Jean Valjean, the chief protagonist, is transformed from a misanthropic and potentially violent ex-convict to a man capable of heroic love and self-sacrifice. The force that transforms him is love. The Bishop of Digne offers Valjean unconditional love, trusting the former criminal with his life and giving him all that he can. Valjean finds inspiration for an entirely new life from this example. He learns to put another person first when he raises Cosette as his own daughter, and he endures moral trials, such as risking his life to rescue Marius, who loves Cosette and whom Valjean hates. On a broader scale, the workers and students on the barricade fight for social transformation, to create a new France without injustice and poverty.

Human Rights

Closely related to the theme of transformation is that of human rights. This is what the barricade is about and what the students, workers, and downtrodden poor of Paris want. The novel offers many examples of the violation of human rights. Valjean steals a loaf of bread because he has hungry children to feed. The law punishes him for nineteen years because of this petty crime, and Valjean finds little peace at the end of his term. The police inspector Javert pursues him almost to the grave for the theft of a coin. Fantine loves a man who abandons her, and she ends up as a prostitute. She sacrifices her child, her looks, and her body just to survive. Even worse, when she does defend her human dignity and accuses a bourgeois gentleman of assault, the police arrest her. As the novel presents it, the aim of revolution is to create a society in which all individuals have equal rights and in which poverty itself is undesirable.

Class Conflict

The central struggle is also a class conflict: revolution mobilizes the have-nots against the haves. The working class of Paris is presented as an ominous force, ready to throw up a barricade at a moment's notice. The barricade is where the life-and-death struggle of the disenfranchised and the government takes place. The students and workers join and fight to create a new and better nation, even at the cost of their lives. Enjolras, their leader, puts it eloquently when he says: "[This] is the hard price that must be paid for the future. A revolution

Topics for Further Study

- Investigate current prison conditions in the United States and compare today's prison experience to Valjean's as described in the novel.

- Consider the ethical issues surrounding imprisonment that the novel raises in book two, chapter seven ("The inwardness of despair"). Does Hugo see prison as an effective means of punishing criminals? Does prison reform criminals, according to Hugo, or does it make them more violent? How does the author suggest prisoners should be treated? Use examples from the book to support your answers.

- Investigate the economic, legal, and social definition of poverty in the United States today and compare it to the conditions of poverty in Paris as described in the novel.

is a toll-gate. But mankind will be liberated, uplifted and consoled. We here affirm it, on this barricade."

Justice and Injustice

Another major question the novel considers is whether the legal institutions of the state exact true justice. While he is in prison, the convict Jean Valjean considers the question of whether he has been treated fairly. Readers must wonder if his crime, stealing a loaf of bread to feed his family, really merits the punishment he receives: four years of imprisonment that stretch to nineteen when he tries to escape. Valjean asks himself "whether human society had the right to … grind a poor man between the millstones of need and excess—need of work and excess of punishment. Was it not monstrous that society should treat in this fashion precisely those least favored in the distribution of wealth…?" He comes to the conclusion that, although he did commit a reprehensible crime, the punishment is out of proportion, and he develops an intense hatred for society as a whole. Fantine meets the same fate when she defends herself against attack. As a prostitute, she is on the bottom rung of society; the law offers her no protection.

Only respectable people with money appear to have any legal rights.

Meaning of Life

Valjean's great discovery, the one that transforms him, is that the meaning of life lies in love. His love is twofold, both the generalized love for one's fellow creatures that the Bishop of Digne shows toward him and the specific love for another person that he feels for Cosette. Summing up this philosophy at the end of his life, Valjean says to Cosette and Marius, "Love one another always. There is nothing else that matters in this world except love."

Style

Structure

In some ways the novel is structured traditionally. It has a rising action, that is, the part of the narrative that sets up the problems that are to be resolved. This consists of Valjean's life up to the point when he saves his enemy Marius by carrying him through the sewers of Paris to safety. The climax, or turning point, when the conflict reaches its peak, is the suicide of the police detective Javert. Caught between his rigid belief in the absolute power of law and his conclusion that he has a moral obligation to break the law and free his savior, Valjean, Javert solves his dilemma by killing himself. The denouement, or winding-down of the story, which describes the outcome of the primary plot problem as well as resolving secondary plots, includes Marius's recovery, the marriage of Cosette and Marius, the revelation of Valjean's true story, and the young couple's visit to Valjean's deathbed.

But the narrative's many departures from the main plot are important to the novel as well. The novel includes separate sections on the sewers of Paris, the criminal underworld, the convent, Parisian street slang, the Battle of Waterloo, revolutionary societies, and the barricades. Hugo is telling more than the story of one man; he is telling the story of Paris. His digressions, although they do not forward plot development, give the reader information about the novel's themes, such as human rights, justice and injustice, class conflict, and the city. He is primarily concerned not so much with narrating a story but with critiquing society and presenting his notions of reform.

Point of View

The story is told from a third-person omniscient point of view. Omniscient narrators have a god's-eye or all-knowing view, knowing more than their characters do. The narrator breaks in several times to equate himself with the author. For example, at the beginning of the Waterloo episode, the narrator says: "On a fine May morning last year (that is to say, in the year 1861) a traveller, the author of this tale, walked from Nivelles in the direction of La Hulpe." And in describing Paris, he states: "For some years past the author of this book, who regrets the necessity to speak of himself, has been absent from Paris." Although generally there is a distinction between the author and the narrator of a work, this device blurs the boundary. The novel is a vehicle of expression for the author's social views. Whenever the narrator is not describing the actions, thoughts, and speech of the characters, the voice of authority emerges. This includes the discussion of Parisian street urchins, the sewers, the underworld, and the barricades. The narrator pulls back from the characters to look at the broader scenario. Here is a typical example of this device, describing the barricade: "And while a battle that was still political was preparing in that place that had witnessed so many revolutionary acts; while the young people, the secret societies, and the schools, inspired by principle, and the middle-class inspired by self-interest, were advancing on each other to clash and grapple … there was to be heard the sombre growling of the masses: a fearful and awe-inspiring voice in which were mingled the snarl of animals and the words of God, a terror to the faint-hearted and a warning to the wise, coming at once from the depths, like the roaring of a lion, and from the depths like the voice of thunder."

Setting

The setting for most of the novel is Paris around 1830, a character in its own right. The narrative devotes almost as much space to it as to the protagonist, Valjean. It is a dark, gloomy, and sinister place, full of plague-carrying winds and polluting sewers, rotting old districts and slums. Its secretive aspect is a blessing, though, for Valjean, who seeks refuge in dark corners. The narrow alleys lend themselves, too, to the building of barricades. The narrative also presents Paris as a microcosm, reflecting the world as a whole: "Paris stands for the world. Paris is a sum total, the ceiling of the human race…. To observe Paris is to review the whole course of history…." Paris also has its places of beauty and tranquillity, such as the

Luxembourg Garden on a fair day, but even here discontent lurks, in the form of two hungry boys wandering in search of food.

The novel presents Paris in all its wretchedness and grandeur. The urban environment has power over those who live in it. Some characters, such as Thénardier, an innkeeper who gets involved with the worst criminal elements of the city, are corrupted by Paris's temptations and hardships. Others, like Gavroche, the street urchin who is Thénardier's son, demonstrate courage and compassion in spite of their circumstances. For Valjean, Paris is both a refuge and a testing-ground. Hugo ranges over many aspects of the city in his portrayal of it, from the convents to the argot, or slang, spoken on the streets, from the heart of the city to its half-tamed outskirts, from rooftops to sewers. The sewer system of Paris symbolizes the dark underside of the city, where its secret history is stored: "that dreadful place which bears the impress of the revolution of the earth and of men, in which the remains of every cataclysm is to be found, from the Flood to the death of Marat." (Marat was a leader of the French Revolution who was assassinated.) Most of all, the citizens of Paris make up its character. The novel presents a sprawling picture of the people: criminals, orphans, students, the middle class, and others.

Symbolism

The novel employs symbolism, the use of one object to represent another, on a grand scale. Paris represents the world as a whole. Gavroche symbolizes the heroism of the average individual. The city sewers represent the seamy underside of Paris, filled with scraps of history, both good and evil, that have been discarded and forgotten, but not destroyed. The sewers also represent Valjean's passage through hell to redemption. He carries Marius to safety on his back through their passages like a martyr bearing a cross. A pair of silver candlesticks, stolen from the Bishop, serves for Valjean as a symbolic reminder of where he has come from and how he should act. Such leitmotivs, or recurring themes, woven through the text add depth and meaning.

Romanticism

Romanticism was an artistic and intellectual movement of the late eighteenth and early nineteenth century that put the individual mind at the center of the world and of art. Romanticism valued emotional and imaginative responses to reality, the individual's interior experience of the

"Conquerors of the Bastille," an engraving by Francois Flamena illustrating the French Revolution of 1789.

world, which it perceived as being closer to truth. It evolved partly as a reaction to the Enlightenment's emphasis on restraint, simplicity, logic, and respect for tradition. *Les Misérables* is a characteristic Romantic work in both theme and form. In theme, the novel assaults the traditional social structure, glorifies freedom of thought and spirit, and makes a hero of the average individual, such as Gavroche the street urchin, who dies with courage on the barricade. In form, the novel values content over structure, offers passionate rhetoric rather than classical restraint, and ranges freely over many subjects.

Historical Context

Romanticism

Romanticism was an intellectual and artistic movement that swept Europe and the United States in the late-eighteenth to mid-nineteenth centuries. This movement was preceded by the Enlightenment, which emphasized reason as the basis of social life. The Enlightenment also promoted universal, formal standards, dating back to Greek and Roman classicism, for greatness in art. The artists, philosophers, writers, and composers of the Ro-

Compare & Contrast

- **1830s:** Under public pressure, French legislators reformed prisons to some extent. They abolished some of the more barbaric forms of punishment that were practiced under the *Ancien Régime,* such as torture and hanging, and offered education for petty offenders.

  1850s: As a result of unemployment caused by industrialization, crime rates rose in France and the prison population increased. Inmates were not allowed to speak to each other. Riots and suicides took place in prisons.

  Today: Due in part to poor economic conditions in France, prison populations are on the rise again, with an increase in the number of convicts serving time for drug-related crimes. With a prison population that is steadily increasing, overcrowding is a problem, and many inmates find themselves sharing a cell with as many as five other prisoners.

- **1830s:** France was beginning to become an industrialized nation, a process that would transform its economy, workplace, working class, and political landscape.

  1850s: Increasing industrialization brought wealth to France as well as increased unemployment. Lack of work drove thousands of poor women to prostitution and many of the urban poor to crime.

  Today: After rapid consolidation of industries in the 1970s, many French manufacturing jobs were eliminated, resulting in high levels of unemployment. Currently, many young people have difficulty finding permanent work. However, recent changes in the French school system have expanded educational opportunities for students, in an effort by the government to create an employable workforce.

- **1830s:** Antigovernment protesters set up barricades in Paris after Charles X published three ordinances calling to abolish freedom of the press, dissolve Parliament, and limit voting rights to 25,000 landed proprietors. The 1830 revolution successfully removed Charles from the throne; succeeding him was Louis Phillippe.

  1850s: A bloody protest occurred in Paris in 1848, removing Louis Phillippe from power and creating a provisional government that extended the right to vote and set up national workshops to combat unemployment. After another violent clash, this government was in turn replaced by the Second Republic, with an assembly dominated by the middle class.

  Today: After violent student protests and nation-wide strikes in May of 1968, new French leaders shifted toward a more liberal form of government, trying to balance a market economy while preserving social-democratic principles. Today, France is joining with other European nations to create the European Union, a community which will share a common currency and create a formidable trading bloc.

---

mantic movement rejected these standards and instead valued the individual imagination and experience as the basis of art and source of truth. Nature, the state of childhood, and emotion, rather than logic or scientific investigation, were considered the primary sources of eternal truth.

Victor Hugo was one of the leading writers of the Romantic movement in France, and *Les Misérables* was one of its major works. The novel is Romantic in style and theme. It is written in a sweeping, emotional manner, taking the experience of the individual as the starting-point for discovering truths about French society.

Revolution

France in the nineteenth century was in a constant state of political and social unrest. In 1789, the newly formed National Assembly created a document called the "Declaration of the Rights of Man," establishing the right to liberty, equality, property, and security, and adding that every citizen had a duty to defend these rights. After King Louis XVI was executed on January 21, 1793, a period of confusion and violence followed. Many people, the innocent along with the guilty, were executed in the aftermath of the Revolution.

With the bloody departure of the monarchy, the legislature appointed a five-man Directory to power in 1795. But conspirators, including Napoleon Bonaparte, staged a coup d'état, or surprise overthrow of the state, in 1799. Napoleon became dictator and remained in power until he was completely defeated at the Battle of Waterloo in 1815. This is when Hugo's novel *Les Misérables* begins.

From 1815 until 1830, France was ruled by Louis XVIII and then Charles X under the Second Restoration. During this time the French used a constitutional monarchy where the king governed alongside an elected parliament. This was a comparatively tranquil and prosperous period, but it ended in the Revolution of 1830, when Charles X published ordinances dissolving Parliament, limiting voting rights to land owners, and abolishing freedom of the press. Charles was forced from the throne and replaced by Louis Philippe, the "citizen king," who had fought in the French Revolution. This was a triumph for the middle class, but it left the working-class and poor out in the cold.

The insurrection of 1832, the first Republican uprising since 1789, started to stir at the burial of Lamarque, a Revolutionary hero. Republicans shouted, "Down with Louis Philippe!" The barricades went up, and a violent clash ensued. The forces on the barricades, composed mainly of students and workers, lacked public support, and the rebellion was put down by government forces.

In 1848, a new wave of revolution swept across Europe, triggered by the political unrest of bourgeois liberals and nationalists, crop failures several years in a row, and economic troubles. In France, Louis Philippe was driven from his throne. After a bloody struggle between the working-class and the middle-class provisional government in Paris, the Second Republic was established, with a mainly middle-class national assembly and Louis Napoleon, who was related to Napoleon I, as president.

Hugo was sympathetic to the 1848 revolution, became a representative in the assembly, and initially supported Louis Napoleon. However, in 1851 the president assumed control of France in a military coup d'état, and in 1852 the population voted to disband the republic and reestablish the empire. Hugo was disillusioned with both the French people who were willing to exchange freedom for stability and with Napoleon III, who had traded in his republican opinions to become a dictator. Criticizing the government and Louis Napoleon publicly, Hugo was forced to leave France, first for Belgium and then for the Channel Islands. *Les Misérables,* which Hugo composed from the late 1840s to 1862 during his exile, integrated his feelings about the political situation, his memories of the barricades of 1848, and his republican ideals. The novel denounces the degradation of the urban working-class and society's mistreatment and neglect of the poor, especially women and children.

Industrialization

The continuing industrialization of France in the 1850s and 1860s created wealth for the country, but it also created unemployment as machines replaced manual laborers in many jobs. This in turn led to an increase in crime. Poor working women turned to prostitution as a means of survival, working under the scrutiny of a Police Morals Bureau, which considered them corrupt. The character of Jean Valjean was drawn from a historical person, a petty thief named Pierre Maurin who spent five years in prison for stealing bread for his sister's children. Hugo draws a clear distinction in the novel between those who choose crime because they are corrupt and those who are driven to it by poverty and desperation. On the one hand, there is Thénardier, who is by nature "highly susceptible to the encroachments of evil." On the other, there is Valjean, who stole only to save his family, and Fantine, who suffered for protecting her own child. The narrator blames society's indifference and injustice for the situation of those who fall into the latter category.

Critical Overview

Publishers bid against each other for the right to publish *Les Misérables,* no doubt sensing that the novel would be a great success. It had been awaited for years. The author's exile to Guernsey only increased his international reputation and the suspense of waiting for his next major work. Hugo received an unheard-of 300,000 francs as advance payment for the novel. But the publishers regained their investment and more when the book came out.

Les Misérables appeared in 1862, published by LaCroix of Brussels and Paris. It appeared simultaneously in Paris, London, Brussels, New York, Berlin, St. Petersburg, and other European capitals. Published initially in five parts, divided into ten volumes, the novel was released in three separate installments in April, May, and June. Hugo's family and friends gave it a huge buildup in the press, advertising its release for a month in advance in all the major papers of Europe. Rumors that it might be banned in France built up the suspense even more. The book-buying public gave it an enthusiastic reception. Booksellers in Paris lined up to buy the second installment in such great numbers that police were needed to manage the crowd. It was an enormous success for its publishers and its author. Adèle Hugo, the author's wife, wrote that groups of workers shared the cost of the ten volumes in order to pass it from hand to hand and read it. The critic Saint-Beuve commented that Hugo "had snatched the greatest popularity of our time under the nose of the very government that exiled him. His books go everywhere: the women, the common people, all read him. Editions go out of print between eight in the morning and noon."

The book's critical reception, on the other hand, was mixed. Some of his contemporaries perceived Hugo's style as long-winded, digressive, melodramatic, and full of unlikely coincidences. Others found his sweeping, passionate prose, championing of social issues, and ideals of justice and morality inspirational.

On the negative side, many critics disliked the novel's digressions from the main plot, especially the long account of Waterloo. Adolphe Thiers, a historian, expressed the strong opinion that the novel was "detestable. The spirit is bad, the plan is bad, and the execution is bad." The writer Barbey D'Aurévilly found the novel vulgar and full of improbabilities, and criticized it for its socialist views. Hippolyte Taine, a critic and historian, thought the novel was insincere and its success was a flash in the pan.

On the positive side, the poet Charles Baudelaire offered praise for the work's poetic and symbolic qualities. The English novelist George Meredith, though he thought it was drawn in oversimplified terms, called it "the masterwork of fiction of this century—as yet. There are things in it quite wonderful." The great Russian novelist Fyodor Dostoevsky considered *Les Misérables* superior to his own *Crime and Punishment,* and saw Hugo as a champion of the idea of spiritual rebirth.

Walter Pater was of the opinion that Hugo's works were among the finest products of the Romantic movement.

In the first half of the twentieth century, Hugo's reputation as a novelist waned. This was in part because of changes in the tastes of writers and readers. First the Realist, then the Modernist writers swept through the literary scene, and it is characteristic of such movements that they debunk what has come before in an effort to break new ground. *Les Misérables* in particular achieved its blinding success partly because of the moment in time when it was released. It was the long-awaited work of a national hero returning from exile, but that historical moment passed, along with Hugo's great influence over national opinion.

But many writers, including André Gide and Jean-Paul Sartre, acknowledged his lasting influence. Hugo's works are still widely read today, and he has modern defenders. The literary critic Victor Brombert, for example, comments: "The dramatic and psychological power of Hugo's novels depends in large part on the creation of archetypal figures.... The sweep of his texts and the moving, even haunting images they project are a function of the widest range of rhetorical virtuosity." *Les Misérables* has passed into modern legend in its well-known and popular adaptations for film and the stage, and it is arguably the most important Romantic novel of the nineteenth century.

Criticism

Anne-Sophie Cerisola

In the following essay, Cerisola, a former teacher at the Lycee Français de New York and a current instructor at New York University, outlines some of the biographical background that led to Hugo's great work; Cerisola also discusses the author's ambition of creating not only a great story, but also a novel that would be an epic of its time, thus explaining the story's complicated narrative approach.

Victor Hugo took seventeen years to write *Les Misérables,* his vast fresco of individual and collective destinies, which was published in 1862 when he was sixty years old. The novel is the parallel story of the redemption of Jean Valjean and France—and to a larger extent, the story of humanity's political and social progress. Above all,

What Do I Read Next?

- Victor Hugo's other major works include the novel *The Hunchback of Notre Dame,* published in 1831, and the poetry collection *Contemplations,* released in 1856, which he wrote at about the same time as *Les Misérables.* Some critics consider the latter, written after the drowning death of his daughter, his best poetry.

- Fyodor Dostoevsky's *Crime and Punishment,* first published in 1866, tells the story of Raskolnikov, a man who commits a brutal murder and then can escape neither his own conscience nor the detective who pursues him.

- Published in 1940, *Native Son,* a novel by Richard Wright, is the story of Bigger Thomas, a poor black boy raised in the Chicago slums. Wright describes how Bigger's fear of white society, and its fear of him, turns him into a criminal.

- *In the Belly of the Beast* is an insider's account of prison life written by the controversial Jack Henry Abbott, a convict. Abbott was released after he published the book in 1991, at the urging of a group of writers including Norman Mailer. Shortly thereafter, he killed a man in a bar brawl and was sentenced to life imprisonment.

- Marie Henri Beyle Stendhal offers a detailed account of the Battle of Waterloo in *The Charterhouse of Parma,* published in 1839. The main theme of this novel is the struggle of the individual against a conformist society.

- Charles Baudelaire's 1857 *The Flowers of Evil* is a collection of poems centered on life in Paris. One of the major poetry collections of the century, it bridged the Romantic and Modernist movements. Six of the poems that were considered too erotic and decadent were banned in France until 1949. Baudelaire was Hugo's contemporary and often reviewed his work.

Hugo intended *Les Misérables* to be a novel about the people, and for the people, and he largely succeeded.

When *Les Misérables* was published, it appeared simultaneously in Paris, London, Budapest, Brussels, Leipzig, Madrid, Milan, and Naples, and was translated into many other languages. The novel's phenomenal success has continued ever since, and understandably so: it is a gripping story well told. As the critic Kathryn Grossman put it, "a plot as full of twists and turns as the treacherous labyrinths—sewers, conscience, streets—Hugo describes." Grossman also reminds us, "in France, Hugo's supporters had prepared the event with a massive publicity campaign. [The book] appeared first in serial form on April 3, 1862. Yet the magnitude of the public's response surprised even the most committed Hugo partisans. According to reports at the time, no one had ever seen a book devoured with such fury: public reading rooms rented it by the hour. By April 6, the book was sold out in Paris."

The novel's power derived from its simple message. Man was not inherently evil, he was made so by an unjust society. In the preface to the novel, Hugo wrote emphatically: "So long as the three problems of the age—the degradation of man by poverty, the ruin of woman by starvation, and the dwarfing of childhood by physical and spiritual night—are not yet solved ... books like this cannot be useless." Jean Valjean was the perfect illustration of this principle. Valjean was not by nature a criminal. The motive which led him to steal bread, the origin of his fall, was not evil. He was seeking to provide food for hungry children, his sister's offspring, only out of desperation. But his years of prison hardened him. "He had for his motives," says Hugo, "habitual indignation, bitterness of soul, the profound feeling of iniquities endured, and reaction even against the good, the innocent, and the just, if such exist." The story of his conversion is exemplary. As Monsieur Madeleine of Montreuil-sur-mer, he is the good industrialist, the admirably just and efficient mayor, the caring philanthropist. Forced back into his true identity by the revelation of the imminent exile to the galleys of the innocent Champmathieu, who has been identified as Jean Valjean, he reluctantly fights again with his demons. From this ordeal, minutely analyzed in the chapter "A Tempest in a Brain," he emerges triumphant, saves Champmathieu in time and goes again to the galleys. After his escape, his life is a long record of care and self-sacrifice to Cosette, his adopted daughter. He triumphs even when faced with Marius's love for Cosette, and is able not only to dominate his jealousy but to save the life of Marius (the famous episode of the sewers) and make possible Marius's marriage with Cosette.

Moreover, Hugo draws constant analogies between Valjean's spiritual progress and humanity's striving toward freedom and social justice. The fight for justice and freedom is led by Marius's group of radical friends, the "Friends of the Underdog," and in particular Enjolras, whose speech on the barricades echoed most of Hugo's ideas:

> "the nineteenth century is grand, but the twentieth century will be happy. Men will no longer have to fear, as now, a conquest, an invasion, a usurpation, a rivalry of nations with the armed hand … they will no longer have to fear famine, speculation, prostitution from distress, misery from lack of work, and the scaffold, and the sword, and the battle, and all the brigandages of chance in the forest of events.… Men will be happy.… Oh! the human race shall be delivered, uplifted, and consoled! We affirm it on this barricade."

However, the young radicals die on the barricades and, as one critic noted, Hugo sometimes seems pessimistic about the outcome of the fight: "The dismal, lurid, grotesque imagery with which Hugo consistently depicts les misérables drives home a powerful point. Despite all the talk about progress, nothing has changed for a large swath of humanity. Conditions may have improved for some individuals and their offspring. But each new generation of the poor and uneducated faced the same physical, psychic, and moral disintegration."

Because he wrote *Les Misérables* late in his life, Hugo also wanted to leave a personal testimony on his own political fights. One of the central characters in the novel, Marius, passes through an intellectual evolution closely similar to the author's: at first strongly royalist, then Bonapartist, later Republican. He fights for his convictions on the barricades. Hugo was born in 1802 to a royalist mother and a republican father who was one of Napoleon's generals. By the time he was a year old

his parents were not living together anymore. Hugo sought fulfillment in and through art, as he was often left by himself. As one of his biographers noted, "Hugo was terribly precocious. He began writing complete plays, echoing his fondness for popular drama, at the age of fourteen; he devoured Walter Scott's historical novels as soon as each translation rolled off the press; and he penned his first work of fiction—whose black rebel hero foreshadowed Jean Valjean—when he was sixteen; finally, he composed poetry that gave him national recognition, including a royal pension, before he had turned eighteen."

At first aesthetically and politically conservative, within years he backed the new school of innovators—Lamartine, Musset, Nodier, Vigny—who were labeled romantics. In 1830 his first play, *Hernani,* broke completely with dramatic conventions. Hugo became the leader of this group of writers, most of them democrats in a regime that killed civil liberties. However, only the 1848 Revolution—the model for the insurrection described in the novel—spawned a republic, which Hugo supported vigorously. He was even elected to the Parliament, on the left. The Republic did not last long. Louis-Napoleon Bonaparte, whom Hugo had first supported, overthrew the young republic three years later in 1852 and became emperor. Hugo, who never hid his own republicanism, had to flee abroad to avoid arrest. It was from exile that he wrote *Les Misérables.*

Since his earlier work, Hugo believed in the importance of the illusion of reality, what he called verisimilitude. Very often in the novel, Hugo pretends that he is copying from notes left by Myriel or Valjean. He quotes pseudo-newspaper articles and letters that came into his possession, everything suggesting authenticity. Indeed, he always worked a great deal on sources, and at least two characters of the novel, Bishop Myriel and Valjean, were inspired by real people whose stories Hugo had read. Finally, Hugo was careful to have each character speak according to the language of his or her social class; so much so that when the novel came out he was accused by some critics of being "low." For example, Gavroche, the street urchin, always speaks slang, including his words to the two little orphans he has just met and for whom he buys some bread.

Finally, like *The Hunchback of Notre-Dame,* Hugo's earlier historical novel, *Les Misérables* multiplies the digressions—on Waterloo, on slang, on the sewers—in an effort to give the historical background of the story. According to one critic, "stripped of all its digression, *Les Misérables* would still be an interesting book, containing an essentially great lesson, but it would be much less a book extraordinarily representative of the nineteenth century. In its final form it gives us not only the lesson of Valjean, but it gives us some of the great deeds and ideas of the century." Hugo justified his all-encompassing approach by saying he wanted to create a contemporary work of fiction that would rival such great national verse epics as Homer's *Iliad* and *Odyssey* and John Milton's *Paradise Lost.*

The strong political content of the novel divided the critics of the time. While popular opinion was virtually unanimous, the many critical assessments—by about one hundred and fifty reviewers in 1862 alone—fell into two camps. Political, social, and religious conservatives assailed the author's intellectual integrity, his motives, his intentions: to blame society for human suffering was, according to them, to deny individual responsibility and to undermine existing institutions. The more progressive, republican critics, on the other hand, defended the novel as profoundly moral. Imbued with the New Testament notions of grace, charity, and self-sacrifice, the novel depicted the struggles of human conscience with temptation and the eventual triumph of duty over passion, of freedom over nature.

Critics were also uncertain about the genre and the composition of the book. Indeed, Hugo's ambitious goal complicated the structure of the book. There is very little linearity and numerous echoes and parallels, while the narration goes back and forth in time. The effect is a little disorienting for the reader who has problems following the narration, as if Hugo were playing with his reader's patience. In addition to this unconventional composition, it defies any attempt at classification. The mingling of literary styles—*le melange des genres*—was a hallmark of French romanticism since the 1820s. As a consequence, *Les Misérables* is a blend of epic, myth, dramatic and lyrical components; grotesque and sublime; satire and romance; comedy and tragedy; realism and romanticism which led many critics to describe the novel as a "monster." Maybe it is, and yet, it still makes people dream.

Source: Anne-Sophie Cerisola, in an essay for *Novels for Students*, Gale, 1999.

Edward Sagarin

In the following excerpt, Sagarin argues that Valjean fails as a symbol of redemption because his crime—stealing a loaf of bread for his sister's children—was an act of altruism.

[What delineates Jean Valjean in *Les Misérables*] is the essential innocence of the man. If he were innocent only in the sense of having been falsely accused, his would be a different tale, and probably one with far less significance for us. Jean Valjean does indeed commit the act that sends him to the galleys and that is the beginning of his downfall. Hugo's supreme indictment of society—for this *is* an indictment of society (he was a forerunner of Zola and other novelists who saw themselves as social critics)—lies in the nature of the act which his hero has perpetrated and for which he is imprisoned. Literally, Jean Valjean is guilty of stealing a loaf of bread.

It would appear that such an act would ordinarily evoke only sympathy and hence require no further mitigation in order for an author to exculpate his "criminal" and to paint him as the purest and most saintly of all beings (one is almost compelled to use quotation marks around *criminal,* so that Hugo's relentless efforts to remind the reader of Valjean's goodness are rendered with integrity). To this end, the taking of the loaf of bread is an almost perfect transgression, and the breaking of the law is justified or at least extenuated by the forces of hunger, poverty, and the execrable social conditions that followed the counterrevolution in France. But Hugo goes even further than this, and in so doing betrays a weakness not only in the literary work but in the social criticism: it is not for himself and his own stomach that Jean Valjean commits a theft. He does not even so much as expect to taste a morsel of the stolen bread. It is for his sister's children, young, fatherless, and hungry, that he becomes a thief. So two factors are here at work, and as they follow the reader throughout the five volumes that make up this novel, they detract from each other rather than act symbiotically to strengthen the motifs: there is the social indictment, and there is the criminal as saint.

Starting with the criminal as victim, Hugo continues with the criminal (or more accurately the ex-convict) as the embodiment of virtue. He is the penitent incarnate, but he has never done wrong and has nothing for which to repent. Over and over he redeems himself. Without a blemish on his past, however, the redemption is ill-placed. What emerges, from the viewpoint of the social critic, and in contrast with other great literary images of the transgressor, is a series of unintended ambiguities, with messages not as clearly drawn as are even the one-dimensional characters who inhabit the novel.

If Jean Valjean is going to be painted as pure and saintly, and he is, the theft from the bishop and a subsequent incident with a little boy from whom he takes a coin are the blemishes—these, and not the stealing of the loaf of bread. Through the many years to follow until the last moments of his life, and through the countless pages and the episodes, coincidences, acts of strength, heroism, and sacrifice, there will be nothing but these two acts that are short of Christlike purity. What is Hugo telling us, then, when so good a person as his hero steals first from the bishop and then from the boy Gervais? That it is prison that brings out all that is worst in man, that turns the potentially best into the most wretched, that leaves one bitter and angry, seeing all humanity, even a man of God and a child, as enemy....

In the message of Hugo, it is kindness, in its most extreme and unexpected form, that alone can bring reform or even instant rehabilitation, not through guilt or expiation but through rebirth and resurrection. Love, Victor Hugo is telling us: love, and the wretched mass of humanity will be redeemed. Man is essentially good, more than good, he is pure and heavenly, he needs only to be shown the other cheek and he will embrace and kiss it, not rebuff and repel it. Jean Valjean is the embodiment of this, but how universal, or how convincing even in his own instance, is a matter of dispute....

[After Jean Valjean's encounters with the bishop and Gervais, we] are given a glimpse of a man in the process of conversion, of the forces of good and evil struggling within him, each seeking victory over the other, the classic theological battle for possession of a man's soul between the devil and God's angels....

[Hugo catches] his character in the very act of change, at the moment of duality when he is traveling from evil to good and both are present as adversary forces. He is neither one person nor the other, neither the convict hardened, gloomy, and bitter against the world nor the redeemed man who has had a vision of the beauty that resides in the good and is beckoned to it. He is neither in the pure sense, because he remains both, as anyone at a moment of change must be. For Hugo, he is one of the two persons (or personalities) in his impulses, instincts, and habits, and he is the other in the intellect which is freeing him (or seeking to do so) from the nineteen years of the constant formation of an evil self. When his intellect sees what his habits have brought him to, he recoils, he denies that it is he (the eternal evasion of responsibility, it was not I, it was something in me, something that drove me), he repents and seeks to undo the act. It is Schopenhauer's eternal enmity between the worlds of will and idea, and it is a forerunner of Freud and the struggle between the unconscious and the intellect. In Valjean, the idea and the intellect will triumph.

Now he must run, run endlessly, for as a second offender, he will, if seized, be returned to the galleys for life. Hugo implies some condemnation of the judicial and penal systems, their harshness and cruelty, but essentially they are tangential to his story and even occasionally interfere with it. The galleys are not filled with Jean Valjeans but with men whose delicts are far more serious than the theft of a loaf of bread, and there is not a great deal that Hugo has to say about these men or their conditions of servitude. Here and there a word suggests suffering and cruelty, but Hugo seems to have known little about the actual conditions prevailing for prisoners, and his book falls short as an important indictment. If it is not an example of successful rehabilitation, for there was no evil in the protagonist but only in the society that condemned him, it nevertheless contradicts the strongly believed tenet that prison itself corrupts. All that is necessary for Jean Valjean to make his way in society is to conceal that he is an exconvict and, as the event with the child makes him, a fugitive as well.

Had Valjean been a different person, or had there been others from the galleys like him, he might have symbolized what Hugo seems haltingly to be suggesting at times: the criminals are the saints, and their jailers are the sinners. But Thénardier and many others are evil criminals, and aside from Valjean himself there are none that epitomize goodness. Only one man has risen, and in the end he is one who had never fallen.

André Maurois has written glowingly of this work. He praises its literary qualities, the excellent prose, the historical frescoes (the description of the Battle of Waterloo, and a more detailed one of the barricades on the streets of Paris in 1832). It is, however, a narrow view, for while *Les Misérables* has these virtues, Maurois ignores its faults—how ill-drawn the characters are, how absurd the plot, how unsubtle the unweaving of the story, as one compares it with the works of the giants of the French novel who came just before Hugo and during his lifetime: Balzac, Stendhal, Gautier, and particularly Flaubert. But then Maurois finds in it great moral qualities, the painful quest of heroism and sanctity.... It is an interesting evaluation, and heroism and sanctity are indeed here present—frequently, selflessly, passionately, unmistakably. No reader can fail to discern the message. There is satisfaction in finding in another these qualities that one cannot attain oneself, but a reader must wish that there really were base passions in Valjean, and that he had actually conquered them and not merely overcome a momentary bitterness that arose because of the inhuman treatment he was accorded following the theft of the single loaf. If only there had been sin, there might have been redemption. Valjean never rises from the basest passions because he had never descended. The thefts of the bishop's silver plates and of the child's two-franc coin, which he sought to return: these and the loaf of bread are all that we have against him; for these he must spend a lifetime of expiation.

Yet there is expiation. I am not sure, as Maurois contends, that this is the sort of book that gives one "greater confidence in life and in himself." Maurois writes of *Les Misérables* that it speaks more to man of "his liberty than of his slavery." Yes and no, but it depends largely upon the willingness of the reader to suspend confidence in the universality of almost all other characters and utilize the hero as symbol of humanity. For Valjean does have liberty to rise, despite the pursuit by Javert, innumerable social pressures, and the social conditions that caused hunger and virtual thralldom.

Victor Hugo evidently gave great importance to the loaf of bread, and *Les Misérables* has left a legacy to the language of irony, that in the world of unequals he who steals a million dollars becomes a prime minister or an industrial tycoon while he who steals a loaf of bread ends up in prison. Jean Valjean spent nineteen years as a galley slave for his theft, about which Hugo writes in one of the passages in which he departs from his role of novelist and becomes essayist, social commentator, or historian:

> This is the second time that, during his essays on the penal question and condemnation by the law, the author of this book has come across a loaf as the starting-point of the disaster of a destiny. Claude Gueux [in the short story "*Claude Gueux*"] stole a loaf, and so did Jean Valjean, and English statistics prove that in London four robberies out of five have hunger as their immediate cause....

Here is Hugo as the critic of society: it is a world populated by prisoners of starvation, and it drives good men to crime. It is a world of cruelty and injustice, and it determines the destiny of men such as Jean Valjean. His, the author's and the hero's, is a cry from the depths of despair. Yet the message of Hugo actually is that all that is good in man cannot be destroyed by the prison air..., not *all* that is good, and not in *all* good men. It can only be driven beneath the surface as one hardens in the struggle for survival.

If this is a story, or even the story, of man rising to heights from the lowest depths, it is also a story of man seeking to escape from a past, to conceal it, to find a manner of starting life anew without pursuit from others and without the cloak that must be worn if one's stigma is to remain invisible. In the first instance, one almost wishes that the rise to heights were to places somewhat less lofty. Maurois is understating when he draws attention to the inability of the reader to fulfill a similar quest for heroism and sanctity. The fact is that Jean Valjean is just too good to be true, and this becomes literal for the reader who cannot immerse himself only in the man as symbol and wants to see him as a living person and to be confronted with greater verisimilitude with his fate.

Hugo's artistry, nonetheless, with all its shortcomings, does present us with an individual who captures our interests; very much as in the old-fashioned cinemas that were continued from week to week, as the hero or heroine hung from the cliffs while the enemy was in hot pursuit, so we read breathlessly and applaud inwardly as Jean Valjean narrowly escapes doom.

Jean Valjean is a sympathetic symbol, but more than a symbol. At times he does emerge as a meaningful personality, even if no one else in the novel has the same good fortune. As symbol, however, Valjean is never at the lowest depths, never has been, and here Hugo fails us. Essentially, Valjean was not converted, especially since his first crime had not been anything other than an act of sacrifice, of altruism, of goodness. Raskolnikov [in Dostoevsky's *Crime and Punishment*] did murder, he killed the pawnbroker and her sister with a hatchet; he planned the murder, and his was an act of baseness. And ... Lord Jim [in Conrad's *Lord Jim*] did abandon ship, as no captain or mate ever should, leaving aboard the sinking vessel the men under his command in contravention of his vows and the moral order of the sea. Moll Flanders [in Defoe's *Moll Flanders*] stole and stole and stole.

But what Hugo has given us is more of a condemnation of society (as his aside on the subject of four out of five English crimes would indicate), and for that reason his novel cannot rank as a study in human redemption. There was really no crime, or so little of one. Valjean had never been a Raskolnikov; Raskolnikov could never have been canonized by Dostoevsky.

Like Lord Jim, Jean Valjean is seeking to escape from a past, but there the analogy ends. Lord Jim never wants to be faced by anyone who has learned of his misdeed because it was an act of infamy; it is really from himself that he wishes to find refuge. An impossible task: there are no worlds without mirrors. So while Lord Jim's secret protects him from inner persecution, Valjean's secret must guard him from the outer world, for two reasons: first, because the world will demand a penalty if he is apprehended and his identity disclosed; and second, because the world will never cease condemning an exconvict.... [In the world of Hugo, man,] once condemned, is forever condemned; he may be released from the bagnes, the galleys, the walls and bars, but he remains always in prison once he has been there. There is no Christian world that forgives anyone, not even this man for whom there is nothing to forgive. One pays forever, and at best can live only by concealment. The biography is there and cannot be rewritten, but it does not have to be told, or it can be falsified (and the two are essentially one). In this sense, if there is a message that Hugo wants us to learn from the life of Jean Valjean, the book is still very much alive. Ask any exconvict, in France or the United States and probably most other countries of the world, and they will tell you that the world of Jean Valjean remains almost unchanged among us. If these exconvicts were to be sanctified, it would give them as little solace as it did Hugo's central figure, for where is the audience that would believe the glorifiers, or perform the canonization rites, except perhaps a century and a half after their death?

The departures that the author takes from his novel in order to offer social commentary often have only tangential reference to the plots and subplots of the book, but they are significant in themselves. Hugo is, as it were, reminding himself that he is writing a story of the wretched, not of one individual, and even if the two clash it does not concern him. "All the crimes of the man begin with the vagabondage of the lad," he states..., although it was hardly true of Jean Valjean and there is little evidence of it in the criminal underworld elements with whom Valjean comes into contact at certain points in his adventures.

A passage that refers to the underworld, the literal criminal underworld though it might be equally applicable to the world of fear of exposure in which Jean Valjean lives, summarizes perhaps as well as any in this novel what Hugo has to say about crime:

> The social evil is darkness; humanity is identity, for all men are of the same clay, and in this nether world, at least, there is no difference in predestination; we are the same shadow before, the same flesh during, and the same ashes afterward; but ignorance, mixed with the human paste, blackens it, and this incurable blackness enters man and becomes Evil there....

It is more than Jean Valjean that Hugo is discussing when he writes that the social evil is darkness, it is humanity. If only humanity could accept the brotherhood of man, know that we come from nothing and will return to nothing, that the short time between need not be wretched for the millions of poor, *les misérables,* then we could live in harmony and love on earth. Have no illusions: we are not predestined, Calvinism notwithstanding, to eternal damnation or endless bliss. We all have the same future, the darkness of the grave, and if we could lift ourselves from the ignorance that does not accept this, we could bring light into a world of somber shadows. This is Hugo's hope for salvation, but it is a meager hope, and in the end only Jean Valjean finds this salvation, only one unusual soul among millions of ordinary folk. Our sins are greater than thefts of loaves of bread for the hungry and the young, and we will not be able to fulfill en masse the hopes that Hugo expresses so eloquently in this passage.

Source: Edward Sagarin, "Jean Valjean: For Stealing a Loaf of Bread," in his *Raskolnikov and Others: Literary Images of Crime, Punishment, Redemption, and Atonement*, St. Martin's Press, 1981, pp. 60-76.

The Southern Literary Messenger

In the following excerpt from a review of Part I of the novel, in contrast to most critics of the period following the initial publication of Les Misérables, *this anonymous reviewer gives the novel unqualified praise.*

[Les Misérables] is the greatest and most elaborate work of Victor Hugo's fruitful genius.... A novel, in the ordinary acceptation of that term, [Fantine] is *not.* The ordinary novel, according to Carlyle, is a "tale of adventures which did *not* occur in God's creation, but only in the Waste Chambers, (to be let unfurnished,) of certain human heads, and which are part and parcel of the Sum of

No-things; which, nevertheless, obtain some temporary remembrance, and lodge extensively, at this epoch of the world, in similar still more unfurnished chambers." These productions have wonderful plots and still more wonderful machinery. *Fantine* has simply dramatic situations, and therefore *Fantine* is no novel. *They* are remarkable for many words and few ideas; every page of *Fantine* contains some beautiful thought, poetically expressed, or some brilliant passage upon Life, Law, Religion, or Philosophy; hence *Fantine* is not a novel. People with waste chambers, (to let unfurnished,) need not read it; it was never written for them. But to the thinker it will be a solace and delight, albeit its lessons may excite some saddened reflections in sympathetic minds.

We have stated that *Fantine* had not the plot of the ordinary novel; but dramatic situations, instead. Let us add, that the work is composed of a series of brilliant pictures, boldly touched off by a master-hand, as in the case of the great works of Niccola Poussin and Claude Loraine.... There is not in the literature of fiction a finer portraiture than that given of [M. Charles François Bienvenu Myriel, Bishop of D—]. His every trait of character, objective and psychological, is elaborately depicted. It is, for several pages of the book, a lone sketch, nothing to heighten the interest thereof save two old virtuous ladies of his household; who are about as important to the theme, as the occasional and indifferent tree in some of Raphael's paintings. It is quite as powerful and much more elaborate, yet not quite so fearful or mysterious, but far more genial and beautiful in type than, Byron's grand portrait of *Lara;* and equally well sustained in power throughout. But the character of Lara is dark and gloomy; that of M. Myriel radiant with spiritual beauty. We are permitted to look, not only upon the objective form and actions of the man, but as if his mind were spread open to view, we have a full revelation of his psychology—we gaze into the divine depths of his immortal soul. Indeed so beautiful is the moral portraiture of that simple but good man, that one of our contemporaries has pronounced such a being an impossibility! We cannot think so—and if mistaken, our historic lessons, standard of ideal virtue, and belief in the true, beautiful and good, must have rested upon shifting sands.... But conceding the supposed fact, that we err—surely it is highly creditable to the genius of M. Hugo, that out of the depths of his contemplation he could create an Ideal Character, so perfect as to be an impossibility in humanity; a concession which, however, must greatly reflect upon, and detract from, the boasted grandeur of the human soul.

But, be this as it may, two personages of opposite opinions are brought in contact with the Bishop—one, a Senator, and the other, a Conventioner, persecuted by the ruling power which succeeded to the French Revolution. The former is a kind of little Atheist—a scoffer at the established forms of religion, after the manner of Voltaire. The latter is a bold intellectualist; a master of the syllogistic forms of logic; a dogmatic denunciator of legitimacy and royalty; and a mystic in Deism. In detailing the particulars of M. Myriel's interviews with these men, Victor Hugo has carried to its highest point of delicacy, that civilization in Art, which pervades modern French authorship. The Atheist's sneers against revealed religion, is treated with respectful silence, or returned only with Christian pity. The bold sallies and loud declamations of the old Conventioner, are met with pastoral humility until he is half subdued. And when death is about to close his eyes, the good Bishop is his only friend—the only witnesser of his spirit's flight. It is as if the Lion had made of the Lamb its confidant and friend. This is the place to remark, however, that Senator and Conventioner, are simply machinery whereby lessons upon life, history, and morality are promulged; as with many of the seemingly nonessential characters in Goethe's *Faust....*

[We] do not hesitate to pronounce [*Les Misérables*] the ablest novel—after Goethe's *Welhelm Meister*—of this century.

Certain supercilious young gentlemen, of most questionable principles, and certain publicists of still more questionable morals, think it fashionable and brilliant to decry *Les Misérables* as an immoral book; simply because they have not the brains to understand it. To us, it is a Bible in the fictitious literature of the nineteenth century. To them, it is merely a translation of a French novel; and all France is but *their* second Sodom: we know that France is *not* morally worse than America. To them, it is a production by Victor Hugo; to us it is a protest of genius against universal crimes—the plea of one who advocates, in the face of obloquy and contumely, the cause of the Life-Wretched. To them, it is a proclamation of war against society; to us, it is a grand sermon in behalf of primitive Christianity—a splendid endeavour to have Christendom permeated by the rules and regulations of the "Church and House Book of the Early Christians," and of the "Law-Book of the Ante-Nicene Church." To them, it is massive, grand, unusual, and incomprehensible; to us, it is beautiful as the *Iliad* of Homer—real as a play by Shakespeare. *Les Misérables* is an event—it is a new jewel in the literary crown of our century....

[*Les Misérables*] should awaken the conscience of society from its dismal lethargy of evil. For it is profound, straight-forward, and marvelously eloquent. "But then, it is a French novel"—say its critics. So much the better, is our response; because it is greater than all of the English novels, gathered together and massed into one, which have appeared during the past quarter of a century. "But," repeat its critics, "it contains exaggerations." No doubt of it; we admit the fact. But are there not exaggerations in all novels? Was there ever one printed that contained them not? Are there not ... more absurdities and vulgar caricatures in [Dickens's] *Great Expectations,* than there could be found in so many of such books as *Les Misérables,* as would sink the Great Eastern? *A French novel!* Is this phrase used as a term of reproach, applicable to the literature of the most civilized and cultivated empire upon the globe? If so, is the novel, or its ignorant assailant, to be blamed—and which? Why the latter. Who is the French Novelist, and what is the French Novel? The one, is a scholar of genius and refinement; the other, a reflex of life and society. What English writers—what American writers—can be compared with such authors, in points of power and art, as Victor Hugo, Alfred de Musset, Alphonse Karr, Edmund About, Emile Souvestre, Octave Feuillet, Alexandre Dumas, Michelet and Sue? Here are no contortionists—no forced humorists—no retailers of vulgar and far-fetched wit—no writers of dreary, idealess wilderness-pages; but gentlemen of power, large and well digested observation, polished wit, noble satire, keen irony, and great Philosophy.... [To] such as find fault with Hugo's humble characters, we would say: first remove Reynold's Dunghill, or clean out Dickens's Augean stables. If they think that the Frenchman crushes society, why, let them the more enjoy Thackeray's crunching and mastication of it. Or if they dislike Jean Valjean, because he was a reformed criminal, then let them revel in the irreclaimable hideousness of Bulwer's Villains. For there are no graceless scamps or vagabonds in the chambers of M. Hugo's mind. His most infamous creation has some principle of homogeneity left; but the vagabond of one

English novel, like the sinner of Jonathan Edwards' theology, is past redemption. In short, the French novel is civilization; the English novel affectation—semi-nude barbarism. It is not, however, much to the credit of our vaunted enlightenment, that the greatest of recent Fictions—this very *Les Misérables*—should have been but poorly received by the press.... [It] is safe to say, at the least, that another so grandly brilliant a book, of its class, will not appear in the lifetime of the youngest of this generation!

Source: T.W.M., in a review of "Les Misérables—Fantine," in *The Southern Literary Messenger,* July, 1863, pp. 434-46.

Sources

Victor Brombert, *Victor Hugo and the Visionary Novel,* Harvard University Press, 1984.

Matthew Josephson, *Victor Hugo: A Realistic Biography of the Great Romantic,* Doubleday, 1942.

Joanna Richardson, *Victor Hugo,* St. Martin's Press, 1976.

For Further Study

Elliot Grant, *The Career of Victor Hugo,* Harvard University Press, 1945.
　　A very basic and useful study of Hugo's main novels and poetry.

Richard B. Grant, *The Perilous Quest: Image, Myth, and Prophecy in the Narration of Victor Hugo,* Duke University Press, 1968.
　　Hugo described himself as a "prophet" among men, as a translator of myths. This book analyzes this theme by examining Hugo's major novels.

Kathryn M. Grossman, *Les Misérables: Conversion, Revolution, Redemption,* Twayne, 1996.
　　Aimed specifically toward students, this work praises the novel as a book that "enables us to escape into the adventures of others: it brings us back to ourselves."

John Porter Houston, *Victor Hugo,* Twayne, 1988.
　　A good introduction to Hugo's life and works.

Patricia Ward, *The Medievalism of Victor Hugo,* Pennsylvania State University Press, 1975.
　　Hugo was fascinated by the mysteries and secrets of medieval times. Although *Les Misérables* cannot really be called a Gothic novel, some of its episodes, like those in the sewers, belong to the genre.

One Hundred Years of Solitude

Gabriel García Márquez

1967

In the mid-1960s, journalist and fiction writer Gabriel José García Márquez was little known outside his native Colombia, having never sold more than seven hundred copies of a book. Everything changed, however, after he had a sudden insight while driving his family through Mexico. In an instant, he saw that the key to the imaginary village of Macondo he had been creating in short vignettes was the storytelling technique of his grandmother—absolute brick-faced description of extraordinary events. He turned the car around and drove straight home, where he proceeded directly to a back room. There he wrote while his wife, Mercedes Barcha, sold, mortgaged, and stretched credit to keep the family going. Gradually the entire neighborhood was involved in helping to bring forth what has since been recognized as a masterpiece. After eighteen months, a hefty tome of thirteen hundred pages was sent to the publishers. The result was *Cien años de soledad,* later translated into English as *One Hundred Years of Solitude.* The first printings sold out before they could be shelved. Today, the novel has been translated into more than thirty languages and there are a number of pirated editions. The exceptional achievement of *One Hundred Years of Solitude* was highlighted in the citation awarding García Márquez the 1982 Nobel Prize in Literature.

Often compared to William Faulkner's Yoknapatawpha County in its scope and quality, García Márquez's Macondo is revealed in several of the author's short stories and novels. The most central of these is *One Hundred Years of Solitude,* which relates the history of several generations of the Buendía family, the founders of this imaginary Colombian town. Interwoven with their personal struggles are events that recall the political, social, and economic turmoil of a hundred years of Latin American history. In addition to establishing the reputation of its author, *One Hundred Years of Solitude* was a key work in the "Boom" of Latin American literature of the 1960s. The worldwide acclaim bestowed upon the novel led to a discovery by readers and critics of other Latin American practitioners of "magical realism." This genre combines realistic portrayals of political and social conflicts with descriptions of mystical, even supernatural events. García Márquez is known as one of its foremost practitioners, although he claims that everything in his fiction has a basis in reality. Nevertheless, it is his inventive portrayals of his homeland which have made him one of the most acclaimed writers in the modern world.

Gabriel García Márquez holding the Nobel Prize.

Author Biography

In 1928, the year when more than one hundred local strikers were massacred, García Márquez was born in Aracataca, Colombia. His first years were spent with a large extended family in his grandfather's house in Aracataca. This environment contributed greatly to his future career as a writer. His grandfather, Colonel Nicolás Ricardo Márquez Mejía, took him to the circus, told him stories, and admonished him against listening to the tales of women. His grandmother, Tranquilina Iguarán de Márquez, told him fantastically superstitious stories with such a deadpan style that he was more often scared than not. It was this style that the author used to such great success in his masterpiece, *One Hundred Years of Solitude.* After his grandfather died, García Márquez went to live in Sucre, Colombia, with his parents, telegraph operator Gabriel Eligio García (a Conservative frowned on by the family) and Luisa Santiaga Márquez de García.

He won a scholarship to the Liceo Nacional de Zipaquirá, a high school near Bogotá. He then entered the National University in the capital city of Bogotá to study law. After liberal political leader Jorge Gaitán was assassinated in 1948, civil war broke out and he had to transfer to the University of Cartagena. Disliking law and encouraged by the writing of Franz Kafka (especially *Metamorphosis*), he took up writing. He left school and began working for several newspapers, including *El Espectador* in Bogotá.

A 1955 serialization of a shipwrecked Colombian almost brought García Márquez journalistic fame. The journalist's account of the sailor's story, however, scandalized the government. Fearing reprisal, the newspaper's editors sent him to Europe but military dictator General Gustavo Rojas Pinilla shut down the *El Espectador* for other reasons. Bereft of his steady source of income, García Márquez worked as a freelance writer in Paris. Meanwhile, friends rescued his novella *La hojarasca* (translated as *Leaf Storm*) from a drawer. Published in 1955, it drew little attention. Although Rojas stepped down in 1957, it was still unsafe for the journalist to return home. He moved to Caracas, Venezuela, and, in 1958, he married the "the most interesting person" he had ever met: Mercedes Barcha, whom he first encountered in 1946, when she was thirteen. Their first child, Rodrigo, was born in 1959; their second, Gonzalo, in 1962.

In 1959, García Márquez went to Cuba, where he befriended its socialist leader, Fidel Castro. He set up *Prensa Latina,* a Cuban press agency, in Bogotá, and reported for them from Cuba and New York. (These Cuban connections later caused visa problems for García Márquez with America as

Cuban-American relations soured.) García Márquez then settled in Mexico City in 1961, where he worked in film and advertising. Finally solving his Macondo puzzle in 1965, he sequestered himself for eighteen months and emerged with *One Hundred Years of Solitude*. After its success, the family moved to Barcelona, Spain, where his study of Spanish dictator Francisco Franco contributed to the 1975 novel *El otoño del patriarca* (translated as *The Autumn of the Patriarch*). After that novel, García Márquez swore he would be silent until Chilean dictator Augusto Pinochet, leader of a military coup against the elected government in 1973, stepped down. Fortunately, he recanted; subsequent novels, including *Crónica del muerte anunciada* (1981, translated as *Chronicle of a Death Foretold*), *El amor en los tiempos del cólera* (1985, translated as *Love in the Time of Cholera*), and *El general en su laberinto* (1989, translated as *The General in His Labyrinth*), were published to great acclaim.

In 1982 the exiled native son was awarded the Nobel Prize and was welcomed home to Colombia with honors. Currently, he divides his time between Mexico City and Bogotá and continues to write fiction, nonfiction, and screenplays, as well as a weekly news column.

Plot Summary

The Founding of Macondo

One Hundred Years of Solitude by Gabriel García Márquez tells the story of the Buendía family and the fictional town of Macondo. The first part of the book's opening line, "Many years later, as he faced the firing squad, Colonel Aureliano Buendía was to remember that distant afternoon when his father took him to discover ice," serves to catapult the reader into the future, while the second phrase pushes the reader into the past. From this point onward, however, the book moves in fairly straight forward chronological order, with only occasional forays into the past or the future.

The first chapter introduces José Arcadio Buendía, the founder of Macondo; his wife, Úrsula; and the gypsy Melquíades, who brings inventions to Macondo. José Arcadio and Úrsula also have two sons introduced in the opening chapter. The older, José Arcadio, is large, strong, and physically precocious. The younger child, Aureliano, is quiet, solitary, and clairvoyant.

One of the more difficult features of the book is that the characters share the same names. That is, in each generation of Buendías, there are characters named José Arcadio and Aureliano, just as there are female characters called Remedios, Amaranta, and Úrsula. The characters named alike share similar characteristics. For example, the Arcadios are physically strong and active, while the Aurelianos are intellectual, with some psychic ability.

The early chapters also introduce the village of Macondo and its founding. In the days before the founding of Macondo, José Arcadio and Úrsula (who are cousins) marry. However, Úrsula fears that the result of incest will be the birth of a child with a pig's tail. Consequently, she is opposed to consummating their marriage. When Prudencio Aguilar announces to the town that José Arcadio's masculinity is suspect, it results in two things: first, José Arcadio consummates the marriage in spite of Úrsula's protests; and second, he kills Prudencio Aguilar. The dead man continues to visit the Buendías until they decide to leave their town and start anew by founding the town of Macondo.

The Growth of Macondo

In the beginning, the town is young; it is a place where no one is over thirty years old and no one has died yet. Except for occasional visits from Melquíades and his troop of gypsies, the three hundred inhabitants of Macondo are completely isolated from the rest of the world. Although José Arcadio leads a band of townspeople on a mission to try to establish contact with the outside world, he is unsuccessful. Later, Úrsula sets off to find her son José Arcadio, who has unexpectedly run away with the gypsies. Although Úrsula does not find her son, she finds a route to another town, connecting Macondo to the world. As a result, people begin to arrive in Macondo, including a governmental representative, Don Apolinar Moscote. Aureliano falls in love with Apolinar's beautiful child, Remedios.

Another new arrival to the town is the orphan Rebeca. The family adopts her and raises her as a sister to their daughter Amaranta and grandson Arcadio, the missing José's illegitimate son by Pilar Ternera. Meanwhile, the village contracts a plague of insomnia and memory loss. The people of Macondo resort to placing signs everywhere to remind themselves of the names of things. Of course, they also forget how to read. Through the intervention of Melquíades (who died in the previous chapter, only to return because he was bored) the town is saved.

Not only does Melquíades return from the dead, the ghost of Prudencio Aguilar returns to keep José Arcadio company. José Arcadio is overcome with nostalgia and goes mad. Úrsula ties him to a tree in the courtyard, where he remains, speaking in a language that no one understands.

After the insomnia plague, another outsider, Pietro Crespi, arrives. He comes to Macondo to give music lessons. Both Rebeca and Amaranta fall in love with him; the result of this love is tragedy as the two women engage in plots and revenge. Even after Rebeca rejects Pietro in favor of the returned José Arcadio, there is bad blood between the two women.

Another tragic love story is that of Aureliano and Remedios. Although no more than a child, Remedios is engaged to Aureliano. He waits patiently for her to mature enough so that they can marry. They do so, but the marriage is short-lived; little Remedios dies of blood poisoning during her first pregnancy.

After Remedios' death, Aureliano becomes Colonel Aureliano Buendía, a soldier for the Liberal Party and a leader in a civil war between the Liberals and the Conservatives. The Colonel loses all of his battles, but seems to live a charmed life otherwise. He survives numerous assassination attempts and one suicide attempt, fathers seventeen sons with seventeen different women, and becomes Commander-in-Chief of the revolutionary forces. In a return to the opening sentence of the novel, the colonel faces a firing squad, but is not killed.

The Buendías at War

The middle portion of the book includes accounts of the seemingly endless civil wars and of the activities of Aureliano Segundo and José Arcadio Segundo, the twin sons of the late Arcadio. When the wars are finally over, Colonel Aureliano Buendía retires to his home, where he leads a solitary life making little gold fishes. His solitude increases and he is overcome with nostalgia and memories. After recalling once again the day that his father took him to see ice, he dies.

Meanwhile, Americans arrive in the prospering town of Macondo to farm bananas. The farm workers eventually launch a strike against the American company, protesting their living conditions. Soldiers arrive and slaughter some three thousand workers. José Arcadio Segundo is present at the slaughter and narrowly escapes with his life. When he attempts to find out more about the massacre, however, he discovers that no one knows that

it even happened. No one has any memory of the event except for himself, and no one will believe that it really occurred. Likewise, the official governmental account of the event is accepted: "There was no dead, the satisfied workers had gone back to their families, and the banana company was suspending all activity until the rains stopped."

The Decline of Macondo

The rains, however, do not stop. Instead, they continue for another four years, eleven months, and two days. Over this time, the rain washes away much of Macondo. When it clears, Úrsula, the last of the original Buendías, dies. She takes with her the memories of the founding of the town and the relationships among people. This failure of memory leads to the union of Amaranta Úrsula, great-great-granddaughter of the original José Arcadio Buendía, to Aureliano, great-great-great grandson of the same man. Aureliano, the bastard child of Amaranta Úrsula's sister Meme, had been raised by the family since his birth. Nevertheless, only his grandparents, Fernanda and Aureliano Segundo, knew the secret of his parentage. His match with Amaranta Úrsula recalls the original Úrsula's fear of incest: the marriage of one of her aunts to one of her cousins led to the birth of a child with the tail of a pig. Likewise, Amaranta Úrsula's relationship with her nephew Aureliano results in the birth of a child with the tail of pig, thus bringing the story of the Buendías full circle.

In the closing chapter, Amaranta Úrsula dies giving birth, and her son is left in the street, to be devoured by ants, due to the carelessness of Aureliano. Aureliano's reaction is surprising:

> And then he saw the child. It was a dry and bloated bag of skin that all the ants in the world were dragging towards their holes along the stone path in the garden. Aureliano could not move. Not because he was paralyzed by horror but because at that prodigious instant Melquíades' final keys were revealed to him and he saw the epigraph of the parchments perfection placed in the order of man's time and space: *The first of the line is tied to a tree and the last is being eaten by the ants.*

In the final pages of the novel, Aureliano finally is able to read the manuscripts left by Melquíades years earlier. As he does so, he realizes that what he is reading is the story of his family. As he finishes the text, a giant wind sweeps away the town of Macondo, erasing it from time, space, and memory.

Characters

Mauricio Babilonia

Always accompanied by yellow butterflies, Mauricio gains access to Meme through the roof over the bathtub, where a man once fell to his death watching Remedios the Beauty. He is mistaken as a chicken thief one night by a guard set by Fernanda and shot. Paralyzed, he dies "of old age in solitude."

Amaranta Buendía

Daughter of Úrsula and José Arcadio Buendía, Amaranta is a lively girl until she discovers that her foster sister Rebeca has won the heart of Pietro Crespi. She becomes bitter and withdraws into solitude, doing all she can to prevent Rebeca's wedding. Even after Rebeca forsakes Pietro for José Arcadio, she continues holding grudges against both of them. She allows Pietro to woo her, only to drive him to suicide when she ultimately rejects him. She thrusts her hand into burning coals with remorse, and the black bandage she wears from that day serves as a symbol of her solitude. Instead of accepting the love of Pietro or Gerineldo Márquez, she indulges in furtive, incestuous gropings with her nephew, Aureliano José. She dies a virgin.

Amaranta Úrsula Buendía

A fifth-generation Buendía and daughter of Fernanda and Aureliano Segundo, Amaranta Úrsula finishes her education in Belgium. There she marries a rich aviator named Gaston. She returns home to find only Aureliano left at the house. Unaware that he is her nephew, she begins a secret relationship with him. When Gaston leaves, the two give in to their passion and live as husband and wife until she dies in childbirth.

Colonel Aureliano Buendía

The second son of Úrsula is Colonel Aureliano, who begins the story and remains in the limelight almost until the book's climax. He is a quiet boy who takes to the alchemical laboratory with enthusiasm and becomes a wealthy silversmith famed for his little golden fishes. Born into the world "with his eyes open," he has premonitions throughout his life. These later enable him to avoid several assassination attempts. He becomes a man of action after the execution of the Liberal agitator Dr. Noguera, when the soldiers become downright abusive of innocent citizens. Seeing enough abuse, Colonel Aureliano gathers twenty-one men and declares war on the Conservatives. He starts and loses thirty-two wars. While on the warpath he has seventeen sons by seventeen different women, in addition to his son by Pilar Ternera. (His wife Remedios, with whom he fell in love when she was nine, dies during her first pregnancy.) At the height of his power, he stands with a chalk circle marked around him, where no one may enter. He dies while urinating against the tree where his father was tied up. Colonel Aureliano is forever "stupefying himself with the deception of war and the little gold fishes."

Aureliano José Buendía

The son of Colonel Aureliano by Pilar Ternera, the second Aureliano is adopted by Amaranta after she blames herself for the accidental death of little Remedios. He awakens to manhood while in the bath with her. When their caresses threaten Amaranta's virginity, he leaves with his father but returns years later "sturdy as a horse, as dark and long-haired as an Indian, and with a secret determination to marry Amaranta." His death comes when he ignores Pilar's pleas to stay indoors and goes to the theater. While attempting to flee from the soldiers searching for revolutionaries, he is shot in the back by Captain Aquiles Ricardo. In return, the Captain is filled with bullets discharged by a line of four hundred townsmen.

Aureliano Segundo Buendía

The third Aureliano is one of the twin sons of Arcadio and Santa Sofía de la Piedad. Aureliano Segundo is a glutton who holds wild parties and bathes in champagne. The passion he shares with his mistress Petra Cotes overflows to ensure he is rich in animals and money. He is mostly good humored and tells his livestock, "Cease, cows, life is short." In answer to family criticisms, he papers the entire house with monetary notes. He brings Fernanda del Carpio home as his lawful wife but he lives with Petra Cotes. He moves home during the rains, but after they cease he returns to Petra. The rains bring ruin and poverty, during which he and Petra discover true love with each other. Unfortunately, Aureliano falls ill at this time, but he manages to collect enough money to send Amaranta Úrsula to school in Belgium before he dies.

Aureliano Buendía (IV)

Son of Meme and Mauricio Babilonia, Aureliano is a sixth-generation Buendía and a bastard. Due to his scandalous birth, he grows up in deeper solitude than the rest of the family. He is kept in a single room for the first few years of life, and never leaves the house until he is grown. His occupation is learning all that is required to translate Melquíades's manuscript. He winds up being the sole occupant of the house when Amaranta Úrsula and Gaston arrive from Belgium. Unaware that Amaranta Úrsula is his aunt, he falls in love with her. He ignores the Catalonian bookseller's recommendation to leave the city and thus witnesses its demise. As a hurricane approaches to wipe out the city, Aureliano translates the manuscript.

Aureliano Buendía (V)

The child of Aureliano and Amaranta Úrsula survives his mother's death. The last Buendía has realized Úrsula's fear of the family's inbreeding—he has a pig's tail. Left on the floor by his grieving father, the child is eaten by the ants that have taken over the house. The vision stupefies Aureliano because it presents the key to understanding the parchments of Melquíades: "The first of the line is tied to a tree and the last is being eaten by the ants." With this key, he quickly takes up the parchments which, like the baby's skin, are slowly being obliterated.

José Arcadio Buendía

José Arcadio is the patriarch of the family and founder of the town of Macondo. After he marries his cousin Úrsula, he becomes a subject of amusement in their hometown of Riohacha because people believe she is still a virgin. After a cockfight, he takes his spear and kills Prudencio Aguilar because of his insults. With this original sin on their conscience, the first Buendía couple ventures into the wilderness with some followers to found a new city. This "New World" begins as a paradise where death is unknown. Melquíades the gypsy introduces "science" to the town, and later death when he inhabits the first grave. But by then, José Arcadio is too busy "searching for the mythical truth of the great inventions" with the toys he wastefully purchased from the visiting gypsies. Eventually, José Arcadio goes mad and speaks only Latin after the reappearance of Prudencio Aguilar's ghost; the family must tie him to the chestnut tree.

José Arcadio Buendía (II)

The first son of Úrsula, José Arcadio "was so well-equipped for life that he seemed abnormal." His hormones drive him to the bed of Pilar Ternera, who conceives Arcadio. Not wanting to face fatherhood, José Arcadio leaves with the gypsies. He travels the world and returns as a giant, illustrated from head to toe. His foster sister Rebeca

Media Adaptations

- One Hundred Years of Solitude has been adapted for the stage as *Blood and Champagne. One Hundred Years of Solitude: A Study Guide,* by Brenda K. Marshall, is available on audio cassette. Read by F. Murray Abraham, it includes dramatic readings from the novel.

finds him irresistible, and they marry shortly after his return. When the soldiers put his brother against the cemetery wall for execution, José Arcadio steps out with guns drawn. Captain Carnicero thanks him for intervening and then joins Colonel Aureliano's forces. Shortly thereafter, José Arcadio is shot to death in his own bedroom by an unknown person.

Arcadio Buendía

See José Arcadio Buendía (III)

José Arcadio Buendía (III)

The illegitimate son of José Arcadio (II) and Pilar Ternera is known simply as Arcadio. Arcadio suffers from not having a father who acknowledges him. Although raised by the Buendía family, he never believes he is one of them. He is taught reading and silversmithing by Colonel Aureliano, and receives some attention from Melquíades. But when Melquíades dies, he becomes a "solitary and frightened child." He is a bit of monster. Not knowing that Pilar Ternera is his mother, he demands to have sex with her. She tricks him and tells him to leave his door unlocked. Then she pays half of her life savings to Santa Sofía de la Piedad to be his lover. Colonel Aureliano makes him civil and military leader of the town. He abuses his position until Úrsula attacks him with a whip. He is executed by the Conservatives when they retake Macondo.

José Arcadio Segundo Buendía (IV)

The twin of Aureliano Segundo, José Arcadio Segundo becomes a foreman for the Banana Company. For this association, his sister-in-law Fernanda bars him from the house. The working conditions, however, lead him to side with the workers and he is part of their last fatal demonstration. The only survivor, he can convince no one that over three thousand men, women, and children were murdered. When the soldiers hunt him down he hides in the room of Melquíades's manuscript. There he remains for the rest of his life, pausing only to pass on what he knows to Aureliano (IV), who then takes his place in the room.

José Arcadio Buendía (V)

Fernanda has decided that her son, José Arcadio, will become the Pope. Accordingly, he is sent away to school and then to Rome. From Rome he writes about theology but he is actually living in a garret and waiting for his inheritance. When Fernanda dies, he returns to a nearly empty house. He expects to find money, but instead finds a letter where Fernanda tells him the truths left out of her letters. He is murdered by four children whom he had used as bodyservants and then expelled from the house.

Meme Buendía

See Renata Remedios Buendía

Rebeca Buendía

She is the daughter of parents who are supposedly related, but are nevertheless unknown to the Buendía family. She carries their bones in a bag when she is dropped off at the house with a rocking chair. The family adopts her and she is raised as a sister to Amaranta. She sucks her fingers, eats dirt and whitewash, and is "rebellious and strong in spite of her frailness." Her engagement to Pietro Crespi starts a feud with Amaranta. When José Arcadio shows up in all his hugeness, however, she marries him instead and turns him into a laboring man. She is happy until he is killed and she returns to dirt and whitewash, forgotten by all except Amaranta. Amaranta prays for Rebeca to die first and spends her days sewing Rebeca's shroud, but Rebeca outlasts her and dies alone in her house.

Remedios Buendía

A fourth-generation Buendía, Remedios is the daughter of Arcadio and Santa Sofía de la Piedad. Remedios the Beauty serves as the femme fatale of the novel, as her beauty kills a number of suitors. People think she is either stupid or innocent, for she often shrugs off civilized behavior and walks around the house naked. One day, while hanging sheets up to dry, she ascends to heaven.

Remedios the Beauty

See Remedios Buendía

Renata Remedios Buendía

Meme is the daughter of Fernanda and Aureliano Segundo. Although she seems to accept her mother's plans for her life, she is a rebel who more closely resembles her father. Unlike the rest of the Buendías, "Meme still did not reveal the solitary fate of the family and she seemed entirely in conformity with the world." She loves a mechanic named Mauricio Babilonia, with whom she has the bastard Aureliano (IV). For her sin she is banished to a convent, where she lives out her days in silence and solitude.

Úrsula Iguarán Buendía

Úrsula is the Buendía matriarch who even in death "fought against the laws of creation to maintain the [family] line." She is obsessed with the idea that a son begotten with José Arcadio (a near cousin) will have a pig's tail. Nevertheless, she has three children without the feared tail. When her husband José Arcadio loses himself in his scientific experiments, Úrsula starts a candy pastry business that makes the family rich and gives them a grand house. When her firstborn disappears, she searches for him but brings back immigrants instead. Through such luck, she succeeds in making the town prosper. Throughout her one hundred fifteen-plus years she rules the family—even disciplining her ruthless dictator sons. Her long life gives her insight that time is a wheel, for events keep repeating themselves. She becomes blind, but knows her house and her family so well that nobody notices—though her manner of walking around with her "archangelic arm" out is curious. Gradually she shrinks and becomes a plaything for her great-great-grandchildren.

Fernanda del Carpio de Buendía

Fernanda is the daughter of a fallen nobleman, who has been raised to believes she is a queen. As the "most beautiful of the five thousand most beautiful women in the land," Fernanda is brought Macondo to be "Queen of Madagascar" at the carnival. Aureliano Segundo makes her his wife, but he keeps a mistress and nobody else in the family likes her. She tries to rule the house but succeeds only when Amaranta dies. She is a bitter woman with a mysterious illness, so she corresponds with "invisible doctors" who eventually attempt "telepathic surgery." Unable to direct their telepathy properly—because in her prudishness she was never able to properly describe the location of her problems (uterine)—they are unable to cure her and cease corresponding. She is forever praying, keeping up appearances, and keeping to her extraordinary family planning calendar. In the end, she dies wearing her queen costume. Her son finds her body four months later with no signs of putrefaction.

Petra Cotes

The lover of Aureliano Segundo, she makes money by raffling off animals. She causes Aureliano Segundo's animals to reproduce at an incredible rate. After he dies, she secretly helps Fernanda keep food on the table.

Bruno Crespi

Pietro invites his brother Bruno to help him with his business. Bruno manages the whole affair while Pietro pursues first Rebeca and then Amaranta. Eventually, Bruno inherits the works, marries Amparo Moscote, and opens a theater where all the national hits perform.

Pietro Crespi

"The most handsome and well-mannered man who had ever been seen in Macondo," Pietro Crespi comes to the house to set up the pianola. He settles in Macondo and opens a shop of wonderful mechanical toys and instruments. He wants to marry Rebeca but the jealous Amaranta declares she will kill her first. When Rebeca marries her foster brother José Arcadio, Pietro turns to Amaranta, who encourages and then refuses him. On All Souls' Day his body is found amidst a racket of clocks and music boxes, a suicide.

Colonel Gerineldo Márquez

Colonel Márquez is Colonel Aureliano's right hand man. When he is placed in charge of the city, he spends his afternoons wooing Amaranta She refuses him too.

Melquíades

Melquíades is the death-defying, plague-exposed, all-knowing King of the Gypsies. He introduces science and death to Macondo, and gives the first José Arcadio an alchemical laboratory. When he eventually dies, he haunts a room in the Buendía household, where he helps successive members of the family with his manuscript. The last adult Aureliano (IV) discovers that the manuscript is the history of the family—and his decoding of it is the novel.

General José Raquel Moncada

General Moncada is the leader of the Conservative forces who becomes great friends with his adversary Colonel Aureliano. After the war, he succeeds in making the city a municipality and himself the first mayor of Macondo. Despite overseeing "the best government we've ever had in Macondo," he is executed by Colonel Aureliano when the next war breaks out.

Don Apolinar Moscote

Apolinar Moscote is sent by the government to be magistrate in the town of Macondo. He arrives quietly and begins to exert control. When he demands all houses be painted blue, José Arcadio—the founder of the city—ushers him out. When Apolinar returns with soldiers and his family, José Arcadio says he and his family are welcome but the soldiers must leave and the people can paint what color they chose. Apolinar complies but eventually introduces more government control and then becomes a figurehead for the army captain.

Remedios Moscote de Buendía

The first Remedios is the daughter of the first city magistrate. Colonel Aureliano falls in love with her when she is only nine, and chooses her for his wife. She becomes a promising young woman who takes care of José Arcadio (I) and even speaks a little Latin with him. She is killed by the blood poisoning during her first pregnancy, and Amaranta feels responsible because she had hoped for something to postpone Rebeca's wedding. The daguerreotype of fourteen-year-old Remedios becomes a shrine for the family.

Father Nicanor

Father Nicanor uses a levitation trick to attract people's attention and purses to the building of a new church. He discovers José Arcadio Buendía's mysterious language is Latin and tries to convert him until José Arcadio's "rationalist tricks" disturb his faith.

Nigromanta

Nigromanta is the last Aureliano's mistress. When Amaranta Úrsula dies and he gets horribly drunk, she "rescued him from a pool of vomit and tears." She cleans him up, takes him home, and erases the number of "loves" he owes her.

Dr. Alirio Noguera

Quack doctor Alirio Noguera is a revolutionary recruiter. He hopes to place people throughout the nation who will rise up and kill all the conservatives. He tries to convert Colonel Aureliano. His execution disturbs Colonel Aureliano because it lacked due process.

Santa Sofía de la Piedad

When her lover Arcadio dies, Santa Sofía moves in with the family and helps Úrsula with her candy pastry business. She is regarded as a servant by Fernanda and often sleeps on a mat in the kitchen. She is the mother of Remedios the Beauty, Aureliano Segundo, and José Arcadio Segundo. She "dedicated a whole life of solitude and diligence to the rearing of children," whether they were hers or not. After Úrsula dies, Santa Sofía loses her capacity for work and leaves the house, never to be heard from again.

Pilar Ternera

Priestess of the city and second matriarch, she sits at the edge of town reading her tarot cards and letting prostitutes use her rooms. She waits for the man promised her in the cards. She bears the children of both Colonel Aureliano and José Arcadio (II), and helps arrange liaisons for several other Buendías. After a hundred years in Macondo, "there was no mystery in the heart of a Buendía that was impenetrable for her."

Aureliano Triste

One of the seventeen Aurelianos born to the colonel outside Macondo, Aureliano Triste inherited his grandfather's inclination for progress but his grandmother's success. He builds a canal, brings the train to Macondo, and sets up an ice factory.

Visitación

Visitación is an Indian queen who renounced her throne to escape the insomnia plague. She finds refuge as a family servant. Unfortunately, the plague arrives with Rebeca and the town is gripped by insomnia until Melquíades arrives with the antidote.

Themes

Solitude

The dominant theme of the novel, as evident from the title, is solitude. Each character has his or her particular form of solitude. Here solitude is not defined as loneliness, but rather a fated seclusion by space or some neurotic obsession. In fact, the

danger of being marked by solitude is its affect on others. "If you have to go crazy, please go crazy all by yourself!" Úrsula tells her husband. One form of solitude is that of madness—the first José Arcadio's solitude is being tied to a tree, speaking in a foreign tongue, and lost in thought. The ultimate expression of solitude, however, is Colonel Aureliano's achievement of absolute power, an "inner coldness which shattered his bones." Consequently, he orders a chalk circle to be marked around him at all times—nobody is allowed near him. Amaranta is another extreme example. Her coldness is the result of power achieved by denial—her virginity. Obstinately, she keeps her hand bandaged as a sign of her "solitude unto death." All the other characters have lesser forms of these two extremes: they become "accomplices in solitude," seek "consolation" for solitude, become "lost in solitude," achieve "an honorable pact with solitude," and gain "the privileges of solitude." The saddest expression of solitude is probably the last. The final Aureliano "from the beginning of the world and forever [was] branded by the pockmarks of solitude." He is literally alone because of the scandal his mother caused Fernanda. He is imprisoned in the house for most of his life until there is no one left to pretend to guard him. He has nothing to do but decipher the parchments of Melquíades. In the process "everything is known" to him—even the obliteration of the world of Macondo.

Love and Passion

Love involving persons afflicted by solitude is not a happy experience for those in the novel. The largest symbol of doomed love is Remedios the Beauty, for anyone who pursues her dies. Often the pursuit of the beloved takes the form of writing. Love poems and letters are rarely sent. Rather, they accumulate in the bottom of trunks and then eventually kindle fires. The chase can lead to animosity between siblings and the death of the innocent. Simple passion, on the other hand, often brings happiness to those involved. Aureliano Segundo's passion for his mistress Petra Cotes, in fact, creates fertility and wealth for the family. Nevertheless, consummation is tricky and often dangerous, as it can involve peering through holes in the roof, threatening the removal of chastity pants, or abiding by strange calendars. In its mildest forms, love is a "physical sensation ... like a pebble in his shoes." At its worst, love drives a man to suicide, "his wrists cut by a razor and his hands thrust in a basin of benzoin." In the end, the only Buendía baby "engen-

Topics For Further Study

- Examine aspects of the Buendía House, considering one or more of the following: how it reflects a certain theme or character personality; how its literal construction relates to the construction of the novel as a whole. Or, with some research and based on your own experience, what conclusions can you draw about family life in nineteenth-century Latin America from the Buendía House?

- Bartók's compositions heavily influenced the novel. Explore the life and works of this composer and write an essay relating his music to this work of literature.

- García Márquez told Rita Guibert, "What I most definitely am is anti*machista. Machismo* is cowardly, a lack of manliness." Find out what the code of machismo is as developed by the conquistador and then relate it to García Márquez's reactions as evidenced in the novel. Be sure to explain the significance of the found suits of armor in the novel.

- Alchemy, or the "science" of transmuting one element into another, has led to several scientific and industrial discoveries. Investigate the history of Alchemy as practiced in the past, then relate it to the scientific pursuits as followed by characters in the novel.

- Compare *One Hundred Years of Solitude* to *Almanac of the Dead* by Native American writer Leslie Marmon Silko. Her book revolves around the piecing together of an almanac that escaped the fires of the Inquisition's book burnings in Mexico. Investigate how the novels explore many of the same colonial and environmental themes.

- A reference to the environment and its degradation at the hands of humans is a not so subtle theme of the book: macaws are traded for trinkets and songbirds are replaced with clocks; the site of the Banana Company's crop is a field of stumps. Gradually, of course, the voracious jungle takes everything back. Research the current state of the environment in Colombia and argue whether García Márquez's vision of the final transformation of Macondo is positive or not.

---

dered with love" kills its mother, is eaten by ants, and brings an end to the world of the novel.

Fate and Chance

The plot of the novel is very simple, García Márquez told Rita Guibert: it is "the story of a family who for a hundred years did everything they could to prevent having a son with pig's tail, and just because of their very efforts to avoid having one they ended up by doing so." The plot is very much like the classic tragedy *Oedipus Rex* (one of García Márquez's favorites), where the effort to prevent a prophecy ends up guaranteeing its fulfillment. In a link with another fundamental western text, the fate of the women in the novel is Eve's fate. They bear the pain of birth, knowing in advance their children will be dictators, bastards, and eventually possess a pig's tail. Úrsula's attempt to avoid taking part in this fate is not only circumvented, but her efforts prompt her family's expulsion from home under the shadow of a murder. Thus the cycle of violence, incest, and procreation is begun. Plans by her descendants to alter this course fail. For example, Fernanda decides the fate of her children only to have them hate her for it. Men, for all their creation and destruction, are but steps toward ending what Úrsula had begun. This is set forth in the greatest declaration of fate in the novel, the epigraph of Melquíades's manuscript: "The first of the line is tied to a tree and the last is being eaten by the ants."

Time

Playing a role in the development of fate is the nature of time. Throughout the novel, time moves in ways that are nonlinear. When Úrsula sees Aureliano Triste planning for the railroad just as his grandfather José Arcadio planned Macondo's development, it "confirmed her impression that time was going a circle." She makes similar observations about her great-grandson José Arcadio Segundo, whose actions resemble those of her son Colonel Aureliano. As Úrsula ages, time becomes mixed up for her, as she relives events from her childhood. Later, José Arcadio Segundo and the last Aureliano discover that the first José Arcadio was not crazy, but understood "that time also stumbled and had accidents and could therefore splinter and leave an eternalized fragment in a room." Pilar Ternera, who has witnessed all the years of the Buendía family's history, knows that the circular nature of time ensures that the family cannot avoid their fate: "A century of cards and experience had taught her that the history of the family was a machine with unavoidable repetitions, a turning wheel that would have gone on spilling into eternity were it not for the progressive and irremediable wearing of the axle." The family's time is limited, even as Aureliano sees how all of it "coexists in one instant" in the manuscript. As he finishes reading the pages, he knows that "everything written on them was unrepeatable since time immemorial and forever more, because races condemned to one hundred years of solitude did not have a second opportunity on earth."

Death

The first line of the novel foreshadows a large role for death in the novel. Death is described as a black mark on a map, and until Melquíades dies, Macondo has no such mark. Thus unknown to the spirits, it is left alone by the world—except for a few accidental discoveries. After that first mark of blackness, death is as constant a theme as solitude and each character has their particular death. The greatest death is that of the patriarch José Arcadio; it is marked by flowers falling from the sky. After that, death becomes a haunting presence, made ever more physical as the degree of decay increases. Burial ceremonies become arduous treks through rain and mud or something one does alone. For example, Fernanda lays herself to rest. Amaranta is the person most familiar with the rites of death. She sees death personified as "a woman dressed in blue with long hair, with a sort of antiquated look, and with a certain resemblance to Pilar Ternera." She is told that she will die once she has finished her own shroud, so she works slowly. When she is finished, she tells the whole community to give her any messages they wish ferried to their dead. Ama-

ranta earlier reveals that she loved Colonel Aureliano the best by the way she prepares his body for burial. She does this in solitude.

Knowledge and Ignorance

In the beginning, José Arcadio was a beneficent and wise leader who disseminated the simple knowledge necessary for creation. His community prospers by following his agricultural instructions and the trees he plants live forever. But then his mind is awakened to the world by the science brought by the Gypsies. His madness begins in the fact that there is so much to know and so many wonderful instruments to invent. In his fascination with mechanical objects he represents the hope of someday having machines do all the work. "Right there across the river there are all kinds of magical instruments while we keep on living like donkeys," he proclaims to his wife. Úrsula keeps working like an ant while José Arcadio sits, depressed at their lack of instruments. When she stirs him, he goes so far as to teach his children the rudiments of reading and writing before he is lost again in "searching for the mythical truth of the great inventions." Knowledge can distinguish man from beast, but it is dangerous without the activity needed to keep human civilization going. The proper mix of knowledge and activity (represented by the vivacity of guests and the fight against the ants' encroachment) is never struck. As the book nears its end and knowledge is ascendant, the lack of activity speeds decay and hastens death.

Style

Climax

The Hungarian composer Bela Bartok fascinates García Márquez and so the author constructed his novel along this composer's line. For example, he configured his climax so it would land five-sevenths of the way through the book—when the strikers are massacred—just as Bartok would have done in a musical composition. From this point on it is denouement and decay until the waters come to wash the earth clean. Also, in similar ways to a musical composition, many characters have a motif or theme which accompanies their presence, such as Mauricio Babilonia's butterflies.

Foreshadowing

The novel opens with the suggestion that the Colonel Aureliano will, at some point, face the firing squad. This is a technique called foreshadowing and it is used throughout the book to emphasize the simultaneity and inevitability of events. The example of Colonel Aureliano's firing squad is also used as a memory motif. Another example of foreshadowing occurs when Fernanda says of Mauricio Babilonia, "You can see in his face that he's going to die," even though she has not yet discovered he is the one romancing her daughter Meme. The guard Fernanda posts to catch a suspected "chicken thief" shoots and paralyzes him.

Narration

The detached, matter-of-face narrative voice in the novel was drawn from his grandmother, according to García Márquez:

> She did not change her expression at all when telling her stories and everyone was surprised. In previous attempts to write, I tried to tell the story without believing in it. I discovered that what I had to do was believe in them myself and write them with the same expression with which my grandmother told them: with a brick face."

Knowing this, the function of the narrator becomes even more difficult to interpret, as one might want to argue that the novel is Úrsula's story. The narrator seems to be the omniscient and omnipresent Melquíades, whose manuscript foretells the Buendía family history and cannot be read for one hundred years. The last Aureliano is finally able to decipher the story after he sees his son eaten by ants. Thus the reader is deciphering a work translated into English from a decoded Spanish translated from the Sanskrit with "even lines in the private cipher of the Emperor Augustus and the odd ones in a Lacedemonian military code."

Burlarse de la Gente

Critic Gordon Brotherston, in his *The Emergence of the Latin American Novel,* wondered whether the novel's conclusion "could be just a sophisticated example of the ability to use literature to make fun of people (*burlarse de la gente*) which [the last] Aureliano had discovered on meeting [Gabriel] Márquez and other friends in The Golden Boy." The novel does make fun of people, especially politicians and writers. It satirizes the chaos of Latin American history, as well as the gullibility of people so easily taken in by circus freaks and politicians. Mostly, it makes fun of the reader, who in the act of reading realizes that he or she is a Buendía who is reading the parchments of Melquíades and ignoring the child being eaten on the floor.

Hyperbole

Hyperbole is a technique of exaggeration that is not intended for literal interpretation. The best example of hyperbole comes in the description of José Arcadio, Úrsula's eldest son. Rather than say he becomes a grown man, José Arcadio is given all the conceivable gargantuan attributes. "His square shoulders barely fitted through the doorways." He has a "bison neck," the "mane of a mule", and he has jaws of iron. He eats whole animals in one sitting. His presence "gave the quaking impression of a seismic tremor."

Magic Realism

A term first used by Alejo Carpentier, magic or magical realism is a uniquely Latin American style of writing which does not differentiate fact from illusion or myth from truth. With its ghosts, magical gypsies, raining flowers, voracious ants, and impossible feats, *One Hundred Years of Solitude* is a seminal example of magic realism. García Márquez has explained that this type of writing is a natural result of being from a people with a vibrant ancestry. In an interview for *Playboy,* he said:

> Clearly, the Latin American environment is marvelous. Particularly the Caribbean.... To grow up in such an environment is to have fantastic resources for poetry. Also, in the Caribbean, we are capable of believing anything, because we have the influences of [Indian, pirate, African, and European] cultures, mixed in with Catholicism and our own local beliefs. I think that gives us an open-mindedness to look beyond apparent reality."

Motif

Motifs are recurring images or themes and are used throughout the novel to close the gaps of the narrative. Seemingly unrelated episodes become connected through the use of these recurring motifs. In addition, motif reinforces the circularity of the novel. As the story is spun, each motif is seen again and again, but in different combinations. One example might be the unusual plagues of insects that appear throughout the novel, from the scorpions in Meme's bathtub to the butterflies that follow Mauricio Babilonia to the ants which continually infest the house.

Men in black robes pass through like a march of death whenever they are needed to justify the actions of the government. Numbers recur—there are twenty-one original founders and twenty-one original revolutionary soldiers. The motif that accentuates the futility of human activity reaches a crescendo in the solitude of Colonel Aureliano, who makes fishes, sells them, and with the money

Men working on a banana plantation.

he earns he makes more fishes. Locked in this circle, Colonel Aureliano seals himself in the workroom, coming out only to urinate. Bodily functions (e.g., drunkenness usually ends up in vomit and tears) are also a motif. Amaranta enters this cycle with sewing, for her theme song is that of the weaver, the spider. She sews and unsews buttons. She, like the mythic Penelope, buys time by weaving and unweaving her shroud. Memories are an essential motif, recurring at their barest every time we hear about Colonel Aureliano facing the firing squad. Úrsula embodies memories and as they fade, so does she. José Arcadio Buendía reads and rereads the parchments. All the while time is passing or not passing, it is always a Monday in March inside the room of Melquíades' manuscript. All of the motifs are games of solitude used by the characters to pass the one hundred years.

Historical Context

Origins of the Colombian State

Knowing the history of the country of Colombia can provide considerable insight into the political battles that take place all throughout *One Hundred Years of Solitude*. The original inhabitants of present-day Colombia were conquered by the Spanish in the 1530s and incorporated into the colony of New Granada, which also encompassed the territories of modern-day Panama, Ecuador, and Venezuela. The area lay under Spanish rule for almost three hundred years, developing a culture and population that blended Spanish, Indian, and African influences. In 1810, Simón Bolívar led the Mestizo (mixed-race) population in a struggle for independence from Spain. It was achieved with his victory at Boyaca, Colombia, in 1819. The new republic of Gran Colombia fell apart, however, when Ecuador and Venezuela formed separate nations in 1830. The remaining territory assumed the name the Republic of Colombia in 1886. In 1903 the area that is now Panama seceded, helped by the United States, who wanted control of a canal along the isthmus between the Atlantic and Pacific Oceans.

Political strife was rampant in nineteenth-century Colombia and parties formed under Liberal and Conservative banners. These parties corresponded to the followers of President Bolívar and his vice-president and later rival, Francisco Santender, respectively. Their essential conflict was over the amount of power the central government should have (Conservatives advocated more, Liberals less). The two parties waged a number of

Compare
&
Contrast

- **Colombia:** The third most populous nation in Latin America, Colombia has a population of approximately 38 million, 95 percent of whom live in the mountainous western half. The per capita percentage of Gross Domestic Product (GDP) is around $5,400. Since the 1950s there has been such rapid urbanization that 73 percent live in cities. The population is 95 percent Catholic.

- **United States:** The population of the U.S. numbers near 270 million, with per capita percentage of GDP around $28,000. Most of the population lives in cities, with increasing migration to the suburbs and the southwest regions of the country. There is no dominant religion, although Judeo-Christian faiths are in the majority and the single largest denomination is Roman Catholic.

- **Colombia:** Immigration to Colombia is negligible. The violent clashes of guerilla troops and the government's army, as well as drug violence, make it an unattractive destination. Internal displacement from this violence is significant. In 1997, 2 families were displaced every two hours.

- **United States:** Despite the recent anti-immigrant fervor in the United States, millions of immigrants the world over hope that the U.S. is their final destination. Of those immigrants from Latin America, Colombians are the most numerous.

- **Colombia:** In 1995, Colombia spent $2 billion on defense, or 2.8% of Gross Domestic Product (GDP). In 1997, they bought $60 million worth of weapons from the US.

- **United States:** The world's greatest arms dealer has spent slightly less on defense in the 1990s than in the 1980s. In 1997, defense spending was 3.4% of GDP, or approximately $267 billion dollars.

- **Colombia:** In 1995, Colombia, Venezuela, and Mexico formed the Group of Three trading alliance. Each country alters its tariffs in favor of the other two members. This alliance took the place of the 1960s effort of LAFTA (Latin American Free Trade Agreement) and responds to the Southern Cone Common Market (formed by Argentina, Brazil, Paraguay, and Uruguay).

- **United States:** In response to the trade block taking shape in Europe, the United States, Canada, and Mexico form the North American Free Trade Agreement (NAFTA). Implemented in 1994, it is blamed by many labor activists for job losses in the United States. Meanwhile, environmentalists say that the effects on Mexico have been more pollution and downward wage pressure.

- **Colombia:** When the international banana conglomerates wound down, Colombian farmers turned to traditional agriculture. Because of poor transportation facilities, however, some farmers face a several-day race against vegetable decay to bring crops to the capital markets. Faced with such poor prospects, it is not surprising that many farmers enter the cocaine trade, in which traders pick up the produce.

- **United States:** Some farmers in the United States grow marijuana for the black market as a way of subsidizing their income, which has diminished as consumers demand low-cost food and politicians cut farm subsidies. Still, the number of farm bankruptcies in the 1990s has far surpassed the records of the 1980s.

---

wars, but the civil war from 1899 to 1902 was incredibly violent, leaving one hundred thousand people dead. In the novel, this history of constant political struggle is reflected in the career of Colonel Aureliano Buendía.

The United Fruit Company

The United States influenced Colombian history at the beginning of the century with their assistance in Panama's secession, and American interests continued their influence for many years thereafter. While petroleum, minerals, coffee, and cocoa are now considered Colombia's main exports, at the start of the twentieth century bananas were the country's chief export. The United Fruit Company (UFC) was the most notorious company invested in this trade. Based in the United States, the UFC gradually assumed control of the Banana Zone—the area of banana plantations in Colombia. The UFC would enter an area, build a company town, attract workers, and pay them in scrip redeemable only in company stores. UFC would then leave as soon as the workers unionized or the harvest began to show fatigue from over-cultivation.

The culminating event of this industry occurred in October of 1928, when thirty-two thousand workers went on strike, demanding things like proper sanitary facilities and cash salaries. One night, a huge crowd gathered in the central plaza of Cienaga to hold a demonstration. Troops, who were being paid by UFC in cigarettes and beer, opened fire on the crowd. Gernal Cortes Vargas, in charge of the troops that night, estimated forty dead. Another observer, however, estimated four hundred lying dead in the square and totalled fifteen hundred dead of wounds incurred there. He also noted an additional three thousand people with non-fatal injuries. Whichever the real numbers, the incident was officially denied by the government and was not included in the history textbooks. This denial is reflected in the novel when José Arcadio Segundo cannot convince anyone that the massacre of strikers he witnessed actually occurred.

Twentieth-Century Political Conflicts

Social and political division in Colombia intensified throughout the 1930s and 1940s. The next period of Colombian history, "the Violence," began after the Liberal mayor of Bogotá, Jorge Eliécer Gaitán, was assassinated. The Liberal government was overthrown, and General Gustavo Rojas Pinilla took control of the government. Both parties sent their paramilitary forces sweeping through the various sectors under their control. Many people were displaced during the fighting. Rojas began a period of absolute military rule, and Congress was subsequently dissolved. It was during Rojas's rule that García Márquez was forced to leave the country because of an article he had written.

When Rojas fell to a military junta in 1957, the Liberal and Conservative parties agreed on a compromise government, the National Front. This arrangement granted the two parties equal representation within the cabinet and legislature, as well as alternating occupation of the Presidency. While this arrangement lessened the direct political rivalry between the two parties, there came a rise in guerilla insurgencies. This was the atmosphere of García Márquez's home country during the time he was writing *One Hundred Years of Solitude*.

Since then, guerilla factions of the 1970s have given way in the 1980s and 1990s to a coordinated network of drug cartels, struggling farmers, and indigenous tribes. Violence has often marked the political process, as guerillas and drug lords attempt to influence elections and trials with violent threats. In 1990, after three other candidates were assassinated, César Gaviria Trujillo was elected president. During his administration the people of Colombia approved a new constitution, aimed at further democratizing the political system. The drug trade has continued to pose problems for the government, however. When the Medellin drug cartel was broken up in 1993, the Calí cartel grew to fill the vacuum. The government of Liberal Ernesto Samper Pizano, elected in 1994, has attempted to combat drug traffickers and thus improve relations with the United States. Popular support for these efforts has not always been forthcoming, particularly by small farmers who are economically dependent on the drug trade.

Critical Overview

Mexican novelist and critic Carlos Fuentes was amazed by the first three chapters of *One Hundred Years of Solitude* that García Márquez sent him for review. Once published, the novel was snatched up by the public, selling out its first printing within a week. Critics were on their feet, fellow novelists took their caps off, and everyone wanted to talk to García Márquez about the story. Printers could not keep up with the demand for what Chilean poet Pablo Neruda called, in a March 1970 issue of *Time*, "the greatest revelation in the Spanish language since the *Don Quixote* of Cervantes." American novelist William Kennedy similarly wrote in the *National Observer* that the book "is the first piece of literature since the Book of Genesis that should be required reading for the entire human race."

Early reviews of the novel were almost uniformly positive, with praise for the author's skill and style. Paul West, in the *Chicago Tribune Book World*, observed that the novel "feeds the mind's eye non-stop, so much so that you soon begin to feel that never has what we superficially call the surface of life had so many corrugations and configurations…. So I find it odd that the blurb points to 'the simplicity …' [of the writing]." Paradoxical as it may seem, many commentators agreed. García Márquez's delivery is so elegantly crafted that despite being bombarded by information, the reader simply wants more. For West, the novel is "a verbal Mardi Gras" that is "irresistible." Given this type of exuberance, the crusty review by D. J. Enright, in *The Listener,* is striking. He found the depiction of civil war and the thud of rifle butts upsetting. He noted that "these are no happy giants or jolly grotesques" and added that "the book is hardly comic." He concluded by calling the novel a "slightly bloated avatar of the austere [Argentinean writer] Jorge Luis Borges."

In contrast, *New York Times* critic John Leonard stated that the novel is not only delightful, it is relevant. "It is also a recapitulation of our evolutionary and intellectual experience," he observed. "Macondo is Latin America in microcosm." He then compared the author with other great writers, including Russian-American Vladimir Nabokov (author of *Lolita*) and German Gunter Grass (author of *The Tin Drum*). Other reviewers have compared García Márquez to a whole range of writers, the most prominent of which is American Nobel laureate William Faulkner. Faulkner's fictional Yoknapatawpha County is similar in scope and depth to García Márquez's Macondo. In addition, the comparison of the Buendías to other famous families started with the Karamazovs of Dostoevsky and Faulkner's Sartoris clan, and moved to the family of black humorist Charles Addams.

In addition to receiving praise for its individual virtues, *One Hundred Years of Solitude* has been hailed for its role in alerting the world to the literature and culture of Latin America. In reflecting on Latin American enthusiasm for the novel, *New York Review of Books* contributor Jack Richardson stated that it is "as if to suggest that the style and sensibility of their history had at last been represented by a writer who understands their particular secrets and rhythms."

While attention has been given to the novel's historical relevance, most criticism has focused on its technical aspects. Writing in *Diacritics,* Ricardo Gullon explained how the novel demonstrates the author's technical mastery: García Márquez's "need to tell a story is so strong that it transcends the devices he uses to satisfy that need. Technique is not a mere game; it is something to be made use

of." Another aspect of the author's technique was noted by Gordon Brotherston in his *The Emergence of the Latin American Novel.* The novel often, and not always in flattering ways, refers to other novels. In doing so, the world of literature is made more real and the real world made literature.

The use of myth in the novel provides another opportunity for critical comment. Roberto González Echevarría, in *Modern Language Notes,* explained the ease of mythmaking in Latin America. He noted that the key to the success of *One Hundred Years of Solitude* is the novel's awareness of the way the New World was "written into existence" through chronicles of the first European settlers. The Spanish crown gathered these eyewitness accounts into a huge archive begun by King Charles V. Echevarría points out the references García Márquez makes to these chronicles, as well as the resultant self-reflexivity imposed on the reader that is only exaggerated by the last scene. His conclusion is that, "In terms of the novel's ability to pass on cultural values … [though] it is impossible to create new myths, [we are brought] back once and again to that moment where our desire for meaning can only be satisfied by myth."

Academics have written on the novel precisely because García Márquez is capable of doing what others have failed to do. Gene H. Bell-Villada writes, in *From Dante to García Márquez,* that García Márquez is able to do for the banana strike what Tolstoy did for Napoleon's invasion of Russia. For example, he avoided "a serious flaw of [Miguel Angel] Asturias's banana trilogy" by not including a Yankee protagonist. Instead, he presented silent Yankee caricatures. The closest he comes is a "rare utterance" from Mr. Brown "relayed to us secondhand, via an unreliable source." Bell-Villada then continues to examine the ways in which the facts of the banana strike are actually used in the novel— even if stretched a little.

When Bell-Villada interviewed García Márquez for *Boston Review,* he told him that his novel is required reading for many political science courses in the United States. García Márquez responded that he was not aware of this, but he was startled to see his book listed in a bibliography for an academic study of Latin America by the French economist Rene Dumont. When asked about the strike scene, García Márquez noted that people now allude to "the thousands who died in the 1928 strike." Wistfully, he added, "As my Patriarch says: it doesn't matter if something isn't true, because eventually it will be!"

Criticism

Diane Andrews Henningfeld

Henningfeld is an associate professor at Adrian College. In the following essay, she explores the layers of meaning in the novel, noting the ways in which García Márquez intertwines myth, history, and literary theory to create a work that is at once readable and complex.

Gabriel García Márquez's masterpiece, *Cien años de soledad* was published in Buenos Aires in 1967. The English translation, *One Hundred Years of Solitude,* prepared for Harper and Row by Gregory Rabassa, appeared in 1970. Several noted Latin American writers applauded the book even before its publication, and post-publication response was universally positive. The novel has been translated into twenty-six languages and continues to enjoy both popular and critical acclaim.

García Márquez was born in Aracataca, Colombia, on March 6, 1928. For the first eight years of his life, he lived with his grandparents. He credits his grandmother for his ability to tell stories, and for giving him the narrative voice he needed to write *One Hundred Years of Solitude.*

One Hundred Years of Solitude is a novel that is at once easily accessible to the reader and, at the same time, very difficult to analyze. The book has an effective plot that propels the reader forward. Simultaneously, the book functions on no less than five or six different levels. Any reading concentrating on one level may not do justice to the others. Consequently, *One Hundred Years of Solitude* is a book that demands careful and multiple readings.

Mario Vargas Llosa, the Peruvian writer, calls *One Hundred Years of Solitude* a " 'total' novel, in the tradition of those insanely ambitious creations which aspire to compete with reality on an equal basis, confronting it with an image and qualitatively matching it in vitality, vastness and complexity." Other critics have commented on the multi-layered nature of the book, noting that García Márquez intertwines myth, history, ideology, social commentary, and literary theory to produce this "total" novel. Although the book needs to be considered as a whole creation, it may also be helpful to examine a few of these layers individually in order to deepen appreciation for the whole.

One of the most common ways of viewing the novel is through myth. In *One Hundred Years of Solitude,* García Márquez weaves references to classical and Biblical myths. Myths are important stories that develop in a culture to help the culture understand itself and its relationship to the world. For example, nearly every culture has a myth concerning the origin of the world and of the culture. In addition, myths often contain elements of the supernatural to help explain the natural world. *One Hundred Years of Solitude* opens with the creation story of Macondo. Certainly, there are echoes of the Biblical Garden of Eden in the opening lines: "The world was so recent that many things lacked names, and in order to indicate them it was necessary to point." In addition, the years of rain that fall on Macondo and the washing away of the village recall myths of the great flood, when all civilization was swept away.

Scholars who study myth have identified characters who fulfill certain functions in myths across cultures. These character-types are often called "archetypes" because they seem to present a pattern. For example, the patriarch is a male character who often leads his family to a new home and who is responsible for the welfare of his people. José Arcadio Buendía is a representative of this type. Other archetypal characters in the novel include the matriarch, represented by Úrsula, and the virgin, represented by Remedios the Beauty. Petra Cotes and Pilar Ternera, with their blatant sexuality and fertility as well as their connection to fortune telling, serve as archetypal witches.

Further, many myths have patterns that repeat themselves over and over. Likewise, the novel presents pattern after pattern, from the language García Márquez uses to the repetitive nature of the battles fought by Colonel Aureliano Buendía, to the naming of the characters. Indeed, the repetitions form the structure of the book.

Finally, many myths take as their starting point violence and/or the breaking of an important taboo. Certainly, the novel does both. The town of Macondo is founded and the history of the Buendías launched as the result of violence and incest. When José Arcadio and Úrsula Iguarán marry, she refuses to allow the marriage to be consummated because they are cousins. She fears that she will give birth to a child with the tail of a pig. Prudencio Aguilar makes jokes about José Arcadio's manhood and as a result, José Arcadio kills Prudencio, an act that finally forces José Arcadio and Úrsula to leave their town and found Macondo.

García Márquez also incorporates personal, local, national, and continental history into his novel.

What Do I Read Next?

- More information about García Márquez can be found on an internet site run by "The Great Quail" at http://rpg.net/quail/libyrinth/gabo/.

- Based on his studies of Francisco Franco, dictator of Spain, García Márquez's 1975 work *El otoño del patriarca* (translated in 1977 as *The Autumn of the Patriarch*) further develops the themes of power and solitude. The novel is technically dazzling and is often described as a prose poem.

- Revealing an affection for Daniel Defoe's 1722 *A Journal of the Plague Year,* García Márquez embellished on the facts of his parents' marriage in his 1985 novel *El amor en los tiempos del cólera* (translated in 1988 as *Love in the Time of Cholera*).

- The 1968 collection of García Márquez stories called *No One Writes to the Colonel and Other Stories* contains themes or ideas later developed in *One Hundred Years of Solitude.*

- Miguel Angel Asturias, a 1967 Nobel prize winner from Guatemala, wrote a trilogy on United Fruit Company. He focused on the exploitation of Indians on banana plantations. In English, the titles of the three novels are *The Cyclone* (1950), *The Green Pope* (1954), and the *Eyes of the Interred* (1960).

- *Terra Nostra,* a 1975 novel by Carlos Fuentes—Mexican novelist, critic, and friend of García Márquez—has been compared to One Hundred Years of Solitude. The comparison comes at several intersections: one is the use of the New World chronicles and the two novels' language concerning the Spanish Conquest; another point is the use of the archive or historian. Fuentes uses the greatest Spanish writer, *Don Quijote* author Miguel de Cervantes, instead of a gypsy.

- No venture into Latin American literature can begin without the collection of poems *Canto General* (*General Song,* 1950), by Nobel laureate Pablo Neruda of Chile. Within that collection is the poem "La United Fruit Co."

- The person of Melquíades is often interpreted as the Argentinean writer Jorge Luis Borges. Master storyteller of the magic realism genre and director of the Argentine national library, Borges, like Melquíades, was a purveyor of knowledge. There are similarities between several of his stories and the character of Aureliano (IV). For example, as in the story "The Aleph" from *The Aleph and Other Stories* (1970), Aureliano's glimpse of history is instantaneous.

- The term magic realism was applied to the new literature of Latin America by Cuban novelist Alejo Carpentier in the late 1940s. His masterpiece is *The Lost Steps* (1953) where he defines Latin American reality as a blending of primeval myth, Indian story, and the imposition of Spanish civilization. It is this cultural blending that makes possible the fantastic yet believable elements of magic realism.

- Another magic realist is the Chilean Isabel Allende, who is best known for her 1982 novel *The House of Spirits.* The niece of assassinated Chilean President Salvador Allende, the author is more up front with her examination of South American political realities as well as the role of women in that reality.

- A Peruvian magic realist is Mario Vargas Llosa, who tells the story of a prophet who incites the people of Brazil to revolt in *The War of the End of the World* (1981). Led by the prophet, the people found the city of Canudos, where history and civilization is turned upside down—there is no money, tax, or property. It is pure revolution.

- Set in Mexico, *Like Water for Chocolate* (1989) is Mexican writer Laura Esquivel's contribution to magic realism. The story concerns a daughter who is destined to stay at home to care for her mother. Her lover marries her sister so as to be near—and this leads to passionate tragedy.

The village of Macondo is clearly modeled on the village of his childhood, Aracataca. Indeed, the name of the banana plantation just outside of Aracataca was Macondo. In addition, many of the episodes of the novel are based on events from García Márquez's life with his grandparents. For example, the opening episode of José Arcadio taking his sons to see ice is certainly modeled on a similar incident in young García Márquez's life, when his grandfather took him to see ice for the first time.

Other critics have noted the ways in which the founding of Macondo mirrors Colombian settlement by Europeans. Just as the early residents of Macondo are cut off from the rest of the world, the early colonists were also extremely isolated. In addition, the institutions of civilization, such as the government and the church, moved slowly, but inexorably, into Colombia, just as they do into Macondo. Apolinar Moscote and Father Nicanor Reyna are recognizable representatives of these institutions; their appearance in Macondo signals a shift from the Edenic, Arcadian days of the founding.

The middle part of the novel traces the course of a long civil war, fought between the Liberals and Conservatives. Colonel Aureliano Buendía is one of the leaders of the Liberal cause. The civil war in the novel follows closely the long years of civil war in Colombia when the Liberals and Conservatives battled for control of the country. Many critics have pointed out the parallels between the fictional Aureliano Buendía and the historical General Rafael Uribe Uribe, the military leader of the Colombian Liberals.

Finally, García Márquez incorporates into his novel the American intervention into Latin America. During the late nineteenth and early twentieth centuries, the United Fruit Company, an American concern, began operating large scale banana plantations throughout Latin America. In 1928, a strike by workers over living conditions and contract violations led to a massive massacre. Newspapers differ in their accounts and it is difficult to arrive at a final figure for the number killed. Further, the governmental bureaucracy, intent on maintaining the flow of American dollars into Colombia, covered up the massacre. The fictional account of the slaying of the strikers in *One Hundred Years of Solitude* reads remarkably like the accounts of the historical 1928 Cienaga strike.

Finally, *One Hundred Years of Solitude* is a novel written within a particular literary context. Three important literary terms are often used in discussion of the novel: magic (or magical) realism; intertextuality; and metafiction. Knowing something about each of these devices is important for an understanding of the literary task García Márquez set for himself in *One Hundred Years of Solitude.*

Magic realism is a term first used to describe the surreal images of painters in the 1920s and 1930s. Defining the term in literature has caused some controversy among literary scholars. However, according to Regina James in her *One Hundred Years of Solitude: Modes of Reading,* "In current Anglo-American usage, magic realism is a narrative technique that blurs the distinction between fantasy and reality." Certainly, *One Hundred Years of Solitude* offers many examples of magic realism according to this definition, although not all critics would agree with the definition. Part of the effect of magic realism is created by the completely neutral tone of the narrator. He reports such things as gypsies on flying carpets, the insomnia plague, the ascension of Remedios the Beauty, and the levitation of Father Nicanor with no indication that these occurrences are the least bit out of the ordinary, just as the inhabitants of Macondo respond to the events. On the other hand, the residents of Macondo respond to items such as magnets and ice with great wonder, as if these were the stuff of fantasy. García Márquez himself argues that the reality of South America is more fantastic than anything "magical" in his writing. Further, as he writes in his Nobel acceptance speech, "The Solitude of Latin America,"

> Poets and beggars, musicians and prophets, warriors and scoundrels, all creatures of that unbridled reality, we have had to ask but little of imaginations, for our crucial problem has been a lack of conventional means to render our lives believable. That is the crux of our solitude.

Another important term for the study of *One Hundred Years of Solitude* is intertextuality. Julia Kristeva, the French philosopher, created this term to describe the way that every text refers to and changes previous texts. Most obviously, a text can do this through allusion, by directly referring to a previous text through names of characters, incidents in the plot, or language, for example. As Regina Janes points out in her book, *One Hundred Years of Solitude: Modes of Reading,* the novel "adopts the narrative frame of the Bible and the plot devices of *Oedipus Tyrannos* and parodies both." That is, *One Hundred Years of Solitude* follows the structure of the Bible: it begins with an idyllic creation in a garden-like setting, where all the people are innocent. The movement of the plot is away from the moment of creation and toward the moment of Apocalypse, when all of Macondo is swept away. Second, in *Oedipus the King,* the entire tragedy is foretold by the oracle at Delphi, which tells Oedipus's parents that their son will murder his father and marry his mother. While the characters in the play take actions to prevent this, each action they take merely ensures that it will happen. Likewise, the fate of the Buendía family is sealed with the incestuous marriage between José Arcadio and Úrsula. What Úrsula fears most occurs in the closing pages of the book: the last Buendía child is born with the tail of a pig, the result of the marriage of Aureliano Babilonia (who does not know his parentage) to his aunt, Amaranta Úrsula.

Finally, *One Hundred Years of Solitude* is an excellent example of metafiction, a work of fiction that takes as its subject the creation and reading of texts. From the moment that Melquíades presents José Arcadio with the manuscript, members of the Buendía family attempt to decipher it. These attempts parallel the attempts of the reader to decipher the text of *One Hundred Years of Solitude.* Further, during the insomnia epidemic, José Arcadio's labels illustrate the metafictional quality of the novel: "Thus they went on living in a reality that was slipping away, momentarily captured by words, but which would escape irremediably when they forgot the values of the written letters." As readers, we participate in the creation of a fictional reality; in this sentence, García Márquez reminds us that the "reality" of the Buendías is no more than "momentarily captured" words. The "reality" of the Buendías ends when the reader closes the book.

Even more explicitly metafictional is the conclusion. In the last three pages, Aureliano finally deciphers the manuscript left by Melquíades, and suddenly understands that he is reading the history of his family. As he reads, he catches up to the present and then reads himself into the future at the moment Macondo is destroyed. At the same instant, readers of *One Hundred Years of Solitude* realize that Melquíades' manuscript is the novel they are reading themselves. The wind that wipes out the "city of mirrors (or mirages)" is the turning of the final page. At that moment, the reader participates in the destruction of Macondo.

As should be obvious, *One Hundred Years of Solitude* is a book that changes with reading; a second or third reading will be very different from the first. The multiple paths a reader takes through the novel, reading it as myth, as history, as metafiction, provide a rich and complicated stew, one that can be savored again and again.

Source: Diane Andrews Henningfeld, in an essay for *Novels for Students,* Gale, 1999.

L. Robert Stevens and G. Roland Vela

In the following excerpt, Stevens and Vela discuss how Márquez deals with the problem of "distinguishing between illusion and reality" by fusing the two instead of treating them as separate entities.

The technical difficulty of distinguishing between illusion and reality is one of the oldest and most important problems faced by the novelist in particular and by mankind in general. In art, philosophy, or politics, western man has traditionally made great conscious efforts to keep illusion separated from fact while admiring and longing (at least superficially) for a transcendental way of life. The irony of this longing resides in the fact that western man's scientific and technological achievements are in great part due to his ability to separate fact from fiction, myth from science, and illusion from reality. It is a paradox of western culture that it draws its psychological strength from a spiritual-mythical well while its muscle is drawn largely from science and technology.

In *One Hundred Years of Solitude,* Gabriel García Márquez deals with the paradox very successfully by not trying to solve it at all. That is to say, the perceptions of reality which appear in the novel are all *prima facie* perceptions and, as a consequence, become indistinguishable from reality. For example, when Meme falls in love with Mauricio Babilonia she finds herself attended ever after by a swarm of yellow butterflies. The question whether they are real or imaginary butterflies is the wrong question. Márquez makes it evident that he places little value on such questions and that there is, in a way, no inherent value in real butterflies as opposed to imaginary butterflies in the world which he describes and, by extension, perhaps in our world as well.

The butterflies are there, *prima facie,* and the distinction between symbol and actuality is broken down and declared void by the lyrical fiat of his style. The technical result of this method and the value of this view is that the conventional distinction between figurative and literal language is impossible to make and pointless beside. Conventional literary terms are inadequate to describe this fusion of both literal and metaphorical language.

We who are trained to compartmentalize our minds into fact and fancy, business and God, myth and science, are prone to wonder over the nature of these butterflies, their origin, and their significance. In reality, however, the question is presumptuous and has validity only in our narrow-minded world with its forty-hour work week and our constant, energy-consuming, watchful stand to keep fancy and reality separated in our minds.

When we are told that it rained for four years, eleven months, and two days, we need not ask ourselves whether this could be so; rather we soon come to accept it as a given quantity and eventually, through the art of García Márquez, we come to accept all things in the novel as they are. This, we are soon convinced, is also a workable view of reality. Multiplying such details with profound ingenuity, Márquez gradually brings the reader's skeptical biases into harmony with the spiritual and intellectual life of his townsfolk. When José Arcadio is shot,

> A trickle of blood came out under the door, crossed the living room, went out into the street, continued on in a straight line across the uneven terraces, went down steps and climbed over curbs, passed along the Street of the Turks, turned a corner to the right and another to the left, made a right angle at the Buendía house, went in under the closed door, crossed through the parlor hugging the walls so as not to stain the rugs … and came out in the kitchen, where Ursula was getting ready to crack thirty-six eggs to make bread.

There is no question as to how this episode is to be taken, only the simple declaration that it happened. This blood which defies the laws of physics is neither symbolical, miraculous, nor scientifically credible. It is simply a fiat of reality in Macondo. Are such events also possible in our own world? Perhaps they are more real in the Colombian *cienega grande,* yet, on the other hand, people who believe in the day of judgment and the resurrection of the dead, except for a certain narrowness of mind, should have little trouble with a stream of blood that does not coagulate in one minute and that travels uphill.

One of the elements constituting this poetic vision of things is the mythopoeic. The village of Macondo is a microcosm and the one hundred years recounted in the novel is a compression of the whole history of man. The village begins *ex nihilo,* rises to a golden age, and falls away into oblivion. Everything that can happen in our world happened there. A village was founded, children begotten, revolutions spawned, technology developed, lust, love, death, and beatitude were all enacted with the luxuriant and unending variety that suggests the inexhaustibility of the individual experience of human events. Márquez's myth has its own cosmology, "going back to before original sin." The world began the "day that Sir Francis Drake attacked Riohacha," and it is of no consequence that Drake set sail and lived a lifetime prior to this day. In the golden age of Macondo nobody died, and all men lived in a sacred and eternal present tense. As time passed knowledge accumulated, but wisdom was still the property of the few, and political power belonged, even as in our world, to the cheat and the liar. As the world aged, it was overtaken by a great insomniac sickness which resulted in a loss of memory. In fear that their loss would bring chaos, the people of Macondo put up signs to remind themselves of the identity of things; "table, chair, clock, door …," and on main street they placed the largest of all the signs against their forgetfulness, *DIOS EXISTE.* In giving things names, they also gave them reality; in having José Arcadio Buendía to give things their names, Garcia Márquez gives him the function of Adam, the first man, and he simultaneously seems to tell us that anything which may be forgotten by man may lose its existence and, perhaps, its *reality.*

Márquez gives a sort of sacredness to all experience by breaking down the wall between the sacred and the profane, as he has broken down the wall between fact and fiction, and by refusing to intellectualize his characters. Remedios the Beauty, for instance, remains utterly chaste—not because she is pious, but because she is simple and does not know the thoughts of men. But what does it matter whether her innocence came by piety or ignorance? In either case, she ascends into heaven while hanging sheets in the backyard, and who is to gainsay her ascension? Márquez, whose point of view in the novel is somewhat like God's, has declared it so. In short, the writer has created in Remedios a natural piety which may be thought of as pure without puritanism— simultaneously sacred and profane.

Time also has mythopoeic significance in the novel. Everything ages and moves toward its own end. Life, regardless of its particular reality, is a transient condition, at best. Márquez's point of view in the novel is the point of view of God: all time is simultaneous. The story of Macondo is at once complete from beginning to end, and, at the same time, it is the story of only one out of an infinite number of worlds each with its own story. More than that, it is the story of José Arcadio

Buendía, one out of an infinite number of men but one who is more the father of man than Adam himself, for if Adam's sin was to eat the fruit of the tree of knowledge, José Arcadio's was to live too much and too long. He lived from the beginning of time until the world became old. Onc has the feeling that if the world had not become old, José Arcadio would not have died—but he and his descendants would never have deciphered the parchments of the ancients, never have acquired knowledge. "What's happening," Ursula notes, "is that the world is slowly coming to an end...." When the great apocalypse does befall Macondo however, it falls not in fire or flood, but rather it creeps in as the rot and decay of antiquity. When Aureliano Babilonia deciphers the parchments of Melquíades which contain all the knowledge and all the secrets of the ancients, he finds that "Melquíades had not put events in the order of man's conventional time, but had concentrated a century of daily episodes in such a way that they co-existed in one instant." The simultaneity of all time cannot be achieved literally by the novelist, and therefore he must create the illusion of it. This Márquez does by creating a microcosm of Macondo and giving it a microhistory while the individuals involved are as real as we.

In the last analysis, "time" is one of the major themes of the novel, as its title suggests. By setting all things in the context of their mortality, by dramatizing the apocalyptic nature of antiquity and decay (some say the world will end in flood, some say in fire, Márquez says it will die of old age), Márquez induces in us a rich reverence for all of his characters and events. There are great depths of bitterness in this novel—bitterness for the death of the old woman clubbed to death by the soldiers' rifle butts, for the treachery of the government and the North American fruit company, for the trainload of massacred townsfolk whose corpses "would be thrown into the sea like rejected bananas." Yet time and decay spread over these bitter incidents in such a way as to mellow and sanctify them. All of history occurred in Macondo, and it became holy through Melquíades's recitation of it in the sacred parchments; in like manner Márquez transforms the common experience of our world into something magical by his telling of it in the novel. Time bestows its blessing; all things are made holy because they have existed.

A second element of Márquez's view of life, beyond the mythopoeic, is the concept that man is naturally a scientist. The wisdom of the people who live in Macondo is a composite of folk wisdom, hearsay, legend, superstition, and religion—all indiscriminately mixed. And yet Márquez builds into the novel a clear sympathy for a certain quality of knowledge. We might think of this sympathy as an instinct for science. José Arcadio Buendía has it, as do each of his descendants who, in successive generations, lock themselves away in Melquíades's room to search for knowledge and truth. This science itself is a mixture of alchemy and occultism, but in it there is a feature which separates it from the popular wisdom of the town: its profound belief that reality is infinitely more wondrous than the most inventive of illusions. It is true that in José Arcadio the love of science exists in undisciplined comradeship with the folk wisdom....

José Arcadio was crude and ignorant in his methodology, but a true scientist in his heart. His fascination with magnets, ice, the sextant, and the geography of the world make it clear that in spite of his own inability always to separate superstition from science, the great yearning of his heart was to *know* things. In many ways García Márquez sees him as the archetype of all scientists, for do they not all share his dilemma? Which scientist could ever truly separate his own illusions from his empirical knowledge? Which scientist could ever know that his methodology is pure and perfected? How much of modern science is old illusion given a new name? The common characteristic shared by true scientists, however, is their great wonder at the profound mystery of reality. And if this be so, then to the brotherhood of Copernicus, Galileo, and Newton, old José—with his poor sextant and his undeterred will to find a system for identifying the exact stroke of noon—eternally belongs.

It is this instinctive awe of reality that separates the first from the second generation of gypsies. Melquíades—a combination of Wandering Jew, picaro, Mephistopheles, and God—is a huckster, true enough, but beyond his slight-of-hand and his alchemy he is a man of great wisdom. It is easy from the vantage point of a highly developed technological culture, to think of Melquíades and José Arcadio as being naive, having too many gaps in their learning to be true scientists. There are loose ends in their knowledge which make them seem provincial. Should we judge them thus, however, we would betray only our own provinciality, for all science has loose ends. There must have been something of the gypsy too in Albert Einstein, for his paradox of the clock is really not different from Buendía's visualizing the air and hearing the buzzing of sunlight. García Márquez perceives it all as a vital and organic whole, as though the jungle itself [were] a Gothic artifact, creating, nourishing, destroying, and regenerating in great, broad brush strokes and in infinitely delicate detail. Márquez's way of seeing things is compatible with both myth and science, but it is neither thing in itself. It has the analytical curiosity of science coupled with the synthetic method of myth. The result is a technique which puts him in the tradition of Unamuno, Gallego, and Lorca, and it may reveal him as one of the most inventive novelists of our day—not because others have failed to explore this artistic fusion of myth and science, symbol and surface, but because of Márquez's ingenuity and the profusion of his imaginative details.

The view of Gabriel García Márquez is a view of life as it is—complex, changing, indefinite, and difficult to understand. It is a view of reality richer and more exciting than any cross-section of any of its parts could ever reveal.

Source: L. Robert Stevens and G. Roland Vela, "Jungle Gothic: Science, Myth, and Reality in *One Hundred Years of Solitude*," in *Modern Fiction Studies,* No. 2, Vol. 26, Summer, 1980, pp. 262–66.

Birutė Ciplijauskaité

Ciplijauskaité describes the ways in which García Márquez uses foreshadowing throughout One Hundred Years of Solitude *to tie different aspects of the novel together.*

The constant use of foreshadowing and premonition stands out as one of the basic structural elements of *One Hundred Years of Solitude.* All such elements, including cyclical reiteration, paradox and parallelism, are tightly interwoven with the main themes of the book; as a consequence, they can be studied as integral parts of the "story" as well as of the "discourse," where syntactic and semantic aspects are interrelated. A major portion of the book obeys the rule of ambiguity ... more generally referred to as "magic realism" when applied to the Latin American novel and short story.

The realm of the fantastic ... lies between the real-explicable and the supernatural, with a continuous fluctuation of boundaries and an uncertainty intensified by the total absence of the narrator's guiding point of view. García Márquez suggests that this will also be a characteristic of his book: on the first page, stressing the importance of imagination in José Arcadio Buendía, the founder of Macondo, he writes, "his imagination always went beyond the genius of nature and even beyond miracles and magic." He causes the whole story to "float" by disrupting the natural temporal sequence and making even spatial relations uncertain. [Mario Vargas Llosa in *Historia de un deicidio,* 1971.] The constant intertwining of the real and material with the fantastic and spiritual fosters ambiguity and permits a myth to be born. (According to García Márquez, [in "García Márquez de Aracataca a Macando," M. Vargas Llosa, 1969] a similar blend was present in the atmosphere in which he grew up: "For lack of something better, Aracataca lived on myths, ghosts, solitude and nostalgia.") Technically, the use of ellipsis together with chronological leap, both forward and backward, produces a seldom-experienced density of statement which invites both literal and symbolical readings. [R. Barthes in "Introduction a l'analyse structurale des récits," *Communications,* 1966.] (García Márquez said once he would have liked to be the author of *La peste* whose economy of devices he admired. If one considers that the density achieved by Camus represents a chronicle of the human destiny of a city during a period of nine months, one may be even more surprised to find that García Márquez compresses into a similar number of pages the hundred-year history of a whole tribe and, figuratively, a whole continent. The absurd arrived at has the same poignancy in both authors; the difference in the presentation derives from the rational and civilized character of the French and the overflowing vitality of the Latin Americans.) Repetitions with variations are extremely effective in producing this density: the variants convey essential developments and at the same time establish paradigmatic relations within and between the symbolic patterns of the text....

Ambiguity in the novel is further intensified by the transposition and confusion of senses and sensations (Melquíades speaks "lighting up with his deep organ voice the darkest reaches of the imagination"; Rebeca "spits hieroglyphics"; José Arcadio sees a "route that ... could only lead to the past" and then perceives the sea colored with disillusionment). Such devices as synesthesia, oxymoron and the like in most cases allow more than one interpretation....

Structurally, the fantastic element helps to create and maintain suspense; its semantic function ... is its very presence in the work. And what could be more fantastic in the case of *One Hundred Years of Solitude,* asks Vargas Llosa, if not the fact that it is a story of a story told in reverse? An unusual aspect of it—with a distinctly twentieth-century flavor—is that it contains within itself not the account of its writing, but rather one of its reading and interpretation. Thus, all events in the novel gain added significance as clues for a final deciphering. A structuralist can easily discover a careful system of signs and codes in this never-totally-revealed universe full of premonitions.

Vargas Llosa took nearly seven hundred pages to outline a few essential characteristics of García Márquez's work. It would seem vain to attempt here a complete analysis of even one aspect. The role of foreshadowing is of primary importance in the novel, and only a long essay could do it justice. These lines will barely serve as an introduction to what begins the book as technique and ends it as theme. It should be noted that throughout the greater part of the story a single character may embody both technique and theme. The very first image the reader encounters, one periodically reiterated, provides a glimpse of the future (which then is not fulfilled): Colonel Aureliano Buendía in front of a firing squad. Aureliano is the first and the greatest seer of the Buendía family, and one who attains mythical stature. His supernatural qualities are suggested when Ursula hears him cry in her womb; his first spoken words are a premonition: "the boiling pot is going to spill" ([la] olla de caldo hirviendo ... "se va a caer.") At this point, with the introduction of the husband's and the wife's characters the dicotomy in their reactions becomes clear: what frightens Ursula seems a "natural phenomenon" to José Arcadio. Much later, while awaiting his execution, Aureliano formulates what could be considered a theory of premonitions, which is related to a vital theme of the novel: the natural versus the artificial. Amazed at the fact that on this occasion he has no premonition of his pending execution, he concludes that only a natural death warrants a supernatural sign. As it happens no one dares carry out the orders leading to his "artificial" end; thus, the lack of a premonition of death in his mind becomes in the mind of the reader a foreshadowing of life.

Another interesting use of the foreshadowing technique is found in the account of Amaranta's death. In this case, a premonition takes on human form and visits her personally, leaving exact instructions. This fantastic situation is even further exploited as it is raised to the level of superstition: knowing she is to die, Amaranta announces publicly her willingness to collect and deliver the "mail for the dead" on behalf of the whole village. An even greater degree of complexity is achieved by the narrator's comment that "it seemed a farce".... The paradox is taken further, however: it is Amaranta herself who, looking and feeling perfectly

well, directs to the very end the preparations for her own funeral.

It might be noted that the manner of presentation of each premonition exemplifies the basic technique of the novel itself: in rhythmically repeated "fore-flashes" of the main characters' deaths is included a short synopsis of the strongest emotions and impressions of their lives. The same interruptive technique is used throughout the novel to record cardinal stages in the life and death of the tribe and the whole village. The opening sentence of the novel renders Aureliano's first distinctly remembered impression as he awaits his last; as the book closes, the last Aureliano in the family line receives the final impression of his life as he reads about the first. Life and literature become one, and both seem destined to sink into oblivion.

The importance of foreshadowing becomes evident when we analyze the first chapter more closely. In it can be found most of the major themes and devices of the novel. Like the entire book, the introductory chapter forms a perfectly circular structure, a circle that runs counter to the clock. There is also a complete integration of various temporal levels: what the colonel glimpses of the past in the first sentence (which is itself a fore-flash) closes the chapter as a living experience in the present tense. Fire and ice unite as opposites, forming a paradox, a device constantly used throughout the novel. The importance of the word—the Verb, the Creation—is stressed at both the opening and the close: Macondo is so new to the world that names have to be invented to designate objects, says the narrator in his first description of the town. At the end of the chapter we see José Arcadio groping for words when confronted with what for him is a new phenomenon—ice. The novel itself closes with a character reading the last line, which for the first time releases the book's full meaning.

The circle—and the premonition—can also be found in the symbol of the child with a tail. What appears in the first chapter as superstitious fear (thereby opening the gates to the realm of the fantastic) is finally justified in the last. The whole novel in some way anticipates the fulfillment of this oracle. Another use of foreshadowing can be found in the first pages: i.e., the prediction by Melquíades that the whole tribe of Buendías will be extinguished. Melquíades's life comes full circle within the limits of this chapter: it starts with his first arrival in Macondo and ends with the news about his death, just as the book itself develops from the arrival of the Buendías in Macondo to the written news of their final extinction.

It may be worthwhile to note that the first character introduced in this book is Melquíades, a fantastic figure constantly fluctuating between the real and the supernatural: he "was a gloomy man, enveloped in a sad aura, with an Asiatic look that seemed to know what there was on the other side of things.... But in spite of his immense wisdom and his mysterious breadth, he had a human burden, an earthly condition that kept him involved in the small problems of daily life." The physical description of him, in turn, intensifies the temporal distortion: he wears "a velvet vest across which the patina of centuries had skated." And one of the first "wonders" he brings is called "*fierros,*" not "*hierros mágicos,*" an archaic form of the word which also suggests his agelessness. While indulging in magic, he is able to give the most lucid explanations about recent progress in the scientific world. (One of the most delightful examples in his conversation with Ursula about his being a demon, where he explains to her the odor of the devil from a chemical point of view. His blindness and the increased lucidity it brings about foreshadow Ursula's last years when the role of intuition is emphasized. It leads, moreover, to another principal theme in the novel: that of insanity versus sanity, which is developed with regard to several members of the family.

Melquíades bears within himself the main theme of the novel: he returns from the kingdom of the dead, renouncing immortality, because he is unable to endure solitude. The book closes with the reading of his scriptures. Only at this point does the reader realize that Melquíades was not only a character but the narrator himself. In one of his first appearances in the novel, he even gives a definition of what the book turns out to be—"fantastic stories"—suggesting, moreover, that there are always several interpretations to a phenomenon: on the same page we see him through four different pairs of eyes, interpreted four different ways. Thus, the figure of Melquíades points to everything in this novel being a language of signs and patterns, a "récit indiciel" with intricate metaphorical relationships. [Barthes, 1966.]

The first chapter makes full use of such structural elements as paradox, which is essential in the presentation of the theme of the absurd (José Arcadio sets out to look for the sea, gets lost in the jungle and founds Macondo; while seeking to communicate with the city, he discovers the sea; Ursula, seeking her son, discovers the road to civi-

lization); parallelism (José Arcadio as a symbol of the village and Ursula, of the home); antithesis (José Arcadio embodying imagination, Ursula embodying common and practical sense; the two sons who become archetypes for the entire descendency divided between an emphasis on physical enjoyment of life and the anguish of imagination); repetition as the essence of the story, summarized by Pilar Ternera at the end: "the history of the family was a machine with unavoidable repetitions." The repetition may be associated with the symbol of mirrors perceived by José Arcadio in the dream which determines the founding of Macondo, transposed once we understand that the mirrors do not reproduce the image an infinite number of times but instead a mirage which is impossible to repeat....

Many secondary themes are also introduced in this chapter and later developed more fully: the first notion of religion is, significantly, mixed with superstition; the only reference to the civil government is especially important for it underscores its inefficiency. José Arcadio's desire to invent a "memory machine" is a precursor of the long episode of the "insomnia plague"; his interest in developing arms for "solar warfare" hints at the future revolution and the mythical exploits of Colonel Aureliano Buendía. The principles of self-government and equality are established by José Arcadio's distribution of land and sun, thus, introducing the important roles nature and climactic conditions are to play. José Arcadio's expedition wrestling with the fierce forces of the jungle provides one of the earliest glimpses of the jungle's power and makes convincing its final invasion of the Buendías' family house in the last chapter.

Nature also serves to introduce the eternal dichotomy between the natural state of man and civilized man, illustrated in the first chapter by the two tribes of gypsies. The first are simple and honest and want to share their knowledge. Those that follow, "purveyors of amusement," come to cheat and loot. The theme of solitude and isolation is opposed to that of friendship and is brought out by emphasizing the desire to communicate, which is as strong in individual characters as it is within the village community as a whole.

There is, finally, in these first pages of the novel an early intimation of one of the most exuberant of the later epistles: Aureliano Segundo's "papering" the walls of his house with money clearly echoes José Arcadio's announcement in the first chapter that "we'll have gold enough and more to pave the floors of the house." (The paradox attached to the theme of gold is that we see José Arcadio on the first page and Aureliano Segundo toward the end of the book desperately searching for it without success while at the peak of the fortune a saint's figure [to whom Ursula lights candles and prays] is discovered containing a treasure of gold. A further paradox can be seen in the fact that Ursula's hiding place is indicated in the first chapter and later repeated, but when the whole house and garden are dug up during the search, nobody looks under her bed.) A strong parallelism can be observed between the fall and rise of the family and of the village, which is symbolized at the end of the book by the return of the first tribe of gypsies we met in Chapter I: The development of the village has completed a full circle between the two comings, and the villagers have returned to a state where they can again be awed by innocent, primitive magic.

A powerful imagination is the prime characteristic defining José Arcadio. It too comes full circle: in the first chapter we see him teaching his children "by forcing the limits of his imagination to extremes," interrupting his task only to greet the arrival of gypsies who bring even more imaginary inventions. At the end, the last descendants receive instruction from Aureliano Segundo who uses an English encyclopedia without being able to read it; he draws on his imagination to invent instructions.

There is a distinct gradation among the first "wonders" acquired by José Arcadio from the gypsies, a gradation further developed in later chapters. He begins by exploring the fields around Macondo with a magnet in search of gold for personal purposes (prosperity that will be achieved through Ursula's fabrication of candied animals and later through the proliferation of real animals during Aureliano Segundo's reign); then he passes on to convert a magnifying glass into a weapon of war (war will eventually involve the whole country through his son's revolutionary opposition to the government); with the compass and the sextant his imagination crosses seas and frontiers—as his last descendants will do in actuality. Finally, alchemy transports him to a realm of irreality, which is later repeated as several members of the family end their lives "liberated" from the limits of time, space and social convention.

Only the all-important element of time remains to be examined in the first chapter. Again a technique is introduced which is used throughout the novel. The compression of time is evident: fourteen years of life are packed into fourteen pages. This is achieved mainly by fragmenting and juggling various temporal levels, a process which can be summarized as follows: future with the present, in which five different stages are marked by the successive arrivals of the gypsies, introducing the great theme of transformations; the past alone, which contains allusions to an even more remote past; and present, past and future together. On all these levels, further divisions as well as interrelations between real time and imaginary time could be established. One remark by Ursula deserves mention: almost ready to die, she complains that "time was slower before." In fact, José Arcadio and his men need four days to conquer twelve kilometers in the first chapter; in the last, Gaston is contemplating the establishment of airmail service to Macondo. The speed of events becomes frantic at the end, when the sudden whirlwind of destruction prevents Aureliano Babilonia (note the change in name) from finishing the deciphering of the manuscript. Almost at the exact center of the novel Ursula utters, "it's as if time had turned around and we were back at the beginning." From this point on, one can add to the reading in progression another reading in regression. The tempo increases, but the quickened passing of time only brings omens of degeneration and destruction. All human efforts are revealed to be futile, all hopes absurd in the face of the ultimate predestination. But precisely at this point, where written time ends, the cycle is reinitiated—in the reader's imagination.

Source: Biruté Ciplijauskaité, "Foreshadowing as Technique and Theme in *One Hundred Years of Solitude*," in Books Abroad, No. 3, Vol. 47, Summer, 1973, pp. 479–84.

Sources

Gene H. Bell-Villada, an interview with Gabriel García Márquez in *Boston Review,* Vol. VIII, No. 2, April, 1983, pp. 25-7.

Gene H. Bell-Villada, "Banana Strike and Military Massacre: *One Hundred Years of Solitude* and What Happened in 1928," in *From Dante to García Márquez: Studies in Romance Literatures and Linguistics,* edited by Gene H. Bell-Villada, Antonio Gimenes, and George Pistorius, Williams College, 1987, pp. 391-403.

Gordon Brotherston, "An End to Secular Solitude: Gabriel García Márquez," in his *The Emergence of the Latin American Novel,* Cambridge University Press, 1977, pp. 122-35.

Claudia Dreifus, an interview with Gabriel García Márquez in *Playboy,* February, 1983.

D. J. Enright, "Larger Than Death," in *The Listener,* Vol. 84, No. 2160, August 20, 1970, p. 252.

Roberto González Echevarría, "*Cien años de soledad:* The Novel as Myth and Archive," in *Modern Language Notes,* Vol. 99, No. 2, 1984, pp. 358-80.

Rita Guibert, an interview with García Márquez in *Seven Latin American Writers Talk to Rita Guibert,* translated by Frances Partridge, Alfred A. Knopf, 1973, pp. 305-37.

Ricardo Gullon, "Gabriel García Márquez and the Lost Art of Storytelling," translated by José G. Sanchez, in *Diacritics,* Vol. I, No. 1, Fall, 1971, pp. 27-32.

William Kennedy, review of *One Hundred Years of Solitude,* in *National Observer,* April 20, 1970.

John Leonard, "Myth is Alive in Latin America," in *New York Times,* March 3, 1970, p. 39.

Pablo Neruda, quoted in *Time,* March 16, 1970.

Jack Richardson, "Master Builder," in *The New York Review of Books,* Vol. XIV, No. 6, March 26, 1970, pp. 3-4.

Paul West, "A Green Thought in a Green Shade," in *Book World—Chicago Tribune,* February 22, 1970, pp. 4-5.

For Further Study

Claudette Kemper Columbus, "The Heir Must Die: *One Hundred Years of Solitude* as a Gothic Novel," in *Modern Fiction Studies,* Vol. 32, No. 3, Autumn 1986, pp. 397-416.

Explores García Márquez's novel for its gothic aspects and compares it to Bram Stoker's *Dracula,* Mary Wollstonecraft Shelley's *Frankenstein,* and Emily Bronte's *Wuthering Heights.*

William Faulkner, *The Portable Faulkner,* edited by Malcolm Cowley, Viking Press, 1977.

This volume presents the entire legend of Yoknapatawpha. The creation of this fictional place is not unlike the creation of Macondo by García Márquez and the two are often compared. It is said that García Márquez read Hemingway as an antidote to Faulkner.

Jean Franco, "Gabriel García Márquez," in his *An Introduction to Spanish American Literature,* Cambridge University Press, 1969, pp. 343-347.

Franco offers a brief but worthwhile overview of García Márquez's major themes in *One Hundred Years of Solitude.*

Carlos Fuentes, *The Buried Mirror: Reflections on Spain and the New World,* Houghton (Pap), 1993.

Renowned Mexican novelist Carlos Fuentes gives a brief history of Hispanic history. The tone of the work is very reflective with a hint of apology for Spanish history. It is clearly a reaction to the Spain-bashing which accompanied the quincentennial.

Gabriel García Márquez, "The Solitude of Latin America," in *Gabriel García Márquez and the Powers of Fiction,* edited by Julio Ortega, University of Texas Press, 1988, pp. 87-92.

García Márquez's 1982 Nobel Prize acceptance speech is essential background reading for any student studying *One Hundred Years of Solitude.*

Regina Janes, "At Home in the Pope's Grotto: *One Hundred Years of Solitude,*" in her *Gabriel García Márquez: Revolutions in Wonderland,* University of Missouri Press, 1981, pp. 48-69.

Janes analyzes the structure of the novel and insists that its reliance on history and biblical framing holds it together.

Regina Janes, "Liberals, Conservatives, and Bananas: Colombian Politics in the Fictions of Gabriel García Márquez," in *Gabriel García Márquez,* edited by Harold Bloom, Chelsea House Publishers, 1989, pp. 125-146.

Janes provides the student with a lucid explanation of how the intricacies of Colombian politics figure in the novel.

Regina Janes, *One Hundred Years of Solitude: Modes of Reading,* Twayne, 1991.

In a book-length study of *One Hundred Years of Solitude* designed for the student, Janes offers literary and historical contexts, as well as well-developed biographical, mythic, and literary readings of the novel.

Gerald Martin, "On 'Magical' and Social Realism in García Márquez," in *Gabriel García Márquez: New Readings,* edited by Bernard McGuirk and Richard Caldwell, Cambridge University Press, 1987, pp. 95-116.

In an important essay, Martin argues that critics should "revise the impression of a novel whose two levels, magical and realist, mythical and historical, are entirely inseparable, since after the death of Úrsula they slowly but surely begin to come apart."

Stephen Minta, *García Márquez: Writer of Colombia,* New York, 1987.

This is the first biography of the writer.

Bradley A. Shaw and Nora G. Vera-Godwin, eds., *Critical Perspectives on Gabriel García Márquez,* University of Nebraska Press, 1986.

Shaw and Vera-Godwin present a variety of useful essays, most notably one on magical realism in *One Hundred Years of Solitude* by Morton P. Levitt.

Anna Marie Taylor, "Cien años de soledad: History and the Novel," in *Latin American Perspectives,* Vol. II, No. 3, Fall, 1975, pp. 96-111.

Explores the value of historical consciousness in the novel by García Márquez and its political relevance.

Mario Vargas Llosa, "García Márquez: From Aracataca to Macondo," in *Gabriel García Márquez,* edited by Harold Bloom, Chelsea House Publishers, 1989, pp. 5-20.

Vargas Llosa, a noted Latin American writer in his own right, is widely regarded as the foremost expert on García Márquez. This essay provides important background for the student of *One Hundred Years of Solitude.*

Raymond Williams, "*One Hundred Years of Solitude* (1967)," in his *Gabriel García Márquez,* Twayne, 1984.

Noted scholar Raymond Williams provides a chapter-length introduction to the novel, providing not only an excellent overview of the book, but also succinct summaries of a variety of critical approaches. The rest of this clearly-written and informative book offers useful information on García Márquez's life and career.

The Outsiders

S. E. Hinton
1967

S. E. Hinton irrevocably altered the course of juvenile literature in America with her first novel. *The Outsiders* was published when she was seventeen and was her stark answer to the fluffy high school stories about proms and dates typical of the 1960s. "Where is reality?" she asked in an essay explaining her motivation in the *New York Times Book Review.* In other narratives for teens, she could not find "the drive-in social jungle ... the behind-the-scenes politicking that goes on in big schools, the cruel social system," or the teenagers who lived in those settings. In contrast, her story was real, graphic, emotional, and true to the challenges of being a teenager in twentieth-century America. In addition, it was an exciting narrative that captured teenagers' attention. It drew a wide audience, particularly boys who were reluctant readers. Thirty years after its publication, the novel remains immensely popular and has sold more than four million copies in the United States. Its adaptation to film was a great success as well.

The novel is the story of a traumatic time in the life of a recently orphaned fourteen-year-old boy named Ponyboy Curtis. He lives on the East Side, a member of the lower class and a gang of "greasers." Quiet and dreamy, Ponyboy has conflicts with his older brother and guardian, Darrel, who keeps the family together. The greasers— whom Ponyboy distinguishes from "hoods"—are the heroes of the tale. Set against them are the upper-class socials, or Socs, who enjoy drinking, driving nice cars, and beating up greasers. The cir-

cumstances of this social situation result in the death of three teens. The story explores the themes of class conflict, affection, brotherly love, and coming of age in a way that young people readily appreciate. This novel's portrayal of disaffected youth has been criticized for its violent content, but it is now regarded as a classic of juvenile literature. It can be considered one of the first examples of the "young adult" genre, and after its publication literature for teens gained a new realism, depth, and respect for its audience.

Author Biography

Born in 1950, Susan Eloise Hinton was raised in Tulsa, Oklahoma. She was an avid reader as a child and experimented with writing by the time she turned ten. Her early stories were about cowboys and horses, and she preferred plots with rough riding and gunfights. When Hinton reached her teens, however, she could not find anything pleasing to read. Adult literature was still a bit too complicated for her, while literature for teens consisted of innocent tales about girls finding boyfriends. To please herself, she decided to create a different fictional universe from these annoying "Mary Jane goes to the prom" novels. She wanted to create a realistic story about being a teen. Additionally, like her character Ponyboy, she wanted to record some events of her high school years. She took inspiration from real events and people to create a story of class warfare between teens. After working on the novel for a year and a half and through four rewrites, she let a friend's mother read it. The mother liked it enough to refer her to an agent, Marilyn Marlow of the Curtis Brown Agency. A contract offering publication arrived during Hinton's high-school graduation ceremonies.

The Outsiders was published in 1967, when the author was just seventeen. Susan Eloise shortened her name to S. E. Hinton so that boys would not know the author was female. It was published to critical acclaim, won several awards, and became a cult classic among teen readers. The success of *The Outsiders* enabled Hinton to go to The University of Tulsa, where she earned a B.S. in Education in 1970. While in school she met her future husband, David Inhofe, who encouraged her to write her second novel, *That Was Then, This Is Now* (1971). Over the next decade, she published a new novel every four years. In 1975, she published *Rumble Fish,* and *Tex* in 1979. Although she was

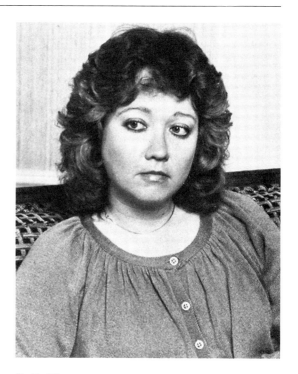

S. E. Hinton

no longer an adolescent herself, Hinton was still able to bring her sympathy for teens and insight into their lives to her work. She only published one work in the 1980s, 1988's *Taming the Star Runner,* and in the 1990s she has focused more on picture books for younger readers than on novels.

Other than her writing, Hinton is kept busy by a family life and her son, Nicholas David. She has also served as a consultant on the film adaptations of her novels and has even appeared in minor roles. She continues to write and lives in Tulsa. Her pivotal role in the development of young adult fiction was recognized in 1988, when the American Library Association awarded her the first Margaret Edwards Young Adult Author Achievement Award for her body of work.

Plot Summary

The Greaser Gang

The Outsiders opens with the recollections of Ponyboy Curtis, the narrator of the story. He tells the reader in the first paragraph that he is a "greaser," from the poor neighborhood of his hometown. In the second paragraph, however, he explains that he is different from other greasers in his love of movies and books. Ponyboy is day-dreaming after a Paul Newman movie when he is jumped by a gang of upper-class rich kids, known as socials, or "Socs." It is only the intervention of his two brothers and their friends that saves Ponyboy from being badly injured. The greasers have good reason to fear the Socs, a group of whom beat their friend Johnny so badly that he began to carry a switchblade wherever he went. Partly for this reason, Ponyboy's oldest brother Darry yells at him for going to the movies unaccompanied, and Pony relates that he feels that he can never please Darry.

On the next night, Pony and Johnny accompany Dallas Winston, the most hardened member of their gang, to a drive-in movie. There Dally begins to harass two Soc girls who are there without dates. After one of the girls, Cherry Valance, tells Dally to leave them alone, he leaves she and Ponyboy strike up a conversation. Dally returns, and when Johnny tells him to leave the girls alone, Dally stalks off for good. Later Two-Bit will join them, scaring Johnny in the process. Later Cherry asks, and Pony tells, why Johnny seems so jumpy and scared. After hearing how the Socs nearly killed Johnny, Cherry tells Ponyboy that "things are rough all over," but he does not believe her.

Greasers vs. Socs

After the movie, Cherry and Ponyboy share their thoughts on the differences between Greasers and Socs, and Ponyboy is surprised to find that they have similarities, too. The three greaser boys are walking Cherry and her friend Marcia to Two-Bit's car when they are spotted by the Socs. In order to avoid a fight, Cherry and Marcia agree to go home with the Socs and Two-Bit also goes home. Johnny and Ponyboy remain at the lot and talk about how things should be different before falling asleep. After Pony arrives home late, Darry confronts, then slaps him. Pony runs out of the house, and he and Johnny go to the park so Ponyboy can cool off before returning home.

In the park, Johnny and Ponyboy are accosted by drunken Socs. After they try to drown Ponyboy, Johnny kills one of them with his knife. The two decide to run away, and Dally helps them by telling them where to hide and giving them money and a gun. They hop a train to their hideout, a church in the country. There they cut and bleach their hair to disguise their identities. Pony feels that in losing his hair style, he has lost his identity, a feature that made him a greaser: "Our hair labeled us greasers, too—it was our trademark. Maybe we couldn't have Corvairs or madras shirts, but we could have hair."

Ponyboy and Johnny pass a lonely and bored four or five days at the church, reading to each other from *Gone with the Wind*. One morning the two boys watch a sunrise, which reminds Ponyboy of a Robert Frost poem, "Nothing Gold Can Stay," though he feels that the poem's deeper meaning escapes him. The next morning, Dally arrives and tells them that Cherry Valance will testify on their behalf. This prompts Johnny to say that they will turn themselves in. Dally tries to talk Johnny out of it, not wanting jail to harden him, but Johnny is determined. They are on their way back to the church when they realize that it is on fire and that a group of kids is trapped inside.

Hoods and Heroes

Ponyboy and Johnny manage to rescue all the kids in the church, but Pony faints after Johnny pushes him out the window. When he wakes up in ambulance, one of the teachers tells him that in spite of Dally's heroism in pulling Johnny from the flames, Johnny is in critical condition. Pony tells the disbelieving teacher that he and Johnny are wanted for murder. At the hospital, Pony is reunited with his brothers; when he sees Darry crying, he realizes the depth of Darry's love and concern for him.

Because of the publicity, Ponyboy realizes that he and his brothers could be separated. He also finds out that Sandy, Soda's girlfriend, has left town, and it is implied that she is pregnant. Later, Pony and Two-Bit encounter Randy, one of the Socs, who is tormented by his part in what has happened. He tells Pony that he could never have gone into the fire to rescue someone as Ponyboy and Johnny did. Two-Bit and Ponyboy then go to the hospital, and Pony realizes that Johnny is dying. Johnny's eyes glow when Pony tells him he's being called a hero, but when Johnny's mother comes to see him, he passes out from the strain of trying to refuse her visit. When Pony and Two-Bit then visit Dally in his room, Pony thinks of Dally as his buddy for the first time. Later, Two-Bit and Pony run into Cherry Valance, who assures them the score-settling rumble with the Socs won't involve weapons. She angers Pony when she says she won't visit Johnny in the hospital because he killed Bob. When Cherry weeps, Ponyboy tells her they both see the same sunset.

The rumble begins later that night when Darry squares off against an old friend of his from high school. Dally runs up to join the rumble and helps Pony fight one of the Socs. He then takes Pony to see Johnny at the hospital to tell him of their victory. Johnny tells them that fighting does no good and then instructs Ponyboy to "stay gold" before he dies. The one thing he loves gone, Dally runs out of the room in agony. After Ponyboy arrives home, the gang gets a call from Dally, who has just robbed a store. They arrive at the vacant lot in time to see Dally killed in a shootout with the police, and Pony faints at the scene of Dally's death.

"Staying Gold"

Ponyboy is still recovering when he is visited by Randy, who leaves when he realizes that Ponyboy is trying to deny that Johnny is dead. Pony plans to confess to killing Bob at the hearing inquiring into the incident, but he is not questioned about it. Pony and his brothers are granted permission to remain together, but Pony continues to have trouble recovering. He tries to write an essay so he can pass English, but finds all the possible topics either meaningless or too painful. After Pony and Darry argue again, Soda uncharacteristically explodes in anger, and Ponyboy learns that Sandy was cheating on Soda. She will not answer Soda's letters, and the baby she is carrying is not his. Ponyboy has been oblivious to Soda's pain, and after Soda tells them that without each other, they'll end up like Dally, they vow to fight less often.

Shortly after the family reconciliation, Ponyboy picks up Johnny's copy of *Gone with the Wind*. Inside, he finds a letter from Johnny, in which he tells Pony to let Dally know that it was worth it to rescue the children from the church, and that Pony can be whatever he wants to be in life, even though he is a greaser. Ponyboy finally realizes what it means to "stay gold." He begins to write his English theme, thinking of all the kids who need to know there is good in the world. He begins with the day that he walked out of the Paul Newman movie, forever changed by all that has happened since.

Characters

Randy Adderson

Randy is Bob's best friend and takes his death very hard. Before the rumble, he has a talk with Ponyboy about all that has happened. He has decided that violence is wrong because "it doesn't do any good." He stays out of the rumble and later comes to visit Pony when he's sick. His words lead Pony to realize that "the other guy was human too."

Johnny Cade

Beaten by his father and ignored by his mother, he stays around town only because he is the gang's pet, "everyone's kid brother." Johnny reminds Pony of a "little dark puppy that has been kicked too many times and is lost in a crowd of strangers." He was jumped once by the Socs and beaten very badly. Since then he has carried a blade and has become even more suspicious and jumpy. Johnny and Pony are friends by default. They are the youngest in the gang and also the most sensitive. They are quiet around the older boys and reflective between themselves.

Johnny echoes Pony's frustration at their predicament in life, scared of being beaten or killed and not able to change anything about it. Johnny was considered dumb by his teachers, and yet he realizes things that completely pass by Pony. While Pony reads from *Gone with the Wind* about Southern gentlemen riding into certain death, Johnny sees Dally. And when Pony recites Robert Frost, Johnny understands the meaning of the poem. They have to stay gold, stay young, and stay true to themselves. It is this message that Johnny sends to Pony in his final letter and the one Pony is left to struggle with.

Darrel Curtis

Darry has been taking care of the family ever since Mr. and Mrs. Curtis died in a car wreck, eight months before the start of the novel. A judge allows the brothers to stay together under twenty-year-old Darry's supervision—so long as they stay out of trouble. Rather than go to college on a football scholarship, Darry has to go to work in order to keep the three together and Pony in school. He has had to give up a lot and has become an adult too fast. "Darry's hard and firm and rarely grins at all." A big and powerful young man, Darry has "eyes that are like two pieces of pale blue-green ice.... He doesn't understand anything that is not plain hard fact. But he uses his head." Darry takes his custodianship very seriously by keeping a tight hold on Pony.

Ponyboy often has conflicts with his oldest brother, not realizing how similar the two are. Darry is different from the other greasers; as Two-Bit says, "the only thing that keeps Darry from being a Soc is us." He is the leader of the gang by mutual consent and respect. He wears his hair short like a Soc and he is clean shaven. While Darry likes fighting for the athletic challenge of it, Pony realizes that Darry is too smart to stay around the greasers forever. "That's why he's better than the rest of us, [Pony] thought. He's going somewhere." Pony finally comes to understand his brother really does love him.

Darry Curtis

See Darrel Curtis

Ponyboy Curtis

The story is Ponyboy Curtis's narrative about his experience seeing three young men die. Pony is a good student, a track star, and a greaser. It is this latter distinction, rather than his orphan status, which brings him trouble. In addition, he is a solitary, sensitive boy who likes movies, watching sunsets, and reading. His consumption of these poetic pursuits often foils his common sense. Thus, his desire to see movies without the distracting fidgets of friends or brothers leads to his lonely walk home from the cinema and his run in with a group of Socs. Luckily for him, his brothers and the gang hear his cries for help and he doesn't receive anything like the beating that spooked Johnny.

A great deal of the tension in Pony comes from his attempts to figure out his oldest brother Darry. He complains to Two-Bit, Johnny, and Cherry that his brother doesn't like him. He believes that Darry resents him because he had to turn down a football scholarship to college in order to support him. Everyone tries to tell him otherwise, but Pony doesn't believe in Darry's love for him until he is injured in the fire. Even so, he only comes to understand his brother after their fighting drives Sodapop, the middle brother, to tears.

The beauty of Ponyboy's character is that though he emerges strong and confident at the end of the book, it is not the result of becoming a tough hood but of remaining true to himself. The positive tone is not so much because the Socs are beaten (this time), or that the boys will remain together, or that Ponyboy recovers from his injuries. Instead, the resolution is excruciatingly personal. When he scares off a bunch of Socs with a broken bottle, he considers his act no big deal: "anyone else could have done the same thing." This scares Two-Bit, because none of the gang wants Pony to become just another greaser. However, Two-Bit relaxes when he sees Pony stoop down and clean up the glass shards so that no one will get hurt. Ponyboy has, as Johnny would say, stayed golden. The real denouement of Pony's character growth is the resolution of tension between him and Darry. It tries to come once, when he hugs him at the hospital, but does not arrive until they chase down Soda. The

Media Adaptations

- *The Outsiders* was made into a film starring C. Thomas Howell, Matt Dillon, Ralph Macchio, Patrick Swayze, Rob Lowe, Diane Lane, Tom Cruise, and Emilio Estevez. The 1983 Warner Brothers film, directed by Francis Ford Coppola, was a huge success and remains a popular film.

- Fox-TV adapted the novel as a television series in 1990.

- *The Outsiders* was also made into a filmstrip with cassette in 1978 by Current Affairs/Mark Twain Media, and as an audiocassette for Random House, 1993.

three have a heart-to-heart talk and when Darry says "Sure, little buddy," thus calling Pony by the name reserved for Soda, Pony knows everything will be okay. "I reckon we all just wanted to stay together."

Sodapop Curtis

Ponyboy's older brother is sixteen going on seventeen and a high school dropout. He is the caregiver and peacemaker of the Curtis brothers. Soda is "movie-star kind of handsome, the kind that people stop on the street to watch go by." Bubbly like his name, Soda is "always happy-go-lucky and grinning" and the type of person who doesn't drink alcohol because "he gets drunk on just plain living." He listens to everyone, "understands everybody," and is Pony's confidante. Soda enjoys teasing Darry and is the only one who would dare do so. He also gives Darry backrubs after he has tried to carry too much roofing material at work. However, being caught between Darry and Pony is draining. He also has to suffer in silence when his girlfriend, Sandy, is shipped to Florida.

Paul Holden

In the big confrontation between Socs and greasers after Bob Sheldon's death, Darry is put forth as the rumble starter. Paul steps up to answer for the Socs. While in high school, the two were

A scene from The Outsiders.

friends and teammates on the football team. Now Paul shows hatred, contempt, and pity for his old friend.

Johnnycakes

See Johnny Cade

Marcia

She is a friend of Cherry's who seems like a good match for Two-Bit when they meet at the drive-in. However, social reality will keep them from getting together.

Two-Bit Matthews

See Keith Matthews

Keith Matthews

The funny guy of the gang who always has to make his "two bits" worth of smart remarks. His specialty is shoplifting, which he does for the challenge of it. He likes "fights, blondes, and for some unfathomable reason, school."

Buck Merrill

Dally's Rodeo partner is the source of the cash Johnny and Pony use to hide out after the killing of Bob Sheldon.

Steve Randle

Soda's best friend and another greaser, Steve works part-time at the gas station where Soda works full-time. His specialty is cars. Between Soda's looks and Steve's mechanical aptitude, their station is the most popular in town. Ponyboy only likes Steve because of Soda; Steve treats Pony like a tagalong when Soda brings him on their escapades.

Sandy

Soda's girlfriend who, later in the novel, leaves for Florida. It is implied that she is pregnant, and Soda has offered to marry her. But she returns his letters unopened and Soda discovers someone else is most likely the father.

Bob Sheldon

The rich, handsome, and arrogant Soc who is responsible for the serious damage done to Johnny one night. Bob is also Cherry's boyfriend; although she doesn't want to see him when he has been drinking, she says otherwise he is sweet and friendly. He has a set of rings he wears to make his hitting all the more damaging. Johnny kills Bob to save Pony.

Curly Shepard

Tim's younger brother, "an average downtown hood, tough and not very bright." He and Pony have a mutual respect for each other after they once burned each other on a dare. Like Darry does for Pony, Curly's older brother Tim keeps an eye out for his sibling. While Pony and Curly are in similar positions—they are being brought up and protected by powerful older brothers—Curly is always in and out of the reformatory.

Tim Shepard

The leader of another gang of Greasers who ally themselves with Darry's gang. He "looked like the model JD you see in films and magazines" and is "one of those who enjoy being a hood." Tim demands the discipline and code one normally imagines a gang to have. That is, his gang is not a loose group of childhood friends like Darry's. He has broken a few of Dally's ribs in one of the regular fights they have just for fun. Nevertheless, he and Dally are good friends. When the rumble is scheduled, it is Tim who brings in his troops and another gang to bring the greaser total to twenty.

Mr. Syme

Ponyboy's English teacher, whose assignment leads to the narrative of the novel. He is concerned about Pony's slumping grades, and "you can tell he's interested in you as a person, too."

Cherry Valance

See Sherri Valance

Sherri Valance

Cherry is a pretty, red-headed Soc whom Pony and Johnny meet at the drive-in. Although she responds negatively to Dally's crude come-ons, she tells Pony that she could easily fall in love with him. Cherry hates fighting and serves as a go-between for the two groups. She doesn't succeed in stopping the fighting, but she does help increase understanding. She delivers two important revelations to Pony. The first is that Socs are not without their own problems, and the other is that rich people are capable of watching sunsets, just as Pony does.

Dally Winston

See Dallas Winston

Dallas Winston

"The real character of the gang," Dally was arrested his first time at the age of ten. He spent three years on the "wild side" of New York and likes to blow off steam in gang fights. He is the most dangerous member of the bunch—not even Darry wants to tangle with him—but he is still a part of their greaser "family." The local police have a large file on him, and he has just gotten out of jail at the opening of the novel. While "the fight for self-preservation had hardened him beyond caring," there are two things that have meaning for him: jockeying on ponies (the "only thing Dally did honestly") and Johnny.

In Tulsa, lacking a rival gang, Dally hates the Socs. Fighting them is frustrating, however, because he knows that beating them doesn't take away any of their social advantages. During fights he takes particular care to look out for Johnny, and so he helps the boys after the murder even though it could return him to prison. Johnny returns Dally's care with a devoted admiration. Consequently, Johnny views him as a heroic gentleman of courage, like those in *Gone with the Wind*. When Johnny is dead the rest of the gang realizes he was Dally's breaking point. Having lost the one thing he really cared about, Dally sets himself up for death. After robbing a store, he threatens the pursuing cops with an empty gun. He dies in front of his friends in a hail of bullets.

Jerry Wood

One of the few adults in the novel, Jerry Wood is a teacher at the scene of the fire. He stays by

Topics For Further Study

- Reflect on the significance of the title—who are the outsiders, and what are they outside of? What does it mean to be an outsider and why has this become a twentieth-century phenomenon? Support your arguments with examples from recent history.

- There are two famous novels with similar titles to Hinton's story. Both concern young men, circumstantial murder(s), and existentialism (the philosophy that the individual is solely responsible for his fate). The two novels are Richard Wright's *The Outsider* and Albert Camus's *The Stranger* (published in England as *The Outsider*). Compare Hinton's novel with one of these other "outsider" stories.

- Many people deny that social or economic class plays a significant role in American society or government. Using examples from this novel and other teenage books or films (such as *The Breakfast Club* and *Pretty In Pink* through the recent *Clueless*), argue whether you think this is true or false.

- Compare and contrast *The Outsiders* with another story of gangs, such as *Boys in the Hood* or *West Side Story*. Compare specific events, characters, and themes.

- Juvenile crime and "youth predators" have become an obsessive political issue over the last decade. Are youth today really more violent than twenty or thirty years ago? Do some research into the phenomenon of youth violence and some of the following topics: trying youths as young as twelve as adults; incarcerating teens with adults; and increasing security at school versus increasing education spending increases. Good sources to start with are the National Center for Juvenile Justice (http://www.ncjj.org) and the Center on Juvenile Justice and Criminal Justice (http://www.cjcj.org).

Pony in the ambulance and the hospital and listens to his tale.

Themes

Class Conflict

Issues of American economic class are confronted head on by the portrayal of the rival gangs as rich and poor. The rich Socs "jump greasers and wreck houses and throw beer blasts for kicks, and get editorials in the paper for being a public disgrace one day and an asset to society the next." The poor greasers, conversely, "steal things and drive old souped-up cars and hold up gas stations and have a gang fight once in a while." Each group views the other as the enemy and "that's just the way things are." But circumstances will at least reveal to a few that everyone is human—although there will still be a rivalry.

Cherry offers her opinion that it is not just a difference in money: "You greasers have a different set of values. You're more emotional. We're sophisticated—cool to the point of not feeling anything.... Rat race is a perfect name for [our life]." This leads Pony to wonder if perhaps it is just natural for the two classes to be separate and unequal—a fact that haunts Johnny's decision to turn himself in. He knows that the courts stereotype all greasers as juvenile delinquents. Still, Ponyboy comes to understand that Socs and Greasers have similarities: "It seemed funny to me that the sunset she saw from her patio and the one I saw from the back steps was the same one. Maybe the two different worlds we lived in weren't so different. We saw the same sunset."

That is as far as the bridge is going to extend between the two worlds. Cherry warns that in public she will have to appear to ignore him as usual, "it's not personal or anything." Pony then says Two-bit is smart for throwing away a false phone number Marcia gave him: "he knew the score." To give her credit, Cherry does act as a go-between in terms of the rumble, but there is no hint of change. Indeed, Cherry's help may simply be an attempt to appease her own conscience. Finally, all contact is lost after Bob's death. Cherry cannot bear to resume the effort of bridging the gap with the group who killed her boyfriend—despite the fact that Bob brought it on himself.

In sum, the portrayal of class that Hinton makes simply outlines the facts. There is no attempt to suggest a way of bringing the classes together. Nor is there a criticism of either side, because both sides are at fault. The only optimism this novel offers is that members of the two sides can learn to understand one another, even if they still fight. In the end, greasers will be greasers and Socs will be Socs.

Search for Self

Ponyboy has all the worries of a boy his age; is he strong, brave, or handsome enough to match up to the masculine ideal? In Pony's case, the ideal is a cross between Soda and Darry. He wants to be handsome and appealing to everyone but he also wants to be tough, full of sense, and a good fighter. He is none of these things. Everyone in the gang is cautious around Pony because they already recognize that he is something special in his own right. As Two-bit says, in response to a headline, "Y'all were heroes from the beginning." Pony doesn't seem to understand this, however. When others tell him they are impressed by his rescue of the children, Pony shrugs and says that anyone would have done the same. But not everyone would have rushed into a flaming building to rescue someone they didn't know; few also have the courage, to hold off a gang of Socs. The brilliance of this last episode is how it reveals Pony is learning something which he sensed at the rumble, but only confronts in the writing of the tale.

In this last confrontation, Pony makes the Socs back down with a broken bottle, giving every appearance of having become a young tough hood. Two-Bit witnesses this and is concerned: "Ponyboy, listen, don't get tough. You're not like the rest of us and don't try to be...." But tough hoods don't get hurt, Pony thinks in response. They also do not pick up glass shards off the street, which Pony proceeds to do. This relieves Two-Bit, who suddenly realizes Pony is still himself, although he won't take anymore trouble from the Socs. In other words, he can act tough enough to survive, but it is just an act—Pony is still the one who remains considerate,

stays gold, reads poetry, and picks up the glass. "I didn't want anyone to get a flat tire."

Loyalty

The tenderness with which the gang regards its respective members is endearing. They are all tough guys, but they all really care about each other. It is a gang community of greasers that wants, subtly, to change their group. They will do it through the youngest and brightest members, Johnny and Pony. Darry wants his younger brother to amount to something and Dally wants Johnny to have a better life. "I just don't want you to get hurt," Dally says when Johnny speaks of turning himself in. "You get hardened in jail. I don't want that to happen to you."

In some ways, then, the group understands the cycle of violence and wants it to stop. Unfortunately, they do not have the family, financial, or community support to make changes, and they realize that they must be satisfied with each other. By this standard the novel ends happily. It is this communal love that enables Johnny to survive a rough home life and die peacefully. "Dally was proud of him. That was all Johnny had ever wanted." Dally's loss of the one person he cares about drives him to a fatal confrontation with police. It is this same community recognition that Pony seeks, and finally gets, from Darry. The brothers realize that "if we don't have each other, we don't have anything." There is some hope that together they will be okay.

Style

Narration

Ponyboy narrates the story in retrospect, under the guise of having to write out a theme for English class. This presentation of a story by one of the characters involved is called first-person narrative. A first-person narrative is easily identified by the use of "I" in telling the story. Having one of the characters tell the story can make the story more immediate for readers, because they easily can put themselves in the narrator's place.

A first-person narrator also means a limited perspective, however. Ponyboy can only describe his own thoughts and can only relate events he has witnessed or heard about. This limited perspective lends itself very well to the themes of class conflict that appear throughout the book. At the beginning of the story, Pony can only sympathize with other greasers. A third-person narrator ("he/she said") who knows about all of the characters could tell the reader what Cherry or Randy or even Sodapop was thinking. Instead, Pony has to learn to understand other people's feelings all by himself. This understanding is an important part of his coming of age.

Characters

Hinton is a character writer instead of an idea writer. She develops her characters in depth and then lets them create the story. Consequently, the opening of the book is a very detailed introduction to each character. By the end of the book, the reader knows each character in intimate detail. In addition, the characters' names are particularly descriptive. "Ponyboy," for instance, creates an image of a youth becoming a cowboy. Sodapop's name reflects his own bubbly personality. Even "Dallas Winston," the combination of a Texas city and a famous cigarette brand, invokes bygone days of Western heroics and toughness. This invocation ties in with Hinton's fascination with that earlier rough and violent era.

Description and Diction

The brief detail used in the book is rather startling in its effectiveness. Just as Ponyboy can "get [Dally's] personality down in a few lines" of a drawing, he can sum up his friends in just a few words. Johnny, for instance, is "a little dark puppy that has been kicked too many times and is lost in a crowd of strangers." The speed of slang adjectives adds another dimension to description. "Greasers. You know, like hoods, JD's," for example, gives Mr. Wood a short but precise description of the boys' background.

The scene of heroic rescue is full of delightful phrasing. The comparison of the burning church to hell might be expected, but the simile of falling cinders as biting ants is rather novel. Adding realism to tension occurs in a truism: "I picked up a kid, and he promptly bit me." And a reaction to Two-Bit's drinking, "I'd hate to see the day when I had to get my nerve from a can," sounds like a wise saying. Hinton is successful in using youth slang in her prose style and this success makes the narrative more believable.

Allusions

Allusions are references to other works of literature or art. A narrator can use them to explain a character or situation by comparing it to something already known by the reader. Ponyboy refers to several other works of literature to make comparisons as well as to avoid lengthy explanations. For instance, he refers to Charles Dickens's novel *Great Expectations,* another tale of class conflict: "That kid Pip, he reminded me of us—the way he felt marked lousy because he wasn't a gentleman or anything, and the way that girl kept looking down on him." While Johnny and Ponyboy are hiding out at the church, they discuss two works: the novel *Gone with the Wind* and the poem "Nothing Gold Can Stay." Johnny sees echoes of the Southern gentlemen's gallantry in Dally's coolness, and the sunrise reminds Ponyboy of the poem. It is only later, with Johnny's help, that Pony comes to understand the meaning of the poem. In this way, an allusion has helped illustrate the coming of age theme of the novel.

Imagery

Imagery is using visual images, sometimes called symbols, to reinforce themes or represent deeper meanings. The novel does not contain many symbols, because the story is simply a recounting of what happened. There is one overriding image in the story, however, one which is important to the main characters and the main theme. The image is that of a sunrise or sunset. Once again, the myth of the cowboy is suggested. Our heroes should ride off safely into the sunset, just like the heroes of Western movies. Unfortunately, not all of the gang will make that ride. Sunsets also figure in the novel because Pony likes to watch them. This signifies that he is a sensitive boy who appreciates beauty. But he is not alone in his appreciation. He discovers that a Soc, Cherry, is capable of watching a sunset. Given the chance, so is Johnny. The sunrise that Johnny and Pony share at the church prompts recitation of a Robert Frost poem, "Nothing Gold can Stay." That poem sums up the meaning of the sunset in this story and is the theme Pony is trying to develop for his English teacher. For Johnny and Pony, the phrase comes to mean that good things don't last. Sunsets are short, and blissful escapes into abandoned churches end in fire. But it is possible, Pony proves, to remain true to one's self and thereby "stay gold."

Historical Context

The Rise of Youth Culture

In the United States, the period from 1945 to 1963 was termed the "Baby Boom" because of the

C. Thomas Howell, Tom Cruise, and Emilio Estevez in a movie still from The Outsiders.

sharp increase in the number of children during those years. By 1958, one-third of the country's population was fifteen years old or younger. The years after World War II had also seen an increase in wealth throughout the United States. By the time they became teenagers in the late 1950s and early 1960s, therefore, many of these "Baby Boomers" had plenty of spare cash to spend. Companies competed to attract the dollars of these new consumers. The film, music, television, and fashion industries created products especially for the increasingly influential teen market. Rock 'n' roll became the most popular music on the radio, and movies also reflected this new focus on adolescents. Actors James Dean and Marlon Brando became idols for portraying teenage antiheroes in *Rebel without a Cause* (1955) and *The Wild One* (1954). Paul Newman, whose looks Ponyboy admires as "tough," followed in the footsteps of these actors by playing similarly cool characters in the films *The Hustler* (1961), *Hud* (1963), and *Cool Hand Luke* (1967).

Teenagers' increased spending power also gave them a new measure of independence from their parents. Rebellion against adult authority became a notable theme in many teen films. Loud rock 'n' roll music became another way for teens to defy their parents' values. Some adolescents' rebellion turned violent, and teenage gangs sprouted in urban areas. The increase in the numbers of young people meant an increase in juvenile delinquents as well. These "JDs" became an urgent concern for law enforcement in the 1950s and 1960s. As *The Outsiders* demonstrates, however, not all of these delinquents were from poor neighborhoods. Children from supposedly "good families" also became dropouts, gang members, and drug or alcohol abusers.

The Vietnam War and the Protest Movement

Teenagers were not the only Americans who challenged authority in the 1960s. The public in general had begun to question U.S. involvement in Vietnam's war against communist rebels. The United States had been providing military advisors to this southeast Asian country since the 1950s. In 1964, however, the number of U.S. troops in Vietnam doubled. By 1967, almost half a million Americans were fighting in Vietnam. Nevertheless, many citizens had doubts as to the effectiveness and morality of American involvement. Protesters turned up in the thousands for antiwar demonstrations. The protesters came from all walks of life: groups included those made up of students, clergy, scientists, and women.

Compare
&
Contrast

- **1967:** Romanticized movies of teen rebellion give way to upbeat musicals extolling a life of beach parties, fast cars, and teen relationships.

  1990s: One of the most popular genres for teens is the horror movie, in which a group of teens is pitted against a homicidal maniac. The 1996 film *Scream* becomes one of the top grossing releases of the year, earning over $100 million in box office receipts.

- **1967:** The Beatles lead the "British Invasion" of American music as they dominate the pop charts. Their 1967 album *Sgt. Pepper's Lonely Hearts Club Band* uses several experimental recording techniques and influences countless pop and rock artists.

  1990s: Popular music has broken down into countless genres, with no one type dominating the market. Rap, "alternative," rhythm and blues, pop, rock, and movie soundtrack albums all reach number one at various times during the decade.

- **1967:** Dropout rates show a sharp increase, and by the late 1960s over 7.5 million students have left high school before graduating. In 1967, 15 percent of white students are dropouts, as opposed to almost 30 percent of black students (Hispanic rates were not recorded at this time).

  1990s: In 1996, the overall dropout rate remains steady at five percent, or about 500,000 students yearly. Dropout rates for both black and white students have decreased, to 6.7 and 4.1 percent respectively; the Hispanic dropout rate remains higher, at 9 percent. Low income students have the highest dropout rate of any group: 11.1 percent.

- **1967:** In an America torn by political protest, race riots, and growing recreational drug use, teenage gangs seem a minor menace in comparison. Schools are relatively safe, as violent confrontations most often occur between gangs outside of school property.

  1990s: Teenage gang violence is an increasing problem for both urban and rural communities. Gang violence often erupts inside schools and sometimes involves innocent bystanders. Easy access to drugs and guns leads to deaths inside school buildings and on school grounds.

- **1967:** The People's Republic of China explodes its first hydrogen bomb, raising U.S. concerns and Soviet fears of another contender in the nuclear arms race.

  1990s: A clear sign that nonproliferation treaties have failed to stop the spread of nuclear weapons, in 1998 first India and then Pakistan conduct nuclear tests and declare themselves nuclear states.

The year 1967 featured many notable protests. University of Wisconsin students destroyed university property while running recruiters from Dow Chemical (the makers of the defoliant napalm) off campus. The week of April 15 saw anti-war demonstrations in New York and San Francisco bring out 100,000 and 20,000 people respectively. A protest at the Pentagon led to arrests of several notable people, including poet Allen Ginsberg and pediatrician Dr. Benjamin Spock. The Reverend Martin Luther King, Jr., proposed a merging of the civil rights movement and the anti-war movement. He declared the U.S. government "the greatest purveyor of violence in the world."

Race Relations in the 1960s

Although all of the "greaser" characters in *The Outsiders* are white, the prejudice they endure recalls that suffered by African Americans and other nonwhites during the same era. Several laws and court decisions of the late 1950s and early 1960s had outlawed public segregation. Nevertheless, discrimination was still part of daily life for many blacks in the 1960s. In some southern cities, public school integration had to be enforced by federal troops. Black students who attended previously all-white schools often faced ridicule and even physical abuse from their classmates. (This calls to mind how Ponyboy is called a "hood" by his lab partner when he uses a switchblade to dissect a worm in biology class.)

Despite the political gains made by the civil rights movement, practical gains for African Americans lagged far behind. According to census statistics of the 1960s, almost one-half of non-white households were below the poverty line, compared to one-fifth of white households. Unemployment rates among nonwhites were more than double that of whites, at 7.3 percent. "White flight" occurred as white middle-class families moved from the city to the suburbs. As a result, many companies and stores moved out of the cities as well, leading to a decline in investment in infrastructure. The poor families left behind, both black and white, often ended up with poorer schools, fewer government resources, and decaying neighborhoods. Thus, while political segregation was outlawed, economic segregation was still in place.

Race riots sometimes erupted in these impoverished neighborhoods, often provoked by incidents of police brutality. The most devastating of these incidents was the Watts riot that took place over six days in 1965. The Los Angeles police required the assistance of the California National Guard to halt this disturbance, which left thirty-four dead, thousands injured, and over forty million dollars of property damage. In 1967, race riots erupted in several U.S. cities, leaving eighty-three dead and several hundred injured. These riots were different from the "rumbles" portrayed in *The Outsiders,* which are essentially conflicts between rival gangs. These race riots of the 1960s, on the other hand, usually began as conflicts between white police and black residents. As the conflict grew, rioters targeted innocent bystanders and property as well. Shops were looted and burned, even those owned by black families living in the neighborhoods. One result of these riots was the Anti-Riot Act, which was added to the Civil Rights Bill of 1968.

Critical Overview

Although *The Outsiders* has been a favorite with teens ever since its publication in 1967, adult critics have been more cautious in their assessments. Initial reviews debated the supposed "realism" of this startling new work, as well as the skill of its young author. Thomas Fleming, for instance, questioned Hinton's portrayal of the Soc–Greaser conflict. He noted that in his hometown it was the poor kids who beat up the rich ones, not the other way around. Nevertheless, he added in his *New York Times Book Review* assessment that "Hinton's fire-engine pace does not give the reader much time to manufacture doubts." Nat Hentoff similarly observed in *Atlantic Monthly* that the plot of the book was "factitious," or forced and artificial. He praised the author, however, for addressing issues of class that were absent in previous books for teens: "Any teenager, no matter what some of his textbooks say, knows that this is decidedly not a classless society." *School Library Journal* contributor Lillian Gerhardt similarly hailed Hinton's portrayal of class rivalry: "It is rare-to-unique among juvenile books ... to find a novel confronting class hostilities which have intensified since the Depression."

In another early review, William Jay Jacobs favorably compared *The Outsiders* with a popular classic from the 1950s, J. D. Salinger's *Catcher in the Rye.* Other critics have observed similarities between Hinton's Ponyboy and Salinger's Holden Caufield. "But as much as the sensitive, thoughtful Ponyboy resembles Holden, his [environment] is irrevocably different," Jacobs noted in *Teachers College Record.* "All around him are hostility and fear, along with distrust for the 'system'." The critic did fault some of the dialogue as "false" and the themes as a bit too "profound" for "hoods." Nevertheless, he noted that the novel had a more mature tone than most first novels, and had "relevance for today's [society]."

By 1970, *The Outsiders* had already been identified as a powerful influence on young adult literature. Many critics questioned whether it and other examples of the "New Realism" were a positive influence on teens. Attempts to ban the book were made in various places. As a result, many reviews of the time were particularly negative. For instance, a *Times Literary Supplement* critic worried that young readers "will waive literary discriminations about a book of this kind and adopt Ponyboy as a kind of folk hero for both his exploits and his dialogue." Other critics faulted the slang dialogue and sometimes moralizing tone. In his *Children's Book News* review, Aidan Chambers noted that the book was flawed because it was written with self-indulgence "and could profitably have been cut." Nevertheless, reviewers could not deny the appeal the book had for teen readers. As Chambers added, the first-person narrative had "interesting qualities," such as compassion and lots of action.

Critics have also recognized, however, that the strength of *The Outsiders* lies in its characters. In her 1969 work *Children's Reading in the Home,* May Hill Arbuthnot praises the book's "incisive portraits of individual boys growing up in a hostile environment.... The characters are unforgettable." Alethea K. Helbig and Agnes Regan Perkins made a similar observation in their 1986 work *Dictionary of American Children's Fiction.* They remarked that while some of the incidents in the plot seem unbelievable, "they hold up well during reading, probably because the author makes Pony's concerns and the warm relationship between the brothers seem very real." Cynthia Rose likewise stated in *Monthly Film Bulletin* that Hinton's "characterisation of the emotional claustrophobia and relentlessly limited prospects of the poor white world—where sacrifice so often defines love—is her most impressive literary achievement."

Hinton's novel has maintained its popularity for over thirty years, leading later critics to analyze its appeal. In a 1986 *Nation* article, Michael Malone suggested that it was because *The Outsiders* conforms to the popular myth of "the tragic beauty of violent youth." He observed that rather than being realistic, Ponyboy's language and story belong to a mythic or ideal world where teens anguish over their problems without adults to hinder or help them. Nevertheless, Malone added that Hinton's ability "to evoke for her audience how teen-agers feel about those clashes [of ideals] is indisputable." On the other hand, critic Michele Landsberg called Ponyboy's many poetic descriptions, particularly those of the greasers' appearance, "simply absurd." She explained in her *Reading for the Love of It* that Hinton's book "flatters the egos of young male readers with its barely-subliminal sexual praise, and lets them escape into the fantasized glory of attention and approval from an older teenage tough."

Other critics have found true literary merit in the novel, however, merit that explains its long-lasting popularity. As Jay Daly observed in his *Presenting S. E. Hinton:* "It has nothing to do with the age of the author, and little to do with the so-called 'realism' of the setting. It does, however, have very much to do with the characters she creates, their humanity, and it has everything to do with her honesty." "One of Susan Hinton's significant achievements in *The Outsiders* is to hold up for scrutiny

young people from economically, culturally, and socially deprived circumstances," John S. Simmons claimed in *Censored Books: Critical Viewpoints.* "In Ponyboy Curtis, his brothers Sodapop and Darry, and his 'Greaser' companions, Hinton has introduced readers, most of whom have probably been from white, middle class origins, to the desires, the priorities, the frustrations, the preoccupations, and above all, the *anger* of those young people who may live in the seedier parts of town but who have established a code of behavior which reflects (to the dismay of some) their sense of dignity and self-worth.... Most important, they believe in, trust, and support each other, all sentiments which can be universally admired despite the circumstances in which they are displayed."

Hinton herself has always known the key to her success. "Teenagers should not be written down to," she wrote in the *New York Times Book Review* upon the publication of *The Outsiders.* As a result, Hinton is an amazingly popular writer amongst teens and, especially, reluctant readers. Librarians and teachers use her books frequently for reading assignments. Hinton sums up the attraction to her action packed gang thrillers, saying: "Anyone can tell when [a teen's] intelligence is being underestimated. Those who are not ready for adult novels can easily have their love of reading killed by the inane junk lining the teenage shelf in the library." So she has gained the devotion of teen readers by following her own advice: "Earn respect by giving it."

Criticism

Jane Elizabeth Dougherty

Jane Elizabeth Dougherty is a doctoral candidate in English at Tufts University. In the following essay, she examines The Outsiders *as a coming-of-age novel, focusing on Ponyboy's choices between growing up too soon and never growing up.*

David Ansen has called *The Outsiders* "the prototypical young adult' novel." Written when S. E. Hinton was sixteen, it is widely credited with ushering in a new era of "realism" in the writing of young adult novels. Yet Hinton's book also contains haunting lyricism; indeed, the tension between dreamy romanticism and hard-knock realism is part of what the book is about. In the early pages of the novel, Ponyboy Curtis tells us of his two brothers: "Darry's gone through a lot in his twenty years, grown up too fast. Sodapop'll never grow up at all. I don't know which way's the best. I'll find out one of these days." In Ponyboy's relationship with his two brothers and with Johnny Cade and Dallas Winston, he experiences the differences between growing up too soon and never growing up. By the end of *The Outsiders,* he has found some tentative answers to the question of which way of being is best.

Ponyboy portrays himself as dreamy and sensitive, not very realistically-minded, and the other characters respond to him this way as well. His idealism enables him to connect with Cherry Valance and with Johnny Cade; makes him fear Dallas Winston; causes him to admire his friend Two-Bit; and creates clashes with his hard-headed, realistic brother Darry. When Ponyboy meets Cherry, he realizes that they are both outsiders in their respective groups, the greasers and the Socs. Both of them are dreamy romantics who watch sunsets, and Ponyboy realizes that, like him, Cherry has green eyes. Of Two-Bit, who is older than Ponyboy, he says more than once that he admires Two-Bit's ability to "understand things." Like Two-Bit and the others in the gang, Pony is also protective of his friend Johnny's innocence, and they connect emotionally because they are both innocent. Pony is the youngest member of the gang, called "kid" by the others, and Johnny has not allowed his abysmal home life or his brutal beating by the Socs to kill his basic goodness. Pony writes of Johnny:

> I don't know what it was about Johnny—maybe that lost-puppy look and those big scared eyes were what made everyone his big brother. But they couldn't, no matter how hard they tried, take the place of his parents. I thought about it for a minute—Darry and Sodapop were my brothers and I loved both of them, even if Darry did scare me; but not even Soda could take Mom and Dad's place. And they were my real brothers, not just sort of adopted ones. No wonder Johnny was hurt because his parents didn't want him. Dally could take it—Dally was of the breed that could take anything, because he was hard and tough, and when he wasn't, he could turn hard and tough. Johnny was a good fighter and could play it cool, but he was sensitive and that wasn't a good way to be when you're a greaser.

Ponyboy thinks of Dally and Johnny as opposites, but in the course of the story, each shows himself willing to sacrifice for others. Johnny calls Dallas "gallant," like a foredoomed Southern soldier in *Gone With the Wind,* because when he was arrested for something he knew Two-Bit had done,

What Do I Read Next?

- Hinton's second book, *That Was Then, This Is Now,* was published in 1971 after she overcame a serious writing block. The story concerns two foster brothers moving in opposite directions: one becomes successful with school and girls while the other falls into drugs and crime.

- Hinton's 1975 novel *Rumble Fish* continues to deal with youths and gangs. In this story, Rusty James struggles to earn a tough reputation.

- The 1979 work *Tex* is Hinton's most seamless novel. The story is set in California, where a traveling father has left his two sons in each other's care. As with her other stories, this one is action-packed.

- The classic *Catcher in the Rye* by J. D. Salinger (1951) relates two days in the life of an idealistic boy after his expulsion from school. Holden Caufield's disillusionment with the world is more profound than Ponyboy's, but comparable.

- A novel by Pulitzer-Prize winner Paul Zindel, 1969's *The Pigman* is about two sophomores who are outsiders in their own community. John and Lorraine pass the time by pulling pranks. It is during one of these pranks that they meet the "pigman" and are led to betray the friendship they have created.

- For a real change of pace, a story where the "outsider" takes her revenge is Stephen King's *Carrie* (1974). It is a brilliant book of horror set in the tense world of adolescent rivalry.

he didn't betray his friend and took the punishment himself. On hearing this story, Pony comments:

> That was the first time I realized the extent of Johnny's hero-worship for Dallas Winston. Of all of us, Dally was the one liked the least. He didn't have Soda's understanding or dash, or Two-Bit's humor, or even Darry's superman qualities. But I realized that these three appealed to me because they were like the heroes in the novels I read. Dally was real. I liked my clouds and books and sunsets. Dally was so real he scared me.

In spite of his original fear and dislike for Dally, a fear which he understands is motivated by his own idealism, Ponyboy comes to realize all that Dally has done for him. It is Dally who makes sure that Johnny and Pony are able to run away after Johnny accidentally kills Bob. Dally saves Ponyboy from the burning church, and tries to save Johnny as well. Ponyboy also realizes that in spite of his cold exterior, Dally has been deeply scarred by his experiences, and is trying to spare Johnny the same trauma:

> "Johnny," Dally said in a pleading, high voice, using a tone I had never heard from him before, "Johnny, I ain't mad at you. I just don't want you to get hurt. You don't know what a few months in jail can do to you. Oh, blast it, Johnny"—he pushed his white-blond hair back out of his eyes—"you get hardened in jail. I don't want that to happen to you. Like it happened to me...."

> I kept staring out the window at the rapidly passing scenery, but I felt my eyes getting round. Dally never talked like that. Never. Dally didn't give a Yankee dime about anyone but himself, and he was cold and hard and mean. He never talked about his past or being in jail that way—if he talked about it at all, it was to brag. And I suddenly thought of Dally ... in jail at the age of ten ... Dally growing up in the streets ...

Ponyboy realizes that, to Dally, Johnny's innocence represents his own lost childhood. When Johnny dies a hero after having saved the kids from the burning church, Dally says bitterly that it is useless to care about other people, that caring for others is not worth it, and that Pony is going to need to toughen up too. Yet Dally's own inability to completely turn off his emotions leads him, in his agony over Johnny's death, to rob a liquor store and then wave an unloaded gun at the police. In this final gesture of his life, Dally finds a way both to end the torment of his emotions and to try to prove, one last time, how tough and violent he is. Ponyboy tells us that both Johnny and Dally died "gallant," but each of them has died gallantly for a different reason: Johnny because he never grew up and remained frozen in his youthful idealism, and Dally because he grew up too soon and lost his innocence in the struggle to survive.

Ponyboy struggles for a long time afterward, trying to make sense of these two deaths. The gang begins to worry about him becoming hardened; when Pony pulls a broken bottle on some Socs, Two-Bit and Steve react by telling him not to get tough like the rest of them. But Ponyboy tells himself, as Dally told him, "that if you got tough you didn't get hurt." It is only near the end of the book that Johnny's voice takes over, telling Ponyboy in a letter that it was worth it to save those kids, that he should "stay gold" and continue to look at the world through a child's eyes. It is only after reading Johnny's letter to him that Ponyboy begins to accept Johnny's death.

Ponyboy's discovery of Johnny's letter is one of two reconciliations at the end of the book. Like Dally and Johnny, Soda and Darry are initially represented as opposites of each other. In his youthful idealism, Pony had believed that Darry was simply a hard-headed, and hard-hearted, realist who did not love him. As Jay Daly writes, "innocence/youth/idealism carried to such extremes is not youth/innocence/idealism at all. It is usually a more selfish, and sometimes dangerous thing. Look at Ponyboy's selfish attitude toward Darry early in the book. This is an attitude that is innocent of the most elementary awareness of another human being." At the end of the book, Soda is forced to confront the reality of his first love's betrayal at the same time his brothers involve him in yet another argument. Upon witnessing the pain he has been causing both his brothers, Pony finally realizes that Darry can feel as scared, hurt, or lost as the rest of them; that he has asked Darry to understand him without trying to do the same; and that Darry has sacrificed for his younger brothers. It is only then that the Curtises finally reach a reconciliation. Soda and Darry represent different kinds of voices than Johnny and Dally; they have found ways to survive without losing their goodness, their "goldness." They have done this in part by sacrificing for and taking care of Ponyboy.

In fact, Ponyboy cannot fully honor Johnny's wish that he stay gold. He has seen too much, and his own awareness of both the existence and the cost of his innocence makes it impossible for him to continue as he was before the deaths of Bob, Johnny, and Dally. But Ponyboy, like Darry and Soda, begins to stay gold by helping others: he writes that suddenly his story "wasn't only a personal thing to me. I could picture hundreds and hundreds of boys living on the wrong sides of cities.... There should be some help, someone should tell them before it was too late." Thus Ponyboy's narrative finds a way to reconcile the stories of Johnny and Dally, of Soda and Darry, by pointing out that they are all outsiders, all caught between never growing up and growing up too soon, all redeemed, even if only in death, by the sacrifices they, and by extension we as readers, have made for others.

Source: Jane Elizabeth Dougherty, in an essay for *Novels for Students*, Gale, 1999.

John S. Simmons

In the following excerpt, Simmons attempts to explain the lasting populatrity of The outsdiers, and why it sometimes is a candidate for banning.

Before we can begin to write a book rationale for our classroom or school library, two conditions should apply: (1) we know the book extremely well, and (2) we believe that this book makes a significant contribution to our curriculum and to students. Writing a rationale for why a book ought to be in the curriculum requires a knowledge of the goals and objectives of the curriculum, the skills, abilities and interests of students, a knowledge of students' literary and popular culture backgrounds, and a knowledge of the broader area of study in which the book is to be used. It is also helpful to know how frequently the title is used in similar situations, what reviewers have had to say about it in professional journals and in the popular press, and what awards the title has won, if any. Much of this material should be available locally; for example, in the school's curriculum guides. Much of the information, however, must be culled from a variety of sources such as textbooks, monographs and journals related to teaching or educational materials. *The Book Review Index,* published by Gale Research Company since 1965, provides an index of reviews appearing in more than 200 periodicals. Readers who are particularly concerned about children's and young adult literature should consult the annotated list of reference and bibliographical resources described in "Familiarity with Reference" (Kenney 48–54). All of these sources add to the rationale writer's own justifications for using a specific title. And since rationales frequently don't get written until a work has been challenged, the rationale writer should also be familiar with the concerns that have been expressed about the work in the local community. This information should be available in a written complaint filed by a local community member but may also need to be acquired through an interview. The local newspapers are another obvious source for community viewpoints on the controversial material. At the state and national level, the rationale writer should consult the *Newsletter on Intellectual Freedom* which keeps track of what titles have been challenged and why they have been challenged.

A rationale explains why a title is valued in the curriculum. It provides reasons for having a book in the public school library or for using it in the classroom. It does not provide all of the support that is needed. A book may be attacked for reasons that are not included in an essay. For support, teachers and librarians should consult with their educational association or union, their local, state, and national subject matter organization and one or more of the anti-censorship coalitions or committees mentioned earlier. Most state professional organizations have such committees. A number of states also have intellectual freedom coalitions made up of union representatives, subject matter organizations, librarians, and school administrators.

The titles that are discussed in this book were chosen on the basis of frequency of challenge. Lee Burress listed over 800 titles that were challenged between 1950 and 1985, in *The Battle of the Books.* That list came from 17 surveys of censorship pressures carried out by various scholars. In addition, several titles were added to the list of frequently challenged books from more recent reports, especially from the ALA *Newsletter on Intellectual Freedom.* One person who was asked to write an essay complained because his favorite censored book was not on the list. The reason is fairly clear; that book is very rarely assigned in the schools, so it is almost never challenged. We could not practically provide essays on 800 or 900 titles, so we chose the books that are most often reported by teachers or librarians as objects of attack. Indirectly, therefore, this list of titles is an index of books that are used in the schools.

If we examine the list of challenged titles, it is clear that most are twentieth century books, that most are by American authors, and that a disproportionate number are by non-Caucasian writers and deal with non-Anglo Saxon characters (disproportionate, that is, in comparison with the total number of books published in the U.S.). There is a strong suggestion here that racism lies behind the challenges. It is frequently disguised under charges that the books contain obscene or pornographic language. So far as the present writers know, no book used in the public schools has been found by a court to be obscene.

Another reasonable conclusion that maybe drawn from the list is that good books are more likely to be challenged than are books of little value. Every library, bookstore and supermarket contains many books with the same kind of language as may be found in the challenged list of books. The great majority of those books are ephemeral or superficial. There is little in them, therefore, to question the values of this society, to challenge readers to question their own values or way of life. The essays in this collection provide specific support for a rather select list of titles which are frequently challenged. They also serve as models for the development of rationales for use in the public schools.

The present volume is different from our earlier collection, *Celebrating Censored Books,* in two significant ways. It is expanded. The earlier volume focused on the so-called "dirty thirty." This volume doubles the number of works discussed and includes a selection from the earlier volume. In addition to essays written by teachers and professors of literature, *Censored Books: Critical Viewpoints* includes essays by poets, novelists and dramatists-authors of adult and adolescent literature.

The central charge to these reviewers was direct and simple: Why should anyone read this book? Why should it be recommended? They were asked to express their impressions of the text, of the concepts and emotions that readers might experience, of the personal and social understandings that might be achieved. A second concern addressed the question, Why is this book under attack? The reviewers were asked to consider the censorial challenges to the text in relation to its perceived merits. Another consideration suggested to reviewers was pedagogic, that is, classroom application.

The essays included in *Censored Books: Critical Viewpoints* provide, in effect, a defense of these frequently challenged books, a rationale for ensuring access to them for readers and support for teaching them. This collection does not, however, propose a curriculum for the English language arts classroom nor is it a cultural literacy list. The editors are not arguing that everyone must read all of these books. Rather, we strongly advocate the right of readers to select literary materials in an open marketplace of ideas and of teachers to select classroom materials in keeping with appropriate teaching objectives.

The collection is organized in two sections. The first, "Perspectives: Censorship by Omission and Commission," offers six author's views. Arthur Miller considers historical attempts to "revise" Shakespeare's *King Lear* in conjunction with current omissions of segments of his plays from school texts. He reflects on current censorship practices against an international backdrop. John Williams focuses on acts of omission—publishers censoring,

that is, not publishing—works by African-American authors. The nature and force of censorship attacks and their impact on authors is revealed by Norma Fox Mazer. She introduces censorship by commission, that is, the act of self-censorship, encouraged by publishers so as not to offend the public. Similarly, Rudolfo Anaya reflects on cultural discrimination that proscribes Hispanic-American writers and the effect of self-censorship on the expression of their life experiences. The last two essays in this section, by Mary Stolz and Lee Bennett Hopkins, encourage broad understanding of censorship challenges. They illustrate their insights with a wide selection of diverse fiction and poetry that has been challenged, from picture-story books to mature adolescent novels.

The second section, "Challenging Books," provides responses and defenses of individual books. Arranged alphabetically by the title of the text, they provide a varied perspective. Some are oriented to social issues, others to personal transactions with the text, and others to teaching concerns. They provide diverse, thoughtful approaches, suggesting that there is no one best way to prepare a rationale for a book or a particular situation. The array is enlightening.

But as these essays enlighten, we hope that they will stir the reader to take a deeper look at the whole question of intellectual freedom for our youth. We, as educators and parents, must constantly remind ourselves and our students that the constitutional guarantees of separation of church and state, freedom of speech and of the press, even the right to congregate to exchange ideas are not given by God but must be won anew with each generation. With the ever escalating calls for accountability in public education, the growing diversity in the school population and the concomitant rise in controversial materials designed to address the needs of all of our youth, (and let's not forget the increasingly organized religious right) we cannot expect or even hope that the number of censorship attempts directed to our public schools will diminish anytime soon. Our future depends upon our youth having the opportunity to grapple with ideas in their reading, their viewing and their interactions with each other and their adult mentors. We can opt for no less if we are to have an educated public capable of dealing with the culturally pluralistic and diverse nature of our world.

A glance at the young adult section of almost any mall bookstore these days will reveal a generous number of novels by the widely heralded writers of the moment: Robert Cormier, Judy Blume, Norma Fox Mazer, Lois Duncan, and Richard Peck, to name but a few. Standing right there beside them, almost assuredly, will be S.E. Hinton's *The Outsiders*—which is quite remarkable when one stops to consider the fact that the life spans of most young adult novels, even the initially popular ones are brief indeed. Most of the highly popular works of the mid to late 60s—*The Outsiders,* appeared in 1967—are now long forgotten. But *The Outsiders,* written when its author was 17 years old and making her maiden voyage on the publication waters, continues to hold the attention of the teenage reading audience as well as the English Education gentry. It would be hard to imagine a college or university instructor of a Literature for Adolescents course not calling attention to this novel somewhere along the line.

The question, then, is *why* this relatively short, rather simply written novel about a fourteen year old boy from the other side of the tracks in a moderately large, unnamed town has remained on the high interest list for so long—25 years. What follows is an attempt to answer that question....

Briefly stated, the American young adult long fiction genre has gone through three discernible evolutionary stages during this century. For the first 40 or so years, it provided little more than escape and recreational reading matter for the children and teenagers of that period. The Hardy Boys novels, along with the adventurous, picaresque, contrived, melodramatic works of Zane Grey, Edgar Rice Burroughs, and William Heyliger held the interest of boys, especially those who fantasized about their exploits on the gridiron, the diamond, the jungle, or the battlefield. For girls, the career and love sagas (although not necessarily in that order) of Emily Loring, (Sue Barton, girl nurse), Daphne du Maurier, Grace Livingston Hill, and Carolyn Keene (the Nancy Drew series) provided a wealth of entertaining books. In that pre-television era, such "light" reading preoccupied millions of young people in their search for escape from the world of homework and tedium. Escape yes, literary study no, in the eyes of classroom teachers, librarians, and teacher educators alike. For just about all of those professionals, a loosely defined set of "classics," largely written by Victorian era novelists and poets, served as objects of serious classroom study.

During the next three decades, however, a "new" kind of young adult novel began to emerge. Writers such as John R. Tunis, Paul Annixter, Fred Gipson, Esther Forbes, and Maureen Daly continued to include substantial doses of action, suspense, and adventure in their novels, but they also attempted to portray the world of the adolescent in a more realistic, self conscious manner. As Stephen Dunning said of *this* young adult novel, "It pretends to treat life truthfully." As the more credible young adult novel appeared on bookshelves everywhere, teachers, especially those in the junior high schools, began to consider their *teachable* aspects, as did the growing number of university faculty members who called themselves English Educators....

Since the young adult novel has developed more recently as a *serious* literary endeavor, it comes as no surprise that the representation of ostensibly unsavory characters and settings should emerge only after other types had been featured. Main and supporting characters in the novels of Tunis, Annixter, Daly, *et. al.* were from suburban, rural, or historical backgrounds. Thus one of Susan Hinton's significant achievements in *The Outsiders* is to hold up for scrutiny young people from economically, culturally, and socially deprived circumstances. In Ponyboy Curtis, his brothers Sodapop and Darry, and his "Greaser" companions, Hinton has introduced readers, most of whom have probably been from white, middle class origins, to the desires, the priorities, the frustrations, the preoccupations, and above all, the *anger* of those young people who may live in the seedier parts of town but who have established a code of behavior which reflects (to the dismay of some) their sense of dignity and self-worth. As developed by their author, there is little which has been considered contemptible, callous, or even objectionable about the Curtis brothers and most of their friends. Faced with poverty and limited opportunity, they maintain a certain determined optimism and aspiration for a better life. Most important, they believe in, trust, and support each other, all sentiments which can be universally admired despite the circumstances in which they are displayed. Hinton's novel is not "rigidly wholesome" nor "insistently didactic" as were many young adult works of preceding decades. It offers a number of *complex* human beings whose strengths and limitations are left to the readers themselves to infer and judge.

Breaking from the pattern of third person omniscient narrators which characterized the majority of earlier young adult novels, Hinton has presented her story from her protagonist's angle of vision. As with Salinger's *Catcher in the Rye* (1951), wherein we view the world from the perspective of the disturbed, vulnerable teenage Holden Caulfield. Hinton establishes the 14-year-old Ponyboy as both protagonist and narrator. It is through *his* eyes that readers view the events and analyze the individuals who make up this novel. His naivete, lack of sophistication and commitment to an established lifestyle give the novel its tone. Amazingly, the author, a teenage female, has created a credible teenage male protagonist/narrator. In doing so, she has contributed significantly to the new realism of the contemporary young adult novel mentioned earlier.

In his 1958 study, Dunning pointed out that one of the major weaknesses of the young adult novels of that era was the authors'; unrealistic depiction of adults and their relationships with adolescents, especially their sons and daughters. Hinton has dealt with this problem quite decisively; she virtually excluded adults from the narrative. This is truly a novel of the teenager, by the teenager, and for the teenager. It is devoid of significant adult characters, and the few that are included serve the most perfunctory of purposes. Thus the focus here is on the young people, particularly the two rival gangs: the Greasers (Ponyboy's) and the Socs (a group of upper middle class individuals whose main goals in life seems to be to embrace hedonism and to wreak havoc on the Greasers, although not necessarily in *that* order. In *The Outsiders,* adults would only serve as a nuisance, and the author does not allow that to happen.

Hinton does provide an element of mature influence, however, in the person of Ponyboy's older brother, Darry. A reluctant school dropout, Darry has assumed the responsibility of parenting his two younger brothers in the face of the untimely, accidental death of their mother and father. At age 20, Darry has taken on an adult role and, given his limited education and financial resources, does the best he can. It is through his character that readers perceive the fight for survival in an underclass situation. But Darry, perhaps more than the other Greasers, accepts his lot stoically and with dignity. He asks for neither material aid nor sympathy. To provide what is needed for family survival, he works longer hours and enforces house rules. In Darry, Hinton has added a note of prophecy to her story. As have countless young single parents of America's 1990s, he has become an adult before his time.

The theme of human fragility is given eloquent voice in *The Outsiders.* Violent confrontations with their rivals place the well-being of both gangs in constant jeopardy. The absence and indifference of parents lead most of the Greasers to the conclusion that they must pretty well fend for themselves. Death and serious, sometimes disabling, injury are possibilities which the latter group faces as a matter of course. During an interlude in which Ponyboy is hiding out with his friend Johnny, a fugitive from the recent murder of a Soc, he recites Frost's poem "Nothing Gold Can Stay" to his distracted friend. The poem has a profound impact on Johnny, who relates it to his own imperiled youth. Later, as he is on *his* deathbed, Johnny's last words are, "Stay gold, Ponyboy. Stay gold...." In an environment, where the concern with survival is omnipresent, the joy and promise of youth are both perceived with irony by Ponyboy and his Greaser cohorts, a far cry from the idyllic teenage days described in so many novels written in the decades before Susan Hinton's first literary effort. As teachers attempt to introduce their classes to a meaningful example of the ironic in literature, they may well look to *The Outsiders.*

The dour tone of *The Outsiders* prevails throughout although the novel is punctuated with examples of humor, selflessness, courage, and humanitarian acts. Despite their heroic quest for dignity and self-determination, both Darry and Ponyboy reflect an alienation from conventional middle class values largely through no fault or their own. Their contempt for the Socs and their lives of luxury, as well as their distrust of public institutions, particularly the law, may stamp them as undesirables in the eyes of some witnesses. It is an aspect of Susan Hinton's creative acumen that most thoughtful readers, both secondary school students and contributors to *ALAN Review,* do not demean these two young people for their attitudes toward middle class mores nor their stubborn adherence to the Greaser code of street-wise self reliance. Their alienation does not result in anti-social, self-destructive behavior and their restrained optimism/hope for better days is made believable by the author's subtle portraiture. While there seems to be little hope for a privileged but emotionally disoriented Holden Caulfield at the end of *Catcher in the Rye,* Ponyboy and Darry exit the book with their heads held high and their eyes on the future. In establishing, most convincingly, her characters' ability to cope, Hinton has led her readers to accept that positive outlook.

In one further stratagem Hinton has assisted the opening of new doors to her young adult novelist successors. The "life goes on" spirit reflected in the ending of *The Outsiders* stands in sharp contrast with the young adult novels of earlier decades.

All of the Horatio Alger-style books of the era before the 1940s included the Hollywood boy-gets-girl endings, which remain with us through endless TV dramatic offerings. Many of the well-written novels of the second phase described earlier were mixed, with the protagonist suffering some losses, usually minor, and some gains, usually crucial. As he leaves his readers, Ponyboy gives a few hints that he'll be okay, but there is no evidence that the quality of life, for either him or those around him, will improve to any degree, any time soon. "That's life" is what Susan Hinton seems to be saying in providing this ending to her book. Clearly, this perspective is consistent with the rest of the tale.

Undoubtedly, *The Outsiders* is, to a degree, a period piece, as indeed are the overwhelming majority of today's young adult novels. Paul Newman is probably a sex symbol only to the over-50 theater patrons. Other cigarette brands have replaced Kools among those widely smoked and advertised in this country. Affluent youngsters stopped wearing madras shirts long ago, and few, if any, 1990s teenagers are impressed by the Beatles or their hair style. Moreover, such words as "rumble," "chicken," "punkout," and "greasers" are terms long absent from teenage patois. The themes described above, however, are with us now and probably forever, and Susan Hinton has treated them with sensitivity. Thus, at least in this precinct, *The Outsiders* possesses a considerable dollop of literary merit. Yes, the book is still being read, taught, and discussed a quarter century after its publication. This is a solid reflection of its merit.

Source: John S. Simmons, "A Look Inside A Landmark: *The Outsiders*" in *Censored Books: Critical Viewpoints,* edited by Nicholas J. Karolides, Lee Burress, and John M. Kean, The Scarecrow Press, Inc., 1993.

Jay Daly

In this excerpt, Daly argues that The Outsiders *is a revolutionary piece of young adult fiction which focuses on idealism rather than realism.*

In April 1967 the Viking Press brought out a book called *The Outsiders,* by S. E. Hinton, and the world of young adult writing and publishing would never be the same. This is not an exaggeration. In more ways than one, *The Outsiders* has become the most successful, and the most emulated, young adult book of all time.

The situation was ripe, in the mid-sixties, for the arrival of something like *The Outsiders,* although no one knew it at the time. There had been a "young adult" genre for many years, dominated by books like Maureen Daly's *Seventeenth Summer,* dreamy-eyed stories of carefree youth where the major problem was whether so-and-so would ask our heroine to the prom in sufficient time for her to locate a prom gown. Or there were cautionary tales to warn us that, if we were not good, and we all know what "good" meant, we would never get to the prom at all.

Into this sterile chiffon-and-orchids environment then came *The Outsiders.* Nobody worries about the prom in *The Outsiders;* they're more concerned with just staying alive till June. They're also concerned with peer pressures, social status, abusive parents, and the ever-present threat of violence. What in the world was this? It certainly wasn't the same picture of the teenage wonder years that the "young adult" genre projected (and no one ever lived). Welcome to real life.

There is a perception now that *The Outsiders* was published to immediate teenage accolades, but such was not the case. In fact, because the book was so different from what the publishers considered "young adult" material, it was at first sent out with the general trade, or adult, releases, where it disappeared into the murk. It was only gradually, as the word from the hinterlands drifted in, that the publishers realized the book was finding its word-of-mouth fame among the very teenagers whose lives it depicted. The rest, as they say, is history.

The grass-roots success of *The Outsiders* paved the way for writers like Paul Zindel, Richard Peck, M. E. Kerr, Paula Danziger, and Robert Cormier. It set off a wail of controversy from those who thought that there was enough real life in real life without also putting it into books. It caused many lesser writers to make the mistake of wandering off in search of the "formula" for her success, and it sent publishers scurrying off in search of other teenaged writer-oracles; everyone wanted a piece of "the next S. E. Hinton." In truth, of course, there is no formula, and it is not likely that there will be "another" S. E. Hinton.

There are now perhaps ten million copies of Hinton books in print. *The Outsiders,* itself now twenty years old, no longer a teenager, continues to be the best selling of all Hinton's books. Clearly there is more to this than the novelty of its publication in those pre-Hinton, Mary-Jane-Goes-to-the-Prom years. In fact there is something in *The Outsiders,* as there is in the other Hinton books, that transcends the restrictions of time and place, that speaks to the reader directly. It has nothing to do with the age of the author, and little to do with the so-called "realism" of the setting. It does, however, have very much to do with the characters she creates, their humanity, and it has everything to do with her honesty. Her characters are orphans and outlaws and, as the song says, "to live outside the law you must be honest." If there is a formula to S. E. Hinton books it is only this: to tell the truth.

There is also something that is quintessentially American about S. E. Hinton. Her books are all set in the real American heartland, the urban frontier, and her characters are American pilgrim-orphans, believers in the dream of perfection, of an American paradise on earth. Francis Ford Coppola, who filmed and cowrote, with Hinton, the screen versions of *The Outsiders* and *Rumble Fish,* called her "a real American novelist," straight out of the tradition that runs from Herman Melville right up through J. D. Salinger, and beyond. The myth of the American hero, of the outlaw-individualist, of the "gallant," lives on in the eyes of Ponyboy Curtis and Johnny Cade.

None of this would matter, though, if it were not based on real characters. None of this would count if we did not believe that her books tell the truth, not so much about beer parties and gang fights, but about what it feels like to be a teenager, caught between childhood and adulthood, always on the outside looking in at a world that is very far from being a paradise on earth.

[Most of the controversy about *The Outsiders* came about because it] grew to be identified with something called "The New Realism" in young adult writing. The term—New Realism—was added later, but the fear—that books for teenagers were getting a little too realistic for their own good—was beginning to be heard more and more frequently during the time after the publication of *The Outsiders.* Indeed there are many who fix the point at which young adult writing changed, and changed utterly—from the cautionary Mary-Jane-Goes-to-the-Prom book to the attempt at serious and authentic portrayal of life as it is—with the publication of *The Outsiders.* Such a radical change could not be expected to go unchallenged....

The irony is that, while the debate team focused on the gangs and the violence, the smoking and the beer drinking—all dreaded evidence of the New Realism—the major thrust of *The Outsiders* had nothing to do with realism at all. The real message of the book is its uncompromising idealism. The real reason the book struck such a responsive chord in its young readers (and continues to strike that chord) was that it captured so well the ideal-

ism of that time of life. Of all the young adult novels of that period, *The Outsiders* is by far the most idealistic, the least concerned with the strictly realistic. In its search for innocence, for heroes, for that Garden of Eden that seems to slip further away as youth fades into adulthood, *The Outsiders* is a book for dreamers, not realists. And youth is the time of dreamers.

On its surface at least, *The Outsiders* is indeed a novel about the friction between social classes, in this case between the greasers and the Socs. It is also about the hunger for status, for a place in the pecking order, both inside and outside these groups. And it is about the violence that is so much a part of that particular place and time of life. These concerns are not, however, what make the book come alive. The book comes to life through its characters and situations, their almost painful yearnings and loyalties, their honesty.... With all the talk of clichés and melodrama, why does this book continue to speak to new generations of young readers? Idealism alone, after all, is not enough. Nor is sincerity. Think of all the sincere, idealistic books in dustbins and yard sales around the country. The continuing popularity, the continuing interest derives, I think, from the fortunate combination of achievements by the young Susie Hinton in three essential categories: the hand of the storyteller....; the continuing credibility of the characters; and the honesty, the sincerity... embodied in the themes of the book, each of which reduces, finally, to the yearning to "stay gold."

The orphans of *The Outsiders* are outlaws and dreamers. They're like "that tragic boy," Peter Pan, in J. M. Barrie's turn-of-the-century play. The Boy Who Would Not Grow Up. Peter Pan, and his group of orphans, the lost boys, rejected by their parents, make their own world of heroics and adventure. They have their own Never Land, where they belong. Wendy, like Cherry with her busy-ness, cannot prevent herself from changing, until she suddenly turns around to discover that she is "old, Peter. I am ever so much more than twenty." Peter Pan, on the other hand, stays pure; he never grows up. He stays gold.

Likewise do the lost boys in *The Outsiders* form their own, more perfect world in the world of the gang. They dream of the perfection they know must exist, their Never Land, that perhaps they even once had and lost, where things are gold, where Johnny Cade can find his "ordinary people," where Ponyboy's parents remain golden and young. The striking thing about these orphans is that they use it to their advantage; they are dreamers and they use their abandonment to feed their dreams. Life intervenes, of course, and their dreams will never come true, but that's only because they have such high standards. They want perfection. Like Peter Pan, they want to stay gold forever.

Ponyboy recites [the Robert Frost poem "Nothing Gold Can Stay"] for Johnny.... The poem captures a feeling that is important to Ponyboy, though he's not sure of all of it. "He meant more to it than I'm gettin," he says, "I always remembered it because I never quite got what he meant by it." Ponyboy, who has the capacity to be a little slow when it serves to advance the story, needs Johnny to validate the poem for him, in his letter at the end of the book. "[H]e meant you're gold when you're a kid, like green. When you're a kid everything's new, dawn. It's just when you get used to everything that it's day." The only way to stay gold, then, is to stay a kid, or at least to retain that childlike wonder, that innocence, which continues to make the world new. The key to staying gold then, in Johnny's view, is to stay, like Peter Pan, a child.

If this is indeed the case, then it creates problems. To stay at a Peter Pan level of innocence is to be retarded (in all senses of the word). All of us are in fact more like Wendy than like Peter; we lose gradually that limber quality of youth, the idealism and innocence, the ability, so to speak, to fly. To the extent that we retain some of this capacity we are blessed, but to retain it fully is impossible. Not just because "nothing gold can stay," but also because it would be unnatural to do so. Innocence cannot escape coming to terms with life, which does not necessarily mean being corrupted. The opposite of innocence is—not corruption, of course—but knowledge.

Worse yet, innocence/youth/idealism carried to such extremes is not innocence/youth/idealism at all. It is usually a more selfish, and sometimes dangerous, thing. Look at Ponyboy's selfish attitude toward Darry early in the book. This is an attitude that is innocent of the most elementary awareness of another human being. When he sees Darry cry, and feels his hurting inside, it is suddenly a loss of innocence, a falling into knowledge of the real world, but it's a far better condition he falls into than that he left behind.

It is no accident that those literary heroes who stay gold, who retain their innocence unnaturally, lead lives whose effect upon others is often far from innocent. There is something inhuman about them.

Think of Melville's Billy Budd, or Lennie in Steinbeck's *Of Mice and Men.* Their very innocence tends to lead them always toward, in Lennie's words, "another bad thing." It's as if they can't help but hurt people in the end. J. M. Barrie, once again, at the end of *Peter and Wendy,* describes his creation Peter, who would not grow up, as forever "young and innocent," but then he also adds, "And heartless."

The Frost poem is in fact not so much about the fleeting nature of youth, or even life, as it is about the Fall. Notice those repeating verbs, "subside ... sank ... goes down." The loss of Eden, of that state of perfection of which the "gold" of the poem is but a cruel reminder, this is the real knowledge in the poem, as it is in *The Outsiders.* When Ponyboy remembers his parents, it is always in a kind of misty Garden of Eden setting ... It's been only eight months since they died, but already they seem to have entered into a golden mythology. The book's idealism invents that place "in the country" of sunsets and ordinary people, but in fact—after the Fall—such a place cannot exist, not in this life.

Which brings us to the one way of staying gold that works. It is the only way of achieving the perfection that was promised. It involves memory, and the shifting of emphasis in Frost's last line from "gold" to "stay." Nothing gold can *stay.* Rather than agree that Ponyboy's image of perfection cannot exist in this world, the book agrees only that it cannot stay here. By dying Johnny stays gold in a way he could never have achieved in life. Even Dally becomes a gallant in death, frozen in time forever under the streetlights of the park like a carved figure from Keats's "Ode on a Grecian Urn."

Most of all, Ponyboy's parents stay perfect parents in a world sadly lacking in parental perfection. They will be young and golden and love him always. His mother in particular remains "beautiful and golden," perfect in a way she could not have remained in life. It is an irony that only by abandoning him could she become for him that symbol of perfection that Ponyboy, and all the others, so desperately need. In the words of the Keats poem: "She cannot fade, though thou hast not thy bliss, / For ever wilt thou love, and she be fair!"

In the pages of *The Outsiders,* and in Ponyboy's memory, she remains, as the song goes, forever young. She stays gold. It's a cruel sort of perfection, but for the idealistic heroes of all the Hinton books (up until *Tex*), who prize perfection so highly, it's the only kind of Paradise they know.

Source: Jay Daly, in his *Presenting S. E. Hinton,* Twayne Publishers, 1987, 128 p.

Sources

May Hill Arbuthnot, in her *Children's Reading in the Home,* Scott, Foresman, 1969, pp. 174-75.

Aidan Chambers, review of *The Outsiders, Children's Book News,* Vol. 5, No. 6, November-December, 1970, p. 280.

Jay Daly, in his *Presenting S. E. Hinton,* Twayne Publishers, 1987.

Thomas Fleming, a review of *The Outsiders,* in the *New York Times Book Review,* Part II, May 7, 1967, pp. 10, 12.

Lillian V. Gerhardt, a review of *The Outsiders,* in the *School Library Journal,* Vol. 13, No. 9, May, 1967, pp. 64-65.

Alethea K. Helbig and Agnes Regan Perkins, "The Outsiders," in their *Dictionary of American Children's Fiction, 1960-1984: Recent Books of Recognized Merit,* Greenwood Press, 1986, pp. 495-96.

Nat Hentoff, a review of *The Outsiders,* in the *Atlantic Monthly,* December, 1967, pp. 401-402.

Susan Eloise Hinton, "Teen Agers Are for Real," *New York Times Book Review,* August, 1967, pp. 26-29.

William Jay Jacobs, "Reading the Unreached," *Teachers College Record,* Vol. 69, No. 2, November, 1967, pp. 201-202.

Michele Landsberg, "Growing Up," in her *Reading for the Love of It: Best Books for Young Readers,* Prentice Hall Press, 1987, pp. 201-28.

Michael Malone, "Tough Puppies," in the *Nation,* Vol. 242, No. 9, March 8, 1986, pp. 276-78, 280.

Review of *The Outsiders,* in the *Times Literary Supplement,* October 30, 1970, p. 1258.

Cynthia Rose, "Rebels Redux: The Fiction of S. E. Hinton," in *Monthly Film Bulletin,* Vol. 50, No. 596, September, 1983, pp. 238-39.

John S. Simmons, "A Look Inside A Landmark: *The Outsiders,*" in *Censored Books: Critical Viewpoints,* edited by Nicholas J. Karolides, Lee Burress, and John M. Kean, The Scarecrow Press, Inc., 1993.

For Further Study

David Ansen, "Coppola Courts the Kiddies," *Newsweek,* April 4, 1983, p. 74.
   A review, mostly negative in tone, of Francis Ford Coppola's film version of *The Outsiders.*

Children's Literature Review, Volume 23, Gale, 1991, pp. 132-50.
   A collection of interviews, articles, and reviews on Hinton and her works.

Nicholas Emler and Stephen Reicher, *Adolescence and Delinquency: The Collective Management of Reputation,* Blackwell, 1995.
   After examining the theoretical perspectives on juvenile delinquency by sociology and psychology and dismissing them as based on nineteenth-century thinking, Emler and Reicher ask questions about the context of delinquent behavior in terms of social dynamics. Their questioning leads them to an analysis of identity construction as pursuit or avoidance of delinquent behavior. Finally, they offer solutions through a notion of "reputation management."

Stephen Farber, "Directors Join the S. E. Hinton Fan Club," *New York Times,* March 20, 1983, Section 2, Page 19, Column 2.
   An article which tries to account for the sudden appeal of Hinton's books as sources for movie ideas, including quotes from Francis Ford Coppola and Hinton herself.

Randall K. Mills, "The Novels of S. E. Hinton: Springboard to Personal Growth for Adolescents," in *Adolescence,* Vol. XXII, No. 87, Fall, 1987, pp. 641-46.
   An article which examines how teachers may use Hinton's novels to help students explore issues of personal growth.

Wayne S. Wooden, *Renegade Kids, Suburban Outlaws: From Youth Culture to Delinquency (The Wadsworth Contemporary Issues in Crime and Justice),* Wadsworth Publishing/ITP, 1994.
   Wooden's book is full of qualitative research into youth culture and teen social groups of suburban Los Angeles and it is very accessible to students interested in sociology. He investigates everything from "mall rats" to violent "gangbangers" and skinheads to try to understand what makes "good kids" turn "renegade."

The Pearl

John Steinbeck
1947

Whether by prayer, quest, or lottery ticket, humans have long expressed their dreams of a better life. Many are the tales about this phenomenon and, more often than not, the tales end in tragedy for the pleasure seeker. This longing for something better is the theme of John Steinbeck's 1947 *The Pearl*.

Steinbeck was disillusioned in the aftermath of World War II. He realized that none of his heroes—the GI, the vagrant, or the scientific visionary—could negotiate survival in a civilization that created the atomic bomb. Repentance, as attempted by his characters in his novel *The Wayward Bus* (1947), was not enough. Fittingly, he reflected his disillusionment through a legend about a man who finds the Pearl of the World and is eventually destroyed by greed.

The legend tells of an Indian pearl diver who cannot afford a doctor for his son's scorpion sting. In this anxious state, he finds the Pearl of the World and is able to get medical help for his boy. Calculating the profit from the gem, the diver dreams of a better life—a grand wedding, clothes, guns, and an education for the boy. But his dream of leaving his socio-economic station leads to ruin. As he attempts to escape those that want to take the pearl from him, he is tracked by professional hitmen and tragedy ensues. No pearl is worth the price Kino and his wife pay, so they throw the pearl back. Their story is a warning to restless dreamers yearning for an easy or magical solution to their problems.

John Steinbeck

Author Biography

Steinbeck was the son of flour mill manager and Monterey County Treasurer, John Ernst, and a school teacher, Olive Hamilton, who lived in the Salinas Valley of California. Like other families in the valley, the Steinbecks thought themselves rich because they had land; unfortunately, they could hardly afford to buy food. There were four children but John Ernst Steinbeck, born in 1902, was the only boy. As a youth he spent much of his time exploring the valley which would become the backdrop to his fiction.

After graduating from Salinas High School in 1919, Steinbeck enrolled at Stanford University and attended intermittently until 1925. He worked to pay his tuition and was forced to take time off to earn money for the next term. This proved invaluable; he worked for surveyors in the Big Sur area and on a ranch in King City. This latter location became the setting for *Of Mice and Men*. Oftentimes he worked for the Spreckels Sugar Company, thereby, receiving firsthand experience of contemporary labor issues.

The most important learning experience, however, was a summer class in biology in 1923 at Hopkins Marine Station in Pacific Grove. Stein-

beck's exposure to biology led him to develop general theories about the interrelationship of all life. Edward F. Ricketts, a marine biologist, whom he met in 1930, would help him with this. Steinbeck adopted his idea that people could only be fully human once conscious of "man's" place within the entirety of creation. Humans were but one animal in life's web. From there, Ricketts and Steinbeck diverged as the latter mixed socialism with biological theory to grow his literary vision: man should act in concert with others to live happily and for the good of all creation. Essentially, Steinbeck's theory was a biological twist to the growing movement of 1930s "Proletarian Realism."

Keeping with his theory, Steinbeck fictionalized human society by observing its groupings rather than by selecting an individual. Observations of group behavior showed how humans could intelligently guide their own adaptation and natural selection. Typically, his characters begin in harmony with nature but then evil, in the form of corrupt politics or greed, upsets their order. Salvation is possible when the individual sees the rationality of cooperation and agrees to act, or adapt, to being part of a group, or phalanx. Failing to work together leads to tragedy. This theory would see Steinbeck through his greatest writing. Shortly thereafter, his inspirational friend, Ricketts, died in a train accident. In 1947, his parable, *The Pearl*, was published.

Steinbeck secured fame and fortune with the immensely popular novel, *Of Mice and Men* (1937). He followed this with his best known novel, *The Grapes of Wrath*, which won the Pulitzer Prize in 1940. He won the Nobel Prize for Literature in 1962. He died of heart failure in 1968. He had three wives (Carol Henning, Gwyn Conger, and Elaine Scott) and two children (Tom and John).

Plot Summary

The Pearl opens in Kino's home in La Paz, Mexico. The sun is beginning to lighten the day, as the "tiny movement" of a scorpion catches Kino's and his wife Juana's eyes. The scorpion is heading towards Kino's and Juana's son, Coyotito.

Kino slowly reaches out to grab the scorpion, while Juana whispers magic to protect Coyotito, but the scorpion strikes anyway. The swelling of Coyotito's flesh marks the beginning of a series of events that will not only destroy the family's home, but will take them away from their family and community.

Kino and Juana take their wounded baby to see a doctor in a "city of stone and plaster." Since Kino and Juana are desperate to find help for their baby, they swallow their pride and appeal to the town doctor, who is a member of a race that has "beaten and starved and robbed and despised Kino's race."

The doctor, a fat man whose eyes rest in "puffy little hammocks of flesh," refuses to help Coyotito, saying that he is a doctor, "not a veterinary." Kino shows the doctor's servant his money, but it is not enough to interest the doctor. In frustration, Kino strikes the doctor's gate with his bare fist and splits open his knuckles.

Although Coyotito is beginning to heal, Juana and Kino are determined to find a way to secure the doctor's help. Juana prays to find a pearl with which to hire the doctor to cure the baby. Kino is singing the "Song of the Pearl that Might Be" as he dives into the ocean in search of oysters and pearls. He finds an isolated oyster, cracks it open, and discovers what soon becomes known as the "Pearl of the World." The family's bad luck seems to be changing, for the swelling is also going out of Coyotito's shoulder.

News that Kino had found the Pearl of the World travels so quickly through the city that many people are becoming jealous of Kino before he and his family have even had time to celebrate. Kino tells his brother, Juan Tomas, that now he and Juana will be married in a church, the family will have new clothes, a rifle, and that Coyotito will learn to read.

The local priest pays Kino a visit and reminds him to give thanks to Him who "has given thee this treasure." Kino feels alone and unprotected in the world. Then the doctor arrives to "help" cure Coyotito. Both Kino and Juana are reluctant to let the doctor near their child, but the doctor claims that the poison of the scorpion goes inward and can wither a leg or blind an eye. Kino does not want to risk harm to Coyotito, so he allows the doctor to give Coyotito a white powder in a capsule of gelatin. The baby grows sicker; in a few hours the doctor returns to give Coyotito ammonia, which helps the baby's stomach.

Kino tells the doctor he will pay him after he sells his pearl. The doctor sees Kino's eyes look toward the pearl's hiding place in the floor. After the doctor leaves, Kino finds a new hiding place for the pearl. He tells Juana he is afraid of "everyone" now.

After Kino stabs a night prowler, Juana begs him to return the pearl to the ocean, calling the pearl evil. Kino replies that Coyotito "must go to school. He must break out of the pot that holds us in."

It is not easy to sell the pearl, however, as the pearl buyers all work for the same employer and have conspired to offer Kino 1,000 to 1,500 pesos for the pearl that is probably worth at least 50,000 pesos. Kino, angered, says he will go to the capital to sell the pearl.

Kino is attacked again that night, and Juana tries again to persuade Kino to get rid of the pearl. Kino tells her that he is a man and that no one will take their good fortune from them.

Early on the morning they are to leave for the capital, Juana tries to throw the pearl back into the ocean. Kino strikes her face, kicks her, and rescues the pearl. Then Kino is attacked again, and ends up killing his attacker. Kino and his family flee for their lives.

Their canoe has been splintered and their home set on fire, so the family seeks temporary refuge in Juan Tomas' home. Juan tells Kino he should sell the pearl and "buy peace for yourself." Kino refuses. "The pearl has become my soul," he says. "If I give it up I shall lose my soul."

Kino's family leaves during the night, carefully covering their tracks behind them. Despite their care, they know that inland trackers are pursing them. They travel as rapidly and stealthily as they can until nightfall, when Kino tells Juana and Coyotito to hide in a cave. Kino hopes to steal a rifle from one of the trackers before the moon rises.

Coyotito cries out, waking two of the trackers and causing the watchman with the rifle to shoot. Kino leaps on the man and kills him, but something is wrong. Coyotito is dead.

Kino and Juana return to La Paz, Kino with a rifle, and Juana with their dead baby wrapped in a blood-crusted shawl. They pass Juan Tomas. They pass their ruined canoe, and make their way to the water. Then Kino returns the pearl, which is now "gray and ulcerous," to the ocean.

Characters

Apolonia

A woman with a big jiggling stomach, Apolonia is the wife of Juan Tomas. She has four children and her family is a little better off than Kino's.

She helps them when the robbers burn down the hut. As the nearest female relative to Kino's family she must lead the mourning. Her presence of mind after discovering Kino and Juana are alive, is crucial to their remaining undiscovered.

Coyotito

Coyotito is Kino and Juana's son. When he is stung by a scorpion, the resulting medical emergency prompts the parents to reach beyond their station in life. The mother will not let her only child languish and demands they go to the Doctor. His refusal of admittance leads them to pray for the means—not to heal the child—to gain the Doctor. Their prayers are answered and they have a Pearl with which they can buy a better future for the child. However, the death of the baby, whose cries could have been those of a coyote pup, finally ends Kino's fantasy: no rise in future prospects was worth the loss of his baby.

The Doctor

The "lazy" Doctor of the village is a man who thinks only of Europe and dreams, with "eyes rolled up a little in their fat hammocks," of returning there. It is to this colonial Doctor that Kino goes to seek help for his baby. However, because his pearls at that time were so poor, the Doctor would not look at the boy of a "little Indian." His attitude towards Kino, not the Indians, changes when he hears that Kino has a great Pearl—the same poor man who had come to him. "He is a client of mine," says the Doctor who then dreams of returning to Paris with the proceeds from the sale of the pearl. He then makes a house call and cures the boy. He appears to be kindly and generous, but he watches Kino closely for indications of the Pearl's hiding place. Seeing one, he sends some men back in the dead of night to steal the pearl. The Doctor represents quackery. He uses the people's lack of choice and power against them and, thereby, furthers their ignorance.

The Gate Keeper

The Doctor's servant is a man of Kino's race. He tries as much as possible to do the Doctor's bidding and thereby distinguish himself from his kind. His efforts go so far as a refusal to speak in the old language. When Kino comes to the Doctor for medical help, it is the Gate Keeper that refuses him. Kino offers worthless pearls as payment but the Gate Keeper declares the Doctor has gone out. "And he shut the gate quickly out of shame." The Gate Keeper, though economically in a better po-sition, still feels the shame of his people's oppression but does nothing to alleviate them. Instead, he enjoys the power he gets from his position. Later, when Kino has the Pearl, this servant is responsible for telling the Doctor that Kino is the same man who had been at the gate—thus betraying his people again.

Juan Tomas

Kino's brother and nearest neighbor, Juan looks out for Kino. He stands by him when he goes into town for the Doctor and to sell the pearl. When the robbers burn down Kino's hut, he hides the family and enables them to escape by borrowing needed items.

Juana

Kino's wife, Juana, is even more simple than Kino. Her reactions are those of the instinctual mother, and her life is devoted to her duties to her husband and child. "She could stand fatigue and hunger almost better than Kino himself. In the ca-noe she was like a strong man." She says Hail Marys and utilizes ancient magic to ward off evil. Her prayers bring the pearl into existence. With the Pearl in hand, however, Coyotito is fine. Her thoughts about the Pearl thus turn practical. They can be married in the church and have nice clothes, but they do not need to have everything. Realizing that Kino wants everything, she begins to see their possession of the Pearl of the world as a harbinger of evil. She begs Kino to throw it away, even becomes so bold as to attempt it herself. For this, Kino hits her.

She performs her duties and follows Kino. Simple as she is, her mind has awakened to the real danger. Her boy survives the scorpion but they may not survive Kino's pearl. As soon as Kino said he was a man and would do the bidding of the Pearl, she went along. "Juana, in her woman's soul, knew … that the sea would surge while the man drowned in it. And yet it was this thing that made him a man, half insane and half god, and Juana had need of a man; she could not live without a man." She, there-fore, silences her doubt. "Sometimes the quality of woman, the reason, the caution, the sense for peser-vation, could but through Kino's manness and save them all." That may be, but Juana, until the bitter end, does her best to maintain their confinement in ignorance and just barely survives.

Kino

The protagonist of the fable is a Mexican-Indian named Kino. He is a primitive character who will fail to benefit from the opportunity chance has afforded him to become enlightened. Kino has been perceived as colonial subject, simpleton, and oppressed man. His people were not always subjugated; at one time, they had control over their destiny, created songs, and lived in peace with their surroundings. But Kino represents his a subsequent generation—one profoundly affected by oppression and exploitation—and when the Doctor comes to him, Kino stands "in the door, filling it, and hatred raged and flamed in back of his eyes, and fear too, for the hundreds of years of subjugation were cut deep in him." Kino is aware of his subjugation but he has no way of dealing with it. He is like a caged animal and exhibits the signs of stress that accompany confinement. Unfortunately, he is not a great man about to lead his people out of the dark.

Kino is an average man in his community with a quiet life diving for pearls that he sells to his colonial overlords. After his son is stung by a scorpion and the doctor refuses to treat him, he goes as usual to the pearl beds hoping that he will find a pearl so magnificent that he will be able to rise in social and economic standing. He discovers the talisman he feels he needs for such a rise in fortune; however, harassment from his oppressor and his own stubbornness foil his ability to take advantage of the Pearl.

Kino hides the pearl and attempts to sell it himself. In conversations with his brother he stops just short of revealing that the pearl buyers have been cheating the people. Everyone could have benefited from his find but he decides to risk his life to sell the pearl for a lot of money in the city. Yet when he is prevented in going to the city because of vandalism and violence, he is profoundly changed. The damage done to his boat, his escape route, is the last straw. "The killing of a man was not so evil as the killing of a boat." Seeing this assault, "[h]e was an animal now, for hiding, for attacking, and he lived only to preserve himself and his family." Yet he maintains some humanity for it never occurred to him, due to tradition, to steal someone else's boat.

The Pearl Buyer

There is only one Pearl Buyer in La Paz but there are many fingers to this one grasping hand. His representatives sit in separate offices giving the appearance of a competitive market. Each pearl buyer's goal is to buy for the main owner at the lowest price. It is each "man's function to break down a price, [and] he must take joy and satisfaction in breaking it as far down as possible ... a pearl

buyer was a pearl buyer, and the best and happiest pearl buyer was he who bought for the lowest prices." Keeping these sentiments enables the pearl buyers to forget that there is really only one and, therefore, they are better able to fool the people. On the day that Kino comes to sell his pearl, all the buyers know in advance what the price will be.

Kino approaches one of the pearl buyers; he is interchangeable with any other pearl buyer as the embodiment of the real Pearl Buyer. This "stout slow man" perfectly symbolizes the closed market in his habitual action of juggling a coin on his hand. "The fingers did it all mechanically, precisely," but when confronted by the pearl of the world the system breaks down. The fingers fumble the coin just as the stacked market bids far too low for the Pearl. The greed of the Pearl Buyer, who assumes Kino will take what he offers, causes them to lose the Pearl altogether.

The Priest

The Catholic Priest is a "graying, aging man with an old skin and a young sharp eye. Children he considered these people, and he treated them like children." He is another symbol of the powers keeping Kino's people down. He encourages his congregation to be submissive to authority. Hearing about Kino's luck, the priest tries to recall whether he has done service to that family and calculates how far the Pearl might go toward repairing the church. He does not remember Kino as a man but as one of his children. The priest reminds Kino of his duty to the church.

The Trackers

Like the Gate Keeper, these two men are Indians who are in the employ of the Europeans. They are regarded as subhuman and not too far above bloodhounds. They find Kino's marks and lead the Watcher to within feet of his hiding place. Kino kills them easily after killing the Watcher.

The Watcher

The merchant of the city has employed a man with a gun, horse, and two professional trackers to find Kino and the Pearl.

Themes

Good and Evil

Kino's belief that evil is in the night is not unusual. But one of his many foibles is that he sees

Topics for Further Study

- Consider the following quote from *The Pearl:* "An accident could happen to these oysters, a grain of sand could lie in the folds of muscle and irritate the flesh until in self-protection the flesh coated the foreign body until it fell free in some tidal flurry or until the oyster was destroyed." Augment this description with that of a biology text or book on marine life and interpret Steinbeck's pearl as a trope for human development.

- Pretending that you are Kino or Juana (knowing only what they know), come up with a plan to relieve the deplorable situation of the community. Be sure to stay true to the characters as they are presented.

- There are many references throughout the story to colonialism and race. Also, Kino embodies the trope of the noble savage and all the dialogue is stereotypically that of the newly colonized (despite the fact that we know the Indians speak an indigenous language and the Europeans speak Spanish). Are these necessary components to the story? Whether you answer yes or no, why do you think Steinbeck made use of those additional tensions?

- What is the significance to the following line from the story: "The thin dog came to him and threshed itself in greeting like a wind-blown flag, and Kino looked down at it and didn't see it."

- Find out more about Steinbeck's literary theory. Does he uphold or betray that theory in this story?

---

himself alone in a world of struggle between good and evil. He does his best to keep good coming his way. In his mind he hears the music of his personal struggle. The Song of the Family hums in his mind when things are as they should be. The waves lapping the shore in the morning and the sound of Juana grinding corn or preparing the meal are part of this song. But when the wind shifts or a representative of the oppressing class nears, then he hears the strains of the Song of Evil, "the music of the enemy, of any foe of the family, a savage, secret, dangerous melody." Kino listens and reacts to these songs. When the scorpion begins to come down the rope toward the baby, he hears the Song of Evil first. However, when the priest enters he is confused despite hearing the song he heard for the scorpion. He has been taught that the priest is good and so he looks elsewhere for the source of evil. This melodic tool, whatever its source, is one of many tools that Kino has in his possession but that he fails to fully utilize.

Juana is more sophisticated yet more esoteric in her view of good and evil. She is the one who prays for protection against actions. She prays the ancient magic and the new Catholic prayers to ward off the scorpion. She does the same when she wishes for a way to pay the Doctor. She sees that the Pearl is the source of evil and that men are only evil because of the pearl.

Because Kino chose to fight alone and Juana chooses to let him, evil wins. The Song of Evil plays loudly in the silence following the deaths on the mountain—one accidental, three brutal. But instead of succumbing to Evil, Juana and Kino together trudge home, past the burnt spot where their house stood. "[T]hey were not walking in single file, Kino ahead and Juana behind, as usual, but side by side." As they walk together, the Song of the Family revives becoming "as fierce as a cry." Kino even offers to let Juana throw the pearl but she declines. He must silence the cause of his insanity. He throws the pearl and as it settles, the Song of Evil "drifted to a whisper and disappeared." Evil is banished but good has not triumphed as is indicated by the bloody package inside Juana's shawl.

Knowledge and Ignorance

The Doctor, the Priest, and the Pearl Buyer do their part to keep the peasants ignorant and docile. They use whatever methods the can to accomplish this—financial instability, religious ceremonies and threats of eternal damnation, or lack of economic choice. When the Pearl is discovered, however, each power controller makes the mistake of thinking he knows how to have his way with the finder. Due to this mistake, they do not allow any knowledge to escape but they alienate Kino from them. In other words, by insisting that he stay ignorant of their ways they harbor resentment and defiance. Kino is ignorant, not mentally deficient.

They answer his reticence with force and are met with force.

The doctor uses an overbearing self-confidence to trick Juana and Kino into thinking their child might be still at risk from the sting of the scorpion. Kino suspects the white powder may be fraudulent but he certainly will not risk his son's life and deny the doctor. He believes in the doctor because the doctor treats the Europeans who are stronger than the Indians. They are strong in part, he reasons to himself, because of the doctor. What choice does he have but to give way? The priest is not much different. He views the Indians as children and keeps them that way by educating them only enough to be scared of the evil they will face without his help. Religions, especially Catholicism, used the devil as a tool to bring the conquered into submission. Religious reasoning was also used on slaves to make them submissive. On the one hand, the people learn enough from the priest to blend his prayers with their ancient superstitions. On the other, they are not any better for the interaction.

Lastly, the pearl buyers are the best at the charade; they have the Indians at their mercy economically. The pretense of an open market and the price wars they fake lead the Indians to think they are getting a fair shake. In this way, the Indians also believe that they are active participants in the economic order. The Indians are illiterate and cannot know how the modern world works. They are kept ignorant to be exploited.

Individual vs. Society

Kino and his people have lost their ability to function as an effectual group. The only time they come together is to form an audience to be witness to what will happen to Kino. Before European rule, they were able to act as a functional society, going so far as to create songs—which they no longer do. Their social mechanisms have been worn down by the new religious institution and, more crucially, by the new economic system. These two institutions encourage the Indians to behave as individuals who will compete with each other in making ends meet alone. Social and tribal sharing is discouraged at every turn. The narrative dramatizes this by depicting the absence of cordial social interaction amongst the Indians.

Conversely, the pearl buyers act in concert for the benefit of one man and to exert their control over the gullible Indian populace. By this comparison, Steinbeck is criticizing the market system in a way that is consistent with his other literary works. Steinbeck feels capitalism leads to monopolies. Steinbeck is also criticizing his own theories of the phalanx. In his writing before the war, he believed that only by voluntary cooperation could people live happily and at peace. The war, however, showed him that people are easily tricked, bought, or coerced into working for a group when the alternate choice is to be a part of an oppressed class. The latter group, Kino's, is unable to pull together because they have been divided by their oppression.

They attempted to break the monopoly a few times when they sent single men to the big city but those men never returned. They did not try with a group of men who could have defended themselves. Kino will try this route of solitude and he will be defeated. He should have taken his brother or another man in a canoe to the city. Instead, he went with his wife and child over land and paid an ultimate price.

Style

Allegory

An allegory takes many forms. One form of allegory is that of a type of fiction more or less symbolic in feature intending to convey a meaning which is not explicitly set forth within the narrative. Allegories usually involve a journey that a character makes toward spiritual growth. Kino's story is an allegory: his journey affords him a small amount of personal growth and a variety of lessons to meditate on. The plot is simple: a man finds the Pearl of the world but he does not gain happiness and throws it back. Within this narrative are many hidden meanings. The story tells us that man is in the dark and needs to wake up. Therefore, the opening shows Kino waking in the night, which is allegorical, but because the Cock has been crowing for some time we know that he has been trying to gain a consciousness—literally wake up—to his people's plight.

Another message is that journeys should be made in communion, not just the company, of another. Kino should be in a leadership position amongst his people because of his fortuitous discovery. But he is not leading them. He tries to sell the Pearl, which could have ruptured the economic system and provided economic opportunity for his people. Instead he falls prey to doubt and decides to go for the big city leaving his people ignorant of his mission. Kino decides to make his own way

Mexican coastal town.

and is followed by his wife. He returns with her, but they are still alone and everything is the same as before.

Symbolism

The story is full of symbolism of the talismanic, allegorical, and ironic kind. The Pearl itself is a symbol of escape for the poor man, but it also symbolizes the effects of greed on man. Worse than that, Steinbeck sets up the Pearl to embody the whole of the European Conquest of the Americas. He does this by saying that Pearl bed in which it was found, is the same pearl bed that raised the King of Spain to be the greatest in the world. Historically, then, this pearl bed represents the gold, silver, and raw resources that Spain extracted from the New World at the height of that nation's empire. Now, this same pearl bed lures in a victim of that colonialism to dream of an easy escape from poverty.

The pearl is a talisman: an object that comes to be interchangeable with a man or an idea. At one point Kino views the Pearl as his soul and vows to keep it. For Kino, the success of the Pearl's sale will indicate his success. The Pearl stands opposite to the canoe that at once stands for his family and is a sure bulwark against starvation. When he makes it known that he will pursue wealth by ven-

turing on his own to the great city, his canoe is sabotaged. This is a crime greater than homicide for it is a direct assault on Kino's family—worse than burning down the house.

Irony arises in the name of the village: La Paz or peace. The town is only peaceful because the majority of the people are demoralized. Their peace is one of an oppressed people. The Pearl stirs up this peace and only bloodshed restores calm.

The Indians are constantly presented as innocent primitives further duped by the superstition of the Catholic Church. They are also, and Kino especially, compared to animals. In their daily habits of fishing and gathering they are like the hungry dogs and pigs described as searching the shore for easy meals. More exactly, Kino howls, the trackers sniff and whine, the baby's yelps sound like its namesake—the Coyote. Animals have roles as well. The Watcher's horse raises the European above the Indians; this advantage is used to conquer the hemisphere.

Metaphor

While the story has its symbols and large allegorical sentiments, every facet of the tale is transcribed into metaphor. Even the minds of the Indian people are as "unsubstantial as the mirage of the Gulf." Further, they are clouded as if the mud of the sea floor has been permanently disturbed to block their vision. Even the city as seat of the colonial administration is given metaphorical animation: "A town is a thing like a colonial animal. A town has a nervous system and a head and shoulders and feet."

In a moment of foreshadowing, Kino watches as two roosters prepare to fight. He then notices wild doves flying inland where later Kino will prepare to fight his pursuers. Juana is like an owl when she watches Kino sneaks down the cliff. Earlier, when the watering hole was described, feathers left by cats that had dragged their prey there are noticed. Those with feathers die. On the other hand, Kino is no longer an animal. Instead, when Kino kills the men who are tracking him he is a machine. He is efficient and without noise, like the cats playing with their doomed prey. He is killing to survive. The metaphor that is mixed in with this scene of tension and action is in keeping with the style of the rest of the work, while also lending it a realistic dimension.

Historical Context

America after World War II

The Peace Treaty signed on February 10, 1947 officially ends World War II. America emerges as a world superpower. It is capable of an incredible industrial capacity and, in addition, America commands the most powerful military in the world: the greatest navy, the largest standing army, the best Air Force, and the only nuclear arsenal. The United States military becomes even stronger when Congress passes a law unifying the Air Force, Army, and Navy under one secretary of defense. Adding another weapon to America's might, Congress creates the Central Intelligence Agency.

Culturally, American literature, music, art, movies, and eventually television gain popularity around the world. The isolationism of the pre-war days is gone and the city of New York emerges as a world center. Visitors to the city experience the tastes and sights of the capital of American publishing, the infant television industry, and the glamour of Broadway shows. They view Abstract Expressionism, maybe bump into a Beat Poet, and revel in the sound of Bebop or blues.

Supply and Demand Economics

With the end of the war, the rationing of goods ends and people demand to be supplied with goods that were unavailable during the war. Industry scurries to provide these goods. One immediate demand is housing. The soldiers coming home are taking advantage of the GI Bill of Rights to attend college. They use the same rights again to procure financing for adding their tract house to that other New York invention—the suburban sprawl. The military industrial complex quickly re-tools to offer pre-fabricated housing components, appliances, and civilian cars and trucks. All of this consumption, however, wreaks havoc on economic forecasts. Price controls are abandoned too quickly and inflation rises. As men re-enter the work force, pressure to raise wages increases and strikes happen frequently.

President Harry Truman's popularity declines drastically with inflation's rise and the liberal coalition formed under Roosevelt—which had brought together business and government so effectively to fight a war—unravels. Fortunately, the worldwide demand for goods is so great and the capacities of America and Canada so vast that boom times are bound to come. Republicans aim to push back the New Deal legislation at a time when the Marshall Plan was being hammered out to help resuscitate Europe. The Democrat coalition begins splitting apart over the thorny issue of civil rights. The Southern Democrats strengthen their alliance with the Republicans to weaken the New Deal and delay action on civil rights legislation.

Despite a presidential veto, the Labor Management Relations Act of 1947 (the Taft-Hartley Act) passes. This law outlaws 'closed shop' agreements—where the employer hires only those persons who belong to a specific union. Further, the law demands that workers must first vote by secret ballot before striking. Perhaps most fundamentally, the law made labor unions liable to court action for contractual violations brought on by strike actions.

The Cold War

Tense relations developed between the United States and their Russian allies late in the war as they raced to see who would dominate Japan. But it is not until after the war that the growing tensions would come to be known as the Cold War. In 1947, American Bernard Baruch uses the term to label the conflict between Russia and the United States that is just short of war. The Cold War re-

Compare
&
Contrast

- **1947:** Jackie Robinson becomes the first black American to play baseball in the major leagues when he joins the Brooklyn Dodgers. Rookie of the year and lead base stealer in the National League, he is a hero to blacks and a symbol of integration.

  Today: Affirmative Action is all but discontinued while blacks retain their predominate role as sports heroes.

- **1947:** Its troops tired of harassment by Jewish settler militias, Britain turns over the "Palestine problem" to the United Nations which allows the creation of the State of Israel months later.

  Today: There is still no peace in Palestine.

- **1947:** Britain releases its colonial jewel, India. In the aftermath, three nations are born: India, Pakistan, and Bangladesh.

  Today: Raising the nuclear stakes worldwide, India and Pakistan have conducted nuclear tests and declared themselves nuclear states. Diplomats from China to Moscow fear an arms race.

- **1947:** The Cold War begins leading to tense relations between the two largest nuclear powers.

  Today: The Cold War is over but war hawks on both sides continually threaten to restart the arms race.

sults in technological races, political influence in lesser countries (from Central America to the Middle East), and curious exchanges at the United Nations. Both nations break the sound barrier in 1947. With the detonation of a Soviet atom bomb in 1949, an arms race begins. Later, Sputnik would cause a furious investment in math and sciences so that America arrives at the Moon first.

Disturbing domestic legislation is enacted early in the Cold War. Truman hands down Executive Order 9835, which requires the Department of Justice to compile a list of subversive organizations that seek to alter the United States "by unconstitutional means." The list includes a whole range of groups like the Ku Klux Klan, the Communist Party, the Chopin Cultural Center, the Committee for the Negro in the Arts, the League of American Writers, the Nature Friends of America, and the Yugoslav Seaman's Club. Truman's order seeks investigation of those persons affiliated with those groups who might have infiltrated the United States government. Of the 6.6 million persons investigated, as a result of this program, not one case of espionage is uncovered. However, this activity paves the way for such later witchhunts as McCarthyism in the 1950s.

Critical Overview

The long term critical reputation of John Steinbeck rises and falls on the relevance and apparent ability evinced in his greatest two novels, *Of Mice and Men* and *The Grapes of Wrath.* However, his endurance as a great American writer is also found in his lesser works such as *The Red Pony* and *The Pearl.* The latter, Steinbeck called, "a black and white story like a parable" and the felicity with which he crafted the work claims its readers to read it again and again. Indeed, for many critics this story has revealed the bedrock of Steinbeck's personal and political philosophy.

John S. Kennedy was one such early friend who summed up Steinbeck's literary philosophy as a "reverence for life." That was the reason for his popularity, said Kennedy, he wrote of "life and living." This critic was not about to simply say Steinbeck was a naturalist or social realist and, thereby, repeat again that he was a champion of the working man. In fact, Kennedy refutes these claims. Steinbeck was too sentimental in his regard of humanity to be a realist. Thematically, Kennedy rather likes Steinbeck's work until he comes to *The Pearl.*

Harris Morris provides a close reading of Steinbeck's use of allegory and symbolism and chronicles the publication history of the fable. The title, for example, went from being "The Pearl of the World" to "The Pearl of La Paz." The overstatement of irony involved in a title "The Pearl of Peace" was unnecessary and finally the title shortens to its present form. Morris makes a great deal of Steinbeck's role as a modern fabulist who wrapped his tales in realism knowing the modern world would view any imitation of Aesop as childish. Therefore, he "overlays his primary media of parable and folklore with a coat of realism, and this was one of his chief problems." Then, through a discussion of the use of animal allusions, night, day, and the journey, Morris finds that the effort to overlay realism actually exaggerates the allegorical tendencies while undermining the "realistic aspects of the hero."

For Todd M. Lieber, Steinbeck has remained true to his basic themes throughout his work and he does not see anything new in this parable. Instead, Lieber is interested in Steinbeck's reliance on talismanic symbols to bring his characters to his larger theme of "becoming aware of the individual's relation to the whole." Talismans are objects "that men believe in or go to for some kind of non-rational fulfillment." Throughout Steinbeck's works, characters come to identify with places and with objects as a part of their becoming conscious; "identification results when man transfers part of his own being to his symbols, when an object becomes suffused with human spirit so that a complete interpenetration exists." This is done most successfully in the parable where the pearl becomes an "emotional prop" and "a principle of right action in the world." Lieber views Steinbeck in some awe as a writer able to "penetrate to the sources of human thought and behavior and present in the form of some objective correlative the archetypal and mythopoeic knowledge that lies deep in the mystery of human experience." The talisman psychology being one of those correlatives.

A very different approach was that of Peter Lisca who notices Steinbeck's disillusionment with the "Kiwannis, Rotary Club, Chamber of Commerce definition of noble character." He sees that Kino finds himself possessed of the means to buy into that world but he also finds "his house burned down, his wife physically beaten, his only son killed, and the lives of three men on his soul." Rather than continue toward dissipation, Steinbeck has the man and wife make a true escape. Kino had been seeking to escape the low-level economic and

social position but willingly returns to that same "repressive society" though "at a higher level." Lisca decides, as Steinbeck perhaps intended, that the "primitive" man's position is the right one to occupy. From there, they see the basic violent and destructive logic of those who repress them. "They return to their village, throw the Pearl of Great Price back into the sea, and return to the edge of unconsciousness, an unthinking existence governed by the rhythms of sun and tide."

Criticism

Elyse Lord

Elyse Lord teaches writing at the University of Utah. In the following essay, she argues that, while The Pearl *literally dramatizes the plight of a man who is caught between the material world and the spiritual world, the novel insists upon a more symbolic reading, too.*

Perhaps the most outspoken critic of *The Pearl* has been Warren French, who criticized author John Steinbeck for using a traditional tale (the legend of the Indian boy who accidentally finds a large pearl) to make his "cautionary points" about the dangers of materialism. According to French, Kino's struggles would be more meaningful to readers of the *Woman's Home Companion,* where the story was first published, than to Mexican listeners of the original folk tale. French's criticisms are only partially valid.

Kino's discovery that the economic value of the pearl is controlled by a few powerful men can be read as a critique of a capitalistic economic system that embraces material values. Naively, Kino believes that he will be a rich man because he has discovered the "Pearl of the World." He plans to finance a church wedding, to purchase clothes, a rifle, and an education for Coyotito. Yet, when he tries to sell his pearl in La Paz, he receives an offer of only 1,500 pesos. So Kino sets out for the capital in order to find traders who will pay him the full value of the pearl. By challenging the status quo in La Paz, he sets off a chain reaction of events that will force him to reevaluate what he defines to be "valuable."

Juana is less naive about the value of the pearl than Kino is, at least initially. She is quick to grasp that the pearl, if given more value than, say, human relationships, can bring both greed and misery. "This thing is evil," she cries. "This pearl is like a sin! It will destroy us.... Throw it away,

What Do I Read Next?

- Another compelling fable by a famous author is *Animal Farm*. Published in 1945 by George Orwell, this satire is a story about farm animals who attempt to take over a farm and operate it collectively. They chase off the exploitative humans but end up under a dictatorship of pigs.

- Also published in 1947 was Steinbeck's novel, *The Wayward Bus*. Like *The Pearl*, this allegorical tale concerns characters who must shed the evil they have contracted. They are not even as successful as Kino and Juana.

- Steinbeck again returned to myth when he created the family saga of the Trask family of the Salinas Valley. *East of Eden* is their story as a modernization of the biblical story of Cain and Abel. Steinbeck regarded the novel as his crowning achievement but his critics have been a bit reluctant to say the same of this overt allegory.

- Ernest Hemingway's short novel of 1952, *The Old Man and the Sea,* is a story about a Cuban fisherman named Santiago. He has not caught anything for weeks and then he snags a great big fish. His battle to hold onto the fish leaves him too tired to do anything but tie the fish to the boat. Sharks eat away its flesh leaving him a worthless skeleton and a good story.

- Fable telling has never fallen out of style but lately old tales have been retold according to ideologies, re-translations, or rediscoveries. Angela Carter reworked several fairy tales into a collection called *The Bloody Chamber* (1979). Her versions of several well-known tales are realistic, feminist, and a heroine replaces the hero.

Kino." Kino refuses to throw away the pearl, because he wants to use the pearl to purchase social status and freedom from oppression for his family and community.

The novel also contrasts the value of the pearl with the value of Kino's family, specifically of Coyotito. The narrator says that for Kino and Juana, the morning that Kino will sell his pearl is "comparable only to the day when the baby had been born." Because the statement follows a paragraph foreshadowing that the pearl will destroy the family, because the reader is likely to believe that there is no greater moment than the birth of a child to a father, the narrator's observation seems ironic. How can one compare the monetary value of the pearl with the value of one's family? It is no coincidence that Coyotito sacrifices his life when Kino insists upon keeping the pearl. Coyotito's sacrifice (death) provides further evidence that French is right. Steinbeck is critiquing materialism and its values.

After Kino has killed a man and the family has been forced to flee, Juana says, "Perhaps the dealers were right and the pearl has no value. Perhaps this has all been an illusion." On a material level, she may be conceding that the pearl really does not have any monetary value. On a spiritual level (if one defines spirit to be a human being's essence), Juana may be suggesting that, even if the pearl's monetary value is 50,000 pesos, it is still of no value to the family, which craves spirit, not matter. Juana's questioning of the value of the pearl mirrors the questioning of the value of the pearl that occurs throughout the novel. Again, this is consistent with a reading of the story as a critique of materialism.

When Juana suggests the pearl may have no value, Kino replies, "They would not have tried to steal it if it had been valueless." In this ironic moment, both the narrator and readers will see that Kino's logic is flawed. He is assuming that thieves steal valuable things, which may or may not be true, and which is only relevant if someone is willing to pay the thieves for their stolen items. Kino must become more sophisticated, more aware of the evil that man is capable of, more aware of the forces that render him and his family helpless.

Again, Kino's naive nature provides support for French's criticism that the novel makes "cautionary" points that are more meaningful to readers in the United States than in Mexico. Contemporary readers in industrial societies *are* probably more likely to see the irony in Kino's logic than readers from less-industrialized countries. Contemporary readers who have a basic understanding of economic principles are also more likely to see that Kino's major conflict is whether or not he will accept or reject the social, economic, (and by extension, materialistic) values that currently determine his choices in life.

However, at this point, the novel begins to resist French's literal reading. By not recognizing the impact of the forces of capitalism upon their lives, by not recognizing their own powers, Kino and Juana unwittingly bring about their own downfall. They lose their home and their canoe. They are forced to flee La Paz, to leave behind their families and friends.

The lessons that Kino and Juana will learn now take the form of an allegorical journey. (An allegory is a story in which the objects, people, or actions represent a meaning that can be found outside of the story.) Because Kino and Juana have not recognized their own power (they have, for example, relinquished their own very capable authority as healers to the less capable doctor), because they have not shown an awareness of the material values and powers that are dominating their lives, they are thrust into a dark (and very symbolic) night in order to be educated.

The responses of readers to the symbolism of Kino's and Juana's journey and to the symbolism of Kino's and Juana's education will take a variety of forms. The suggestive symbols in the novel, particularly the symbols of the pearl and of the journey, ask readers to move beyond French's tidy interpretation of the novel into a more psychological and fluid realm.

Not surprisingly many critics *do* view the return of the pearl to the ocean at novel's end to be a rejection of the material world in favor of the spiritual world. However, this interpretation largely ignores the symbolism of the pearl, which is linked in many ways throughout the story to Kino. Most strikingly, the pearl has, as Kino tells his brother, Juan Tomas, become his soul. "If I give it [the pearl] up I shall lose my soul," he says.

To follow the logic of this symbolism, when Kino rids himself of the pearl, he is ridding himself of his soul. How will readers respond to this?

Peter Lisca offers one interpretation. Kino's definition of the soul, says Lisca, is "not the usual religious definition of 'soul,' but human consciousness and potential, those qualities that cause man to separate himself from the rest of nature." When Kino renounces the pearl, he therefore "refuses the option of attaining his soul (a distinct identity) ... preferring to *undefine* himself ... thus going back to the blameless bosom of Nature in a quasi-animal existence." Other interpretations are possible, even suggested. The novel gives readers room to decide for themselves.

Jungian critics (followers of the Swiss psychiatrist Carl Jung), with their interest in archetypes (images that occur in the unconscious minds of all humans) offer a satisfying complement to French's interpretation of the novel. Because the Jungians believe in the notion of "universal" symbols, and because they find these symbols in *The Pearl,* they equate Kino's family's journey with the symbolic journey of the soul. More specifically, they suggest that both Juana and Kino undergo initiations into adulthood, and that these initiations would be recognizable, as symbols, to cultures in Mexico, in the United States, and in many other countries.

As Deborah Barker points out, Joseph Campbell has documented that the archetypal hero's journey often takes the familiar pattern of departure, initiation, and then return. The initiation may involve a symbolic death, which then requires a symbolic rebirth. In the context of *The Pearl,* the loss of his son, home, and canoe would symbolize Kino's death, while the return of the pearl to the bottom of the sea would symbolize rebirth. This pattern of departure, initiation (symbolic death, symbolic rebirth), and return recurs throughout stories around the world.

According to Barker, Juana's initiation is a little different from Kino's. Juana undergoes a "rite of disenchantment" through her journey. At the start of the story, says Barker, Juana appears as a "submissive figure trailing after her husband with a devotion nearly dog-like." At the conclusion of the story, Juana has been elevated to a status equal to Kino's as the two return to town "side by side." In other words, Juana, as archetype, leaves La Paz as a young girl, is initiated into the "disenchantments" of womanhood, and then becomes a woman transformed. Barker reads Juana's journey primarily as a soulful one, in keeping with the notion that the meaning of the story is not solely thematic, but can be found in its images and in the patterns of its images. Again, these images recur in other stories throughout the world, thus Barker would probably disagree with French's suggestion that the novel holds localized appeal to readers of the *Woman's Home Companion.*

Another Jungian approach to *The Pearl* reads the characters in the story as symbolizing different aspects of the human psyche. Jung was concerned not just with archetypes, but with the ongoing struggle between the conscious and the unconscious. To a Jungian psychologist, harmony is achieved only when one is able to successfully confront the reality of one's unconscious.

Joseph Timmerman provides an example of a Jungian interpretation of the novel that is concerned with the ongoing struggle between the conscious and the unconscious. Timmerman reads Kino's journey as a confrontation with his own shadow (the part of his unconscious that is socially unacceptable, his darker side.) In order for Kino to access his shadow self, he must listen to the female part of his unconscious (known as his anima). Juana, who is portrayed as intuitive and wise, symbolizes Kino's anima. Juana (Kino's anima) helps Kino to express his unconscious desires, as when she forces him to, in Timmerman's words, "brave the civilized world of the doctor." As the novel progresses, she becomes Kino's "guiding power," as his anima would.

Keeping the novel's rich symbolism in mind (from this very brief discussion), one is perhaps better prepared to appreciate the themes in the novel without feeling bound by them. A thematic analysis reveals that the novel does dramatize man's struggle to know what to value, a struggle that is complicated by his trapped position between the material and the spiritual world. While this reading is consistent with the reading that Steinbeck is critiquing materialism, it can not be taken as the "definitive" interpretation of the novel. The novel contains another symbolic level that will resonate within each reader's unconscious.

When Steinbeck wrote in his preface, "If this story is a parable [an allegory that makes a moral point], perhaps everyone takes his own meaning from it and reads his own life into it," he was not making an idle suggestion. Meaning in *The Pearl*, as some of the psychoanalytical readings have already demonstrated, extends far beyond the realm of a materialist critique.

Source: Elyse Lord, in an essay for *Novels for Students*, Gale, 1999.

Earnest E. Karsten

In the following excerpt, Karsten examines two of Steinbeck's major themes and their manifestations in The Pearl.

Before advancing to thematic material, it may be well to establish immediately what we hold as the structure of the novel. Although the structure could be shown schematically, let us use words. Each chapter contains a central incident which has both cause and effect, tying together the action. In Chapter I the central incident is accidental, the scorpion's stinging Coyotito, and results in the need to find a pearl with which to pay for a doctor's treatment. The discovery of the pearl, the fruit of purposeful action for something good and the central incident of Chapter II, has the effect of making Kino everyone's enemy, the townspeople's becoming a threat to Kino and his family. Chapters III and IV have as central incidents the attacks upon Kino for possession of the pearl. These attacks are both physical as well as emotional (the doctor's "treatment" of Coyotito) or intellectual (the pearl buyer's attempt to take advantage of Kino's ignorance), and they arise from a human evil, greed. These incidents result in the growing conflict between Kino and Juana over the pearl. In Chapter V the turning point is reached in the central incident of that chapter, the destruction of what we call *existence* for Kino, caused by purposeful action for an evil goal. The effect of this incident is Kino's forced emigration from the community. The central incident of the final chapter is the death of Coyotito, again, as in the first chapter, an accidental incident, which results in Kino's return to the community and the destruction of the pearl.

With this structure in mind, let us turn now to the central theme. Just as the pearl is an "accident," so is man's existence, and that existence has meaning within human relationships, basic of which is the family. Just as the Pearl is good or becomes invested with evil because of the ways men use it, so man himself appears, becomes, emerges as good or evil because of the ways men use other men, nurturing or destroying the human relationship between them, validating or invalidating the meaning of their existence.

We have attempted to trace two manifestations of this theme through the novel. The first follows Steinbeck's use of music as a symbolic representation of the theme paralleling the basic story. The second manifestation is found in Steinbeck's use of description to suggest the relationships between Kino and his community and between the community and the town as social embodiments of the theme again paralleling the basic story.

Steinbeck has established three main songs that are named: the Songs of the Family, of Evil, and of the Pearl. Schematically, these three melodies can be envisioned as originating on three separate planes, with the Song of the Family in the middle and the Song of Evil on a parallel plane, but imminent. From a plane below both, the Song of the Pearl is created and, as the story itself progresses, moves forward to become one with the Song of the Family, then to transcend it and join with the Song of Evil....

As symbolic representation, the musical parallel must now be related to the central theme. Within the human relationship where Kino's life has meaning, the Song of the Family is warm, clear, soft, and protecting. Herein the Song of the Family represents completeness. It continues to have these qualities as long as the Song of the Pearl does not overwhelm it. As Steinbeck writes, "they beautify one another." When the human relationship is threatened and destroyed (the crisis: Juana attempts to toss away the pearl, Kino strikes her, Kino is attacked and commits murder, Juana realizes the irrevocable change and accepts it to keep the family together, and the change is manifested in the destruction of the old ties of boat and home, and the pearl becomes both life and soul for Kino), the Song of the Family is interrupted and then becomes secondary to the Song of the Pearl. But because life's meaning is now dependent upon the pearl rather than upon human relationships, the Song of the Pearl becomes the Song of Evil opposed to the Song of the Family, which is now harsh, snarling, and defensive—a fierce cry until the Song of the Pearl is stilled and the human relationships are restored within the original community.

Through the suggestive power of Steinbeck's description, the second manifestation of the theme becomes clear: the close harmony in the human relationships within Kino's community and the parasitic relationship between that community and the town....

Even in what might be termed indirect description, Steinbeck has pictures of the parasitic relationship between the community and the town. In the first instance of metaphors from the animal world, Steinbeck reports how an ant, a social animal working for the good of its colony, has been trapped by an ant-lion, living near the ant colony to prey upon it for his individual needs. In the same way the individuals of the town have built "traps" to take advantage of the ignorance of the Indians and to prey upon them for whatever they have of wealth, labor, or services. Next the author cites the example of the hungry dogs and pigs of the town which scavenge the beach searching for dead fish or seabirds, the latter here representing the Indians who live off the sea and who for all general purposes are *dead* because they have no power to resist, while the former represent the greedy townspeople. In a third metaphor Steinbeck describes the fish that live near the oyster beds to feed off the rejected oysters and to nibble at the inner shells. Perhaps this is the most forceful of the metaphors, for the author seems to be saying that the Indians,

the rejects of modern society, thrown back after having been despoiled of their wealth by that society, are the prey of the townspeople who live nearby and who scavenge even upon the hopes, dreams, and souls of these people. Finally in the metaphor of the large fish feeding on the small fish, Steinbeck supplies a simple restatement of this parasitic relationship between the town and the community, and perhaps a picture of the inevitability of such a relationship in nature....

In Kino's community all have a sense of responsibility to one another and a respect for the humanity of each. Coyotito's scream attracts the neighbors' sympathetic attention as well as curiosity, and the neighbors accompany Kino to the doctor's when the community makes one of its few incursions into the town. Upon the doctor's refusal to treat the child, the neighbors will not shame Kino and abandon him so that he will not have to face them. The discovery of the pearl brings them again, this time to share the joy and dreams; yet, they are more concerned for Kino than they are interested in the pearl. The neighbors again come to Kino when the doctor appears to inflict temporary illness upon Coyotito. They also go with Kino when he attempts to sell the pearl as a necessary sign of friendship; and both before and after the visit, Juan Tomàs emerges from the group to represent the thinking of the community. During the crisis, Kino could escape; but he will not commit sacrilege against the community by taking another's boat. Although the neighbors demonstrate concern at the fire and grief over the supposed deaths of Kino and his family, Kino's relationship with the community has been destroyed because of the murder; and he must leave to protect the community and his brother ("I am like a leprosy.")

The town, on the other hand, is like a separate organism, walled off from the life of the community, yet living only to drain off that life....

In general, the townspeople as presented in the novel suggest the characteristics of parasitism, especially the retreat from strenuous struggle, the passive mode of life. In addition, the pearl buyers, as agents of a single unnamed, never introduced individual, show another characteristic, that of retreat from independent endeavor. Finally, the doctor symbolizes the unmistakable degeneration that results from parasitism.

Up to this point in the story, we can easily see that Kino's community nurtures human relationships and validates the meaning of existence for its members, whereas the town, as far as the community is concerned and Kino in particular, has consistently sought by its manipulation of men to invalidate the meaning of existence, and it succeeds by forcing Kino to leave the community. From this point the images became animalistic, because the human relationships that gave meaning to Kino's existence as a man have been left behind. The pursuers personify the animostity of the town, which in its greed and as an example to others seeks now to destroy utterly the outsider who has defied it. Their destruction and the consequent salvation of the family, although at the sacrifice of one of its members, re-establish the humanity of and the meaning of existence to Kino and Juana only because they return to the community to begin life again by destroying the pearl.

Besides the central theme as noted above and these various expressions of it, Steinbeck has included additional themes. Let us conclude with a discussion of one of these, the treatment of man and woman in their basic roles and essential natures. Immediately we see expressed, in the reactions of Kino and Juana to the scorpion's attack, the author's statement of these roles. Kino, full of rage and hatred, acts as the avenger of the family, since, as protector, he was unable to act before the scorpion struck; Juana, on the other hand, full of caution, fulfills the role of comforter and healer for the family. And we must note that each has acted separately, not simultaneously, on instinct—first Kino, then Juana, while Kino stands by helplessly having already played his part.

Later, after the pearl has been found, it is Kino who envisions the future in the pearl, who sees what it will provide for the family, and who soon becomes tenacious of what he hopes can be his. Juana quietly watches this tenacity increase to the point of obsession and urges the healing of the family by casting away the source of infection—the pearl.

The tension caused by the growing conflict between the two roles, Kino now as provider and Juana as preserver, begins slowly during the first attack upon Kino. It has its first expression in Juana's remarks that the pearl would destroy them all, even Coyotito. But she relaxes, and the tension subsides as she realizes that they are "in some way one thing and one purpose." With the second attack in the night the tension increases. Juana strives to preserve the family, but Kino, resolute in his plan for the future, opposes her with his whole being, indeed with the very essence of manhood, in the words "I am a man." Juana is driven, although instinctively as a woman to heal the family, nevertheless in reality to act for the man to protect the

family. This appropriation of the man's role by Juana, her rebellion against Kino's decision not to destroy the pearl and her attempt to do so herself, has its counterpart in the interruption of the Song of the Family....

The unfortunate conflict in roles has made both Kino and Juana aware of each other in a new way, and this awareness is reflected in a change in Juana's role during the flight and the final return to the community. For she becomes a sharer in, rather than a follower of, Kino's planning. When the trackers make their appearance, it is Juana who goads Kino into overcoming his "helplessness and hopelessness." And again a little later when Kino suggests he go on alone while Juana and Coyotito lie hidden in the mountains, Juana says that they will stay together, and Kino submits to her strength and resolve. After the final, terrible moment of the flight, as husband and wife face the tragedy of Coyotito's death, they find renewed strength in one another. With that strength they share the difficulties of the return to the town, walking side by side, and of the re-establishment of a meaningful existence within the community.

Source: Ernest E. Karsten, Jr., "Thematic Structure in *The Pearl,*" in *English Journal,* Vol. 54, No.1, January, 1965, pp. 1–7.

Harry Morris

In the following excerpt, Morris examines the relationship between realism and allegory in The Pearl.

[Nothing] more clearly indicates the allegorical nature of *The Pearl* as it developed in Steinbeck's mind from the beginning—as the various titles attached to the work—*The Pearl of the World* and *The Pearl of La Paz.* Although the city of La Paz may be named appropriately in the title since the setting for the action is in and around that place, the Spanish word provides a neat additional bit of symbolism, if in some aspects ironic. In its working title, the novel tells the story of The Pearl of Peace. When this title was changed to *The Pearl of the World* for magazine publication, although the irony was partially lost, the allegorical implications were still present. But Steinbeck had apparently no fears that the nature of the tale would be mistaken when he reduced the title to merely *The Pearl....*

Steinbeck knew that the modern fabulist could write neither a medieval *Pearl* nor a classical Aesopian Fox and Grapes story. It was essential to overlay his primary media of parable and folklore with a coat of realism, and this was one of his chief problems. Realism as a technique requires two basic elements: credible people and situations on the one hand and recognizable evocation of the world of nature and of things on the other. Steinbeck succeeds brilliantly in the second of these tasks but perhaps does not come off quite so well in the first. In supplying realistic detail, he is a master, trained by his long and productive journeyman days at work on the proletarian novels of the thirties and the war pieces of the early forties. His description of the natural world is so handled as to do double and treble duty in enrichment of both symbolism and allegory. Many critics have observed Steinbeck's use of animal imagery that pervades this novel with the realistic detail that is also one of its strengths....

Kino is identified symbolically with low animal orders: he must rise early and he must root in the earth for sustenance; but the simple, pastoral life has the beauty of the stars, the dawn, and the singing, happy birds. Yet provided also is a realistic description of village life on the fringe of La Paz. Finally, we should observe that the allegory too has begun. The first sentence—"Kino awakened in the near dark"—is a statement of multiple allegorical significance. Kino is what modern sociologists are fond of calling a primitive. As such, he comes from a society that is in its infancy; or, to paraphrase Steinbeck, it is in the dark or the near-dark intellectually, politically, theologically, and sociologically. But the third sentence tells us that the roosters have been crowing for some time, and we are to understand that Kino has heard the cock of progress crow. He will begin to question the institutions that have kept him primitive: medicine, the church, the pearl industry, the government. The allegory operates then locally, dealing at first with one person, Kino, and then with his people, the Mexican peasants of Lower California. But the allegory works also universally, and Kino is Everyman. The darkness in which he awakes is one of the spirit. The cock crow is one of warning that the spirit must awake to its own dangers. The allegorical journey has often been called the way into the dark night of the soul, in which the darkness stands for despair or hopelessness. We cannot describe Kino or his people as in despair, for they have never known any life other than the one they lead; neither are they in hopelessness, for they are not aware that there is anything for which to hope. In a social parable, then, the darkness is injustice and helplessness in the face of it; in the allegory of the spirit, darkness concerns the opacity of the moral substance in man.

The social element is developed rapidly through the episode of Coyotito's scorpion bite and the doctor's refusal to treat a child whose father cannot pay a substantial fee. Kino's helplessness is conveyed by the fist he crushes into a split and bleeding mass against the doctor's gate. This theme of helplessness reaches its peak in the pearl-selling attempt. When Kino says to his incredulous brother, Juan Thomás, that perhaps all three buyers set a price amongst themselves before Kino's arrival, Juan Thomás answers, "If that is so, then all of us have been cheated all of our lives." And of course they have been.

Kino is, then, in the near dark; and, as his misfortunes develop, he descends deeper and deeper into the dark night of the soul. The journey that the soul makes as well as the journey that the living Kino makes—in terms of the good and evil that invest the one and the oppression and freedom that come to the other—provides the allegorical statement of the novel.

In the attempt to achieve believable situations, create three-dimensional characters, Steinbeck met greater difficulties that he did not entirely overcome. The germ-anecdote out of which he constructed his story gave him little more than the bare elements of myth....

[In] Steinbeck's source [are] all the major elements of his expanded version: the Mexican peasant, the discovered pearl, the belief that the pearl will make the finder free, the corrupt brokers, the attacks, the flight, the return, and the disposal of the pearl. But there are also additions and alterations. The episodes of the doctor and the priest are added; the motives for retaining the pearl are changed. While the additions add perhaps some realism at the same time that they increase the impact of the allegory, the alterations tend to diminish the realistic aspects of the hero.

In these alterations, employed perhaps to add reality to a fable, Steinbeck has diminished realism. Narrative detail alone supplies this element. The opening of chapter three, like the beginning paragraph of the book, is descriptive.... Symbol, allegory, and realistic detail are again woven satisfactorily together. The large fish and the hawks symbolize the doctor, the priest, the brokers, and the man behind the brokers, in fact all enemies of the village people from time prehistoric. Allegorically these predatory animals are all the snares that beset the journeying soul and the hungering body. Realistically these scenes can be observed in any coastal town where water, foul, and animal ecology provide these specific denizens.

Somewhere in every chapter Steinbeck adds a similar touch.... All these passages operate symbolically as well as realistically, and some of them work even allegorically.

Kino's flight may be seen as a double journey, with a third still to be made. The journey is one half spiritual—the route to salvation of the soul—and one half physical—the way to freedom from bodily want.

The Indian boy of the germ-story had quite falsely identified his hold on the pearl with a firm grasp on salvation, a salvation absolutely assured while he still went about enveloped in flesh and mortality: "he could in advance purchase masses sufficient to pop him out of Purgatory like a squeezed watermelon seed." Kino also holds the pearl in his hand and equates it with freedom from want and then, mystically, also with freedom from damnation: "If I give it up I shall lose my soul." But he too has mistaken the pearl. The chances are very much more likely that with freedom from want his soul will be all the more in danger from sin. The Indian boy becomes free only when he throws the pearl away, only when he is "again with his soul in danger and his food and shelter insecure." The full significance of Kino's throwing the pearl back into the sea now becomes clear: the act represents his willingness to accept the third journey, the journey still to be made, the journey that Dante had still to make even after rising out of Hell to Purgatory and Paradise, the journey that any fictional character has still to make after his dream-vision allegory is over. Kino, Dante, Everyman have been given nothing more than instruction. They must apply their new knowledge and win their way to eternal salvation, which can come only with their actual deaths.

Kino is not defeated. He has in a sense triumphed over his enemy, over the chief of the pearl buyers, who neither gets the pearl nor kills Kino to keep him from talking. Kino has rid himself of his pursuers; he has a clear road to the cities of the north, to the capital, where indeed he may be cheated again, but where he has infinitely more opportunity to escape his destiny as a hut-dwelling peasant on the edge of La Paz. He has proved that he cannot be cheated nor destroyed. But his real triumph, his real gain, the heights to which he has risen rather than the depths to which he has slipped back is the immense knowledge that he has gained about good and evil. This knowledge is the tool that he needs to help him on the final journey, the inescapable journey that everyman must take.

A final note should be added concerning some parallels between Steinbeck's novel and the anonymous fourteenth century *Pearl*.

The importance of the medieval *Pearl* for a reading of Steinbeck's novel is centered in the role of the children in each. Coyotito can, in several ways, be identified with Kino's "pearl of great value." The pearl from the sea is only a means by which Coyotito will be given an education. For the doctor, who at first refused to treat Coyotito, the child becomes his means to the pearl, i.e. the child is the pearl to him. But more important than these tenuous relationships is the fact that with the death of Coyotito the pearl no longer has any significance. The moment the pursuer with the rifle fires, Kino kills him. Kino then kills the two trackers who led the assassin to him and who were unshakable. This act gives Kino and his family unhindered passage to the cities of the north, where either the pearl might be sold or a new life begun. But the chance shot has killed Coyotito, and though Kino and Juana are now free, they return to the village near La Paz and throw the pearl back into the sea. Thus the sole act that has altered Kino's determination to keep the pearl which has become his soul is the death of his child; and, as I read the allegory, Kino and Juana turn from the waterside with new spiritual strength, regenerated even as the father in the medieval *Pearl*.

However, I do not think that anything overmuch should be made of [the] similarities. Possibly the mere title of Steinbeck's allegory brought memories to his mind of the fourteenth century poem. He may have gone back to look at it again, but he may have satisfied himself with distant evocations only. For myself, whatever likenesses I find between the two works serve only to emphasize the continuing tradition of true allegory and the modern writer's strong links with the past.

Source: Harry Morris, "*The Pearl:* Realism and Allegory," in *English Journal,* Vol. 52, No. 7, October, 1963, pp. 487–505.

Sources

John S. Kennedy, "John Steinbeck: Life Affirmed and Dissolved," in *Steinbeck and His Critics: A Record of Twenty-five Years,* edited by E.W. Tedlock, Jr. and C.V. Wicker, University of New Mexico Press, 1957, pp. 119-34.

Todd M. Lieber, "Talismanic Patterns in the Novels of John Steinbeck," in *American Literature,* May, 1972, pp. 262-75.

Peter Lisca, "Escape and Commitment: Two Poles of the Steinbeck Hero," in *Steinbeck: The Man and His Work,* edited by Richard Astro and Tetsumaro Hayashi, Oregon State University Press, 1971, pp. 75-88.

Harry Morris, "*The Pearl:* Realism and Allegory," in *English Journal,* Vol. LII, No. 7, October, 1963, pp. 487-505.

For Further Study

Carlos Baker, "Steinbeck at the Top of His Form," in *New York Times Book Review,* Vol. 97, November 30, 1947, pp. 4, 52.
> In this favorable review, Baker finds parallels between *The Pearl* and the "unkillable folklore of Palestine, Greece, Rome, China, India," and western Europe.

Debra K.S. Barker, "Passages of Descent and Initiation: Juana as the 'Other' Hero of *The Pearl,*" in *After The Grapes of Wrath, Essays on John Steinbeck,* edited by Donald V. Coers, Paul D. Ruffin, and Robert J. DeMott, Ohio University Press, 1995, pp. 113-23.
> Barker argues that Juana undergoes a trial "equal to or perhaps more momentous" than Kino's as she evolves from the role of "Helpmate" to that of "The Sage."

Warren French, "Dramas of Consciousness," in *John Steinbeck,* Twayne Publishers, 1975, pp. 126-30.
> French defines parable, and maintains that *The Pearl* does not fit the definition of a parable because it contains too many loose ends.

—, "Searching for a Folk Hero," in *John Steinbeck's Fiction Revisited,* Twayne Publishers, 1994, pp. 106-12.
> French describes the novel as offering a "high-minded lesson for materialistic cultures that certainly could not have been true."

Maxwell Geismar, "Fable Retold," in *The Saturday Review,* Vol. 30, November 22, 1947, pp. 14-15.
> Geismar criticizes the novel as a work of propaganda rather than art.

Sunita Jain, "Steinbeck's *The Pearl:* An Interpretation," in *Journal of the School of Languages,* Vol. 6, Nos. 1-2, 1978-1979, pp. 138-43.
> In this positive review, Jain interprets the central drama in the story to be "Kino's education into manhood through the knowledge of good and evil."

Ernest E. Karsten, Jr., "Thematic Structure in *The Pearl,*" in *English Journal,* Vol. 54, No. 1, January, 1965, pp. 1-7.
> Karsten relates the novel's themes to its organization, focusing his analysis on the Songs of Family, of Evil, and of the Pearl, on the theme of human relationships, and on the essential roles of men and women.

Sydney J. Krause, "*The Pearl* and 'Hadleyburg': From Desire to Renunciation," in *Steinbeck's Literary Dimension: A Guide to Comparative Studies Series II,* edited by Tetsumaro Hayashi, The Scarecrow Press, Inc., 1991, pp. 154-71.
> Krause says that critical responses to the novel depend on how one interprets its conclusion, which he sees optimistically as revealing how Kino's weaknesses have become his strengths. Krause classifies

the novel as belonging to the "pessimistic-naturalist" tradition of Twain's "The Man That Corrupted Hadleyburg."

Howard Levant, "The Natural Parable," in *The Novels of John Steinbeck, A Critical Study,* University of Missouri Press, 1974, pp. 185-206.
> Levant analyzes Steinbeck's narrative methods, focusing on the novella's simple structure, which, he believes, provides a necessary balance to Steinbeck's complex material.

Peter Lisca, "The Pearl," in *The Wide World of John Steinbeck,* Rutgers University Press, 1958, pp. 218-30.
> Lisca offers an interpretation of *The Pearl* as both a "direct statement of events," and "as a reflection of conscious or unconscious forces dictating the imagery in which it is presented."

—, in *John Steinbeck: Nature and Myth,* Thomas Y. Cromwell, 1978.
> Critical look at Steinbeck's theoretical use of biological theory and mythical components in his fiction.

Michael J. Meyer, "Precious Bane: Mining the Fool's Gold in *The Pearl,*" in *The Short Novels of John Steinbeck, Critical Essays with a Checklist to Steinbeck Criticism,* edited by Jackson J. Benson, Duke University Press, 1990, pp. 161-72.
> Meyer analyzes critical responses to the novella, in particular how they interpret the ambiguity in the tale, then offers his own interpretation: the parable acknowledges that only on his way toward death is man able to "discover who he really is."

Harry Morris, "*The Pearl:* Realism and Allegory," in *English Journal,* Vol. 52, No. 7, October, 1963, pp. 487-505.
> Morris investigates the appearance and reception of allegory in the past four hundred years of literature, responds to those who criticized the novella because it is an allegory or because it is anti-materialist, and concludes that Kino is a remarkable hero because he is an allegorical Everyman.

Orville Prescott, "Books of the Times," in *New York Times,* November 24, 1947, p. 21.
> Prescott praises *The Pearl* for its simple style and powerful emotional impact, and compares it to Kipling's Mowgli story, "The King's Ankus."

John Steinbeck, "Nobel Prize Acceptance Speech," in *Faulkner O'Neill Steinbeck,* edited by Alexis Gregory, Helvetica Press, Inc., 1971, pp. 205-08.
> In this speech, Steinbeck considers the human need for literature, and agrees with Faulkner that the "understanding and the resolution of fear are a large part of the writer's reason for being."

John Steinbeck and Edward F. Ricketts, in *Sea of Cortez: A Leisurely Journal of Travel and Research,* Viking, 1941.
> This work is the result of a marine expedition that Steinbeck undertook with his friend Ed Ricketts in 1940. It provides more insight into Steinbeck's biological theories. The expedition takes place in the Gulf of California where a story like *The Pearl* might easily take place.

The Sun Also Rises

Ernest Hemingway

1926

Ernest Hemingway's first novel, *The Sun Also Rises,* remains, as F. Scott Fitzgerald said, "a romance and a guidebook." It also became, in the words of critic Sibbie O'Sullivan, "a modern-day courtesy book on how to behave in the waste land Europe had become after the Great War." *The Sun Also Rises* successfully portrays its characters as survivors of a "lost generation." In addition, the novel was the most modern an American author had yet produced, and the ease with which it could be read endeared it to many. But for all its apparent simplicity, the novel's innovation lay in its ironic style that interjected complex themes without being didactic. Generally, the novel is considered to be Hemingway's most satisfying work.

The material for the novel resulted from a journey Hemingway made with his first wife, Hadley Richardson, and several friends to Pamplona, Spain, in 1925. Among them was Lady Duff Twysden, a beautiful socialite with whom Hemingway was in love (the inspiration for the novel's Lady Brett Ashley). There was also a Jewish novelist and boxer named Harold Loeb (source of Robert Cohn) whom Hemingway threatened after learning that he and Lady Duff had had an affair. Lady Duff's companion was a bankrupt Briton (like Mike Campbell). The trip ended poorly when Lady Duff and her companion left their bills unpaid. The ending of the novel is only slightly more tragic, yet it recovers those precious values which make life livable in a war-wearied world: friendship, stoicism, and natural grace.

Author Biography

One of the greatest authors of American literature, Hemingway had modest beginnings in the town of Oak Park, Illinois, where he was born to Dr. Clarence and Grace Hall Hemingway in 1899. Young Hemingway pursued sports with his father and arts with his mother without distinction. In 1917, after graduating from high school, he took a junior position at the *Kansas City Star* where he was given a reporter's stylebook that demanded brief, declarative, and direct sentences. Hemingway became the master of this style and adapted it to literary demands.

In 1918 he volunteered for service in World War I and served as an ambulance driver on the Italian front. This experience later served as the source material for *A Farewell to Arms*. His legs were wounded and he was sent home. His convalescence took place over several months at the family cabin in Michigan. When he recovered, he took a position as companion to a disabled boy in Toronto in 1920. There, he again entered the world of writing through the *Toronto Star*. After marriage to Hadley Richardson, he became a Parisian correspondent with the paper.

He and his wife left for Paris where Hemingway associated with those known as the "Lost Generation" (James Joyce, Ezra Pound, Gertrude Stein, and Ford Madox Ford). His first publishing success was a short story entitled "My Old Man" in 1923. For the next few years he continued to meet literary figures (F. Scott Fitzgerald among others) and edited a journal with Ford Madox Ford. In 1925 he began work on *The Sun Also Rises* which reflected his life in Paris among the "Lost Generation." He also wrote *The Torrents of Spring* at the same time. Both were published the following year.

With the success of *A Farewell to Arms* in 1929, Hemingway traveled quite a bit. He frequented Cuba, Florida, and France, contributed money for ambulance service in the Spanish Civil war, and also covered the war for *The North American Newspaper Alliance*. In 1940 he married his third wife, Martha Gellhorn, and published *For Whom the Bell Tolls*. Hemingway and Gellhorn then went to China where he became a war correspondent with the United States Fourth Infantry Division. There he met Mary Welsh, whom he married in 1945.

Hemingway continued to publish until 1952 when *The Old Man and the Sea* crowned his extraordinary career. He received the Pulitzer Prize

Ernest Hemingway

in 1953 for this story. Unfortunately, by the mid-1950s his adventurous life had taken its toll. Hemingway became depressed and spent time in various hospitals. Finally, he returned from a stay in the Mayo Clinic on June 30, 1961, to his home in Ketchum, Idaho. There he used a favorite gun to commit suicide on July 2.

Plot Summary

Book I

The Sun Also Rises is set in Paris and Spain in the 1920s and depicts the lives of a group of young American and English expatriates living in the aftermath of World War I. Often read as a representation of the now familiar "Lost Generation," Hemingway's story revolves around the impossible love affair between the war-damaged American journalist Jake Barnes, the novel's narrator, and Lady Brett Ashley, a former nurse in a hospital Jake was in during the war.

Jake begins his narrative by introducing Robert Cohn, one of his friends in Paris. A one-time boxing champion at Princeton, Cohn, as he is generally called, is now the author of a rather "poor novel" and is living in Europe with his fiancee,

Frances. Lamenting the fact that his life is quickly passing by and that he is not really living it, Cohn tries to recruit Jake for a voyage to South America. Jake, however, will not join him. He knows first-hand that traveling to another country does not make a difference and tells his friend that "you can't get away from yourself by moving from one place to another."

Shortly after parting from Cohn, Jake picks up a prostitute walking in front of a cafe. He buys her a drink and takes her out to dinner. Riding in a cab to the restaurant, the girl, Georgette, touches Jake but he pushes her away. He later explains that he was wounded during the war. After dinner, they go to a club where several of Jake's friends have gathered. When Brett arrives, Jake notices that Cohn cannot keep his eyes off her. Jake and Brett soon leave the club and find a cab. As they drive, Jake kisses Brett but she turns away. She tells him that she loves him but cannot bear to go through "that hell again."

They proceed to the Cafe Select and are introduced to Count Mippipopolous, a man who, Brett later confirms, is "quite one of us." Jake leaves early and returns home. As he prepares for bed, he undresses and looks at himself in the mirror. "Of all the ways to be wounded," he thinks. Unable to sleep, he thinks of his accident and how he would probably never have minded had he never met Brett. He cries and finally falls asleep.

The next day, Cohn tells Jake that he might be in love with Brett. When asked what he knows about her, Jake tells him that Brett is a drunk and that she is engaged to Mike Campbell, presently is Scotland. That evening, Jake receives a visit from Brett and the Count. He is feeling "pretty rotten" and Brett sends the Count on an errand so they can be alone. Jake asks Brett if they could live together but she tells him that she would just "*tromper*" him with everyone. She then announces that she is going to San Sebastian and that, when she returns, Mike will be back.

When the Count returns from his errand, they finish off three bottles of champagne and go out for dinner. After some dancing at Zelli's, Brett tells Jake that she is feeling miserable and would like to leave. Immediately, Jake gets the feeling that he is going through something that has happened before. They bid goodnight to the Count and leave together. Outside her hotel, Brett tells Jake not to come up. They kiss, Brett pushes Jake away and they kiss again. Brett then turns and enters the hotel.

Book II

Jake does not see Brett again until her return from San Sebastian. Nor does he see Cohn, who has reportedly gone to the country for a couple of weeks. Upon Brett's return, arrangements are made for everyone to join Jake and his friend, Bill Gorton, on their fishing trip to Spain. Brett worries that this excursion might be rough on Cohn, revealing that they were together in San Sebastian. Jake and Bill meet Cohn in Bayonne and travel on to Pamplona but, at the last minute, Cohn backs out of the fishing trip, deciding instead to meet Brett and Mike in San Sebastian. Jake and Bill spend five days fishing, drinking and playing bridge in Burguete, then return to Pamplona to meet Brett, Mike, and Cohn.

After witnessing the unloading of the bulls, Cohn remarks that "it's no life being a steer." This comment starts Mike, who is drunk and who knows of the affair with Brett, on a long tirade against Cohn. He figures Cohn should enjoy being a steer, since they never say anything and are always hanging about. He asks Cohn why it is that he does not know when he is not wanted and why he follows Brett around like a steer. That night, Jake is unable to sleep. He is jealous of what happened to Cohn. He likes to see Mike hurt him but wishes he would not do it because he feels disgusted with himself afterwards.

On the first day of the fiesta of San Fermin, Jake, Brett and the others are led into a wine shop by a group of men dancing in the street. All eat, drink, sing and have a good time, except Cohn, who passes out in a back room. The following afternoon, Jake and Bill are introduced to Pedro Romero, a young bullfighter. Later, they see that Pedro is a "real one"—his bullfighting gives real emotion whereas the others only fake danger. After the bullfight, Brett says she thinks Pedro lovely and comments on his tight green trousers.

The next morning, Montoya, owner of the hotel where the "real ones" stay, seeks Jake's advice concerning the American ambassador's request to meet Pedro. Montoya fears the influence such a meeting might have on the young bullfighter and Jake agrees that Montoya should not pass along the message. Later that day, Jake finds himself sitting in the dining room with Brett, his friends and Pedro. Montoya enters the room and starts to smile at Jake but then notices Pedro sitting at a table full of drunks. He leaves the room without even nodding.

A little while later, Brett tells Jake that she is mad about Pedro. Jake advises her not to do anything but then agrees to help her find the young bullfighter. When Cohn finds out that Brett and Pedro are together, he calls Jake a pimp and boxes him and Mike to the ground. He then finds Brett and Pedro and beats the bullfighter badly. Later that night, he apologizes to Jake and explains that he could not stand Brett's cool behavior toward him. He tells Jake that he will be leaving in the morning. On the last day of the fiesta, Jake and the others learn that Brett has gone off with Pedro.

Book III

The fiesta over, Jake, Bill and Mike all leave Pamplona. They drive together as far as Bayonne, then go their separate ways. Jake plans a quiet week in San Sebastian but a telegram from Brett shortens his stay. He joins her in Madrid and there learns that she has sent Pedro away. She tells Jake that she realized Pedro should not be living with anyone and that she did not want to be "one of these bitches that ruins children." She then tells him that she will go back to Mike. They arrange for tickets out of Madrid and stop for drinks and dinner. Afterwards, they go for a ride in a taxi. Sitting close to Jake, Brett says: "Oh, Jake, we could have had such a damned good time together." Jake's response ends the novel: "Yes, isn't it pretty to think so?"

Characters

Lady Brett Ashley

Lady Brett Ashley best encapsulates the beauty of being "lost." She represents the dead aristocracy and constantly fends off the long-dead notions of romance best captured in the melancholy of Robert Cohn. Yet she also represents the future and the new feminism of the 1920s; she is an amoral socialite who lost her first love and husband to dysentery in the War, divorced her second because he was abusive but gave her a title, and is working on a third. She is the interesting woman of intelligence from the nineteenth century that Henry James would want to make into a portrait. Lastly, she is an inspiration to otherwise impotent writers because she "was damned good-looking ... [and] built like the hull of a racing yacht." Consequent to all these ingredients and the fact that she is in love with Jake, Brett is the moving force of the novel's action. She is also Hemingway's denunciation of all bohemians.

Media Adaptations

- Using a screenplay by Peter Viertel, Twentieth Century-Fox adapted *The Sun Also Rises* to the big screen. The movie was released in 1957 and was directed by Harry King. The film stars Tyrone Power, Ava Gardner, and Errol Flynn.

- Directed by James Goldstone and starring Elisabeth Borgnine, *The Sun Also Rises* was adapted for television in 1985.

Jake Barnes

The narrator of the story is Jake Barnes. Like his Biblical namesake Jacob, Jake has trouble sleeping because he wrestles nightly with his fate. He is an American living in Paris as a newspaper correspondent. He was rendered impotent by a World War I wound and is thus unable to consummate his love with Brett. Both his physical condition and his terse manner embody the sterility of the age. Jake forgets the war by immersing himself in the meticulous details of life. He has a calculated view of the events in the story and is sure to relate minutiae, such as how much things cost, who owes whom, how to bait the hook, and what is in the packed lunch. His method for living and being at ease with the world is not unlike the Count's. He states his philosophy, which is the new moral for a world disillusioned by war, as "you paid some way for everything that was any good. I paid my way into enough things that I liked, so that I had a good time. Either you paid by learning about them, or by experience, or by taking chances, or by money. Enjoying living was learning to get your money's worth and knowing when you had it."

Jake Barnes is Hemingway's first and best attempt to explain to others the mannerisms which enable constructive living with an accompanying disillusionment. Exaggerating this position, Jake is a man to whom things happen. Through no fault of his own, he was a victim of war; he suffers a wound that prevents a normal life. His story is an

A scene from The Sun Also Rises, *starring Ava Gardner and Tyrone Power.*

effort, not so much to react to the world, but to sort out in a visible manner an explanation for his life and a solution to his quandary. He discovers a coded style of "hardboiledness" which he uses to pull off the appearance of living with the war. Along with this, he turns to the relational exchanges embodied in money as his emotional salve. Consequently, his meticulous record of what is spent and how is a reassurance. He grows less and less troubled as he perfects his code among those who are more lost, get less for their money, and are not wounded. Only the Count (who also has physical scars) has an understanding of this and, therefore, he is the only other character who does not appear troubled.

Belmonte

An historical figure, Belmonte was one of the greatest matadors of all time. He is shown in the story as aging and past his prime. This is ironic in the extreme since it is the matador who fulfills the ideal of the hero. Yet, showing a hero in decline makes him all the more human. Belmonte, despite his pain, maintains his dignified poise and provides yet another example of the novel's moral: no matter how you choose to live in this senseless world, live with style.

Mrs. Braddocks

Mrs. Braddocks "was a Canadian and had all their easy social graces." She is attempting to revive pre-war dancing events. At the moment she simply gathers people about her for dinner before they go on their nightly clubbing.

Brett

See Lady Brett Ashley

Michael Campbell

A bankrupt Scotsman who is engaged to Brett, Mike Campbell grows weary of Cohn always hanging around Brett. He takes advantage of Cohn's inferiority complex to needle him. He is made painfully aware that Brett does not love him when she goes off with the matador.

Frances Clyne

Frances believes that she is in love with Cohn. She is ready to sacrifice anything to be with him. Cohn, in his new success as a novelist, would rather seek adventure. Realizing that Cohn has no intention of marrying her, she insults him and leaves for England.

Robert Cohn

The novel opens with Robert Cohn, a mediocre writer and middleweight boxing champion at Princeton with a "hard, Jewish, stubborn streak." He is the representation of all that was supposedly destroyed in the war. Therefore, he must be exiled from the group that is busily reshaping the world.

He is a friend and tennis partner to Jake. Born rich and married rich, he was unhappy until his wife left him. Now free, he decides to pursue happiness in the form of editing a magazine. But when that fails, he moves to Paris with his assistant, Frances, and writes. The success of his first novel goes straight to his head as he lives out his dreams of chivalry and romance; Frances becomes his mistress. From this point, his role is one of decline in the eyes of his associates for, as Brett says, he is not "one of us." From the moment of Brett's judgment, the other men seek ways of being rid of him. Jake succeeds by letting Cohn exile himself.

Cohn's love for Brett and his expression of that love is meant as criticism of the romantic. He represents the American values of love, idealism, and naive bliss that were soundly exploded in World War I. Therefore, Cohn is Hemingway's satirical portrait of the last knight who would defend the old faith and ideals. This knight absurdly undergoes overt humiliation under the guise of a love for a lady and brings upon himself verbal wrath and abuse. Cohn's actions are the last gasp of those values yet his survival is a bitter reminder of their beauty in not too dissimilar ways from Jake's more physical reminder in the form of his wound.

Bill Gorton

One of the few positive characters in the novel arrives in Paris at the start of Book II. Bill Gorton has come to accompany Jake on a fishing expedition but finds he must also buoy his friend's spirits. Bill believes in "a simple exchange of values" and living for the moment. This philosophy prompts him to say, in sight of something that would bring ease, "let's utilize it."

Georgette Hobin

See Georgette Leblanc

Georgette Leblanc

A prostitute, Georgette Leblanc is very cynical and does her utmost to hide her defect—her teeth. She shares a knowledge with Jake that everyone is "sick" in their way but she is not brought into the group.

Count Mippipopolous

The Count has a very simple philosophy of life—get your money's worth and know when you have. He owns a chain of sweet shops and is charmed by Lady Brett, who thinks he is one of them. The Count knows through experience and age what the others are trying to figure out—how to live well.

Montoya

Montoya is the owner of a hotel in Pamplona where Jake habitually stays while in town for the fiesta. He recognizes that Jake is a fellow aficionado—one who is capable of appreciating the ritual bullfight. He is the truest devotee of bullfighting and all the matadors try to stay in his hotel. Montoya does what he can for those matadors who show promise as the "real thing."

Pedro Romero

The stock hero of the tale, Romero is handsome and brave. His beating at the hands of the annoying boxer, Cohn, shows him to be just a man who has a talent for bullfighting.

Themes

Morals and Morality

Reflecting on his friends and especially on Robert Cohn, who is becoming a major annoyance, Jake reflects on his moral code, "That was morality; things that made you disgusted afterward. No, that must be immorality." Jake is more interested in his own concerns and, secondarily, Brett's. Cohn was fortunate enough to have a holiday with Brett but he is not smart enough to accept that it meant nothing. Because Cohn cannot create his own version of the group's code, he becomes the subject of persecution. Jake is bothered by it but he is more disgusted when he knowingly violates the code of aficionado by setting up Brett with Romero. This disrupts his friendship with Montoya and with Cohn. Respect is betrayed and lost. The garbage that is visible at the end of the fiesta only compounds his self-disgust. However, instead of leading to an epiphany he simply decides to develop his own code of style more thoroughly. That style is a hard-boiled self-centeredness.

Brett is lost throughout the novel. She is disgusted with herself and those around her, especially Jake—through no fault of his own. The only moment she exerts herself in terms of morality is to

Topics for Further Study

- After doing some research on bullfighting and its surrounding festival, explain the novel according to your findings discussing whether or not the British title of *Fiesta* was more or less appropriate. Is the bullfight the focus of the novel? Back up your claims by examining each character's reaction to the spectacle.

- Thinking about the role that the matador plays in the novel, what is the role of a hero in a world disillusioned by war? Would you agree with cultural anthropologist Joseph Campbell that his role (and Joseph Campbell does emphasize the need for rejuvenating masculine heroic ritual) is to reconnect people into a "coordinated soul"? As he says in *The Hero with a Thousand Faces,* "It is not society that is to guide and save the creative hero, but precisely the reverse." Lastly, do you think Hemingway was working with this idea in mind?

- Compare *The Sun Also Rises* with Jack Kerouac's *On the Road.* How does the spokesman for the "lost generation" compare with that of the "beat generation"?

- Given the conditions of agrarian life in the dust bowl of the early part of this century, what arguments can you make for linking the "greats" of the "lost generation" to their birth-region? Except for Ezra Pound (Idaho), they are all from the Midwest—F. Scott Fitzgerald (MN), Ernest Hemingway (IL), Sherwood Anderson (OH), Sinclair Lewis (MN), and T.S. Eliot (MO).

- Would Hemingway, or any character in his novel, approve of a female matador? Provide evidence from the novel or from other Hemingway novels or short fiction to support your assertion.

get rid of Romero. Throughout the novel, Brett defies conventional morality by having short, meaningless affairs. Because of her self-centeredness and unhappiness, she is unable to stop this self-destructive behavior and is often passive to events.

The affairs are meant to escape her unsatisfactory relationship with Jake, whom she truly loves but who is unable to physically consummate their relationship.

Meaning of Life

The theme of life's meaning turns from the question of essence, "what it was all about," to existence, "how to live in it." However, the reason for this polarity is the inability of the main characters to rise above that mediocrity. They must reject the life of the hero as impossible for themselves. "Nobody ever lives their life all the way up except bullfighters." To which Cohn replies, "I am not interested in bullfighters. That's an abnormal life." Cohn's idea of life is romantic—a life of literary fame and adventure with a beautiful mistress who happens to have a title. But the group despises Cohn's notions and Brett finally judges that he is "not one of us." Instead, the key to life is a development of one's ability to wisely utilize the full worth of one's money. This can take many forms but only Jake, the Count, and to a certain extent Bill Gorton, are able to do this. Brett, and especially Mike Campbell (who is ever an "undischarged bankrupt"), will never be happy even if they become rich because they are incapable of utilizing money well.

Bill relies on exchange value and use. When he first enters the narrative he wishes to buy Jake a stuffed dog, "Simple exchange of values. You give them money. They give you a stuffed dog." Bill's philosophy is to use money to buy moments as well as to show one's stature. His motto is "Never be daunted." Possibilities for bliss, such as a pub or a bottle, must be utilized to their full potential.

Jake, meanwhile, is developing a more sophisticated attitude full of tabulating expenses which keeps his mind off his main problem of impotence. "I paid my way into things that I liked, so that I had a good time. Either you paid by learning about them or by experience, or by taking chances, or by money. Enjoying living was learning to get your money's worth and knowing when you had it. You could get your money's worth. The world was a good place to buy in." Then he adds that he might change his mind in five years. In other words, "the lost generation" can get their kicks by a wise expenditure of money (even if they are not rich) until a semblance of reality has been reconstructed and the war is in the past. A possible future philosophy is hinted at when Jake reads Turgenieff and knows he will remember what he reads as if it was his experience. That is, Turgenieff writes truthfully about experience in a way Hemingway agreed with. "That was another good thing you paid for and then had." But payment here is the effort of reading literature which you can then use to recover from war.

Style

Narrative

The first-person narration of Jake Barnes is sometimes referred to as a "roman à clef." A roman à clef is a story understandable only to those who have a "key" for deciphering the real persons and places behind the story. The story of Jake Barnes resembles the real events of the summer of 1925 in the life of Hemingway and his friends. Still there is enough difference that no "key" is needed for understanding. That is to say, the novel stands on its own whether or not the reader knows on whom the character Lady Brett Ashley is based. In addition, Jake Barnes is not Hemingway because in real life Hemingway was married when he went to Pamplona. Jake is a blending of several real people as well as a fruition of Hemingway's theoretic code-hero. There is enough similarity for comparisons but the novel is in no way an autobiographical event. It is a story attempting to speak truths to the present generation.

Dialogue

Hemingway's dependence on dialogue is just one mark of his modernity. Henry James, for example, felt dialogue was the climax of a scene and was to be used sparingly. Hemingway creates whole scenes solely from dialogue. However, Hemingway's dialogue made the story an easy and fast read with effects similar to news writing. The author seems to disappear as the narrator allows his contact with others to balance out the story. It becomes a group conversation rather than a narration. Hemingway's ability with this feature delighted many critics. Conrad Aiken remarked, "More than any other talk I can call to mind, it is alive with the rhythms and idioms, the pauses and suspensions and innuendoes and shorthands, of living speech. It is in the dialogue, almost entirely, that Mr. Hemingway tells his story and makes the people live and act." The use of dialogue is one of the key features of Hemingway's style.

Hero

Hemingway's solution to the ennui, or disillusioned nausea, that marked his "lost generation" was the encouragement of each person in their path to being a hero. However, as is clear in the novel, his theory did not include bravery in war or sport but insisted that the individual create a moral code. One must "never be daunted."

Jake Barnes and friends are the best examples of Hemingway pursuing his theories. Succeeding Hemingway heroes do have the humanity to inspire our sympathy and imitation. This code-hero was defined eloquently by Robert Penn Warren and Cleanth Brooks while discussing Hemingway's "The Killers." They said that the code-hero "is the tough man, ... the disciplined man, who actually is aware of pathos or tragedy." Lacking spontaneous emotion, the code-hero "sheathes [his sensibility] in the code of toughness" because "he has learned that the only way to hold on to 'honor,' to individuality, to, even, the human order ... is to live by his code." Romero provides the clearest example not through his bullfighting but through his ability to ignore the bruises Cohn gives him in order to perform as he is capable. The success of the fiesta depends on his ability to do so. Brett and Jake also satisfy this definition. Brett decides she cannot corrupt the young bullfighter but will continue to live in style hiding her frustrated love. Jake decides he has to live according to his own code with the help of his stoicism.

Idiom

The heavy use of dialogue, the terse, staccato sentences, and the minimalist tightness that characterizes descriptions and emotional expenditure are the marks of the style or idiom that Hemingway made his own. According to this idiom, carefully chosen language can relate fictional authenticity in such a way that it will never ring false, the goal being to carefully construct a world that has certitude and leave the uncertain unsaid. Thus the language appears often to refer to ideas beyond what is actually written. However, only the written words are to be trusted and only they are true. The effect of this new style is similar to Biblical genesis: reconstruct from the rubble of war a civilization of beauty and simplicity.

The bareness of the intention is best revealed on the fishing expedition. "Once in the night I woke and heard the wind blowing. It felt good to be warm and in bed." Two sentences were used where previous writers would have expended chapters. Fur-

Bullfighting is a popular attraction in Spain.

thermore, it is an incredibly simple and stark contrast to the sleepless nights of Paris and it directly calls to mind the howls of the "Waste Land."

Historical Context

The Lost Generation

Writers, horrified by the stranglehold of business and the uselessness of Prohibition, expatriated to Paris where the favorable exchange rate enabled them to work for a newspaper or magazine. Yet these writers usually spent most of their time sitting in cafes lost in the aftermath of a war for which they refused responsibility. Disillusioned, they discussed their inherited nineteenth-century values and the provincial and emotional barrenness of America. Fortunately, they found comfort in an older generation. Hemingway, armed with letters of introduction by Sherwood Anderson, joined this group who flocked to Gertrude Stein's Salon, Sylvia Beach's Shakespeare and Company bookstore, the apartment of James Joyce, *the transatlantic review* offices of Ford Madox Ford, or Samuel Putnam's office. The older writers cultivated the members of what Stein labeled, after overhearing her mechanic, as "the lost generation."

Of the elders Stein, who was the bridge between past and present, and Ezra Pound, whom Hemingway tried to teach boxing in return for tutelage, were the most important influences on Hemingway.

"The Lost Generation" succeeded in poking through the rubble of civilization and manufacturing art anew. From war's negation comes affirmation as a means to live with disillusion. T.S. Eliot wove the old myths together into a poem of epic influence, "The Waste Land." A new poetry was created by e.e. cummings. F. Scott Fitzgerald, John Dos Passos, Hart Crane, and Glenway Westcott were members of this generation who helped rejuvenate the arts. The most important contribution of "The Lost Generation" was to prove the resiliency of culture and set it moving again with the hopeful idealism that would mark American literature in the 1930s.

The Roaring Twenties

In the Europe of the mid-1920s, life was returning to normal and cities were being reconstructed after the devastation of World War I. Tensions, which still existed between France and Germany over border issues, were quiet, as France became isolated. The French war effort had depended on American loans and their repayment depended on reparations from Germany. These repa-

Compare & Contrast

- **1920s:** Thomas Hunt Morgan proves his theory of hereditary transmission through experiments with fruit flies and publishes *The Theory of the Gene* in 1926. Coincidentally, Herman Joseph Mullar proves that X-rays can produce genetic mutations.

  Today: It is no longer speculation that genes provide the source code for life and can be mutated by radiation. In fact, Morgan's groundbreaking experiment is now an exercise in college biology rooms. Moreover, armed with lessons in genetic engineering, biotechnology firms are literally changing the fabric of nature by gene manipulation and the techniques of cloning.

- **1920s:** The "Noble Experiment" of Prohibition is in full swing. Backers hope it will make America better by forcing its people to be sober. Instead, average citizens flout the law by patronizing illegal establishments run by the Mafia. Bootlegging is a billion-dollar industry.

  Today: The "War on Drugs" is mounted to stop the sale of hard drugs and urban deterioration in the United States.

- **1920s:** The tuna industry is in a crisis as albacore disappears off the California coast. The industry begins harvesting the lower quality yellow-fin tuna.

  Today: The entire fishing industry is in a crisis with vast areas of the oceans fished out. Whole strata of the aquatic food chain have disappeared with lower-level fish, like jellyfish, producing record numbers for lack of predators. The situation is so bad that normally friendly nations (like Great Britain, Canada, Spain, and Portugal) have almost come to blows over fishing rights.

- **1920s:** The Spanish ritual of bullfighting is confined to Spain and parts of Latin America. It is purely a male domain.

  Today: The popularity of bullfighting continues to rise and many Americans venture to Pamplona for the bull run. There have been several female matadors and recently a female champion.

---

rations were recovered with difficulty because Britain and the United States were hesitant to force matters. Still, Germany was potentially the most powerful nation in Europe and was quietly being given favorable loan terms by the United States. The French economy worsened when the franc was stabilized at 20% of its pre-war value. This had the effect of making France a collector of gold and brought adventure-seeking Americans, with moderate sums of dollars, to take advantage of exchange rates.

New Leaders

Though a long way off, the leaders who would play a large role in World War II came to power. Josef Stalin assumed his 27-year dictatorship in the Soviet Union. He de-emphasized world revolution in favor of repressing and terrorizing Soviet citizens and Russian neighbors. The Politburo, meanwhile, expelled Leon Trotsky and Grigori Zinoviev. In Italy, Benito Mussolini assumed control of the country and the Fascist party became the party of state without opposition. Chiang Kai-shek succeeded Sun Yat-Sen and began to unify China. In Japan, Yoshihito died and his son became Emperor Hirohito (a role which he retained until his death in 1989).

Economics

For members of the upper middle class or the rich, the twenties were indeed the era of prosperity, debauchery, and bootlegging. For the rest of humanity, life was still a struggle. The 1921 musical "Ain't We Got Fun" encapsulates the period saying, "The rich get richer, and the poor get children." Coal miners in America stretched their meager 75-cents-per-hour wages (roughly $7.50 in 1995 dollars) to feed their families. Public-school teachers made slightly less at $1000 a year. Labor movements were met with brutal force but there were few improvements. The Ford Motor Company introduced an 8-hour day and a 5-day week. The picture for blacks in America was especially hard with 85% of blacks living in the segregated south and 23% of them illiterate. Great numbers of blacks began migrating north to the cities with lasting demographic effects.

Meanwhile, labor relations in Britain were tantamount to class war. A general strike crippled the nation as coal miners belonging to the Trade Union Congress demanded, "Not a penny off the pay; not a minute on the day." Many workers sympathetic to the miners (railwaymen, printers, dockworkers, construction workers, and others) went on strike as well. At the root of the problem was the decision by Chancellor of the Exchequer Winston Churchill to return to the gold standard. That decision had the effect of cheapening import prices and thus forcing mine operators to cut wages so as to compete with German and Polish imports. Economist John Maynard Keynes considered Churchill's decision "silly." Matters nearly erupted in violence as the Royal Navy trained its guns on strikers who tried to prevent the off-loading of ships at the docks.

Critical Overview

Already prepared for his style by the short story collection *In Our Time* and the subject matter by a short story, "The Undefeated," Hemingway's readers asserted that *The Sun Also Rises* more than satisfied expectations. The novel was appreciated for its modern "ease" and quickly became the novel of the "lost generation." More recently, the novel has helped rejuvenate Hemingway's reputation. Critical attention to the novel can categorized as follows: early surprise and discussion of plot (focusing on the bullfighting, Europe, or "the lost generation"); the alternative morality Hemingway provides in the face of disillusionment; the facts of impotency and gender in the novel; and finally, where the novel fits into Hemingway's reputation.

Except for Allen Tate's, the first reviews were glowing, congratulatory, and painfully aware of the ubiquitous war fatigue. Conrad Aiken, in the *New York Herald Tribune,* was struck first and foremost by the bullfighting which he compared to "half a course of psycho-analysis." "One is thrilled and horrified; but one is also fascinated, and one cannot have enough." Aiken observes that the novel "works up to, and in a sense is built around, a bullfight." In addition, he is unaware of anyone using dialogue better than Hemingway does. A reviewer for the *New York Times Book Review* said, "It is a truly gripping story, told in a lean, hard, athletic narrative prose that puts mere literary English to shame. Hemingway knows how ... to arrange a collection of words which shall betray a great deal more than is to be found in the individual parts." Lawrence S. Morris, in *The New Republic,* saw the novel as "one stride toward that objectification" which the current generation needed after rejecting its inherited myths. Tate wrote negatively, in *The Nation,* that the significance of Hemingway's subject matter "is mixed or incomplete." Furthermore, the habit of throwing stones at the great "is disconcerting in the present novel; it strains the context; and one suspects that Mr. Hemingway protests too much. The point he seems to be making is that he is morally superior ... [to] Mr. Mencken, but it is not yet clear just why."

James T. Farrell wrote a 1943 reaction, in the *New York Times,* to a novel that was supposedly "the definite account of a war-wearied lost generation." He explained the novel's popularity as a result of the pacifism of the post-war generation ready to challenge those values that had brought that war. Hemingway's novel, therefore, was right on time. "He arrived on the literary scene the absolute master of the style he has made his own; his attitudes were firmly fixed at that time, and he said pretty much what he had to say with his first stories, and his first two novels." Philip Young was more succinct, saying the novel is "still Hemingway's *Waste Land* and Jake is Hemingway's Fisher King."

Criticism became more analytical through the 1950s and gradually dissected Hemingway the man. Mark Spilka, in *Twelve Original Essays,* tried to find the moral of the story by focusing on its love theme. He concluded that Pedro is the hero of the story. Therefore, the lesson is that a hero is someone "whose code gives meaning to a world where love and religion are defunct." Carlos Baker focused on the geography because "place and the sense of fact ... [as well as the] operation of the sense of scene" is Hemingway's style, nothing more. Earl H. Rovit felt otherwise, in *Landmarks of American Writing.* He likened the novel to a "Newtonian world-machine" which rendered the metaphor of our age—which is explosion—conscious for the first time. For this reason the novel continues to "provoke our thought." Terrence Doody, in *The Journal of Narrative Technique,* was moved to say Hemingway did not know what he was doing with his narrator Jake Barnes. He added that the "naive contact with the world" the Hemingway style enables is clearly not sufficient since Faulkner and Fitzgerald are now preferred.

Sam S. Baskett picked up on the debate over Jake Barnes for his review in *The Centennial Review,* asking what sort of moral center Hemingway, spokesman for a generation, had come up with. Baskett answered this question by noting the value that characters have for themselves is a function of their regard for Brett—their godhead. Thus, Jake is the hero because he understands how to "live as a moral being" through writing his story and ignoring Brett. Andrew Hook's review, in *Ernest Hemingway: New Critical Essays,* is also interested in the moral center which is imposed, contrary to the novels that follow where the hero makes the choice, on Jake. Hook found that in this novel Hemingway "risks challenging the very codes and values" of the rest of his fiction and his life.

Criticism of the 1980s summed up Hemingway or discussed issues of gender. Nina Schwartz, in *Criticism,* analyzed the novel as an attempt to return "man to the center of a humanistic universe" by allowing Jake to control the signifiers. The crucial act here is Jake's displacement of his own desire to his favorite hero, Romero. Woman, or Brett as love object, assumes the most powerful position as castrator of "the very mythos of castration." The woman becomes the author of the men and the Bull of their ritual. Sukrita Paul Kumar more simply declared woman as the hero of the novel, not Jake or Romero. Kumar said the novel "paves the way for complete androgynous relationships through an acceptance and absorption of the new values as well as the new female ideal." Sibbie O'Sullivan's article, in *Arizona Quarterly,* defended Hemingway against charges of misogyny: he respected the new woman being created in the 1920s. O'Sullivan took inspiration from Jake's idea that you had to love a woman to befriend her and showed that Brett "is a positive force ... who makes an attempt to live honestly."

Lastly, John W. Aldridge summarized up Hemingway's modern reputation in *The Sewanee Review.* The dark side of the author is forgiven and his first novel is held up as a continuing inspiration for us not to "give up [our] hold on the basic sanities."

Criticism

Jeffrey M. Lilburn

Jeffrey M. Lilburn, M.A. (The University of Western Ontario) is the author of a study guide on Margaret Atwood's The Edible Woman *and of numerous educational essays. In the following essay, he discusses the mutually destructive nature of Jake and Brett's relationship as well as the characters who, critics contend, might provide Jake with a model of behavior.*

Set in Paris and Spain shortly after the end of World War I, *The Sun Also Rises,* for many the finest of Hemingway's longer works, is frequently described as a novel that captures the mood of an age. Its publication in 1926 forever identified the author with a generation and, even today, it is difficult, if not impossible for many readers and critics to consider Hemingway's works without drawing on the wealth of biographical information available on the now-famous expatriate artists of the 1920s. Centered around Jake and Brett's doomed love affair, the novel portrays the disillusionment and shift in values that resulted from the wartime experiences shared by a generation. In an essay emphasizing the historical context of the novel, Michael S. Reynolds explains that the end of the war signaled the end of a 20-year period during which the stable values of 1900 had eroded: "home, family, church, and country no longer gave the moral support that Hemingway's generation grew up with. The old values—honor, duty, love—no longer rang ... true...." According to Linda Wagner-Martin, this loss of promise after the war led to the wasteland atmosphere evident in the works of Eliot and Dreiser. Similarly, *The Sun Also Rises* is frequently read as a record of the "Lost Generation," a term attributed to Gertrude Stein that refers to the aimless and damaged youth who survived the war. Although many critics have recognized that such an interpretation is limiting and that to read Hemingway's novel as a "paean to the lost generation" is, as Reynolds argues, to miss the point badly, Stein's epigraph continues to influence many readers' imaginations.

What Do I Read Next?

- Bullfighting often disgusts people as cruel treatment of animals. Whether or not you feel that way, it is worth learning more about the sport or art form. Try reading "The Spanish Fiesta Brava: Historical Perspective" by former matador Mario Carrion on his homepage at http://coloquio.com/toros.html.

- "La Historia de las Plazas de Toros en Espana—Research Paper," by Jason Westrope, is a very good historical discussion of bullfighting. It is in English and can be found at http://www.arch.usf.edu/people/students/westrope/portfoli/D5doc.htm.

- "The Undefeated" is Hemingway's first short story about bullfighting and can be found in his collection of 1925 entitled *In Our Time*.

- Hemingway's posthumously published love letter to the Paris of the 1920s is entitled *A Moveable Feast* (1954). The book is full of Parisian scenes as well as character sketches of his famous friends: Gertrude Stein, James Joyce, Ezra Pound, Ford Madox Ford, and F. Scott Fitzgerald.

- Set far away from Hemingway's stage, Sinclair Lewis' *Babbitt* (1922) has a similar satirical bent. Rather than strike at the aristocrats, Lewis was after the normalcy of business that America seemed to prefer in reaction to the disruption of the war. The name Babbitt has become synonymous with impoverished cultural spirit. While many despise Babbitt, many aspire to his wealth.

- *The Great Gatsby* (1925), by F. Scott Fitzgerald, another Midwesterner, is second to *The Sun Also Rises* as manifesto for the 1920s. It is the story of a young stockbroker named Nick Carraway who watches his neighbor, Jay Gatsby, become betrayed by his own dreams. The novel reveals the disillusionment of the time but offers little, beyond the character of Carraway, in the way of solution.

A frequently discussed aspect of Hemingway's work is his suggestive writing style. When *The Sun Also Rises* first appeared, it was, Wagner-Martin explains, considered a "new manifesto of modernist style and was praised for its dialogue and its terse, objective presentation of characters." The modernist method was understatement, "a seemingly objective way of presenting the hard scene or image." There was, Wagner-Martin continues, "no sentiment, no didacticism, no leading the reader." This understated style, and the narrator's apparent toughness of attitude, can sometimes conceal pain, emotion, and desire. A typical example of this understated style is Jake's attempt, late in the novel, to justify Mike's drunken and, at times, vicious behavior towards Robert Cohn. Jake tells Brett that Cohn's presence in Pamplona has been hard on Mike, suggesting but leaving unsaid what is equally obvious: that Cohn's presence, not to mention Mike's and Pedro's, has also been very hard on

him. According to James Nagel, Jake's love for Brett and the pain of their having to be apart "underscores everything he relates."

Early in the novel, Cohn tells Jake that he longs to get away, to travel to South America, to be elsewhere. Presenting himself as someone who knows that "you can't get away from yourself by moving from one place to another," Jake advises Cohn to start living his life now, in Paris. However, as Jake's narrative unfolds, it becomes evident that he has not yet learned to live according to his own advice. Tormented by thoughts of his injury and by his love for Brett, Jake spends many sleepless hours inhabiting the elsewhere of an imaginary past—the past he and Brett could have had, the past that continues to be a source of pain and frustration every time they are together. Evidence of this ongoing frustration is easy to find. In response to Jake's attempt at intimacy in the cab, for example, Brett turns away and tells him that she does not "want to go through that hell again." Likewise, when Brett tells Jake that she is "so miserable," he immediately gets the feeling that he is about to go through a nightmare that he has been through before and must now go through again.

The mutually destructive nature of Jake and Brett's relationship has led several critics to point to the scene in which Jake acknowledges that all he really wants is to know "how to live in it"—it referring to the world, to the new and ever-changing post-war reality and, as Kathleen Nichols suggests, to the world of emotional relationships. Consequently, critics have also identified characters in the novel who might provide Jake with a model of behavior. Robert Fleming, for example, suggests that Count Mippipopolous is an early prototype of the character type known as the "code hero" or "tutor"—a type whose minor flaws "are outweighed by his strict observation of a code." The Count illustrates courage and grace under pressure, maintains his self-respect in relation to Brett and, Fleming argues, imparts to Jake lessons "that will help [him] toward a philosophy of life." Another critic, Scott Donaldson, proposes that it is Bill Gorton, through humor directed at ideas and institutions, not human beings, who provides a model of behavior that can be emulated. Jane E. Wilson looks to yet another character, discussing the significance of the Englishman, Wilson-Harris, in association with the regenerative fishing trip to Burguete. She believes that Jake's relationship with Harris is "one of the keys to the meaning of the fishing episode and its beneficial aspects."

The character most often identified as a model of behavior is the young bullfighter, Pedro Romero. Early in the novel, Jake tells Cohn that "nobody ever lives their life all the way up except bullfighters." The appearance of an actual bullfighter later in the novel thus commands attention. Pedro is described as a "real one"—a bullfighter who does always "smoothly, calmly, and beautifully" what others could do only sometimes. Allen Josephs, who has explored how the art of *toreo* (the bullfight) lies at the heart of *The Sun Also Rises,* cites the work of H.R. Stoneback who is himself citing Hemingway's *Death in the Afternoon,* to show that "the bullfight is meant to convey an emblem of moral behaviour." To be moral, conduct must be "rooted in courage, honour, passion, and it must exhibit grace under pressure...." Josephs believes that all of the characters who make the pilgrimage to Pamplona "are measured—morally or spiritually—around the axis of the art of *toreo.*" He identifies

Pedro, the creator of the art, as the character closest to perfection.

Robert Cohn, by contrast, is rarely included in discussions about models of behavior. On the contrary, Cohn's behavior continually sets him apart from the rest of the group. The recipient of insults and abuse from several characters in the novel, Cohn is also frequently mistreated by critics. Josephs, for instance, has accused Cohn of being a "moral bankrupt who is completely out of place at the fiesta." It is important to remember, however, that Jake may not be providing an accurate picture of the man who spent a week in Spain with Brett. Jake even acknowledges this possibility, noting that he may not have "shown Robert Cohn clearly." He tries, briefly, to improve his incomplete portrait but continues to highlight moments and events that cast Cohn in a negative light. From the very beginning of the novel, Jake's depiction of Cohn seems partial. He mentions that Cohn was once middleweight boxing champion of Princeton, but then strips the achievement of any value by noting that he is not "very much impressed" by this title. Similarly, on the first day of the fiesta, Jake notes that, while everyone else is drinking and having a good time, Cohn is passed out alone in a back room, sleeping on wine casks. Jake also pokes fun at Cohn's lack of acumen when the latter fails to understand a banner bearing the slogan "Hurray for the Foreigners!" As a result, when Mike verbally attacks Cohn, accusing him of following Brett around like a steer and of not knowing when he is not wanted, the accusations seem justified.

Sibbie O'Sullivan has described Cohn as a character who "lives in the waste land but does not adhere to its values." Jake's portrayal of Cohn appears to suggest that Cohn's values are out of date and out of place. However, Cohn's negative depiction is complicated by the frequent references to the fact that he is Jewish. Comments such as Mike's, who tells Jake that "Brett has gone off with men, but they weren't ever Jews," have led several critics to address the issue of anti-Semitism in the novel. Michael Reynolds believes that the depiction of Cohn does betray Hemingway's anti-Semitism but argues that to fault him "for his prejudice is to read the novel anachronistically." He believes that the novel's anti-Semitism "tells us little about its author but a good deal about America in 1926." Barry Gross, on the other hand, dismisses critics who dismiss Cohn's treatment in the novel as commonplace and wonders whether we should not expect our great writers "to rise above the regrettably commonplace of their society, es-

pecially writers who made careers out of being critics of … all that *they* considered regrettably commonplace in American society."

Like other characters in the novel, Brett Ashley has also been identified as a model of behavior—but not for Jake. Instead, Brett's daring and
unconventional lifestyle has led several critics to
identify her as a new kind of woman. Although she
is not, as James Nagel has pointed out, the first representation of "a sexually liberated, free-thinking
woman in American literature," she is, Reynolds
explains, "on the leading edge of the sexual revolution that produced two types of the 'new woman':
the educated professional woman who was active
in formerly all male areas and the stylish, uninhibited young woman who drank and smoked [and]
devalued sexual innocence…". But more than a
model of behavior or a representation of something
new, she is, like Jake, an individual trying to learn
how to live her life. She is, like Jake, trying to get
over what could have been.

Whether or not Jake and Brett do successfully
overcome their attachment to the past they could
have shared remains a topic of debate. The fact that
Jake travels to Madrid to meet Brett is, for some,
a sign that their relationship has not changed. James
Nagel argues that the journey is evidence of Jake's
continued love for Brett and that he "is resigned to
the pain that continued association with her is likely
to bring." But the continuation of their relationship,
or at least, the continuation of their relationship as
it has existed until now, becomes questionable in
light of Jake's response to Brett's lament about the
good time they could have had together: "Isn't it
pretty to think so?" The novel's famous last words
can be read as signaling a change in Jake's outlook.
Donald Daiker reads them as the "coup de grace
which effectively and permanently destroys all possibilities for the continuation of a romantic liaison
between them." To Kathleen Nichols, the response
shows that, instead of lamenting what could have
been, Jake can now "calmly and ironically comment on how 'pretty' it is to think [his relationship
with Brett] would have been so good." By no means
a happy or even compensatory ending, Jake's response does suggest the possibility of a relationship with Brett that is not burdened by unrealistic
ideas about an imaginary past.

Source: Jeffrey M. Lilburn, in an essay for *Novels for Students,* Gale, 1999.

Ira Elliott

*This excerpt explores Jake's fractured male
identity and the ways in which he relates to homosexual men in the novel.*

My project is to consider the ways in which
Jake Barnes's male identity is called into question
by the genital wound he suffered during the First
World War, and the ways in which his fractured
sense of self functions in relation to homosexuality and the homosexual men he observes at a *bal
musette* in the company of Brett Ashley. Jake's attitude toward the homosexuals—the way he de-
grades them and casts them as his rivals—will, I
believe, reveal the extent to which sexual categories
and gender roles are cultural constructions. Close
readings of several key passages in the novel will
at the same time uncover the reasons behind Jake's
own inability to openly accept, if not fully endorse,
the potentialities of gender/sexual mutability.

I take as my starting point the recent work of
theorist Judith Butler, whose influential book *Gender Trouble* maintains that "the heterosexualization
of desire requires and institutes the production of
discrete and asymmetrical oppositions between
'feminine' and 'masculine,' where these are understood as expressive of 'male' and 'female.'"
[*Gender Trouble: Feminism and the Subversion of
Identity,* 1990.] This process suggests that "the gendered body is performative," and, in fact, "has no
ontological status apart from the various acts which
constitute reality." Insofar as "the inner truth of
gender is a fabrication," "genders can be neither
true nor false, but are only produced as the truth
effects of a discourse of primary and stable identity." The notion of a "primary and interior gendered self" is, therefore, a cultural construction
which creates the "illusion" of such a disguised
self. That gender is itself a kind of "performance
of drag.… *reveals the imitative structure of gender
itself—as well as its contingency*" (Butler's emphasis). [Butler, 1990.]

With respect to the "crowd of young men,
some in jerseys and some in their shirt-sleeves" that
Jake encounters at the *bal musette,* external signs—
that is, behavioral or performative acts—lead Jake
to "read" the men as homosexual. The various signs
by which their homosexuality is made known are
these: their "jerseys" and "shirt-sleeves," their
"newly washed, wavy hair," their "white hands"
and "white faces," their "grimacing, gesturing, talking." While it may be argued that the idea of performativity ("grimacing, gesturing, talking") is
here conflated with the notion of the homosexual

as a morphological "type" ("newly washed, wavy hair"; "white hands" and "white faces") created by a congenital condition, I maintain that what may at first seem to be morphological is in fact performative: these men are "types" not owing to natural physical features, but rather because they have created themselves as a "type" in order to enact (perform) the role of homosexual.

Their casual dress and careful grooming suggest a "feminine" preoccupation with physical appearance. Their hair appears to be styled ("wavy"), like a woman's, while their "white hands" suggest delicacy, their "white faces," makeup or powder. Just as the feminized Jew of the novel, Robert Cohn, is mocked for his excessive barbering, the homosexuals are scorned for their obvious concern with appearance. Rather than exhibiting the reticence and rigidity associated with masculinity, they are overly and overtly expressive, uninhibited in the use of their bodies and voices. Jake's "diagnosis" is confirmed, his own masculinity momentarily consolidated, by the policeman near the door of the bar, who, in a gesture that bonds the two "real" men and marginalizes the homosexuals as "other," looks at Jake and smiles.

But what is it, really, that Jake "reads"? It is not the sexual orientation of the men but rather a set of signs, a visual (and aural) field—the body—upon which is inscribed, and through which is enacted, their otherwise concealed sexuality. The young men have their homosexuality "written" on their faces and on their bodies. They "perform" their sexuality through facial expressions and physical gestures. Just as Jake's wound remains unnamed, so, too, homosexuality is never mentioned; both are instead disclosed through, in the words of Arnold and Cathy Davidson, "sexual and textual absences." The reader, like Jake, "must read the ostensible sexual preference of the young men from the various signs provided and thereby decode covert private sexuality from overt public sociability." ["Decoding the Hemingway Hero in *The Sun Also Rises*" in *New Essays on The Sun Also Rises*, edited by Arnold E. and Cathy N. Davidson, 1987.] Homosexuality is therefore not simply a matter of erotic object choice and same-gender sex. It is also a way of being, for the performativity of the young men indicates—is, in fact, predictive of—their bedroom behavior....

Jake objects not so much to homosexual behavior (which is unseen) but to "femininity" expressed through the "wrong" body. Gender-crossing is what troubles Jake; the rupture between a culturally-determined signifier (the male body) and signified (the female gender) disrupts the male/female binary. But what if the young men had not crossed the gender line, if their behavior were "in accord" with their sex, if they, in short, acted the way Jake expects men to act? He would then have no "signs" of their homosexuality.

The perception that the young men are enacting the "wrong" gender leads to the conclusion that they are inauthentic, that the projection of a "feminine" persona is a parody, a send-up of the female's "proper" role. Just as their presumed sexual deviation is a "deviation from the truth," a behavioral "error," so the way they act in public is a deliberate "deviation" from the "truth" of their gender. Although one could argue that the men are "camping" in order to destabilize the notion of fixed (naturalized) gender characteristics—that theirs is a conscious deployment of gender for strategic political ends—Jake cannot allow for the possibility that they might truly *be* the way they *act*. He cannot believe that these men are *really* like that ("feminine") because they are male....

Jake's inability to perform sexually corresponds to the homosexual's inability to perform his "correct" gender. Jake's sexual inadequacy and the homosexual's gender transgression are therefore conjoined: neither can properly signify "masculinity."...

It is also notable that "it is not Brett who elicits Jake's obvious and immediate attraction" [Davidson and Davidson, 1987] when she enters the bar, but rather her homosexual companions: "I was very angry. Somehow they always made me angry. I know they are supposed to be amusing, and you should be tolerant, but I wanted to swing on one, any one, anything to shatter that superior, simpering composure." The urge to physically assault the homosexual man—what we now call "gay bashing," which many theorists argue constitutes an attack on the "feminine" rooted in misogyny—quite clearly derives from Jake's anger; but what, precisely, is he so angry about? The source of his rage is in part his frustration at being unable to categorize the homosexual within the male/female binary. That these men represent and enact gender nonconformity violates the cultural boundaries established to demarcate appropriate social and sexual behavior. Any attempted remapping of these culturally agreed upon borders exposes the arbitrariness of their frontiers, which in turn calls for a rethinking of the ontological groundwork of sex/gender itself. At the same time, his anger is self-hatred displaced onto the homosexual, for Jake has lost (physically and psychologically) his signifying phallus. What's more, the tolerance he knows he should have for the homosexuals may also be the same tolerance he hopes Brett will have for him and his sexual failing.

In a cultural system that authorizes a single mode of self-presentation for each gender, transgressing the binary law of male/female constitutes a crime. Just as homosexuality is often constructed as "a crime against nature," so, too, this crime, or sin, against naturalized gender performance must be punished: Jake wishes "to shatter that superior, simpering composure" which he sees as a homosexual or "feminine" trait. Robert Cohn's manner is also described as "superior." To whom or what the homosexual is "superior" is not expressed, but Jake apparently believes that they are, or think that they are, "superior" to him. He is also disturbed by their "simpering composure," though one may wonder whether it is their composure itself which troubles Jake, or its simpering nature. In either case, the ostensibly heterosexual man here feels threatened by the homosexual's acceptance and assertion of his presumably "incorrect" gender behavior. If he is superior to Jake, then it is axiomatic that Jake is inferior to him, for Jake himself hopes that he signifies what he is not, namely, the potent and powerful heterosexual male.

What Jake is unable or unwilling to acknowledge (disclose) is that his relationship to women resembles that of the homosexual. Though for different reasons, both Jake and the homosexual man do not relate to women in accordance with the demands of a heterosexual/heterosexist culture. What Jake desires but cannot do is to perform sexually with women, the same performance rejected by the homosexual. While the homosexual rejects heterosexual performance, he does so in favor of an alternative. Jake, on the other hand, is bound by a "masculine" signification and desire which is "untrue"—he cannot *do* what his appearance suggests he can. The homosexual signifies differently, Jake not at all, and so the homosexual is seen as "superior."

Jake's body stands, as it were, between himself and his desires; the homosexual's "perverse" desire, however, circumvents the "natural" physical act. It is therefore not the homosexual's denial or disinterest in women which offends Jake but the renunciation of naturalized male desire. When he looks at the homosexual man, what Jake sees is the body of a male that does not perform as a "man";

when he regards himself what he sees is the body of a male that lacks the sign of "manliness." This tends to support Jonathan Dollimore's observation [in his *Sexual Dissidence: Augustine to Wilde, Freud to Foucault,* 1991] that "the most extreme threat to the true form of something comes not so much from its absolute opposite or its direct negation, but in the form of its perversion.... [which is] very often perceived as at once utterly alien to what it threatens, and yet, mysteriously inherent within it."...

In the following chapter (4), Jake's affiliation with the homosexual and with gender reversal is even more pronounced. While undressing for bed, he sees himself in the mirror: "Undressing, I looked at myself in the mirror of the big armoire beside the bed. That was a typically French way to furnish a room. Practical, too, I suppose. Of all the ways to be wounded. I suppose it was funny. I put my pajamas on and got into bed." While the digression concerning the armoire might at first appear to be an attempt to avoid seeing himself or talking about what he sees, it is actually a symbolic corollary of Jake's wound. Just as the armoire represents "a typically French way to furnish a room," so the penis is "typical" of the male body. Whereas the armoire is "practical," however, Jake's member is not (at least in relation to his sex life); rather, it is all "furnishing." In relation to the female, the homosexual's sex is similarly "furnishing." That Jake regards his wound as "funny" recalls his earlier observation that homosexual men "are supposed to be amusing," though clearly neither are a source of much humor. Both are instead ironic objects of derision.... That which is present signifies absence—not of desire but of ability. The mirror reflects appearance; it does not reveal essence. At the same time, the "external signs" which it presents can, if "read" correctly, provide the clues necessary to apprehend "inner truth." In Jake's case, that "truth" is his fractured sense of masculine identity. In holding the mirror up to himself, what Jake discovers is his close affiliation with the homosexual men.

Inasmuch as Jake considers himself to be heterosexual, the novel posits the site of sexuality in gendered desire rather than sexual behavior. What distinguishes Jake from the homosexual men is gender performance and erotic object choice. By this logic, it follows that sexuality is determined by gender identification rather than sexual activity. Jake's sex can no longer penetrate a woman (and so all sexual relations are apparently ruled out), but he remains heterosexual by virtue of his desire. If the men from the bar discontinued same-gender sex, they would presumably remain homosexual. Sexual identity issues not from the sex act but from covert desire or overt social behavior....

It remains unclear, however, whether Jake's masculinity is in question because of the lost body part (morphology) or because of his inability to express what is regarded as masculine—that is, heterosexual performativity. This loss is later seen in relation to homosexuality itself, when Jake's wound is directly linked to homosexual identity.

This linkage occurs about midway through the novel, during the fishing trip Jake takes with his friend Bill Gorton before the fiesta. The fishing episode is one of what Wendy Martin calls Hemingway's "pastoral interludes, in which his male characters seek relief from social tensions," part of a tradition in American fiction "that begins with Cooper and Brackenridge and extends through Hawthorne, Melville, and Twain." ["Brett Ashley as New Woman in *The Sun Also Rises*"] This "pastoral interlude" is also a "set piece" profoundly colored by the homoerotic element.... In *The Sun Also Rises* the physical battle between male rivals is most overtly expressed in the bullfight, where two such signifiers are the man and the bull. And just as Jake is a spectator at the bullfight rather than a participant, so, too, he can only look on as other men (Robert Cohn, Mike Campbell, Pedro Romero) compete for the affections of Brett Ashley. The arena where "real" men compete—whether the bullring or the bedroom—is for Jake a foreclosed area of emotional and psychic involvement.

Whether "greenwood," bullring, or battlefield, these episodes are intense moments of male bonding, which for Mario Mieli (and I concur) is always an expression of a "paralysed and unspoken homosexuality, which can be grasped, in the negative, in the denial of women." [*Homosexuality and Liberation: Elements of a Gay Critique,* 1980.] While alone and apart from the world, Bill teases Jake by asking him if he knows what his real "trouble" is: "You're an expatriate [Bill explains]. One of the worst type.... You've lost touch with the soil. You get precious. Fake European standards have ruined you. You drink yourself to death. You become obsessed by sex. You spend all your time talking, not working. You are an expatriate, see? You hang around cafés." Jake's association with the old world places him within the shadow of European decadence, which is seen as a performance, a role unbecoming to him. That he has "lost touch with the

soil" suggests that Jake is estranged from enduring values, for "the earth abideth forever." Jake has become "precious," "ruined" by "fake European standards," so that his very identity has been compromised, if not corrupted, by foreign influences. Similarly, Jake's body has been corrupted by a foreign object, perhaps a mortar shell. This has in turn transformed his corporeal existence into something foreign or other—not quite a "whole" man but certainly not a woman. Jake has come to inhabit the demi-monde, the world of the outcast, the lost, the homosexual—the decadent other *par excellence*. What's more, like Lawrence's, Hemingway's "anxieties about homosexuality were conjoined with class antagonism" [Dollimore, 1991]—his antipathy for the rich, the "mincing gentry."

Jake, like the homosexual, is a habitué of cafés, where one "does" very little except talk, and the homosexual, the female, and the Jew are constructed as overly discursive. (Another of Hemingway's fears was that writing—talking—was unmanly, for it is not "doing.") The gay man, however, is like a woman in that he "hangs around" and doesn't work much. His only "work" is night-work related to sex, just as the "proper" work for a woman is to serve her man. Even Brett, the independent Modern Woman, exists only in relation to men—Jake, Mike, Robert, Pedro, Count Mippipopolous, the homosexuals.

Bill goes on to say that Jake doesn't work, after all, and that while some claim he is supported by women, others insist that he's impotent. A man who is supported by women is of course not a "real" man, but what Bill means by "impotent" is ambiguous. He may believe that Jake is sexually impotent or that as a decadent American who has adopted "fake" European standards he is psychically impotent. In either case, the link between nonnormative sexuality and decadence is clear. Jake responds to Bill by saying, "I just had an accident." But Bill tells Jake, "Never mention that.... That's the sort of thing that can't be spoken of. That's what you ought to work up into a mystery. Like Henry's bicycle." Once again, just as homosexuality is the love that dare not speak its name, so Jake's "accident" should not be discussed. "Henry's bicycle" is a reference to Henry James and the "obscure hurt" he suffered while a teenager—either a physical wound which rendered him incapable of sexual performance or a psychic "hurt," the realization of his homosexuality. [R. W. B. Lewis, *The Jameses: A Family Narrative,* 1991.] The failure to perform in the culturally prescribed way (heterosexually) is therefore figured as "de-masculiniz-ing."

Jake and Bill then banter about whether Henry's wound was suffered while riding a bicycle or a horse, with attendant puns on "joy-stick" and "pedal." When Jake "stands up" for the tricycle, Bill replies, "I think he's a good writer, too." He adds that Jake is "a hell of a good guy":

> Listen you're a hell of a good guy, and I'm fonder of you than anybody on earth. I couldn't tell you that in New York. It'd mean I was a faggot. That was what the Civil War was about. Abraham Lincoln was a faggot. He was in love with General Grant. So was Jefferson Davis. Lincoln just freed the slaves on a bet. The Dred Scott case was framed by the Anti-Saloon League. Sex explains it all. The Colonel's Lady and Judy O'Grady are Lesbians under the skin.

That Jake opts for the tricycle over the horse as the instrument of Henry's "unmanning" implies that the modern world of the machine has had a negative, disruptive effect on traditional male/female roles. When Bill acknowledges that Henry, in spite of his wound, was "a good writer" (could still perform as an artist), he is also reassuring Jake that he can still perform as a good friend and "proper" man—fishing, eating, drinking. Jake will not be banished from the homosocial realm where all "good guys" go to escape from the debilitating influence of women.

While Jake may now occupy an uncertain place between the genders, Bill continues to be "fonder" of him than anybody. Defending himself from any potential "charge" of homosexuality, Bill quickly adds that had they been in New York, he wouldn't be able to voice his affection for Jake without being a "faggot"; European decadence makes it possible to speak the unspeakable. Without belaboring Bill's mock history of the Civil War, we should remark that "sex explains it all." The "truth" of the self is revealed, after all, in sex; and homosexuality (in this instance, lesbianism) is inscribed in the body, concealed "under the skin." If we recall that male homosexuality may be "read" in external signs, it appears here that lesbian sexuality is not similarly marked by gender nonconformity, that concealed lesbian identity cannot be discerned through observing performance but only by unmasking what is hidden in the body, under the skin. This seems to suggest that lesbianism is congenital, while male homosexuality is performative.

The novel concludes with the justly famous scene of Jake and Brett together in a cab: "'Oh, Jake,' Brett said, 'we could have had such a damned good time together.' Ahead was a mounted

policeman in khaki directing traffic. He raised his baton. The car slowed suddenly pressing Brett against me. 'Yes,' I said. 'Isn't it pretty to think so?'" Earlier in the novel, Georgette pressed against Jake while in a cab, and now Brett is thrown against the body of a man who desires more than he can do; he wants not just "pressing" but penetration. Once again the symbolic policeman is present, but this time he isn't smiling; he and Jake are no longer members of the same "club." This time his raised baton is a rebuke. The policeman, a "manly" authority figure, is not only "mounted" (and perhaps "well-mounted") on a horse (suggesting a "stud" or "stallion" while recalling Henry's "accident"), but also a uniformed presence whose "raised" baton is suggestive not only of an erect phallus but also of the baton of a conductor or military officer, two whose role is to orchestrate the performance of others, though Jake can no longer perform.

The sun, almost always figured as "male" (and in most Indo-European languages grammatically of the "male gender"), "ariseth" and "goeth down," as does a male. The earth, a female/maternal signifier, "abideth forever," and "the soil," it will be recalled, is what Jake has "lost touch" with. As Arnold and Cathy Davidson note, "Jake's last words readily devolve into an endless series of counter-statements that continue the same discourse: 'Isn't it pretty to think so?' / 'Isn't it pretty to think isn't it pretty to think so?'" This "negation," as the Davidsons call it, closes the novel and returns us to its title, for "only the earth—not heroes, not their successes or their failures—abideth forever." [Davidson and Davidson, 1993.] The use of so "feminine" a word as "pretty" further underscores Jake's mixed gender identification as well as the "feminine" qualities of life which abide forever.

Source: Ira Elliott, "Performance Art: Jake Barnes and 'Masculine' Signification in *The Sun Also Rises,*" in *American Literature,* Vol. 67, No. 1, March, 1995, pp. 77–91.

Robert W. Cochran

In this excerpt, Cochran disagrees with the body of criticism which finds The Sun Also Rises *overtly cynical, focusing instead on the circularity of the human condition.*

Emphasis in the considerable body of criticism in print on *The Sun Also Rises* rests with the cynicism and world-weariness to be found in the novel. Although Lionel Trilling in 1939 afforded his readers a salutary, corrective view, most commentators have found the meaning inherent in the pattern of the work despairing. Perhaps most outspoken is E. M. Halliday, who sees Jake Barnes as adopting "a kind of desperate caution" as his *modus vivendi.* Halliday concludes that the movement of the novel is a movement of progressive "emotional insularity" and that the novel's theme is one of "moral atrophy." ["Hemingway's Narrative Perspective," in *Sewanee Review,* 1952.] In his "The Death of Love in *The Sun Also Rises,"* Mark Spilka finds a similarly negative meaning in the novel. Thus Spilka arrives at the position that in naming "the abiding earth" as the hero of the novel, Hemingway was "perhaps wrong … or at least misleading." [*Twelve Original Essays on Great American Novels,* 1958.]

But if Hemingway was misleading in so identifying the novel's hero, he was misleading in a fashion consistent with his "misleading" choice of epigraph from Ecclesiastes and consistent with the "misleading" pattern he incorporated in the text of his novel. Far from indicating insularity and moral atrophy, the novel evidences circularity and moral retrenching. Much Hemingway criticism—always excepting Trilling's—demonstrates the reaction of conventional wisdom to healthy subversion of that brand of wisdom. Hence the often truly sad gulf which Trilling laments between the pronouncements of Hemingway "the man" and the artistically indirect achievement of Hemingway "the artist." ["Hemingway and His Critics," *Partisan Review,* 1939.] Jake Barnes, to deal with the central character of but one of Hemingway's novels, is far more than the "desperately cautious" mover through life which Halliday calls him. Like the Biblical Preacher, Jake is a worldly wise accepter of the nature of the human condition. That condition is, to be sure, a predicament, for as Hemingway more than once baldly stated, life is tragic. But recognition of the tragic nature of life is by no means necessarily a cause for despair. If any readers of *The Sun Also Rises* become misdirected, they are certainly not misled by Hemingway.

The opening verses of the Book of Ecclesiastes are ambiguous, and the individual reader's responses to these and subsequent verses are varied. One must assume that Hemingway found the dominant tone of Ecclesiastes right for his artistic purposes, but one hastens to recognize the distinct possibility that that overall tone is not one of world-weariness (although the temptation to think so is great at many junctures) but of worldly wisdom. In reading the epigraph from Ecclesiastes which Hemingway provides, one is struck by the omission of all occurrences of "Vanity of vanities." Most Hemingway critics appear to regard these omissions as ironically absent, as evidence, that is, of Hemingway's application of his celebrated "iceberg" principle—in this instance of a knowledge shared between the author and reader of the bulk of the iceberg which floats beneath the surface. But is it not just as likely that the omissions are made not in the service of irony, but quite simply in the service of exclusion? The so-called "Hemingway Code" is designed, I suggest, not to provide a means of survival in a life which is a vain endeavor to discover meaning, but rather to provide a means of survival which itself is meaning. This I take to be the import of that passage in the novel, so readily identified as important, but so potentially "misleading," in which Jake thinks,

You paid some way for everything that was any good. I paid my way into enough things that I like, so that I had a good time. Either you paid by learning about them, or by experience, or by taking chances, or by money. Enjoying living was learning to get your money's worth and knowing when you had it. You could get your money's worth. The world was a good place to buy in. It seemed like a fine philosophy. In five years, I thought, it will seem just as silly as all the other fine philosophies I've had.

Perhaps that wasn't true, though. Perhaps as you went along you did learn something. I did not care what it was all about. All I wanted to know was how to live in it. Maybe if you found out how to live in it you learned from that what it was all about.

Certainly Jake is not rejecting life, any more than Count Mippipopolous ("'one of us,'" Brett insists) is "dead." Nor is love dead in *The Sun Also Rises;* it is, rather, unattainable—or better, never to be consummated. All of which is to say that *The Sun Also Rises* is a far less bitter and a far more mature book than is *A Farewell to Arms.*

In any event, nothing in the passage actually chosen and printed as the second of the two epigraphs for *The Sun Also Rises* is in contradiction to Hemingway's assertion that the abiding earth is the hero of his novel. There can be no denying, however, that circularity such as that contained in the epigraph may be employed by an author to suggest meaninglessness. Perhaps it may even be said that our usual response to circularity is that it suggests meaninglessness.… But when in a literary work circularity is demonstrated to be the pattern of life, the response of the reader is to be governed by the artist's presentation; whether the author is complaining about what he regards as an inescapable fact of life or whether he is stating what he regards as an unalterable fact must emerge from the work itself.

And so to the text of *The Sun Also Rises*. To begin with, let us not forget that, as John Rouch says, "Jake Barnes is telling the story in retrospect. Because Jake has lived through these events, he is well aware of what is going to happen." And let us further agree with Rouch that "... Jake knows that the essential story is contained between the two cab drives of Jake and Brett." ["Jake Barnes as Narrator," *Modern Fiction Studies*, 1965–66] Let us add to these observations of Rouch, the second of which so clearly intimates a coming full circle, Jake's thoughts after he has framed his telegram to Brett, who awaits his aid in the Hotel Montana in Madrid: "That seemed to handle it. That was it. Send a girl off with one man. Introduce her to another to go off with him. Now go and bring her back. And sign the wire with love. That was it all right. I went in to lunch." Echoing Rouch, I would point out that here Jake is not only "well aware" but perfectly aware of the position he is in. The ironic tone of Jake's words is equal to the irony of his situation, and his going in to lunch is a simple demonstration of his ability to function rather than to dwell morbidly on the cruelty of Fate's dealings with him.

Rouch speaks further of a change in Jake, but what can that change be? Not only does Jake tell the story in retrospect, knowing all along "what is going to happen," but at no point in the novel does Jake announce that he has undergone a change. One must concede, however, that after he has been hit by Cohn, Jake does experience a change in perspective, a change which provides emotional preparation, since it falls between the passage "The fiesta was really started.... The things that happened could only have happened during a fiesta. Everything became quite unreal finally and it seemed as though nothing could have any consequences. It seemed out of place to think of consequences during the fiesta" and the sentence early in Book III, "The fiesta was over." This change in perspective, this new light of unfamiliarity and objectivity, is explained by reference to a "phantom suitcase." Mark Spilka has seriously battered that suitcase in a totally unconvincing attempt to equate Jake and his suitcase with Robert Cohn and his Princeton polo-shirt; in an attempt to make Jake, like Cohn, "a case of arrested development." But Jake is emphatically not a case of arrested development; as he says in another connection, he " 'just had an accident.' " Cohn wishes he could " 'play football again with what I know about handling myself, now.' " Can it be seriously proposed that Jake too wishes to play another football game, so that he

may once more enjoy such a sobering experience as being "kicked in the head early in the game"?

Jake's thoughts after he has sent the telegram to Brett at the Hotel Montana do not support Rouch's contention that Jake undergoes a change. Indeed, Jake's advice to Cohn to give up the romantic notion that he can further his experience of "life" by taking a trip to South America is placed very early in the novel precisely to establish that Jake the character, like Jake the narrator, has long since learned in a broad and fundamental way "how to be": " 'Listen, Robert, going to another country doesn't make any difference. I've tried all that. You can't get away from yourself by moving from one place to another. There's nothing to that.' "...

Jake Barnes is especially privileged, both as narrator and as character: even before the events reported in the novel took place, he understood what was acceptable and supportable in life in the post-World War I era.

As Trilling so admirably explained in his corrective essay of 1939,

> Everyone in that time had feelings, as they called them; just as everyone has "feelings" now. And it seems to me that what Hemingway wanted first to do was to get rid of the "feelings," the comfortable liberal humanitarian feelings: and to replace them with the truth.

> Not cynicism, I think, not despair, as so often is said, but this admirable desire shaped his famous style and his notorious set of admirations and contempts. The trick of understatement or tangential statement sprang from this desire. Men had made so many utterances in such fine language that it had become time to shut up. Hemingway's people, as everyone knows, are afraid of words and ashamed of them and the line from his stories which has become famous is the one that begins "Won't you please," goes on through its innumerable "pleases," and ends, "stop talking." Not only slain men but slain words made up the mortality of the war. ["Hemingway and His Critics."]

The Sun Also Rises serves a corrective function, then, or better, several corrective functions, among them that articulated by Trilling and that implicit in Bill Gorton's parody of editorials of the 'Twenties on the nature of American expatriates in Paris. But, as Malcolm Cowley has stated, "In 1926 one felt that he was making exactly the right rejoinder to dozens of newspaper editorials then fresh in the public mind; in the 1960's these have been forgotten." [Introduction to *The Sun Also Rises*, 1954.]

In addition to the corrective functions underlined by Trilling and Cowley, *The Sun Also Rises* contains a positive and timeless message with respect to the value of some kind of religious observance. If traditional religion no longer seems to apply to human problems, within the world of the novel the values of fishing and of bull-fighting remain. Such a statement smacks of the hysterically obvious in a discussion of Hemingway's work, of course, and unquestionably no further discussion of the experience of Jake, Bill, and the Englishman Harris on the Irati is required. Nor need one pursue the general value of the bull-ring as the place of experiencing the moment of truth. But what seem to me the most important uses of circularity in the novel revolve about the symbolic distinction drawn between France and Spain, first in the opening three paragraphs of Chapter X, and finally in the last chapter of the novel:

> The waiter seemed a little offended about the flowers of the Pyrenees, so I overtipped him. That made him happy. It felt comfortable to be in a country where it is so simple to make people happy. You can never tell whether a Spanish waiter will thank you. Everything is on such a clear financial basis in France. It is the simplest country to live in. No one makes things complicated by becoming your friend for any obscure reason. If you want people to like you you have only to spend a little money. I spent a little money and the waiter liked me. He would be glad to see me back. I would dine there again some time and he would be glad to see me, and would want me at his table. It would be a sincere liking because it would have a sound basis. I was back in France.

> Next morning I tipped every one a little too much at the hotel to make more friends, and left on the morning train for San Sebastian. At the station I did not tip the porter more than I should because I did not think I would ever see him again. I only wanted a few good French friends in Bayonne to make me welcome in case I should come back there again. I knew that if they remembered me their friendship would be loyal.

> At Irun we had to change trains and show passports. I hated to leave France. Life was so simple in France. I felt I was a fool to be going back into Spain. In Spain you could not tell about anything.

In Spain, one of course "could not tell about anything" because in Spain one encounters a Montoya. But, important as Montoya is to Hemingway's establishing that Jake has *aficion* and that Pedro Romero's greatness must be nourished and protected for the rare phenomenon it is, the fiesta at Pamplona and the total religious realm of bull-fighting is described in such a way as to stress its elemental force in providing the integrity, the unity, the never-ending cyclical pattern at the heart of Spanish life.

The Spanish waiter who is so contemptuous of the "sport" of running before the bulls is not unlike the American editorial writers who fail to understand expatriates. The waiter may be said to be Hemingway's spokesman for the uninitiated reader, the reader who views bull-fighting as a bloody, inhumane, pagan slaughter of a brute victim in service of a brutal, "inhuman" human desire. And Jake's nearly complete lack of interest in the Tour de France is another telling instruction by indirection that in Hemingway fishing and bull-fighting are to be regarded as far more than the mere "outdoor sports" which Spilka wishes to dismiss them as.

Therefore, like the monastery at Roncevalles, which Bill and Harris agree is "remarkable" but not "the same as" the fishing on the Irati, traditional religious values are "nice" but no longer viable as the values inherent in bull-fighting are viable—for spectator as well as participant. With respect to the observance of religious practices within a church, Jake and Brett are in the position of Matthew Arnold in his poem "The Grande Chartreuse," a position of respectful alienation.

With respect to bull-fighting, Brett has had no initiation prior to the Pamplona festival of the novel. It is she, then, and not the *aficionado* Jake who must represent the in-group in being put to the test. Desperately in need of some meaning for her life, Brett reaches a kind of nadir of promiscuity in going off to San Sebastian with Robert Cohn. Labelled a "Circe" by Cohn, Brett is, within one page of text of the novel, first debarred from a church during the San Fermin religious procession and then kept from participating in a dance, so that she may serve as "an image to dance around." Wishing to enter the church and wishing to dance, Brett is denied the privilege of entering into either ritualistic activity. In concert with her wearing her hair in a mannish bob, these details symbolize Brett's lack of spiritual fulfillment.

Because she is unfulfilled, when the handsome young Romero captures her fancy Brett is in grave danger of becoming the bitch she feels herself to be, but more significantly she may destroy for a time the entire meaningful cycle of life and death which is bull-fighting in Spain. In the novel, particular definition of this cycle begins not with announcement of the death of an as yet unnamed runner before the bulls and not with the waiter's contemptuous judgment following the runner's death, but rather with that remarkable paragraph immediately following the conversation between

Jake and the waiter. A notable example of the bare Hemingway style, the paragraph is not, as it may at first blush appear to be, ironic in tone. Rather, the style complements the ritualistic activities it reports, investing the death of Vicente Girones with a dignity which this simple farmer could not possibly have achieved through some other manner of dying.

And the succeeding paragraph provides the tension which builds the basic conflict of the novel, for in this paragraph we are immediately informed that the bull "who [not "which"] killed Vicente Girones ... was killed by Pedro Romero as the third bull of that same afternoon." We are also told that Pedro presented the ear of Bocanegra to Brett, and that Brett "left both ear and handkerchief, along with a number of Muratti cigarette-stubs, shoved far back in the drawer of the bed-table that stood beside her bed in the Hotel Montoya, in Pamplona." By her callous indifference to the cycle of life and death into which Romero has permitted her to intrude, Brett has broken the circle, has momentarily robbed Vicente Girones of the significance of his death. The Hotel Montoya is, for the moment at least, corrupted.

Hemingway's having Jake identify the bull and report what became of the bull's ear before he has him describe the bull-fight in which the ear is taken is a master stroke. When the moment of the kill is described, the classic moment of perfection—that of the tableau on the Grecian Urn or of the scene at the death of Old Ben in Faulkner's *The Bear*— is conveyed as a moment of supernal, eternal beauty. The viewing of that divine spectacle is an utterly spiritual, a fully religious experience.

What remains, then, is for Brett to prove herself sensitive to this religious meaning. By thoughtlessly discarding the bull's ear in a drawer full of cigarette butts, Brett has profaned a religious structure; she has been guilty of sacrilege. To be worthy of Jake, to provide the measure of the moral worth of the group, she must atone for the sin of sacrilege. Her promiscuity is not her sin; it is her search. And her affair with Romero is not her sin: so long as the encounter is brief, Brett has been, as Jake suggests, "'probably damn good for him.'" By giving Romero back to bull-fighting, his seriousness and discipline intact, Brett in effect removes the bull's ear from the bed-table drawer and restores it to its rightful place in the religious ritual of which it is a part.

Brett's famous words describing her satisfaction in being strong enough to give Pedro his free-

dom are therefore neither extravagant, nor, in the total context of the novel, small compensation for what the Lost Generation has lost. Brett indeed is not "'one of these bitches who ruins children,'" and the capacity for moral discrimination required to make such a decision indeed is "'sort of what we have instead of God.'" At this point of development in Hemingway's novel one is reminded of the brilliant insight provided by William Styron's Peyton Loftis: "'Those people back in the Lost Generation ... They thought they were lost. They were crazy. They weren't lost. What they were doing was losing us.'" [*Lie Down in Darkness,* 1957.]

Still, in the flush of her considerable moral victory, Brett is swept on to her final—and this is extravagant—lamentation: "'Oh, Jake,' Brett said, 'we could have had such a damned good time together.'" Giving "them" "irony," if not "pity," Jake responds, "'Yes. Isn't it pretty to think so?'" In this truly concluding line, Hemingway cuts the sweetness of self-pity and avoids the curse of an up-beat ending (a curse very clearly drawn down upon Tyrone Power and Ava Gardner in the final scene of the movie version of the novel) by having Jake remain steady in his realistic, anti-romantic conception of life as it is.

Life can be made worse by human beings who "behave badly." Robert Cohn characteristically behaves badly: he wonders if one might bet on the bull-fights; he falls asleep in the midst of gaiety; his tennis game falls apart when he is a moonsick calf in a world of bulls and matadors; he does not fight when he is insulted, then later hits Jake, his "best friend." And Brett begins to behave badly, for the integrity of bull-fighting as a religious ritual is dependent upon a valuing of the bull's ear as a symbol of significant victory in a direct confrontation of life with death.

Phillip Young writes of the novel's ending, "Soon it is all gone, he is returned to Brett as before, and we discover that we have come full circle, like all the rivers, the winds, and the sun, to the place where we began. This is motion which goes no place." [*Ernest Hemingway,* 1952.] But Geoffrey Moore is surely correct in speaking of the "queer, twisted but nonetheless real sense of standards in Brett." [*Review of English Literature,* 1963.] Life and the bull-fight go on, and Jake will be welcome at the Hotel Montoya, as before, for Brett's release of Pedro Romero guarantees that Vicente Girones will not have died in vain.

Explicitly termed "values" in *The Sun Also Rises* are understated, but they are not undermined.

Traditional values are scrutinized and found inadequate, but the values of the group are tested and found adequate to the demands made on those values by life. The ending of the novel is of course not beamingly optimistic, but neither is it bleakly pessimistic. Life has not, as Young says, "become mostly meaningless." The moral success of Brett and the comprehensive worldly wisdom of Jake have upheld and enhanced life's meaning in a (war-torn—"The soldier had only one arm") world which is otherwise mostly meaningless.

Source: Robert W. Cochran, "Circularity in *The Sun Also Rises*," in *Modern Fiction Studies,* Vol. XIV, No. 3, Autumn, 1968, pp. 297–305.

Sources

Conrad Aiken, "Expatriates," in *New York Herald Tribune Books,* October 31, 1926, p. 4.

John W. Aldridge, "*The Sun Also Rises*—Sixty Years Later," in *The Sewanee Review,* Vol. XCIV, No. 2, Spring, 1986, pp. 337-45.

Carlos Baker, in *Hemingway: The Writer as Artist,* third edition, Princeton University Press, 1963, p. 379.

Sam S. Baskett, "'An Image to Dance Around': Brett and Her Lovers in '*The Sun Also Rises*'" in *The Centennial Review,* Vol. XXII, No. 1, Winter, 1978, pp. 45-69.

Cleanth Brooks Jr. and Robert Penn Warren, "'The Killers', Ernest Hemingway: Interpretation," in *Understanding Fiction,* edited by Cleanth Brooks, Jr. and Robert Penn Warren, Appleton-Century-Crofts, Inc., 1959, pp. 306-25.

Terrence Doody, "Hemingway's Style and Jake's Narration," in *The Journal of Narrative Technique,* Vol. 4, No. 3, September, 1974, pp. 212-25.

James T. Farrell, "Ernest Hemingway, Apostle of a 'Lost Generation'," in *The New York Times Books Review,* August 1, 1943, pp. 6, 14.

Andrew Hook, "Art and Life in *The Sun Also Rises,*" in *Ernest Hemingway: New Critical Essays,* edited by A. Robert Lee, Vision Press, 1983, pp. 49-63.

Sukrita Paul Kumar, "Woman as Hero in Hemingway's *The Sun Also Rises,*" in *The Literary Endeavour,* Vol. VI, Nos. 1-4, 1985, pp. 102-08.

"Marital Tragedy," in *The New York Times Book Review,* October 31, 1926, p. 7.

Lawrence S. Morris, "Warfare in Man and among Men," in *The New Republic,* Vol. XLIX, No. 629, December 22, 1926, pp. 142-43.

Sibbie O'Sullivan, "Love and Friendship/Man and Woman in *The Sun Also Rises,*" in *Arizona Quarterly,* Vol. 44, No. 2, Summer, 1988, pp. 76-97.

Earl H. Rovit, "Ernest Hemingway: *The Sun Also Rises,*" in *Landmarks of American Writing,* edited by Hennig Cohen, Basic Books, Inc., 1969, pp. 303-14.

Nina Schwartz, "Lovers' Discourse in *The Sun Also Rises:* A Cock and Bull Story," in *Criticism,* Vol. XXVI, No. 1, Winter, 1984, pp. 49-69.

Mark Spilka, "The Death of Love in *The Sun Also Rises,*" in *Twelve Original Essays on Great American Novels,* edited by Charles Shapiro, Wayne State University Press, 1958, pp. 238-56.

Allen Tate, "Hard Boiled," in *The Nation,* Vol. CXXIII, No. 3206, December 15, 1926, pp. 642, 644.

Phillip Young, in *Ernest Hemingway,* Rinehart & Company, Inc., 1952, p. 244.

For Further Study

Donald A. Daiker, "The Affirmative Conclusion of *The Sun Also Rises,*" in *Modern American Fiction: Form and Function,* edited by Thomas Daniel Young, Louisiana State University Press, 1989, pp. 39-56.
    Daiker asserts that a close reading of Book III reveals that *The Sun Also Rises* is an affirmative book.

Scott Donaldson, "Humor in *The Sun Also Rises,*" in *New Essays on* The Sun Also Rises, edited by Linda Wagner-Martin, Cambridge University Press, 1987, pp. 19-41.
    Revealing that Hemingway started his writing career trying to be funny, Donaldson discusses the author's use of humor in *The Sun Also Rises.*

Barry Gross, "Dealing with Robert Cohn," in *Hemingway in Italy and Other Essays,* edited by Robert W. Lewis, Praeger, 1990, pp. 123-30.
    Gross discusses the depiction of Robert Cohn and the issue of anti-Semitism in *The Sun Also Rises.*

Robert E. Flemming, "The Importance of Count Mippipopolous: Creating the Code Hero," in *Arizona Quarterly,* Vol. 44, No. 2, Summer, 1988, pp. 69-75.
    Flemming contends that the Count may be an early prototype in Hemingway's fiction of the character type known as the "code hero."

Ernest Hemingway, in *Death in the Afternoon,* Touchstone Books, 1996.
    Contains Hemingway's own discussion of his favorite sport—bullfighting. The book explains the ritual and provides pictures.

Allen, Josephs, "Toreo: The Moral Axis of *The Sun Also Rises,*" in *Critical Essays on Ernest Hemingway's* The Sun Also Rises, edited by James Nagel, G.K. Hall & Co., 1995, pp. 126-40.
    Josephs explores how and why the art of *toreo* lies at the heart of *The Sun Also Rises.*

Albert Kwan, "*The Sun Also Rises* and *On the Road,*" at http://www.atlantic.net/~gagne/pol/ontheroad.html, 1998.
    World War II created a group of artists with similar disillusions to those of the Lost Generation. This group came to be know as the Beat Generation and

in Albert Kwan's essay Ernest Hemingway and Jack Kerouac are compared.

Kenneth S. Lynn, in *Hemingway,* Fawcett Books, 1988. In an attempt to be objective about Hemingway, Kenneth Lynn is seen by some fans as a bit harsh in this biographical account. It is an unusually balanced work for a Hemingway biography and it is not afraid to reveal some of the darker things about the famous writer.

James Nagel, "Brett and the Other Women in 'The Sun Also Rises'," in *The Cambridge Companion to Hemingway,* edited by Scott Donaldson, Cambridge University Press, 1996, pp. 87-108.
   In this discussion of the women in *The Sun Also Rises,* Nagel argues that, in order to come to terms with his emotional devastation, Jake tells his story— a cathartic reiteration that focuses on Brett and the women who surround her.

Kathleen Nichols, "The Morality of Asceticism in *The Sun Also Rises:* A Structural Reinterpretation," in *Fitzgerald/Hemingway Annual,* edited by Matthew J. Bruccoli and Richard Layman, 1978, pp. 321-30.
   Nichols contends that the solution Jake finds to his problems might be called a secularized morality based on the Catholic ideal of asceticism.

Sibbie O'Sullivan, "Love and Friendship/Man and Woman in *The Sun Also Rises,*" in *Arizona Quarterly,* Vol. 44, 1988, pp. 76-97.

O'Sullivan proposes that the novel may be read as a story about the cautious belief in the survival of the two most basic components of any human relationship: love and friendship.

Michael S. Reynolds, "The Sun in Its Time: Recovering the Historical Context," in *New Essays on* The Sun Also Rises, edited by Linda Wagner-Martin, Cambridge University Press, 1987, pp. 43-64.
   Arguing that *The Sun Also Rises* is "anchored in time," Reynolds places the novel in its historical context.

—, in *The Sun Also Rises: A Novel of the Twenties,* Twayne Publishers, 1988.
   A book-length study of the themes, characters, and symbolism of the novel.

Linda Wagner-Martin, "Introduction," in *New Essays on 'The Sun Also Rises',* edited by Linda Wagner-Martin, Cambridge University Press, 1987, pp. 1-18.
   Wagner-Martin discusses various biographical, historical and textual issues in this introduction to a volume of essays on *The Sun Also Rises.*

Jane E. Wilson, "Good Old Harris in *The Sun Also Rises,*" in *Critical Essays on Ernest Hemingway's* The Sun Also Rises, edited by James Nagel, G.K. Hall & Co., 1995, pp. 185-90.
   Wilson discusses the fishing trip to Burguete and argues that Jake's relationship with Harris is the key to understanding the meaning of the episode.

A Tale of Two Cities

Charles Dickens
1859

A Tale of Two Cities occupies a central place in the canon of Charles Dickens's works. This novel of the French Revolution was originally serialized in the author's own periodical *All the Year Round.* Weekly publication of chapters 1-3 of Book 1 began on April 30, 1859. In an innovative move, Dickens simultaneously released installments of the novel on a monthly basis, beginning with all of Book 1 in June and concluding with the last eight chapters of Book 3 in December. Dickens took advantage of the novel's serial publication to experiment with characterization, plot, and theme. He described the work in a letter to his friend John Forster, cited in Ruth Glancy's *A Tale of Two Cities: Dickens's Revolutionary Novel,* as "a picturesque story rising in every chapter, with characters true to nature, but whom the story should express more than they should express themselves by dialogue." The novel that emerged from his experimentation is now regarded as one of Dickens's most popular and most innovative works.

Dickens's work was very popular with the reading public when it was first published. One review in the magazine *Athenaeum* stated that *A Tale of Two Cities* had attracted the praise of a hundred thousand readers. On the other hand, a whole set of critics, most notably Sir James Fitzjames Stephen writing in *Saturday Review,* criticized the novel precisely for its popularity. "Most of the critics writing in the intellectual and literary journals of the day considered popular success a good reason to condemn a work," explains Glancy. "If the

Charles Dickens

public liked it, they certainly could not be seen to approve of it at all." Modern critical opinion, however, has given the novel an important place among Dickens's most mature works of fiction.

Author Biography

From the time he was twenty-one, Charles Dickens knew he would not be the great actor he had imagined, nor even the journalist he next attempted to be. Instead, he felt he was destined to become a great novelist. He not only had experiences with the same joys and tragedies his characters would have, but he also had the great talent to make his readers feel and see all these experiences in detail. The second of eight children of John and Elizabeth Dickens, Charles was born on February 7, 1812, in Portsmouth, England. His early childhood was a happy one. Though plagued by frequent illnesses, his first years were also filled with exciting stories told to him by his parents and his nurse.

However, when Dickens was twelve, his family moved to London, where his father was imprisoned for debts he could not pay. Charles was forced to go to work pasting labels on bottles at a bootblack factory. Although this job lasted less than a year, he often felt hungry and abandoned, especially compared to his sister Frances, who continued studying at the Royal Academy of Music, where she was winning awards. For Dickens, the injustice was almost more than he could stand, and his suffering was multiplied by his mother's delight about the job that he always remembered with hatred.

Although his critics are the first to say that *Great Expectations* is not directly autobiographical, Dickens's own words tell us that he resented having to work in the factory, where he dreamed of the better life he felt he deserved, much as Pip is eager to leave Joe's forge. Also, Dickens's essay "Travelling Abroad" describes a small boy who rides in a coach with Dickens past his grand house, Gad's Hill. Although the boy in the essay does not know Dickens or that this is the great author's house, he remarks that his father has told him that hard work will earn him this house, which Dickens had also admired for years before finally being able to afford it in 1856. Dickens's familiarity with youthful expectations and later-life remembrances of them are clear in this reflection.

Likewise, Dickens's first love for Maria Beadnell so impressed him by its horrible failure that even years later he could barely speak of it to his friend and biographer, John Forster. All that Dickens had written about her he later burned. He believed that Maria had rejected him because of social class differences, since Dickens had not yet established his writing career at the time and Maria's father was a banker. Decades later, his character Miss Havisham would burn, shooting up flames twice her size, in compensation for her cold heart.

Dickens's marriage to Catherine (Kate) Hogarth, the daughter of a newspaper editor, in 1836 produced ten children. Their union ended in separation in 1858, however. By the time *Great Expectations* was published in 1860, Dickens had known his mistress Ellen Ternan—an actress he had met when he became interested in the stage— for several years, and he established a separate household in which he lived with Ternan. It would not be until after the author's death, however, that Dickens's daughter would make the affair public. Ternan was twenty-seven years younger than Dickens, a fact that resembles the age difference between the happy, later-life couple Joe and Biddy in *Great Expectations*. Dickens protected his privacy because he was worried about his reputation as a respected writer and the editor of *Household Words,* a family magazine. Such turmoil and ecstasy in Dickens's intimate relationships have since been compared to the misery and bliss of couples in his novels.

If anything, Dickens's descriptions of suffering were and still are his chief endearing quality to readers who find them both realistic and empathetic. Beginning with *Bleak House* in 1852, Dickens is widely acknowledged to have entered a "dark period" of writing. Yet he seemed to enjoy his continuing popularity with readers and to ignore his critics' remarks that his stories were too melodramatic. While readers have long accepted that tendency, they have also warmed to Dickens's love of humor.

Critics suggest that the part of Dickens's life that is most reflected in *A Tale of Two Cities* is his personal relationships with his wife and Ellen Ternan. In 1855, he reestablished contact with his childhood sweetheart Maria Beadnell, but he was very disappointed with their meeting and depicted his disillusionment in the 1857 novel *Little Dorrit.* A quarrel with his publishers Bradbury & Evans over his mistress's reputation led Dickens to turn to a new publishing house, Chapman & Hall, to publish *A Tale of Two Cities.* Some critics suggest that Dickens's depiction of Lucie Manette in *A Tale of Two Cities* and the behavior of the two principal characters, Sydney Carton and Charles Darnay, toward her, reflects his own attitude toward Ternan.

Dickens died of a brain aneurysm in June 1870. Although he had expressly wished to be buried at his country home, Gad's Hill, his request was disregarded, apparently owing to his fame. Instead, he was buried in the Poets' Corner of Westminster Abbey, London.

Plot Summary

Book One: Recalled to Life

On a cold November night in 1775, Mr. Jarvis Lorry, who works for Tellson's Bank, tells a messenger who stops his mail coach to return with the message, "Recalled to Life," in *A Tale of Two Cities.* That evening in a Dover hotel he meets Miss Lucie Manette, a young woman whom Lorry brought to England as an orphaned child many years earlier and whom he is now to return with to

France to recover her father, recently released from prison after eighteen years.

In Paris, Mr. Lorry and Miss Manette arrive at the wine shop of Madame and Monsieur Defarge. In a top floor garret room above the shop, working away at a shoemaker's bench, sits an old, white-haired man, too feeble and too altered to recognize his daughter. With the help of Lorry and Defarge, Lucie takes Dr. Manette away in a carriage to return him to London.

Book Two: The Golden Thread

On a March morning in 1780, Mr. Charles Darnay is being tried at the Old Bailey for treason. In the court as witnesses are Dr. Manette and his daughter Lucie, who testifies that on the night five years earlier when she was returning with her father from France, the prisoner comforted her and her father aboard the boat on which they crossed the channel. Darnay is acquitted after the counsel for the defense, Mr. Stryver, befuddles a witness by presenting Mr. Sydney Carton, who so closely resembles Mr. Darnay that the witness is unable to stand by his story. Mr. Jerry Cruncher, messenger for hire, rushes the news of the acquittal to Tellson's Bank, as he was instructed to do by Mr. Lorry. Outside the courtroom, everyone congratulates Darnay on his release.

In France, meanwhile, both the abuses of the aristocracy and the furor of the oppressed grow. Monseigneur, the Marquis St. Evremonde, "one of the great lords in power at the court," drives off in a gilded carriage and runs over a child. He tosses a gold coin to the child's grieving father, Gaspard. Someone throws a coin at the carriage, but when the Marquis looks to see who, he sees only Madame Defarge, knitting. She knits into a scarf growing longer by the day the names in symbols of those who will later die at the hands of the revolutionaries. Later at his chateau, the Marquis asks if "Monsieur Charles" has yet arrived from England. Charles Darnay, the nephew, tells the Marquis that he believes his family has done wrong and that he wishes to redress the wrongs of the past. The Marquis, who scorns Darnay's suggestions, is later found stabbed to death in his bed.

Lucie and her father live in a London apartment with her maid, Miss Pross. Darnay prospers as a teacher in France and visits England frequently. He speaks of his love of Lucie to Dr. Manette, who grants his permission for a marriage, although he refuses to hear until the wedding day the secret of his identity which Darnay tries to tell him. Sydney Carton, self-described wastrel and un-successful suitor, tells Lucie he is "a man who would give his life, to keep a life you love beside you."

At the Defarge wine shop, local anger over the execution of Gaspard and the news that Lucie Manette is about to marry Charles Darnay, a French Marquis, grows. All the women knit.

After Lucie and Darnay go off to honeymoon, Mr. Lorry discovers Dr. Manette making shoes, lapsed into an absent mental state which lasts for nine days while Lucie is away. On the tenth day of Dr. Manette's mania, he recovers, converses with Mr. Lorry about a "friend" who suffered similarly, and agrees to have the things of his old occupa-tion—his shoemaking bench and tools which he had returned to in his distress—destroyed for his mental well-being.

On a July evening in 1789 Lucie Darnay, now the mother of a six-year-old girl, sits and worries over the future. Mr. Lorry speaks of the run on Tell-son's Bank as a consequence of the turmoil in Paris. There citizens storm the Bastille to free its seven prisoners. Among them are Madame and Monsieur Defarge, who find Manette's old cell. The people of St. Antoine hang a man named Foulon, who had once told the starving people to eat grass. They seek out aristocrats with a frenzy. One evening they burn down the chateau of the Marquis.

> The château was left to itself to flame and burn. In the roaring and raging of the conflagration, a red-hot wind, driving straight from the infernal regions, seemed to be blowing the edifice away. With the ris-ing and falling of the blaze, the stone faces showed as if they were in torment. When great masses of stone and timber fell, the face with the two dints in the nose became obscured: anon struggled out of the smoke again, as if it were the face of the cruel Mar-quis, burning at the stake and contending with the fire.

In August of 1792, Mr. Lorry is about to em-bark on a trip to Paris to organize accounts there. Darnay learns from him that the bank has been holding an unopened letter addressed to "Monsieur Heretofore the Marquis," whom he says he knows. The letter from Monsieur Gabelle, a servant, begs St. Evremonde/Darnay to come to France to free him from the mob who hold him. Darnay resolves to leave for France, for his honor demands it. He leaves a letter to Lucie, but he does not tell her his identity or purpose.

Book Three: The Track of a Storm

On his way to Paris, Darnay is captured, im-prisoned, charged with being an aristocratic emi-grant, now to suffer the justice of the revolution. Lucie and her father have also hastened to France to meet Mr. Lorry at Tellson's Paris bank. Dr. Manette uses his influence as one formerly im-prisoned to calm the revolutionaries and to have Darnay's life spared during the Reign of Terror when the King and Queen and 1100 others lose their lives to the guillotine. Yet shortly thereafter, Darnay is again arrested, charged by the Defarges and "one other."

Miss Pross and Jerry Cruncher, with the Manettes in Paris, come upon a man on the streets whom they identify as Miss Pross's lost brother. Sydney Carton then pursues the man's identity to reveal that he is John Barsad, who had been in-volved in Darnay's trial in England and who had spied for the English. Carton uses this knowledge as leverage to persuade Barsad, a turnkey at the prison, to work for him.

At the second trial, Darnay is denounced by the Defarges and "the other," who is no other than Dr. Manette himself! Defarge tells how when he stormed the Bastille, he found in Manette's old cell a paper in Manette's hand in a crevice in the wall. He proceeds to read the paper. Manette's story dates to 1857 when he was summoned by two men, the twin St. Evremondes, to attend to a dying peas-ant woman and a dying, peasant boy, wounded fighting in her defense. The woman had been raped by the two men. They tried to pay Manette off, but he refused; when he tried to write to authorities re-garding their case, they destroyed his letter and threatened to kidnap his wife. He then denounced them and their descendants (and thus Charles Dar-nay). Darnay is condemned to die within 24 hours.

After Carton takes Lucie home, he visits the Defarges, where Madame Defarge reveals that the woman in Manette's story was her sister. He re-turns to the Manettes that evening to find that Dr. Manette has this time been unsuccessful in freeing Darnay. Carton instructs Lorry on plans to have the Manettes escape Paris the next day. "The moment I come to you," he says, "take me in and drive away." Carton enters the prison and Darnay's cell with the help of Barsad. He drugs Darnay, then ex-changes clothes with him. Barsad carries Darnay out; Carton remains behind. The Manettes, Darnay, and Mr. Lorry all escape in a carriage. Miss Pross and Jerry Cruncher also devise a plan of escape. While Cruncher goes for a carriage, Madame Defarge, armed with a gun and a knife, comes to the apartment to execute Lucie and her daughter, confronts Miss Pross, and dies of a gunshot in the ensuing struggle. Miss Pross and Cruncher escape, the former forever after deaf. Carton is executed as Darnay, willingly giving his life for the one he loves.

Characters

John Barsad

See Solomon Pross

Sydney Carton

Sydney Carton is a dissipated English lawyer who spends a great deal of his life drunk. Although he has a brilliant legal mind, his alcoholism keeps him from becoming a success. He first enters *A Tale of Two Cities* in 1780, during Charles Darnay's trial for espionage. Darnay is acquitted because of his uncanny resemblance to Carton, thus casting doubts on the testimony of his accusers. Carton works in an unofficial partnership with another lawyer, C. J. Stryver. Although Carton's legal mind was mostly responsible for Darnay's acquittal, his coarse manners and habitual drunkenness contrast with his double's refinement and politeness. Carton falls in love with Lucie Manette and, when she marries Darnay, asks to be considered a friend of the family with the privilege of visiting them from time to time. His devotion to Lucie is the major factor in his decision to take Darnay's place in prison and be guillotined in 1793.

Understanding the character of Carton is difficult for the reader. We know nothing of his past life or of the reasons that have kept him single into his forties (the age at which he enters the novel). His only major weakness is his alcoholism, which in Victorian times was regarded as a character flaw rather than a disease; his redeeming grace is his love for Lucie, which persuades him to sacrifice himself so that she and her family can escape. Ironically, Carton does this by passing himself off as Darnay and taking his place on the scaffold.

Carton is Darnay's alter-ego in several senses of the phrase. He is English, while Darnay is French; coarse-mannered, while Darnay is polite; and alcoholic, while Darnay is temperate. They are united only in their mutual love for Lucie Manette. But it is Carton in the end who succeeds in rescuing the Darnays—Lucie, her husband, and their lit-

Media Adaptations

- Dickens made a lot of money by reading selections from his works aloud before an audience. His own version of *A Tale of Two Cities,* which he prepared but never actually performed, was entitled *The Bastille Prisoner. A Reading. From "A Tale of Two Cities". In Three Chapters.* It was published by William Clowes of London, probably in the early 1860s. The text of *The Bastille Prisoner* can also be found in *Charles Dickens: The Public Readings,* published in Oxford by the Clarendon Press, 1975.

- The 1935 MGM film *A Tale of Two Cities,* featuring Ronald Colman as Sydney Carton, Basil Rathbone as the Marquis St. Evremonde, and Elizabeth Allan as Lucie, received Academy Award nominations for Best Picture and Best Editing. It is still regarded as the best film version of Dickens's novel.

- Burbank Films animated *A Tale of Two Cities* and released it in 1984. The film is available on videocassette,

- PBS television's *Masterpiece Theatre* produced *A Tale of Two Cities* in 1991. It featured James Wilby, Serena Gordon, and John Mills in leading roles, and it is available on videocassette.

- *A Tale of Two Cities* was recorded as a radio play by BBC Radio 4, featuring Charles Dance as Carton, John Duttine as Darnay, Maurice Denham as Dr. Manette, and Charlotte Attenborough as Lucie. It was released in the United States in 1989 by Bantam Doubleday Dell Audio, 1989.

tle daughter—from the fate planned for them by the Revolutionary authorities. On the scaffold Carton has a vision in which he sees that through his execution he creates a memory that Lucie and Darnay will preserve for generations to come. Carton foresees that his namesake, Sydney Darnay, will become a famous judge, fulfilling the career that Carton wanted for himself but could not get. At the

Still from the 1935 movie A Tale of Two Cities, *starring Ronald Colman (right) as Sydney Carton.*

end of *A Tale of Two Cities,* Carton becomes a Christ-figure, a godlike being who redeems the blood shed in the name of freedom and brotherhood. Through his heroic self-sacrifice, Carton redeems the sins of the St. Evremondes in a way that the purer Darnay could not do.

Jerry Cruncher

Jerry Cruncher is the literal symbol of Dickens's theme of resurrection in *A Tale of Two Cities.* Cruncher is a "resurrection man"—he steals fresh corpses from graveyards and delivers them to medical schools so that students can study human anatomy. His values are upside-down; he regards body-snatching as honest work and prayer as weakness. He also works as a porter for Mr. Jarvis Lorry's bank, Tellson's, and helps make Sydney Carton's rescue of the Darnays successful. In the end, Cruncher is impressed by Carton's sacrifice and by the Darnays and resolves to reform.

Charles Darnay

Charles Darnay, or St. Evremonde, is the nephew and heir of the Marquis St. Evremonde, the wicked aristocrat who is responsible for the imprisonment of Dr. Manette. However, Charles has renounced his wicked uncle's fortune, has adopted his mother's maiden name, and has taken a posi-

tion as a tutor in the French language in England. Darnay is caught up in the events of the French Revolution. In 1781, while trying to help a woman that his family had injured, he is arrested as a spy and placed on trial in England. There he meets Lucie Manette and marries her; they have several children. Darnay is caught in France in 1792 while trying to help a former family servant; he is arrested and sentenced to be executed on the basis of a letter written by Dr. Manette during his years of imprisonment (1757-1775). He is rescued by his English double, Sydney Carton, who takes his place and is executed in his stead.

Like his wife Lucie Manette, Charles Darnay is a largely passive character. Although his manners and behavior are impeccable and his intentions are well-meant, he is incapable of performing the important tasks to which he commits himself. Both his arrests take place while he is in the process of trying to extract friends or former servants from difficulties. Darnay is also like Dr. Manette because of the time he spends unjustly confined in prison. It takes Carton's sacrifice to release Darnay from the cycle of arrests.

Some critics believe that Dickens viewed Darnay as a version of himself. The character shares the author's initials (C.D.) and his relationship with Carton may reflect a split in Dickens's own psyche between his heroic, honorable side and his baser nature.

Lucie Darnay

Lucie Manette, Dr. Manette's daughter, at the age of seventeen discovers her father's existence in a French jail. As an infant she was carried off to England by Mr. James Lorry and is raised there in the belief that her father is dead. She travels with Mr. Lorry once again in 1775 to rescue Dr. Manette. Later she marries protagonist Charles Darnay and gives birth to young Lucie, their daughter. Like many other Victorian literary heroines, Lucie tends to give the impression that she is frail and delicate; she faints easily and is earnestly committed to the salvation of her husband and to the future of her children. Lucie is primarily a passive character whose purpose is to be the object of devotion of Sydney Carton, Charles Darnay, and Dr. Manette.

Some critics have suggested that Dickens's portrayal of Lucie is based in part on his own feelings for the actress Ellen Ternan and that Lucie is an idealized version of Ellen. Others see her as an expression of his memories of his childhood friend Lucy Stroughill, or a version of the heroine Lucy of Dickens's 1856 play *The Wreck of the Golden Mary.* "Golden-haired" Lucie Manette, according to these interpretations, is an expression of the light (the name Lucie is derived from a word meaning "light") that opposes the darkness and hatred of the Revolutionary figures, especially Therese Defarge. Like the light, Lucie is largely passive; she does not transform herself, but those who are illuminated by her love are transformed themselves. It is Lucie's affection that makes Sydney Carton resolve to sacrifice himself for her family's safety. Lucie is a catalyst; she does not change anything herself, but she is the cause of change in others.

Ernest Defarge

Dickens presents the husband of the vengeful Madame Defarge, Ernest Defarge, as another force in the Revolution; a less driven, but still flawed, example of the French common people. Ernest Defarge had served Dr. Manette as a servant before the doctor was imprisoned by the Marquis St. Evremonde and has some affectionate feelings for him when he is released. Defarge later becomes an important Revolutionary leader. However, Defarge exploits Dr. Manette's insanity, opening his prison to curious gapers who want to gawk at the unfortunate madman. Unlike his wife, Ernest Defarge is not interested in pursuing Lucie Darnay and her daughter to their deaths. At the end of the book, Carton foresees Defarge's own death on the guillotine at the hands of his revolutionary companions.

Madame Therese Defarge

Madame Defarge is the symbol of the evils brought forth by the French Revolution. Her entire family was destroyed by the St. Evremonde clan; her sister was raped by the Marquis St. Evremonde—Charles Darnay's uncle—and her brother died at the aristocrat's hands. Because of this tragedy, Defarge has conceived an intense hatred for the St. Evremondes, including Charles Darnay himself, as well as the rest of the aristocratic class. Madame Defarge plots the downfall of the St. Evremondes and other aristocrats with almost infinite patience, working the names of those whom she hates into her knitting. She plots Darnay's arrest in 1792 and the eventual deaths of his entire family, demonstrating the depths of her hatred. Madame Defarge represents the uncontrollable forces of the French Revolution. She is killed in a struggle with Miss Pross, Lucie's nurse, when her pistol goes off accidentally.

Charles St. Evremonde

See Charles Darnay

Marquis St. Evremonde

The Marquis St. Evremonde parallels the animalistic evil of Madame Therese Defarge. He is the image of the uncaring aristocrat of the *ancien regime.* He was responsible for both the imprisonment of Dr. Manette and for the rape of Therese Defarge's sister and the death of the rest of her family. He is also responsible for the death of Gaspard's young son, whom he runs down in his coach. Dickens stresses the Marquis's lack of humanity and predatory nature by comparing him to a tiger.

Jarvis Lorry

Jarvis Lorry is the representative of Tellson's Bank, an old, established English institution. He serves partly as a means of progressing the plot and partly as a symbol of English middle-class virtue. It was Mr. Lorry who rescued the infant Lucie Manette and took her to safety in England when her father was arrested and her mother died. It is Mr. Lorry who goes to retrieve Dr. Manette after his eighteen years in prison. Finally, it is Mr. Lorry who aids Carton in his deception of the French authorities in order to rescue the Darnays from Revolutionary France. Mr. Lorry serves as well as a way of introducing one of the novel's major themes: the idea of imprisonment and redemption. He dreams of literally "resurrecting" Dr. Manette, who has been buried alive for nearly twenty years; yet Mr. Jarvis confines himself in the jail-like recesses of Tellson's.

Dr. Alexandre Manette

Dr. Manette is one of the central characters in *A Tale of Two Cities.* He was imprisoned at the start of the story because he had tried to bring the crimes of two of the St. Evremondes, members of a noble family, to public trial. The St. Evremondes have conspired to keep Manette in prison for eighteen years and this confinement is one of the major plot points of the novel. The doctor's incarceration has cost him his sanity. He can only remember his cell number. When he is first rescued from his prison he believes he is a cobbler, and when he comes under stress his insanity reasserts itself. He first begins to revive when the sight of his daughter Lucie recalls memories of his dead wife. He collapses into insanity again when he discovers his son-in-law is a member of the hated Evremonde clan, and still again when Darnay is imprisoned in Paris and threatened with beheading.

Dr. Manette's major function is to set the plot of *A Tale of Two Cities* in motion, but some critics consider his sane and insane personalities to represent the Victorian literary fascination with duality. His dual personas also illustrate the social split taking place in France during the "Terror," and the differences between Paris and London, the two cities of the title. Some critics also suggest that Manette's character reflects the author's own personality. They trace parallels between Manette's career as a physician and his selflessness in reporting the abuses of the nobility with Dickens's career as a journalist and advocate for social improvement. They also see similarities between Manette's creation, in his madness, of a world in which he is only a cobbler and Dickens's creation of secondary worlds in his novels.

Lucie Manette

See Lucie Darnay

Miss Pross

Miss Pross is Lucie Manette Darnay's nurse, then her companion and nurse to her daughter Little Lucie during the traumatic months spent in Revolutionary Paris. She is also the sister of the English spy Solomon Pross (John Barsad). In some ways Miss Pross is a stereotypical Englishwoman;

she is blunt-spoken, nationalistic, and short-tempered, but she is also good-hearted and devoted to Lucie. She opposes the darkness of the revolutionary Madame Therese Defarge. In a climactic struggle, Miss Pross kills Madame Defarge while trying to keep her from discovering that the Darnays have fled from Paris.

Solomon Pross

Solomon Pross is the brother of Miss Pross, Lucie Manettte's nurse. He works as a spy under the name John Barsad, first for the English and then for the French government. Carton foresees in his final vision that Barsad will be caught and executed during the "Terror."

C. J. Stryver

C. J. Stryver is the quasi-law partner of Sydney Carton. He makes his living by exploiting Carton's legal mind. Unlike Carton, Stryver is motivated and active, but he is also unprincipled and in the end unredeemed. He courts Lucie Manette briefly and, after she chooses Darnay, pretends that he had rejected her.

The Vengeance

The Vengeance is Madame Therese Defarge's chosen companion. As her title suggests, her entire identity is swallowed by her desire for revenge on the aristocratic class.

Themes

Order and Disorder

The story of *A Tale of Two Cities* takes place during the turbulent years of the French Revolution. Dickens stresses the chaos of Revolutionary France by using images of the ocean. He calls the Paris mob a "living sea," and compares Ernest Defarge to a man caught in a whirlpool. Defarge and his wife are both at the center of revolutionary activity in Paris, just as their lives are at the center of the whirlpool. Order breaks down once again in the second chapter of the third book, "The Grindstone." "Dickens deliberately set Darnay's return to Paris and arrest at the time of the September Massacres," writes Ruth Glancy in *A Tale of Two Cities: Dickens's Revolutionary Novel,* "a four-day execution of 1,089 prisoners from four Paris prisons, condemned in minutes each by ... 'sudden Courts of Wild Justice.'" Contrasted to the chaos of Paris is the order of England: Dr. Manette's peaceful home in Soho is a place of refuge for Darnay, Carton, and Mr. Lorry, while even Tellson's Bank serves as a center of calmness in the whirlpool of Revolutionary Paris.

Death and Resurrection

Death, burial, and resurrection are themes that Dickens returns to again and again in *A Tale of Two Cities*. The first book of the novel, "Recalled to Life," traces the resurrection of Dr. Manette, who has been held in prison for almost twenty years. Prisons, for Dickens, are symbolic of the grave— a comparison that he makes throughout his works, and which may be related to his father's imprisonment in the debtors' prison at Marshalsea. Mr. Lorry, who travels to Paris in 1775 to secure the doctor's release, views himself as literally digging up Dr. Manette's body. He fancies that the doctor has been buried for so long that he will fall to pieces upon being liberated: "Got out at last, with earth hanging around his face and hair, he would suddenly fall away to dust." Even the doctor's daughter Lucie, whom he has never seen, believes that the person who will emerge from the prison will be a ghost rather than a living man. Like a man brought back to life, Manette cannot quite shake the hold his burial and rebirth has on his mind. He reverts to his cobbling—a sign of his madness contracted in prison—during periods of stress, but he is finally redeemed by his daughter's love and his own forgiveness of Darnay for the crimes of the St. Evremondes.

Other characters are also absorbed in Dickens's death imagery. Jerry Cruncher, the Tellson's Bank messenger, is also a "resurrection man"—a person who steals fresh corpses from graveyards and sells them to medical schools for use as anatomy specimens. Charles Darnay is imprisoned and released twice in the course of the novel; the second time, it takes another death, Sydney Carton's, to secure Darnay's freedom. Madame Defarge, consumed by a desire for vengeance, finds her death in a tussle with Miss Pross. In addition, in his final moments Carton foresees the deaths of a large number of minor characters, including the spies Barsad and Cly, the revolutionary leaders Defarge and the woman known as The Vengeance, and the judge and jury who condemned Darnay to death. Revolutionary anarchy and hatred consume these people, but the Darnays, Dr. Manette, Mr. Lorry, and especially Carton, are redeemed through their love and self-sacrifice.

Topics for Further Study

- Investigate contemporary accounts of the French Revolution, concentrating on the "Terror"—the months between the summers of 1793 and 1794—and compare them to Dickens's own version of the story.

- Compare the character of Maximilian Robespierre, the most powerful man in France during the "Terror," to that of the fictional Madame Defarge.

- Many critics consider Sidney Carton and Charles Darnay as two sides of a single character. Some of them have suggested that this split in the novel reflects the split in Dickens's own life: at the time he was writing, his marriage was breaking up and he was consorting with a younger woman. What evidence is there for this in the novel?

- The title of the book *A Tale of Two Cities* refers to the two cities of Paris and London. Compare and contrast Dickens's presentation of the two. Why did the author consider them central to his story?

- Dr. Manette is often said by other characters in *A Tale of Two Cities* to be "resurrected"—to have been rescued from the grave and brought back to life. Trace the way this theme of "resurrection" occurs throughout the novel.

- Research the history of the Chartist Movement and other reform movements in Victorian Britain. What parallels does Dickens draw between the abuses of the French Revolution and the kind of society that opposed reform in England during his own life?

Memory and Reminiscence

A Tale of Two Cities is a historical novel, about events approximately seventy years past when Dickens wrote the work. For the author in *A Tale of Two Cities,* memory is often a trap, pulling people into an abyss of despair. Madame Defarge's hatred of aristocrats in general and St. Evremonde in particular is based on her memory of the rape and deaths of her siblings at his hands. However, it can also be a force for redemption. It is Dr. Manette's memory of his dead wife, seen in his daughter's face, that begins his process of resurrection from the grave of his prison and madness. "Darnay … listens to the voices from his past," states Ruth Glancy in *A Tale of Two Cities: Dickens's Revolutionary Novel;* "his desire to right the wrongs of his family is primarily due to his mother's reliance on him to do so." Perhaps most interesting, however, is Sydney Carton and his relationship to memory. His colleague C. J. Stryver calls him "Memory Carton" for his brilliant legal mind. Dickens's portrayal of Carton, however, shows him inspired by the memory of his love for Lucie to renounce his passive life. "When Carton dies with the words 'It is a far, far better thing that I do, than I have ever done,' he is renouncing the mental prison that has prevented him from making something of his life," writes Glancy; "he is living dynamically, as Doctor Manette does, and even if for him the action will soon be over, its repercussions will be felt for as long as the Darnay family survives."

Style

Setting

The chief characteristic of *A Tale of Two Cities* that sets it apart from Dickens's other novels is its historical setting. Most of the author's works comment on contemporary English society; *A Tale of Two Cities* does this, too, but not as directly as, say, *David Copperfield* or *Great Expectations.* Dickens contrasts late eighteenth-century Paris and London both to advance the plot and to draw conclusions about the nature of freedom and the redeeming power of love. The novel begins in England, and most of the first book takes place in that country. In the second book, chapters alternate between the English and the French settings, and the third is set almost entirely in France. "At the beginning of the novel," writes Ruth Glancy in *A Tale of Two Cities: Dickens's Revolutionary Novel,* "Dickens paints a grim picture of both countries. They both had kings who believed in their divine right to rule. English spirituality had deteriorated into communing with spirits and other superstitious practices…. France, he says, was less given over to such spiritual revelations, but had instead a clergy that inflicted cruel punishments for minor offenses." In England mi-

nor legal offenses were often punished with hanging. At the end of the novel, Dickens contrasts the two countries in the persons of Frenchwoman Madame Defarge and Englishwoman Miss Pross; in the struggle, however, he portrays not the triumph of one country over another, but the triumph of love over hatred.

Antithesis

One of the most notable devices that Dickens uses in *A Tale of Two Cities* is the contrast of thesis and antithesis. The opening words of the novel introduce this conflict. Most of the major themes of the novel are summed up in these lines: "It was the best of times, it was the worst of times, it was the age of wisdom, it was the age of foolishness, it was the epoch of belief, it was the epoch of incredulity, it was the season of Light, it was the season of Darkness, it was the spring of hope, it was the winter of despair." Characters mirror and oppose each other. For example, Madame Defarge's experiences mirror those of Dr. Manette. Defarge's sister is raped and her brother is murdered by the Marquis St. Evremonde; Manette witnesses the crime and is imprisoned by the aristocratic criminal. Ernest Defarge and Mr. Lorry mirror each other; they both regard themselves as businessmen and they both care for Dr. Manette. However, while Defarge becomes consumed by hate and will eventually die under the guillotine, Mr. Lorry is redeemed by his love for the Darnays and escapes France in their company. These conflicts, which Dickens pursues throughout the novel, are resolved by Sydney Carton's sacrifice for love of Lucie. He concludes with a positive statement of goodness: "It is a far, far better thing that I do, than I have ever done; it is a far, far better rest that I go to, than I have ever known."

Doppelganger

The device of the *doppelganger,* or identical double, is central to *A Tale of Two Cities.* Charles Darnay and Sydney Carton are physically nearly identical, and some critics suggest that they are psychologically two sides of the same psyche. When Darnay is accused of spying and placed on trial in England, his lawyer, C. J. Stryver, secures his release. Stryver discredits the prosecution witness, who upon seeing Carton can no longer swear that Darnay was the man he saw spying. The climax of the novel, in which Carton takes Darnay's place on the execution grounds, is dependent on their close physical resemblance. The fact that both Carton and Darnay are in love with the same woman—Lucie

Manett—echoes the physical resemblance between the two. In other ways, however, the two are opposed. Darnay, for instance, is consumed with the need to undo the evils that his uncle, the Marquis St. Evremonde, has inflicted on people. He makes his nearly-fatal trip to Paris in order to try to rescue Gabelle, a former family servant, but he is unsuccessful; he is caught, imprisoned, and sentenced to be executed. On the other hand Carton, who reveals to Lucie that he has previously lived a life of idleness, is successful in his bid to release Darnay from prison. Ironically Darnay, who has lived an upright, moral life, is successful only as a passive figure in his marriage. Carton, who has lived an immoral life of drunkenness and idleness, is successful in his activity, although the price of his success is his life.

Historical Context

Although *A Tale of Two Cities* takes place in a time some seventy years before Dickens was writing the novel, it does indirectly address contemporary issues with which the author was concerned. During the 1780s—the period in which the novel was set—England was a relatively peaceful and prosperous nation. Its national identity was caught up in a long war with France, which the French Revolution first interrupted, then continued. The ideals of the French Revolution were imported to England by political and literary radicals such as William Wordsworth and Samuel Taylor Coleridge. Many people, especially the English aristocracy and middle classes, feared these revolutionary values, seeing in them a threat to their prosperous and stable way of life. However, although there were social inequities in England as well as in France, England also had a long tradition of peaceful social change. In addition, the country's political leaders were very successful at uniting all classes of society in the struggle against Revolutionary France and its successor, the Empire under Napoleon Bonaparte.

Despite these successes, fears of revolutionary rhetoric and struggle persisted in England down to Dickens's own day. Other changes also embraced the country; the Industrial Revolution created a new wealthy class and brought a previously unknown prosperity to England. That same industrialization, however, also created an underclass of laborers who relied on regular wages to survive. "Overcrowding, disease, hunger, long hours of work, and

Illustration by H. K. Browne, from Dickens's A Tale of Two Cities, *published by Chapman and Hall, 1859.*

mindless, repetitive labor," explains Ruth Glancy in *A Tale of Two Cities: Dickens's Revolutionary Novel,* "characterized the new life for this new class of urban poor." This underclass was largely scorned or ignored by society. It had no rights, it could not vote in elections, and it could not legally form unions for its own protection. In addition, Glancy states, "many members of the upper classes feared even educating the poor, in case they would then become politically aware and eager to better themselves when it suited many people to have them as cheap labor." The English tradition of peaceful protest, expressed by public marches and meetings, continued throughout the early nineteenth century, but it was interrupted as the century progressed by riots and the destruction of property. "People feared that a revolution as horrifying as the French one could after all happen in England," Glancy declares. "A few political thinkers believed that such a revolution was actually the answer to Britain's problems, but most people, like Dickens, feared the actions of the mob, having seen the bloody outcome of the 1789 revolution."

The revolution that Dickens and many others feared in 1850s England did not arrive, in part be-

Compare & Contrast

- **1780s:** At the end of the period known as the Enlightenment, most educated people believed that the universe was essentially knowable and operated by fixed laws capable of being understood by human beings.

  1850s: With the publication of Charles Darwin's *The Origin of Species* (1859), conservative Victorians launched a backlash of religious fervor that spoke against scientific progress.

  Today: With technological advances such as space travel and cloning, modern science appears to be able to correct almost any problem. As specialization within science increases, however, few people can know very much about a variety of sciences.

- **1780s:** French thinkers and *philosophes* such as the Marquis de Montesquieu recommended an enlightened system of government with powers balanced and divided among different bodies.

  1850s: After decades of political stagnation, England began to liberalize its franchise by extending the right to vote to all male citizens regardless of how little property they might own.

  Today: With the collapse of Communist governments worldwide, the democratic model established by the United States—on which the French Revolution was based—has become the model for most national governments.

- **1780s:** The science of anatomy was in such a primitive state that new bones were still being discovered in the human body. The German Romantic poet Johann Wolfgang von Goethe discovered one, later known as the intermaxillary bone, in 1784.

  1850s: By this time in England, Jerry Cruncher's trade of body-snatching had been extinct for over twenty years, thanks to Parliament's Anatomy Act (1832).

  Today: Modern medical science can replace portions of human anatomy with artificially-made bones, or through transplant surgery substitute animal organs for human ones that fail. Because of the success of transplants, a need for human organs has resurrected the trade of body-snatcher.

- **1780s:** English sailors on board H.M.S. *Bounty* mutinied in the South Pacific when their captain Bligh cut their water ration in order to water his cargo of breadfruit trees. The sailors concealed themselves on Pitcairn Island and remained undiscovered for years.

  1850s: Seafaring European explorers had identified most land masses and other Europeans were beginning to press into the continental interiors of Australia, North America, and Africa.

  Today: Modern satellite technology can map the entire world within the space of a few days. Very few corners of the earth are still unknown to Europeans or their cultural descendants, the North Americans.

- **1780s:** During the French Revolution, drinking was commonplace among all classes of society.

  1850s: A "temperance movement" centered in Protestant countries (mostly English commonwealth and the United States) vilified alcohol consumption and tried to eliminate drinking on moral grounds.

---

cause of the efforts of various reform parties. Although groups such as the Chartist movement had struggled for better conditions for English workers as early as the 1830s, by the 1850s many of the reforms they had sought were still not in place. The 1832 Reform Bill, introduced by Lord John Russell, had smoothed out some of the inequities in the parliamentary system, but it still left thousands of working poor disenfranchised and discontented. It was not until 1867 that Benjamin Disraeli introduced a Reform Bill that nearly doubled the number of voters throughout England, Wales, and Scotland. This reform, passed late in Dickens's life, helped smother the fears of bloody revolution that dogged the English upper and middle classes. "There was no bloody revolution," explains Glancy, "but Dickens and others deplored the snail's pace that the government took to achieve peaceful reform through the parliamentary process. If the time of the Revolution in France was 'the epoch of belief ... the epoch of incredulity,'" she concludes, "so too were the 1850s in Britain."

Critical Overview

A Tale of Two Cities is perhaps the least characteristic of Charles Dickens's works. Unlike both his earlier and his later novels, which are largely concerned with events within the Victorian society in which he lived, *A Tale of Two Cities* is set during a period some seventy years earlier. It shows both France and England in an unflattering light. Perhaps because the novel is so uncharacteristic of the author, it remains among the author's most popular works with readers who do not generally enjoy Dickens. On the other hand, it is often rated the least popular Dickens novel among Dickens fans.

While *A Tale of Two Cities* was immensely popular with the reading public on its original serialization in 1859, its critical reception was mixed. "One feature that appears from the outset," explains Norman Page in his essay "Dickens and His Critics," "is a polarisation of responses, the novel being found either superlatively good or superlatively bad." According to Ruth Glancy in *A Tale of Two Cities: Dickens's Revolutionary Novel*, most contemporary critics routinely dismissed the type of popular literature that Dickens wrote as being unworthy of ranking as art. The most famous and the most caustic of the early critics of *A Tale of Two Cities* was Sir James Fitzjames Stephen, who wrote a very harsh review of the book in the December 17, 1859, issue of *Saturday Review.* "After condemning the plot—'it would perhaps be hard to imagine a clumsier or more disjointed framework for the display of the tawdry wares which form Mr. Dickens's stock in trade'—Stephen dismissed *A Tale of Two Cities* as a purely mechanical effort, producing grotesqueness and pathos through formula writing and trickery," explains Glancy. "He objected particularly to the 'grotesqueness' of the speech of the French characters, whose French-

sounding English he considered 'misbegotten jargon' that 'shows a great want of sensibility to the real requirements of art.'" "It has been suggested," continues Page, "that ... Stephen was motivated more by political than by literary considerations, and it is true that one line of his attack is directed at Dickens's disparagement of eighteenth-century England in relation to the present, and his hostile portrayal of the French aristocracy of the same period."

Stephen's attack, politically motivated or not, sums up most of the criticisms that later scholars have levelled at the novel: (1) as history, it is flawed; (2) it is mechanical and unrealistic in its construction; and (3) it is very uncharacteristic of Dickens. Many late nineteenth- and early twentieth-century critics, including the important Dickens scholar George Gissing and Dickens's fellow-journalist and novelist G. K. Chesterton, followed Stephen's lead in criticizing the novel. According to Page's essay, Chesterton objects to Dickens's portrayal of the Revolution as an elemental act of emotion rather than recognizing the importance of intellectual ideas. Page also reveals that in Gissing's review of the novel, construction has "ceased to be a virtue and has become a constraining and excluding factor." After Dickens's death in 1871, writes Page, "the novelist Margaret Oliphant dismissed it as unworthy of Dickens and suggested that it 'might have been written by any new author, so little of Dickens there is in it.'" Other critics considered its characters and its staging unrealistic and objected to its lack of humor.

Stephen's opinion, although influential, was not universally accepted. Favorable reviews of *A Tale of Two Cities* appeared in London newspapers, including the *Daily News,* the *Daily Telegraph,* the *Morning Post* and the *Morning Star,* throughout the month of December, 1859. Many of Dickens's own literary friends, acquaintances, and contemporaries, including John Forster, Thomas Carlyle, Wilkie Collins, and Mark Twain (Samuel Clemens) also praised the novel. Modern critics also largely praise the novel, concentrating on its psychological portraits and its status as historical fiction. Glancy reports that the work "has achieved new status and new serious study," and concludes that "its continuing presence on school reading lists and in films and plays ... attests to its lasting popularity ... with the many readers who find in *A Tale of Two Cities* the full range of Dickens's dramatic and narrative power."

Criticism

George V. Griffith

Griffith is a professor of English and philosophy at Chadron State College in Chadron, Nebraska. In the following excerpt, he discusses Dickens's obsession with duality in the book and the parallels implied between the era of the French Revolution and the author's own time.

In a preface to *A Tale of Two Cities* Dickens described how the idea for the novel came to him when he was playing a role in 1857 in a theatrical production of *The Frozen Deep,* a play written by his friend Wilkie Collins. In the play a man involved in a love triangle sacrifices his life to save the rival suitor of the woman he loves. Dickens's account of the origins of the novel points to Sydney Carton as the central character of *A Tale of Two Cities,* although other evidence suggests that other ideas might have played as large a role in the birth of the book. In notebooks as early as 1855 there appear references to the fate of people released after long imprisonment and to the phrase "Buried Alive," which was for a time Dickens's working title for *A Tale of Two Cities.* "Recalled to Life" became his title for Part I of the novel. This evidence places Dr. Manette's imprisonment center stage. An argument for either character as focal misses Dickens's craft in bringing those two characters—and others—together in the theme of resurrection and renewal, life, death and rebirth in this story of the French Revolution.

The secrecy shadowing the opening chapter, best expressed in the cryptic message "Recalled to Life," attends the effort to retrieve Dr. Manette from the French prison where he has been "buried" for eighteen years. Three times Dickens repeats the following exchange:

> "Buried how long?"

> "Almost eighteen years."

> "I hope you care to live."

> "I can't say."

Dr. Manette, a man figuratively returned from the grave and given life again, is the first of many characters in the novel whose life story is the story of death and rebirth. Charles Darnay, on trial for his life at the book's opening, is acquitted; then in France, not once but twice, he is retried, each time to be rescued from a near certain death by guillotine. He is rescued first by Carton, then by Dr. Manette, then again by Carton, who speaks the words of the Anglican funeral service, "I am the Resurrection and the Life." Carton himself is figuratively brought to life by his heroic role in the novel. In his first appearance, at Darnay's trial, Carton is the Jackal to Stryver's Lion, a man whose promise has ended in a dissolute alcoholism and idleness. When he describes himself to Lucie as a "self-flung away, wasted, drunken, poor creature of misuse," she asks: "Can I not recall you ... to a better course?" Indeed she does. In his self-sacrificing devotion to Lucie he finds redemption, giving his life that Darnay might live, the savior saved.

Dickens extends the "Recalled to Life" theme to the secondary characters, sometimes in comic ways. Jerry Cruncher, for example, is a "Resurrection Man," the term given to those who robbed the graves of the freshly buried to keep the anatomy schools supplied with corpses. Cruncher's efforts to retrieve the body of Roger Cly following his burial are stymied when he discovers an empty casket. Cly's death and burial as an Old Bailey spy, complete with an enraged London mob, is a fraud, a means of his escaping England with John Barsad. Cly, too, then, is "buried" and resurrected. The aristocrat Foulon tries the same trick in Paris, but the enraged French mob will not be fooled. "Resurrected" from a staged death, he is then killed, his mouth stuffed with grass in fitting vengeance for his once having told the hungry peasantry to eat grass.

The larger canvas on which Dickens works is the story of the two cities of the title, the historical account of the French Revolution about which Dickens also thinks in terms of death and renewal, for the Revolution is the death of the *ancien regime* and the birth of the Republic, the bloody and fiery renewal of France. In the same preface in which he spoke of the genesis of the novel in his participation in Collins's play, Dickens also expressed his gratitude to Victorian historian Thomas Carlyle, whose *The French Revolution* (1837) Dickens once claimed in a letter to have read "for the 500th time." From Carlyle, Dickens took both numerous specific details about the Revolution and a more general view of history. Carlyle viewed history as a grand succession of eras, often in cycles of destruction and reconstitution. In history there was always a revelation of a divine moral order at work in the world. The French Revolution, the single most significant recent event in the lives of those like Carlyle and Dickens who were born in the Napoleonic aftermath, offered abundant lessons regarding the presence of the past. Horrified by the Terror of

1793, the English read the lesson that corruption breeds corruption, that extremes are followed by extremes. The earlier generation of English writers, typified by the Romantic poet William Wordsworth, were stirred by the ambitious idealism of the Revolution. To Dickens, by contrast, although he evoked sentimental ideals in Carton's sacrifice to save the life of a rival lover, there was nothing romantic or idealizing about what death was necessary to recall to life a nation.

The avenging revolutionaries are as dreadful as those whom they overthrow. Dickens allots a single chapter to recounting the rape of the young peasant girl, Madame Defarge's sister, at Darnay's second trial when Defarge reads from the account of the affair which Dr. Manette had written in 1857. Only three chapters sketch the proud indifference to the suffering of the peasantry of Monseigneur St. Evremonde, Darnay's uncle, leading to his murder. The remaining French chapters unroll in all their gruesome predictability the equally barbarous French mobs of the Revolution. In other words, Dickens is more horrified by the sins of the Revolutionaries than by the sins of the aristocrats which give birth to revolution. Except for the Defarges, who are given names and more singular identities, the Revolutionaries are seen collectively, all of them named "Jacques." St. Antoine, a place name for a Paris suburb, is personified, given a collective identity. In the Carmagnole, the frenzied dance in the Paris streets which follows Darnay's acquittal in his first French trial, all identities merge into one destructive force. Finally, characters have identities not as persons but as awful functions in the Revolution, as in the case of Vengeance, who accompanies the Defarges.

With death and life so closely linked in the renewal theme, Dickens found a strategy for his presentation. He presents, beginning with the title, complementary and contradictory pairs of places, characters, events, and ideas. London and Paris, the former apparently a safe haven, the latter a hell, are more similar than they seem. Darnay is tried in both cities. The mob at Cly's "burial" is as frenzied as the ones in Paris. At the Manettes' apartment in Soho, a thunderstorm disrupts an outdoor Sunday dinner, driving the Manettes inside for safety while people hurry in the streets, their footsteps "the footsteps destined to come to all of us."

Characters are doubles of each other. Carton resembles Darnay, in the beginning physically but not morally, in the end reversed. Darnay himself, having renounced his birthright, is a ghost of the

What Do I Read Next?

- Simon Schama's *Citizens: A Chronicle of the French Revolution* (1989) is a modern account of the people and events of the French Revolution that show how the rational goals of the Revolution mix with irrational elements of the same period.

- *The Pickwick Papers* (first serialized 1836-1837), Charles Dickens's tremendously popular first novel, concentrates on the relationship between middle-class Mr. Pickwick and his lively Cockney servant Sam Weller.

- *A Christmas Carol, in Prose: Being a Ghost Story of Christmas* (1843) is Dickens's perennially popular story about how the spirits of Christmas turn an old miser's outlook back to humanity.

- Dickens's *Great Expectations* (1861) is the story of a young man's slow advancement in society against the backdrop of mid-Victorian England.

- *War and Peace* (1866) is Leo Tolstoy's study of Russian society during the period of the Napoleonic Wars and the French invasion of Russia.

Evremondes. Darnay's father and uncle are twins, indistinguishable in their awful pride. Dr. Manette has two selves, the imprisoned man who flees the horror of his imprisonment by reducing his life to work on a shoe bench, and the rescued man who several times regresses to his former self.

Even Dickens's style reflects his obsession with duality. The famous opening passage almost traps Dickens, like a repeated melody which he cannot stop:

> It was the best of times, it was the worst of times, it was the age of wisdom, it was the age of foolishness, it was the epoch of belief, it was the epoch of incredulity, it was the season of Light, it was the season of Darkness, it was the spring of hope, it was the winter of despair, we had everything before us, we had nothing before us, we were all going direct to

Heaven, we were all going direct the other way—in short, the period was so far like the present period, that some of its noisiest authorities insisted on its being received, for good or for evil, in the superlative degree of comparison only.

The key note struck is contradiction, but the passage also points to the similarity between the age of the French Revolution and Dickens's own. His story insists that all ages are one in the call of duty and the threat to civility and virtue. His most virtuous characters in the book—Lucie, Darnay, Carton, Manette, Lorry—are self-sacrificing, but, unlike the Revolutionaries, who insist on self-sacrifice for the sake of Revolution, Dickens's virtuous ones give of themselves for another individual. For Dickens the grand sweep of historical events is still dwarfed by the power of personal relationships in which life, death, and renewal are less ambiguous, as the Revolution disappears before Carton's final words: "It is a far, far better thing I do than any I have ever done; it is a far, far better rest I go to than any I have ever known." Dickens's apparent solution to the problem of a world so troubled that it spawns vengeful revolution is a call to a moral renewal in our personal relationships which would make such revolutions unnecessary.

Source: George V. Griffith, in an essay for *Novels for Students,* Gale, 1999.

Leonard Manheim

In the following excerpt, Manheim uses Lucy and Dr. Manette as examples of roles female and male characters play in A Tale of Two Cities.

Lucie is basically only one more in the line of Dickensian virgin-heroines whom the critic Edwin Pugh [in *The Charles Dickens Originals,* 1925] felicitously called "feminanities." Yet, as Professor Edgar Johnson clearly saw [in his book *Charles Dickens: His Tragedy and Triumph,* Vol. II, 1952], there was a subtle distinction.

> Lucie ... is given hardly any individual traits at all, although her appearance, as Dickens describes it, is like that of Ellen, "a short, slight, pretty figure, a quantity of golden hair, a pair of blue eyes," and it may be that her one unique physical characteristic was drawn from Ellen too: "a forehead with a singular capacity (remembering how young and smooth it was), of lifting and knitting itself into an expression that was not quite one of perplexity, or wonder, or alarm, though it included all the four expressions." ... The fact that Lucie and Dr. Manette at the time of his release from the Bastille are of almost the same age as Ellen and Dickens does not mean that the Doctor's feeling for his daughter is the emotion Dickens

felt for the pretty, blue-eyed actress, although the two merge perhaps in his fervent declaration [in his letter protesting the scandal, a letter which he "never meant to be published"] that he knows Ellen to be as "innocent and pure, and as good as my own dear daughter."

But Lucie fails to fit into the pattern of the unattainable dream-virgin of the earlier novels in at least one other respect. Most of Dickens' earlier heroine-ideals do not marry until the last-chapter summation of the "lived-happily-ever-after" pattern. Lucie is married, happily married, through much of the book. She maintains a household for her husband and her father, and she finds room for compassion, if not love, for the erring Carton. What is more, she has children, two of them. Yet she seems never to grow older. She was seventeen in 1775; she is, to all intents and purposes, seventeen in 1792. In the interim she has allegedly given birth to two Dickens-ideal infants, two of the most sickening little poppets we could possibly expect from one who, despite his experience as the father of ten children, still sought desperately to re-create infancy and childhood in an image which would affirm his own concept of unworldly innocence. Let the reader take a firm grip on himself and read the dying words of the little son of Charles and Lucie Darnay, who died in early childhood for no other reason, it must seem, than to give the author another opportunity to wallow in bathos.

> "Dear papa and mamma, I am very sorry to leave you both, and to leave my pretty sister; but I am called, and I must go!"

> ....

> "Poor Carton! Kiss him for me!"

Poor Carton, indeed! Poor Dickens! Little Lucie is not much better, for in Paris, after her father's condemnation, when her mother is mercifully unconscious and unaware of Carton's presence, she cries out in sweet childish innocence to friend Sydney:

> "Oh, Carton, Carton, dear Carton! ... Now that you have come, I think you will do something to help mamma, something to save papa! Oh, look at her, dear Carton! Can you, of all the people who love her bear to see her so?"

Out of the mouths of babes! At this point there is obviously nothing for Sydney to do but head straight for the nearest guillotine.

But Sydney is not to be left wholly without his own dream girl. Just as the purified Darnay is permitted to live out his life with the "attained" (and untainted) Lucie, so the dying Carton is accompanied to his execution by the virgin-victim, the innocent seamstress whom he solaces and strengthens until the final moments of their love-death, although her first glance had revealed that he was not the man Darnay whom she had previously admired.

Since the pattern of attainability is characteristic of the primary "virgin" in this novel, the figure of the *decayed virgin,* the older freak and enemy, is markedly absent from it. A few novels back, Dickens had had such characters in the immortal Sairey Gamp (*Martin Chuzzlewit*) and Mrs. Pipchin (*Dombey and Son*); he was to have the most horrifying of them all in his very next novel (*Great Expectations*) in the person of Miss Havisham. Here Miss Pross, although she has many of the elements of the "freak" in the best Dickensian tradition, is all benevolence, with her red-headed queerness overshadowed by her devoted love and affectionate care of the virgin-queen to whom she is a substitute mother, with no flaw except her unconquerable belief in the virtue and nobility of her erring brother Solomon. Just as she, the benevolent mother-protectress, is herself merely an aged virgin, so her counterpart and rival is the childless wife (also a devoted, albeit vindictive, sister), Thérèse Defarge. The word *rival* is used advisedly, for while there is no sign of overt rivalry between the two during nine-tenths of the novel, Dickens goes out of his way to bring them face to face at the end. He strains all of his plot structure to bring Mme. Defarge to the Manette dwelling on the day of the execution to have Miss Pross left there alone to face her. Then a melodramatic physical encounter ensues between the two women, neither of whom can, in any sense of the words, speak the other's language. Lucie's bad angel falls dead (accidentally, of course, by her own hand), but the good angel is not unscathed, and if, in her later life, her "queerness" is augmented by the ear-trumpet which she will no doubt use, yet all will know that she came by this crowning, though no doubt humorous, affliction in a good cause.

Although the category of mother-figure is limited, there is no lack of father-counterparts, for the law-as-father has become blended with the fear of condemnation by society, which thereby also becomes a symbolic father-figure. Society and its moral sanctions constitute the only fly in the ointment of adolescent happiness in a sinful love. We have noted that, as a propitiatory gesture, Charles's wicked father-enemy is not his father (as he well might have been) but his thoroughly aristocratic twin-uncle, who, being French, is more villainous than any British father-enemy might have been. Mr. Stryver, in his vampirish relationship with Carton,

is another figure of the worthless "father" who sucks the blood of his talented "son." And since Dickens almost always maintains a balance between evil and virtuous figures in all categories, we have, on the benevolent side, Mr. Lorry, another unmarried "father," the only living figure in the gallery of scarecrows who inhabit Tellson's Bank. Midway between the two classes is the hagridden Ernest Defarge, whose every attempt at benevolence is thwarted by his vengeful wife and her abettors, the allegorically named *Vengeance* and the members of the society of Jacques. This last-named group produces one brilliantly sketched psychopath, the sadistic, finger-chewing Jacques Three.

The one remaining father-figure is the most interesting, complex, and well-developed character in the whole novel, Dr. Manette. Since he could not have been much more than twenty-five years old when he was torn from his newly-wedded English wife to be imprisoned in the Bastille for nearly eighteen years, he must have been less than forty-five when we first met him in Defarge's garret. And Dickens, let it be remembered, was forty-five when he wrote of him. Here is his portrait:

> A broad ray of light fell into the garret, and showed the workman, with an unfinished shoe upon his lap, pausing in his labour. His few common tools and various scraps of leather were at his feet and on his bench. He had a white beard, raggedly cut, but not very long, a hollow face, and exceedingly bright eyes. The hollowness and thinness of his face would have caused them to look large, under his yet dark eyebrows and his confused white hair, though they had been really otherwise; but they were naturally large, and looked unnaturally so. His yellow rags of shirt lay open at the throat, and showed his body to be withered and worn.

Of course the appearance of great age in a middle-age man is rationally explained by the suffering entailed by his long, unjust imprisonment. Yet, nearly eighteen years later (the repetition of the number is meaningful), when he has become the unwitting agent of his son-in-law's destruction and has been unable to use his special influence to procure Charles' release, he is pictured as a decayed mass of senility.

"Who goes here? Whom have we within? Papers!"

The papers are handed out and read.

"Alexandre Manette. Physician. French. Which is he?"

"This is he;"

this helpless, inarticulately murmuring, wandering old man pointed out.

"Apparently the Citizen-Doctor is not in his right mind? The Revolution-fever will have been too much for him?"

Greatly too much for him. Carton envisions his complete recovery, but we have some difficulty in believing it.

In the interim, however, he is pictured as a stalwart, middle-aged medical practitioner. His sufferings have caused a period of amnesia, with occasional flashes of painful recollection, as in the scene in which he hears of the discovery of a stone marked D I G in a cell in the Tower of London. We never know, by the way, whether his recollection at this moment is complete and whether he has, even furtively, any recall of the existence of the document of denunciation found by M. Defarge. The aspects of conscious and repressed memory are here handled with great skill by Dickens. Generally, his amnesia is reciprocal; he cannot recall his normal life during the period of relapse, or vice versa, especially when his relapses are triggered by events and disclosures which bring up memories of his old wrongs. His reversion to shoemaking for a short time after Charles proposes marriage to Lucie and again for a longer time following Lucie's marriage and Charles's final revelation of his long-suspected identity foreshadow the great disclosure which is to make him the unwitting aggressor against the happiness of his loving and beloved daughter.

When we consider Dr. Manette's conduct, however, we find that, whether Dickens consciously intended it to be or not, the doctor of Beauvais is a good psychiatrist, at least in the handling of his own illness. His shoemaking is superficially pictured as a symptom of mental regression and decay, but in its inception it must have been a sign of rebellion against madness rather than a symptom thereof. He relates that he begged for permission to make shoes as a means of diverting his mind from its unendurable suffering. Shoemaking, truly an example of vocational therapy, was the only contact with reality that his distracted mind, otherwise cut off from reality, possessed. It was, therefore, a means of bringing about his recovery. Lucie fears the shoemaking, but she realizes that her loving presence, coupled with the availability, if needed, of the vocational contact with reality, will serve to draw him back to normal adjustment. It would seem, then, that the act of Mr. Lorry and Miss Pross, carried on furtively and guiltily, of destroying his shoemaker's bench and tools after his spontaneous recovery from the attack following Lucie's wedding, was a great error, an error against

which the doctor, giving an opinion in the anonymous presentation of his own case by Mr. Lorry, strongly advises. For when he once again falls into a state of amnesia and confusion, after the realization of the damage he has done to Charles and his impotence to remedy that damage, he calls for his bench and tools, but they are no longer to be had, and he huddles in a corner of the coach leaving Paris, a pitiful picture of mental decay from which we can see no hope of recovery despite the optimistic vision of Carton's last moments.

The basic aim of this paper has been, of course, psychological interpretation; but the psychological critic has sometimes been accused of neglecting the critical function of evaluation, and possibly a few concluding words might be added on that score.

In a lecture on criticism given at Harvard in 1947, E. M. Forster [as recorded by V. S. Pritchett in an article on E. M. Forster, published in the *New York Times Book Review,* December 29, 1968] distinguished beautifully between the function and method of creation and the function and method of criticism.

> What about the creative state? In it a man is taken out of himself. He lets down, as it were, a bucket into the unconscious and draws up something which is normally beyond his reach. He mixes this thing with his normal experience and out of the mixture he makes a work of art.... After this glance at the creative state, let us look at the critical. The critical state has many merits, and employs some of the highest and subtlest faculties of man. But it is grotesquely remote from the state responsible for the works it affects to expound. It does not let buckets down into the unconscious. It does not conceive in sleep or know what it has said after it has said it. Think before you speak, is criticism's motto; speak before you think is creation's. Nor is criticism disconcerted by people arriving from Porlock; in fact it sometimes comes from Porlock itself.

What Mr. Forster has set forth can best be understood in the light of the road which has been taken by psychological, particularly psychoanalytic, criticism in the more than twenty years which have elapsed since the delivery of that lecture in 1947. The psychoanalytic critic of today would like to think that he comes from Xanadu rather than Porlock. He cannot claim that he consistently writes before he thinks, but his thinking is to some extent based on material which the bucket lowered into the depths has brought up for him.

What can he say about the permanent literary value of the work which he is discussing? He cannot of course undertake to give any absolute final judgment; it will hardly be suitable for him to do what so many academic critics do, that is, to report the state of critical opinion in the "in-group" that usually passes critical judgment in academic circles. I have suggested elsewhere that the function of the psychoanalytic critic in evaluation is to prognosticate rather than to judge. I can do no better than to quote here my preferred authority, Norman Holland [as quoted from *The Dynamics of Literary Response,* 1968]:

> Saying a literary work is "good," then, from the point of view of our model, is predicting that it will pass the test of time; that it "can please many and please long"; that it is a widely satisfying form of play; or, more formally, that it embodies a fantasy with a power to disturb many readers over a long period of time and, built in, a defensive maneuver that will enable those readers to master the poem's disturbance.

A Tale of Two Cities does, it seems to me, give every indication, even apart from its past history, that it "can please many and please long." Its use of the dynamic scapegoat pattern with the employment of the pattern of multiple projection, which it has been my aim to point out in this essay, does indeed embody a fantasy, a fantasy which was disturbing to Dickens and is still undoubtedly disturbing to many readers, and has used that device of multiple projection as the defensive maneuver that enables readers to master that disturbance. In that sense, there seems to be little doubt about the continuance of the perennial popularity of this often maligned but still frequently read novel of Dickens' later period.

But all of that is really by the way. Criticism of the kind which I have attempted is designed to furnish information rather than critical judgment, even of a prognostic nature; it is the kind of criticism which was described by Arthur Symons in his introduction to the *Biographia Literaria* of Coleridge:

> The aim of criticism is to distinguish what is essential in the work of a writer. It is the delight of the critic to praise; but praise is scarcely part of his duty.... What we ask of him is that he should find out for us more than we can find out for ourselves.

Source: Leonard Manheim, "A Tale of Two Characters: A Study in Multiple Projection," in *Dickens Studies Annual,* 1970, pp. 225-37.

Jack Lindsay

In the following excerpt, Lindsay shows how events in Dickens' personal life strongly influenced the plot and characters of A Tale of Two Cities.

Charles Dickens was in a driven demoniac state of mind when the idea for *A Tale of Two Cities*

came to him. The bracelet he sent to Ellen Lawless Ternan had fallen into the hands of his wife Kate; and he was determined to end his marriage and to seduce Ellen. But he was in the midst of the rehearsals which had finally brought himself and Ellen together; and he could not pause to think. Amid Kate's tears, Forster's disapproval and a generally unnerving situation, he carried on in his furious possessed fashion, determined to have his own way and yet to keep his hold on the public; and in the midst of this spiritually and physically racked condition, as he was holding back his agony of mind by acting and producing *The Frozen Deep,* the central idea of the novel burst upon him.

So much we know from his own statement. It is clear then that we should be able to find the imprint of his ordeal, his tormented choice, in the novel. One would expect writers on his work to concentrate on this problem; but so abysmally low is the standard of Dickens criticism that no one has even seriously raised the question at all.

Where then is the imprint of the situation to be traced? By solving this point we can begin to understand what the novel itself is about, and the part it plays in Dickens' development. One general aspect of the selection of theme is at once obvious. The deep nature of the breach he is making with all customary acceptances is driving him to make a comprehensive effort to grasp history in a new way. So far (except for *Barnaby Rudge*) he has been content to use certain symbols to define his sense of basic historical conflict and movement. Yet all the while the influence of Carlyle, both in his *French Revolution* and his prophetic works like *Past and Present,* has been stirring him with the need for a direct statement of the historical issue as well as a symbolic one; and now, as he is coming close to a full confrontation of his opposition to all ruling Victorian values, he feels the need to set his story of conflicting wills in a manifestly revolutionary situation: that on which he had so long pondered as holding the clue to the crisis of his own world.

He had read and re-read Carlyle's history, till its theme and material were richly present in his mind; and now he wrote to the master asking for a loan of the cited authorities. The story goes that Carlyle jokingly sent him all his reference-books, 'about two cartloads.' And in the novel's preface Dickens wrote:

> It has been one of my hopes to add something to the popular and picturesque means of understanding that

terrible time, though no one can hope to add anything
to the philosophy of Mr. Carlyle's wonderful book.

But though this need to make a general re-
consideration of the nature of historical movement
and change was certainly central in the impulse that
Dickens felt, he had to fuse the overt theme with a
more immediately personal nexus of emotion and
imagery before it could take full grip of him. In the
midst of his domestic misery and frenzied play-act-
ing he did not feel simply an intellectual need to
revalue history. The desire to break through ob-
structions and to mate with Ellen could turn into
the desire to write about the French Revolution only
if some image or symbol made him feel a basic coincidence between his own experience and the Revolution. What then was this image?

It was that of the Imprisoned Man in the
Bastille. The Lost Man who has been jailed so long
that he has become an automaton of oppressed misery; who has forgotten even the source of his
wrong, the cause of his dehumanizing misery; who
needs to break out of the deadly darkness of stone
in order to become human again, to learn the truth
and regain love.

Here then is the core of the novel. The origi-
nally-intended title was *Recalled to Life*. Though
Dickens dropped this for the whole novel, he kept
it for the first part, and it expressed the originating
emotion of the story. *A Tale of Two Cities* is built
up from the episode of Dr. Manette's unjust imprisonment; and its whole working-out is concerned with the effects of that unjust deprivation of
light and joy: effects which entangle everyone
round the Doctor and recoil back on his own head
in unpredictable ways. The Doctor's fate is thus for
Dickens both a symbol of the Revolution, its deeds,
causes, and consequences, and of himself, immured
in a maddening cell of lies and cruelties, and seeking to break through into the truth, into a full and
happy relationship with his fellows. It was the de-
mented sense of environing pressures, of an unjust
inescapable mechanism, which caught Dickens up
in the midst of his wild mummery and gave him a
sense of release when he determined to write the
novel.

It has been pointed out (by T. A. Jackson) that
there is a close underlying similarity between the
plot of *A Tale* and that of *Little Dorrit* (the preceding novel in which Dickens had at last fully
marshalled his condemnation of Victorian society).
Both Dorrit and Manette are imprisoned for a score
of years; both are released by forces outside their
control and then continue tormented by their jail-

experience. Dorrit is haunted by fear of social exposure, which comes finally in the collapse of Mer-
dle (the exposure of the theft basic in the economic
system). Dorrit thus from one angle embodies
Dickens's deep fears of the past, fears of being exposed, fears of being driven back on the terrible
moment of loss which therefore threatens to return
in exacerbated form. He also embodies the bad conscience of a whole society which dares not contemplate truly its origins. But in Manette the symbolism goes much deeper. The experience of
oppressive misery has not merely twisted him, as
it twisted Dorrit; it has broken down the whole system of memory in his psyche. The problem then is:
What can restore consciousness? what can connect
the upper and the hidden levels of the mind again?
Manette is kept going by a blind exercise of the
craft learned in the cell of oppression, and only the
intrusion of events from the Revolution can bring
him back to an active consciousness and release
him from his obsession. But the drama of objecti-
fying in action the pattern of memory, the repeti-
tion-compulsion which must be broken, inevitably
brings its shocks, its apparent evocation of forces
as destructive as those working from the traumatic
level. The test lies in the way that evocation is
faced, the way it works out. So Manette finds that
the bitterness engendered by his sufferings as an
innocent wronged man has tangled him up in a net
(inside a larger reference of social action and reaction, guilt and innocence) from which escape is
possible only after a great sacrifice has been made.
The old must die for the new to be born; man cannot attain regeneration without accepting its sacri-
ficial aspect. In the story this appears in the struggle between Darnay and Carton for Manette's
daughter, and the solution that mates Darnay and
the girl, yet sends Carton to a regeneration in death.

In this dire tangle of moral consequences we
see Dickens confronting his own confused situation and trying to equate his own moment of painful
compelled choice with the revolutionary moment
in which a definite break is made with the old, amid
violent birthpangs, and makes possible the rebirth
of life, the renewal of love and innocence.

The lacerated and divided state of Dickens's
emotions at this moment of choice is revealed by
the device of having two heroes who are practically
twins in appearance and who love the same girl.
Both Carton and Darnay are generous fellows, but
one is morally well-organized, the other is feck-
lessly a misfit. The latter, however, by his devoted
death reaches the same level of heroic generosity
as his rival; indeed goes higher. His gesture of re-

nunciation completes the ravages of the Revolution with its ruthless justice, and transforms them into acts of purification and redemption, without which the life of renewed love would not be possible.

Thus, in the story, Dickens gets the satisfaction of nobly giving up the girl and yet mating with her. He splits himself in the moment of choice, dies, and yet lives to marry the beloved, from whom the curse born out of a tainted and divided society is at last removed. And at the same time he is Manette, the man breaking out of a long prison-misery, who seeks only truth and justice, and whose submerged memory-drama projects itself as both the Carton-Darnay conflict and the socially-impinging dilemma that disrupts and yet solves that conflict.

There are thus a number of ambivalences in the story; and Dickens shows himself divided in his attitude to the Revolution itself. His petty-bourgeois fear of mass-movements is still alive; but the fascination of such movements, which stirred so strongly in *Barnaby,* is even keener than the fear. On the one hand he clings to the moral thesis to defend the Revolution: the Old Regime was vilely cruel and bestialized people, it could not but provoke excesses in return as the bonds slipped. But this thesis, to which Carlyle had sought to give a grandiose religious tang, now merges for Dickens with a deeper acceptance:

> Crush humanity out of shape once more under similar hammers and it will twist itself into the same tortured forms. Sow the same seed of rapacious license and oppression over again and it will surely yield the same fruit according to its kind.

> Six tumbrils roll along the streets. Change these back again to what they were, thou powerful enchanter Time, and they shall be seen to be the carriages of absolute monarchs, the equipages of feudal nobles, the toilets of flaring Jezebels, the churches that are not my Father's house but dens of thieves, the huts of millions of starving peasants.

This passage begins with the simple moral statement; but the tumbrils, conjured up as mere counterpoises to the feudal carriages, become emblems of a great purification sweeping away the reign of the old iniquity. They express a ruthless *transformation* of society and are far more than an allegory of cruel tit-for-tat. Rather, they appear as forces of triumphant righteousness.

Throughout the book there runs this ambivalent attitude to the Revolution, shuddering, yet inclining to a deep and thorough acceptance. Not a blank-cheque acceptance, but one based on the subtle dialectics of conflict revealed by the story of Manette. For that story, symbolizing the whole crisis and defining its tensions in the depths of the spirit, makes a serious effort to work out the process of change, the rhythms of give-and-take, the involved struggles with their many inversions and opposed refractions, the ultimate resolution in death and love, in the renewal of life.

The working-out of the clash of forces is in fact more thoroughly done than in any previous work of Dickens. The weakness lies in the comparative thinness of characterization. The strain of grasping and holding intact the complex skein of the story is too much for Dickens at this difficult moment of growth. But his instinct is, as always, right. He needed this strenuous effort to get outside himself: no other way could he master the difficult moment and rebuild his foundations. After it he could return to the attack on the contemporary world with a new sureness, with new thews of drama, with new breadths of comprehension. The great works, *Great Expectations* and *Our Mutual Friend,* were made possible. (I am not here dealing with those works; but it is interesting to note that the imprisonment-theme finds its completion in the contrasted and entangled themes of Miss Havisham and the old convict, the self-imposed prison of the traumatic moment and the socially-imposed prison of the criminal impulse, both merging to express the compulsions of an acquisitive society.)

A Tale is not a successful work like the two novels that followed it, but they would never have been written without it. An inner strain appears in the rigidity of tension between the thematic structure and the release of character-fantasy. Such persons as Manette, however, show a new persistence of psychological analysis, and the Defarges show what untapped sources of dramatic force Dickens could yet draw on. The final falsification of the book's meaning came about through the melodrama based on its material, in which the emphasis put on Carton sentimentalized away all the profundities.

Lucie is meant to represent Ellen Ternan; but at this stage Dickens knows very little about the real Ellen, and Lucie is therefore a stock-heroine. Charles Darnay, the winning lover, has the revealing initials *Charles D.* Dickens with his love of name-meanings can seldom resist leaving at least one or two such daydream-admissions among the names of a novel. Ellen was acting as Lucy in *The Frozen Deep* at the time when the novel's idea came.

Source: Jack Lindsay, "*A Tale of Two Cities,*" in *Life and Letters,* September, 1949, pp. 191-204.

Sources

Ruth Glancy, *A Tale of Two Cities: Dickens's Revolutionary Novel,* Boston, MA: Twayne Publishers, 1991.

Norman Page, "Introduction," *A Tale of Two Cities* by Charles Dickens, edited by Norman Page, Rutland, VT: Charles E. Tuttle Co., Inc., 1994, pp. xxiii-xxxii.

Sir James Fitzjames Stephen, *A Tale of Two Cities, Saturday Review,* December 17, 1859, pp. 741-43; reprinted in *The Dickens Critics,* edited by George H. Ford and Lauriat Lane, Jr., Ithaca, NY: Cornell University Press, 1961, pp. 38-46.

For Further Study

Cates Baldridge, "Alternatives to Bourgeois Individualism in *A Tale of Two Cities,*" *Studies in English Literature, 1500-1900,* Vol. 30, Autumn, 1990, pp. 633-54.

A Marxist reading which sees the book as sympathetic to the collectivist ideology of the Revolution.

Thomas Carlyle, *The French Revolution: A History,* 2 volumes, Boston, MA: Little, Brown, 1838.

This work by the famous Victorian author and critic is traditionally credited with providing the inspiration for Dickens's scenes of Revolutionary life in France during the period covered in *A Tale of Two Cities.*

Dickens Studies Annual, Vol. 12, Southern Illinois University Press, 1983.

A collection of essay ranging across an array of topics about the novel.

John Drinkwater, "The Grand Manner: Thoughts upon *A Tale of Two Cities,*" *Essays of the Year,* London: Argonaut, 1929-1930, pp. 3-14.

In this essay, Drinkwater examines the manner in which *A Tale of Two Cities* reveals Dickens's creative talent.

K. J. Fielding, "Separation—and *A Tale of Two Cities,*" *Charles Dickens: A Critical Introduction,* London: Longmans, Green, 1958, pp. 154-68.

A biographical essay that examines the similarities between Dickens's own failing marriage and the separation and loneliness of Dr. Manette.

Lawrence Frank, *Charles Dickens and the Romantic Self,* University of Nebraska Press, 1974.

Sees Darnay, not Carton, as the novel's focus and relates the character to Dickens's life.

—— "Dickens's *A Tale of Two Cities:* The Poetics of Impasse," *American Imago,* Volume 36 (1979), pp. 215-44; reprinted under title "The Poetics of Impasse," *Charles Dickens and the Romantic Self* by Lawrence Frank, Lincoln, NE: University of Nebraska Press, 1984, pp. 124-50.

Frank looks at the characters of Sidney Carton and Charles Darnay in *A Tale of Two Cities* psychoanalytically, seeing Carton as Darnay's doppelganger trying to bring the Frenchman to be aware of his guilty feelings toward Dr. Manette.

Barton R. Friedman, "Antihistory: Dickens's *A Tale of Two Cities,*" in *Fabricating History: English Writers on the French Revolution,* Princeton, NJ: Princeton University Press, 1988, pp. 145-71.

Friedman provides a useful guide to further criticism of Dickens's novel and draws parallels between the work and the genre of the Gothic Romance.

Michael Goldberg, *Carlyle and Dickens,* University of Georgia Press, 1973.

Analyzes the influence of Carlyle and his *The French Revolution* on Dickens.

Albert D. Hutter, "Nation and Generation in *A Tale of Two Cities,*" *PMLA,* Vol. 93, May, 1978, pp. 748-62.

A psychological reading in which the clash of aristocrats of the *ancien regime* and the revolutionaries is also a clash of parents and children.

Leonard Manheim, "A Tale of Two Characters: A Study in Multiple Projection," in *Dickens Studies Annual, Vol. I,* edited by Robert B. Partlow, Jr., Southern Illinois University Press, pp. 225-27.

Relates Darnay and Carton biographically to Dickens, viewing them as projections of Dickens's idealized self.

Andrew Sanders, *The Companion to* A Tale of Two Cities, Unwin Hyman, Ltd., 1988.

Chronologically arranged annotations to allusions in the novel likely not to be known by modern readers.

Glossary of Literary Terms

A

Abstract: As an adjective applied to writing or literary works, abstract refers to words or phrases that name things not knowable through the five senses.

Aestheticism: A literary and artistic movement of the nineteenth century. Followers of the movement believed that art should not be mixed with social, political, or moral teaching. The statement "art for art's sake" is a good summary of aestheticism. The movement had its roots in France, but it gained widespread importance in England in the last half of the nineteenth century, where it helped change the Victorian practice of including moral lessons in literature.

Allegory: A narrative technique in which characters representing things or abstract ideas are used to convey a message or teach a lesson. Allegory is typically used to teach moral, ethical, or religious lessons but is sometimes used for satiric or political purposes.

Allusion: A reference to a familiar literary or historical person or event, used to make an idea more easily understood.

Analogy: A comparison of two things made to explain something unfamiliar through its similarities to something familiar, or to prove one point based on the acceptedness of another. Similes and metaphors are types of analogies.

Antagonist: The major character in a narrative or drama who works against the hero or protagonist.

Anthropomorphism: The presentation of animals or objects in human shape or with human characteristics. The term is derived from the Greek word for "human form."

Antihero: A central character in a work of literature who lacks traditional heroic qualities such as courage, physical prowess, and fortitude. Antiheroes typically distrust conventional values and are unable to commit themselves to any ideals. They generally feel helpless in a world over which they have no control. Antiheroes usually accept, and often celebrate, their positions as social outcasts.

Apprenticeship Novel: See *Bildungsroman*

Archetype: The word archetype is commonly used to describe an original pattern or model from which all other things of the same kind are made. This term was introduced to literary criticism from the psychology of Carl Jung. It expresses Jung's theory that behind every person's "unconscious," or repressed memories of the past, lies the "collective unconscious" of the human race: memories of the countless typical experiences of our ancestors. These memories are said to prompt illogical associations that trigger powerful emotions in the reader. Often, the emotional process is primitive, even primordial. Archetypes are the literary images that grow out of the "collective unconscious." They appear in literature as incidents and plots that repeat basic patterns of life. They may also appear as stereotyped characters.

Avant-garde: French term meaning "vanguard." It is used in literary criticism to describe new writing that rejects traditional approaches to literature in favor of innovations in style or content.

B

Beat Movement: A period featuring a group of American poets and novelists of the 1950s and 1960s—including Jack Kerouac, Allen Ginsberg, Gregory Corso, William S. Burroughs, and Lawrence Ferlinghetti—who rejected established social and literary values. Using such techniques as stream of consciousness writing and jazz-influenced free verse and focusing on unusual or abnormal states of mind—generated by religious ecstasy or the use of drugs—the Beat writers aimed to create works that were unconventional in both form and subject matter.

Bildungsroman: A German word meaning "novel of development." The *bildungsroman* is a study of the maturation of a youthful character, typically brought about through a series of social or sexual encounters that lead to self-awareness. *Bildungsroman* is used interchangeably with *erziehungsroman,* a novel of initiation and education. When a *bildungsroman* is concerned with the development of an artist (as in James Joyce's *A Portrait of the Artist as a Young Man*), it is often termed a *kunstlerroman.* Also known as Apprenticeship Novel, Coming of Age Novel, *Erziehungsroman,* or *Kunstlerroman.*

Black Aesthetic Movement: A period of artistic and literary development among African Americans in the 1960s and early 1970s. This was the first major African-American artistic movement since the Harlem Renaissance and was closely paralleled by the civil rights and black power movements. The black aesthetic writers attempted to produce works of art that would be meaningful to the black masses. Key figures in black aesthetics included one of its founders, poet and playwright Amiri Baraka, formerly known as LeRoi Jones; poet and essayist Haki R. Madhubuti, formerly Don L. Lee; poet and playwright Sonia Sanchez; and dramatist Ed Bullins. Also known as Black Arts Movement.

Black Humor: Writing that places grotesque elements side by side with humorous ones in an attempt to shock the reader, forcing him or her to laugh at the horrifying reality of a disordered world. Also known as Black Comedy.

Burlesque: Any literary work that uses exaggeration to make its subject appear ridiculous, either by treating a trivial subject with profound seriousness or by treating a dignified subject frivolously. The word "burlesque" may also be used as an adjective, as in "burlesque show," to mean "striptease act."

C

Character: Broadly speaking, a person in a literary work. The actions of characters are what constitute the plot of a story, novel, or poem. There are numerous types of characters, ranging from simple, stereotypical figures to intricate, multifaceted ones. In the techniques of anthropomorphism and personification, animals—and even places or things—can assume aspects of character. "Characterization" is the process by which an author creates vivid, believable characters in a work of art. This may be done in a variety of ways, including (1) direct description of the character by the narrator; (2) the direct presentation of the speech, thoughts, or actions of the character; and (3) the responses of other characters to the character. The term "character" also refers to a form originated by the ancient Greek writer Theophrastus that later became popular in the seventeenth and eighteenth centuries. It is a short essay or sketch of a person who prominently displays a specific attribute or quality, such as miserliness or ambition.

Climax: The turning point in a narrative, the moment when the conflict is at its most intense. Typically, the structure of stories, novels, and plays is one of rising action, in which tension builds to the climax, followed by falling action, in which tension lessens as the story moves to its conclusion.

Colloquialism: A word, phrase, or form of pronunciation that is acceptable in casual conversation but not in formal, written communication. It is considered more acceptable than slang.

Coming of Age Novel: See *Bildungsroman*

Concrete: Concrete is the opposite of abstract, and refers to a thing that actually exists or a description that allows the reader to experience an object or concept with the senses.

Connotation: The impression that a word gives beyond its defined meaning. Connotations may be universally understood or may be significant only to a certain group.

Convention: Any widely accepted literary device, style, or form.

D

Denotation: The definition of a word, apart from the impressions or feelings it creates (connotations) in the reader.

Denouement: A French word meaning "the unknotting." In literary criticism, it denotes the resolution of conflict in fiction or drama. The *denouement* follows the climax and provides an outcome to the primary plot situation as well as an explanation of secondary plot complications. The *denouement* often involves a character's recognition of his or her state of mind or moral condition. Also known as Falling Action.

Description: Descriptive writing is intended to allow a reader to picture the scene or setting in which the action of a story takes place. The form this description takes often evokes an intended emotional response—a dark, spooky graveyard will evoke fear, and a peaceful, sunny meadow will evoke calmness.

Dialogue: In its widest sense, dialogue is simply conversation between people in a literary work; in its most restricted sense, it refers specifically to the speech of characters in a drama. As a specific literary genre, a "dialogue" is a composition in which characters debate an issue or idea.

Diction: The selection and arrangement of words in a literary work. Either or both may vary depending on the desired effect. There are four general types of diction: "formal," used in scholarly or lofty writing; "informal," used in relaxed but educated conversation; "colloquial," used in everyday speech; and "slang," containing newly coined words and other terms not accepted in formal usage.

Didactic: A term used to describe works of literature that aim to teach some moral, religious, political, or practical lesson. Although didactic elements are often found in artistically pleasing works, the term "didactic" usually refers to literature in which the message is more important than the form. The term may also be used to criticize a work that the critic finds "overly didactic," that is, heavy-handed in its delivery of a lesson.

Doppelganger: A literary technique by which a character is duplicated (usually in the form of an alter ego, though sometimes as a ghostly counterpart) or divided into two distinct, usually opposite personalities. The use of this character device is widespread in nineteenth- and twentieth-century literature, and indicates a growing awareness among authors that the "self" is really a composite of many "selves." Also known as The Double.

Double Entendre: A corruption of a French phrase meaning "double meaning." The term is used to indicate a word or phrase that is deliberately ambiguous, especially when one of the meanings is risqué or improper.

Dramatic Irony: Occurs when the audience of a play or the reader of a work of literature knows something that a character in the work itself does not know. The irony is in the contrast between the intended meaning of the statements or actions of a character and the additional information understood by the audience.

Dystopia: An imaginary place in a work of fiction where the characters lead dehumanized, fearful lives.

E

Edwardian: Describes cultural conventions identified with the period of the reign of Edward VII of England (1901-1910). Writers of the Edwardian Age typically displayed a strong reaction against the propriety and conservatism of the Victorian Age. Their work often exhibits distrust of authority in religion, politics, and art and expresses strong doubts about the soundness of conventional values.

Empathy: A sense of shared experience, including emotional and physical feelings, with someone or something other than oneself. Empathy is often used to describe the response of a reader to a literary character.

Enlightenment, The: An eighteenth-century philosophical movement. It began in France but had a wide impact throughout Europe and America. Thinkers of the Enlightenment valued reason and believed that both the individual and society could achieve a state of perfection. Corresponding to this essentially humanist vision was a resistance to religious authority.

Epigram: A saying that makes the speaker's point quickly and concisely. Often used to preface a novel.

Epilogue: A concluding statement or section of a literary work. In dramas, particularly those of the seventeenth and eighteenth centuries, the epilogue is a closing speech, often in verse, delivered by an actor at the end of a play and spoken directly to the audience.

Epiphany: A sudden revelation of truth inspired by a seemingly trivial incident.

Episode: An incident that forms part of a story and is significantly related to it. Episodes may be either self-contained narratives or events that depend on a larger context for their sense and importance.

Epistolary Novel: A novel in the form of letters. The form was particularly popular in the eighteenth century.

Epithet: A word or phrase, often disparaging or abusive, that expresses a character trait of someone or something.

Existentialism: A predominantly twentieth-century philosophy concerned with the nature and perception of human existence. There are two major strains of existentialist thought: atheistic and Christian. Followers of atheistic existentialism believe that the individual is alone in a godless universe and that the basic human condition is one of suffering and loneliness. Nevertheless, because there are no fixed values, individuals can create their own characters—indeed, they can shape themselves—through the exercise of free will. The atheistic strain culminates in and is popularly associated with the works of Jean-Paul Sartre. The Christian existentialists, on the other hand, believe that only in God may people find freedom from life's anguish. The two strains hold certain beliefs in common: that existence cannot be fully understood or described through empirical effort; that anguish is a universal element of life; that individuals must bear responsibility for their actions; and that there is no common standard of behavior or perception for religious and ethical matters.

Expatriates: See *Expatriatism*

Expatriatism: The practice of leaving one's country to live for an extended period in another country.

Exposition: Writing intended to explain the nature of an idea, thing, or theme. Expository writing is often combined with description, narration, or argument. In dramatic writing, the exposition is the introductory material which presents the characters, setting, and tone of the play.

Expressionism: An indistinct literary term, originally used to describe an early twentieth-century school of German painting. The term applies to almost any mode of unconventional, highly subjective writing that distorts reality in some way.

F

Fable: A prose or verse narrative intended to convey a moral. Animals or inanimate objects with human characteristics often serve as characters in fables.

Falling Action: See *Denouement*

Fantasy: A literary form related to mythology and folklore. Fantasy literature is typically set in non-existent realms and features supernatural beings.

Farce: A type of comedy characterized by broad humor, outlandish incidents, and often vulgar subject matter.

***Femme fatale*:** A French phrase with the literal translation "fatal woman." A *femme fatale* is a sensuous, alluring woman who often leads men into danger or trouble.

Fiction: Any story that is the product of imagination rather than a documentation of fact. Characters and events in such narratives may be based in real life but their ultimate form and configuration is a creation of the author.

Figurative Language: A technique in writing in which the author temporarily interrupts the order, construction, or meaning of the writing for a particular effect. This interruption takes the form of one or more figures of speech such as hyperbole, irony, or simile. Figurative language is the opposite of literal language, in which every word is truthful, accurate, and free of exaggeration or embellishment.

Figures of Speech: Writing that differs from customary conventions for construction, meaning, order, or significance for the purpose of a special meaning or effect. There are two major types of figures of speech: rhetorical figures, which do not make changes in the meaning of the words, and tropes, which do.

***Fin de siecle*:** A French term meaning "end of the century." The term is used to denote the last decade of the nineteenth century, a transition period when writers and other artists abandoned old conventions and looked for new techniques and objectives.

First Person: See *Point of View*

Flashback: A device used in literature to present action that occurred before the beginning of the story. Flashbacks are often introduced as the dreams or recollections of one or more characters.

Foil: A character in a work of literature whose physical or psychological qualities contrast strongly with, and therefore highlight, the corresponding qualities of another character.

Folklore: Traditions and myths preserved in a culture or group of people. Typically, these are passed on by word of mouth in various forms—such as legends, songs, and proverbs—or preserved in customs and ceremonies. This term was first used by W. J. Thoms in 1846.

Folktale: A story originating in oral tradition. Folktales fall into a variety of categories, including legends, ghost stories, fairy tales, fables, and anecdotes based on historical figures and events.

Foreshadowing: A device used in literature to create expectation or to set up an explanation of later developments.

Form: The pattern or construction of a work which identifies its genre and distinguishes it from other genres.

G

Genre: A category of literary work. In critical theory, genre may refer to both the content of a given work—tragedy, comedy, pastoral—and to its form, such as poetry, novel, or drama.

Gilded Age: A period in American history during the 1870s characterized by political corruption and materialism. A number of important novels of social and political criticism were written during this time.

Gothicism: In literary criticism, works characterized by a taste for the medieval or morbidly attractive. A gothic novel prominently features elements of horror, the supernatural, gloom, and violence: clanking chains, terror, charnel houses, ghosts, medieval castles, and mysteriously slamming doors. The term "gothic novel" is also applied to novels that lack elements of the traditional Gothic setting but that create a similar atmosphere of terror or dread.

Grotesque: In literary criticism, the subject matter of a work or a style of expression characterized by exaggeration, deformity, freakishness, and disorder. The grotesque often includes an element of comic absurdity.

H

Harlem Renaissance: The Harlem Renaissance of the 1920s is generally considered the first significant movement of black writers and artists in the United States. During this period, new and established black writers published more fiction and poetry than ever before, the first influential black literary journals were established, and black authors and artists received their first widespread recognition and serious critical appraisal. Among the major writers associated with this period are Claude McKay, Jean Toomer, Countee Cullen, Langston Hughes, Arna Bontemps, Nella Larsen, and Zora Neale Hurston. Also known as Negro Renaissance and New Negro Movement.

Hero/Heroine: The principal sympathetic character (male or female) in a literary work. Heroes and heroines typically exhibit admirable traits: idealism, courage, and integrity, for example.

Holocaust Literature: Literature influenced by or written about the Holocaust of World War II. Such literature includes true stories of survival in concentration camps, escape, and life after the war, as well as fictional works and poetry.

Humanism: A philosophy that places faith in the dignity of humankind and rejects the medieval perception of the individual as a weak, fallen creature. "Humanists" typically believe in the perfectibility of human nature and view reason and education as the means to that end.

Hyperbole: In literary criticism, deliberate exaggeration used to achieve an effect.

I

Idiom: A word construction or verbal expression closely associated with a given language.

Image: A concrete representation of an object or sensory experience. Typically, such a representation helps evoke the feelings associated with the object or experience itself. Images are either "literal" or "figurative." Literal images are especially concrete and involve little or no extension of the obvious meaning of the words used to express them. Figurative images do not follow the literal meaning of the words exactly. Images in literature are usually visual, but the term "image" can also refer to the representation of any sensory experience.

Imagery: The array of images in a literary work. Also, figurative language.

***In medias res*:** A Latin term meaning "in the middle of things." It refers to the technique of beginning a story at its midpoint and then using various flashback devices to reveal previous action.

Interior Monologue: A narrative technique in which characters' thoughts are revealed in a way that appears to be uncontrolled by the author. The interior monologue typically aims to reveal the inner self of a character. It portrays emotional experiences as they occur at both a conscious and unconscious level. Images are often used to represent sensations or emotions.

Irony: In literary criticism, the effect of language in which the intended meaning is the opposite of what is stated.

J

Jargon: Language that is used or understood only by a select group of people. Jargon may refer to terminology used in a certain profession, such as computer jargon, or it may refer to any non-sensical language that is not understood by most people.

L

Leitmotiv: See *Motif*

Literal Language: An author uses literal language when he or she writes without exaggerating or embellishing the subject matter and without any tools of figurative language.

Lost Generation: A term first used by Gertrude Stein to describe the post-World War I generation of American writers: men and women haunted by a sense of betrayal and emptiness brought about by the destructiveness of the war.

M

Mannerism: Exaggerated, artificial adherence to a literary manner or style. Also, a popular style of the visual arts of late sixteenth-century Europe that was marked by elongation of the human form and by intentional spatial distortion. Literary works that are self-consciously high-toned and artistic are often said to be "mannered."

Metaphor: A figure of speech that expresses an idea through the image of another object. Metaphors suggest the essence of the first object by identifying it with certain qualities of the second object.

Modernism: Modern literary practices. Also, the principles of a literary school that lasted from roughly the beginning of the twentieth century until the end of World War II. Modernism is defined by its rejection of the literary conventions of the nineteenth century and by its opposition to conventional morality, taste, traditions, and economic values.

Mood: The prevailing emotions of a work or of the author in his or her creation of the work. The mood of a work is not always what might be expected based on its subject matter.

Motif: A theme, character type, image, metaphor, or other verbal element that recurs throughout a single work of literature or occurs in a number of different works over a period of time. Also known as *Motiv* or *Leitmotiv*.

Myth: An anonymous tale emerging from the traditional beliefs of a culture or social unit. Myths use supernatural explanations for natural phenomena. They may also explain cosmic issues like creation and death. Collections of myths, known as mythologies, are common to all cultures and nations, but the best-known myths belong to the Norse, Roman, and Greek mythologies.

N

Narration: The telling of a series of events, real or invented. A narration may be either a simple narrative, in which the events are recounted chronologically, or a narrative with a plot, in which the account is given in a style reflecting the author's artistic concept of the story. Narration is sometimes used as a synonym for "storyline."

Narrative: A verse or prose accounting of an event or sequence of events, real or invented. The term is also used as an adjective in the sense "method of narration." For example, in literary criticism, the expression "narrative technique" usually refers to the way the author structures and presents his or her story.

Narrator: The teller of a story. The narrator may be the author or a character in the story through whom the author speaks.

Naturalism: A literary movement of the late nineteenth and early twentieth centuries. The movement's major theorist, French novelist Emile Zola, envisioned a type of fiction that would examine human life with the objectivity of scientific inquiry. The Naturalists typically viewed human beings as either the products of "biological determinism," ruled by hereditary instincts and engaged in an endless struggle for survival, or as the products of "socioeconomic determinism," ruled by social and economic forces beyond their control. In their works, the Naturalists generally ignored the highest levels of society and focused on degradation: poverty, alcoholism, prostitution, insanity, and disease.

Noble Savage: The idea that primitive man is noble and good but becomes evil and corrupted as he becomes civilized. The concept of the noble savage originated in the Renaissance period but is more closely identified with such later writers as

Jean-Jacques Rousseau and Aphra Behn. See also Primitivism.

Novel of Ideas: A novel in which the examination of intellectual issues and concepts takes precedence over characterization or a traditional storyline.

Novel of Manners: A novel that examines the customs and mores of a cultural group.

Novel: A long fictional narrative written in prose, which developed from the novella and other early forms of narrative. A novel is usually organized under a plot or theme with a focus on character development and action.

Novella: An Italian term meaning "story." This term has been especially used to describe fourteenth-century Italian tales, but it also refers to modern short novels.

O

Objective Correlative: An outward set of objects, a situation, or a chain of events corresponding to an inward experience and evoking this experience in the reader. The term frequently appears in modern criticism in discussions of authors' intended effects on the emotional responses of readers.

Objectivity: A quality in writing characterized by the absence of the author's opinion or feeling about the subject matter. Objectivity is an important factor in criticism.

Oedipus Complex: A son's amorous obsession with his mother. The phrase is derived from the story of the ancient Theban hero Oedipus, who unknowingly killed his father and married his mother.

Omniscience: See *Point of View*

Onomatopoeia: The use of words whose sounds express or suggest their meaning. In its simplest sense, onomatopoeia may be represented by words that mimic the sounds they denote such as "hiss" or "meow." At a more subtle level, the pattern and rhythm of sounds and rhymes of a line or poem may be onomatopoeic.

Oxymoron: A phrase combining two contradictory terms. Oxymorons may be intentional or unintentional.

P

Parable: A story intended to teach a moral lesson or answer an ethical question.

Paradox: A statement that appears illogical or contradictory at first, but may actually point to an underlying truth.

Parallelism: A method of comparison of two ideas in which each is developed in the same grammatical structure.

Parody: In literary criticism, this term refers to an imitation of a serious literary work or the signature style of a particular author in a ridiculous manner. A typical parody adopts the style of the original and applies it to an inappropriate subject for humorous effect. Parody is a form of satire and could be considered the literary equivalent of a caricature or cartoon.

Pastoral: A term derived from the Latin word "pastor," meaning shepherd. A pastoral is a literary composition on a rural theme. The conventions of the pastoral were originated by the third-century Greek poet Theocritus, who wrote about the experiences, love affairs, and pastimes of Sicilian shepherds. In a pastoral, characters and language of a courtly nature are often placed in a simple setting. The term pastoral is also used to classify dramas, elegies, and lyrics that exhibit the use of country settings and shepherd characters.

Pen Name: See *Pseudonym*

Persona: A Latin term meaning "mask." *Personae* are the characters in a fictional work of literature. The *persona* generally functions as a mask through which the author tells a story in a voice other than his or her own. A *persona* is usually either a character in a story who acts as a narrator or an "implied author," a voice created by the author to act as the narrator for himself or herself.

Personification: A figure of speech that gives human qualities to abstract ideas, animals, and inanimate objects. Also known as *Prosopopoeia*.

Picaresque Novel: Episodic fiction depicting the adventures of a roguish central character ("picaro" is Spanish for "rogue"). The picaresque hero is commonly a low-born but clever individual who wanders into and out of various affairs of love, danger, and farcical intrigue. These involvements may take place at all social levels and typically present a humorous and wide-ranging satire of a given society.

Plagiarism: Claiming another person's written material as one's own. Plagiarism can take the form of direct, word-for-word copying or the theft of the substance or idea of the work.

Plot: In literary criticism, this term refers to the pattern of events in a narrative or drama. In its simplest sense, the plot guides the author in composing the work and helps the reader follow the work. Typically, plots exhibit causality and unity and have a beginning, a middle, and an end. Sometimes, however, a plot may consist of a series of disconnected events, in which case it is known as an "episodic plot."

Poetic Justice: An outcome in a literary work, not necessarily a poem, in which the good are rewarded and the evil are punished, especially in ways that particularly fit their virtues or crimes.

Poetic License: Distortions of fact and literary convention made by a writer—not always a poet—for the sake of the effect gained. Poetic license is closely related to the concept of "artistic freedom."

Poetics: This term has two closely related meanings. It denotes (1) an aesthetic theory in literary criticism about the essence of poetry or (2) rules prescribing the proper methods, content, style, or diction of poetry. The term poetics may also refer to theories about literature in general, not just poetry.

Point of View: The narrative perspective from which a literary work is presented to the reader. There are four traditional points of view. The "third person omniscient" gives the reader a "godlike" perspective, unrestricted by time or place, from which to see actions and look into the minds of characters. This allows the author to comment openly on characters and events in the work. The "third person" point of view presents the events of the story from outside of any single character's perception, much like the omniscient point of view, but the reader must understand the action as it takes place and without any special insight into characters' minds or motivations. The "first person" or "personal" point of view relates events as they are perceived by a single character. The main character "tells" the story and may offer opinions about the action and characters which differ from those of the author. Much less common than omniscient, third person, and first person is the "second person" point of view, wherein the author tells the story as if it is happening to the reader.

Polemic: A work in which the author takes a stand on a controversial subject, such as abortion or religion. Such works are often extremely argumentative or provocative.

Pornography: Writing intended to provoke feelings of lust in the reader. Such works are often condemned by critics and teachers, but those which can be shown to have literary value are viewed less harshly.

Post-Aesthetic Movement: An artistic response made by African Americans to the black aesthetic movement of the 1960s and early '70s. Writers since that time have adopted a somewhat different tone in their work, with less emphasis placed on the disparity between black and white in the United States. In the words of post-aesthetic authors such as Toni Morrison, John Edgar Wideman, and Kristin Hunter, African Americans are portrayed as looking inward for answers to their own questions, rather than always looking to the outside world.

Postmodernism: Writing from the 1960s forward characterized by experimentation and continuing to apply some of the fundamentals of modernism, which included existentialism and alienation. Postmodernists have gone a step further in the rejection of tradition begun with the modernists by also rejecting traditional forms, preferring the anti-novel over the novel and the antihero over the hero.

Primitivism: The belief that primitive peoples were nobler and less flawed than civilized peoples because they had not been subjected to the tainting influence of society. See also Noble Savage.

Prologue: An introductory section of a literary work. It often contains information establishing the situation of the characters or presents information about the setting, time period, or action. In drama, the prologue is spoken by a chorus or by one of the principal characters.

Prose: A literary medium that attempts to mirror the language of everyday speech. It is distinguished from poetry by its use of unmetered, unrhymed language consisting of logically related sentences. Prose is usually grouped into paragraphs that form a cohesive whole such as an essay or a novel.

Prosopopoeia: See *Personification*

Protagonist: The central character of a story who serves as a focus for its themes and incidents and as the principal rationale for its development. The protagonist is sometimes referred to in discussions of modern literature as the hero or antihero.

Protest Fiction: Protest fiction has as its primary purpose the protesting of some social injustice, such as racism or discrimination.

Proverb: A brief, sage saying that expresses a truth about life in a striking manner.

Pseudonym: A name assumed by a writer, most often intended to prevent his or her identification as the author of a work. Two or more authors may work together under one pseudonym, or an author may use a different name for each genre he or she publishes in. Some publishing companies maintain "house pseudonyms," under which any number of authors may write installations in a series. Some authors also choose a pseudonym over their real names the way an actor may use a stage name.

Pun: A play on words that have similar sounds but different meanings.

R

Realism: A nineteenth-century European literary movement that sought to portray familiar characters, situations, and settings in a realistic manner. This was done primarily by using an objective narrative point of view and through the buildup of accurate detail. The standard for success of any realistic work depends on how faithfully it transfers common experience into fictional forms. The realistic method may be altered or extended, as in stream of consciousness writing, to record highly subjective experience.

Repartee: Conversation featuring snappy retorts and witticisms.

Resolution: The portion of a story following the climax, in which the conflict is resolved. See also *Denouement*.

Rhetoric: In literary criticism, this term denotes the art of ethical persuasion. In its strictest sense, rhetoric adheres to various principles developed since classical times for arranging facts and ideas in a clear, persuasive, appealing manner. The term is also used to refer to effective prose in general and theories of or methods for composing effective prose.

Rhetorical Question: A question intended to provoke thought, but not an expressed answer, in the reader. It is most commonly used in oratory and other persuasive genres.

Rising Action: The part of a drama where the plot becomes increasingly complicated. Rising action leads up to the climax, or turning point, of a drama.

Roman a clef: A French phrase meaning "novel with a key." It refers to a narrative in which real persons are portrayed under fictitious names.

Romance: A broad term, usually denoting a narrative with exotic, exaggerated, often idealized characters, scenes, and themes.

Romanticism: This term has two widely accepted meanings. In historical criticism, it refers to a European intellectual and artistic movement of the late eighteenth and early nineteenth centuries that sought greater freedom of personal expression than that allowed by the strict rules of literary form and logic of the eighteenth-century neoclassicists. The Romantics preferred emotional and imaginative expression to rational analysis. They considered the individual to be at the center of all experience and so placed him or her at the center of their art. The Romantics believed that the creative imagination reveals nobler truths—unique feelings and attitudes—than those that could be discovered by logic or by scientific examination. Both the natural world and the state of childhood were important sources for revelations of "eternal truths." "Romanticism" is also used as a general term to refer to a type of sensibility found in all periods of literary history and usually considered to be in opposition to the principles of classicism. In this sense, Romanticism signifies any work or philosophy in which the exotic or dreamlike figure strongly, or that is devoted to individualistic expression, self-analysis, or a pursuit of a higher realm of knowledge than can be discovered by human reason.

Romantics: See *Romanticism*

S

Satire: A work that uses ridicule, humor, and wit to criticize and provoke change in human nature and institutions. There are two major types of satire: "formal" or "direct" satire speaks directly to the reader or to a character in the work; "indirect" satire relies upon the ridiculous behavior of its characters to make its point. Formal satire is further divided into two manners: the "Horatian," which ridicules gently, and the "Juvenalian," which derides its subjects harshly and bitterly.

Science Fiction: A type of narrative about or based upon real or imagined scientific theories and technology. Science fiction is often peopled with alien creatures and set on other planets or in different dimensions.

Second Person: See *Point of View*

Setting: The time, place, and culture in which the action of a narrative takes place. The elements of setting may include geographic location, characters' physical and mental environments, prevailing cultural attitudes, or the historical time in which the action takes place.

Simile: A comparison, usually using "like" or "as", of two essentially dissimilar things, as in "coffee as cold as ice" or "He sounded like a broken record."

Slang: A type of informal verbal communication that is generally unacceptable for formal writing. Slang words and phrases are often colorful exaggerations used to emphasize the speaker's point; they may also be shortened versions of an often-used word or phrase.

Slave Narrative: Autobiographical accounts of American slave life as told by escaped slaves. These works first appeared during the abolition movement of the 1830s through the 1850s.

Socialist Realism: The Socialist Realism school of literary theory was proposed by Maxim Gorky and established as a dogma by the first Soviet Congress of Writers. It demanded adherence to a communist worldview in works of literature. Its doctrines required an objective viewpoint comprehensible to the working classes and themes of social struggle featuring strong proletarian heroes. Also known as Social Realism.

Stereotype: A stereotype was originally the name for a duplication made during the printing process; this led to its modern definition as a person or thing that is (or is assumed to be) the same as all others of its type.

Stream of Consciousness: A narrative technique for rendering the inward experience of a character. This technique is designed to give the impression of an ever-changing series of thoughts, emotions, images, and memories in the spontaneous and seemingly illogical order that they occur in life.

Structure: The form taken by a piece of literature. The structure may be made obvious for ease of understanding, as in nonfiction works, or may obscured for artistic purposes, as in some poetry or seemingly "unstructured" prose.

Sturm und Drang: A German term meaning "storm and stress." It refers to a German literary movement of the 1770s and 1780s that reacted against the order and rationalism of the enlightenment, focusing instead on the intense experience of extraordinary individuals.

Style: A writer's distinctive manner of arranging words to suit his or her ideas and purpose in writing. The unique imprint of the author's personality upon his or her writing, style is the product of an author's way of arranging ideas and his or her use of diction, different sentence structures, rhythm, figures of speech, rhetorical principles, and other elements of composition.

Subjectivity: Writing that expresses the author's personal feelings about his subject, and which may or may not include factual information about the subject.

Subplot: A secondary story in a narrative. A subplot may serve as a motivating or complicating force for the main plot of the work, or it may provide emphasis for, or relief from, the main plot.

Surrealism: A term introduced to criticism by Guillaume Apollinaire and later adopted by Andre Breton. It refers to a French literary and artistic movement founded in the 1920s. The Surrealists sought to express unconscious thoughts and feelings in their works. The best-known technique used for achieving this aim was automatic writing—transcriptions of spontaneous outpourings from the unconscious. The Surrealists proposed to unify the contrary levels of conscious and unconscious, dream and reality, objectivity and subjectivity into a new level of "super-realism."

Suspense: A literary device in which the author maintains the audience's attention through the buildup of events, the outcome of which will soon be revealed.

Symbol: Something that suggests or stands for something else without losing its original identity. In literature, symbols combine their literal meaning with the suggestion of an abstract concept. Literary symbols are of two types: those that carry complex associations of meaning no matter what their contexts, and those that derive their suggestive meaning from their functions in specific literary works.

Symbolism: This term has two widely accepted meanings. In historical criticism, it denotes an early modernist literary movement initiated in France during the nineteenth century that reacted against the prevailing standards of realism. Writers in this movement aimed to evoke, indirectly and symbolically, an order of being beyond the material world of the five senses. Poetic expression of personal emotion figured strongly in the movement, typically by means of a private set of symbols uniquely identifiable with the individual poet. The principal aim of the Symbolists was to express in words the highly complex feelings that grew out of everyday contact with the world. In a broader sense, the term "symbolism" refers to the use of one object to represent another.

T

Tall Tale: A humorous tale told in a straightforward, credible tone but relating absolutely impossible events or feats of the characters. Such tales were commonly told of frontier adventures during the settlement of the west in the United States.

Theme: The main point of a work of literature. The term is used interchangeably with thesis.

Thesis: A thesis is both an essay and the point argued in the essay. Thesis novels and thesis plays share the quality of containing a thesis which is supported through the action of the story.

Third Person: See *Point of View*

Tone: The author's attitude toward his or her audience may be deduced from the tone of the work. A formal tone may create distance or convey politeness, while an informal tone may encourage a friendly, intimate, or intrusive feeling in the reader. The author's attitude toward his or her subject matter may also be deduced from the tone of the words he or she uses in discussing it.

Transcendentalism: An American philosophical and religious movement, based in New England from around 1835 until the Civil War. Transcendentalism was a form of American romanticism that had its roots abroad in the works of Thomas Carlyle, Samuel Coleridge, and Johann Wolfgang von Goethe. The Transcendentalists stressed the importance of intuition and subjective experience in communication with God. They rejected religious dogma and texts in favor of mysticism and scientific naturalism. They pursued truths that lie beyond the "colorless" realms perceived by reason and the senses and were active social reformers in public education, women's rights, and the abolition of slavery.

U

Urban Realism: A branch of realist writing that attempts to accurately reflect the often harsh facts of modern urban existence.

Utopia: A fictional perfect place, such as "paradise" or "heaven."

V

Verisimilitude: Literally, the appearance of truth. In literary criticism, the term refers to aspects of a work of literature that seem true to the reader.

Victorian: Refers broadly to the reign of Queen Victoria of England (1837-1901) and to anything with qualities typical of that era. For example, the qualities of smug narrowmindedness, bourgeois materialism, faith in social progress, and priggish morality are often considered Victorian. This stereotype is contradicted by such dramatic intellectual developments as the theories of Charles Darwin, Karl Marx, and Sigmund Freud (which stirred strong debates in England) and the critical attitudes of serious Victorian writers like Charles Dickens and George Eliot. In literature, the Victorian Period was the great age of the English novel, and the latter part of the era saw the rise of movements such as decadence and symbolism. Also known as Victorian Age and Victorian Period.

W

Weltanschauung: A German term referring to a person's worldview or philosophy.

Weltschmerz: A German term meaning "world pain." It describes a sense of anguish about the nature of existence, usually associated with a melancholy, pessimistic attitude.

Z

Zeitgeist: A German term meaning "spirit of the time." It refers to the moral and intellectual trends of a given era.

Cumulative Author/Title Index

Cumulative
Nationality/Ethnicity Index

African American

Angelou, Maya
  *I Know Why the Caged Bird
    Sings*: V2
Baldwin, James
  Go Tell It on the Mountain: V4
Ellison, Ralph
  Invisible Man: V2
Gaines, Ernest J.
  *The Autobiography of Miss Jane
    Pittman:* V5
Hurston, Zora Neale
  *Their Eyes Were Watching
    God:* V3
Kincaid, Jamaica
  Annie John: V3
Morrison, Toni
  The Bluest Eye: V1
Naylor, Gloria
  The Women of Brewster Place: V4
Walker, Alice
  The Color Purple: V5
Wright, Richard
  Black Boy: V1

American

Alvarez, Julia
  *How the García Girls Lost Their
    Accents:* V5
Anderson, Sherwood
  Winesburg, Ohio: V4
Angelou, Maya
  *I Know Why the Caged Bird
    Sings:* V2
Bradbury, Ray
  Fahrenheit 451: V1

Card, Orson Scott
  Ender's Game: V5
Cather, Willa
  My Ántonia: V2
Chopin, Kate
  The Awakening: V3
Cisneros, Sandra
  The House on Mango Street: V2
Clemens, Mark
  *The Adventures of Huckleberry
    Finn:* V1
Cormier, Robert
  The Chocolate War: V2
Crane, Stephen
  The Red Badge of Courage: V4
Dick, Philip K.
  *Do Androids Dream of Electric
    Sheep?:* V5
Didion, Joan
  Democracy: V3
Dorris, Michael
  A Yellow Raft in Blue Water: V3
Ellison, Ralph
  Invisible Man: V2
Erdrich, Louise
  Love Medicine: V5
Faulkner, William
  The Sound and the Fury: V4
Fitzgerald, F. Scott
  The Great Gatsby: V2
Gaines, Ernest J.
  *The Autobiography of Miss Jane
    Pittman:* V5
Gardner, John
  Grendel: V3
Gibbons, Kaye
  Ellen Foster: V3

Guest, Judith
  Ordinary People: V1
Hawthorne, Nathaniel
  The Scarlet Letter: V1
Heller, Joseph
  Catch-22: V1
Hemingway, Ernest
  A Farewell to Arms: V1
  The Sun Also Rises: V5
Hinton, S. E.
  The Outsiders: V5
Hurston, Zora Neale
  Their Eyes Were Watching God: V3
Kesey, Ken
  *One Flew Over the Cuckoo's
    Nest:* V2
Keyes, Daniel
  Flowers for Algernon: V2
Kincaid, Jamaica
  Annie John: V3
Kingsolver, Barbara
  The Bean Trees: V5
Knowles, John
  A Separate Peace: V2
Lee, Harper
  To Kill a Mockingbird: V2
Lowry, Lois
  The Giver: V3
Mason, Bobbie Ann
  In Country: V4
Morrison, Toni
  The Bluest Eye: V1
O'Connor, Flannery
  Wise Blood: V3
Plath, Sylvia
  The Bell Jar: V1

Potok, Chaim
  The Chosen: V4
Rölvaag, O. E.
  Giants in the Earth: V5
Salinger, J. D.
  The Catcher in the Rye: V1
Steinbeck, John
  Of Mice and Men: V1
  The Pearl: V5
Tan, Amy
  The Joy Luck Club: V1
Twain, Mark
  *The Adventures of Huckleberry
    Finn*: V1
Tyler, Anne
  *Dinner at the Homesick
    Restaurant*: V2
Vonnegut, Kurt, Jr.
  Slaughterhouse-Five: V3
Walker, Alice
  The Color Purple: V5
Wharton, Edith
  Ethan Frome: V5
Wright, Richard
  Black Boy: V1

Asian American
Tan, Amy
  The Joy Luck Club: V1

Asian Canadian
Kogawa, Joy
  Obasan: V3

British
Austen, Jane
  Pride and Prejudice: V1
Blair, Eric Arthur
  Animal Farm: V3
Brontë, Charlotte
  Jane Eyre: V4
Brontë, Emily
  Wuthering Heights: V2
Conrad, Joseph
  Heart of Darkness: V2
Dickens, Charles
  Great Expectations: V4
  A Tale of Two Cities: V5

Forster, E. M.
  A Passage to India: V3
Golding, William
  Lord of the Flies: V2
Hardy, Thomas
  Tess of the d'Urbervilles: V3
Marmon Silko, Leslie
  Ceremony: V4
Orwell, George
  Animal Farm: V3
Shelley, Mary
  Frankenstein: V1

Canadian
Atwood, Margaret
  The Handmaid's Tale: V4
Kogawa, Joy
  Obasan: V3

Colombian
García Márquez, Gabriel
  Love in the Time of Cholera: V1
  One Hundred Years of Solitude:
    V5

Dominican
Alvarez, Julia
  *How the García Girls Lost Their
    Accents*: V5

French
Hugo, Victor
  Les Misérables: V5

German
Remarque, Erich Maria
  All Quiet on the Western Front: V4

Hispanic American
Cisneros, Sandra
  The House on Mango Street: V2

Jewish
Bellow, Saul
  Seize the Day: V4

Malamud, Bernard
  The Natural: V4
Wiesel, Eliezer
  Night: V4

Mexican
Esquivel, Laura
  Like Water for Chocolate: V5

Native American
Dorris, Michael
  A Yellow Raft in Blue Water: V3
Erdrich, Louise
  Love Medicine: V5
Marmon Silko, Leslie
  Ceremony: V4

Nigerian
Achebe, Chinua
  Things Fall Apart: V3

Norwegian
Rölvaag, O. E.
  Giants in the Earth: V5

Romanian
Wiesel, Eliezer
  Night: V4

Russian
Dostoyevsky, Fyodor
  Crime and Punishment: V3

South African
Gordimer, Nadine
  July's People: V4
Paton, Alan
  Cry, the Beloved Country: V3

West Indian
Kincaid, Jamaica
  Annie John: V3

Subject/Theme Index